WILLIAM FRIDAY

WILLIAM FRIDAY

FRIDAY

Power, Purpose, and American Higher Education

WILLIAM A. LINK

The University of North Carolina Press *Chapel Hill & London*

The paper in this book meets the guidelines
for permanence and durability of the
Committee on Production Guidelines for
Book Longevity of the Council on Library
Resources.

Unless otherwise indicated, illustrations are
courtesy of William Friday.

Frontispiece photograph
by Bill Bamberger

The publication of this volume was aided by
the generous support of Archie K. Davis,
Myra Neal Morrison, The Mary Duke
Biddle Foundation, Carolina Power and
Light Company, and Wachovia Bank of
North Carolina, and by the Fred W.
Morrison Fund for Southern Studies.

Library of Congress
Cataloging-in-Publication Data

Link, William A.

William Friday: power, purpose, and
American higher education / William A.
Link.

   p.   cm.

Includes bibliographical references and
index.

ISBN 0-8078-2167-5

1. Friday, William C. (William Clyde). 2.
University of North Carolina at Chapel
Hill – Presidents – Biography. I. Title.

LD3942.7.F75L56   1995

378.1′11 – dc20

[B] 94-5723

CIP

99 98 97 96 95

5 4 3 2 1

FOR PERCY, MAGGIE, AND JOSIE

A new North Carolina generation

The research and writing of this volume

were made possible by a generous grant from the

WILLIAM R. KENAN, JR. CHARITABLE TRUST

Contents

Illustrations

Introduction

THIS book is the product of a set of circumstances that an earlier generation of Americans might have described as providential. In November 1989 Matthew N. Hodgson, then director of the University of North Carolina (UNC) Press, took me aside at a bookstall at a Southern Historical Association meeting in Lexington, Kentucky. Would I be interested, he asked, in writing a biography of William Friday, recently retired after three decades' service as president of the University of North Carolina? Like most people from North Carolina, I was acquainted with Bill Friday as a public figure; though I had seen him speak on several occasions, we had never met. His accomplishments – in shepherding UNC through a period of growth, turbulence, and uncertainty – as well as his influence over state and national affairs are all well known. I knew of the unusual public affection that Friday enjoyed among North Carolinians and many Americans and of the esteem, respect, and even adulation that college and university faculty and administrators often expressed for him. And I realized that few figures in post-1945 North Carolina, and in recent America, were more worthy of a biography. Still, my first reaction to Hodgson was skeptical. Chiefly because I was then completing another book, I feared committing myself. I had other concerns as well. Would I have access, I wondered, to all of Friday's papers? Would Friday and his associates be forthcoming in interviews? Most important, would I have the courage to write Friday's biography wherever the story might lead?

Not all of my fears were immediately dispelled, though most were. In time, I became convinced of the possibility of writing a full, fair, and properly contextualized biography of Bill Friday. A biography of a living person such as Bill Friday, if produced with complete access to his papers and with his cooperation, offered an extraordinary opportunity. My first meetings with Friday confirmed Hodgson's assurances. Although the biography was not Friday's idea, he agreed to cooperate and also to help to ensure that the book would be written without outside interference. Friday's cooperation meant that I would possess the advantages of a rich documentary record and the ability to verify and enlarge that record through interviews. With Hodgson (and subsequent UNC Press director Kate Douglas Torrey) agreeing to broker the project, and with the generous support of the Frank H. Kenan family, I also enjoyed complete editorial freedom.

Hodgson proved as good as his word; never did he or anyone else interfere in the research, conceptualization, or writing of this biography. I hope that I have done justice to a story that I found engrossing and that my treatment of Friday's career in higher education will stand the scrutiny of my peers in the historical profession and the test of time. The conclusions that I have reached herein are entirely my own. Although Friday cooperated fully, he never attempted to influence my judgment. Nor did he read any portion of this biography before it appeared in print.

Five years after that initial meeting with Matt Hodgson – including nearly forty hours of interviews with Friday – the fruit of the unusual circumstances that converged during the fall of 1989 is this book. It is the story of an extraordinary man and an extraordinary period in the history of American higher education.

THE decades after World War II were the most tumultuous ever experienced by American colleges and universities. Everywhere, higher education underwent a period of sustained expansion in enrollments, faculties, and facilities. Congress's passage in June 1944 of the GI Bill, which eventually subsidized a college education for 2.2 million World War II veterans, has been described by one scholar as "the most important educational and social transformation in American history."[1] But the GI Bill simply inaugurated a larger and more significant revolution in American higher education. Between 1946 and 1980 enrollments at colleges and universities exploded, from 2 million to 12 million students, while faculty increased from 165,000 to over 685,000. By the 1990s total employment in American higher education increased to more than 2 million people. In the two decades after 1945, the number of colleges and universities grew by 48 percent. Post–World War II America experienced undreamed-of access to and unprecedented support for higher education. More than a third of the nation's youth attended colleges and universities, while Americans, by the 1990s, were spending about 3 percent of GNP on higher education; in both of these areas, the United States led the world. Public funds, both state and federal, financed this post-1945 expansion: in 1980 states were spending $21 billion and the federal government over $14 billion in support of higher education. The importance of public colleges and universities grew accordingly. In the 1940s roughly equal numbers of students were enrolled in private institutions and public colleges and universities. In the mid-1950s, however, public higher education enrolled a majority of all students; in the 1970s three-quarters of American students attended state-supported colleges and universities.[2]

Conflict, as well as growth, also characterized post-1945 American higher education. In the 1960s students challenged expanded but also depersonalized universities and offered a general critique of racial inequity at home and Vietnam-style intervention abroad. The rush during the postwar years to expand facilities occasioned debate about the allocation of public resources. Flagship public universities sought to transform themselves into research universities; in this quest they were aided by the infusion of new funds from the federal government. Teachers' colleges remade themselves into comprehensive colleges and universities: between 1960 and 1980 student enrollments at comprehensive colleges grew from 500,000 to nearly 3 million. With expanded enrollments and influence, they possessed increased political clout. Expanded access to higher education increased the possibilities of political intervention, while the problem of equity, whether racial or class, remained a nagging concern.[3]

In the post-1945 era, the expansion of higher education was no less turbulent in North Carolina. The University of North Carolina had been a major factor in the state's political, economic, and cultural history for most of the twentieth century. Opening its doors in 1795, UNC remained for over a century a sleepy college not unlike other southern state universities. Then, a succession of presidents – Edwin A. Alderman in the 1890s, Francis P. Venable and Edward K. Graham in the early 1900s, Harry Woodburn Chase in the 1920s, and Frank Porter Graham in the 1930s and 1940s – remade the institution. UNC adopted a new civic ideal of service to state development and, especially after World War I, became a leading southern forum for the expansion of the liberal state and, after World War II, an active agent of political and economic development.[4] The university's research facilities were major factors in industrial recruitment and growth; world-class higher education facilities in the Research Triangle area served as magnets for development. Business came to depend on UNC expertise and resources; farmers could not survive the competitive environment of post-1945 American agriculture without the support of agricultural extension and research at UNC land-grant campuses.

At the same time, UNC development mirrored the most significant tensions and contradictions of North Carolina's evolution after World War II. Paul Luebke's study of modern North Carolina politics describes a twentieth-century division in the state between modernizers who sought to promote economic development through the use of the liberal state and traditionalists who opposed state intervention.[5] As an intellectual and political base for Luebke's modernizers, UNC became a lightning rod for the ire of the state's traditionalists. After the creation of a three-campus UNC system through consolidation in 1931, the university, firmly aligned with Luebke's modernizers and by far the largest and most prestigious agency of higher education in the state, became a major, and sometimes controversial, force.

Raised in depression-era Gaston County, Bill Friday reached adulthood in a distinctive culture of civic responsibility that prevailed at UNC during the 1930s, 1940s, and 1950s. As a young veteran and State College graduate, after entering the UNC Law School in 1946, he began a career as an educational administrator. In his twenties Friday became a fast learner, studying at the feet of UNC legends such as Frank Porter Graham, William D. Carmichael Jr., and Robert Burton House. When Gordon Gray succeeded Graham in 1950, Friday became his protégé and successfully blended the opposite administrative styles of Graham and Gray.

After his election as Gray's successor in 1956, Friday became the longest-serving UNC president of the twentieth century, an important actor in recent North Carolina history, and a major leader of post-1945 American higher education. There have been few figures more important in the recent history of colleges and universities than Bill Friday – and no better example of this era of rapid educational change. Friday ranks among contemporary university presidents such as James Conant, Theodore Hesburgh, and Clark Kerr in their central role in the refashioning of the function of higher education in modern American society.

As the following pages show, Friday's unique leadership and contributions arose from a native intelligence, an innate political ability, an informal and nonbureaucratic style, and, perhaps above all, a simultaneously gregarious and sensitive personality. As UNC president, he was guided by two overriding and sometimes conflicting considerations. The first was to further the twentieth-century public mission of the University of North Carolina. UNC, he always believed, served a civic responsibility: to aid in the economic and political modernization of the state. UNC was deeply immersed in the political structure and in the most significant public debates about North Carolina's future. The second consideration, however, ran against the first, and that was to protect the inhabitants of the multicampus system – chancellors, faculties, and students alike – from outside intrusion. The inclination of the North Carolina political power structure toward intervention and politicization of higher education constituted one example of outside intrusion, efforts by the federal government to determine the path of desegregation another. Balancing these considerations required subtlety and political skill, and the UNC president's role became to articulate the university's larger mission and to protect it from outside interference. During the 1950s and 1960s Friday made the case for expanded public support while fending off antiliberal and anti-intellectual sentiment; during the 1970s and 1980s he resolved the seemingly intractable problem of desegregating UNC and maintaining the confidence of the local campuses and the state's political leadership.

READERS should be warned that this is not biography in the usual sense. Because the career of Bill Friday embodied the historical development of higher education in North Carolina and the nation, recounting the story of his life is intertwined with the life of the American university during the latter half of the twentieth century. Indeed, it is no exaggeration to say that it would be impossible to give proper account of Friday's contribution to post-1945 public life without contextualizing it within developments at UNC and the state and nation as a whole. By virtue of his management style, which was personal and usually most effective in behind-the-scenes consultations, Friday often appeared in the background of the flow of events even when he was centrally involved.

A major theme in Friday's life – and the source of the subtitle of this book – lies in the commitment, on the part of both UNC and Friday, to power and purpose. By the 1950s UNC had become a power center for the state's political, cultural, and economic leaders. Not only were many of them UNC graduates, but also the university's 100-member Board of Trustees was composed of a cross section of the state's most powerful. University affairs dominated public life. Few sessions of the General Assembly in the decades after 1945 were not absorbed in issues arising from the state's public university system. Public interest in the university remained strong; the state's major newspapers avidly covered higher education issues throughout the 1950s, 1960s, and 1970s. While a power center, the twentieth-century University of North Carolina also became a center of purpose – an extension of the Progressive Era commitment to making the university a training ground for socially responsible leadership. University leadership would be, according to this view, crucial in the social and economic transformation of North Carolina from a backward and poor into an urban-industrial state.[6]

For most of his life, Bill Friday has been drawn to the sources of power and to the avenues by which it can be purposefully exercised. As UNC president, few people in the state had greater influence in public affairs than he. As a young man, Friday sought out and identified the sources of power; as a university leader, he was propelled into the UNC presidency at an early age in part because of a close association with university leadership. Subsequently, as UNC president, he maintained and expanded public support in the state and extended its national reputation. But Friday had little interest in power for its own sake; like the corporate entity of the university, he sought to fashion power toward a larger purpose – providing civic-minded leadership for North Carolina.

The life of Bill Friday serves as a metaphor for the tangled history of the university and state since the Great Depression. Today, as for most of the twentieth century, North Carolina strongly supports a prominent and widely respected public university system but, as a state, consistently ranks low in literacy, public expenditures for elementary and secondary schools, and Scholastic Aptitude Test (SAT) scores. If North Carolina is a state proud of the cosmopolitanism and dynamism of the Research Triangle Park and the National Humanities Center, it is also home to a prevalent strain of anti-intellectualism and widespread suspicion of change. And if it is a beneficiary of economic progress fueled by a tradition of public leadership, the state also offers scenes of poverty that rival those anywhere in the country. The tension between modernity and traditionalism that these sharply contrasting images of North Carolina suggest was central to the experience of Bill Friday himself, for the life and times of Bill Friday are also the life and times of modern North Carolina.

Drawn to Power

I

CHAPTER 1 *The Barefoot Son of the Mayor of Dallas*

WILLIAM Clyde Friday was born on July 13, 1920, in Raphine, Virginia, a Shenandoah Valley village so small that it did not merit mention in that year's federal census as an incorporated town. Nestled in the hills of northern Rockbridge County, Raphine was home to Friday's mother, Mary Elizabeth "Beth" Rowan Friday. After teacher training farther north at Harrisonburg State Normal (now James Madison University), Beth traveled at her father's urging to the hill country of Gaston County, North Carolina, to enroll in Linwood College, a four-year Associate Reformed Presbyterian (ARP) school that had existed since 1914 at the foot of Crowders Mountain southeast of Gastonia. Beth's father, William Henry Rowan, insisted that his children attend ARP schools, and she was no exception. Only a few years before the college closed its doors in 1921, a young veteran, David Lathan "Lath" Friday, began courting Beth, pursuing her even after she had returned to Raphine to teach school. Married on July 15, 1919, at Old Providence Church, the Rowans' family church, the Fridays took up residence in Lath's hometown of Dallas, in Gaston County. During the latter stages of her pregnancy and childbirth in the summer of 1920, Beth, following prevailing custom, was with her family in Raphine.[1]

WHEN Beth and Lath married, Raphine was a prosperous country town. Like other bustling communities in the first decade of the twentieth century, it was the product of the railroad revolution. The town was situated on the border between Rockbridge and Augusta Counties almost 2,000 feet above sea level, at the summit of the watershed of the James River, flowing southeast, and the Shenandoah River, flowing north. Raphine dated its existence to 1862, when James E. A. Gibbs, inventor of a sewing machine that stitched feed sacks, purchased a tract of land and built a home and the nucleus of a village, which he named from the Greek for "to sew." Raphine did not acquire real permanence until 1883, when the Valley Railroad, linking Staunton and Lexington, was completed. In the 1880s and 1890s new railroad-dependent businesses came to Raphine, including a sawmill, a grain elevator, a creamery, a drugstore, and two general stores. This was an era before hard-surfaced roads, and villages like Raphine offered the only link to the outside world for surrounding rural communities. By 1906 the community was prosperous enough to organize a bank; even in the middle of the recession that began the following year, a newspaper described it as "one of those prosperous little towns in this section of the valley that seems not to have yet struck the hard times."

Beth's father operated one of Raphine's general merchandising stores. In 1908 a local newspaper reported that William Rowan, "re-stocking and ready for an increased volume of business," had purchased a village lot, where he planned to locate a "handsome residence." By World War I, Rowan's business, depending on a farm-to-market railroad trade, was linked with a nucleus of entrepreneurs. The Rowans were well known in northern Rockbridge County, not only for their large home in Raphine but also for their moral rigor. The townspeople shared their principles; an early local historian once bragged that there had never been any whiskey legally sold in the village. Bill Friday described William Rowan – unlike his brothers, who were tall – as a "frail, little short fellow." But this did not mean that William lacked in physical presence; with a wide mustache and, like his daughter Beth, red hair, he cut an impressive figure.[2]

A devout and, his grandson remembered, "very strict" adherent of Associate Reformed Presbyterianism, William Rowan remained unwavering in his adherence to biblical standards. The Rowans were a "farm people, tithing people," Bill Friday recalled, whose links to Rockbridge County and the Valley extended to the colonial period. In 1779 James Rowan, a Scots-Irish Presbyterian, migrated to America in the human stream that had taken hundreds of thousands of Ulster Scots to North America. His son, James Rowan III, married Ann Elizabeth Walker sometime in the early nineteenth century. Their grandson and Beth's father, William Henry Rowan, was born in 1864, and he married Maggie Strain, a hatmaker and an Illinois native five years his junior.[3]

At night William Rowan supervised the saying of prayers by the entire family, and he insisted that private faith accord with public piety. Every Sunday the Rowans attended Old Providence Church, an ARP structure in Rockbridge County located on a knoll surrounded by farmland. There they assumed their place in the family pew for the hour-and-a-half services. After

Mary Elizabeth Rowan Friday and David Latham Friday, 1919.

church, the Rowans, as strict Sabbatarians, permitted no work, cooking, or play. Sunday was a day of prayer and meditation; William Rowan observed the Sabbath rigidly. All of the eggs that the chickens laid on Sundays went to the church; indeed, whatever the farm produced on the Sabbath was the church's property. Almost sixty years later, Bill Friday remembered the Rowan patriarch calculating at the end of each week "every dime he made that week" so that he could put 10 percent of it in an envelope to give to the church.[4]

LATH Friday hailed from very different roots. His ancestors were Palatine Germans who were among the waves of German and Scots-Irish immigrants that swarmed down the Carolina backcountry during the mid-eighteenth century. In 1744 the first white migrant, a German, arrived in the basin surrounding the tributaries and main branch of the South Fork of the Catawba River in the southwestern North Carolina Piedmont. Over the next two decades the South Fork country would attract scores of other settlers, one of whom was Nicholas Freytag II. Descendants of Nicholas and other German and Scots-Irish settlers, Lath Friday's forebears lived in the South Fork basin in what later became Gaston and, to the north, Lincoln Counties.[5]

For the most part, the Fridays were river basin folk, yeoman farmers who were neither desperately poor nor obviously rich. Yet they were also what Bill Friday called "public people." Lath's grandfather, Marion D. Friday, was a county magistrate and county commissioner. Nonetheless, Lath's immediate family broke the pattern of livelihood and residence that had prevailed over the past two centuries. His father, David Franklin Friday, was born in 1864, the third of eight children. He became what Bill Friday later described as "a part-time county judge, merchant, [and] farmer." A physically imposing man, David "loomed large," commanding public respect. After the death of his first wife, David F. Friday married Lath's mother, Sudie Hooper, and she bore four children and raised the five children from David's first marriage. Although her husband died before Lath reached manhood, Sudie lived into her late eighties.[6]

Like many of their contemporaries in the late nineteenth- and early twentieth-century Carolina Piedmont, the Fridays were attracted to that region's expanding towns. Lath was born in Hardin, a small village in northwestern Gaston County, and as a boy attended a one-room schoolhouse. But in 1910, at age fourteen, he moved with his family into the town of Dallas after the death of his father. Working in a cotton mill as a young adolescent, Lath Friday finished the ninth grade at the newly established Dallas High School. If his parents had tested tradition by participating in the move from farm to town, he and his siblings expressed even greater restlessness with old ways. Two of his half brothers, Ed and Grady, became merchant-entrepreneurs, operating gas stations, barbershops, fuel oil supply companies, monument businesses, and various other part-time enterprises. Yet Lath maintained little contact with the rural Fridays, although an extended family of 150 to 200 would gather annually for a family reunion in Gastonia.[7]

After attending Dallas High School, Lath enrolled in a thirty-day summer session for teachers at the university in Chapel Hill and immediately returned to Gaston County to teach school in 1915. His career was forever changed by America's entry into the world war two years later. In 1918, at age twenty-two, he became a self-taught accountant, serving as a payroll auditor on the project to construct Fort Jackson, in Columbia, South Carolina. Thereafter he joined the army and was stationed at Fort Jackson as a member of a field artillery unit. But before Friday could be transferred to Europe, the armistice of November 1918 was signed and he was mustered out. With a high school degree and training in one summer school session at the University of North Carolina, Lath talked his way into a job as a clerk and secretary to the general manager of the Cocker Machine and Foundry Company in Gastonia. Job in hand, he successfully wooed Beth Rowan.[8]

Bill Friday – named for Lath's brother, William Clyde, who died in the great influenza epidemic of 1918 – grew up in a household dominated by his father.[9] Bill remembered Lath as a physically powerful man; Lath had worked hard in his childhood, and that "muscle power" stayed with him for the rest of his life. In many ways, Lath was a bundle of contradictions. Most people remembered him to be gregarious; his son John characterized him as an "extremely aggressive" salesman. As his granddaughter explained, however, Lath was "bigger than life." Endowed with a good sense of humor, he occasionally liked to play practical jokes. But he was "very careful" with children and "deeply sensitive" and was known for his generosity and affection for people. His grandchildren later remembered Lath as a "very good" grandfather who always came armed with presents and a "big pocketful of change" to give away.[10]

Like many of his contemporaries, Lath enjoyed hunting and fishing; he also read detective stories, played golf, and strummed the banjo. He was, according to one account, a "bon vivant" who enjoyed the good life. With a trademark cigar in his mouth (his son described him as an "inveterate cigar smoker"), portly, and friendly, he attracted the attention of other men. One person in the textile business who met him in his prime recalled his "big smile" – he was a "very friendly" man who "knew everybody." Handsome, personable, and well kept, Lath was outgoing but not a glib talker. To Bill Friday, who favored his father in facial features and physical build, Lath was "extrovertish in every way."[11]

A skillful salesman, Lath rose quickly up Cocker's ranks. Working with that company for thirty-three years successively as office manager, general manager, vice president, and member of the board of directors, he traveled frequently, selling large textile machinery – the warpers, slashers, and creels that put starch into yarns and prepared them for weaving – to the textile factories of the Southeast. The machines were huge and expensive – as much as $100,000 apiece – and by selling three of them, Lath could provide work for his company for six months. After the Walter Kidde Manufacturing Company bought out Cocker in 1942, he worked with them as southern sales manager for textile machinery. Meanwhile, in 1944, Friday founded Friday Textile Machine and Supply Company and later served as president of the Gastonia Belting and Supply Company.[12]

Driven toward public service, Lath fervently believed in the value of civic contribution. By the late 1920s the growing Friday family, which eventually numbered four boys and one girl, had moved into a house facing the Dallas courthouse square, and there were few town activities in which Lath was not involved. Dallas citizens elected him alderman, and he served for five years. Subsequently elected mayor, an office he also held for five years, he supervised the construction of the village's first water system and paved sidewalks. When the draft was reinstituted during World War II, Friday was appointed to the draft board of Gaston County and served in that capacity through the Vietnam War. A leader in the Dallas Baptist Church, he was a long-standing deacon who was elected chairman of the board of deacons.[13]

Although never educated beyond high school, Lath Friday sat on the school board for twenty years and strongly valued education. In business he experienced feelings of frustration and inadequacy because he did not have a college education. Lath was "limited by his lack of education," recalled John Friday, but he "made the most of what he had." He reached the conclusion, as Bill Friday noted, "that whatever he did, he was going to get these children into college some way, somehow." Lath had a "hunger" for education, according to his son, and he sought to fulfill himself through his children. Eventually, all of his five children completed college; three of his sons would finish law school. For him, the educational ethic was rooted in a work ethic; life revolved around hard work and personal drive. "I love to work," he told a reporter in 1967; he would not know what to do if he had to sit down and rest. Lath learned this work ethic at an early age; according to Bill Friday, he lived a "hard life" growing up, and "in terms of the great American tradition of commitment to work, none was better than his."[14]

The youngest of nine siblings and half siblings, Lath was under the influence of two strong women who also lived on the courthouse square: his mother, Sudie Friday, and his unmarried sister, Lelia Friday. Lelia was a strong personality. In the mostly male world of textiles, she became a successful seller of leather belting and knew the industry thoroughly. John Friday said that when he became a superior court judge, he profited from Aunt Lelia's extensive political contacts. In a later era, he observed, she would have been elected governor or senator. After her husband's premature death, Sudie Friday grew into a "very dominant woman," according to her grandson Bill, and an authority figure, especially for her youngest surviving child. As a widow, she supported herself by selling Charis corsets, which were used to correct back problems, and she traveled all over Gaston County to visit local doctors. Lath often acceded to Sudie's wishes, and on important issues he was "indecisive" and frequently made excuses.

Lath's work habits exacted a high price. Bill Friday remembered his father's restlessness, a quality he ascribed to insecurity. Lath lived a stressful life and was, in many ways, compulsive. As a salesman, he spent much of his time on the road, and, although his job required it, he seemed to thrive in transit. Lath enjoyed that high-energy lifestyle. But from the point of view of his wife and five children – Bill, David ("Dave"), Rutherford ("Rudd"), John, and Mary Elizabeth ("Betty"), who arrived in quick succession between 1920 and 1928 – the traveling and frequent absences contributed to family stress. With Lath often away from home, John Friday recalled, the children were able to see him "on the weekends, if we were lucky." Lath, perhaps because of his absences, was "not particularly warm with his children." He did not enjoy a normal relationship with his family, according to Bill, and life was difficult for Beth.[15]

THE history of Dallas, North Carolina, was interconnected with the economic changes of the post-Reconstruction era. In establishing Gaston County, the state legislature in December 1846 provided for a seat in the center of the new county. Named for George Mifflin Dallas, vice president during the Polk administration, the new community by the time of the Civil War boasted a courthouse, post office, and hotel. But the coming of the railroad network completely altered Gaston County and Dallas's status as an urban center. The extension of the Wilmington, Charlotte, and Rutherfordton Railroad in 1872 bypassed Dallas because the town commissioners refused to appropriate funds to build bridges across several creeks, while many of the town's citizens feared that the trains would awaken them and frighten their livestock. Instead, the railroad engineers curved the line south, through a cow pasture that was named Gastonia Station. Eventually known as Gastonia, this new town became the epicenter of an economic revolution in Gaston County. During the 1880s Gastonia eclipsed Dallas as the county's economic center; by the end of the century it had become a hub of the industrial revolution reshaping the Carolinas.[16]

The impact of these changes on Dallas was less dramatic. In the decades before and after World War I, the town's population grew steadily though not explosively – from 417 residents in 1880 to slightly less than 1,500 in 1930; during the same period Gastonia's population swelled from 236 to over 17,000. By 1930, moreover, the spread of urbanization countywide diminished the importance of Dallas as a population center; it ranked seventh in size out of the nine towns in Gaston County. Much of the Dallas citizenry worked out of town; the morning bus to Gastonia was always crammed with commuting workers. Three textile mills, owned by the Robinson, Webb, and Moore families, operated on the east side of town, and industrial life melded with the traditional ways of the sleepy small town. Bill Friday remembered that, on the

The Barefoot Son of the Mayor of Dallas : 9

surface, the professional classes – teachers, ministers, drugstore merchants, and lawyers – ran the town, yet they depended completely on farming and, to a growing extent, on the textile business. "It was all mills," he said. Every morning he awoke at six to the blowing of the mill whistle that summoned workers to the seven o'clock shift. The mills' dominance was best exemplified by the fact that a mill superintendent occupied the largest house in town.[17]

Although surrounded by a changing social landscape, Dallas retained a rural ambience. Not until well after World War I were the sidewalks and streets paved; as was true for most early twentieth-century Piedmont towns, the line dividing farm and town was blurred. Everybody knew everybody, recalled one resident, and the townspeople "probably knew everybody's business, too." No one locked their doors, according to another account, and there was a "warm and kindred" feeling and a "very comfortable atmosphere" to the town. Dallas, said John Friday, was a "good place to grow up," with a "very warm relationship" among the townspeople. There was, nonetheless, a well-established social hierarchy in which mill workers lived on the town's periphery, the middle- and upper-class townspeople in the center. This hierarchy extended throughout the county, as the town classes of Dallas, Gastonia, and other communities intermarried.[18]

Although nostalgia probably tainted memories, residents recalled few acute social conflicts. The Loray strike of 1929, in which the Communist-led National Textile Workers' Union unsuccessfully attempted to organize Gastonia's largest mill, created a genuine crisis in Gaston County. Friday vividly remembered his father, who was virulently antiunion, driving him through the Loray community to show him the guns stacked up in the center of the street. The strike was "a very pivotal event," but its chief impact on Dallas was to "harden lines" against unions. It was a "bitter time." When he later associated with Frank Porter Graham, who had publicly defended the Gastonia strikers, some in the community regarded Bill Friday as a "kind of scalawag."[19]

In contrast to that explosion of social tensions in Gastonia, paternalism in relations between the classes and between the races characterized life in the small-town atmosphere of Dallas, where relations among classes appear to have been harmonious; according to one resident, the community was "one big happy family." Few of Gaston County's African Americans lived in Dallas, but for those who did the canon of segregation and paternalism was well defined. Strictly separated from the townspeople and the mill workers residing on the edge of town, the black community supplied menial laborers and domestic servants for Dallas whites. In what they viewed as "an understood and charitable kind of relationship," white families established direct connections with black families, but always with the implicit understanding of inequality. Dallas whites identified with African Americans primarily through black women who served as domestics, and they "looked after" their people.[20]

CONTEMPORARIES of Bill Friday said much more about his father's impact on the young boy than about his mother's. Frequently separated from Lath because of his traveling but surrounded by numerous Friday in-laws – including the strong-minded Sudie and Lelia Friday – Beth, an outgoing person herself, developed a different set of interests, including the local women's club, reading, and, above all, music. Later in life, she would even run, though unsuccessfully, for the town council. Her contemporaries remembered Beth's strong interest in music as a piano teacher and, later, her twenty-five years' service as organist at the local Presbyterian church. Music was her "outlet," according to her son, and "all the burdens of the world vanished when she got to playing." She enjoyed the "triumph of her life" when she was able to buy a baby grand piano.[21]

Lath, in contrast, conveyed expectations of practical accomplishment upon his progeny. Bill's seventh-grade teacher, Wilma Thornburg, recalled that Lath had "a great influence" on his oldest son. Dalton Stowe, a classmate of Bill's, was more direct: although he derived personality traits from both sides, his "fine leadership ability and concern about education" were derived from Lath. Friday, he believed, was "well tutored" by his father. The degree of paternal influence doubtless had much to do with the burdens of a growing family; with five children born in the space of eight years, Beth supervised the young children, while Lath assumed more responsibility for the oldest. Increasingly, he tried to provide guidance to Bill and the rest of the boys; he pushed them to "do better than he'd done." Under Lath's tough instruction, Bill and the other children became imbued with a work ethic and moral responsibility that characterized both the Rowans and the Fridays.[22]

Religion became a major influence on Bill Friday at a young age. At home, his family practiced a form of Christianity that was not as strict as either the Rowans' Sabbatarianism or the rural Protestant background of the Fridays. Although Beth remained a lifelong Presbyterian, the family attended Dallas Baptist Church, which attracted, according to John Friday, most of the town's "solid citizens." The church was fundamentalist and antievolutionist. The two ministers who served during Friday's boyhood, W. T. Baucom and especially his successor, Hubert Huggins, were both biblical literalists. Organizations such as the Baptist Young People's Union, which met every Sunday evening, occupied much of Bill's time into later adolescence.[23]

For young Friday, the town's social center, aside from church, was the nearby court square. On Saturday nights in the courthouse, an itinerant projectionist who traveled from community to community showed movies at a dime a person; most of the townsfolk did not easily get to Gastonia's theater. On the way out, Friday and other boys often slid down the banisters leading up the courthouse stairs. Every Halloween a party was held in the courthouse for the town's youth. The court square, which had a tennis court that the boys could play on, was "our playground," Friday said. There, Friday and his friends often engaged in ball play and marbles within sight of his home, a house that Lath had moved from another location in the village to a prominent position across from the courthouse. In the evenings, Friday and his friends played "Fox and Dogs," in which the boys, the dogs, chased one of their group, the fox. Not far from the courthouse was the town soda shop, where Bill Friday and his brothers also gathered to socialize. Friday was thus "busy with the things boys were busy with"; that included swimming in the summers at the railroad culvert. Like much of the small-town South, sports among smaller children were often integrated. Blacks and whites, recalled Thornburg, would play "just as if they were white." Dallas children frustrated efforts by the local women's club to beautify the court square.[24]

FRIDAY's warmest boyhood memories were of the three summers he spent with his Rowan grandparents in Raphine. The first of these summers occurred in 1930, when Bill was nearly ten years old. By the 1930s the flush times of World War I had passed in Raphine. As hard-surfaced roads such as Lee Highway, which traversed the Valley from one end to the other, were constructed, railroad traffic declined, and smaller farm-to-market centers like Raphine declined in favor of larger towns such as Lexington, Staunton, and Roanoke. The Raphine that Bill Friday remembered was already frozen in time. During the last decade in which railroads served the village, a small diesel three-car train still traveled through and was the object daily of "great excitement" among the children. Friday recalled Raphine as "filled with older people" who maintained large, freshly painted homes. Yet it was also a community that had come to view outsiders and change suspiciously.[25]

That first summer Bill went to Raphine alone, but in the next two years Dave, the Fridays' second child, joined him. Although their trips ended thereafter with the death of William Rowan, the Raphine experience left a deep impression on Bill and Dave, who received strict instruction in the values of thrift, hard work, and Protestantism. Grandpapa Rowan took his grandson Bill in hand. He put him to work in his store, which sold everything from high-laced shoes to horse collars, from hats to flour. For the customers, Friday sliced pieces from rounds of cheese, measured out and cut portions of chewing tobacco from whole slabs a foot long and a half-inch thick, and picked out cookies for children from boxes that contained one hundred of them. At other times, he did everything from tethering horses to sweeping the store. He would accompany Grandpapa when he went out into the countryside to collect delinquent bills, and Friday recalled that his grandfather sometimes packed a pistol. When business was slow, Rowan dispatched his grandson to his brother Warren's farm, about two miles outside of Raphine, where Friday shocked wheat, picked apples, and bagged wool from sheared sheep. To a boy raised in the industrial Piedmont, these Raphine experiences were "astounding," and Grandpapa's influence on Friday was considerable.[26]

William Rowan was unswerving in the example he set for his grandsons. He was a "stickler for cleanliness" and had an obsession with order. Friday recalled that he would punish the boys by sending them down to a darkened basement; simply the thought of that punishment terrified them. Yet Grandpapa's harsh discipline was also loving, and he taught Bill a deep respect for responsibility and duty. Rowan's insistence on personal, moral, and religious rigor left a lasting impact.

During their visits the boys attended Bible school as well as services at Old Providence Church – where nine Rowans are today buried – and they would seat themselves in the family pew. After the service, the family would climb into Grandpapa's car, a Whippet model, for the return trip home. Rowan "never understood that you drove it any way except wide open," and he "would just fly down" the county roads; the Friday boys waited eagerly for the weekly "ski run" in Grandpapa's car. The locals used to say that there were baskets at every sharp curve to pick up what was left of the Rowans. At the same time, the Friday boys "grew to fear" Sundays, for the Rowans prohibited not only work but also any kind of play, including swimming and baseball.[27]

Friday had many diversions in Raphine. Once a week, he would ride with Grandpapa to shop for supplies in Lexington or Staunton; Bill was given an allowance, and he would often spend it on ice cream at McClure's drugstore in Lexington. There was ample time for play and exploration in the Valley's diverse, even engrossing landscape. A few miles to the north, in Augusta County's Cyrus Hall McCormick Meadow, Friday began playing baseball with his friend Bill McCormick and others, and there developed an interest that would carry him through much of his adolescence. In addition, he was befriended by local townspeople such as Gibb Blackwell, the village blacksmith, and Postmaster Jimmy Wilson and his brother Tommy. On occasion, Friday accompanied Jimmy Wilson on deliveries to the rural reaches of Rockbridge, an exciting experience for the boy. Riding throughout the countryside,

Dallas School, October 1927. Friday is in bottom row, third from the right.

Friday was astounded to travel on back roads that lacked bridges; as he and the Wilsons forded rivers, he was exposed to the world of rural Virginia.[28]

WILLIAM Rowan's strong influence reinforced Lath's unrelenting instruction that Bill should distinguish himself from the crowd and rise above his position. Lath insisted on educational excellence, which to him meant leadership, not necessarily bookish scholarship. And it was toward leadership that Bill strived. Friday presented himself well in school. Dalton Stowe, who first met him in the fifth grade, remembered him as well dressed, "neat, clean, and very friendly." But he was no bookworm. Wilma Thornburg, who began teaching in Dallas High School in 1924, noted that Friday was a "likeable little ol' boy" in whom she recognized no great academic potential. He had a "real gift for making friends," without any "show" to him, and he was "most dependable." "We'd be as smart as Dalton," Friday was said to have told one of his classmates, "if'n we'd studied."[29]

By the time Bill reached the junior high grades, the diffident schoolboy had begun a social and intellectual maturing. Beginning in the fifth grade, Friday moved down the street to the Dallas High School; the fifth and sixth grades occupied the bottom floor, the seventh through eleventh grades the upper floor. There, in seventh grade (1932–33), on his return home from a Raphine summer, he first discovered the world of learning. The combination of his father's emphasis on education and the instruction of teachers such as Wilma Thornburg created a challenge that, he recalled, brought on an intellectual awakening. Friday's experience in the seventh-grade class was crucial. In

Wilma Thornburg he encountered a woman with a lively wit and keen intelligence who was childless and poured her energies into her students. According to John Friday, she instilled a "real sense of learning and of what school was all about"; she set high expectations for her students. Bill Friday remembered Thornburg as the sort of teacher "that would make you feel embarrassed if you came to class and hadn't studied your lessons." She would not do so meanly by humiliating students in front of the class. Often she waited until it was just the two of them, then say, "Now William, you know that you can do better than that." Soon "Billy," as she called him, was ashamed to appear in class without having completed his homework. In her own determined fashion, she communicated the message that if her students "had the ability to do something," they would be expected to "be something" and to make themselves "useful." Thornburg had "an excellent way," recalled Friday's contemporary Bob Summey, as a communicator, disciplinarian, and motivator. She urged many of her students to think of broad horizons and about the possibility of preparing themselves to attend college. Thornburg inspired an achievement mentality by pushing Bill beyond a point where his parents "couldn't go." By adolescence Friday had become a leader of his peers: for four years he was elected class president in the tiny Dallas High School, whose classes each numbered about twelve students, and contemporaries noted that he possessed exceptional political and leadership abilities.[30]

Bill Friday's early maturing manifested itself in other arenas. At the urging of his father, he participated in competitive declamation, or debating, contests. The spread of high schools in North Carolina in the first decades of the twentieth century was accompanied by the popularity of declamation contests. Lath Friday, who had taken part in such competitions during high school, retained an "intense interest" in debating. He insisted that all his sons participate every autumn in countywide declamation contests sponsored by the American Legion, an organization in which he was active. Lath believed that it was of "enormous value to you to be able to get up on your feet," and so Bill and his brothers began debating in high school. Home from school for lunch, Bill said, "nothing would do but I had to go upstairs and practice that speech with him" and "work at it and work at it" in preparation for the competition. Although his father instilled a discipline and drive in his son, Bill later remembered debating with a grimace – it was against "every impulse I had some days" – and recalled the stresses of the occasions and the antipathy that he developed toward them. His father became a "drillmaster," honing and refining his speaking skills. With the routine of practice five days a week, the speeches became so "chiseled" in his mind that, decades later, Friday could almost deliver them from memory.[31]

By the seventh and eighth grades, Friday was also displaying leadership skills through his participation in organized sports. Like many of the smaller high schools of that era, Dallas High School could not afford football, and during the fall and winter months Dallas adolescents played basketball, which became the most popular school sport. The Dallas team competed against the small high schools of Gaston County, but its fiercest opponent was Gastonia High School, whose teams were always bigger and better. Friday recalled playing against Gastonia's Lawrence "Crash" Davis, who starred for Duke University and later became second baseman for the Philadelphia Athletics.[32]

Because the school lacked a gymnasium, the team – composed of Friday, Bob Summey, Ralph Rhyne, John Paul White, and John Puett – played many of its games in rural northwestern Gaston County, in a building constructed to store wheat, cotton, and other crops during the summer. In winter, after the crops had gone to market, the competitors would sweep away the dust and debris and play basketball. With two pot-bellied stoves heating the building on either side of the playing floor, it was not uncommon for Friday, a guard, to feel his feet fly out from under him because of the dust on the floor when he turned suddenly while dribbling. In the early season, when it was still warm enough, the Dallas team even played outside. Despite these conditions, basketball was enormously popular in Dallas, and the high school games were well attended and frequently sold out. One year, when the team, coached by principal Marcus Pasour and physics teacher Phil Edwards, won a tournament at Belmont Abbey College against the smaller high schools of Gaston County, Friday distinguished himself as an all-star.[33]

The common denominator for all of Gaston County's mill communities, however, was their fanaticism about baseball; according to Friday, it was a "way of life," "a fever" in the county. Every mill had a team – Friday estimated that there were at least seventy-five mill teams in a local league, and competition between communities was intense. Any adolescent male who wanted local recognition sought to prove himself on the baseball diamond. Friday, who became an accomplished catcher, loved the game. Outfitted in rag-tag uniforms that did not match, he and his teammates played pickup games, sometimes at the diamond outside one of the town's mills, using worn, tattered baseballs, some of which were repaired with black tape. Friday said that it was "always a struggle on Monday to find somebody to play on that Saturday," but the boys rode around the county to mill towns such as High Shoals and Stanley for games. Unpretentious and tobacco chewing, Friday enjoyed a close male-bonded camaraderie through participation in sports.[34]

By the time Friday was sixteen, baseball had become an obsession. The position of catcher required stamina and durability; catchers' mitts had little padding, and effective catchers caught hard-thrown balls in the webbing of the glove. Considered good enough to have a chance at a professional career, Friday acquired a reputation. Years later, a Dallas resident, who used to watch him play, observed that Friday might have made "something of himself" if he had "kept to baseball." Friday's catching skills attracted the attention of a Dallas coach, Jack Kiser, who persuaded him to play during the summer of 1937 on the first American Legion team in Cherryville, a Gaston mill town. Two other boys joined Friday: Brian Leper, a first baseman, and Rusty Jenkins, a hard-throwing pitcher. Living in the home of a local banker, Ezra B. Moss, Friday joined players from all over the county at the Cherryville High School ballpark. The competition was intense: the Cherryville team not only toured Gaston County, it also traveled as far as Shelby and Charlotte.[35]

Although Lath was proud of his son for his Cherryville experience, Beth was unhappy with it. She realized that this was the last summer that Bill would spend at home before he went to college; she knew "that once I went up there, I was gone forever." According to Bill, Beth was not a sports fan; she was concerned that Bill might neglect his academic work and worried about the physical toll. One of her fears was confirmed on July 4, 1937, when Friday broke his middle finger; despite the bleeding, he continued playing. When Cherryville won the game, the crowd rushed forward to congratulate the team. One fan shook Friday's hand, including his broken finger; as pain shot through his hand, the man slipped him a dollar bill. Working from 7:00 A.M. to noon at the local Rhyne-Hauser Mill – a job arranged by local team boosters – Friday played baseball in the afternoon. He was paid for an eight-hour day while playing baseball three of those hours. It was, he said, his first experience with "subsidized athletics."

In his senior year, Friday's interest in sports led to an early involvement with journalism. In 1937 he worked as a stringer for John Derr, the youthful sports editor of the *Gastonia Gazette*. Derr was a Dallas native, a year or two ahead of Friday; as adolescents in Sunday school together, Derr and Friday organized Christmas caroling parties to serenade the townspeople. Subsequently, Derr went to work as a golf commentator for CBS Sports and helped to found the World Center of Golf at Pinehurst, North Carolina. As sports editor of the *Gazette*, Derr "just pulled me in," Friday said; whenever the Dallas team played, Friday would call in the scores and provide a brief account of them. The experience was a good one. Not only did it expose him to sports journalism, but it also introduced him to a few of the people in the business, such as Jake Wade of the *Charlotte Observer*, whom he met through Derr.[36]

THE adolescent Bill Friday impressed his contemporaries as assertive, polished, and even charismatic. Yet there was a certain duality in his personality.

Open and friendly, Friday was also sensitive and thoughtful. Unlike most men of his time and social environment, he detested violence. He recalled that social life in Gaston and the surrounding counties was violent; the life span of Piedmont people was short, poverty was rampant, and tempers escalated into domestic violence. "The difference," he observed, "between then and now is that you didn't know it all"; there were no television news broadcasts dramatizing it. Nonetheless, guns and killing so repelled Bill Friday that he refused to own a gun and to engage in the traditional male pastime of hunting. With pet dogs as a young boy, killing animals was "too much" for him. His father had trouble understanding Bill's aversion to hunting, but the simple fact was that he "didn't like to kill things" and refused to do it.[37]

Between school, declamation contests, church, and family, Friday had an extremely busy childhood. Free time was built around sports; there was little opportunity for a community of friends. His teens were a "rather lonely series of years." No doubt much of Friday's emotional turbulence resulted from the Great Depression, whose full impact was felt when he was twelve or thirteen. The depression brought the textile industry to a standstill in Gaston County and elsewhere in the industrial Piedmont. The loss of jobs and ensuing hardship created what Friday described as a "poverty of spirit" in which Gaston people "were just lost." Friday's contemporary, Bob Summey, was the son of Dallas's only druggist. His father's drugstore was hurt badly by the hard times, but through its doors came townspeople and rural folk who faced even greater deprivation. Summey vividly recalled the "desperation of people trying to eke out a living."[38]

Although the depression imperiled their financial security, the Fridays did not let on to other Dallas residents. Dalton Stowe, who had it "extremely hard," worked at a paper route into the evening darkness to help his family pay bills and took brown wrapping paper from grocery bags to school on which to write his notes. Bill Friday, he believed, had "the good fortune of having a father" who had "a real good job" and a family that fared well. Despite hard times, Lath displayed his typical flash, driving a big, company-owned car that took him across the South. Bob Summey had been impressed with Lath's cosmopolitanism. For a boy who considered a trip to nearby Lake Lure a major expedition, he was wide-eyed when he overheard Lath tell of business trips to far-off Philadelphia and New York City. Dallas people, believing that Lath had prospered during hard times, circulated rumors of a lavish salary.[39]

That Bill Friday's memories of the depression varied significantly from these perhaps suggests the success with which the Fridays kept their problems to themselves. As a salesman in a collapsed industry, Lath held a marginal job.

With the closing or slowing down of mills across the South, the textile machinery industry and the Cocker Machine and Foundry Company were devastated. Bill and his siblings were well aware of Lath's precarious financial situation. One Christmas during the depths of the depression, Lath, who was ill, called his oldest son to his bedside and gave him an orange and a cheap toy. That, Bill remembered, was all he received. About the same time, Lath lost land between Dallas and Gastonia that he had purchased in the hope of some day constructing a larger home. To young Bill, it seemed that his family came perilously close to losing everything during the depression.[40]

Hard times had a decided effect on the sensitive youth. To help out, Bill took on jobs delivering the *Charlotte Observer* and the *Gastonia Gazette*. He also began to work in his father's Gastonia textile machine shop on Saturdays and in the summer for eighteen cents an hour. In place of the idyllic summers at Raphine, Bill now faced a grueling regime. Arising at 5:30 on Saturday morning – six days a week in summer – he rode eight miles to South Gastonia, carpooling with four others in machinist Bunn Dixon's 1933 Essex. Because the car crept along at twenty-five miles per hour, they needed ample time to be at work by 7:00 A.M. Working fifty-six hours a week, young Friday returned home exhausted and covered with grime. In the summers, work ended at 1:00 P.M. so that baseball games could begin at 3:00; Sunday was the only day off.[41]

Friday's experiences during the Great Depression resembled those of millions of other Americans. What made them different for Bill was their conjunction with stresses at home. The most painful aspect of Friday's adolescence lay in the estrangement of his parents. Serious marital problems had erupted by the time Bill reached college age. Beth and Lath came from two different worlds. Lath was barely removed from rural Piedmont society; he was a man on the move, a glad-hander, a gregarious salesman who was constantly on the go. He was a conspicuous product of the social changes that had catapulted Gaston County from subsistence agriculture into the very center of the southern industrial revolution. In contrast, Beth was a musician whose family roots were sunk in the Valley's cultural environment, whose father was a merchant in a rural and pastoral village that was being bypassed by the economic forces of the day. The Rowans were ARP Presbyterians and adhered to an old-fashioned Calvinism quite unlike the Fridays' Southern Baptist culture. The arrival of one child after another – five offspring in less than a decade – must have only aggravated these underlying differences, as did Lath's frequent absences. The depression placed additional stress on the marriage, and marital conflict embittered Beth generally. By the time he entered college, Bill realized the severity of these problems.[42]

The conflict between Lath and Beth never healed, and, sometime during

Bill's early college years, Lath moved out of the house to live with his mother. The estrangement did not surprise Bill, but it pained him greatly. Remaining in a "gossipy little town" was certainly difficult for both parents, as was the fact that the Fridays separated but never legally divorced and lived across the street from each other. Lath, according to Bill, lacked the emotional strength to follow through with divorce; he could be tough and hard, but he had trouble confronting the marital conflict and never once discussed it with his son. But the dissolving marriage and "the constant struggle of loyalty and identity" exacted an emotional price upon Bill and the other Friday children. The experience of parental separation, according to John Friday, who was in the seventh grade at the time, was "very traumatic." Like other children of separated or divorced parents, Bill Friday "fought thinking about it" but kept wondering why this was happening to his family. He was at an age, late adolescence, when marital breakups make a deep impression; this was also an era in which separation and divorce carried a social stigma. One college classmate, Douglass Allison, recalled that Bill spoke "very affectionately" of his parents and gave no indication that there were any problems at home. Allison only learned of the Fridays' separation years later when he visited Bill's younger brother John in Lincolnton.[43]

With the separation, Bill completed a psychological distancing from his parents. The experience hit him very hard and created what he described as emotional "scar tissue." In college, with difficult conditions at home, Bill returned only infrequently. Instead, he plunged into work in a way "that some people would think abnormal." Subsequently, although his relationship with Lath and Beth was based on "great affection, great caring" and "in a strange way, we were rather close," in another way, Bill remained distant. Moreover, because of his absence from home during college and then the war, he never had the opportunity to spend time with his siblings as they grew into adulthood.[44]

By the time Friday was graduated with ten other members of his Dallas High School class in 1937, a distinct personality had emerged out of his childhood and adolescent experiences. From his mother and her family he acquired strict moral principles, a sense of order, and a sensitivity toward the feelings and behavior of others; from his father, an ability to persuade and a drive for recognition. His own disrupted and emotionally stressful adolescence, in turn, reinforced ingrained work habits and a strong ambition to achieve. His life experiences also made Friday unusually sensitive to the feelings of others; he felt conflict personally, and he was perceptive about human behavior. "One of the reasons that I guess I always enjoyed working with people so much," he said later, was "that I felt I understood the problems they

Dallas High School, May 1937. Friday is in top row, first on the left.

were dealing with." Frequently this sensitivity led him to understand an individual's situation without being told. He could sense it because he "had been there" himself. Rather than "sympathy," he described this quality as "empathy" with the condition of others.[45]

BILL Friday's world widened when he was accepted for admission to Wake Forest College. In the spring of 1937, during Bill's senior year in high school, Lath drove him on a day-long trip across the state from Dallas to Wake Forest, then in Wake County. (Sending a son to the university at Chapel Hill was out of the question for Lath, who strongly believed – like many other Gaston County textile businessmen – that the campus was excessively liberal.) Lath and Bill had been encouraged to make the trip because Hubert Huggins, minister at the Dallas Baptist Church, thought that Bill might qualify for a tuition scholarship. Himself a Wake Forest graduate, Huggins was one of many North Carolina Baptist ministers who composed a Wake Forest recruiting system. Always on the lookout for capable Baptist youth, he urged Lath to visit his alma mater. Arriving at the college, Bill entered Wade Hall for an interview with Daniel B. Bryan, Wake Forest's dean since 1923. As the meeting

The Barefoot Son of the Mayor of Dallas : 21

concluded, Friday recalled, Bryan scrutinized him closely and said, "Son, do you really want to go to college?" When Friday responded that he did, the dean wrote out a fifty-dollar tuition scholarship waiver grant and stuck it in his desk.[46]

Once on the Wake Forest campus, Friday realized that he had left his Dallas life behind him. Years later, when asked if he then had any intention of returning, he quickly and emphatically answered no. In the Dallas of the 1930s few people attended college, and on trips home Friday felt that his entering Wake Forest had created a "social barrier" with ordinary Gaston folk; he always feared offending his old friends by sounding pretentious. Still, Wake Forest College – since moved to Winston-Salem, but then located in northeastern Wake County – was remarkably accessible to North Carolina youths such as Friday. While his $50 scholarship paid half of the $100 tuition, board was available at clubs or with families at rates that varied from $4 to $6 a week; many students also lived in the private homes surrounding the campus.[47]

Arriving in September 1937, Friday and his parents entered the village of Wake Forest from the west, circled the campus, drove beneath the Seaboard Airline trestle, and continued north up U.S. Route 1 to the home of William Royall, who had been a professor of modern languages until his death in 1893; his widow, whose home was located on North Main Street in the village of Wake Forest, took in Friday and several other lodging students. Mrs. Royall, whom Friday described as the "grand dame of the town," had two unmarried adult children, William Jr. and Winifred – known as Mr. William and Miss Winifred. Both of them worked, Mr. William for a cotton mill, Miss Winifred for the college. These were "wonderful, southern people" who were "intellectually driven." Once Lath and Beth had unloaded Bill at the Royalls' and the time had come for them to leave, they drove him around the college once again and then let him out in front of the campus, near Wake Forest's official marker, which contained the school motto, "Pro Humanitat." Watching them drive away in front of that marker, Friday had mixed emotions. Both homesick and sensing problems between his parents, he felt a "total, total loneliness" – as "lonely a feeling as I've ever had." Not knowing a "living soul there," he experienced the acute anxiety and pressure of a first-generation college student; he was on his own. He wondered, "What on earth am I doing here?" He "couldn't quite get hold of it."[48]

Adjustment came quickly, however. At Mrs. Royall's, Friday found congenial classmates: Bill Ellington, his roommate, the son of the Wake County registrar of deeds, and Joe Helsabeck, of Walnut Cove, North Carolina, and his cousin Bill Helsabeck, of King, North Carolina, who occupied the other room. The Helsabecks and Friday shared an interest in sports; all three would participate in intramural athletics. Ellington, who had a girlfriend at home in Raleigh, was an artist who loved to draw; he had little interest in athletics and spent few weekends at Wake Forest. But Friday and the Helsabecks became "fast friends." Friday began to expand his social reach, making new friends with students from around the state, and in the process he discovered that he "could work with . . . total strangers."[49]

As an entering freshman, Bill Friday experienced a process of peer discipline designed to transform him into a Wake Forest gentleman.[50] The college considered training for public service an obligation, and a distinguished teaching faculty constantly emphasized the point. For "a little poor kid" from a little high school who had "never been anywhere in his life," the exposure to the intellectual ferment of Wake Forest was "a dramatic kind of contact." In academics, Friday felt disadvantaged by his training in a small high school; he was "scared to death." As the oldest son of parents who had never attended college – and, for that matter, like most freshmen – Friday was anxious about academic success. He acutely feared failure, becoming a "compulsive worker" during his first semester. Nonetheless, Friday later described himself as "just an average student" who "didn't excel at anything" and was "lucky to get by." But the most significant impact of Wake Forest was in reinforcing his identification with public service. With its strong tradition of activism, the school instilled in him a conviction that education required its students to "give back in some way" the same degree of service and contribution from which they had benefited.[51]

Facing a taxing academic schedule, feeling woefully underprepared, and uncertain about his athletic abilities, Friday mostly concentrated on his studies. For various reasons, he never sought recognition in sports at Wake Forest. Basketball, at which he had excelled in Dallas, interested him enough to join a college intramural league, but he resisted the temptation to participate in intercollegiate athletics. Unlike many of his peers, Friday decided against joining a fraternity. Fraternity rush held little appeal. He realized that attending Wake Forest was expensive and, with four siblings behind him, his parents were "squeezing every nickel they could." Unusually serious and mature for his age, Friday avoided the frivolity of fraternity life.[52]

Friday found outlets other than athletics and fraternities for leadership and recognition. He briefly considered writing for the yearbook and the school newspaper, the *Old Gold and Black*, but "backed off," again fearing that his studies would suffer. By year's end, however, Friday had become involved in student government. Self-discipline through Wake Forest's honor system served as part of a self-governing student body. Student government included two chief agencies, a Legislative Body, representing the entire student body, and a Student Council composed of twelve representative men from each class. While the Legislative Body enacted all laws governing student behavior, the Student Council governed student conduct, disciplined wrongdoing, and reported to the faculty. Below this was another level of student governance – the individual classes – and it was here that Friday began his career in student government. At the end of his freshman year in April 1938, he was approached by some of his classmates to run as part of a ticket that included Bedford Black, a candidate for class president. In a runoff election for the position of class treasurer, Friday defeated his opponent, Ed Rice.[53]

Although Friday had matured considerably at Wake Forest, in the spring of 1938 he contemplated a major decision: to transfer to North Carolina State College of Agriculture and Engineering in Raleigh. In this decision his father played a key role. Lath wanted Bill to join him in the textile machinery business, and he believed that enrolling in the Textile School at State College would provide Bill with a significant career advantage. With only a "fuzzy idea" of becoming a lawyer, Bill relented. The decision to leave Wake Forest "was sort of foreordained since I was the oldest son," and Bill shouldered a self-imposed responsibility toward his family. A few years later, he told a friend at State College that he needed formal training in textiles in the event that he entered his father's business.[54]

Friday left Wake Forest College reluctantly. After a year at the college, he felt that he had only partly appreciated its rich traditions. Wake Forest offered a first-rate liberal arts education; "nobody waltzed through," and students "learned in a hurry." The school further possessed a "family" spirit that guided and protected its students. As he recalled, the student body was neither fantastically rich nor desperately poor. With most of them from similar backgrounds, Wake Forest students realized that they were "part of something that was tremendous." That world of Wake Forest College was, for Friday, not easy to abandon; he had developed a "real affection for the place," and he "really hated" to leave it.[55]

In 1938 the contrast between Wake Forest and State College could not have been starker. Wake Forest was a liberal arts college, whereas State College, established in 1887, had opened its doors in 1890 as the North Carolina College of Agriculture and Mechanic Arts in response to pressure from farmers for improved agricultural education. Although State College subsequently expanded its curriculum to include engineering and diversified its study of agriculture, it made no attempt to provide a liberal arts education. (Indeed, under the UNC consolidation of 1931, which united State College, the Chapel Hill campus, and the Woman's College in Greensboro into a single consolidated University of North Carolina, a large portion of State's liberal arts and humanities faculty was eventually transferred from Raleigh to Chapel Hill.) Wake Forest was located in an isolated village; State College was situated about two miles west of the state capitol. Whereas Wake Forest provided a protective and nurturing environment, State drew a larger student body – over 2,100 in the autumn of 1938 – and offered a more impersonal environment. And unlike Wake Forest, State College had only an infant system of self-governance: its honor system had been abolished in 1935 out of disuse, while student government had become moribund.[56]

The State College student body functioned in isolated pockets. According to Friday, there was no "great organized social structure on campus." Instead, students were divided by those who lived on and those who lived off campus, those who belonged to fraternities and those who did not, and those who were enrolled in agriculture, engineering, and textiles. "There was no sense of large involvement on the campus and the great issues of the time." Spending most of his class time with his peers in textiles, Friday found contacts with other students limited.[57]

Upon arrival in September 1938, Friday faced the immediate problem of housing: of 2,100 students, only 1,000 lived in dorms, 400 commuted, and the remainder lived in fraternity houses or rented rooms. Arriving too late to obtain dormitory space, Friday was forced to knock on the doors of rooming houses surrounding the campus. He and two other students in the same position, A. Douglass Allison and Waverly C. Simpson Jr., were directed to the neighborhood directly north of campus, where, Assistant Dean of Students Charles Romeo "Romie" Lefort told them, two-thirds of the houses accepted student roomers. They "stormed the streets" of the area until they found space at 1714 Park Drive, a home owned by Lawrence E. Hinkle, professor of German at State College. Eventually joining the trio was another student, Bob Furman, from Henderson, North Carolina, who was obsessed with flying and later became a senior chief pilot at American Airlines. The four men occupied an upstairs suite that Hinkle rented to students. It contained a sun porch where Allison and Simpson roomed together, a common living room, and another bedroom occupied by Friday and Furman.[58]

Allison was from Pine Bluff, North Carolina, and, along with his boyhood friend Simpson, formed a "delightful association" with the congenial Friday. Allison remembered him as a "fun fellow" who "accepted everything seriously but . . . could see the humor inside of it." On occasion, Friday and Allison would bowl together at an alley on Hillsborough Street; at other times, they would take out-of-town trips in Allison's Ford V8. Once, when Allison carried a carload of students to Greensboro, Friday sat in the rumble seat. Driving through downtown on Market Street, Greensboro's east-west thoroughfare,

Allison suddenly realized, on a hill, that his brakes were malfunctioning. As they passed through an intersection with cars honking, Allison shouted to his passengers, "Hang on, boys!" Keeping his cool, Friday exclaimed, "Greensboro, here we come!" Once out of danger, he turned to the driver and said, "That's my man, Douglass, what's next?"[59]

At 1714 Park Drive, Mrs. Hinkle served as a surrogate mother to her student boarders. Her husband also took an interest in the students and often sought to engage them in a discussion of current affairs. An avid student of developments then occurring in Europe, Hinkle was later described by Allison as "a very interesting individual." At night, the professor invited Allison, Simpson, and Friday into his living room downstairs, where they sat and talked. Friday, who had studied German at Wake Forest, took an active part in these discussions; according to Allison, he was "most interested in any and all affairs," listened avidly, was analytical in conversation, and showed a noticeable ability to retain information.[60]

There was little time for idleness, however, as the curriculum for entering students was demanding. Friday probably took to heart the advice of *The Technician*, the campus newspaper. The first year, it warned, was the most crucial; it laid "the foundation," and State College was no "easy school." It offered "loafers . . . little chance," hard workers a "place in industry." The Textile School, which Friday entered in the fall of 1938, had existed – first as a department – since 1899. In 1902, when the Textiles Building was constructed, it had a faculty of two, including Thomas Nelson, a young Englishman who had taught at the Lowell Textile School. In 1906 Nelson became head of the Textile Department, and, despite some initial resistance from the textile industry, he made slow progress. In 1925 State College trustees established a Textile School and made Nelson its dean – a position he retained until his retirement in 1943; in the 1920s and 1930s the school enjoyed a close association with the textile manufacturers of the Carolinas. During the depression enrollments grew steadily, from an average of 139 for the period 1928–33 to 334 for 1933–38. Much of that growth reflected the Textile School's reputation among manufacturers; job security drew applicants such as Bill Friday, who recalled that virtually all textile students hailed from mill communities. Because of the increasing need for trained managers and knowledge of specialized technology, moreover, the industry was by the 1930s working closely with the Textile School. Even during the hard times of that decade, according to the school's historian, the industry "readily absorbed" its graduates.[61]

Unquestionably the dominant figure for students like Friday was Dean Nelson. Known to textile students as "Tee Foot," Nelson, a native of Preston, England, was warm and avuncular. On his retirement, the *Textile Bulletin*, praising his forty-eight years at State College, described his "kindly personality and his interest in young textile students." Friday remembered Nelson as the "gentlest, kindest person you ever saw." With most students and faculty recruited directly from industrial mill communities, the school possessed a structure that closely resembled mill-work organization itself. The Textile Manufacturing Department had three faculty members: head J. T. Hilton, assistant professor J. G. Lewis, and instructor G. R. Culbertson. Day-to-day operations of the school were handled by Thomas Roy Hart, who, as director of instruction, "ran the place like it was his." Hart, a former mill superintendent, displayed a management style that emanated from the plant floor.[62]

Friday found the adjustment to the rigid Textile School curriculum difficult. Although he received a smattering of instruction in basic history, English composition, psychology, and mathematics, most of his courses were taught within the Textile School. The 251 textile students in the 1938–39 school year were divided among four departments – textile manufacturing, weaving and designing, chemistry and dying, and research – but the great bulk of them, some 137, were, like Friday, enrolled in textile manufacturing. These students followed a regimented, vocational curriculum and attended most of their classes on the top floor of the new Textiles Building after its completion in 1939. Friday recalled only four courses that were taught outside of the professional school; with a narrow vocational education, he "didn't know anything." Textile students had to take applied courses in the coloring, dying, and design of fabrics, draftsmanship, plant layout, personnel management, and the applied technology of the textile industry. The laboratory requirements, which were time-consuming, involved the operation and management of a small textile factory.[63]

During his first years in the program, to make up for his year at Wake Forest, Friday worked long hours to fulfill the laboratory requirements. Students were expected to learn all aspects of the textile industry, and Friday spent "endless hours" operating weaving and spinning machines. In the morning textile students attended classes; most of their afternoons were filled with lab work. This was "a plodding time" in which Friday learned "by repeating, and repeating, and repeating." More than fifty years later, he recalled making castings in a foundry, a skill that he acquired after the second time he did it but that he was expected to practice for a full semester. After the third time, making castings held little appeal for him.[64]

After tasting the liberal arts program at Wake Forest, Friday soon found the textile curriculum unsatisfying. Partly out of frustration, he took an increasing part in campus affairs. Friday's involvement in student affairs brought him to the attention of Romie Lefort, the assistant dean of students. Lefort kept his finger on the pulse of student life. Unlike his boss, E. L. Cloyd, whom the students thought remote, Lefort was accessible. A practicing Roman Catholic, he had first entered State College in 1928 as a chemical engineering student; he served as president of the junior class, then of the student body during the 1931–32 year. After graduation in 1932 he returned as assistant dean of students, a post he held for nine years. Lefort became Cloyd's eyes and ears. As one student recalled, Cloyd was a "tough old cookie." Friday described him as "a rule-book dean," who, though not unfriendly, "didn't know how to cope . . . at times." One student said that Lefort was a "beautiful" assistant dean; Friday called him a "great humanitarian" who functioned as a "great counter-personality" to Cloyd; students had great affection for him. Lefort had a difficult job, however, because, as Friday put it, "he sat under people who didn't have the vision he had and were afraid to let him loose." Friday, who frequently saw Lefort, felt a natural affinity with him. According to another alumnus, he was a "great guy" who would regularly visit the dormitories. Lefort talked to students "on their level," recalled student body president Paul H. Lehman Jr., and served as a "go-between" for Cloyd. Lefort and his wife, then childless, poured their energies into the nurturing of students, especially those who showed leadership potential. Lefort genuinely liked young people, and he urged them to become involved in student life. "He always sought out the people who were the innovators on campus," remembered Friday, "people who were really doing things, had ideas."[65]

Lefort became what Bill Friday would later describe as a "second father." In Friday, Lefort recognized a leadership potential that he liked to encourage. Friday, he believed, possessed an unusually well-defined conception of public service, and he "had something to offer, and he was going to give his life to it." Lefort saw something in Friday that existed in himself: an ability to converse with people, to communicate empathy for their problems, and to convey integrity and trust. Even as a State College junior, Friday "had the background and the desire" to help others; because of his ability to talk with his peers, he immediately gained their confidence. The more they talked with Friday, Lefort observed, the more they believed in him.[66]

Encouraged by Lefort's example, Friday applied his considerable energies to campus life. Striking up a friendship with State College sports publicists Wade Ison and Dick Herbert, he took on work during his junior year as a "spotter" and general assistant; he would sit beside the announcer and provide him details of the play. Typically, announcers such as Lee Kirby, Phil Ellis, J. D. Clark, and Jim Reid were flanked by two spotters covering the home and visiting teams. Friday almost always spotted for State; he and the other spotter would point the announcers toward key players on the field, indicating whether a pass or a running play was about to occur.[67]

Friday soon became one of the campus's most visible citizens. Early in the 1939–40 year his name appeared on the masthead of *The Technician* as a reporter, and his responsibilities on the paper grew steadily. In November 1939, less than two months after he started writing, Friday was listed as assistant sports editor; in February 1940, his first byline appeared over a column entitled "Sports Comments." By the end of the academic year, in April, when sports editor Arnold Krochmal became ill and entered the college infirmary, Friday took over temporarily as sports editor. While Friday's responsibilities increased at *The Technician*, Krochmal regarded him as an interloper. He later described Friday as always looking "very neat and very dignified"; incorrectly taking him for a fraternity member because of his dress and demeanor, Krochmal remembered that he believed Friday's associations with the "in-boys" had hastened his success on campus. In contrast, Krochmal maintained, Jews like himself tended to enjoy limited access to the inner councils of campus politics.[68]

Already a campus figure through his involvement in broadcasting, Friday found that journalism provided another avenue for leadership. His columns often contained advice to students. He exhorted them to compete in a gentlemanly fashion; in one instance, he criticized "rough stuff" in a freshman game with Wake Forest. On another occasion, when the State College Red Terrors faced the Carolina Tar Heels in a basketball game in February 1940, Friday told State students to treat "our brethren from Chapel Hill" as guests. During the previous football season, he wrote, State fans had earned a reputation for good sportsmanship, "so let's carry it on through the rest of the year."[69]

In his senior year, Friday, as sports editor, continued to encourage proper enthusiasm. "In opening our home season" of football, he urged the students in September 1940, "let's get that State College spirit rolling right away." At the end of the previous year, school spirit was "going strong," but students could "do a lot better this season." Friday's career in sports journalism also became a practice session in personnel management. In November 1940 a staffer facetiously complained in *The Technician* that the newspaper could not "reach the 100% efficiency mark, what with Bill Friday practicing his golf stroke in the middle of the office and papers strewn all over (and I do mean all over) the place." Others, such as assistant sports editor Bob Pomerantz, noted sharper managerial skills. Friday, he later said, "really didn't do much work"; as his subordinate, Pomerantz "did all of the work," although Friday had "a way of motivating people." Often, he would appear to "talk it out"; without imposing anything, "he generally had his way." Pomerantz recalled attending sporting events with Friday, who had a four-door Chevrolet that he drove too fast, but the sports writing largely fell to Pomerantz and others.[70]

Friday became more directly involved in campus politics during his junior year, when he was elected to the State College General Assembly. At its first meeting in January 1940, he was elected speaker of the house of representatives. Remaining active in the assembly during his senior year, he was elected president of the senate and vice president of the assembly. He was chosen for membership in the prestigious Golden Chain and Blue Key societies, both of which recognized student leadership. Meanwhile, along with nineteen other student leaders at State College, he was included in the *College Who's Who* in September 1940. Friday, who had some interest in state and national politics, also became active in organizing a chapter of the Young Democrats Club (YDC) in early 1940 and was elected its first president.[71]

In the spring of 1940, in what *The Technician* described as "one of the closest and most hotly contested elections held in recent years," Friday was named senior class president. In "unusually heavy" voting on May 6, in a mass meeting of 260 members of the rising senior class, he defeated Thomas F. Jackson Jr., another campus leader. Jackson was an electrical engineer from Washington, North Carolina, and the race so aroused State College's textiles-engineering rivalry that Friday won by only two votes (131–129). The post was largely ceremonial – raising funds for the senior class gift and helping to organize commencement – but it pushed Friday further into the limelight.[72]

Chiefly because of his activities on *The Technician* and then in student government, Friday became part of an inner circle of campus leaders. It included Henry B. Rowe of Mount Airy, editor of *The Technician*; P. Dudley "Dud" Kaley of Scranton, Pennsylvania, a fellow textile student and editor of the yearbook, the *Agromeck*; and Paul H. Lehman Jr., of Winston-Salem, who in Spring 1940 was elected student body president. All three were members of Lambda Chi Alpha fraternity and had developed positions of campus leadership through interfraternity contacts. Lehman and Kaley became acquainted with Friday through Rowe; Lehman, whose father was in the textile business, also had a number of friends in the Textile School. The group eventually became a foursome. Once a week, prior to the publication of the student newspaper, they gathered in the basement of the Textiles Building, where *The Technician* was printed on an old flat-bed press. Lehman, who was a chemical engineer, remembered that, after finishing labs at Winston Hall, the chemical engineering building, he and other chemical engineering students such as Rowe and Ralph B. Williams would "whip over" to the newspaper office. On other occasions they met for meals at the student cafeteria. There, Lehman, Kaley, Rowe, Friday, and others would sit and "yak about things around the college, and things that needed to be done, and what our opinions were." Talking together frequently, they became a "close-knit little group" that, as

Friday recalled, "sort of pulled me in." "Everything we did," he said, "we did together."[73]

In addition to their meetings at *The Technician's* offices, they would gather in the evening with other students such as Howell W. Stroup, *The Technician's* business manager Ralph Williams, and textile student W. Aldine "Luke" Thomason at Phifer Fullenwider's State Drug Store across from the dean of administration's house on Hillsborough Street. Next door, Friday sometimes worked as a self-help student at Huneycutt's Clothing Store, but off duty he would often join his friends loitering on a twelve-foot iron rail in front of the pharmacy, where they observed passersby and commented on the day's events.[74] In November 1940 the group was calling itself the "Royal Order of the Rail," and notice of its existence appeared in *The Technician.* Friday recalled the formal organization of the group as a joke, and a newspaper account confirms this. The Royal Order's constitution directed its members to seek out students who had had too much outside work to make averages of "B" or better. The order was to be a truly secret society; officers would be elected by secret ballot, and the ballots would be destroyed immediately. Its projects included steam heating for the pharmacy's iron rail, a petition to Meredith College requesting that buses filled with women pause at the intersection of Hillsborough Street and Oberlin Road for the Royal Order to cheer them, and an annual tapping ceremony at the tap room of the Sir Walter Hotel.[75]

This group, Friday's social nucleus, became known as the "rail birds." None of the members came from wealthy families; like Friday, they focused their energies on the completion of a practical education and, ultimately, on economic security. Nine students listed themselves in the yearbook as members of the Royal Order of the Rail, and their membership transcended disciplines. Friday and Dud Kaley were in textile manufacturing; Howell Stroup from Cherryville, cocaptain of the football team, was in agricultural education; Bruce C. Halsted of Arlington, Virginia, was in electrical engineering; William T. (Tom) Rowland was in architecture; Edwin R. Johnson was in aeronautical engineering; and Lehman, Rowe, and Ralph Williams of Warrenton, North Carolina, were in chemical engineering.[76]

These students shared a common interest in campus life and leadership. Friday remembered that there was not "much developed social life" at State College; most students "had to work, and put in the hours, and get through that place." As Lehman put it, they hailed from backgrounds where "money didn't grow on trees, but . . . they weren't hard-up either." The depression limited their spending power and placed severe constraints on their time. Friday and most of his peers had part-time jobs throughout the academic year as well as summer employment. Howell Stroup, along with LeRoy "Shorty"

Bill Friday and his father at the Southern Textile Exposition, April 4, 1941.
(Courtesy of University Archives, North Carolina State University)

Barnes, worked for the National Youth Administration (NYA) cutting wood and performing other odd jobs for twenty-five cents an hour. Paul Lehman earned $9.35 a week at one summer job, while Stroup paid his tuition by growing 600 bushels of sweet potatoes. Four of the five students who lived with Stroup pooled their money to help put him through school.[77]

Nonetheless, most State College students found time for recreation and fun. In addition to occasional trips with Doug Allison his first year, Friday rode with other friends who had cars. Bruce Halsted owned a 1931 Ford roadster, and he remembered driving Friday to Meredith College to date his future wife, Ida Howell. During his senior year, Friday and Rowe purchased a 1934 four-door Chevrolet that cost them each fifty dollars; according to Romie Lefort, it "got them around" and transported them on their dates. On one occasion, Kaley, Lehman, Friday, and Tom Rowland traveled in the Chevrolet to a "lonely spot where they could see the moon come up." Friday reported to Rowe that it was the "best picnic" he had ever attended, and they stayed out into the wee hours of the morning. The automobile also became known as *The Technician*'s "staff car," although its reliability was questionable. Lehman claimed that the car refused to start when he needed it most. One evening, he and Friday pushed it all over Raleigh, but the "pay-off" came when it stalled on a railroad track with a train coming. The Chevrolet started in time to avoid disaster, but it required considerable pushing and coaxing.[78]

Yet there were limits to Friday's participation in the social life of State College. Lehman described him as neither a "social hound" nor a "party boy." Although most of his friends belonged to Lambda Chi Alpha, Friday scrupulously avoided membership in a fraternity. He did not connect with fraternities, Friday later said; their restrictiveness was alien to his social ideals. Doug Allison offered another explanation. He maintained that Friday, to begin with, lacked time for fraternities. But he "didn't want to become aligned with any one particular organization." Although he was "clean, neat, and box perfect," he was neither a "flashy dresser" nor a "flamboyant person"; rather, Friday was "one of the fellows all the way through." Viewing campus life with unusual maturity, he "saw the whole thing as a whole," pursued his own agenda, and believed that he could "shuffle" one campus organization against another.[79]

Although the Royal Order of the Rail was facetious, Lehman remembered it as an unofficial group of campus leaders. A diverse representation of students belonged to the society; they shared a common view of how campus culture should be changed. For Friday, the fresh memory of the homogeneous, well-structured patterns of student life at Wake Forest made State College campus culture seem disorganized and scattered, and an agenda grew out of conversations with Kaley, Rowe, and Lehman. They agreed that there needed to be better means of reaching, informing, and even uplifting the student body. Lehman believed, as did Friday, that "there was not enough broadening of young people going to a college like that." He described State as a "grass-roots type college," where students had "their noses to the grindstone in textiles, or agriculture, or engineering." Working primarily with Lefort, who encouraged their enthusiasm, Friday and his friends looked for ways to broaden student culture and unify campus life. Friday helped to initiate a separate ceremony for ROTC graduates when they received their commissions during commencement – the first such ceremony in the country. This not only pleased the State College dean of administration, Colonel John W. Harrelson, himself a military man, but it also attracted the attention of the U.S. Army, which wrote to Friday praising him. Because most outside speakers rarely attracted student audiences across disciplinary and school lines, campus leaders sought to invite speakers who could attract a campuswide audience. Lefort applauded these ideas. In January 1941 he traveled with Lehman and Friday to Washington, D.C., where they met with North Carolina senators Robert R. Reynolds and Josiah W. Bailey to obtain their help in attracting speakers.[80]

Within the protective umbrella of his peer group, Friday developed a distinctive political style. Characterized by one of his contemporaries as a "quiet motivator" who avoided "stage center" and operated "within the shadows," he was also known for his integrity and as a "straight-shooter." This contemporary drew a contrast between Friday and Jim Graham, of Rowan County, then a year behind Friday in the School of Agriculture and later state commissioner of agriculture. Whereas Graham was "colorful," "loud and boisterous," and a "damned politician . . . from the day he hit his foot on campus," Friday was low-keyed and "went about his way." But he was also friendly and gregarious, and, as Bob Pomerantz had discovered, could often find ways to promote student participation. As Lefort recalled, Friday's success as a campus leader was linked to his ability to motivate students on his own projects.[81]

While Friday displayed a sociable and disarmingly open manner to many persons, he revealed a different side to his closest friends. Lefort described him as "shy" in a way that brought others "closer to him"; Friday's retiring manner made people take a "second look at him." He possessed the "uncommon" trait of conversing with people in such a way that his peers wanted "to talk with him again." To Lehman, Friday was a "complex" personality who was simultaneously retiring and sociable and "mature for his age, in some respects." Lehman observed a contrast between Friday's outgoing public personality at State College, on the one hand, and his "retiring manner" with close friends

State College commencement, Frank Thompson Gymnasium, June 9, 1941. (Courtesy of University Archives, North Carolina State University)

on the other. At heart, he was a "rather quiet" person who worked most effectively in the security of small groups; here his motivational skills appeared prominently. He had a way of "very quietly, without saying very much, letting people talk themselves into something, and then he would twist their arm at the last minute and get them to do something, without seeming to put any pressure on them." Lehman saw this "interesting knack" as a personality trait that later characterized his career in higher education.[82]

THE spring term of 1941, his last at State College, was a heady time for Bill Friday. Well known on campus, he began to reach out beyond its confines. In April 1940 he had attended, as a member of the Student Council, the annual meeting of the Southern Federation of College Students in New Orleans. There, using his characteristic personal and communication skills, he offered the general assembly plan of student government at State College as a model for other institutions. The same spring, when the North Carolina Federation of Student Governments convened its first meeting, Friday represented State College. Not only did Friday help to establish the organization, he emerged from the group as its first elected president. By his last semester at State College, during the spring of 1941, Friday was also appointed to the NYA's state board, where he first met the distinguished Durham black leader and president of North Carolina College for Negroes, James E. Shepherd.[83]

Student leadership in a state arena also brought Friday into contact with Frank Porter Graham, president of the three-campus University of North Carolina and legendary southern liberal. Most students attending either State College or the university at Chapel Hill had had some experience with Graham, who visited the campuses often, frequently accompanied by his lieutenant, William D. "Billy" Carmichael Jr. Graham and Carmichael could work a crowd effectively; while Graham never forgot a face, Carmichael always remembered names. Graham especially prided himself on his personal associations with the faculty, students, and administration of the three campuses. Graham and Paul Lehman's father had a mutual friend who introduced them while Lehman was a high school student on a trip to Chapel Hill. After chatting and visiting briefly, Graham talked Lehman into attending State College.[84]

Friday recalled vividly the first time that he saw Graham at an all-university meeting, and later on several other occasions. Although there was "nothing particularly significant" about these meetings, the experience made a distinct impression on him. Graham, a "man who was already a legend," was so easily available for "work, talk, and debate." When the Advisory Budget Commission recommended in February 1941 that the legislature enact deep cuts in State

College's budget, Graham solicited student support to lobby against the measure. As senior class president, Friday, at the urging of Billy Carmichael, appointed a twenty-five-member Student Committee on Legislative Action. Friday himself subsequently appeared before a legislative committee, and Graham succeeded in fending off the budget cuts. In this, his "first encounter with the power of persuasion," Friday was deeply impressed.[85]

On the eve of his graduation in June 1941, Friday was universally recognized as a campus leader. That spring, the *Charlotte Observer* had described him as "the mayor of Dallas' barefoot son," and the name stuck on campus, even appearing in *The Technician*. The student newspaper, in January 1941, featured Friday as its "Senior of the Week" and declared him to be "an ideal of every State College student that is really interested in the welfare of State College." Friday had done "an unbelievable amount of work" for campus improvement. He was "exceptionally well known by everybody on campus," according to Doug Allison, who did not know "a single soul who didn't like him." Friday was "very popular, well-known, and respected campus-wide," according to Bruce Halsted. "It seemed like everybody knew him," recalled Katherine Stinson, one of the few women enrolled at State College; "he was involved in so many activities." Everyone assumed that he would become a "successful person."[86]

Friday's last year at State College had been frenetic; he had, as he later said, made a career of everything but his major. Yet the manner in which he threw himself into campus affairs partly reflected the emotional toll of his parents' breakup, and his involvement in campus activities had exacted a price. His academic work was not affected "too much" since he was enrolled in advanced textile courses; as long as he was active in campus affairs, the registrar did not hold him to academic requirements too rigidly. As a result, during his senior year, Friday by his own admission "really didn't do much academic work." He had become a "busy, busy body, really spending far too much time outside the classroom." If on the one hand he realized that he had not done everything that he should have done academically, he also later recognized that he had become "too close, too identified, too involved" in the affairs of student life. He had been "fully consumed by extra-curricular work, and that was wrong."[87]

State College's commencement exercises, held on Monday, June 9, 1941, were bittersweet. Sometime that spring Dean of Administration Harrelson had summoned Friday to his office. When the colonel said that he wanted to break tradition by having Friday become the first student ever to speak at a State College commencement, Friday "nearly fainted dead away." But he agreed nonetheless. As a textile student, Friday had had little opportunity to give speeches; despite his high school debating experience, he "lived in terror" of the graduation exercises. Both of his parents attended the event, and he asked his father to help him, on the day before commencement, to prepare for an address before an audience that would include Governor J. Melville Broughton and Frank Porter Graham. In a closing chapter in his relationship with his father, the two went into Pullen Auditorium, where Friday rehearsed the speech before his father one last time. When the time came for this occasion, Friday later remembered, "I wanted to pay him the compliment of making it all possible for me when I needed it."[88]

Graduation day was hot and sticky, typical weather for North Carolina in early summer. Not long after the 293 graduating seniors marched into Riddick Stadium for the commencement ceremonies at dusk, a thunderstorm blew in over the State College smokestack, bringing a deluge. Students, faculty, and visitors alike ran for cover; the reassembled group convened in nearby Frank Thompson Gymnasium. In the confusion, however, Friday had rolled up his speech and stuck it in the sleeve of his academic robe. As the crowd gathered, graduating students sang "How Dry I Am." The ceremonies then began, with Friday on stage with the visiting dignitaries. While Broughton announced to a cheering crowd plans to build a 10,000-seat indoor arena, Friday was desperately trying to unroll the drenched speech and get it unstuck. Realizing that the talk was a "wet mess" and gripped by a "consuming sense of panic," he looked out on the crowd until he saw his father. Suddenly, his practice session from the day before brought the speech back from memory, and he completed it in five minutes.[89]

With commencement over, Friday realized that one stage in his life had ended. "I don't know that I've ever had a feeling, in my entire life, of such emptiness," he said later. Members of the Royal Order of the Rail, along with other campus leaders, gathered at the fifty-yard line in the center of the field inside Riddick Stadium, still wet from the soaking of that evening's thunderclap. The group, Lehman remembered, "just chatted with each other for a while." Promising to keep in touch yet acknowledging that this was probably the last time all of them would be together, they remained to talk. Like everyone on the State College campus, they realized the likelihood of American involvement in the war and had "no idea where people were going, or whether we would ever come back or what."[90]

That spring Bill Friday and other members of the Royal Order of the Rail, while loitering on Hillsborough Street, had seen military trucks filled with soldiers roll by for a solid hour.[91] A year earlier Nazi armored divisions, in a blitzkrieg, had overrun France. In June 1941, even as the placid graduation ceremonies took place at State College and its graduates contemplated their uncertain futures, the Battle of Britain was raging in the west and the invasion of the Soviet Union was about to occur in the east. In the United States, war clouds were as dark as the early summer clouds in North Carolina.

D ESPITE a distaste for textile manufacturing at State College, Friday, on graduation, took a job with DuPont Corporation's Waynesboro, Virginia, manufacturing plant. Working with DuPont held considerable attraction. Even in 1941, with the defense mobilization, a graduating senior could not easily reject secure employment in one of the textile industry's premier jobs. DuPont was known to prefer students who were clean-cut, WASPs, and campus leaders; the company hired Paul Lehman, who shared these characteristics with Friday, as a chemical engineer. Meeting a DuPont recruiter at Raleigh's Sir Walter Hotel during an interview session sometime in the spring of 1941, Friday signed on with the company at $130 a month – the highest starting salary that the company offered.[1]

Soon after graduation Friday packed up his belongings in his newly purchased 1941 Chevrolet coupé and departed Raleigh for Waynesboro, which was situated in the Valley of Virginia not far from Raphine. Along with nearly forty others recruited from around the country, Friday learned what he later called the "DuPont way." All new trainees began at the bottom; starting positions with DuPont, remembered Lehman, who spent most of his career with the company, were "learning operations." Friday was assigned to the midnight to 7:00 A.M. shift, where he faced a difficult adjustment to the regimen of factory work. Once, when a thunderstorm swept through Waynesboro, sending lightning everywhere, Friday shut down the production process. Almost immediately, he was reprimanded by a supervisor and the machinery was switched back on. This incident and others brought home a hard reality: in place of the "halo effect" of campus leadership, he suddenly found himself a factory worker on the third shift, "trying to sleep at daytime – totally a stranger." For Friday, this was "a great lesson in . . . what life can do to change you."[2] But he waited out the DuPont training program, which lasted ninety days. In Waynesboro, not only did Friday learn the details of a manufacturing process, but he also realized that his vocation lay outside of textile manufacturing. The looming war clouds provided a reason, perhaps something of an excuse, to leave an occupation for which his father had carefully groomed him. It also provided him an opportunity to experiment in other forms of work and leadership more suited to his personality.[3]

During that summer of 1941 Friday reconsidered his future. He was convinced that war was imminent, yet he realized that, unlike most State College graduates, he lacked ROTC training. Sometime in the autumn, State College dean of students E. L. Cloyd called to tell him that Romie Lefort had left to lead the campus ROTC program and that there was an opening in Cloyd's office. Lefort had urged Cloyd to make the call; if Friday was not immediately entering the military, he said, "latch on to him." "Come on down here," Friday remembered Cloyd urging him. "You are going to have to go in the service anyway." Friday leaped at the chance. Though already considering an application to the navy for a commission, Friday enjoyed student affairs and he decided to return to State College, apply for a commission, and wait out the navy's response. He knew that the navy was "looking for anybody that knew the difference between a slide rule and a pencil." Tendering his resignation to DuPont, he explained to the head of the Waynesboro operations that he would have to go to war and needed to return to Raleigh.[4]

Arriving in Raleigh in September 1941, Friday took a job as State's chief dormitory assistant, a position that at least partly filled the vacuum created when Lefort departed Cloyd's office that summer. Taking up residence on the first floor of Ninth (later Clark) Dormitory, with his office in Berry Dormitory, Friday worked closely with students. His duties included supervising dormitory life, which often meant, as Lefort remembered, "keeping the noise down and getting the bad characters out." Friday was also involved in supervising meetings, helping students to stage events and ceremonies, and supporting the operation of *The Technician*. In all of these activities, his experience as a student leader at State College was crucial. Later that year, Friday lived in a Ninth Dormitory room with Mike Andrews, a State College football player whom he had taken in. Andrews remembered him as neat, congenial, and willing to lend his car to students. The students regarded Friday with great affection, which they sometimes expressed by throwing water balloons at him as he left the dormitory. Friday also served as a member of the State College committee on freshman housing, as well as chairman of the committee on dormitory telephones. At the same time, he would often travel with alumni secretary Dan Paul to visit alumni.[5]

Ensign William Friday, Spring 1942.

But Friday realized that his return to State College was only a stopgap. Not on campus "long enough to cause any ripple," he later admitted that he was "just biding time." He had applied for a naval commission in the autumn of 1941, and it was still pending when the Japanese attacked Pearl Harbor on December 7. Friday remembered that Sunday vividly. Continuing his work as a spotter during radio broadcasts, he had driven his Chevrolet coupé to Greenville, South Carolina, with friends for the Shrine Bowl, an annual all-star football game. Returning home, the group had almost reached Sanford when Friday turned the radio on and heard news of the Japanese attack. Unable to believe it, Friday and his companions, who included Raleigh appliance store owner Woodrow Jones and other State alumni, sat in "total silence" as they drove into Raleigh. Soon, at State College, the "whole climate of the place changed," according to Friday, as the campus became "very serious and very sensitive."[6]

With war under way, Friday began an active courtship of Ida Howell, whom he had met the year before, in the autumn of 1940, on a blind date arranged by Paul Lehman. The occasion was the annual Greater University Day, when the student bodies of State College, Carolina, and Woman's College assembled for the State-Carolina football game. Friday, who as senior class president was involved in the opening and halftime ceremonies, was in need of a "sponsor," or a date, to accompany him to Riddick Stadium. Lehman was dating Meredith student Janie Parker, and she proposed to arrange a blind date for Friday with her suite mate, Ida Howell. Bill, recalled Lehman, did not actively date; he was simply "involved in so many other things" that he rarely attended fraternity dances. Not having any particular female interest at the time, Friday was available, as was Ida, who had been dating a State College football player but now was unattached. Ida, who had heard about Bill Friday but had never met him, accepted.[7]

Ida and Bill took part in all of the activities of that busy football weekend, including a parade, football game, and dance on the State College campus. The blind date made no particular impression; Ida later admitted that it was not love at first sight. But the two continued to see each other. Bill remembered visiting Ida at Meredith "to the point of antagonizing" the college's authorities. Male visitors to Meredith, and to all women's colleges of the day, were subject to strict rules. To escape these rules, Meredith students often mingled with State College and Carolina men at one of the drugstores in downtown Raleigh. When Bill traveled north to work with DuPont, his contact with Ida was limited to the telephone, but when he returned, they picked up where they had left off. During the fall of 1941 and spring of 1942 their relationship matured into a love match, and the arrival of Bill's commission from the navy in the spring of 1942 forced the issue. The two decided, like many other couples in those war years, in favor of marriage.[8]

Bill Friday and Ida Howell were very different in some respects. To Lehman, Ida was outgoing – more outgoing, he thought, than Bill – with a good sense of humor. She was candid and acted fearlessly, often without consideration of the consequences. Actually, the lives of Bill Friday and Ida Howell had run in parallel tracks. Ida, at five feet, seven inches – three inches shorter than Bill – was a tall, striking brunette from Lumberton who had overcome extraordinary hardship to obtain a college education. Like Bill, she had suffered financial deprivation during the depression and the emotional deprivation of a parental separation.[9]

Her father, Alphonso Avery Howell, was born in Robeson County and had established a successful lumber business in Sumter, South Carolina. There, he met Pansie Edwins, an energetic schoolteacher and graduate of Winthrop College, from which she was nearly expelled for surreptitiously dancing. Phonso and Pansie were married in 1915, and for about a decade they lived in Sumter, raising a family of four children: Ida, who was born on December 22, 1919; an older brother, Avery; a younger sister, Pansie; and a younger brother, Russell. In the mid-1920s, however, the Howell family began to disintegrate. When Ida was in the first or second grade, Phonso's business in Sumter failed. The stress of hard times fell heavily on the family, as the Howells lost their home and were thrust into poverty. Pansie resumed teaching, taking the children with her to a position near Andrews, South Carolina, while Phonso moved back to Robeson County. Not until Ida began the fourth grade in Lumberton was the family reunited.[10]

Ida's father never recovered from the shock of losing his business, and he carried heavy emotional baggage. The Howell family hailed from the Backswamp neighborhood, in rural Robeson County, located along the Lumber River. Phonso's mother, Willa Purvis Howell, had died of typhoid fever when he was only six, and other members of the family had reared his two youngest sisters; he rarely saw them after Willa's death. Along with a brother and another sister – two other siblings were sent to relatives – Phonso was reared by an emotionally "cold" and "stubborn" father, a schoolteacher and tobacco farmer, and, as Ida put it, a family of "cold disciplinarians." Lacking "love and attention" and emotionally weak himself, he did not express emotions directly, even with his own family. Years later, his daughter admitted that she did not really know the inner workings of his personality. Phonso was often "impatient" when the small children needed to stop frequently during family road trips. According to Ida, he was a bright and educated man with a good mind, but not a reader of books; he did, however, faithfully read the *Charlotte*

Observer. He was a farmer but "never did the work of a farmer," relying instead on tenants, and he refused to work for others, preferring to be his own boss. The stress of economic failure fell heavily upon Phonso Howell. At some point after his return to Robeson County, he became an alcoholic, and drinking bouts would come and go. Meanwhile, his marriage became difficult; Ida described it as "on again, off again." By the time that the mother and children returned to Lumberton, Phonso and Pansie had "sort of split." Although they remained separated for some time, unlike the Fridays, they eventually divorced, and Phonso Howell remarried.[11]

Ida's mother emerged from this experience as a powerful and determined personality. Pansie, with a twin sister and nine other siblings, was born on a farm outside Orangeburg. Her roots were deeply sunk in rural South Carolina society. Of moderate means, her family had supported the Confederacy; one often-told story was that when Sherman's cavalry forces swept through South Carolina in early 1865, they stopped at the Edwins farm. Ida's grandfather, then only three or four years old, approached the officer and asked him, "Are you my papa?" The Union officer answered, "No, but I hope he comes home." He then ordered his men to spare the farm.[12]

The Edwinses, like most people of the land, had a large family. Ida's grandmother and namesake, Ida Miller, bore twelve children, and they kept bees and grew figs, melons, and peanuts. The Edwinses were an affectionate family; in contrast to the Howells, they expressed emotions openly. They were strong people; in the crisis that Ida's mother faced, with her husband unable to provide for the family, Pansie returned to the classroom – she taught English at Lumberton High School, served as school librarian, and even directed drummers in the school band. She loved poetry and English literature, often quoted Shakespeare, and listened to music by a windup gramophone. At night, she read by an oil lamp. But probably her best-remembered characteristic was her concern for people. She was "interested in just everything about people and the development of people," Ida recalled. In time, her impact on generations of Robeson children became legendary. Among Pansie's former students were future jurists David Britt and James McMillan.[13]

Despite the dissolution of her marriage, Ida's mother prevailed. She maintained family unity in the face of her husband's alcoholism. The emotional crisis of the family breakup coincided with the trauma of the Great Depression, and the Howells lived in homes without running water and at the kind of economic peril that threatened many Americans during the decade. Ida remembered vividly, for example, that her mother took her paycheck to the bank one Friday, only to see the bank close its doors on the same day. When the family farm was about to be lost, Pansie agreed to pay the taxes if the

Howells would agree to deed over Phonso's share to her children. After her divorce, Pansie, then in her mid-forties, lived with Ida and Bill in Chapel Hill; she received a degree in school health and then worked as a health educator in Chapel Hill and Rutherfordton. She spent her later years with the Fridays and her grandchildren, who formed a close attachment to her.[14]

Like Lath Friday, Pansie Howell realized that her children's escape from poverty lay in education; she implanted in them high aspirations and gave them unqualified support. From her adolescence, Ida was an achiever. While retaining her mother's emotional resiliency, Ida resembled her father physically; "if you look at me," she once said, "you see him." She was tall for her age and remained taller than many of her male peers. Ida also had her father's facial features, and her hands and feet were large like his. In high school, she served as center and, during her senior year, captain, of the school basketball team. She later described herself as a "pretty good" player who, in a tournament, once shot twenty-four out of twenty-five foul shots.[15]

Ida Howell was also an academic achiever. Valedictorian of her high school class, there was never any question about her attending college, and she was spurred on by her mother's determination and drive. Because of Pansie's struggle and perseverance through adversity, Ida was "given wings" to greater development and emotional and financial security. She was offered a scholarship by the University of California but could not afford the costs of transportation. Instead, she decided to attend Meredith College, where a $100 scholarship reduced the total cost of her education from $450 to $350.[16]

Ida found the restricted social environment at Meredith somewhat oppressive. In addition to the strict regulation of contacts with male students from nearby colleges, there was no dancing at Meredith and most students went to other campuses to dance. And weekly attendance at church was required. Yet Meredith opened up new intellectual avenues for Ida, and her college education was a central element in her emotional and intellectual evolution. A turning point for her came in a religion class, which was required for all students, conducted by an instructor who encouraged the mostly Baptist students to challenge biblical literalism. Although Ida had never been a fundamentalist, the experience of that religion class was eye-opening.[17]

An able student, Ida recalled that she was a good memorizer. But, like Bill Friday, she became committed, urged on by her mother, to securing a practical occupation. Pansie Howell discouraged her from teaching, and, although Ida eventually received a teaching degree from Meredith, she drifted into home economics, a discipline that trained women either in food preparation and management or for the teaching profession. Throughout college Ida struggled to make ends meet, for her $100 scholarship lasted only one year. Her father supported her to the extent that he permitted her and her older brother to manage an acre of tobacco, which yielded perhaps as much as $115 a month split between the two of them. With her mother paying her tuition, Ida earned spending money – $10 to $15 per month – at jobs provided for students by the NYA, first as a secretary in the Baptist Student Union office and then, for the remaining three years, as an NYA laboratory assistant for Ellen Brewer, who headed the Home Economics Department. Always careful with her money, Ida had also long received clothes from two aunts who had married millionaires; their children's castoffs carried her through high school and college.[18]

At Meredith, Ellen Brewer exerted a strong influence over Ida. From a distinguished Baptist family – Brewer's father, Charles Brewer, was president of Meredith – she had studied home economics at Columbia University and then returned to Meredith, where she established herself as a force on the faculty. Unmarried, she made her students her life by providing them with a role model of activism and influence for women outside the home. Her experience in the field also provided her with formidable contacts and influence. Nearing graduation, Ida applied for a job as a home economist with the Carolina Power and Light Company (CP&L) in Raleigh. When Brewer discovered that the company was not going to hire Ida, she called CP&L officials and urged them to reconsider. The next thing Ida knew, she had been offered a good position, even though she had no experience and "should have been out in the boondocks."[19]

For Ida, the CP&L job was ideal. Home economists did many of the things that salesmen did: they sold stoves and refrigerators, they taught customers how to use appliances, and they made arrangements for servicing them. But the attack on Pearl Harbor and the American declaration of war changed things. The total mobilization of national resources meant that appliances such as stoves and refrigerators could no longer be manufactured. With lower sales, CP&L put Ida and other home economists to work on public service projects, and she traveled to women's clubs in the state and explained basic principles of nutrition.[20]

Bill and Ida made arrangements for their wedding hastily; the ceremony took place two days after they were informed of Bill's call to service. Because all the local Baptist ministers were attending the annual state Baptist convention, Bill and Ida secured a Methodist minister and church. The families were summoned, and friends from CP&L and State College were invited by word of mouth. Pansie Howell and two of Ida's siblings arrived, as did Beth and Lath Friday along with Bill's grandmother and aunt. Outfitted in a wedding dress that cost thirty dollars, Ida married Bill on May 13, 1942, in the Hayes-

U.S. Naval Training School, Notre Dame, June 20, 1942. Friday is in front row, eighth from the left.

Barton Methodist Church in Raleigh. Lacking any money to pay for it, the couple decided to forego a reception, but Ellen Brewer intervened and hosted one at her two-bedroom log cabin in the woods near the church.[21]

In May and June 1942, Bill, commissioned as an ensign in the navy's ordnance division, spent three and a half weeks at Notre Dame University, where the navy had established a school to train the thousands of young men it was inducting. There, housed in a dormitory, he learned how to be an officer; the trainees were subject to regular drills and physical conditioning. One day, they even practiced by marching in a war bond parade through downtown South Bend, Indiana. "If the enemy had seen us," Friday said, "they would have invaded Lake Michigan without any fear of attack." Years later, watching Notre Dame play in its football stadium, he could clearly see the cadets marching under a hot Indiana sun. In the same stadium, Friday, who had been part of the second group of naval officers processed at Notre Dame, received his ensign's commission, one among a hodgepodge group of reservists whose blue serge uniforms showed every shade of blue. As Friday's commanding officer said with some disdain, that day every tailor in America had unloaded his material.[22]

From Notre Dame, Friday was stationed for about a month at the Naval Gun Factory in Washington, D.C., where he received specialized training in the components of weaponry – the handling of ammunition, gun mounts, and basic ordnance. Then he was transferred to the Naval Ammunition Depot (NAD) at St. Julien's Creek, near Norfolk, Virginia. Soon after his arrival, his superior, a captain, "lined us up against the wall" and went down the row, asking what each of them – all of whom were reservists – had done in civilian life. When he came to Friday, Bill described his technical education at State College and his DuPont experience. The captain said, "Take one step forward," and Friday realized that he "was in for trouble." As the only reservist trainee with an engineering degree, he was named plant operations manager for the depot. Another navy officer serving with Bill Friday later observed that "whatever you were trained for" before the war was now "rather irrelevant."[23]

Friday was an unlikely person for the job. When he told Romie Lefort of his new responsibilities, Lefort was aghast. His first thoughts, he recalled, were that Friday, whose training was in textile engineering while his own had been in chemical engineering, was ill-suited for a position that would require him to supervise the assembling and disassembling of high explosives. "Oh my Lord," Lefort thought to himself. He could not imagine Friday being in "that sort of work." Ida was also surprised, for she realized that he knew nothing about running an ammunition operation. But most astonished of all was Friday himself. At twenty-two years of age, he was suddenly thrust into a position of major responsibility supervising machinists, lathe operators, wood workers, sheet metal workers, electricians, and steam plant operators. As a maintenance officer, Friday remained on call twenty-four hours a day, directing the manufacturing and loading of naval ordnance. He worked under four lieutenant commanders, all of them prewar noncommissioned officers who had been suddenly elevated by the navy's post–Pearl Harbor expansion. Crusty veterans such as Ashton Smith, in his late sixties and with long experience in gunnery, taught the depot's officers most of what they needed to learn.[24]

Many of the young officers at the St. Julien's Creek depot were, like Friday, "ninety-day wonders" who went immediately from a campus environment into the military. Edward A. Smith had nearly completed Harvard Law School when he joined the navy. Smith was commissioned as an ensign and, after a quick training period, sent to St. Julien's Creek some weeks before Friday. Eager for more active duty, he regarded the assignment as too "tucked away," and he succeeded in obtaining a transfer about a year later. In his first encounter with Friday, Smith took him and another young ensign, Bill Holman, a Seattle attorney whom Friday had befriended, out to practice fire the .45-caliber sidearms that the navy required its officers to possess. Friday "knew what he was doing" with the gun; Holman did not. The difference between their experience with firearms was brought home to Smith when Holman's gun accidentally went off while Smith was retrieving a target on the firing range.[25]

When Ida arrived at St. Julien's Creek sometime in 1942, she and Bill briefly rented an apartment in nearby Portsmouth and then sublet an apartment halfway between downtown Norfolk and the Norfolk Navy Yard. Ida took a job as an assistant director of the Chesapeake and Potomac Telephone Company employee cafeteria in Norfolk, which housed a large defense plant, while Bill arose every morning to take a bus to the St. Julien's Creek depot in Craddock, Virginia. During the war Norfolk became a raucous boom town, with a large military population and a group of civilians lured to the city because of the wartime buildup. Much of Bill's meager ensign's pay and Ida's salary went toward rent in this "rent-crazy" region. Through careful budgeting – they sorted their income into five categories, each with its own envelope – they managed, but by month's end they had "absolutely nothing."[26]

At the telephone company's employee cafeteria, Ida's main responsibilities included planning the meals, purchasing the food, and managing personnel. The cafeteria served continuously 2,400 meals daily. The wartime buildup in the Norfolk area attracted thousands of women into the workforce; because of the rapid turnover during the war, as cafeteria workers were attracted to higher-paying jobs, Ida was constantly besieged by labor shortages; on various occasions, she served food, washed pots and pans, and helped to prepare meals herself. As she recalled, it was the hardest work she ever did, and the experience was "tiring and wearing." In late 1943 Ida quit work and the Fridays moved to the NAD base. They lived in a four-room, newly constructed house across the street from a magazine with three-foot-thick walls that was loaded with tons of high explosives.[27]

Friday worked daily in a tense environment. As the war effort accelerated and American naval forces became engaged in North Africa, Europe, and the Pacific, the St. Julien's Creek depot operated around the clock. Ida and Bill left the base only infrequently, although they socialized with other married officers at occasional dinners and bridge games. But the tension and sense of risk at NAD were constant. The Fridays realized that, living across the street from so much weaponry, an accident could blow them up while they slept. Ida recounted how her husband went down to the docked barges during a hurricane to secure them against the possibility of collision and a disastrous explosion. Working with high explosives constantly, Bill was always on his guard; the environment was "infinitely dangerous." Matches were prohibited; workers wore static-proof shoes and clothing to avoid any possibility of sparks. Some of the highly explosive material would ignite by contact with any kind of moisture, even perspiration. On one occasion, such material blew up in the face of a woman, set her on fire, and eventually killed her. Bill was among the first people to reach her, and the experience, according to Ida, "nearly ruined him." It was impossible to escape, physically and emotionally, the constantly dangerous atmosphere, and NAD workers eventually were numbed by the experience. In the end, the constant stress had a psychological impact, and subsequent decompression was not easy. For years after he left the service, Friday recalled, he immediately became tense whenever someone struck a match.[28]

Another problem at the depot was racial tension. Like the armed forces generally, the navy had long been segregated. Before the war, it had excluded blacks from shipboard duty, except as mess attendants. Yet even mess attendants in the 1930s became increasingly Asian in origin; by Pearl Harbor, the navy had succeeded, according to one military historian, in eliminating "almost all" blacks from that grade of service. In 1939 not one of the more than 10,000 commissioned officers and only 2,800 of the total 116,000 enlisted men were black. This policy continued in the early stages of World War II; Secretary of the Navy Frank Knox was said to have threatened resignation rather than implement integration. Still, the navy exerted aggressive efforts during the war. In April 1942 the navy first used blacks for general labor service; by 1944 it had integrated crews on twenty-five ships.[29]

At St. Julien's Creek, however, integration was the exception rather than the rule. The workforce was segregated by task and by residence; whites lived inside a tall fence surrounding the facility, blacks outside of it. Edward A. Smith, who commanded the eight hundred or so black sailors serving at the St. Julien's Creek NAD, recalled that there were "a lot of problems" related to race on base. Although black sailors believed that they had joined the navy for shipboard duty, they soon discovered themselves working in menial jobs for thirty dollars a month, next to white civilian workers who earned high wages while performing the same work. White workers frequently voiced their resentment of the black seamen, and the adjoining village of Craddock was staunchly segregated; the navy prohibited black seamen from visiting the town. Black seamen instead spent free time in Portsmouth, where they often encountered trouble from local authorities intent on controlling blacks in uniform.[30]

The combination of racial tension and a dangerous work environment meant that the potential for catastrophe was great. Disaster struck at Port Chicago, a naval ammunition depot in San Francisco Bay, on July 17, 1944, when two ships moored at its pier, the *E. A. Bryan* and the *Quinalt Victory*, erupted in a powerful explosion. While the *Bryan* was blown to bits, the force of the blast lifted the *Quinalt Victory* out of the water, turning it around and breaking it up some 500 feet away from its original mooring. A Coast Guard fire barge, the train carrying the explosives, and a 1,200-foot pier were destroyed in the blast, and 320 men lost their lives. The calamity resulted in 15 percent of all black casualties in the navy during World War II. The equivalent of 5 kilotons of TNT, the blast wrought heavy damage throughout the Port Chicago community and was the war's worst home-front disaster. The crisis culminated in a strike by the black workforce to protest working conditions when officials attempted to resume operations. The navy responded by summarily convicting 50 black sailors of mutiny.[31]

Although such a disaster did not occur at St. Julien's Creek, the ever-present racial tensions, which Edward Smith characterized as "seething," eventually boiled to the surface in what Friday called "one hell of a race riot."[32] Blacks were, according to Smith, treated "shabbily." Everywhere in the Fifth Naval District, headquartered in Charleston, South Carolina, the navy's attempt to integrate had resulted in bad feelings among southern white communities, and the black seamen were relegated to a second-class status. With a large detachment of black enlisted men, the St. Julien's depot was literally and figuratively a powder keg; in retrospect, Friday said later, some sort of conflict was inevitable. One night in the late summer of 1944, a big-band touring orchestra arrived for a USO (United Service Organization) show. A squabble developed when the show was made available to the all-white officer corps and the black seamen were excluded. The arrival of the orchestra, what Friday called "an issue rather than a reason," sparked a small riot. Some of the black enlisted men threw their heavy porcelain coffee mugs; as the mugs sailed through the air and damaged cars, other black seamen knifed the tires of parked automobiles. The outbreak was quelled only when the base's marine detachment restored order.[33]

The episode – NAD's first major racial incident – left a deep imprint. Fully aware of the disruptive potential of racial conflict on the war effort and sensitive to the mixed results of the integration experiment, naval officials acted quickly. Within a week of the riot, they cashiered the base's commanding officer, Captain James S. Woods, an older career naval officer. Meanwhile, the navy dealt with the black enlisted men as summarily and, in Friday's view, as unfairly as they treated the black "mutineers" at Port Chicago. Those with any previous disciplinary record – including minor infractions such as being late for train passage – were called before naval investigators; within a day, they were shipped out. The result was a "general, and rather massive, housecleaning." But the housecleaning was done in a "swift, mean way," without much consideration for due process of law. The transferred men received a damning mark on their military records, and the all-black barracks outside the depot's main gate was closed. The handling of the case revealed to Friday how a bureaucracy could easily administer injustice; he would later regard the incident crucial in shaping his attitudes toward personnel management.[34]

The riot prompted the navy to reconsider integration, and this coincided with a changed role for the St. Julien's Creek depot. Toward the end of the war, NAD became less a facility for the production of ammunition; by 1945 larger production and storage centers elsewhere – Crane, Indiana; Hawthorne, Nevada; McAlester, Oklahoma; and Hastings, Nebraska – figured more prominently. These massive plants, all of them located in large inland locations, contained state-of-the-art, fully modernized production equipment. The St. Julien's Creek depot, in contrast, possessed older equipment and an antiquated plant; its production methods were safe but less productive, and the depot increasingly specialized in research and development of new and captured weapons. But even as the war wound down, the danger continued: German and Japanese weaponry, Friday recalled, was "shoddy stuff," hurriedly assembled and consequently dangerous to handle.[35]

Friday's wartime experiences had a profound influence on him. For one thing, the military brought him into contact with a cross section of people from around the country. Many of his fellow officers were trained at Ivy League colleges; Edward Smith had attended Harvard Law School, while another navy acquaintance, Jim Stone, was a Brown graduate. Stone, who was as emotional and impulsive as Friday was cool and dispassionate, often teased Bill about his southern drawl. Friday felt acutely the narrowness of his State College technical training. For him, like many Americans of the World War II generation, the war was an educational experience that dramatized the contrast between the wealth of the nation and the poverty of his own region. He remembered, in particular, feeling the "enormous loss" that resulted from southern poverty.[36]

After the passage of five decades, Friday harbored little nostalgia for his wartime adventures. He had seen firsthand the waste of war. Sensitive to violence and human misery and immersed in a stressful environment, Friday emerged from the conflict with emotional scars. As an officer in a depot that was transporting the weapons of death, he constantly thought that he was killing "more people than anybody else." His responsibility for death troubled him deeply; he later declared that it did not let his conscience rest.[37]

The experience also reinforced Friday's habits of hard work. Rarely had he operated according to set hours. "Whatever the task was, it was there to be done," he recalled, "whatever the need was, it had to be met." But the war years left him with little taste for the military's autocratic style. There was "nothing romantic about it, in my book"; in all, it was a "hard experience," and, though it was "terribly necessary [and] . . . essential," he would not freely repeat it. As a reservist, he had been an interloper in the military bureaucracy; in terms of advancement, he had realized that he was encroaching on career officers and that there was "no place" for him. The strict sense of hierarchy and the "inhibiting influence" of the military chain of command further rankled, for he preferred a freer and more innovative atmosphere in which to work. Having achieved the rank of full lieutenant by war's end, Friday was offered a permanent commission, but he refused it.[38]

In the last months of the war, Friday, "worn out" and "very nervous," with his weight down to 155 pounds, was hospitalized for a few weeks for catarrhal fever in the Portsmouth Naval Hospital. Following his release, he was assigned for several months in the autumn of 1945 to the admiral's staff of the commandant of the naval district in Charleston, where he served as duty officer, a position he later described as "a mustering out kind of experience." Life in Charleston was generally pleasant. Ida's uncle, Charlie Weinheimer, who was married to Pansie's sister, was a school principal there, and the Fridays stayed with the Weinheimers until they found an apartment at Battery Park near the waterfront. Their stay in Charleston was a "sort of recuperating" time for Bill and provided an opportunity to become acquainted with the community.[39]

Like many veterans, Friday eagerly anticipated his discharge. While in Charleston, he and Ida discussed the future. They concluded that both needed more education. Friday now believed that his future lay with the law; he confided to his wife then that he had always wanted to enter that profession. The law would provide him with greater insight into more things. Moreover, he hoped to capitalize on his experience in textile manufacturing by entering the world of corporate finance via a law degree. In the fall of 1945, Friday began sending inquiries to law schools while he read Roscoe Pound's study of the common law and Albert J. Beveridge's biography of Chief Justice Marshall. He applied to Harvard and was turned down. He then telephoned Robert H. Wettach, dean of the University of North Carolina's School of Law, to see if he could apply. When Wettach determined that Friday had a State College diploma, he told him to come to Chapel Hill.[40]

Discharged formally from the navy on February 1, 1946, Bill and Ida packed their belongings into their Chevrolet coupé and left Charleston. After visiting with relatives and friends, they arrived in Chapel Hill on February 7. The village seemed unwelcoming: ice covered the ground, "a fierce, cold wind blew," and the Fridays had to compete for housing with a crush of returning veterans and their wives. After lunch that day at the Carolina Inn, they immediately began searching – just as Friday had done his first year at State College – for residents who were willing to take in roomers. From the center of Chapel Hill, Bill and Ida walked down Cameron Avenue: she took one side, he the other. At the end of the street, near the university power plant, Bill knocked on a door. A woman invited him in and called a friend to ask if she had any room. While waiting, Bill recognized from a photograph the woman's husband – still in military service – as a former State College teacher. The connection gave the Fridays, desperate for shelter, a "talking point"; that, according to Ida, was "all it took."[41]

The woman offered them temporary lodging until an apartment, owned by Chapel Hill Esso distributor "Obie" Davis, became available. The Fridays' new lodgings – and their first introduction to Chapel Hill residence – were spartan: an unceiled attic, one iron bed, a suitcase that served as a dresser, and four nails on a column that held up the roof and served as a closet. Their stay in the Cameron Avenue attic did not last long, however. The landlady did not like the fact that Ida washed her laundry and hung it out to dry in the attic room. After only forty-eight hours as a new student at the UNC Law School in Manning Hall, Friday learned, on meeting a tearful Ida for lunch at the Carolina Inn, that she had packed all of their belongings into their car. "What on earth has happened?" he asked. Ida then explained that guests had arrived at their landlady's and the woman had "literally dumped us into the streets of Chapel Hill."[42]

Their eviction was a low point, for it coincided with Bill's discouraging introduction to the UNC Law School. As in other parts of the university, returning veterans were filling the law school ranks. During the war the law school had become so depleted that, at its nadir, only fifteen students matriculated. Future North Carolina governor and senator Terry Sanford, who attended law school at Carolina just before the war, remembered the intimate atmosphere that prevailed during wartime. Students "knew all the professors and all about them," and most classes were, in effect, seminars. This changed, however, when the war ended. The veterans' mustering out created a tidal wave, as first-year enrollment swelled to forty-five in the autumn of 1945 and then, in February 1946, to over one hundred, the largest first-year class to that time in the history of the law school. The great majority of the new entrants – some 80 percent – were, like Friday, veterans, while Friday's class included the largest number ever of women students. Meanwhile, the law faculty, which had consisted of the "Great Seven" – Robert Wettach, Frank William Hanft, Maurice T. Van Hecke, Albert Coates, Fred B. McCall, M. S. Breckinridge, and John Dalzell – was expanded. Among the newer faculty was Henry Parker Brandis Jr. A native of Salisbury, Brandis had received the LL.B. degree from Columbia University in 1931, practiced law in New York City for two and a half years, and then become an associate director of the UNC Institute of Government. He joined the law school faculty in 1940 but left to serve as a lieutenant commander in the naval reserve from 1942 to 1945. Returning in 1945, Brandis became dean of the UNC Law School in 1949.[43]

Friday's early days in law school were a "very hard grind." While still occupying the Cameron Avenue attic, he made the mistake, in preparation for his first day of classes, of opening his real property casebook. Unfortunately for Friday, the first five cases appeared in Latin, a language that he could not read. This reaffirmed his lack of classical training, and Friday began to wonder about his "brilliant start." Like most veterans, he found the transition to academic life difficult. He discovered, in the absence of required class attendance, the lack of grading until end-of-term exams, as well as the case method of teaching, a "difference of day and night" compared to his State College experience. Even more difficult was decompression from the navy. He often found himself able to concentrate for only thirty minutes at a time before he had to get up and walk around.[44]

Friday was not alone in that decompression, of course. He remembered a law school student, a navy veteran, who had experienced combat duty as a pilot and had won two navy crosses, the highest honor that the service awarded. In the seat in front of Friday, he would methodically but unconsciously tear strips from a newspaper during the course of class, encircling himself with inch-wide pieces. He was "just a bundle of nerves." His case was not atypical; "you could replicate that in half the guys in the room." Most faculty members were sensitive to veteran decompression. Some of them, such as Brandis, had served during the war; others, like William B. Aycock, joined the law school faculty after graduating earlier than the rest of the veterans.[45]

Nonetheless, during the first semester Friday was filled with self-doubt. He wondered whether he had made the right decision in attending law school. The eviction from Cameron Avenue crystallized this crisis of self-doubt. Unable to read the cases in property law, Bill told Ida that he was not "burning" to study the law and that perhaps they should pack their belongings and leave. Ida refused. Although there were other times that spring when Bill believed that he was "going under," the luck of the Fridays eventually changed. Evicted from the Cameron Avenue attic, they drove south on Pittsboro Street, where they found temporary housing for a week with a neighbor of Dickson "Dick" Phillips, a classmate of Bill's at the law school. After a week in the furnished one-room apartment, the Fridays took up permanent residence at Obie Davis's apartment, several blocks north of campus, at 111 North Street.[46]

For both Ida and Bill, the move to Chapel Hill opened new vistas. A small college town that housed a student body of several thousand, Chapel Hill faced a future of expanding enrollment, faculty, and facilities. In 1946, however, the town and campus had a comfortable, personal feel, and a sense of shared purpose that had united the campus since World War I still prevailed. A student of the 1940s remembered Carolina as being located in the middle of "vast forests"; it was "out in the middle of nowhere" and "way out in the country." In glorious isolation, Chapel Hill had a "special magic about it." The 1940s were a heady time for the university, which was in the middle of a golden age. During the presidency of Edward Kidder Graham (1913–18), the University of North Carolina had become a force in the affairs of the state, firmly identifying itself with economic development and progress. High levels of financial support continued under Graham's successor, Harry Woodburn Chase; despite a perilous budgeting situation in the 1930s, UNC–Chapel Hill emerged as the leading public university in the South, with a world-class faculty and a national student body.[47]

There was camaraderie among Carolina students, faculty, and administrators. Members of the faculty, emulating the practice of Frank Porter Graham during his presidency (1930–49), knew students by their first names. There were notable personalities among them, to be sure. Howard Washington Odum, the leading southern sociologist of his generation, was nearing the end of more than three decades in Chapel Hill. Edgar Wallace Knight in education and Paul Green (resigned 1944) and Frederick Koch (died 1944) in drama had been other leading figures on the Chapel Hill campus of the 1940s; they possessed large egos, would debate issues vigorously, but shared a common dedication to the welfare of the university. This was "one big community," according to Bill Friday, with "very dominant uncles and aunts and cousins in it" who were all striving toward the same objective.[48]

The law school faculty – Wettach, Van Hecke, Brandis, Hanft, and Herbert R. Baer – set an example for Friday of public service. Hanft, who taught jurisprudence, held forth every week in a Sunday school class at the University Methodist Church; although Baptists, the Fridays attended Hanft's discussions of the philosophy of religion.[49] Albert Coates, also on the law faculty, had founded the UNC Institute of Government, which was conceived as a center of training for North Carolinians in public service. The Institute of Government was established in 1931, but it received scant support during the depression. Coates sold a Chapel Hill lot on which he and his wife had planned to build a house in order to finance the institute. When a new building was constructed on Franklin Street in the late 1930s and he again faced the problem of scarce funds, Coates simply told the contractor excavating the basement to dig slowly while he raised the money. Not until 1942 did the institute become a formal part of the UNC administrative structure. A member of the law school faculty since 1923, Coates had been always on the alert for talented, public-spirited young men, whom he sought to steer toward public service. With a raspy voice and a strong determination, he often told his protégés that the state was "bad off" and needed their dedication. "My God, boys," he would say, "we've got to work morning, noon, and night, weekdays and Sunday."[50]

And work they did. When the war ended, Coates brought a new cadre of students and recent graduates into the Institute of Government. Bill Cochrane was a Carolina graduate who served in the navy during the war; mustered out in 1944, he fell under Coates's spell. Cochrane headed up the institute's efforts in postwar planning and conducted the first training schools for state prison officials. He later described Coates as "just one of the most extraordinary people I've ever known." When Terry Sanford, another Carolina graduate and Coates protégé, returned from wartime service with the army paratroopers, he completed law school and then was given responsibility for the Institute of Government's program to train state and local police officers. Sanford also operated Boys State, a program designed to develop political leadership among Tar Heel youth, and Friday worked one summer as a counselor in the program. Friday later described Coates as "an institution himself," a "very complex man" with "a lot of humor" but who was "bright and hard driving."[51]

The Chapel Hill campus was filled with veterans; Carolina, remembered Terry Sanford, "was an entirely different kind of campus" in the immediate postwar years. Like Friday, these veterans were keenly aware of the time they had lost during the war and were determined to get on with their lives. Often arriving with families, they were generally in their mid-to-late twenties, but some of them were older. Bill Aycock, who had graduated from State College four years before Friday, had taught high school, received an M.A. in history, and supervised the state NYA program before entering the service. At thirty years of age, he was married and had a small child. Terry Sanford, who lived above Bill and Ida in the North Street apartment house, had already begun a long career in public service. William Dees, also married, remembered that there "wasn't very much playing going on," for this was a "more mature group than you would ordinarily run into in law school." The atmosphere, consequently, was very serious, and students were "ready to do business." These veterans were, Friday maintained, "the hardest working group of people that I've ever been associated with."[52]

Most of his classmates, Friday said, possessed a "clear vision of what they wanted to do." They exhibited a missionary zeal about North Carolina and the university's role in state development. From their ranks would come many of the dominant figures in the post-1945 public life of the state. Along with Friday, they included John R. Jordan Jr., a future state senator and the third elected chairman of the UNC Board of Governors; he would remain a long-time Friday ally. William Dees of Goldsboro had graduated from the University of North Carolina in 1941. He first met Friday during his senior year through the North Carolina Federation of Student Governments. While also serving in the navy, he ran into Friday at the St. Julien's Creek depot, and one evening during the war they ate supper together. Dees later became the first elected chairman of the UNC Board of Governors. Joining Dees in the law school in the autumn of 1945 was Bill Aycock, who in 1957 would become chancellor of the university at Chapel Hill. Other future legislators and state leaders included L. P. McLendon Jr., J. Russell Kirby, H. Patrick Taylor Jr., and Terry Sanford.[53]

Friday soon developed an inner circle of friends. The Fridays and the Sanfords, as neighbors, became close. Although graduating ahead of them, Sanford kept in close touch with Friday, Aycock, Dees, Phillips, and Jordan and their wives. The Aycocks lived about two miles south of town; the Deeses occupied one of the few apartments at the Carolina Inn. Often six or eight of them ate together. Dees, Friday, Aycock, Jordan, and Phillips belonged to a study group in law school; as was true at most law schools, it was a basic unit in which students not only studied but learned the law. The members of the study group and their wives, in turn, socialized regularly.[54]

Friday threw himself into law school activities with his usual energy and drive. Operating at a disadvantage because of his technical training at State College, he was never a superior student. Bill Aycock was ranked first in his class and thus became editor of the *Law Review*; just below him in class standing were associate editors William Dees and Dick Phillips; Jordan was also on the *Law Review* staff. In contrast, Friday was the only member of his study group who was not elected. His contemporaries recalled that he studied hard; Dees would see him frequently at his study desk on the third floor of Manning Hall. Jordan characterized him as a "good" and "thorough" student, despite his absence from the *Law Review*. Friday's downfall, according to Aycock, was examinations; he did not test well. Yet he was generally acknowledged to be a highly intelligent student who contributed intellectually to the study group.[55]

Performance in the classroom had never been among Friday's strengths. He later admitted that he was most interested in the "human side of the law," while commercial and property law held little attraction for him. Hard work, skill with people, and flashes of organizational genius were Friday's attributes: and these qualities certainly emerged during his early days at Chapel Hill. To peers such as Aycock, Friday was "an outgoing person" who genuinely liked people. Friday did not "contrive friendships"; these came naturally. He radiated "friendship by his very presence." People responded to that, as they did to his impeccable standards of personal behavior.[56]

On a much smaller scale than at State College, he became involved in extracurricular affairs. With Sanford and Cochrane, Friday joined the state

Young Democrats Club; they managed the election of O. Max Gardner Jr., son of a former governor, as YDC president. With the group meeting at various locations, including the North Street apartments of Sanford and Friday, Cochrane recalled that, on account of YDC activities, he "saw a lot of Bill." Because the law school had become depleted during the war, it lacked any semblance of student organization. Working with Dean Wettach, Friday helped to reconstruct the UNC Law School Student Association. Wettach gave Friday and other students a room in the basement of Manning Hall, and, during his last year in law school, Friday was drafted as president of the student association.[57]

Meanwhile, Ida Friday was also drawn into Chapel Hill affairs. During the first weeks in Chapel Hill, she encountered a Meredith classmate studying at the UNC School of Public Health who told her about the availability of scholarships. Because of Ida's home economics major and science background, she seemed a natural candidate. Her friend then introduced her to two of the most important members of the School of Public Health, Lucy Shields Morgan and Eunice Nickerson Tyler, who were part of what a recent historian has called a "unique enclave of female academics" at Carolina. Largely through their influence, Ida in May 1946 obtained a two-year fellowship from the General Education Board (GEB), a Rockefeller philanthropy long involved in southern education. Paying her tuition and field training fees plus one hundred dollars a month, the stipend was a godsend to Ida, who took courses during the 1946–47 academic year and then conducted field training work for three months in the Bedford-Marshall Health District, near Shelbyville, Tennessee, where Lucy Morgan's brother, H. A. Morgan, served as the local health officer.[58]

Ida and Bill established a lifelong relationship with Lucy Morgan and Eunice Tyler. Morgan, daughter of the president of the University of Tennessee, Harcourt A. Morgan, and granddaughter of a Louisiana state superintendent of public instruction, taught high school biology in Tennessee, Texas, and North Carolina. In 1937 she received a fellowship to pursue graduate work at Yale University, where she earned the Ph.D. a year later. During World War II the U.S. Public Health Service recruited Morgan to develop public health education in Raleigh and Fayetteville, and in 1942 she joined the UNC School of Public Health in Chapel Hill. At Carolina she attracted scores of students, most of them women from around the South as well as from developing nations who were seeking to build up a public health infrastructure. For public health workers, the influence of Morgan and Tyler was something akin to that of Frank Porter Graham for UNC at large. Public health educators like Ida Friday became experts in community organization and development, but they were not merely technicians. Ida and her public health coworkers were imbued with a liberal faith in the improvability of human-kind; Morgan and Tyler were, for their day, advanced racial liberals, and they helped to establish a cooperative teaching program with North Carolina College for Negroes in Durham that brought blacks, for the first time, into Carolina's classrooms. Their egalitarianism affected Ida, who had grown up in segregated Robeson County. By the time she completed her degree, she had had her sights elevated and her feelings and heart "raised to a different level."[59]

Morgan and Tyler were both intrigued by Ida, and after their first meeting with her, they told her that they wanted to meet Bill. The two professors invited the Fridays to their apartment across from the School of Public Health, and they immediately befriended Bill. The semester had not yet begun, they told Ida, and the GEB fellowship would not become available until the summer. Could she simply come to the School of Public Health and volunteer her time instead, thus gaining some important experience? Friday, jumping at the opportunity, became an office volunteer and "did any and everything needed." Beginning her M.S. degree in public health in the summer of 1946, she completed the program and was graduated on June 8, 1947.[60]

Ida's involvement in public health exposed both Fridays to Chapel Hill's new influences. With support from the GI Bill and the GEB fellowship, they lived comfortably in their North Street basement apartment. Their exposure to the ideas swirling through the Chapel Hill campus, she recalled, "made Bill and me over, both of us." They made it a point to attend every major lecture on campus. Bill accompanied Ida when there was a "special somebody," such as Eleanor Roosevelt or J. Robert Oppenheimer, on campus. As a result, Bill, always a keen listener, absorbed new ideas, information, and attitudes; as Ida said, "a great deal rubbed off."[61]

By the summer of 1948, however, the Fridays faced a major career decision. Taking classes during the previous two summers, Bill completed law school in June 1948. That summer, he and classmates Henry Colton and Woodrow Sims met each day on the top floor of Manning Hall at 8:00 A.M. and prepared for the bar exam; after this grueling regimen, Friday passed the exam and was admitted to the North Carolina bar. But the new crop of lawyers in Friday's class faced an uncertain job market. No swarms of recruiters came to campus, and much of the hiring was done by word of mouth. Friday's intention had been to obtain work in corporate law for a textile manufacturer, and he realized halfway through law school that he would never practice law in a courtroom. He was especially interested in Burlington Industries, then the largest textile company in the world, which maintained a large legal depart-ment. Near the end of his last term at law school, Friday visited Burlington's headquarters at Greensboro, but his interview did not go well. As he remembered it, they turned him away.[62]

Friday hesitated to continue the search for work as a lawyer, chiefly because of limitations on his ability to move. Ida's GEB fellowship obligated her to provide four years of public health service – paid or unpaid – in North Carolina; by the time Bill finished law school, she had served two years. Ida, concerned about where they might live in the state, expressed a strong preference for a community where she could get a job that she enjoyed. After the rebuff by Burlington Industries, Bill and Ida decided that he would look for an interim job that would enable them to remain in Chapel Hill.[63]

That opportunity came when the dean of students at Carolina, Fred H. Weaver, offered Friday a job as his assistant. For years Romie Lefort, who knew Frank Graham well because of his involvement in State College student affairs, had taken "every opportunity" to tell Graham about Friday. "You're gonna miss a bet," he would explain, "if you don't get Bill Friday in your administrative work there." Weaver had known Friday since Bill's State College days, and when Friday entered law school, they often had meals together at the Carolina Inn. Prodded by Graham and Chancellor Robert Burton House, Weaver was also encouraged by Albert Coates, who told him of a "bright young man that's finishing his law degree" who might serve Weaver well as an assistant. When Weaver asked Coates about Friday's abilities, Coates half seriously responded that he was "the kind of man who might be president of the University someday." If Friday was that qualified, Weaver rejoined, why had Coates not hired him on the Institute of Government staff? Coates responded that Friday would be better in administration than research. Weaver then called Friday into his office upstairs in South Building, where the university administration was located, and offered him the job of assistant dean.[64]

Entering into university administration, Friday later said, was the "last thought" in his mind. "There was no premeditation about choosing the University as a career"; that had never occurred to him. Indeed, he did not immediately accept Weaver's offer, saying that he wanted to discuss it with Ida. Walking home from South Building down the shaded lanes of Chapel Hill toward the North Street apartment, he thought about his response to Weaver. The decision was one of the most difficult that Friday ever made. When Ida endorsed the idea, they both realized that it was "quite a gamble," for he was abandoning a legal career to enter into yet another world – the unique world, created by Frank Porter Graham, of the administration of the University of North Carolina. His move to South Building in September 1948 had been accidental, as he later told an interviewer, yet his years on campus would be marked by a meteoric ascent to power.[65]

BILL Friday and Fred Weaver were, in many ways, differing personalities. Raised in Aberdeen, North Carolina, Weaver attended Carolina, where he was graduated in 1937 and where he came under the spell of Frank Porter Graham and the dean of students, Francis Bradshaw. Following graduation Weaver became a teaching fellow in the School of Commerce and then, from 1938 to 1941, an assistant dean of students. He served as a navy pilot in the war, and after his discharge in January 1946 he was appointed dean of men under Bradshaw's successor, Ernest L. Mackie. Weaver became dean of students in September 1948, several weeks before he hired Friday as his assistant. Tall, strikingly handsome, a tennis player, philosopher, and poet, Weaver struck some as "very Ivy League."[1]

Friday, unassuming, modest, and humble, became Weaver's perfect complement, and the two made an effective team. While Weaver was "elegant, tall, and intellectual," a dignified dean, Friday was a low-keyed figure with his ear to the ground, the UNC administration's direct link to the student body. Friday's main concerns were student government and student affairs, and during the next two years – including a stint as the acting dean of students for the 1949–50 year – he immersed himself in student problems. Friday demonstrated a combination of toughness and understanding; as Ida observed, he was firm when he needed to be but was "kind in it." The students were his charges, and he considered it his responsibility to "look after them." Once, he drove a pregnant coed from Chapel Hill – Carolina accepted women in their junior year – to her home in Charlotte Court House, Virginia. On other occasions, Friday dealt discreetly with undergraduates who, exhibiting highspirited energy, became involved in adolescent carousing.[2]

Early in his tenure, he developed a close relationship with William T. Sloan,

Chapel Hill chief of police since October 1935. Sloan, who sent all six of his children to Carolina, was unusually tolerant of student behavior. "The students who come to the University," he once said, "are good boys from good families, and they don't aim to give trouble." His approach was to "go along with the students, to talk with the leaders and to iron out problems before they became big ones." Sloan often made early morning telephone calls to Friday, who arranged for the lenient treatment of students so that no permanent mark would go on their record. After the editor of the *Daily Tar Heel* engaged in a drunken drive around the Old Well, at the center of campus, Friday heard of the incident from Sloan. The next day Friday called the student in and informed him of "a report" to this effect. When the student "changed color," Friday told him: "We're not going to let this happen again, are we?"[3]

There was, however, another side to his work in the dean of students' office, which he called "the unhappy side." On some occasions, Friday delivered bad news about a death in the family – a duty that he never handled easily – while on others he told students that they had flunked out of school.[4] Yet the fit between Friday and student affairs was a good one. He was not a harsh disciplinarian; those who saw student affairs as "cops and robbers," he remembered, were "in the wrong place." He believed that his job meant helping students "find their way" in their adolescent crises as well as in the day-to-day affairs of operating financial aid and student organizations, such as student government, publications, social events, and fraternities. Friday made it a point to befriend student leaders; he met with student body presidents at least twice a year. He viewed his experience as valuable in helping him to determine whether or not he really wanted to make a career in university administration.[5]

Although Chapel Hill during the late 1940s appeared calm and idyllic, there were underlying tensions. In Friday's first year in Weaver's office, the Carolina Forum, a student organization that sponsored outside speakers, invited Communist Party official and *Daily Worker* editor John Gates to campus. But Gates was then under indictment under the Smith Act, which Congress had enacted in 1940, forbidding any persons to advocate the violent overthrow of the government. Despite Chapel Hill's reputation for tolerance and free speech, Gates's invitation tested the administration's patience. On the evening of January 12, 1949, at 6:30 P.M., just before Gates was to speak, Chancellor Robert Burton House, acting without the knowledge of either Friday or Weaver, canceled the speech. When Gates subsequently attempted to speak at a local gasoline station, the attendant chased him off. Finally, facing what the *Daily Tar Heel* called a "continued din of booing and heckling," he delivered a brief address in front of Chapel Hill High School, then on West Franklin Street.[6]

The flood of veterans during the three or four years after the war helped to create an unconventional student body. Along with other young married faculty and staff members, the Fridays had taken up residence in Victory Village, a postwar prefabricated housing development constructed to ease the housing shortage in the late 1940s and 1950s. But Victory Village also included undergraduate veterans, such as football star Charles "Choo-Choo" Justice and his wife. Compared to former UNC student bodies, Friday recalled, the GI classes of 1946–49 were like "left and right." Veterans, most of them in their late twenties and married, were impatient with the closely supervised traditions of student life; they wanted their afternoon beers, Friday said, "and you had better get out of the way." These war-hardened adults were simply unwilling to abide by the old rules, and the university had to adjust to that fact. The student leadership that invited John Gates to campus was composed of "very activist oriented, career-oriented people" who regarded the campus culture of the 1930s as "kid stuff." The challenge for Friday was to keep "some sense of balance," and during this era he often put in eighty-hour work weeks.[7]

By the early 1950s the veteran population was declining and the traditional character of the UNC student body was reasserting itself. Friday himself was aware of the resulting tension between nonveterans and veterans. Richard Jenrette, who entered Chapel Hill in the autumn of 1947, found veterans "more sophisticated," more worldly, and older. The students of Jenrette's age group, in contrast, were interested in fraternities, sororities, and football games – that is, the same activities that had occupied students of the 1930s. "Worldly-wise" and "world weary" students gave way to the postwar hedonists of the 1950s who were avowedly nonpolitical and conservative in their social tastes. Jenrette's age group, he recalled, grew up "in the shadow of these older people."[8]

Friday successfully bridged these tensions. Arnold King, a longtime Carolina faculty member who worked as associate dean of the graduate school, recalled that the students became "very fond" of Friday because of his empathy and his ability to reach out to people and understand them. No one else in the dean's office came close to exhibiting these qualities. Even though he was a State College graduate, noted the student yearbook, the *Yackety Yack*, in 1949, Friday was still "worthy to be an important influence in the life of the Carolina gentleman." When Weaver took a leave of absence during the 1949–50 year for graduate study in American civilization and history at Harvard, Friday served as acting dean, with Ray Jeffries as his assistant dean. At the end of that year, yearbook editors described Friday effusively. He was, they wrote, "to all students a living example of young Carolina leadership." In him, students found "competent and able guidance." As Friday recalled, during his tenure at Fred Weaver's office he became involved in students' lives to an extent that he would never again duplicate.[9]

Friday's work in Weaver's office helped to refine his leadership and administrative styles. Out of his boyhood and adolescent experiences in Dallas he had developed an unusually well defined notion of obligation, a commitment to public service, and a restless drive for recognition. In college, the war, and law school he obtained a measure of that recognition, but he found his true element in the unique setting of a university campus. In June 1949 he returned to deliver the commencement address to seniors at the Dallas High School. Only twelve years earlier, Pleasant E. Monroe, president of Lenoir-Rhyne College in Hickory, had told Friday and other Dallas graduates that the future of human society rested with young Americans. That prediction had proved true, Friday said, and the terrible experience of World War II revealed a darker side: Americans had inadequately developed their "moral and spiritual foundations."[10]

To Friday, the University of North Carolina was crucial in meeting the challenge of developing leadership in the postwar period. Its functioning was a "public business and a public trust," he told the New Bern Junior Chamber of Commerce in June 1949; university administrators had a "responsibility and a privilege" to communicate to the state's citizenry. The university produced graduates who were "men of knowledge, courage, conviction, forthrightness, and integrity; men who want to achieve meaningful and significant gains for human welfare." Observing that North Carolina ranked near the bottom of the national averages in per capita income, wages, and education, he urged that the university lead the state in economic progress. Genuine leadership lay in knowing and understanding, seeking the truth and the right, and faithfulness to the public trust. It did not arise inherently from accumulated wealth. Rather, true leadership became possible only when "free men in a free society" worked, thought, and acted in "the interest and service of their fellow man."[11]

The university administrators who surrounded him in South Building deeply affected Friday's conception of leadership. The UNC administration, in the late 1940s, depended on four key people. Billie Curtis, Frank Porter Graham's secretary, kept the UNC president's records, managed his schedule, and looked after him in "the professional sense." Claude Teague, a Chatham County native who was graduated from the university in Chapel Hill in 1912 and worked as a school principal and superintendent, had become business

Friday with Robert Burton House. (Courtesy of the North Carolina Collection)

manager of the North Carolina College for Women in 1930. In 1943 he joined the university staff as business manager. Robert Burton House, who was graduated from the university in 1916, served as UNC's executive secretary beginning in 1926, dean of administration of the Chapel Hill campus after 1934, and chancellor after 1945. Described by one contemporary as "a very popular ol' corn pone" and a "good inside man," House was folksy and good-humored. He often warmed up for public meetings by playing the harmonica, telling audiences that he had brought his "notes" with him.[12] William D. "Billy" Carmichael Jr., born in Durham in 1900, was graduated from Durham High School in 1917 and then attended the university, where he excelled in athletics. He was business manager of the *Daily Tar Heel* and editor in chief of the student humor magazine *Tar Baby*. Thereafter he left Chapel Hill for New York City, where he earned a small fortune in advertising and on the stock market. In 1940 he returned to Chapel Hill as controller of the consolidated university and Frank Porter Graham's right-hand man.[13]

Friday had become casually acquainted with Billy Carmichael while at State College, but it was during his law school years that he developed a closer working relationship. On this basis, and especially when Friday moved into South Building, he and Carmichael quickly became "working partners." Carmichael served as mentor to Friday. Carmichael's primary strengths were meeting and dealing with people, especially with industrial and financial leaders who did not fully understand Frank Graham and harbored suspicions of his social and racial liberalism. Carmichael liked the give-and-take of meetings and conversation; although he had never given a speech before arriving in Chapel Hill in 1940, he eventually became much in demand across the state as a speaker. Carmichael was also instrumental in obtaining donations from wealthy Tar Heels. He and Graham "complemented each other"; Carmichael never sought to upstage Graham, but he could interpret him to the power structure in finance and textiles. According to Friday, Carmichael understood the public pulse "awfully well."[14]

With his background and interests, it was only natural, as Ida Friday later said, that the UNC faculty would not always like Billy Carmichael. Yet he shone among administrators, legislators, and the business community. One colleague who worked in South Building in the 1950s described him as "very effective" in dealing with the legislature. Carmichael got along "very well" with his peers in university administration because of his geniality, democratic style, and self-deprecating sense of humor. Among administrators and legislators alike, he was regarded as a clever man who often could turn tense conflicts into opportunities for humor. Ida Friday subsequently described his "fine, buoyant, joyful way" that won over people to his cause; according to Bill, he was "a great one for laughter" who exerted "great influence with his humor." Typical of his repertoire were jokes about Roman Catholics; as a devout Roman Catholic himself, he once said that "any convenient telephone booth" could house a convocation of North Carolina Roman Catholics.[15]

Billy Carmichael was a complex personality whose exterior humor and warmth were counterbalanced by introspection. Bill Friday saw a tender spot in Carmichael. Despite his bravado, Carmichael was an "exceedingly sensitive person" and a "very gentle man" who never deliberately hurt anyone. A person of enormous drive and energy, he was a dominant personality who worked himself to "the point of exhaustion." Carmichael, who never permitted anyone to drive while he was in the car, drove so fast that Friday often believed that his life was "hanging by a thread." Only once, when he became sick from food poisoning on a trip to Kinston, did Carmichael give up the wheel, and Friday put him in the back seat to sleep while he drove back to Chapel Hill.[16]

When Friday moved into South Building in the autumn of 1948, the UNC administration bore the imprint of Frank Graham. In March 1931, in response to legislative logrolling by public colleges and a severe fiscal crisis brought on by the depression, the North Carolina legislature, at the urging of Governor O. Max Gardner, had consolidated State College, the university at Chapel Hill, and the North Carolina College for Women (renamed the Woman's College of the University of North Carolina) into a single University of North Carolina. Governor O. Max Gardner, a champion of consolidation, then formed a Commission on Consolidation, and it appointed a survey team. Although many of the survey team's recommendations, such as transforming the campuses at Raleigh and Greensboro into junior colleges, caused a storm of controversy, others – such as transferring the engineering school from Chapel Hill to Raleigh, most business and liberal arts courses from Raleigh to Chapel Hill, most education and home economics programs to Greensboro, and library science training from Greensboro to Chapel Hill – were eventually approved.[17]

By the mid-1930s the UNC office had become closely identified with Graham's administrative and political style. Graduated from the university in 1909, "Dr. Frank" attended the UNC Law School for one year, taught English for a short time at Raleigh High School, and then resumed his law studies and was admitted to the bar. What one biographer calls his "indifference" toward the law prompted Graham to study history, and in 1915 he entered Columbia University, where he received a master's degree a year later. Serving in the marines during World War I, Graham taught briefly at Chapel Hill; in the 1920s he studied at the University of Chicago, the Brookings Institution, and the University of London. Although he never received the Ph.D., he returned to Chapel Hill in 1925 as a member of the History Department and became one of the university's most effective teachers. In June 1930 he was elected president to succeed Harry Woodburn Chase.[18]

The university system that Graham fashioned was theoretically unitary but effectively decentralized. Consolidation abolished any semblance of campus control over budget and program allocations. Campus budget officers dealt with UNC controller Carmichael and his assistant, A. R. "Buster" Shepherd. After consolidation, the campus boards of trustees were abolished and replaced by a 100-member Board of Trustees whose regular business was conducted by a 12-member Executive Committee. Campuses could not initiate new programs without the approval of the president and Board of Trustees. Consolidation also abolished the campus presidencies: Julius I. Foust and E. C. Brooks, previously presidents of North Carolina College for Women and State College respectively, each assumed the title of "vice president"; they and their successors in 1934 became "deans of administration." Graham became UNC president, and Bob House, his Chapel Hill lieutenant, became Carolina's dean of administration. (The university at Chapel Hill never had a "vice president" by that title.)

Yet consolidation was also accomplished with loose control from above. In curriculum, personnel, and other issues considered purely local, State College and the Woman's College enjoyed nearly complete autonomy. The case of Chapel Hill was distinctive; although legally House held the same responsibilities as his counterparts at Raleigh and Greensboro, Graham continued to operate the Chapel Hill campus directly in those matters of interest to him, with the support and cooperation of House. But with Graham frequently absent because of service on various national commissions, the university, according to Arnold King, more or less ran itself. Friday later described Graham's administrative style as a "disaster" when it came to organization, and "everybody knew it." Considerable responsibility fell to Carmichael, House, and Claude Teague, the local business manager; the administration operated by its own bureaucratic momentum, with State College and Woman's College functioning "as if they were independent institutions." Once, after returning from a trip abroad, Dr. Frank called together his advisers and said, "Well, it's time to make some decisions." "Frank," House replied, "the university's running well." "Now just sit down and tell us what you've been doing." That constituted the end of the meeting. Graham was, according to one assessment, "an idea man, but a poor administrator."[19]

Few people in Chapel Hill were not struck by what one contemporary called Graham's "personal touch." It was said that Frank Graham knew a large portion of the Carolina students by name. His Sunday evening open houses were legendary, and he often permitted indigent students to stay at his home during the depression years. Arnold King acknowledged Graham's ability to recognize academic quality; on one occasion he described him as "an authentic genius, perhaps the only one that this state has produced in this century," and the "original architect" of the modern University of North Carolina. He was a "great spirit who moved people," an evangelist and a missionary for causes. Nonetheless, he "wasn't much of an administrator"; without House "on the inside" and Carmichael "on the outside," Graham "would have been just swamped."[20]

At Fred Weaver's office in South Building, Bill Friday was gradually drawn into the operations of the Consolidated Office. Occasionally Weaver lent Friday to Graham, and, on frequent trips around the state, he served as companion and chauffeur for Graham, who did not drive. Friday recalled driving him "all over everywhere" to attend meetings across the state. As Dr. Frank's "chauffeur and the fellow who got the things together," Friday learned about the university's inner workings. En route from Chapel Hill to the state capitol, Graham often liked to stop for a Coca-Cola or a fresh banana in order to boost his energy level. While Friday drove, Graham would sit in the front seat, issuing instructions to the car's other passengers about their strategy once in Raleigh.[21]

The lobbying team included, as Friday called them, the "two major field officers," Carmichael and Teague. At the capitol, they divided up responsibilities. Carmichael and Teague worked in tandem, always with a strategy in mind: "You knew exactly who you were going to see," remembered Friday, "and you'd bide a certain amount of time" and then report back to the others to find out what they had learned. If there was "a weakness somewhere, you went over and tried to plug it." Carmichael talked to the "power structure" of the legislature; Friday found it "amazing to see the man work." Meanwhile, Teague knew and was comfortable with ordinary folk, the "little fellows," the "forgotten legislators" who filled the capitol. A quiet man, Teague was a "superb listener" who could walk into a legislative session and quickly determine political trends, or "what the current rascality was, or who was involved." In a different fashion from Carmichael, Teague complemented Dr. Frank's style.[22]

Graham's most radical idea, journalist Gerald W. Johnson once said, was that the Sermon on the Mount was sound doctrine, and he applied it in his dealings with legislators. Friday later recalled that Dr. Frank would identify his bitterest opponent, ask him to meet him in the capitol rotunda, and then take him by the arm and walk him to the corner. There, he would speak to him "in that quiet voice and make clear his mission." He was always an advocate and always effective, and his manner was disarming. "Even those who hated him," Friday noted, never failed to acknowledge his personal magnetism.[23]

During Friday's first year at South Building, in the spring of 1949, the stunning announcement came of Graham's appointment to the U.S. Senate. In midafternoon of March 22, Billy Carmichael summoned Friday to his office. "I've got to swear you to something, under oath," he said. Governor W. Kerr Scott, Carmichael explained, would appoint Frank Graham to the Senate that evening, at the annual O. Max Gardner Award dinner. Friday's first reaction was that Scott's announcement would destroy the occasion; Carmichael responded that Scott was determined nonetheless. After weeks of urging, Graham had agreed to fill the vacancy created by the death of Senator J. Melville Broughton on March 6. Established by the will of the depression-era governor and founder of the "Shelby dynasty," the O. Max Gardner Award annually recognized a faculty member who had made the greatest contribution to the "welfare of the human race" at a banquet that convened representatives of the faculties of the three UNC campuses. The first Gardner Award would be given that evening to Louise Alexander, a member of the Department of History and Political Science at the Woman's College.

That afternoon before the evening banquet, Carmichael candidly laid out the situation to Friday. After wandering outside South Building, they sat in Carmichael's car and contemplated the future. What did this mean for the university? Who, if anybody, could replace Dr. Frank? Friday had a vivid recollection of that evening's dinner, held at Lenoir Hall in the center of campus. Awaiting Scott's bombshell, he strategically positioned himself in a corner of the room. As the guests finished their meal and Louise Alexander received the award, Governor Scott rose to offer a few comments. Then, in an "almost casual" manner – "just as casually," Friday later said, "as he would say that tomorrow is Wednesday" – he announced Graham's appointment to the Senate. Lenoir Hall erupted into an uproar; the "roof came off the building," and "bedlam" broke loose. The next day few people remembered who had won the Gardner Award.[24]

When the excitement of the moment had subsided, Friday began to consider the implications of Graham's departure. Soon after the Gardner Award dinner, Billy Carmichael intimated to Friday that Friday might accompany Dr. Frank to Washington as part of his staff. Friday himself began to develop expectations, and he later admitted that he "would have gone if he had been asked." A few days after the announcement of Graham's appointment, while Friday was standing in front of South Building facing the Old Well, Graham came up behind him and placed his hand on his shoulder. Everyone around Chapel Hill, he told Friday, was expecting him to invite Friday to become a part of his senatorial staff. "I've thought about this," Graham said. But, he added, he believed that it was "much more important that you stay here and finish what we're doing." Friday stood in stunned disappointment, believing that working in Washington would have been a great experience. "You really wanted to work with Dr. Frank, didn't you?" Ida said to him that day. Although he attended Graham's swearing-in in the nation's capital on March 29, 1949, Friday regretted missing a chance to enter Washington politics.[25]

As it turned out, Graham's belief in the university's need for Friday spared him from what he called the "catastrophe" of the 1950 senatorial primary. Immediately after his swearing-in, Graham announced that he would stand for election to the remainder of the Senate term the following year. His announcement began one of the bitterest campaigns in the history of North Carolina. By February 1950 two candidates, former senator Robert Rice "Our Bob" Reynolds and Raleigh lawyer Willis Smith, had both announced that they would oppose Graham in the primary. Although Graham won a plurality of the votes in the four-way first primary and was only about 5,600 votes short of the nomination, Smith called for a runoff election. In that ballot, held in late June, Smith forces focused on Graham's racial liberalism and ties to

Bill Friday, Ida Friday, and Frank Porter Graham at Graham's U.S. Senate swearing-in ceremony, March 29, 1949.

"subversive" organizations to rally the white vote behind them. As a result, Smith defeated Graham in the second primary by a margin of 20,000 votes.[26]

With Smith leading early, it became obvious to Graham's supporters, who had gathered at the Sir Walter Hotel in Raleigh, that Dr. Frank's senatorial career was over. Friday had worked on Graham's behalf, but he was scrupulous to do so only on his own time. On election night, he and Ida drove to Raleigh with Claude Teague and his wife, Mary Spaugh Teague. Listening to the radio on the way over, they realized that the election was lost; even before they reached the Sir Walter, many of the Graham faithful had left. Marian Graham had prepared little sandwiches for the evening; many of them went uneaten, as Graham partisans did not know what to say or do. By ten o'clock, Graham had conceded defeat.

Among the last to leave, Friday noticed Graham's coat lying on a chair. Picking it up, he looked at Marian: "Isn't it time," he said, "for us to go home?" With "pain and hurt" in his face, Dr. Frank accepted Friday's offer to drive him to Hillsborough, where the Grahams were staying with one of Marian's sisters. On the way out of the hotel, the Teagues, Fridays, and Grahams noticed the gaiety at Smith's headquarters nearby, where some of

Graham's earlier well-wishers had now relocated. They made the thirty-mile drive to Hillsborough in silence. Despite the presence of his most intimate associates, Graham did not, Friday remembered, "utter one word of reaction or outrage." In Hillsborough, Friday walked Dr. Frank and Marian to the door, where Graham turned to Friday and said, "Good night. I'll see you tomorrow." Reviewing the disaster the next day with Bill Joslin, Graham's campaign manager in Wake County, Friday remarked that Dr. Frank had faced a "supreme test" in his relationships toward others and had demonstrated a "true nobility of character." He sought "the fresh start, the new energy, the forward vision," Friday declared at a conference on Graham in October 1983. Because he was "a man at peace with himself sustained by his great inner spirit," he was also a "master of defeat."[27]

For Friday, Frank Graham's defeat exhibited a personal, divisive, and nasty dimension to politics. It educated him about the perils of public life and about the potential for public resentment toward UNC. Friday would not forget that election easily. He had long contemplated politics as an avenue to public service and leadership; even in the distant future, the political world would continue to hold his attention. But the election of 1950 ended any serious aspirations for public office and turned him decisively toward a career in higher education. The experience of that bitter election, he later said, "drove me away from political involvement."[28]

During the interregnum that followed Graham's departure for the Senate, Billy Carmichael served as acting president, and the position was not filled until the Board of Trustees' election of Gordon Gray as president on February 6, 1950. Gray came to that office with strong credentials of public service. The son of Bowman Gray, president of R. J. Reynolds Tobacco Company, Gordon Gray grew up at Graylyn, the second largest private home in the state. "If ever there exists such a thing as an American aristocracy," one historian has written, "Gordon Gray may be said to be a fullfledged member."[29]

Gray's life was one of distinction and accomplishment, demonstrating his ability, with or without wealth. He was a superlative student, graduating first in his class at the exclusive Woodberry Forest School in Virginia and then as valedictorian at Chapel Hill in 1930. After receiving a law degree from Yale University three years later, he worked for a New York law firm until 1935, when he returned to North Carolina to practice law and to establish an empire in radio and newspaper publishing in Winston-Salem. Serving as state senator for three sessions, Gray in 1942 declined an officer's commission, preferring to join the U.S. Army as a private and eventually advancing to the rank of captain. In 1947 he became an assistant secretary of the army; two years later President Harry S. Truman named him secretary of the army.[30]

Regarded as a highly qualified administrator, Gray was named president of the university only after a power struggle within a nine-member trustee nominating committee that was headed by Durham lawyer and UNC trustee Victor S. Bryant. Bryant had favored the election of William De Vane, dean of Yale College and an English literature scholar. Although Friday, who did some staff work for the nominating committee, recalled that Bryant wanted to "move on and get Dr. De Vane to move in," he was opposed by other trustees, especially Billy Carmichael, who preferred a "more administratively public-oriented" candidate. The choice of Carmichael and his supporters was Gordon Gray, and, in the end, they prevailed.[31]

The contrast between Gordon Gray and Frank Graham was too obvious to ignore. Graham was a man of the people, whereas Gray struck many as a cold aristocrat. Graham's style was inspirational and chaotic; Gray was meticulous and methodical, a fervent advocate of systematic management. Graham thrived without formal bureaucracy and with confused lines of authority; Gray insisted on a clear chain of command. UNC's operation had largely depended on Graham's personality; without him, it was a cumbersome, ill-defined, and understaffed operation. Clearly, Gray's mandate was to re-create a system that had relied on the charisma of Dr. Frank.[32]

Gray's personality, in stark contrast to Graham's, was reserved and distant; one observer said that he was both "vain" and "shy." His inauguration, according to a recent historian, ushered in a "new aura of formality and businesslike precision" to university administration. Perhaps inevitably, not long after his inauguration as president on October 12, 1950, an uncomfortable distance lay between UNC administrators and faculty members and Gordon Gray. Most faculty members were "afraid of him," according to Friday, and never "really understood" what he wanted to achieve.[33]

Whereas Graham had always prided himself on his accessibility, Gray seemed cold and remote. Edwin M. Yoder, who arrived in Chapel Hill as a freshman in September 1952, characterized Gray as having a "stiff, formal, rather legalistic" approach in his relations with students. Yoder was struck by the fact that when Gray described the freshman honorary society, Phi Eta Sigma, at an early meeting with freshmen, he confused the order of the Greek letters. The episode was symptomatic, Yoder said, of Gray's "lack of direct, focused contact with undergraduate life." When Yoder was elected editor of the *Daily Tar Heel*, Gray called him into his office for a get-acquainted visit. The encounter struck Yoder as "very strange in that he spent most of his time telling me what he was not saying"; Gray attempted to impress him with "what he did not want to be understood to be saying." According to Yoder, who often saw Gray at student functions, Gray always told the same joke at every gathering. Another anecdote that circulated about Gray was that, in his undergraduate fraternity days, he was so able to concentrate and "so bookish" that he would read a book while a fraternity party went on around him.[34]

Bill Friday joined Gray at the Consolidated Office on April 16, 1951, early in his administration. Looking for an administrative assistant, Gray had been urged by Billy Carmichael to choose Friday. The move to Gray's office, for Friday, meant that the "whole world turned around." Over the next four years he experienced what Arnold King called a "severe discipline" under Gray's tutelage. Gray came from one world, Friday from another: the eager student of administration was still a rough-hewn young man from a mill town and a State College graduate, whereas his new mentor hailed from the Piedmont aristocracy. Friday sensed that he could help Gray to communicate with people in Friday's world, and that was what Friday set out to do. The twosome developed "patterns of working together, just almost by happening," and during their four years together Gray delegated increasingly important responsibilities to his young protégé.[35]

This was so because their backgrounds and operating styles were complementary. Both were tireless workers whose hours knew few limits. A contemporary described Gray as a "workhorse" who was "often at his desk before staff arrived and there long after they had gone home." Gray was accustomed to military-style decision making, a style ill-adapted to university governance; Friday was a team player who had spent four years in the navy. But perhaps most of all, Friday supplied the warmth of personality and charm that supplemented the reserve of Gray. Gray was not an extrovert, remembered Bill Aycock, and Friday became the "friendly side of that office." According to Ida Friday, Gray was a "fine human being," a "very privileged human being," but fundamentally shy. Bill Friday was folksy and outgoing and "met the people at the front door."[36]

Bill Friday's early years in the Consolidated Office were spent as an aide-de-camp to Gray. Carey T. Bostian, then chancellor of State College, described Friday as "just sort of a message boy" during his first years with Gordon Gray. Another State College administrator who had dealings with South Building said that the relationship between Gray and Friday was that of "the master and his aide, rather than of two partners." Arnold King maintained that Gray had a "typical military view" of Friday's job; he wanted someone who "could do a lot of dirty work." This "dirty work" included not only university business but also keeping Gray's schedule and even chauffeuring his wife and children.[37]

Gradually, however, Friday's responsibilities increased, and he became what Gray called his "stout right arm." Gray appointed Friday chairman of the new All-University Council on Student Affairs, which was established to examine issues of student welfare, scholarships, automobile use and parking, and extra-curricular activities. In 1952, when Gray sought to expand fund-raising at the three campuses, he consulted with the alumni-giving director at Yale University, Curtis Fields, about expanding the university's annual giving programs; Yale, then enjoying the most successful development program in the country, was raising a million dollars a year. Gray also employed an outside consultant, Paul Davis, earlier a development officer and adviser to Dwight D. Eisenhower while he was president of Columbia University, to coordinate a development strategy and to report directly to Gray. The UNC president assigned Friday to serve as liaison with Davis and with alumni secretaries Spike Saunders at Chapel Hill, Betty Jester at Greensboro, and H. W. Taylor Jr. at State College. Development work provided Friday with an intricate knowledge of the three campuses and helped him to establish valuable contacts. He also served as Gray's personal representative with UNC trustees and their committees, and in that capacity he became thoroughly acquainted with the power structure governing the university.[38]

Within a few years, Friday had become a campus figure and a leading force within the administration. From Gray he had acquired polish and meticulousness – what John R. Jordan Jr. later called a "board room practicality." Unlike Gray, he appeared at most events of any importance on the Chapel Hill campus, where he continued to maintain contacts with undergraduates. Yoder said that Friday was the first person he met when he went to Carolina in the autumn of 1952. Entering freshmen then attended a freshman orientation at Camp New Hope outside of town, and as they gathered at the campus YMCA to be transported there, the person greeting them was Bill Friday.[39]

Under Gray's tutelage, Friday learned the operation of the UNC presidency. Friday accompanied Gray everywhere, and they frequently discussed university affairs as they drove to various locations around the state. When important visitors arrived on campus, Friday often served as host. In this connection, he first met Generals Omar Bradley, Matthew Ridgeway, and Mark Clark. In these and other capacities, he showed increasing polish and grace. "He was thoughtful and always friendly," recalled Dean W. Colvard, then dean of State College's School of Agriculture. Friday "always seemed to sense what would be on the mind of the person who was going to be involved, and explain in advance what one might expect and what one might be expected to do."[40]

As the relationship between the two men developed, Gray's methodical habits, operating style, and careful attention to detail wore off on Friday. While Graham inspired Friday and others of his generation, Gray defined Friday's method of operation and honed his administrative skills. Friday's memories of Gray are both warm and generous. Gray, he believed, never received adequate credit for his contributions to Chapel Hill. He was "an exceptional person," a "very decent and honorable man" who was "very generous to me." Most of all, Friday said, he was a "great teacher."[41]

As Gray's assistant, Friday participated in efforts to reorganize the university. There had been no attempt to conduct planning since the implementation of consolidation in the 1930s. On the three campuses, chancellors, although theoretically possessing strong powers, faced entrenched interests and a diffusion of administrative units. Meanwhile, the Consolidated Office was badly understaffed and did well to devote its energies to lobbying in the legislature for appropriations. As Gray once told Friday, "administrative chaos" prevailed in the running of the University of North Carolina.[42]

The hiring of Bill Friday as assistant represented an early step in Gray's administrative restructuring; the appointment as provost of Logan Wilson, who had been dean of Sophie Newcomb College of Tulane University, constituted another. But perhaps the best expression of Gray's efforts came in the report of the management engineers, Cresap, McCormick, and Paget, which was begun in 1953 and completed, at a cost of $80,000 – half of which came from a Ford Foundation grant – in June 1954. Containing 367 recommendations, the management report urged that the president be defined as the chief executive officer of the university and the chancellors as CEOs of their campuses. It further recommended a better-defined staff structure, the establishment of a clearer relationship between the Consolidated Office and the chancellors, and the creation of a formal university cabinet that would include the three chancellors and university staff to advise the president. At the campus level, the report proposed an enlarged university bureaucracy composed of vice chancellors, including a staff person responsible for expanded development efforts.[43]

Not all of these recommendations were adopted – for example, the proposal to consolidate Carolina's General College and the College of Arts and Sciences. But, particularly in its advice regarding campus administration, the report served as a blueprint for the coming decades. It also prompted fresh consideration of the university's mission through a series of All-University Conferences involving faculty, administrators, and trustees. Chapel Hill sociologist Howard Odum and his protégé George Lee Simpson Jr. provided much of the leadership for these gatherings. In response to the Cresap, McCormick, and Paget report, the Board of Trustees approved a revamping of the UNC administrative structure, and the changes implemented during Gray's administration during the mid-1950s constituted the basis for the university's subsequent functioning. As a result of the administrative reorganization,

Friday as Gordon Gray's assistant, 1951. (Courtesy of the North Carolina Collection)

moreover, the university for the first time in its history adopted a code that defined relationships between the administrators and faculty of the three campuses, as well as the relationships between the campuses and the UNC administration in South Building.[44]

Like his predecessors, Gordon Gray sought to expand the reach of the university. In the late 1940s the state had inaugurated a Good Health Campaign that envisioned an ambitious statewide expansion of hospitals and public health. The center of this campaign was to be the university's medical school, then only a two-year program. In 1950 a Division of Health Affairs, responsible to the Chapel Hill chancellor, was established to supervise the transformation of the two-year program into a four-year medical school and to develop a major medical center in Chapel Hill. Similarly, Gray also began a bold venture with the development of educational television and WUNC-TV, which began operations in 1954.[45]

Despite a busy schedule, Gray maintained active ties with Washington, and he was drawn increasingly into the affairs of the national government. By 1955 he was serving as chairman of the National Commission on Hospital Care and Financing and as a member of the Ford Foundation's Board on Overseas Training. His most important assignment was the chairmanship of the Personnel Security Board of the Atomic Energy Commission, which investigated disloyalty charges against physicist J. Robert Oppenheimer in the spring of 1954. The case was all-consuming. Gray had to be in Washington during the week; returning to Chapel Hill on Friday afternoon, he would spend the weekend catching up on university business. The findings of the Gray review board, which were released on May 27, 1954, created an uproar in the academic world. The board voted two to one to exonerate Oppenheimer of disloyalty but, because of his past association with leftist organizations and individuals, refused to reinstate his security clearance. Gray cast the deciding vote against Oppenheimer over the objections of scientist Ward V. Evans, who vigorously defended Oppenheimer.[46]

Although Gray's position on the Oppenheimer case reflected public opinion during the age of Joseph R. McCarthy, it became a celebrated example in the academic community of an anticommunist witch hunt. The "academic world never believed in the disloyalty of Oppenheimer," explained Arnold King, and Gray's stock declined thereafter, both nationally and at Chapel Hill. To the Chapel Hill faculty, the Oppenheimer case reinforced an unfavorable comparison of Gray with Frank Graham; the common belief was that Graham would have conducted himself differently in the Oppenheimer case. Although Gray never discussed the Oppenheimer case with Friday, Friday was aware that "it weighed heavily on him."[47]

Meanwhile, serious problems had emerged in intercollegiate athletics. When, in 1953, the rumor circulated that State College was considering employing Jim Tatum, a Carolina graduate, the Maryland football coach, and a symbol of big-time athletics, Gray placed an angry phone call to Chancellor Bostian, telling him that he would not permit Tatum to be hired. But three years later Carolina, seeking to upgrade its football program, signed on Tatum at the insistence of Billy Carmichael – Tatum's first cousin – despite Gray's earlier objections to big-time athletics. The *Daily Tar Heel* opposed Tatum's hiring, describing it as evidence of a "parasitic monster of open professionalism in our midst."[48] Gray and Carmichael, Friday recalled, had a falling out over the Tatum appointment, and, at a New Year's Day meeting, a "very unfortunate kind of confrontation" developed between the two. Meanwhile, some members of the Executive Committee of the Board of Trustees who had been deeply divided about Gray's election in 1950 were growing restive at his frequent absences; many of them believed, according to Friday, that "when you took the job of being president of the university, that was a lifetime commitment."[49]

Gray, as well as Graham before him, had sought curbs on big-time sports at the State College and Chapel Hill campuses. Along with Friday, Gray was present at the formation of the Atlantic Coast Conference (ACC), which was created on June 14, 1953, at the Morehead building on the Chapel Hill campus. The Southern Conference, to which UNC–Chapel Hill and State College belonged, had become unwieldy, and some of its members were openly manipulating conference rules. The creation of the ACC represented an effort to establish an exclusive conference of schools of similar size in the same region that could enforce stricter controls over athletics. Gray, partly in response to National Collegiate Athletic Association (NCAA) sanctions applied to State College basketball and football programs in 1950 and 1953, restructured authority over athletics by sponsoring a Board of Trustees resolution in 1954 explicitly delegating control to the chancellors and holding them accountable for their programs.[50]

Personal affairs further clouded Gray's situation. In 1953, the death of his wife, Jane Henderson Boyden Craige Gray, left him disconsolate and with four sons to raise on his own. Friday, who was present when Gray received the news of his wife's death, described it as a "crushing blow." This combination of professional frustration and personal tragedy made the life of a university president increasingly unattractive. Gray had accepted the presidency, according to Ida Friday, "without fully realizing what it was." To Chancellor Carey Bostian, it had become obvious that Gray was discouraged and disillusioned. Gray grew increasingly discontented with the slow pace of administrative reform at the university, and he was unhappy about his inability to effect changes more rapidly. Decision making at a university was "not anything like he'd ever experienced before anywhere," Friday recalled. "He didn't find here what he thought he was going to find." Discovering that rank and authority meant little and that effective university leadership required persuasion made Gordon Gray very unhappy and convinced him that progress was too slow.[51]

By 1955, only five years into his UNC presidency, Gray was looking for a way out. John Jordan, who knew him casually, was startled when Gray privately declared that he planned to leave the post. Earlier in his presidency, after the death of Willis Smith on June 26, 1953, Gray had rebuffed feelers about an appointment to the U.S. Senate. Less than a year later, when the death of Clyde R. Hoey on May 12, 1954, created another vacancy in the

Senate, Gray called in Friday and suggested that he would be "amenable." The UNC president then told Billy Carmichael the same thing, and Carmichael conferred with Friday. "What do you think this means?" he asked. Friday advised Carmichael to go see Governor William Umstead, a classmate of Carmichael's at Carolina, and urge him to appoint Gray. But Umstead's discovery that Gray, a Democrat, had developed close ties with the Eisenhower administration and had even voted for the president in 1952 immediately ended any consideration of Gray for the Senate.[52]

Gray's resignation on June 10, 1955, to become Dwight D. Eisenhower's assistant secretary of defense for international security affairs came as little surprise to Friday. Although the Board of Trustees' Executive Committee, rather than accepting his resignation, granted him a leave of absence, it finally appointed Provost J. Harris Purks Jr. acting president in November. Earlier in the year, in February 1955, Friday had been appointed secretary of the university, a position that gave him greater access to the trustees.[53]

Gray's departure coincided with a crisis of confidence in the consolidated UNC system. Purks, formerly dean of the College of Arts and Sciences at Emory University, an associate director of the Rockefellers' General Education Board in New York City, and director of the Georgia University Center, had become provost in 1954. Billy Carmichael was in poor health, suffering from a chronic hypertension that would eventually cause his death. With Gray's leaving, Purks became the heir apparent. Yet Purks, an indecisive man, found the acting presidency an unhappy experience. Bill Friday subsequently described him as a man who was "given to a lot of nervous energy"; he was never "really comfortable in the job at all." It was also "pretty evident," according to Arnold King, that Purks was unpopular with enough trustees that he would not be chosen president. Consequently, when the newly created State Board of Higher Education offered Purks the job of executive director effective in March 1956, he accepted.[54]

By early 1956 there were stirrings in the state press and among legislators about the future of UNC consolidation. In the opinion of the *Rocky Mount Evening Telegram*, the departure of Gray and Purks suggested that "no competent educator would accept a position as ill-defined as the University presidency." Perhaps, indeed, the presidency was "a useless appendage" that could be eliminated. Even the *Chapel Hill Weekly* asserted that the "logical, sensible" thing for the legislature to do was to abolish the consolidated structure and turn the operations of the three campuses back to locally controlled boards of trustees.[55]

During this interregnum in presidential leadership, UNC experienced a number of crises that demanded a strong response. On March 27, 1951, the Fourth Circuit Court of Appeals, reversing a lower court decision of October 9, 1950, ordered the University of North Carolina Law School to admit its first black students. Bill Friday, then in the dean of students' office, drove over to the federal district court in Durham to hear the lower court case, which was argued by Thurgood Marshall, attorney for the Legal Defense Fund of the National Association for the Advancement of Colored People (NAACP). Friday followed the case closely, knowing that "it was very significant." Although the district court ruled for the university, Friday realized that integration was only a matter of time.[56]

The inevitability of integration at the graduate level became apparent even to the Board of Trustees. On April 5, 1951, nine days after the court of appeals's ruling, the board passed a resolution to admit black students to the UNC medical school since no separate facilities existed in the state, but it continued to ban black students from entering programs where "equal" facilities existed at all-black public colleges. When the U.S. Supreme Court affirmed the court of appeals ruling, the university was forced to admit five black students to the law school in the summer of 1951, and over the next four years twenty blacks entered graduate and professional programs. By the fall of 1955 there were three black graduate students, two black medical students, and one black law student.[57]

The *Brown* v. *Board of Education* decision, which outlawed school segregation in 1954, brought further changes. In the spring of 1955, NAACP lawyer Conrad O. Pearson of Durham filed suit on behalf of three black applicants to Carolina's undergraduate program – LeRoy B. Frasier Jr., his brother Ralph, and John Lewis Brandon – all of them students at Durham's all-black Hillside High School. For UNC trustees, who preferred the status quo, the *Brown* decision had been "an earthquake and a volcano combined," recalled Arnold King. In late May 1955 the Executive Committee adopted a resolution rejecting the admission of African American applicants as undergraduates. UNC administrators implemented this policy by firmly rejecting the applications of the Frasiers and Brandon and any other blacks who followed them. Carolina officials were also uneasy about the future. They worried that integration would drive away white students, especially women, who might flee to private colleges. They feared that integration would result, as dean of UNC's General College Corydon P. Spruill explained, in the transformation of Chapel Hill from "an open society to one more nearly closed." They wondered where the black students would be housed. On the other hand, administrators such as C. Hugh Holman, dean of Chapel Hill's College of Arts and Sciences, argued in favor of accepting black undergraduates, maintaining that most students welcomed integration.[58]

The example of the UNC Law School, which was desegregated by court order in 1951, was instructive. Dean Henry P. Brandis maintained, in the midst of the 1955 crisis, that the admission of blacks – only two or three blacks were admitted annually to the law school throughout the 1950s – posed "no problem whatever." There were a few "fringe problems" regarding the attendance of black law students at football games, lockers in the gymnasium, and integrated dormitories. The earliest black students in the law school strenuously objected when UNC administrators first housed them in a separate section of Steele Dormitory and then sought to grant them tickets to football games on a segregated basis. Later, some white law students complained when a black student attempted to eat with them in Lenoir Hall. In still another incident, the university barred the holding of a law school dance that permitted black participation; those law students favoring integration responded by renting the ballroom of the Washington Duke Hotel in Durham. By 1955, however, the handful of black law students at Carolina were fully accepted in the classroom and permitted to participate in some activities, such as intramural athletics.[59]

The decision of the three-judge panel in the case of *Frasier* v. *Board of Trustees*, heard in Greensboro in September 1955, left little room for maneuver. Although UNC lawyers claimed that no discrimination on the basis of race had occurred and that the Supreme Court, in the *Brown* decision, had said nothing about higher education per se, the court ruled otherwise. Circuit Judge Morris A. Soper of Baltimore decreed that the university's policy of "refusing to receive and process applications of citizens of North Carolina" on the basis of race was invalid. The university had pursued a policy that was at worst evasive and at best gradualistic, and the district court's order settled the matter. State Attorney General William B. Rodman Jr., who represented the university, told trustees and administrators that further legal resistance was futile. Although he doubted that they would accept his advice, Rodman advised against appeal and urged the immediate admission of black undergraduates. UNC officials did in fact appeal the decision; but when the case came before the U.S. Supreme Court on March 5, 1956, that tribunal, in a thirteen-word statement, affirmed the lower court's ruling. Meanwhile, the Frasier brothers and Brandon had desegregated Chapel Hill in the autumn of 1955 – two days after the district court's decision in *Frasier* – while the first African Americans were admitted to the Woman's College and to State College the following year.[60]

Exposed to Chapel Hill liberalism in the late 1940s, both Bill and Ida Friday had become increasingly convinced that the time had come to end Jim Crow. Yet effectively dealing with the race issue meant educating trustee opinion. While avoiding a public posture on integration, Friday urged that the issue be settled in a court of law. As he saw it, if the question of integration remained exclusively with the Board of Trustees, there was the strong likelihood that the board would remain opposed. In the strained atmosphere of the 1950s, "changing the thought processes" of trustees was "almost impossible in the heat and tension" of the moment. But, with the *Frasier* decision, trustees – many of whom were attorneys – felt obliged to obey the law while realizing that desegregation, at least for the next two decades, would mean a slow trickle of blacks into the university.[61]

Despite some desegregation, integration remained an elusive goal. As William H. Chafe has argued, North Carolina's brand of desegregation in the 1950s brought mostly tokenism. When the Woman's College was integrated with the admission of two black women in the autumn of 1956, the students were limited to a segregated wing of Shaw Dormitory. Elsewhere, black athletes remained barred from competition; Carolina and State College teams would not compete with colleges and universities that were integrated. In general, as Chapel Hill dean and subsequent chancellor J. Carlyle Sitterson noted, "little had been really done" about meaningful integration in the decade after *Frasier*, primarily because of the Executive Committee's segregationist attitudes and the political structure that it represented. Not a single black person was on the faculty; when the first African American was hired in 1966 at Chapel Hill, a special case had to be made to the trustee leadership.[62]

In January 1956, when J. Harris Purks announced his intention to leave effective mid-March, the Executive Committee faced an even more serious crisis: selecting an acting president. Soon Purks had departed. Billy Carmichael was unavailable because of poor health. And William Whatley Pierson, dean of the Graduate School for the three campuses, was considered too aged. The trustees turned to Bill Friday, whose role as Gordon Gray's assistant and as secretary of the university had made him a symbol of continuity. Named acting president on March 15, 1956, Friday found himself in the right place at the right time.[63]

Few people, including Bill Friday, thought that the appointment meant anything more than a temporary stint. "I expect that I will be in this place no more than a few months," he told a reporter in January 1956. A return to the position of secretary of the university, he said, would be "a very happy" thing for him. Friday's appointment put him "on the spot," according to Arnold King; Friday had "no dream" of it. Years later, Ida Friday recalled that she and Bill had had "no aspirations" toward the presidency. When he was named acting president, Bill told her that his primary function was to "hold the fort" by answering the mail and the telephone. Most observers would have agreed with a contemporary who remarked that the trustees did a "very wise thing" in appointing Friday to serve "as a sort of caretaker" in a period of transition, during which the office of the presidency would be "either eliminated or clarified."[64]

Though only thirty-five years old, Friday was respected among trustees for his astuteness and congeniality; he particularly enjoyed the confidence of newly appointed members George Watts Hill Sr. and Virginia Terrell Lathrop. With a reputation for conciliation and mediation, he successfully communicated with a wide range of people and demonstrated an exceptional intuition about human relations. Not long after Friday's selection was announced, Fred Weaver described his "sensitive antennae," which enabled him to "learn things so quickly and to adapt himself so well." Noting that Friday seemed to know about situations before anyone else did, he once told his pregnant wife, Frances, that he wanted to know the sex and weight of his child before Bill Friday had the information. Another colleague in South Building, commenting on Friday's abilities in dealing with people, said he seemed "to know your problems as well as you do, and to have an equally deep concern for them." A profile appearing in the *Greensboro Daily News* characterized Friday as a "relaxed and smiling young man" who was quiet but had "the rare gift of listening well." Although it would astonish him to hear it, the reporter concluded, Friday was a "charmer, in his way perhaps as effective as Dr. Frank Graham." Still another colleague called him a mediator: "I never saw anyone who could walk more easily between disparate factions, calm ruffled feathers, maintain the trust of both sides, and yet not commit himself to a partisan view."[65]

In the early months of his acting presidency, Friday later recalled to a reporter, he was "scared to death" and would have been "foolish" if he were not. His uncle, William Rowan, was equally skeptical. After hearing of the appointment, he wrote to Friday's mother, "Maybe governor, but never president of the university at thirty-five." Problems that had been brewing during Gray's administration, and earlier, came to a head. The vaguely defined administration at the Consolidated Office continued. On his departure, Purks warned Friday about the likelihood of "one short circuit after another." The administrative affairs at South Building, under both his and Gray's presidency, leaked "like a sieve around the president's desk, thus leaving the president both uninformed and powerless." Meanwhile, Friday faced a rash of problems on the three campuses. At State College, the faculty was divided over the location of a new nuclear power reactor – a project promoted by Billy Carmichael – and at Chapel Hill the Division of Health Affairs was afflicted with severe internal conflict between the division's administrator, Henry Clark, and the head of the Carolina medical school, W. Reece Berryhill. According to one account, Friday discovered a "real mess" when he took office in March 1956.[66]

A more immediate challenge, however, came from the Woman's College, where a faculty uprising against Chancellor Edward Kidder Graham Jr. threatened faculty morale and perhaps imperiled the stability of the consolidated system itself. "Sonny" Graham, son of the World War I–era president of the University of North Carolina, was born in Chapel Hill on January 31, 1911. When he was seven, his father died in the great influenza epidemic of 1918; his mother had died two years earlier, and he was raised by his mother's brother-in-law and sister, Louis and Mildred Moses Graves. Graduating from Chapel Hill in 1933, Sonny went on to receive a Ph.D. in history from Cornell and there began an administrative career, serving as its secretary from 1941 to 1947. He became dean of the faculty at Washington University in 1948 but returned to North Carolina two years later as chancellor of the Woman's College.

Even as early as 1950, the Greensboro campus had become an anomaly: as Chapel Hill and State College entered an inevitable future of coeducation, Greensboro remained one of the largest women's colleges in the nation. In the 1930s and 1940s the college had stood in relative isolation and practiced its own customs and rituals of student life. The campus was dominated by unmarried women faculty members who were not involved in scholarship and resented those who were. In contrast, a portion of the faculty, such as Gregory Ivey in art and Marc Friedlander in English, sought to change the institution, and they remained frustrated for much of the 1940s.[67]

Early in his chancellorship, it became apparent that, despite his ambitious plans, Graham lacked the requisite skills in human relations. As one faculty opponent wrote, he had a "genius for doing even the right things in the wrong way." Instead of "gentle finesse and tact," Graham used "blunt, drastic, and even cruel methods." Soon after taking office, he expanded the chancellor's staff by hiring sociology professor Mereb E. Mossman as his dean of instruction, a new position. Mossman's appointment occurred without any general discussion among the faculty; one contemporary later said, "it was just reported to us that this had been done." At the same time, the centerpiece of Graham's agenda was a new general education program that sought to revise the college's curriculum completely. In 1951, when faculty opposition emerged, the curriculum committee blocked its passage, and in late 1953 Graham proposed to bypass the usual channels and seek approval from the entire faculty. When the faculty, in January 1954, vetoed this proposal, Graham began a long slide toward catastrophe.[68]

News of Graham's troubles had filtered to the Consolidated Office by 1954, when President Gray appointed a trustee visiting committee to hear out faculty complaints. Gray appeared before the Woman's College faculty in late February and March 1954 in unsuccessful attempts to restore its confidence in Graham. Another trustee committee, headed by Robert M. Hanes, organized itself and held meetings in October 1955 in the Presbyterian Church of the Covenant, located a few blocks from campus. Because of the polarization of opinion, Hanes sought a neutral ground; the prevailing view, according to a contemporary, was that coming forward at a hearing would put a "hex" on Graham's opponents. At the suggestion of Greensboro alumna and trustee Emily Preyer and apparently without the involvement of the president's staff, Hanes began to conduct hearings on his own. By the time Friday became acting UNC president in March 1956, Graham's position was hopelessly undermined.[69]

Lacking any authority, the Hanes committee, as one contemporary put it, became a "talk fest" that led nowhere. The existence of the committee undermined the authority of the Consolidated Office; the Hanes committee apparently was preparing to fire Graham about the time that Friday took office. Friday persuaded the committee to disband, saying that he would handle the matter personally. This he did by appointing a new committee armed with the full authority of the president's office and composed of some of the university's most respected figures – Billy Carmichael, William Whatley Pierson, and Provost William Whyburn – because he realized that "no one could attack that committee." The Carmichael committee, according to another contemporary, functioned as a "buffer" that would take on the Graham situation without directly involving Friday.[70]

Moving swiftly, Carmichael announced to the Greensboro faculty that his committee would hold hearings for three days – March 8, 9, and 10, 1956 – and that it would hear anyone who came forward. Some 132 faculty members eventually testified; their transcribed testimony ran to more than six hundred pages. It soon became obvious that Graham was doomed as chancellor. Sonny, Arnold King observed, had gotten himself into "deeper and deeper trouble," and it had become "quite obvious, even to his friends, that the time had come for him to go." In addition to his disastrous relations with a large part of the faculty, it had become common knowledge that Graham was involved in an extramarital affair. Meanwhile, the director of buildings and grounds, a Graham opponent, was sifting through Graham's garbage counting beer cans in order to document reports of excessive drinking. For a cloistered women's college in the 1950s, these transgressions were the last straw, and the Carmichael committee, and Friday, sought to handle Graham's departure with discretion and grace. As a Greensboro faculty member recalled, Friday "got rid of Graham" but managed it "very delicately."[71]

In early April 1956 Carmichael and Friday independently presented the evidence to Graham and urged him to resign. Friday, according to King, had "a way of putting a thing to you very effectively and very straight" even while he remained sympathetic. Graham realized that the evidence of his personal transgressions was damning, and he resigned in order to avoid public exposure. His leaving was confirmed during a meeting of the Board of Trustees in Chapel Hill's Gerrard Hall on May 28, 1956. In a six-page report, the Carmichael committee explained the origins of the conflict; without taking sides, it acknowledged that the "bitterness" of the "differences" was crippling the "effective operation" of the college. It urged Graham's resignation and the selection of an interim chancellor who could avoid becoming a party to the "existing factionalism." Graham accepted the committee's recommendation and recognized that a "serious and deep-seated cleavage" made his resignation inevitable. Friday found the experience personally painful. He had urged Graham to resign rather than be fired and "to make it his decision, as much as it was mine."[72]

With Graham's departure, Friday was able to stabilize the situation at Greensboro. Three days after the chancellor's resignation, he told the faculty of Woman's College that "no person, group, faction or division" had emerged victorious; rather, each of them had "lost something" and the college had suffered. Nothing would be done in haste; instead, the faculty needed to pull together and unify. As a gesture of healing, Friday appointed W. W. Pierson as acting chancellor, and his year's tenure, preceding the appointment of Gordon M. Blackwell in 1957, soothed a badly split faculty.[73]

Bill Friday's handling of the trouble at Greensboro confirmed his skills in personal diplomacy and human relations. According to the *Greensboro Daily News*, he had shown "a warm personality, administrative skill, and maturity beyond his years." In several crises, the most prominent of them at Woman's College, he had moved in with determination and resolution, examined the facts, and made "prompt and courageous decisions." His orchestration of Graham's resignation was simply his "nature," his wife recalled, and it demonstrated the same abilities that he had earlier shown in student affairs at Chapel Hill. Many members of the UNC Board of Trustees' Executive Committee were greatly impressed; they recognized that a delicate and potentially embarrassing situation had been handled, as Ida Friday expressed it, "in the very best of ways." The resolution of the problems at Greensboro coincided with the trustees' search for a permanent president in the spring and summer of 1956, and Friday's performance had suddenly propelled him forward as a candidate.[74]

When an advisory committee composed of faculty members from the three campuses made its report to the trustee selection committee in March 1956, Bill Friday emerged as one of 11 finalists out of 109 candidates under consideration. Whereas the committee had regarded Friday in December 1955 as "approachable," "gracious," and disciplined, it also noted his inexperience and lack of scholarly qualifications. By the following May, however, the committee had revised its evaluation, based on Friday's performance as acting president. Faced with "unusually significant and numerous problems," he had shown an ability to work effectively and responsibly, while he had displayed good judgment, a devotion to fairness and orderly procedure, and a decisiveness that was prompt "without being arbitrary." Of those candidates without teaching or scholarly experience, the committee ranked him "by all odds" the highest. Even Governor Luther Hodges said that Friday had done "an outstanding job, with courage and decisiveness that we've needed."[75]

The members of the Executive Committee had been similarly struck in January 1956, when Friday, in a meeting at the governor's office in the capitol, had so impressed them that they appointed him acting president. Yet their selection of Friday was a harbinger of coming problems among the trustees. Before naming him acting president, some trustees had asked for concessions in exchange for their support; apparently they had tried a similar approach with other candidates. When he responded by describing the university's troubled condition and urging action, Friday recalled that he "upset the playhouse." Leaving the meeting, he was so disconcerted by the lack of trustee support that he walked around the capitol building and down to the Smith Bagley monument. Mulling over the matter, he walked up to the double doors of the capitol and contemplated withdrawing as a candidate. Then, thinking better of so rash an action, Friday drove out to State College for a meeting with Chancellor Bostian. While he was in Bostian's office, Hodges called, summoning him back to receive the appointment as acting president. Friday accepted the job with no great sense of elation; he realized what a "monstrous" task lay ahead.[76]

Into the summer and fall of 1956, the selection committee, headed by Victor Bryant, was crippled by internal discord. Bryant again raised the name of William De Vane of Yale College, only to encounter strong opposition for a second time. Some trustees supported candidates with Chapel Hill connections, such as Bill Aycock, Gordon Blackwell, and Alexander Heard. Others endorsed outsiders like John Stuart Allen, executive vice president of the University of Florida; John Tyler Caldwell, president of the University of Arkansas; and Irvin Stewart, president of West Virginia University. Yet the committee proceeded uncertainly, given the low salary ($15,000) that the university could offer. Deadlocked, the selection committee sought a compro-

Friday with Luther Hodges.

mise: it would select Friday as president if he would accept De Vane as his chief academic officer. Concerned about Friday's age – he was only thirty-five, De Vane fifty-eight – the committee members proposed to appoint De Vane as a sort of mentor to the young president.[77]

The plan was presented to Friday at a meeting in Bryant's office in Durham sometime in the autumn of 1956. The day before he had seen UNC trustee Virginia Terrell Lathrop, a journalist and Woman's College alumna. Friday immediately sensed that "something was troubling her very much," but he realized that she "dared not say a word." When the selection committee members presented their proposal to him, he immediately understood that it had been prearranged, and he unequivocally rejected it. "Anybody chosen to be president of the university should have the right to pick his own team," he recalled telling the committee. Refusing any prearranged commitment, Friday said that this was his final answer. When another trustee privately offered support in exchange for concessions regarding the personnel of the UNC Division of Health Affairs, he gave the same response. As Lathrop later told Friday, this was his "finest hour."[78]

Lacking a consensus in favor of another candidate, the selection committee chose Friday on October 18, 1956, and the Board of Trustees ratified its recommendation a week later. The *Daily Tar Heel*, which had endorsed Friday's candidacy in the spring, proclaimed that his selection would promote a new "era of good feelings" among the three UNC campuses. Informing him of the decision, Bryant took him aside. "Who would have thought in January," he said, "that you'd ever be considered for this position in October?" Friday had not campaigned for the job; in many respects, remembered Ida, he was "pushing it away." The night the announcement was made, a number of Friday's friends, including his old professors and peers in the UNC Law School, came to see him. John Jordan recalled that he was driving down Fayetteville Street in Raleigh when he heard the news; Jordan turned the car around and headed for Friday's home in Chapel Hill. There he was joined by Maurice Van Hecke and Herbert Baer of the law school faculty. Characteristically, Jordan recalled, "Bill Friday was just sitting there in the living room reading the local newspaper." Among most Carolina faculty members, however, there was no great enthusiasm about the election of this young and inexperienced man for such a demanding position. A few months later Friday was walking through the Chapel Hill campus, by Bynum Hall, when he came up behind two faculty members. Unfortunately, he overheard them. "After eighteen years of Frank Graham," one of them said to the other, "Good Lord, look what we have now!" That, Friday said later, was "known as administrative orientation."[79]

Bill Friday's selection as UNC president in October 1956 marked the completion of a remarkable ascent to power. No sooner was he in office, however, than Friday confronted a staggering series of challenges to UNC's position of power and preeminence, not only from other public colleges and universities in the state, but also from within North Carolina's political leadership. As a young university president in his thirties and forties, Friday would have little respite from these pressures, and the coming decades would test his abilities to defend, preserve, and extend UNC's educational and political status.

Defender of the Purpose

CHAPTER 4 *The Roaring Lions of Reaction*

O N May 8, 1957, Bill Friday was inaugurated as UNC president in the William Neal Reynolds Coliseum at State College. The event concluded with the pomp and ceremony that usually accompanies such occasions. The 7,000 people in attendance included Friday's family and old friends, as well as most of the state's power structure. Frank Porter Graham and Gordon Gray gave brief tributes, though Friday sensed surprise on their part that such a young man was taking on such a large job. Governor Luther M. Hodges presided, and a combined band from State College, Chapel Hill, and the Woman's College played "God of Our Fathers." As Ida Friday bit back tears, Chief Justice J. Wallace Winborne of the North Carolina Supreme Court administered the oath of office. Pledging "my mind, my heart, my hands, and my strength," Bill Friday told the audience that his administration would bring changed methods and programs but a constancy of purpose. Although a freight train passing through the State College campus on its regular run almost drowned out his address, Friday reaffirmed the university's traditional emphasis on unified administration and institutional autonomy. He announced his belief in the principle of "responsible freedom" that the university had long enjoyed. He promised better faculty salaries, improved facilities, academic freedom, and the provision of a liberal education at all three UNC campuses. The university reached into the distant corners of the state, he declared, by providing leadership in all phases of education.[1]

Observers noted that the ceremony was more subdued than Gordon Gray's inauguration six years earlier. Although Friday's oratory was not "golden," according to the *Raleigh News and Observer*, it was nonetheless "solid." Friday realized that he faced awesome challenges. At the Woman's College, the in-

95

Friday's inauguration as UNC president, May 8, 1957, William Neal Reynolds Coliseum, Raleigh, with Frank Porter Graham (left) and Luther Hodges (right). (Courtesy of the North Carolina Collection)

terim chancellor, William Whatley Pierson, had soothed ill feelings, but faculty morale remained poor. At State College, the vocational schools were resisting Chancellor Carey T. Bostian's efforts to exert campuswide control; clashes over the establishment of a nuclear reactor on the campus continued. And at Chapel Hill, the Division of Health Affairs was in turmoil; the retirement of Robert Burton House and the establishment of a mandatory retirement age of sixty-five for all administrators created a vacuum in campus leadership.[2]

Friday faced not only these but also other new problems. While he succeeded in expanding public backing for UNC and continued to rely on the support of the state's power structure, Friday remained in a largely defensive position. For on a number of fronts the academy's traditional autonomy was undermined, and its ability to maintain the confidence of North Carolinians would undergo extraordinary duress during the coming years. In his first decade of university leadership, Bill Friday confronted two issues that brought UNC's public role into sharp relief – athletics and anticommunism. Both punctuated fundamental questions: how independent was a public university

Ida Friday at Bill Friday's inauguration, May 8, 1957, with Martha Blakeney Hodges. (Courtesy of the North Carolina Collection)

from prevailing cultural and political norms? To what extent should the political culture, as manifested either by the legislature or the public at large, govern UNC's operation? With what degree of independence should a public university pursue the truth and, in the case of athletics, set its house in order? And, in the event that academic policy was unpopular, how could a university president best manage public discontent and political pressure?

Both athletics and anticommunism further demonstrated a disquieting reality of the late 1950s and early 1960s: in North Carolina, the university and public opinion were growing apart. Intercollegiate athletics in the post–World War II years grew increasingly popular; commercialized sports such as football and basketball became multifaceted industries with strong constituencies, while they were increasingly divorced from the academic functions of a university. Efforts to curb excesses won few friends; instead, they deepened public suspicion of academic leadership. More troubling still was anticommunism, a national phenomenon that expressed deeply rooted anxieties in the southern psyche and had become a metaphor for fears about the eroding racial order.

WHEN Bill Friday became acting president of UNC in 1956, the issue of intercollegiate athletics loomed so large as to threaten the stability of the UNC structure. With little success, his predecessors had tried to control intercollegiate sports programs on campus. In 1935, more than two decades before Friday's inauguration, Frank Porter Graham had proposed root-and-branch reforms. Studies by the Carnegie Corporation in 1929 and 1931 criticized the system of subsidized student athletics in existence by World War I. Graham's proposals, announced in the late autumn of 1935 and soon known as the Graham Plan, would prohibit athletic scholarships or any other form of aid based solely on athletic performance. Requiring that athletes sign a pledge stating that they were amateurs, the Graham Plan also would ban any recruiting. Although both the UNC faculty and the Southern Conference, to which both State College and Carolina belonged, adopted these recommendations in early 1936, the Graham Plan evoked strong opposition among alumni chapters and the North Carolina sports establishment; alumni groups in ten cities sent resolutions of protest, and the athletics council of the university unanimously opposed it. Ultimately, the issue nearly cost Graham his job. In December 1936 the Southern Conference reversed itself and permitted the awarding of financial aid according to the sports potential of a student. A year later, the conference reestablished full sports scholarships if they were paid for by off-campus booster organizations.[3]

The failure of the Graham Plan meant the end, for the next two decades, of any meaningful efforts to limit athletics at the University of North Carolina. Gordon Gray's insistence on greater administrative control led him to help to found the Atlantic Coast Conference (ACC) in 1953, but it also resulted in clashes with Billy Carmichael over Carolina's hiring of Jim Tatum as football coach and its commitment to big-time football. In the 1940s an even greater challenge had arisen with the arrival of Coach Everett Case and big-time basketball at State College. Gray wanted greater accountability and control over Case's sports empire – and, later, over the Carolina basketball empire headed by Frank McGuire, who won a national championship in 1957 – by delegating authority over intercollegiate sports to the three chancellors. On January 25, 1954, the UNC Board of Trustees unanimously approved a transfer of responsibility.[4]

Gray's policy, however, simply deferred the question. At State College, the chancellor's office worked with semiautonomous schools of agriculture, engineering, and textiles; historically, the athletics department and the coaches had functioned without close oversight. Neither John W. Harrelson nor Carey T. Bostian, as State College chancellors, could control the freewheeling Everett Case and his alumni supporters. At Chapel Hill, under Bob House, Gray, maintaining Frank Graham's policy, continued to exert direct control over campus affairs, but alumni boosters and sports enthusiasts asserted themselves during the mid-1950s with the hiring of McGuire in 1952 and Tatum in 1956.

Bill Friday was no stranger to intercollegiate sports, and as Gray's assistant he had become well acquainted with the lack of academic control. In 1953, after State College conducted tryouts for fourteen high school recruits, a banned practice, the ACC placed the campus on a year's probation and declared those prospects who had participated in the tryouts to be ineligible. It was in response to this scandal that the UNC trustees, in January 1954, delegated responsibility over athletics to the chancellors. In May 1954, after State College had won the ACC basketball championship and played in the National Collegiate Athletics Association (NCAA) tournament, the NCAA also penalized the Wolfpack by placing the team on probation during the 1954–55 season. Although it won the 1955 ACC championship, State was barred from postseason play. Reports of irregularities in the recruitment of basketball player Ronnie Shavlik prompted another NCAA investigation, but State College was cleared. Then, in 1956, while Friday was still acting president, the NCAA launched another investigation into the recruiting of Jackie Moreland, a six-foot, eight-inch star from Minden, Louisiana.[5]

The NCAA eventually made four charges of rules violations in the Moreland investigation. First, investigators accused State College of paying Moreland's transportation expenses of $80 from Minden to Raleigh. Second, Moreland was allegedly offered a five-year scholarship. Third, the NCAA contended that State College recruiters – assistant athletic director Willis Casey, assistant basketball coach Vic Bubas, and Harry Stewart, secretary of State College's booster organization, the Wolfpack Club – had proposed to give Moreland financial aid beyond an athletic scholarship, to include annual cash payments. And fourth, State College allegedly offered to pay for seven years the educational expenses of Moreland's girlfriend, Betty Clara Rhea, who was attending Centenary College at Shreveport, Louisiana, and who planned eventually to enroll in medical school.

The NCAA began its probe after a furious recruiting war between State College, Centenary College, the University of Kentucky, and Texas A&M University resulted, in September 1956, in Moreland's decision to attend State College. Moreland apparently reached his decision after Bubas, Stewart, and former player Ronnie Shavlik and his wife paid a visit to Louisiana in late August 1956, where they allegedly made the illegal offers of cash payments and aid. One of the losers in the recruiting war was Adolph Rupp, builder of a basketball dynasty at the University of Kentucky. Rupp, who had signed Moreland to a letter of intent and expected him to enroll at Kentucky, urged an NCAA investigation as a way to punish the State College upstarts.[6]

That investigation took place at the highest levels; it involved Commissioner Walter Byers and the governing NCAA Council. Byers personally took charge of the case, traveling to Raleigh during October 1956 to interview Moreland at the Sir Walter Hotel. In late October the NCAA summoned Chancellor Bostian to testify twice, and in November Bostian and State College athletic director Roy Clogston met with the NCAA's compliance committee in Kansas City and with the eighteen-member NCAA Council in Detroit. The NCAA's disposition of the Moreland case was announced on November 13, 1956. Having two years earlier imposed a severe sanction, the NCAA now regarded State College as a renegade institution, and it was determined to discipline the school. The NCAA inflicted the most severe penalty ever imposed: probation for four years, during which time none of State College's intercollegiate teams would be eligible for postseason competition.[7]

Bill Friday was shaken by the announcement. To reporters, he expressed "puzzlement" at the NCAA's decision but said that he was determined to investigate and take whatever action was necessary. Years later, he expressed frustration about the case. "I had never in my life," he said, "gotten into anything that was as perplexing and as bothersome to me as that episode." Much of Friday's frustration lay in his inability to discover the truth, either from closed-mouthed State College officials or from the NCAA, whose investigators took secret testimony and refused to reveal the basis for NCAA decisions. Although Friday's attempts to investigate the situation in Raleigh evoked denials from the State College campus, doubts remained. He subsequently recalled that an NCAA official, visiting Chapel Hill in the midst of the Moreland case, had called and asked him for a meeting to discuss the case. "All I want to tell you is that you are not being told the truth," he said.

Claiming that he possessed irrefutable evidence, the NCAA official assured Friday of State College's guilt.[8]

Nonetheless, Friday remained troubled. Even admitting the likelihood of State College's malfeasance, he lacked confidence in the fairness or accuracy of the NCAA investigation. As he explained in a public statement released on November 13, 1956, UNC officials had, two years earlier, conducted their own inquiry, fully disclosed State College's illegal tryouts, and willingly accepted the ACC's and the NCAA's sanctions. Now, in the Moreland case, Friday had conducted another investigation after charges were circulated in September. But UNC found no violation of NCAA rules and so reported this finding to the NCAA's Committee on Infractions at its meeting in Kansas City on October 22. When the NCAA committee charged State College with rules violations, Friday called Byers and sought to review the NCAA's evidence. That request was denied, as was a request, in November, for a postponement in the NCAA Council's decision. Although the Moreland case focused on State College practices, Friday was actively involved. State College chancellor Bostian recalled that Friday accompanied him to NCAA headquarters in Kansas City, where Friday "did most of the talking" and served, in effect, as Bostian's attorney. NCAA officials, Friday asserted, acted as "judge, jury, prosecutor," and the university "had to abide by what they said." The NCAA bureaucracy was, he remembered, the "final law." Bostian, like Friday, wanted firmer evidence, and the two administrators took the position that they would not fire Coach Case without it.[9]

As the Moreland case dragged on over the next months, UNC officials appealed the NCAA sanctions. Soon after the sanctions were imposed, on November 27, Bostian asked Charles Jordan, Duke University secretary and president of the ACC, for an independent investigation by the conference. After reviewing evidence, the ACC faculty representatives, on December 7, 1956, concurred with two of the NCAA's charges – that State College had offered a five-year scholarship to Moreland and that it had paid his $80 transportation costs – while they ignored the more sensational charges of cash grants and the payments to his girlfriend. ACC commissioner James Weaver, whom Friday had known when Weaver was athletic director at Wake Forest, communicated the ACC's findings to UNC on December 8. Then, a week later, affirming that State College had broken the rules, the conference imposed additional sanctions: a fine of $5,000 (which would be canceled if the ineligible Moreland remained as a student) and a ban on any recruiting for one year. ACC representatives subsequently endorsed these sanctions at a meeting in Greensboro.[10]

Convinced that the case would never be adequately resolved, Friday de-

Bill Friday's UNC administration. From left to right: Donald B. Anderson, William M. Whyburn, William D. Carmichael Jr., William Friday, Claude Teague, and A. H. Shepard Jr. (Courtesy of the North Carolina Collection)

cided in late February 1957 to close the matter formally. At a meeting of the Board of Trustees' Executive Committee, he explained that UNC officials had exhausted every possible means to understand the Moreland affair. Unable to obtain access to the NCAA's evidence, they took the position that there was "no cause for action." The trustees, quickly concurring, supported Friday's actions. At the same time, they reaffirmed the trustees' decision in 1954 to delegate authority over UNC sports to the chancellors. About a week later, he formally reported the closing of the case to Bostian, reminding him of his responsibilities as chancellor to ensure that "no future question may be raised concerning our compliance with all regulations." Yet, as Friday later admitted, the conclusion of the matter was unsatisfactory. In essence, he had "got out a bucket of whitewash, painted over the whole mess, and called it concluded."[11]

Friday's inability to obtain the truth in the Moreland case from either State College or the NCAA strongly shaped his subsequent attitude toward intercollegiate athletics. Friday had experienced a "deep frustration" in his search for a successful resolution. Thoroughly disgusted with the NCAA style of investigation, he was also suspicious of the State College sports establishment while fully cognizant of the entrenched alumni and commercial interests that surrounded it. Moreover, Friday realized that uncontrolled intercollegiate sports threatened a university's academic integrity. Tainting by a corrupt sports establishment might eventually provoke the intervention of external agencies, such as the NCAA or perhaps even law-making bodies, that would seek to limit university autonomy in order to clean up college and university sports programs. All these considerations convinced Friday that if he were to face another issue of administrative control over intercollegiate athletics less equivocal than the Moreland case, he would act decisively.[12]

Friday's fears were soon confirmed. In 1960 the NCAA investigated charges of excessive entertainment for recruits and their parents by Carolina basketball coach Frank McGuire; on January 10, 1961, it placed the team on a one-year probation.[13] Then, in March, there was evidence that North Carolina basketball players were involved in a point-shaving scandal, in which athletes were bribed to increase or reduce the margin of victory; the scandal would eventually implicate as many as fifty players around the country. New York City district attorney Frank S. Hogan charged that Seton Hall College players had shaved points in a game with the University of Dayton at Madison Square Garden on February 9, 1961, that a University of Connecticut player was bribed to shave points in a game against Colgate University on March 1, 1961, and that widespread fixing and point shaving had occurred in as many as twenty colleges and universities. On March 21, 1961, two New York City detectives visited North Carolina, stirring speculation in the local press about point shaving at Carolina and State. On March 29, Louis Brown, a reserve player on the Carolina basketball team, admitted that he had connections with gamblers. When Brown was named as the contact man, he voluntarily withdrew from Carolina, although William Aycock, who had succeeded Bob House as Chapel Hill's chancellor in 1957, announced that Brown would not return without his permission.[14]

In May 1961 the point-shaving scandal spread, as Doug Moe, an All-American at Carolina, became implicated in Brown's operation. Although Moe had accepted no bribes, he had been given a total of $75 in the course of his dealings with Brown on two occasions, in September and December 1960. When Aycock personally investigated the Brown affair on March 22, the day after the visit from the New York detectives, Moe had told the chancellor that he was in "no way" involved in the scandal. During two additional conferences with Aycock, Moe again denied involvement. It was only at a fourth meeting — after a sportswriter called Aycock and told him that Moe had admitted receiving the $75 payment in court testimony — that Moe acknowledged his role in the affair. Aycock moved swiftly. But although he brought Moe's case before the Men's Honor Council at Carolina, the council was unable to question Brown because he had withdrawn from Chapel Hill. Without hearing any testimony from Aycock, the Men's Honor Council absolved Moe, who was due to graduate that spring. Aycock found its decision perplexing, and, on May 3, 1961, he suspended Moe "indefinitely," giving him forty-eight hours to leave campus. The penalty, which was less severe than expulsion, permitted Moe to apply for readmission in the spring semester of 1962.[15]

But the true implications of the point-shaving scandal and intercollegiate athletics at State and Carolina had not yet become fully clear, however. On the morning of Saturday, May 14, 1961, Lester V. Chalmers, the district solicitor for Wake County, telephoned Friday at home. "I need to talk to you," he said.

Friday agreed to meet him at the UNC office, which had moved from South Building to Franklin Street. Chalmers delivered some shocking news. "I've got to tell you a very unpleasant thing," he explained. Gamblers, he recently learned, had paid State College basketball players to shave points at the Dixie Classic tournament game between State and Georgia Tech on December 17, 1960. The point spread was five points, and when State College won the game 82–76, the gamblers later met the players outside Reynolds Coliseum, pressed guns into their stomachs, and demanded that they return the money. The Dixie Classic, a three-day tournament, matched the North Carolina Big Four schools of Wake Forest, State College, Carolina, and Duke against four nationally ranked out-of-state teams. By 1961 the Dixie Classic was at the center of the state's basketball fever. "Are you telling me that gambling has now taken over this event?" Friday asked. Chalmers responded that the evidence so indicated.[16]

Friday subsequently discovered that three State College players had been implicated: Stan Niewierowski, a forward from Brooklyn and the team captain; Anton "Dutch" Muehlbauer, a junior guard, also from Brooklyn; and Terry Litchfield, a six-foot, ten-inch reserve center from Louisville, Kentucky. Through Lou Barshak, a player at Los Angeles State College, gamblers had approached Litchfield at a summer basketball league held in the Catskill Mountains of New York State. Litchfield then made contacts with other State College players. Niewierowski, according to some accounts, induced Muehlbauer to join him. The two starters, according to the warrant with which officers arrested them in mid-May 1961, had received $50 each for State's defeat of George Washington, in a game on December 3, 1960, by more than ten points (it won by twenty). Later, in addition to their participation in the botched point-shaving scheme during the Georgia Tech game, Niewierowski and Muehlbauer both received $1,250 to shave points in a game against Duke on January 7, 1961; State lost by fourteen points (81–67) after leading by a point at halftime. They were also paid $2,500 to throw a game against Carolina on February 15, 1961. The erratic play of Niewierowski and Muehlbauer aroused the suspicion of Coach Everett Case, who asked the State Bureau of Investigation to speak to the State College players the day after the Georgia Tech game about the dangers of gambling.[17]

Friday then went to work to prepare a response for the May 22 meeting of the Executive Committee and full Board of Trustees. State College chancellor John Tyler Caldwell was informed of the impending arrest and indictment of the three State College players; Niewierowski and Muehlbauer had already withdrawn for academic reasons. On May 13 Caldwell refused to permit them to reenroll; he also dismissed Litchfield and told him that he would not be readmitted. Friday imposed an information blackout. He even refused to discuss the matter with his old friend Dick Herbert, sports editor of the *Raleigh News and Observer*. Instead, in what he recalled as a "long and extensive examination," Friday held numerous meetings with Caldwell and Aycock in the UNC office. Both chancellors and Friday were eager to take bold steps to put the scandal behind them. They briefly discussed reviving the Graham Plan but rejected it because of its demonstrated impracticality. A consensus emerged that strong measures were needed to end athletes' involvement in summer camps, that recruiting should be limited to the conference area, and that the number of games should be reduced.[18]

Friday himself was determined to administer bitter medicine. He strongly influenced the chancellors' consultations, according to Aycock, meeting extensively with them and exerting "a right heavy hand" in decision making. If there was a difference of opinion, it had to do with the Dixie Classic. Aycock had little interest in it; Carolina had been an invited participant, while the revenues went to State College. Caldwell, with an avid alumni basketball following and equally vociferous supporters of the tournament within the Raleigh business community, was not eager to end it permanently. Lasting for twelve years, from 1949 to 1961, the Dixie Classic had become known as the most successful holiday college basketball tournament in the country; during those years it had attracted a total of 713,800 spectators to State's Reynolds Coliseum. The tournament was also a moneymaker for State College, bringing annual profits of nearly $31,000 out of a total basketball budget of $70,000. Although Caldwell recalled that he had favored ending it for only a year, Friday maintained that there was "no time context" attached to the decision to end the tournament.[19]

Caldwell kept these reservations, if he had them at the time, to himself. Friday's decision to end the Dixie Classic enjoyed the full participation and concurrence of Aycock and Caldwell, and the three of them were of one mind at every juncture of their discussions. After the Moreland case and the problems at Carolina with Louis Brown and Doug Moe, Aycock recalled, the Dixie Classic scandal was "sort of the tornado on top of the storm." Friday realized, along with the chancellors, that the situation had reached a desperate point when gamblers were themselves visiting Reynolds Coliseum and dealing directly with student athletes. This was "Friday's decision," said Aycock, "because he was the one that was going to have to take the heat for it."[20]

When the Board of Trustees met at North Carolina State's College Union shortly after 11:00 A.M. on May 22, 1961, Friday offered shock treatment for the university's athletic programs. In a seven-page statement that took more than fifteen minutes to read, the UNC president laid out his program. Basketball, he told the trustees, had brought "serious embarrassment" to UNC, and he was determined "to take action that would be clear in its purpose and specific in its application." Significant improvement, he said, had resulted from Gray's delegation of administrative responsibility for athletics to the chancellors in 1954 and from the reaffirmation of this policy in 1957. Aycock had acted boldly at Chapel Hill, and Caldwell, in dismissing the offending players, had proceeded "unhesitatingly and decisively" at State College. Friday then described his consultations with Aycock and Caldwell and reported their consensus about the need for strong action.[21]

Two courses of action were now available, Friday explained. One was to suspend or discontinue participation in intercollegiate athletics for a fixed period of time; the other was to move forthrightly to reform abuses so that sports could be continued. Friday chose the second alternative. In order to save intercollegiate athletics and to "restore sports to sportsmanship," it was necessary to deemphasize athletics. Participation in summer competition, such as the kind that exposed Terry Litchfield to gamblers in the Catskills, would be prohibited. Friday then announced measures that were to be in place for the next five years. While continuing athletic scholarships – for abandoning them completely might well accentuate control by boosters – Friday limited each UNC team to only two out-of-state scholarships. Beginning with the 1961–62 season, basketball competition would be restricted to fourteen games, most of them against ACC opponents – rather than a maximum of twenty-five games permitted by the conference – along with the ACC and NCAA tournaments. In addition, Friday reaffirmed that the coaches' jobs were "expressly assured" and not contingent "upon their obligation merely to win games or to achieve national standing for our teams." But the most dramatic step was Friday's announcement that the Dixie Classic would be discontinued. Holiday tournaments, he said, exemplified "the exploitation for public entertainment or for budgetary and commercial purposes of a sports program which properly exists as an adjunct to collegiate education." Tournaments subjected students, coaches, and colleges to "unnecessary demands and unwise distractions."

Bill Friday simply informed the trustees of these actions. He made it clear that he was not presenting them for approval, because earlier resolutions delegated responsibility for athletics to the local campuses and gave final authority to the president's office. Friday realized that the matter required strong leadership. "If I had turned the thing over to the trustees," he recalled, "I think we'd probably have had four meetings, six committees, and never have gotten to the decision point." Indecision and "exhaustion" would have been the likely results. Instead, he and Caldwell and Aycock decided to act alone; "nobody told us we didn't have the authority to do it, so we did it."[22]

Some trustees at the meeting of the full board objected to the fact that the decision to cancel the Dixie Classic had been made without their consultation. Sam Whitehurst of New Bern urged that trustees study the issue before acting and provide an "opportunity to hear from the people back home." Friday responded pointedly. The nation, he told Whitehurst, was watching to see how UNC acted. "We aren't asking you to approve any of the steps I have indicated to you," he said. The administration had already acted; the decision had already been made. The issue facing trustees was instead "the attitude and philosophy" that they manifested toward the future of intercollegiate athletics. Despite an hour-long discussion on a motion offered by William B. Harrison of Rocky Mount to study the report and to form a trustee committee, the administration had presented trustees with a fait accompli. The question, recalled Friday, had become, "Are you ready to take over the administration of intercollegiate athletics as a Board of Trustees?"[23]

Friday, despite some trustee grumbling, enjoyed the solid backing of the Executive Committee and the chancellors. When trustee Ernest Parker asked why an out-of-conference tournament should be canceled when much of the bribery occurred during conference games, Caldwell responded. Big-time athletics had brought the university national stature; many people enjoyed seeing their institutions in a national ranking. But the real question was whether "the price has been too great." In order to seize "upon the sobering moment," Caldwell explained, trustees should realize that UNC's good name was its "most precious possession." Alumni, university officials, and trustees had to rally around the university and defend its "integrity and moral rectitude and a sound sense of values."[24]

It was a skillful performance by Friday. He had struck a strong blow for academic integrity and prodded along efforts at both State and Carolina to clean up their athletic programs. In the wake of the Dixie Classic cancellation, both Everett Case and Frank McGuire resigned; their departure went a long way toward reforming their programs. At Carolina, Dean Smith succeeded McGuire, who left in August 1961 to coach the Philadelphia Warriors in the National Basketball Association, and Smith began a long and extraordinary career in college basketball. Even more important, the collapse of Everett Case's empire ended more than a decade of uncontrolled athletic boosterism at State College.[25]

Much of the state's leadership praised the decision to cancel the Dixie Classic. Friday now had the opportunity, commented the *Charlotte Observer*, "to grab hold of the tail" that was "wagging the dog." The *Raleigh News and Observer* declared that cancellation was the only way that athletics at UNC could be "salvaged from the scandal that is now shaking its very foundations."

Years afterward a legislator maintained that "most thoughtful people" had supported Friday's decision: sports "had just sort of gotten out of hand," and Friday displayed appropriate leadership by stepping in and doing "what he had to do." Most state leaders also admired Friday's courage. William Snider, then editorialist for the *Greensboro Daily News*, later cited Friday's handling of the Dixie Classic crisis as an example of his ability to put out fires before they started. Even though he faced the wrath of the "marketplace people, the athletic people," Snider said, Friday had acted quickly, decisively, and effectively.[26]

Yet Friday paid a high political price for abolishing the Dixie Classic. Trustee disgruntlement at the meeting on May 22 gave some indication of public opinion about the tournament. It had been hugely popular and had attracted basketball fans from across the state, especially from eastern North Carolina. It was said, according to one fan from Duplin County, that you could tell whether State College had "won or lost on Saturday night by the expressions on the young men's faces on Sunday morning at Sunday School." As Friday later realized, canceling the tournament created "a lot of ill will" that would be directed toward UNC. Although his edict to the trustees ended the matter, he later said that "it nearly came to ending me, too." State agriculture commissioner Jim Graham, in a letter to Caldwell, called the decision a "serious mistake" that amounted to "grabbing at a straw man for an outlet." Another correspondent complained to Friday that it would "hurt and retard" UNC's political support and had been made without consultation with its "leaders and backers."[27]

Although they grudgingly accepted Friday's decision to cancel the Dixie Classic, State College boosters – even Caldwell himself – claimed not to have realized that the tournament was doomed. Caldwell later maintained that he thought that Friday had only suspended it for a year, although he soon realized that the other Big Four schools, especially Carolina and Duke, were happy to be released from the obligation. As Friday eased restrictions on the Carolina and State athletics programs in 1963, when recruiting and the numbers of games played returned to the pre-1961 limits, calls were made to resurrect the Dixie Classic. State College alumni, basketball fans, and the Raleigh business community began to hope that the tournament would be revived. In the spring of 1963 they even attempted to push a resolution endorsing its revival through the state legislature. That measure failed, and, despite the easing of restrictions on State and Carolina's participation in holiday tournaments in May 1964, the political fallout was significant.[28]

State College fans in particular were aggrieved, and they suspected that Chapel Hill was the culprit. "Shall we all bow down three times in celebration of 'the mighty one' to allow a couple of regular season basketball games?" a State College alumnus from Knightdale wrote soon after Friday's easing of the holiday tournament restrictions. Earlier, in a January 1964 TV editorial, Jesse Helms admitted that the scandal surrounding the Dixie Classic was "shocking and heartbreaking," but its cancellation was "not a cure but a revelation of inadequacy to meet a problem." The UNC administration had made the tournament into "a scapegoat in an act of haste and devoid of logic." "You cannot separate a strong athletic policy from a strong educational policy," maintained another sports fan; the two went together like "crackers and cheese." If anything, he believed, what needed reforming at the university were the "pseudo-intellectual groups," the beatniks, the "pinks," Communists, and other suspicious left-wingers.[29]

THE Dixie Classic episode was but one illustration of a widening gulf between the world of the university and the world of the average North Carolinian. Although most residents of the state, on one level, valued academic integrity, on another they were insistent about the importance of intercollegiate sports. Friday intervened drastically in May 1961 by canceling the Dixie Classic and preserving UNC autonomy against the possibility of outside intervention, whether it was that of the NCAA, the ACC, or the North Carolina General Assembly. Yet his intervention tested the limits of public patience and, over time, contributed to an erosion of political support for the University of North Carolina.

The furor surrounding the cancellation of the Dixie Classic was part of a public backlash against universities in general and the Chapel Hill campus in particular that culminated in the most serious challenge to Friday's leadership since he had become president in 1956. In late June 1963 the legislature concluded its longest session to that date, divided by rancorous disputes over the Dixie Classic, the reorganization of the university, and the laborious task of reapportionment in the wake of the Supreme Court's landmark ruling in *Baker* v. *Carr*. In an ugly mood, the legislature, on June 25, 1963, enacted House Bill 1395, an innocuous-sounding measure, which barred any "known Communist" or person who had taken the Fifth Amendment from speaking at public colleges and universities. The passage of the bill stirred up a hornet's nest. Behind its passage lay a growing sense of frustration with UNC among legislators and a belief, widely held among North Carolinians generally, that Chapel Hill was a stronghold of disloyalty.

Fears of communism had long been merged with fears of racial integration; the Speaker Ban bill simply brought those tensions into the open. In the campaign preceding the gubernatorial primary of May 1960, when arch-segregationist I. Beverly Lake opposed Terry Sanford, Lake's manager, state senator Robert B. Morgan, attacked an appearance by civil rights leader Martin Luther King Jr. on the Chapel Hill campus that spring. Further, Morgan claimed that black leaders used the UNC-run educational television station to publicize the sit-in movement that had swept the state and region during the winter and spring of 1960. Later, the Chapel Hill post of the American Legion continued the offensive. After two leftist organizations, the Progressive Labor Club and the New Left Club, obtained campus recognition and sponsored appearances by black activists, the Chapel Hill post, in a resolution written by Colonel Henry Royall, denounced leftist leanings on the Chapel Hill campus and urged a legislative investigation. When Progressive Labor leader Milton Rosen spoke on campus on December 3, 1962, under the auspices of the New Left Club – an event attended by fourteen people – the legionnaires were further aroused, and they adopted two resolutions in June 1963 urging state intervention.[30]

Other North Carolinians contributed to the anti-intellectual chorus. Much of it had a xenophobic tone. In 1960 Jesse Helms began a decade of televised editorials on Raleigh's WRAL-TV that regularly criticized New Deal liberalism. In December 1961 he attacked Abraham Holtzman, a professor of political science at State College, whom he described as a California native who had "little admiration for the South and its traditions." With a "captive audience of young minds," Holtzman espoused liberalism – specifically, he supported federal aid to education – without "rebuttal by other professors with opposing philosophies." Professors such as Holtzman, Helms suggested, were adversely affecting the university's public reputation; its stature was "not enhanced by the public preachments of such men."[31]

When both Friday and Caldwell defended Holtzman's right to free speech, Helms suggested a "head count" of professors of political science and history. If there was an imbalance between conservatives and liberals, then administrators should seek to rectify it. The issue, Helms claimed, was not academic freedom. The search for truth was legitimate, he contended, only insofar as its "substance is sometimes debatable." Helms continued his assault on UNC into late 1962, when he joined the legionnaires' attack on Milt Rosen's visit and criticized an appearance by folksinger Pete Seeger, whom Helms called a "known Communist." In April 1963 Helms, complaining about the "avowed Communists, leftwingers, ultra-liberals in a solid phalanx" who had visited the Carolina campus, asserted that "the matter ought to be looked into."[32]

The reality was that, despite its reputation for tolerance, the Chapel Hill campus had excluded Communists since the late 1940s. In May 1949 the UNC trustees delegated responsibility for screening speakers to administrators. Chancellor House had already banned *Daily Worker* editor John Gates from speaking on the campus in January 1949. Soon afterward, House added loyalty questions to the personnel forms required of all new faculty, and there were no Communists on the faculty in the 1950s. Communist speakers remained banned from campus throughout the 1950s. In 1954, when Gus Hall, general secretary of the American Communist Party, visited Chapel Hill, he was forced to speak in a vacant lot off campus. In 1956 Tom Lambeth, then student chairman of the Carolina Forum, the campus speaker series, quashed a student attempt to invite Junius Scales, a Communist and former UNC student who was convicted under the Smith Act, to speak on campus. Lambeth reached this decision without the explicit approval but certainly with the blessing of administrators. Although Bill Aycock, when he became chancellor, succeeded in removing loyalty oaths from personnel forms, until the 1980s faculty members (as public employees) were still required to sign separate oaths indicating loyalty to both the state and national constitutions.[33]

The real reason for the growing public criticism of Chapel Hill lay elsewhere: anxiety about the mass uprising, during the spring of 1963, of black North Carolinians. Across the state there emerged a movement that largely paralleled the model of nonviolent disobedience spearheaded by Martin Luther King Jr. in Birmingham, Alabama. In Greensboro, street demonstrations lasted most of May and into June 1963, while similar protests occurred in other cities. In Raleigh, the movement became galvanized after the Liberian assistant secretary of state and ambassador to the United States, Angie Brooks, a graduate of Shaw University, returned for a seminar at her alma mater. Along with a student and Allard Lowenstein, a Chapel Hill graduate and longtime activist who was then on the political science faculty at State College, Brooks went to downtown Raleigh, where the management of both the coffee shop at the Sir Walter Hotel and the S&W cafeteria refused to serve her.[34]

An organized movement of street demonstrations erupted during much of May and June 1963. Demonstrators marched down Fayetteville Street, singing freedom songs along the way; before long, activists sought service at segregated hotels, restaurants, and movie theaters. By early May, police were beginning to arrest blacks for trespassing when they entered all-white establishments; black marchers responded by producing even larger groups of protesters. On May 8 police arrested ninety-two blacks as they descended on the state capitol's restaurant, the coffee shop at the Sir Walter Hotel, the S&W cafeteria, and two theaters. Nearly two hundred demonstrators, most of them Shaw students, strained the jails' capacity.[35]

After the mass arrests of May 8, city leaders and demonstrators reached a truce with the creation of a biracial committee. But the truce broke down about a month later, when demonstrators conducted a sit-in on Monday, June 10, 1963. About 8:30 P.M., six blacks attempted to register at the Sir Walter; when they were refused, they sat down in the lobby and the hotel manager called in the police. This began the so-called suitcase sit-ins and resulted in another round of arrests as about thirty more black demonstrators arrived with their suitcases that evening, inviting arrest. With the onset of the suitcase sit-ins, legislators – most of whom took up residence at the Sir Walter for the legislative session – were exposed to the demonstrators on an almost daily basis.[36]

On the evening of June 10, many legislators regarded the demonstrators angrily, convinced that white faculty members were inciting the black upris-ing. Secretary of State Thad Eure, a power in the General Assembly, remem-bered standing in front of the Sir Walter that night when "the motliest Negro group you ever saw" appeared and announced its intention to sleep in the hotel. Jim Phipps, a state representative from Orange County who was stand-ing next to Eure, nudged him and pointed to a white who, he said, was a professor at Chapel Hill. Eure urged Phipps to contact Bill Friday and see if he could, in "some tactful way," ensure that "this doesn't happen again."[37]

Other legislators reached a similar conclusion. T. Clarence Stone, president of the state senate, loudly complained that Carolina faculty members were instigating the demonstrations. Frank Taylor, a UNC trustee from Golds-boro, recognized among the marchers Al Amon, a psychology professor at Carolina, and denounced him for damaging the university's reputation. Other faculty members who took part included Allard Lowenstein and Nancy Adams, who was on the dean of women's staff at Chapel Hill. "If I hadn't already signed the university appropriation bill," Stone was heard to say, "I'd be holding back my pen." His colleagues communicated similar threats. Rep-resentative Phipps, who had seen Taylor, Stone, and Eure, tried to reach Friday by phone on the evening of June 20, but he was out of town. Instead, Phipps talked with Fred Weaver, then secretary of the university, and in-formed him that legislators were upset about faculty participation in the demonstrations and that the UNC educational television bill, then pending, might be endangered. Weaver, however, refused to restrict the political liber-ties of the Carolina faculty; later Friday fully endorsed Weaver's position. When Phipps returned with the news, the angry lawmakers regarded Weaver's response as an insulting brush-off from the UNC administration.[38]

The notion had become commonplace that Chapel Hill liberals and racial protesters were intimately connected and that, as Robert Morgan recalled, the UNC administration "wasn't willing to heed public outcry" about "objection-able" speakers. Much of the legislature's anger, he explained, had to do with

Friday and William Aycock, 1964. (Courtesy of the North Carolina Collection)

the perception of UNC "arrogance" toward public opinion. White faculty members involved in civil rights marches, Jesse Helms told WRAL-TV viewers on June 14, were participating in a host of other causes. "They hate this nation's immigration laws," he intoned, "which require the careful screening of foreigners coming to this country." They favored greater governmental centralization, world government, and deficit spending. "You pull a thread in the torn fabric of the structure of America and the thread endlessly crisscrosses from one stormy issue to another." Allard Lowenstein, Helms said, was an "announced leader and promoter" of the demonstrations; he had been a "close friend" of Junius Scales. This was a man whose life had been "dedicated primarily to agitation and the promotion of strife."[39]

The "accumulated animosity" that focused on the civil rights demonstrations and the university's involvement in them lay behind what Friday would, years later, call the General Assembly's "bad mood, an angry mood, a vengeful mood." Led by T. Clarence Stone in the state senate and Clifton Blue, speaker of the house, a group of legislators, including Representatives Ned Delamar of Pamlico County and Phil Godwin of Gates County, held private discussions in which they agreed that there was a need to assert legislative control over Chapel Hill liberalism. Among these men, there emerged a consensus that the 1941 North Carolina law prohibiting the advocacy of the violent overthrow of the government was insufficient. On Friday, June 21, Helms broadcast an editorial over WRAL praising the decision of Ohio State University to bar

Communists from its campus and the Ohio House of Representatives for passing a bill forbidding them to speak on campus. That weekend Delamar asked Secretary of State Eure to obtain a copy of the Ohio bill, and Eure sent a telegram to Ted Brown, his counterpart in Ohio and an old friend, from the Sir Walter lobby. On Monday, June 24, with a copy of the Ohio bill in hand, Eure visited Attorney General Wade Bruton.[40]

The lawmakers now proceeded according to a well-laid plan. The passage of the Speaker Ban was, Friday later stated, "as planned as anything that they'd ever done in that General Assembly." On June 25 the ban passed in the house in an orchestrated and rapid-fire fashion. Although Godwin subsequently denied any outright conspiracy, he and a small group of legislators proceeded carefully and deliberately. Godwin and Delamar showed the bill to potential supporters, picking up allies; by lunchtime, there were six additional cosponsors, along with Godwin and Delamar. That afternoon, during the waning hours of the 1963 session, Godwin introduced House Bill 1395 and moved that the rules, which normally required a lengthy committee process to consider a bill, be suspended. Few university supporters remained in the house; many of them had gone home. Those legislators still in the house chamber were, as Blue later admitted, "tired and inattentive." After the clerk read the bill, Godwin spoke on its behalf; copies of the measure were not made available. Most of the remaining legislators paid little attention to the Speaker Ban measure, which was grouped with the flood of local bills that usually accompanied the end of a legislative session. To Representative David M. Britt, later state supreme court justice, it had "sounded just like apple pie and everything else a true American would back." Impressed by Godwin's "very forceful remarks," he "didn't pay much attention to it." Nonetheless, he admitted that he and other legislators were "just taken by surprise." Four minutes after Godwin introduced the legislation, Speaker Blue declared it passed by a voice vote. House Bill 1395 was then sent by special messenger to the senate, where Stone, who had become presiding officer after the death of Lieutenant Governor H. Cloyd Philpott on August 18, 1961, rammed it through three readings. Gaveling down the opposition, he ruled the bill passed by voice vote even before opponents had a chance to open their mouths. By three o'clock, barely an hour after Godwin introduced it, the Speaker Ban bill had cleared the General Assembly, and the senate adjourned for the day.[41]

Sailing through the General Assembly along with the usual end-of-session local and pork barrel bills, the new law would embroil the University of North Carolina in a controversy lasting nearly five years. Entitled "An Act to Regulate Visiting Speakers at State Supported Colleges and Universities," it prohibited from speaking at any public college or university anyone who was a "known member" of the Communist Party, who was "known" to advocate the overthrow of the constitution of North Carolina or of the United States, or who had pled the Fifth Amendment in refusing to answer questions about Communist subversion. The law's enactment was a defining moment in the history of post–World War II North Carolina. Its passage and the ensuing controversy also illustrate the relationship between the University of North Carolina and the political power structure of the state, and the ways in which President William Friday sought to manage relations with the political establishment.

By 1963 public tolerance of UNC liberalism was running out, and most observers agreed that the Speaker Ban was directed at Carolina. Both the "civil rights militancy" and UNC's apparent support for it, explained one reporter, seemed "particularly abrasive" to legislators. Ralph Scott described a "spirit of fear and distrust" that made Chapel Hill the "real object" of the law. It was an effort by a well-organized group, he believed, to "discredit the University." The wrath of the legislators, said Louis Round Wilson, Carolina librarian and longtime Chapel Hill figure, boiled over at the civil rights uprising in which blacks "had the nerve to 'demonstrate' in Raleigh and in the new Legislative building." The presence of Chapel Hill students and faculty at these demonstrations was simply the "last straw."[42]

Caught off guard, Bill Friday was engrossed in other, seemingly more pressing issues during the 1963 legislative session and out of town during the suitcase sit-ins. The death of Billy Carmichael two years earlier, in January 1961, meant the loss of Friday's ablest political adviser; his administrative team did not include anyone so skilled in reading the legislative mood. According to one reporter, the lawmakers missed the "continuity" of Carmichael. He could "talk the language of the educators and the legislators" as no one else seemed able to do. Although Friday and Weaver attended virtually every day of the session, they were absent from Raleigh during the events of June 25 and, more seriously, suffered from an important intelligence gap about the maneuvering of Delamar, Godwin, and Stone. No one in the entire university, remembered Bill Aycock, "had the slightest notion" of the impending Speaker Ban. A unique combination of factors – rage at the civil rights revolution, anti-intellectualism, and hostility toward a perceived lack of UNC responsiveness – had caught Friday completely unprepared. "I should have seen," he later reflected, "that the leadership [of the legislature] . . . was not leadership devoted to the University of North Carolina." That leadership was a "negative element," determined to discipline Chapel Hill.[43]

The Speaker Ban, Bill Aycock would say, was the only piece of legislation in the three decades of Friday's UNC presidency "that he didn't know anything about." Not until about 2:45 on the afternoon of June 25, after Grace Mewborn Aycock, wife of the chancellor, heard on the radio that the bill had passed its house readings and notified her husband, did Friday learn of it. Hearing more about the measure after a telephone call to the Institute of Government, Friday telephoned Raleigh to discover that the senate was about to convene in an afternoon session. He and Weaver immediately drove to the capitol; during the trip, they heard a radio newscast about the bill but discovered, upon their arrival, that the senate had passed it and adjourned. After conferring with lawmakers at the Legislative Building, Friday, as he said a few weeks later, "sought out friends" and walked over to the Sir Walter Hotel to see if enough votes could be organized for reconsideration. Meanwhile, he told reporters that he would "do everything possible" to oppose the law, which he described as "totally unnecessary."[44]

At the front door of the hotel, about 5:00 P.M., he ran into state assemblyman David Britt. Recognizing "a very worried look" on Friday's face, Britt asked, "Bill, what brings you over here this time of day?" "You may not realize it," Friday responded, but "all hell's going to break loose as a result of that bill that was passed today." Thinking for a minute, Britt asked, "What bill are you talking about?" Still outside, Friday also encountered Hathaway Cross, a conservative lobbyist. "What are you doing over here?" Cross asked. "You know full well what I'm doing over here," Friday responded. "I came over here to tell you what you were doing to the university with this kind of legislation."[45]

Inside the hotel, Friday conferred with state senators John R. Jordan Jr., Perry Martin, Luther Hamilton, and others, and they agreed that the best strategy was to recall the bill from the enrolling office before it became law. Friday and his supporters worked furiously, pacing the corridors of the Sir Walter until 10:00 P.M. Friday's reception from Stone was icy. "You tell Friday to get out of here," he commented to a bystander when he saw the UNC president, "and to get back over there to run the university." Confronting Friday in person, Stone lectured him about the virtues of the Speaker Ban. Realizing the heavy lobbying by UNC forces, Stone would employ the power of his office to pressure wavering senators to stand firm.[46]

Returning to Chapel Hill late that night, Friday remained home the next day, fearing that his presence at the capitol might anger legislators. When the vote came before the senate to recall the bill, however, it failed to obtain the necessary two-thirds margin by a vote of 25 to 19. Despite vigorous objections by Luther Hamilton and Ralph Scott, another university supporter from Alamance County, Stone permitted the Speaker Ban to be ratified and so to become law. Fifteen senatorial opponents of the ban then registered their objections in a resolution that denounced the "abridgement or denial of free speech" and unwarranted intervention in university affairs.[47]

Governor Terry Sanford was also caught off guard by the passage of the bill. On the afternoon of June 25, he was speaking in Winston-Salem; although his engagement was "one of those things that you didn't have to go to," the end of the legislative session, he thought, had ushered in a more relaxed season. Sanford had wanted to lobby against the Speaker Ban, but when he spoke with Senator Gordon Hanes of Winston-Salem, he encountered what he later described as a typical reaction in the General Assembly. "What difference does it make?" Hanes asked. The bill had made Clarence Stone happy, and he saw no reason to oppose him. If Gordon Hanes failed to recognize the dangers of the Speaker Ban, recalled Sanford, who would?[48]

Sanford said that he would have vetoed the Speaker Ban law "in a second" had he had that power – governors in North Carolina do not – but other legislators later contended that his efforts were only half-hearted. Because Sanford believed that it would have been "terribly resented," he refused to call a special session to repeal the law. John Jordan subsequently claimed that the governor's tepid support for the opponents of the Speaker Ban was "one place Terry Sanford dropped the ball." Despite Sanford's assertions that he lobbied for reconsideration during the evening of June 25, Jordan said, he refused to provide the all-out support that might have provided the two-thirds margin. David Britt, who was not part of UNC's lobbying effort on June 25 and 26, remembered that Sanford was "very cautious" in the late stages of his governorship; he "just rode out the remainder of his term" and took few steps for repeal. In any event, Britt doubted whether more aggressive leadership from Sanford would have made any difference.[49]

Once the Speaker Ban became law, Friday realized, university administrators faced a formidable challenge in seeking repeal or amendment. He communicated with legislators in person and by mail, but opinion seemed to have hardened against repeal now that the law had been enacted. Clarence Stone received numerous letters commending him, as one correspondent expressed it, for "standing up for our concept of the truly American way of life." Meanwhile, Friday also pumped editorialists statewide with information, and the immediate response of the mainstream dailies was to condemn the ban. The *Raleigh Times*, for example, described it as "unworthy of the long tradition of the people of North Carolina." Both in the manner in which it was enacted and in the substance of the law, the Speaker Ban was "shameful" and an "admission of weakness, a terrible and dismaying weakness." It proclaimed to the world that the young people of the state were "so stupid and so impressionable and so weak that just the mere threat that a Communist might make a speech to them could turn them into Communists." Were young North Carolinians really "that weak and that stupid"? The law struck at the autonomy of college campuses and was a "slap in the face" of administrators and trustees; it opened the way for "scheming and unscrupulous meddlers to stick their dirty and ignorant and fearful fingers" into academic affairs.[50]

The *Greensboro Daily News* agreed. The law, it editorialized, was "fundamentally objectionable," not only because of its abridgement of free speech, but also because it was so vague as to be unenforceable. It raised a myriad of questions. What constituted a "known Communist"? What was the definition of a "speaker"? Would visiting dignitaries from Iron Curtain countries qualify? Would Russian ballet dancers invite a ban? Did the banning of "known Communists" and those who had taken the Fifth Amendment mean that all speakers would be required to sign an affidavit before entering the campus? Would any faculty member who had taken the Fifth be fired? A literal enforcement of the law might also lead to an exodus of competent faculty from the UNC campuses. "Screening everybody who strolls through the campus gates" would be "a big job."[51]

Nonetheless, editorial opinion did not necessarily represent public opinion at large. "Do I understand that you are supporting the right of communists to speak on the campus at the University of North Carolina?" one North Carolinian asked Friday. Why should Communists be able to "speak and spread their poison, and be honored at our colleges and university?" a Wilmington attorney wrote. "Should they be honored by the very State they are trying to destroy?" If he was "any judge of the public mood," added Jesse Helms a day after the Speaker Ban became law, "the law banning Communists from our campuses will be greeted by overwhelming approval by the general public." The law was a "vote of no-confidence" in those running the state's public universities and colleges.[52] Despite what one Winston-Salem journalist described as "almost unanimous newspaper criticism of it," popular opinion coalesced behind the Speaker Ban in the summer of 1963. UNC supporters in the legislature soon realized, as one assemblyman later reflected, that they had crashed into a "hornet's nest." Even Friday acknowledged that there was "widespread and disturbing public support" for the law and that it was "an almost impossible task" to repeal it.[53]

Public support for the ban struck close to home: Friday realized that trustee support for repeal or modification was weak. Trustees might not have sympathized with the law, according to J. Carlyle Sitterson, a Carolina historian who later became chancellor at that campus, but many of them "sympathized with the viewpoint that the law was trying to impose." Trustees were reluctant to enter into a "political minefield," recalled Bill Aycock; others saw little wrong with the law. The typical trustee reaction, Aycock observed, was to say, "Let's be quiet about this thing for a while." Facing trustee reluctance, Friday embarked on a campaign to solidify support for repeal. In this effort, he turned to Aycock, partly because he trusted his superior skills as a lawyer and advocate, partly because the Speaker Ban was aimed directly at the Chapel Hill campus. Soon after the bill was passed, according to Aycock, the two men were in "constant consultation" over the matter.[54]

On July 8, two weeks after enactment of the law, the Executive Committee of the UNC Board of Trustees convened, with the Speaker Ban the main order of business. As usual, Friday came well prepared. A week earlier, he had told the chancellors at the regular meeting of the Administrative Council that he favored repeal and would coordinate strategy with the trustees. For the time being, based on a legal analysis provided by Bill Aycock, he would seek to persuade the Executive Committee to follow a narrow construction of the law. That meant, he explained, stating that the law applied to visiting speakers but not to faculty or staff members.[55]

Friday elaborated on this strategy in the Executive Committee meeting. Reviewing the events that had led up to the passage of the Speaker Ban, he maintained that faculty involvement in the civil rights demonstrations had helped to arouse the legislators' anger. Friday explained the potentially disastrous implications of the law, but he raised the more immediate problem of university autonomy. The issue was not the banning of leftist speakers; the real question was UNC's freedom to manage its own affairs. A university lacking academic freedom, he told the committee members, was no university; the Speaker Ban's "fatal contradiction" was that it sought to protect freedom against Communist subversion by fettering "an institution which is the surest guarantor of freedom." Moreover, the law was unenforceable. The Executive Committee responded by offering a vaguely worded resolution that called for enforcement of the law but also requested its repeal.[56]

During the remainder of the summer and the autumn of 1963, Friday attempted to solidify trustee support. He was bolstered by nearly unanimous faculty opposition to the ban. Meanwhile, prior to the full Board of Trustees meeting on October 28, he and Aycock visited North Carolina cities to meet with trustees and urge them, in Friday's words, to assume "a more aggressive attitude." The first of these meetings was held in September 1963 in Greenville, where, according to Aycock, Friday did "all of the talking" but relied on Aycock's legal opinion of the law. They next visited Raleigh, where they met with a group of ten or twenty trustees. Then Aycock visited a group in Charlotte by himself while Friday traveled to Asheville and Wilmington.[57]

Largely because of these efforts, the trustees, at their meeting on October

28, gave Friday solid backing. Victor Bryant had told Friday in early October that the university should resist the Speaker Ban to the fullest extent of its ability and that neither the administration nor the trustees could afford to remain silent. The full board meeting was preceded by a meeting of the Executive Committee, which, after "lengthy discussion," drafted a resolution and named Bryant, Wade Barber, and Watts Hill to steer its passage through the full board. The resolution asserted that the Speaker Ban law violated "an essential principle of university existence," damaged university prestige, and threatened trustee autonomy. To "remove this legislative impairment of intellectual freedom and preemption of the authority and prerogatives of the Board of Trustees," the resolution recommended the creation of a special committee, to be appointed by the governor, to seek changes in the law.[58]

Before adopting this resolution, the UNC trustees heard a strong statement from Bill Aycock. He pointed out that the Speaker Ban law was vague whereas the act of 1941, which made advocacy of the violent overthrow of the government illegal, was specific. Because it prohibited any speech by a whole category of people, the ban was "fraught with uncertainties and ambiguities." Moreover, it was virtually impossible to enforce. What kind of Communists were included? Were only Americans so prohibited, or were any citizens of any Communist nation? By what standard could UNC administrators determine whether a speaker was a "known" Communist or a subversive who had taken the Fifth Amendment?[59]

Even with board support, Friday faced an uphill battle. With the October 1963 trustee resolution, he was now free to become a public advocate of repeal, but he recognized that the Speaker Ban could become an issue during the legislative and gubernatorial elections of 1964. The publicity surrounding his efforts to rally trustee opinion also threatened to alienate legislative opinion, which Friday was attempting to cultivate. In November 1963 state representative and Speaker Ban supporter Phil Godwin complained to Friday that there was "too much being done by the administration on this matter"; he also cited as excessive the statements by some trustees describing promoters of the ban as "little Hitlers and Mussolinis." Friday, ignoring his own attempts to rally opposition, assured Godwin that he had not gone out of his way "to agitate this issue."[60]

Fearing a political backlash, Friday and other university officials awaited the outcome of the Democratic gubernatorial primary. In that contest, the conservative Dan K. Moore defeated the moderate ally of Terry Sanford, L. Richardson Preyer, in a runoff primary in which the black uprising of 1963 and Sanford's racial liberalism had been major issues. Two weeks before Moore's election, on October 21, 1964, Governor Sanford – who had avoided entanglement in the Speaker Ban issue – finally appointed the special committee authorized by the UNC trustees a year earlier. Headed by Waynesville attorney William Medford, the committee eventually would seek a formula for amendment rather than repeal of the Speaker Ban. The basic elements of that formula, the Medford Committee decided at its first meeting on January 8, 1965, included shifting authority over speakers to the trustees and delegating the power to decide the rules governing those speakers to UNC officials.[61]

The Medford Committee, meeting in the winter of 1965, operated under terrific political pressure. Governor Moore was suspicious of Friday and the university administration; as Arnold King put it, Friday and Moore "had no rapport when he [Moore] came into office." The Medford Committee attempted to persuade Moore and legislators that it was operating independently of Friday's staff. In April 1965 committee member Jennings G. King informed Friday that UNC loyalists were having "a certain amount of difficulty" in solidifying support for amending the Speaker Ban law. At least two former supporters of the UNC position had changed their minds, he wrote, because of "a constant pressure from their home districts."[62]

Nonetheless, the report of the Medford Committee, which was delivered to Moore on April 24, 1965, embodied most of the changes that Friday sought. The committee, which met four times between January and April, rejected outright repeal, chiefly because of Moore's opposition. But it recommended amendment of the law to return responsibility for speakers to the UNC administration. The report and even the existence of the Medford Committee were carefully kept from public view. In late May the Board of Trustees passed a resolution urging the General Assembly to adopt the committee's recommendations.[63]

On May 22, about a month after Moore received the Medford report, the governor learned of a telegram sent two days earlier to Friday by Emmett B. Fields, chairman of the accrediting committee of the Southern Association of Colleges and Schools (SACS). In mid-March 1964 a SACS accreditation team had visited Chapel Hill, where faculty spoke frankly about the Speaker Ban. The visiting committee then expressed its concern to Fields. After subsequent trips to North Carolina and consultations with Moore, state government officials, and UNC administrators, the SACS executive council, which was the chief accrediting body of southern colleges and universities, met on May 19, 1965, and determined that the Speaker Ban law interfered with the "necessary authority" of the UNC administration.[64]

Some legislators responded to the SACS threat with bluster. Tom White, a state senator from Kinston and a vocal supporter of the Speaker Ban, believed that UNC should withdraw from an organization "unworthy of being privileged to 'accredit' any kind of educational institution." But the looming threat of the loss of accreditation, and the disastrous consequences that would follow it, spurred Moore to action. Still hoping for repeal, Friday urged the governor to appoint a legislative study commission to examine the law. Although disappointed that repeal now seemed unlikely, Friday realized that a legislative majority opposed even modification. Moore, though a Carolina graduate who "dearly loved" the university, was deluged with constituent mail that ran six to one in favor of the Speaker Ban. According to his count, a solid majority in the legislature opposed any change; although he might have obtained a slight majority favoring change in the senate, amendment faced certain defeat in the house. Clarence Stone, whose position was typical of General Assembly opinion, remained opposed to what he described as "people who would destroy our way of life" whether they were Fidel Castro or a "pink professor." Although Friday reaffirmed his commitment to "responsible freedom" and trustee authority to make educational decisions, he emphasized UNC's willingness to aid the study commission.[65] Realizing that repeal or modification during that year's regular session was politically impossible, the governor endorsed Friday's suggestion. On June 1, 1965, he proposed that the legislature establish a commission composed of nine members appointed by the governor, lieutenant governor, and speaker of the house to examine the law and propose remedies that might be considered in a special legislative session.[66]

To head the legislative commission, Moore appointed his old political ally, David M. Britt, soon to become speaker of the house. The members of the Britt Commission included a representative sampling of the North Carolina political system.[67] After meeting privately in July, the commission conducted televised public hearings on August 11–12 and September 8–9 in the Legislative Building in Raleigh. The hearings attracted widespread press and public attention. Testifying on August 11, Emmett Fields of SACS denounced the "political interference" of the legislature. Yet Colonel William T. Joyner and other conservative members of the Britt Commission challenged the right of an outside group to intervene, and they questioned Fields closely, pointing out inconsistencies in the Southern Association's approach. Although the Tennessee law of 1925 restricting the teaching of Darwinian evolution remained on the books, SACS had taken no action to disaccredit the University of Tennessee. If the legislature could make laws regarding speeding on campus or drunken driving, Britt asked Fields, did it not also have the right to regulate speakers? The answers of the SACS representative did not quiet his critics. An observer sympathetic to changing the law described Fields's performance as "embarrassing." Other opponents of the ban appeared in the August session.

Harvard Law School professor John Dawson, representing the national office of the American Association of University Professors, and William L. Van Alstyne, a Duke University law professor, both testified on August 12 that the law was unconstitutional.[68]

Meanwhile, supporters of the Speaker Ban were well represented. Phil Godwin and Tom White both testified about the appropriateness of what White called this "wholesome law." Godwin, denying that the legislature's motivation had anything to do with the civil rights demonstrations of 1963 or "personal animosity" toward the university, said he was surprised by the extent of opposition. The law, he asserted, did not restrict free speech, only the location of the speech. State senator Robert Morgan, representing the American Legion, told commission members that Chapel Hill had become a center for communism and those sympathetic toward it. Because of the threat of subversion, he maintained, North Carolinians would be better served if those faculty members who threatened to resign left as a result of the law. Morgan and the legionnaires he represented were, moreover, dubious about returning authority over speakers to the trustees.[69]

The Britt Commission's August hearings brought solace to no one. Britt, who recalled that he was seeking a means to "defang" the political problem, was disappointed. So was Moore, who wanted a way out of a politically explosive problem. Friday was no happier. The Speaker Ban issue had consumed much of his time for the previous two years. Although he had rallied trustee support behind outright repeal, subsequent wavering, along with the prospect of legislative opposition, had led him to support modification along the lines proposed by the Medford Committee. But even the minimal Medford formula – which would have given UNC greater flexibility but would have retained the objectionable law – provided no sure path to compromise.[70]

Still, in the summer and autumn of 1965, Friday believed that compromise was possible. In late July, before the public hearings began, Britt Commission member Gordon Hanes urged Friday to propose that the UNC administration assume responsibility for enforcing the Speaker Ban along the lines of the Medford formula. Yet Hanes's approach carried the risk that Friday would become too closely identified with the suppression of free speech. Between the August and September sessions of the Britt Commission, when trustees and commission members sought compromise, this risk became apparent. On August 21 Friday met with university trustee Frank Taylor, a former legislator, who was in communication with Colonel Joyner. In exchange for a trustee resolution embodying the language of the Speaker Ban law, Joyner had suggested, the legislature might enact repeal of the law.[71]

Taylor was convinced that Joyner's offer could provide a solution and pressed Friday, who called a meeting of the Executive Committee on September 3. Friday had strongly objected to the Joyner proposal at the August 21 meeting and, after consultations with the chancellors, drafted a statement to that effect. The Taylor-Joyner compromise, he warned trustees, so contradicted earlier trustee positions that it constituted a "serious procedural problem." In fact, the Medford Committee's proposal was more open-ended about the trustees' role; rather than embracing the Speaker Ban law, the Medford formula would make it palatable to the university community. The real problem, Friday told the Executive Committee on September 3, was the trustees' attitude. Should they listen to Robert Morgan, or others like him, who "would be willing to see the university eroded to maintain this law"? Or should they heed the advice of "reasonable people of the state" and lead them "to a higher ground of conviction"?[72]

Although the Executive Committee endorsed a resolution offered by Virginia Lathrop of Asheville reaffirming its support for the Medford formula, Friday could not have been heartened by trustee uncertainty.[73] The second round of Britt Commission hearings, which followed less than a week after the Executive Committee meeting, was crucial. Speaking before the commission on the morning of September 8 in Raleigh, Friday was joined by Chancellors John Tyler Caldwell (North Carolina State University in Raleigh), Bonnie Cone (University of North Carolina at Charlotte), James S. Ferguson (University of North Carolina at Greensboro), and Paul Sharp (University of North Carolina at Chapel Hill); former Chapel Hill student body president Robert Spearman, at the time a Rhodes Scholar, appeared as well. Other educators, including the president of every public senior college in the state, also testified. All of them offered strong support for academic freedom.[74]

Friday's testimony was the longest and the most impressive. Universities, he told a packed audience, were only "useful and effective" if they remained "free from unnecessary political control." Legislatures should manage UNC affairs through publicly appointed boards of trustees; the faculty and students should be protected in an "atmosphere of intellectual freedom that permits them to chart the scope and direction of their professional activities." Although controversial speakers had occasionally visited the Chapel Hill campus, free speech was basic and indispensable to an academic community. This was not a matter of favoring or opposing communism; the university opposed "all systems of government that suppress the liberties and freedoms of its people."[75]

The university's case, observed the *Greensboro Daily News*, was "stunning in its thoroughness, sweeping in its advocacy of the unhindered search for truth, specific in its response to charges of subversive influence on the campus – and virtually irrefutable in fact and logic." Although the men representing UNC were far from "public performers" – among them, Friday was "reserved and shy," Ferguson, "soft-spoken and unabashedly professorial," and Paul Sharp, "forthright in manner and economic in speech" – they had made their point with "the clarity and passion of deep commitment."[76] But Bill Friday had cracked the door open to compromise. Speaking for himself, Friday declared, he favored repeal, but failing that he would support amendment of the law. If the legislature would renounce its control over campus speakers, he said, the trustees, through the chancellors, would assume responsibility by imposing three requirements: that meetings be chaired by faculty members or administrators, that speakers take questions from the audience, and that differing points of view also be represented.

Friday's proposal coincided with another development: an East Carolina College (ECC) Board of Trustees policy statement, issued on August 31, that was strongly anticommunist but insisted on trustee control over speakers. Robert Morgan, a staunch Speaker Ban defender and chairman of the ECC trustees, endorsed Friday's proposal but insisted that UNC trustees should give some assurance that they would regulate objectionable speakers. In the case of East Carolina, its resolution provided that ECC trustees would not permit Communist speakers unless their appearance served a "college purpose."[77]

There were significant differences between the Friday and ECC proposals: while the former would only impose restrictions to protect free speech, the latter would limit free speech to preserve the original Speaker Ban restriction. Nonetheless, in light of Morgan's comments before the commission on September 8, the way seemed clear for compromise. Morgan's announcement, coupled with Friday's willingness to accept amendment rather than total repeal, according to the *Raleigh News and Observer*, "threw a new cast on the commission's inquiry." After questioning by commission members, moreover, Morgan, who had in his testimony on August 12 refused to consider delegating authority to trustees, indicated that he would support amendment of the ban in a future legislative session.[78]

Assemblyman Britt, consulting with Friday and Weaver, spent the next weeks drafting language to amend the law. As Britt subsequently recalled, he and Friday became "much closer friends . . . during that time than we had before." The report of the Britt Commission, which was transmitted to Governor Moore on November 5, contained three provisions that were central to Friday's conception of a compromise. While the first cleared the university of any "irresponsible radicalism" on campus, the second proposed that the Speaker Ban law be amended to transfer control over visiting speakers from the legislature to the trustees and to grant them the power to establish rules and regulations concerning speakers. The third provision was a specifically worded speaker policy that was drafted by Friday and bore a close resemblance to his September 8 proposals in the commission hearings. Governor Moore made the findings of the Britt Commission public on November 5 and then called for a special session of the legislature on November 15, 1965, to enact changes in the law.[79]

The Britt Commission report, adhering to the basic elements of Friday's solution, was a triumph for the UNC president. A reporter said that Moore delivered the announcement of a special session with a "sense of urgency." Friday was "grinning intermittently" during the announcement; according to another account, he "could hardly conceal his pleasure" as Moore made the announcement. No doubt Friday's good mood reflected a confidence that Moore's support, and that of the dominant wing of the Democratic Party, had been secured. Because he and his staff had written much of the Britt Report, its contents were no surprise, and he acted quickly to formalize trustee support. Moore convened a meeting of the Executive Committee on November 11, 1965, and the full board a day later, and the members gave the compromise their endorsement. The lone dissenter was Tom White, who described himself as a "voice crying out in the wilderness."[80]

The passage of the basic elements of the Britt Commission compromise was all but assured. Despite the continued opposition of hard-line supporters of the Speaker Ban such as Robert Morgan – who, notwithstanding his September 8 announcement, turned against the compromise – Moore's full support guaranteed passage. Moore telephoned every member of the legislature to gain support; one legislator said that the governor had exercised "forceful leadership" in pushing for amendment. Opponents of the amendment were vocal; Morgan, White, and Godwin, for example, endorsed a proposal that would require North Carolina public college and university presidents to submit a monthly accounting of campus speakers, would limit trustee terms to eight years, and would permit "persons of ideologies alien to the U.S. form of government" to speak only "in the furtherance of education." But a large majority fell in behind the Moore administration. Meeting from November 15 to 17, 1965, the state legislature acted quickly. Overcoming last-minute efforts by opponents of amendment to require a statewide referendum to ratify any changes in the Speaker Ban law, the Britt Commission's recommendations were approved, 35 to 13 in the senate and 75 to 39 in the house, becoming law on November 17.[81]

The great majority of the political leadership, tired of the Speaker Ban issue, embraced the Britt proposals, which they viewed as a practical compromise. At its heart was a new speaker policy under which control would be transferred to the trustees. The policy stated that speakers who advocated ideologies or forms of government "wholly alien to our basic democratic institutions" should be "infrequent," only tolerated when it served some clear educational purpose. The key provision of the speaker policy was that the trustees and administrators would exert "reasonable and proper care" in supervising speakers so as to balance the considerations of anticommunism and free speech.

The compromise reflected the Bill Friday style of consensus building. Through a compromise that restored trustee integrity yet also satisfied the political leaders who were keenly suspicious of campus liberalism, Friday found a middle ground that forestalled confrontation and crisis. The *Greensboro Daily News* described the compromise as an "honorable way out of this difficulty" that mixed "respect for fundamental principles with common sense." Passage of this compromise, David Britt told fellow legislators, would still forestall the appearance by a Communist speaker on the Chapel Hill campus for the "foreseeable future." Yet not everyone agreed with this assessment. As an editorialist for the *Raleigh News and Observer* noted, the Britt amendment demonstrated the "utter lack of necessity for this law in the first place." It provided for free speech only to the extent that infrequent appearances by radicals would be tolerated. It made administrators directly accountable to trustees and trustees accountable to the political system. By throwing the burden of responsibility upon the university itself, it threw "some scraps to the roaring lions of reaction."[82]

Reviewing the developments that culminated in the Speaker Ban controversy, Bill Friday later said that he wondered how he survived it physically. As Friday's presidency entered the turbulent 1960s, the crises over athletics and anticommunism revealed the delicate balance between the politically isolated academic community and a university's public obligations. The university was in the political process but not of it. The 1960s brought out latent tensions of ideology and race that had been dramatized in the 1950 Graham-Smith senatorial campaign – "nervousness issues" that set people "on edge."[83]

In late 1965 Friday was far from sanguine about the future. At the cost of considerable time and effort, he had effected a compromise through the Britt Commission that seemed to forestall a loss of SACS accreditation and protect university autonomy. Yet the legislative actions during the special session were, he later recalled, "a step forward coming back." He hoped that UNC administrators would be able to "do pretty much anything under the law, . . . with the way it was phrased." His main concern was to find a way to blunt legislative intrusion, but, as he later admitted, this was an "error in judgment." As events would soon prove, the political compromise struck in the autumn of 1965 was fragile indeed.[84]

ALL over the United States during the mid- and late 1960s presidents of major universities faced a similar predicament, with often disastrous consequences: responding to a rising tide of student activism. Some university administrators, adopting a laissez-faire policy, found themselves enveloped in a crossfire of student demands and mounting frustration by alumni, community, and political leaders. Still others, by overreacting to the student revolt and employing excessive police force to quell it, risked an unraveling of the equilibrium of the academic community. Bill Friday pursued a careful path between these two extremes. Avoiding either passivity or overreaction, he attempted to insulate the university community from outside intervention and to preserve public confidence in it.

At Chapel Hill, the earliest evidence of a new tone of student activism manifested itself in a challenge to the Speaker Ban. In December 1965 leaders of the Students for a Democratic Society (SDS), which was then emerging as a major New Left student organization, planned a challenge. The SDS chapter, founded on the Chapel Hill campus during the spring of 1965, remained small, with a membership that never exceeded twenty-five. It needed a rallying cause; the Speaker Ban provided the perfect issue. On January 3, 1966, the Carolina SDS chapter invited two controversial speakers: Frank Wilkinson, who had served a month in prison because he refused in 1958 to answer questions about his Communist Party membership and who was leading an effort to abolish the House Un-American Activities Committee (HUAC), and Herbert Aptheker, a historian who joined the Communist Party in 1939 and who, in 1965, led a delegation to visit the Vietnamese Communists in Hanoi. On January 21 Roy James McCorkel Jr., a UNC graduate student of sociology and SDS president, telephoned Paul Sharp, who had succeeded Bill Aycock as chancellor in 1965, to tell him about the SDS invitations; Sharp then informed Friday.[1]

On November 12, 1965, the UNC trustees had adopted a general speaker policy that permitted "infrequent" appearances by controversial speakers if they served "the advantage of education." Then, on January 14, 1966, the Executive Committee adopted, subject to approval by the full board, more specific regulations. The committee stipulated that all statutes, including the 1941 law that prohibited speeches advocating the violent overthrow of government, had to be obeyed. Only recognized student, faculty, and university organizations could sponsor and invite outside speakers; student attendance was voluntary. Each chancellor, moreover, could require that a campus officer or ranking faculty member preside at the meeting, that speakers be required to field questions, and that opposing points of view be represented.[2]

A week after learning of McCorkel's action, Friday, proceeding on the assumption that the invitations to Wilkinson and Aptheker could be regulated under the trustees' speaker policy, arranged meetings between himself, Chancellor Sharp, Chapel Hill vice chancellor for academic affairs J. Carlyle Sitterson, and dean of students C. O. "Phil" Cathey. Cathey had already investigated the Chapel Hill SDS and received information from the Federal Bureau of Investigation (FBI) and HUAC. Although he maintained "routine contact" with the FBI and could find nothing disloyal about SDS, he kept the group under close surveillance. But when Cathey consulted with other student leaders, they strongly believed that the visits should be permitted.[3]

Friday, after further conversations with Sharp, requested that the Faculty Advisory Committee, a seven-member group chaired by George Nicholson, consider the matter. Although the committee agreed that the university community would regard a campus speech by Aptheker, a known Communist, as "distasteful," it believed that it would be a serious mistake to ban him or Wilkinson. At a subsequent meeting on January 26, Friday, Fred Weaver, Sharp, Sitterson, and Cathey decided to adopt the Faculty Advisory Committee's proposal for a panel discussion that followed the Executive Committee speaker regulations. Chaired by Henry Brandis, the panel would consist of the speaker, a historian, a sociologist, and a political scientist. The UNC administrators then took the proposal to the Executive Committee for approval.[4]

The Executive Committee reluctantly considered the matter on January 28 at a meeting in Governor Moore's office. Only two months earlier, the trustees had thought that the Speaker Ban issue – and, according to a reporter, "an administrative and public relations headache" – was settled. Now, as they saw it, a small group of campus radicals threatened to upset a delicate equilibrium. Many of them were frightened by the potential for a political backlash. The meeting on January 28 was stormy. It lasted nearly four hours, and serious divisions surfaced. On the one hand, Friday and Sharp endorsed the Faculty Advisory Committee's proposal to permit Aptheker and Wilkinson to speak but also to ensure free discussion and rebuttal. The SDS was a recognized student organization, Friday told committee members. Because it had followed existing regulations regarding speakers, UNC officials "could do no less" than permit the speeches and provide for a panel format. The Britt Compromise called for infrequent visits by objectionable speakers if some educational purpose were served, and a trustee asked Sharp whether the Wilkinson-Aptheker speeches would further this objective. In light of the procedures established to safeguard varying points of view, Sharp responded, he believed that a "very definite" educational purpose would be served.[5]

Hard-line trustees rejected concessions that they believed violated the spirit of the Britt Compromise. The most important hard-liner was Dan Moore, who early in the meeting announced his opposition to any appearances by Aptheker and Wilkinson on the Chapel Hill campus. After heated and prolonged discussion, several motions were proposed and withdrawn. Trustee Shelton Wicker moved that the Executive Committee reject outright the Wilkinson-Aptheker visits; Victor Bryant then offered a substitute motion that trustees recess to a later date. The Bryant motion carried narrowly, 5 to 4.[6]

The issue thereafter became significantly more polarized. Once the invitations were made public, Friday and the trustees were exposed to powerful political pressure. Caught between "public clamor and . . . the academic conscience, which can be fastidious to an irritating point," as *Greensboro Daily News* editorialist Edwin Yoder put it, trustees were in a difficult position. "Those of us who stood up for U.N.C. during the special session," added David Britt, would become the "laughing stock of North Carolina," while those who opposed it would become "heroes for a long time to come." He believed that if Aptheker and Wilkinson appeared on the Carolina campus, the 1967 session of the legislature might well reenact the Speaker Ban and apply it exclusively to Chapel Hill. If Wilkinson and Aptheker spoke at Chapel Hill, Britt Commission member A. Augustus Zollicoffer wrote to Friday, he had made "one hell of an error," and his confidence in Friday and UNC trustees was misplaced. On February 2 Moore turned up the pressure by publicly announcing his opposition to the appearance of either speaker. The SDS invitations, he said, were an attempt "to create controversy for the sake of controversy and not for any legitimate education purpose." The exceptions to the Speaker Ban adopted in November 1965 therefore did not include the Aptheker and Wilkinson invitations.[7]

Student leaders, meanwhile, were unwilling to accept an outright ban of either Wilkinson or Aptheker. Moore's opposition to the invitations reflected a "tremendous amount of ignorance," said SDS president McCorkel at a news conference held on February 2 at the student union building. It was the duty of all North Carolinians, especially university faculty and administrators, to support the First Amendment. Although most students believed that the SDS invitations were deliberately intended to provoke a confrontation, a majority nonetheless supported permitting Aptheker and Wilkinson to speak. The controversial invitations were now embraced by the Carolina Forum and the *Daily Tar Heel*, and, on February 3, four days before the Executive Committee reconvened, Carolina student body president Paul Dickson III released a statement announcing that student government was also officially sponsoring Aptheker's visit, which was scheduled to occur on March 9, 1966.[8]

The Carolina faculty responded to the crisis differently. The younger members, for the most part, vigorously opposed the Speaker Ban. Many of them openly sympathized with the students; some even threatened to resign if free speech were not completely reestablished. In contrast, many older faculty members, such as former dean and professor of economics Corydon P. Spruill, believed that the invitations were "untimely" and the circumstances "inflammatory." Although the consequences of banning Aptheker would be harmful, Spruill felt that the university was being "manipulated as a puppet in this heartless fashion by persons whose seeming purpose" was to "learn how much provocation we can take." Most of the faculty, however, was simply dismayed. The "wolf has appeared," wrote Paul Green, a retired professor of dramatic art, and he was "a hungry one at that." "I'm going to keep hollering just the same," he said, "and fighting as best I can the wolf's taking over."[9]

On February 7, 1966, Governor Moore reconvened the Executive Committee. Some five hundred students gathered for a Chapel Hill rally preceding the meeting to express their strong support for the Wilkinson and Aptheker visits. At the Executive Committee meeting at the governor's office in Raleigh, trustees learned that the Faculty Advisory Committee, a group of younger faculty headed by Nathaniel Rodman, SDS president McCorkel, and a student delegation led by Dickson were waiting to present their cases. Agreeing to receive only the Faculty Advisory Committee and Dickson's delegation, the trustees heard their prepared statements. The faculty group urged that Aptheker be permitted to speak; banning him would inflict "incalculable – and irreparable – harm to the University." Communism was no danger on the Chapel Hill campus; trustee suppression of free speech was "in line with Communist, not American tenets." Should the trustees forbid Aptheker to speak, the faculty delegation warned, the result would be lower campus morale and a victory for the minority who wanted crisis and confrontation.[10]

Paul Dickson, representing the Chapel Hill student government, followed. Dickson, from Raeford, North Carolina, was twenty-four years old, a tall, slender, thoughtful man who had served in the Air Force for three and a half years, with ten months of service in Vietnam. In the autumn of 1965 Chancellor Sharp had demanded Dickson's resignation as student body president because he had taken a coed into a fraternity house on an unauthorized visit and had been charged with a campus code violation. But after a student delegation visited the chancellor's office Sharp reversed himself, and Dickson remained in office.

The student body president displayed equal determination in dealing with the trustees. He had already demonstrated his anticommunism by fighting in Vietnam, he told trustees; Carolina, he said, should be preserved as an "open forum" for diverse views "no matter how unpopular or divergent." Since April 1964, the campus had been host to speakers from all sides of the political spectrum: Mississippi segregationist governor Ross Barnett, Averell Harriman, Herbert Philbrick of the FBI, John Kenneth Galbraith, Hugh Hefner, and Floyd McKissick. The invitation to Aptheker simply followed Chapel Hill's tradition of hearing diverse opinions. Although he disagreed with Aptheker's trip to Hanoi and with his avowed communism, Dickson believed that the man should be permitted to air his opinions, no matter how distasteful. The best defense against communism was to understand it thoroughly. Distancing himself from the SDS, Dickson asserted that an overwhelming majority of the student body supported him. "Ladies and gentlemen," he told the trustees, "there are no traitors among us." The Carolina student body was American, Tar Heel, and "loyal and patriotic." "When we are called by our country," he said, "we shall answer, even in the cannon's mouth."[11]

Friday spoke next. The situation, he said, was acute, for the Speaker Ban controversy had taken a toll. The university community was seriously divided from its political supporters: the views of the governor and most trustees contrasted with those of the Carolina campus. Student leadership was now aroused, perhaps permanently; the faculty, especially the younger faculty, was expressing a new restiveness. Personally, Friday said, he deplored the circumstances surrounding the invitation to Aptheker and Wilkinson, but the university needed a compromise: a panel format, combined with closer supervision of speaker invitations by the UNC administration.

The alternatives to compromise, Friday noted, were grim. Student opinion was now thoroughly mobilized; it was likely that students would mount a full-scale legal challenge to the law. A hard line by trustees would invite constant challenges by more radical and less responsible groups than the students whom Dickson represented. A "deplorable weariness" was now setting in across campus; there would be further erosion of student and faculty morale if the issue were not settled in the right way. The "whole fabric" of the UNC structure was under stress; compromise would strengthen the authority of trustees.[12]

Despite Friday's impassioned appeal, Moore's hard-line position solidified wavering trustees, and well before the meeting's conclusion it had become certain that Friday would be unable to persuade them to permit either speaker on campus.[13] When Friday asked the Executive Committee to consider the possibility of a panel discussion involving more speakers than just Aptheker, he received little support. Instead, after what the meeting's secretary succinctly described as an "extended debate," the Executive Committee instructed UNC administrators to deny the use of university facilities to either Aptheker or Wilkinson. A vote permanently barring Aptheker and Wilkinson carried, 7 to 4; the only trustees supporting Friday were Victor Bryant, Watts Hill Sr., Virginia Lathrop, and Mebane Burgwyn. Then, in a modified resolution, the Executive Committee refined the ban – in an 8-to-3 vote in which Hill switched sides – by canceling the March engagements for the two speakers but leaving the possibility open for subsequent invitations to them. The committee also suspended all invitations to speakers until the full UNC Board of Trustees – which had not yet adopted the speaker regulations endorsed by the Executive Committee on January 14, 1966 – met and ratified the new regulations.[14]

When the committee's decision was released to the public shortly before 8:00 P.M., an uproar ensued. Dickson declared that he was "greatly disturbed." Aptheker threatened no one; his Marxist message was less relevant than "the right to hear this man, and all others who would speak of the broad and dangerous world in which we live." The day after the Executive Committee meeting a sympathetic trustee wrote to Friday that he shared his "grief" and felt like "hanging black crepe over the entrance to all of the buildings of the University and, as a matter of fact, over the State Capitol itself." The *Greensboro Daily News* summarized the editorial opinion of the state's leading newspapers. "Bad for the [Executive] committee" and "bad for the university," the decision suggested that North Carolinians feared free speech.[15]

For his part, Friday was deeply aggrieved by the severest trustee rebuke of his presidency. He remembered the Executive Committee's vote as "quite a shock" and a "sad day." At the time he believed that his two-and-a-half-year campaign to enlist trustee support on the free speech issue had failed. "I just couldn't make it work," he said later; he had run "smack into a stone wall." But Friday kept his frustration to himself, and in the weeks preceding the full Board of Trustees' consideration of the speaker regulations at its regular meeting on February 28, 1966, he explored further compromise. The chancellor at Greensboro, Mississippian James S. Ferguson, urged Friday to end the polarization. "Protest," he wrote a day after the Executive Committee met, was "no longer contained in trust"; it waxed "ever stronger, and the University, already laboring with difficulty to serve 'its owners,' must now divert much of its energy to a struggle with its captors."[16]

Ferguson correctly identified the dilemma confronting Friday: he served two masters, the university community and the leadership and public opinion of North Carolina. What Ferguson called the "Compromise of 1965" – the Britt Compromise – offered a middle position between "impetuous" academics and an impatient public. Yet Ferguson believed that the burden of responsibility lay with the state's political leaders who struck this compromise. They needed to realize that an "honest confrontation of contrary theories" was part of university life; rejecting that struck at the heart of academic integrity. If the Britt Compromise was "truly a compromise and not a ruse, this burden cannot be tossed aside the first time the going gets tough."

Although it had banned Aptheker and Wilkinson, the Executive Committee on February 7 had created a three-man subcommittee, headed by Victor Bryant and including Wade Barber of Pittsboro and Reid Maynard of Burlington, to draft speaker regulations for adoption by the full Board of Trustees on February 28. Bryant, who had voted with Friday at the meeting but had always been independent-minded, drafted a policy on February 9 that widened the gulf between Dickson's position and that of the UNC administration. Bryant's draft required student organizations to obtain prior registration with the chancellor; student groups with an outside affiliation (such as SDS) needed prior approval. Student groups would be required to sign a statement indicating that they were aware of the speaker policy and to notify the chancellor at least ten days in advance before inviting a speaker. The chancellors, in turn, were required to submit proposed invitations in writing to the UNC president; either the chancellor or president could veto the invitation.[17]

The extent to which Friday endorsed Bryant's version of the invitation policy is unclear, and he proceeded, in typical fashion, to reach out to both sides in the controversy. He saw some merit in elements of Bryant's proposal, which offered a formula for returning control of speakers to the UNC administration. In late February 1966 Friday sought wider support by creating a faculty committee to consider Bryant's proposals and offer its own solution to the trustees. Yet to some it appeared that Friday had tilted toward the Bryant draft. Bill Snider, editorialist for the *Greensboro Daily News* and a staunch university loyalist, wrote that Bryant had created a "crisis" that "deeply disturbed" him. Worried that Friday backed the Bryant proposal, he feared that if Friday failed to "come up with a fairly stiff set of regulations the Trustees will impose a completely unacceptable set of rules." Snider regarded the direction of Bryant's proposal as "distasteful" and "one step toward killing the University of North Carolina as a true university." None of the administrators encircling Friday was facing up to the disastrous consequences of these proposals; instead, Snider argued, Friday should stand on principle and state "unequivocally" that he would resign rather than carry out such regulations.[18]

Meanwhile, Friday also kept lines of communication open to the students. Not long after the Executive Committee's decision of February 7, Dickson called Friday to request a conference. The two met and talked outside of the president's home. Friday and Dickson, well before the current crisis, had developed a working relationship; the student body president not only had informed Friday of developments among students, but he had occasionally sought his advice. For his part, Friday came to admire the student leader for his "enormous courage." No one, he subsequently recalled, "communicated the way Dickson did." He and Dickson established a "very unusual personal relationship"; they became "perfectly open with each other" and "understood each other."[19]

Friday said that he and Dickson met regularly during the winter of 1966, though no one else knew of their contacts, and Dickson kept him "fully apprised of every move he was making." After the February 7 Executive Committee meeting, their consultations intensified. Friday informed Dickson about his position; Dickson told Friday about his activities, which he made no attempt to restrain. Friday realized that if "open communication" between students and administrators was not preserved, "real trouble could result." Although he disagreed with some of Dickson's decisions, Friday later noted, it was "never a question of veto." Out of the give-and-take of these conversations, Friday reached a significant conclusion: the political leadership of North Carolina was incapable of resolving the Speaker Ban controversy. The only solution, he now believed, was a court challenge. Friday urged Dickson to begin litigation – even if that meant a court challenge against Friday himself. "I ought to have been fired for what I did," Friday admitted.[20]

As early as February 2, Dickson had informed a reporter for the *Greensboro Daily News* that there was a "good possibility" of a lawsuit if Aptheker was denied permission to speak. On February 8, after the Executive Committee's decision, Dickson and other student leaders created an umbrella organization, the Committee for Free Inquiry (CFI), to challenge the Speaker Ban; Dickson was elected chairman of its steering committee. Although the SDS participated in the CFI, centrist student leaders such as Dickson dominated it, and they rejected direct-action tactics such as strikes and sit-ins that had become popular in the civil rights movement and in Berkeley's Free Speech Movement. "We've got to be cool, calm, and collected," Dickson told students, and in order to prepare for a possible lawsuit, it was imperative first to exhaust all alternatives on campus and with the UNC trustees. "If you go out and demonstrate," Dickson said, "you will play into the hands of our enemies" by creating a furor that would subvert any real progress. Despite SDS's support of immediate direct-action tactics, the CFI endorsed Dickson's strategy.[21]

On February 11 Dickson convened a meeting of Carolina students at Gerrard Hall. Announcing his intention to speak to the trustees at their February 28 meeting, he persuaded the group to support the CFI's nine-member steering committee, on which moderates held the upper hand. Two weeks later at Memorial Hall, the CFI sponsored an open meeting that attracted 1,200 faculty members and students, who adopted a written statement of principle. The students then sought to deliver their statement to J. Carlyle Sitterson, who would be appointed acting chancellor after Chancellor Paul Sharp's departure on February 15, 1966, to become president of Drake University in Iowa. When they discovered that Sitterson lived off campus, student leaders agreed to send a delegation to President Friday's home. Marching across campus, the students delivered the statement to Sitterson, who awaited them at the president's home. Sitterson handed the statement to Friday, then praised the students for their responsible conduct and asked them to delay further action until the trustees' upcoming meeting.[22]

On February 28 the full Board of Trustees, following a two-and-a-half-hour meeting, adopted Bryant's proposed new regulations governing visiting speakers. Prior to the meeting, Friday, Sitterson, Fred Weaver, John Caldwell, and Arnold King had divided up the trustees and lobbied for adoption of Bryant's proposal. Calling his recommendation a "reaffirmation of faith in the university, and in its process of education and the essentialness of freedom of discussion," Bryant faced the lone opposition of Tom White. Bryant told the trustees that the new regulations, including a new policy for inviting speakers, had been "hammered out on the anvil of discussion in many long hours of conference and study." Dickson, given the floor, opposed any restrictions on the right to free speech. Friday spoke on behalf of the regulations and endorsed them, according to one account, "with unusual conviction and authority" and with a tone that was "polite, but edged with steel." He described the new speaker policy as a compromise; it was not in the "best interest" of the university or the state "to protract the issue of visiting speakers longer than necessary."[23]

The student leadership responded quickly. On March 1, 1966, the CFI reissued invitations to Wilkinson and Aptheker to appear on March 2 and 9, respectively; the group reported these invitations to Sitterson. Dickson, urging students to proceed carefully so as to lay the basis for a court challenge, promised that in the event of a ban, Wilkinson would speak on the sidewalk running along Franklin Street; on the other side of the famous campus wall, which Dickson called "Dan Moore's wall of repression," the student audience could stand at McCorkle Place. This would demonstrate to the state how "ridiculous and absurd" the law was.[24]

A joint student-faculty committee on visiting speakers, established by the Board of Trustees on February 28, convened on March 1 to consider the reinvitation to Wilkinson. The committee was composed of three students appointed by Dickson and three faculty members: Corydon P. Spruill, chairman of the faculty; George Nicholson, chairman of the Faculty Advisory Committee; and Arnold Perry, chairman of the committee on established lectures. The committee was sharply divided, but four of the six members recommended that the Wilkinson invitation be vetoed. Unable to agree on a report to Chancellor Sitterson, the committee asked to meet with him the next morning to communicate its opinions. One committee member strongly supported permitting an appearance by Wilkinson; others believed that it should be postponed and still others that it should be unconditionally rejected.

Sitterson occupied an intolerable position. The students had forced the issue; their reinvitations to Aptheker and Wilkinson, he explained days later, had not permitted "any time for much further thought and consideration." Sitterson, a Carolina-trained historian of the South, found any banning of speakers personally repugnant. Returning home for lunch following the meeting with the faculty-student committee, he remembered having become "so sick of this" that he told his wife: "You know, I just can't stand going through this anymore. I think I'm just going to go ahead and admit these speakers." But that afternoon the Faculty Advisory Committee, which Sitterson consulted with for two hours, recommended rejecting the invitations.[25]

The meeting with the Faculty Advisory Committee confirmed Sitterson's belief that it would be impossible for him to defy the trustees. Overruling the Executive Committee, he recalled, amounted to administrative anarchy. Like Friday, he realized that if the administration clashed with the trustees, it would have "created a crisis in the working relationship between the Chancellor and the Board which would have been really untenable." The decision contradicted his "basic principles" and his "concept of what a university should be," as he explained to Victor Bryant, but permitting Aptheker and Wilkinson to speak on campus would lead to the loss of public confidence in the university.[26]

Immediately after his conference with the Faculty Advisory Committee, Sitterson called Bill Friday, then in Raleigh, who fully supported his position. That afternoon, the Chapel Hill chancellor barred Wilkinson from speaking on campus that same day. Two days later, he informed the faculty-student committee that, based on the same considerations, he would also prohibit Aptheker from speaking on March 9. Recognizing that the decision was entirely his own, Sitterson also rejected Dickson's proposal that Wilkinson be permitted to sit in the auditorium while another person read his speech or played it on a tape recorder.

Although he unequivocally banned both speakers, Sitterson was hoping for a cooling-off period. He planned to permit other controversial speakers in the future if only UNC could ride out the current controversy. Yet the subtleties of Sitterson's approach were lost on student activists, who continued to press their case.[27]

On the morning of March 2, speaking from the sidewalk across from the stone wall on Franklin Street that separated the university from the town of Chapel Hill, Frank Wilkinson delivered a ten-minute speech to a group of 1,200 people. Without loudspeakers (their use would have violated a town ordinance against them) and because of crowd and street noise, most students present were unable to hear him. After Dickson asserted that this was a "reasonable way of demonstrating the ridiculousness of the procedures we have to follow," Wilkinson received the loudest applause when he told the crowd that it was his hope "to restore academic freedom to this university."

That evening, 350 students looked on as campus security chief Arthur Beaumont turned Wilkinson away from Carroll Hall. Dickson, who accompanied Wilkinson, asked Beaumont, "Do I understand that we are not to use this building?" "As I understand it," Beaumont replied, "he can't speak on campus." Dickson, armed with a tape recorder, asked if he could play a tape recording of Wilkinson's speech. Beaumont responded that the tape could be played on the auditorium steps but not inside the building. Turning to the crowd, Dickson described the situation as "particularly depressing" because the "important right" to hear Wilkinson was being denied. Roy McCorkel joined in, announcing that the denial of Wilkinson's speech would lead directly to a lawsuit. The group then walked three blocks off campus to Hillel House, which housed the Jewish Student Center, where Wilkinson finally spoke.

Paul Dickson had orchestrated the Wilkinson appearance to maximize public exposure, demonstrate the absurdity of the law, and, most important, lay the basis for a court challenge. Litigation was uppermost in his mind. A reporter described the student government officers, when word arrived about

Sitterson's decision to ban Wilkinson, as "anything but glum." Hearing the news, Dickson rubbed his hands together and yelled, "Man, we've got 'em now." Soon afterward he telephoned Greensboro attorney McNeill Smith and Duke University law professor William Van Alstyne, both of whom had been informally advising the students about a court challenge. The student leadership would, Dickson told reporters, "file suit as soon as we can."[28]

The banning of the two speakers and Wilkinson's dramatic appearance electrified the campus. Yet Dickson faced a challenge in maintaining control over the emerging student movement and ensuring its support for an incremental, legalist strategy. Clearly, the SDS did not favor litigation alone. On March 3, while Dickson was in Greensboro consulting with McNeill Smith, the CFI voted to picket Sitterson's office – a decision that Dickson would have opposed had he been present at the meeting. Able to persuade students to abandon the picketing when he returned, the Carolina student body president also began raising money to help defray legal costs.[29]

The Wilkinson drama was repeated on March 9, when Herbert Aptheker arrived. Dickson escorted him for a noon appearance on campus, where banners proclaimed "Still here, Dan Moore's Chapel Hill Wall" and cameras from NBC's Huntley-Brinkley show were waiting. As students shoved each other to position themselves in front of the television cameras, Dickson and Aptheker attempted to speak in front of the campus Confederate Memorial. But security chief Beaumont again intruded, this time threatening to arrest Aptheker and report Dickson to the Men's Honor Council. Dickson then led Aptheker back to the Franklin Street sidewalk abutting the university wall, where he addressed an audience of more than two thousand. Dickson introduced Aptheker by stating that the Speaker Ban law and UNC policy had already inflicted "great damage" on the university. Again the absence of loudspeakers made it impossible for most of the audience to hear Aptheker, who abandoned his prepared text on the Vietnam War and instead spoke briefly about the Speaker Ban. Later, students, after rebuffs from the local Presbyterian, Baptist, and Methodist churches, received permission to use the Chapel Hill Community Church for an evening speech. Editorialists around the state sympathized with the students. Aptheker's message was "nonsense," said the *Raleigh News and Observer*, but the views of that "Communist bogey-man" would not stand the scrutiny of open discourse. "The best way to deal with such persons," it concluded, was "to let 'em come and squirm in their own holes."[30]

In the aftermath of the Wilkinson and Aptheker visits, Dickson and the CFI pursued their legal challenge. In consultations with student leaders, Sitterson advised that new invitations to Wilkinson and Aptheker might be possible, but that the two speakers were "dead ducks" for that semester and it would be unwise to reinvite them before the upcoming May 28 Democratic primary. In these conversations, Sitterson encouraged the students to invite other controversial speakers. But student leaders rebuffed the chancellor; some of the activists feared that he might approve other speakers and thus deprive them of the basis for a legal challenge. On March 14 Dickson and other student leaders wrote to Sitterson requesting that Aptheker and Wilkinson be permitted to speak on campus on March 23 and 25. When Sitterson did not reply before those dates, they wrote again on March 25, reiterating their request and adhering to the trustees' speaker policy. Three days later Sitterson finally replied, stating that he had referred the matter to the faculty-student committee. When, on March 31, the chancellor again turned down the request, the students filed suit.[31]

Dickson v. *Sitterson* was decided by a three-judge federal district court in Greensboro on February 19, 1968. Declaring that the law failed to establish "clear, narrow and objective standards," the court ruled that the Speaker Ban law and the trustees' regulations were unconstitutional because of their vagueness. The trustees possessed the right to regulate speakers; no one possessed the unlimited right to speak on a college campus. But once the campus admitted speakers, "it must do so under principles that are constitutionally valid." The limitations over legislative or trustee powers were strict when it came to free speech issues. The original Speaker Ban law proscribed "known" Communists, but, the court asked, " 'known' to whom, and to what degree of certainty?" Did the advocacy of the overthrow of established government include the violent overthrow or simply the "advocacy of ideas"? Did pleading the Fifth Amendment encompass self-incrimination? If so, the Speaker Ban's proscription of speakers was not only vague but also violated the protections extended by the amendment in the first place. In order for the speaker regulations to withstand scrutiny, the decision continued, trustees were required to impose a "purely ministerial duty" on administrators supervising the invitation of speakers, or they had to contain "standards sufficiently detailed to define the bounds of discretion." The trustees' speaker policy failed on all these counts. Citing a recent Supreme Court decision that struck down loyalty oaths in New York because of their vagueness, the court held that legislators and trustees were obliged to provide "clear, narrow and objective standards" when limiting free speech.[32]

Actually, by 1968, the environment had so changed that the Speaker Ban had few active supporters. The civil rights movement had passed into a different phase; North Carolina was experiencing a major transition in racial attitudes and practices. A few Speaker Ban stalwarts remained, to be sure, but most legislators were happy to see the issue disappear. As McNeill Smith subsequently wrote, political leaders were "relieved" and even "off the hook" when the Dickson suit was filed because they could say "that the matter was in the bosom of the court and they did not have to comment." The Speaker Ban was a "millstone around everyone's neck," and few mourned its passing.[33]

University administrators and most trustees greeted the court's decision with relief and happily relegated the Speaker Ban to oblivion. It was his hope, Friday declared, that "the opinion released by the three-judge federal court today brings this long and costly controversy to an end." Four days after the *Dickson* ruling, Governor Dan Moore announced that the state would not appeal the decision, adding that the decision nonetheless permitted trustees to ensure that "those invited to speak have something to offer the cause of education as opposed to the creation of sensationalism and discord." On February 26 the Board of Trustees instructed Moore to appoint a special committee, headed by Virginia Lathrop, to study what remained of the speaker policy. On May 27, 1968, the committee recommended and the trustees adopted a much-watered-down approach.[34]

For Friday, the *Dickson* ruling provided the only way out of the Speaker Ban imbroglio, what Sitterson later called an "absolutely unresolvable issue, except finally in the way that it was resolved." The passage of the law had raised fundamental issues not only about academic freedom but also about the hostile climate encircling UNC in the midst of the civil rights revolution. Throughout those years Friday sought mediation and compromise, yet in the end he discovered that mediation in the alienated environment of the mid-1960s was impossible. The Britt Compromise, which Friday at first regarded as workable if distasteful, collapsed with the onset of a determined student uprising, and it was the students, fully aware that three years of political debate had resulted in stalemate, who succeeded in finally eliminating the Speaker Ban. McNeill Smith recalled that in 1963 free speech was "hung on the scaffold"; two years later, with the Britt Compromise, the legislature created "a different, perhaps gentler executioner." In the end, it was the students "who took the rope away."[35]

STUDENT activism in the spring of 1966, and the legal dispute that followed it, offered a prelude to a more serious challenge to Friday's leadership. In the mid-1960s the civil rights movement took a decisive turn with the emergence of a black power movement. By 1969, moreover, leading campuses around the country had experienced major turmoil, as student protests erupted over the heavy-handed control by administrators, the Vietnam War and the draft, and racial equality. Beginning with the free speech movement in Berkeley, California, in 1964 and culminating in a student uprising at Columbia University in 1968, campuses had become increasingly difficult to govern. At Chapel Hill in the spring of 1966, Paul Dickson led a well-coordinated student movement that focused on the specific goal of restoring free speech through the invalidation of the Speaker Ban law.

By 1969, in contrast, the primary issue that concerned UNC student activists, aside from the Vietnam War, was racial equity. The entry of larger numbers of African American students to Chapel Hill had been accompanied by an increasing degree of black militancy. In 1967 black students, led by Preston Dobbins and Reggie Hawkins, transformed the Carolina chapter of the NAACP into the Black Student Movement (BSM). In February 1968 some sixty BSM members marched through campus protesting the killing of three black students in Orangeburg, South Carolina; in April, following the assassination of Martin Luther King Jr., they burned several Confederate flags in front of a fraternity house and orchestrated a brief boycott by campus food workers. In November 1968, when black activist Stokely Carmichael visited Chapel Hill and spoke to 6,700 mostly white students, student union director Howard Henry prohibited the BSM from charging admission; a "free will" offering netted only $700 of the $1,500 promised to Carmichael. The BSM believed that Henry and the UNC administrators had deliberately sabotaged the occasion.

In December 1968 the BSM presented a list of twenty-three demands to the Chapel Hill administration. These included not only increasing the African American presence on campus but also providing better treatment of the university's largely black custodial and cafeteria workforce. The latter stipulation, BSM president Dobbins later said, represented an attempt to establish contacts between black students and the local African American community. After more than a month of consultation on campus, Sitterson responded to the BSM demands on January 24, 1969, during final exams and after many students had left. The chancellor told black student activists that the university could not "in policy or in practice, provide unique treatment for any single race, color or creed." To do so, he said, would be "a step backward, and the university should set its sights upon a better future." At the same time, his response, which had Friday's blessing, urged the "free and frank discussion" of all aspects of campus life and promised that a faculty-student committee would be formed to study the matter.[36]

Within a month, events were outdistancing Sitterson's moderation. On February 7, some 450 white students and faculty members, in a demonstration arranged by the Southern Student Organizing Committee (SSOC), a national organization established in 1964 as a white offshoot of the now all-black Student Nonviolent Coordinating Committee, marched through the campus and town in support of the BSM's demands. For ten minutes, about 100 of the marchers occupied the ground floor of South Building before departing peacefully. On the same day, a group of students attended a meeting of the Faculty Council, the faculty's legislative body, and observed its deliberations. A week later, SSOC organized another rally in the YMCA courtyard, and about 100 students and faculty members jammed the hall of nearby South Building. Meanwhile, on February 5, students at the all-black North Carolina A&T State University in Greensboro had occupied the administration building, and, on February 13, over 50 black students on the Duke campus in Durham conducted a sit-in at Allen Building, the university's administration office. When police attempted to oust the Duke students, who had occupied the building for nine hours, a melee ensued as more than 1,000 mostly white rioting students battled tear gas and the police.[37]

The Duke uprising greatly inflamed the charged atmosphere at Chapel Hill. Students learned from the Duke example, and there was direct contact and cross-fertilization between Duke and Carolina black leadership. In late February, matters came to a head. At that time the faculty-student committee on minorities and the disadvantaged, appointed by Carlyle Sitterson in late January to examine campus life for blacks, dissolved when the three black members resigned, claiming that the other committee members were "not qualified, not knowledgeable about the whole situation." Feeling outnumbered, black students objected to a white-majority committee. Black student leaders at Carolina, moreover, considered Sitterson's response on January 24 an unequivocal rejection of their demands; in the radicalized environment of Spring 1969, they increased the ante. Reinforced by the Duke experience, where the administration gave in to student demands, BSM leaders embraced greater militancy. According to Mickey Lewis, a BSM leader, Carolina activists emulated the Duke example. At Chapel Hill, he said, students "backed the man up against the wall"; the UNC chancellor "had to come through or lose his job." Sitterson, he thought, was "a cool dude, and we're going to have to rap him hard to get anything from him." On February 17, four days after the Duke confrontation, two hundred students gathered and agreed to take more aggressive action. The students then marched to Sitterson's office, where four of them met with the chancellor to discuss their demands, including the elimination of grades, the abolition of ROTC, more effective recruitment of black students, and the establishment of an Afro-American studies program. The meeting ended inconclusively, with Sitterson promising to hold an open meeting with Bill Friday sometime during the next ten days.[38]

The students, however, refused to wait that long. The next day, February 18, the BSM convened another meeting; two black basketball players, Charlie Scott, the first black basketball player at Carolina, and freshman Bill Chamberlain, attended. Complaining that their demands had not received "proper consideration," black leaders threatened to adopt revolutionary tactics, and BSM president Preston Dobbins declared that the group was unafraid of antiriot laws. They also added new demands – that the university recognize the BSM as the sole campus organization for blacks, that it end the use of white mediators to resolve black problems, and that it recognize the right of the BSM to make demands. BSM leaders then set a deadline of February 21 for Sitterson's response; according to Reggie Hawkins, unless their ultimatum was met, "our tactics will change from reform to revolution."[39]

The BSM's noisy militancy, Friday feared, would provoke a public backlash and threats of outside intervention. With Sitterson, he steered a moderate course in a radicalized environment. On February 19 Friday issued a statement warning that he would "promptly" do whatever was necessary to forestall the occupation of campus buildings. There was a need for change, he said, but it should occur only through the democratic process. North Carolinians expected that the university would remain a sanctuary of free and open discussion; Friday would enforce a 1965 law imposing jail terms and fines on persons convicted of obstructing the use of public buildings. While Friday took a hard line, Sitterson issued a statement on the same day urging conciliation; as one editorialist expressed it, he "very wisely . . . considered the substance of the changes insisted on, not the disagreeable manner in which they have been presented." Sitterson reconstituted the disbanded faculty-student committee on minorities and the disadvantaged; he also promised to increase efforts to recruit African American students.[40]

With Friday offering a stick and Sitterson a carrot, the two administrators attempted to satisfy two diverse constituencies: the Chapel Hill academic community, which wanted peaceful compromise, and the state's political leadership, which desired firmness and resolve. What neither Friday nor Sitterson anticipated, however, was the intervention of the mercurial governor, Robert W. Scott. Elected in the previous fall at the age of thirty-nine, Scott was a scion of a family of Alamance County farmer-politicians. His father, W. Kerr Scott, had been a reforming governor from 1949 to 1953; his uncle, Ralph Scott, was an influential leader in the legislature. A loyal State College alumnus (class of 1952), Bob Scott harbored deep suspicions of Carolina, and he was willing to take political advantage of anti–Chapel Hill sentiment.[41]

Governors presided over the UNC Board of Trustees meetings, sometimes with interest, sometimes with indifference. Only slightly more than a month after his inauguration, it was obvious that Scott would be an activist governor concerning UNC affairs, and, faced with the possibility of student rebellion at Chapel Hill, the governor assumed a hard line. On February 20, 1969, he sent a strongly worded memorandum to the presidents of state-supported colleges and universities in North Carolina. It asserted that any students or faculty who threatened public order or harassed organized meetings "in such a manner as to deprive speakers of the right of expression" in the classroom would be arrested. Campuses were not, he said, "places of refuge or asylum" from the law; lawbreakers would be prosecuted.[42]

Scott's stern warning did not depart far from Friday's own statements, but the governor ventured further by threatening state intervention if college or university officials could not control campus conditions. The memorandum detailed thirteen procedures relating to the occupation of buildings and ordered the presidents to follow them strictly. Police officers, Scott contended, did not need permission from college and university officials before they entered a campus to enforce the law. State authorities should consult campus officials as a matter of courtesy, but the views of university authorities were "not controlling and binding." In the event of an occupation of a state-owned building, presidents and chancellors were obliged to call in the police. Failing that, Scott, as governor, would not hesitate to send in the state highway patrol or units of the National Guard, or both, when he had reasonable grounds to believe it was necessary.

There was little doubt that Scott's memorandum, released to the press on Friday, February 21, 1969, was directed toward the rising tension on the Chapel Hill campus. That day, as the BSM's deadline of February 21 passed without action, about thirty-five BSM members, dressed entirely in black, marched from the Alumni Building to the university refectory, Lenoir Hall, chanting "We're gonna burn this place down." They then sequestered themselves in an upstairs private dining room for four and a half hours. Despite their public militancy, however, the black activists did not begin direct-action, "revolutionary" tactics; according to one BSM leader, they were "generally satisfied" with Sitterson's statement of February 19.

Nonetheless, tensions persisted over the weekend. A number of BSM leaders expressed irritation that Sitterson, who had been out of town on February 19, had issued his statement before consulting them. Although Bill Friday supported, even orchestrated, Sitterson's conciliatory overtures, his own hard-line statement of the nineteenth seemed to contradict the chancellor's efforts at conciliation, and Sitterson complained that press coverage had understated his attempts at mediation. Then, on Sunday, February 23, worker grievances at the Pine Room of Lenoir Hall, which was operated by Carolina, exploded. Sixteen or seventeen workers, with the support of the Black Student Movement, staged a walkout when the cafeteria opened for business at 4:00 P.M. As the black workers came from behind the food counters and, to the consternation of University Food Service management, sat down at tables, BSM members blocked the service lines and threw food around the room. The next day, about one hundred food service workers from Lenoir Dining Hall, Chase Dining Hall, and the Monogram Club (in the basement of the Faculty Club) joined the strike, and only Lenoir Hall remained open. The BSM, fully involved in the strike, moved into nearby Manning Hall, which the UNC Law School had recently vacated for new quarters, and there workers and students established a strike center and makeshift eatery.[43]

Almost immediately, the food workers' strike attracted the sympathy and support of some white students. As BSM members and the strikers set up picket lines, they succeeded in turning away food trucks and preventing nonstrikers from reporting to work. On February 27, the Carolina student legislature passed a resolution supporting the strikers. The white Southern Student Organizing Committee participated in the strike, and over the next days sympathetic students, white and black, began to stage "stall-ins" at Lenoir Hall in an attempt to disrupt service by deliberately slowing their progress through the cafeteria line. Not all students supported the strike, however, and a scuffle occurred shortly after 7:00 P.M. on March 4, when some students, including three football players and one ex-marine, broke through the SSOC stall-in. Meanwhile, fighting erupted when one of the boycotters emptied ammonia in one part of the dining room and then refused to permit the windows to be opened; in the ensuing melee, one white student was injured when he was hit on the head by a sugar dispenser. Riot-equipped Chapel Hill police were dispatched to the scene, as fifty BSM members, twenty-five black Chapel Hill residents, and fifty white supporters dashed through the north end of Lenoir Hall, overturning tables as they went. That evening, police with riot gear closed and locked Lenoir Hall and posted guards around it. At Manning Hall, Charlotte physician Reginald Hawkins – father of BSM leader Reggie Hawkins – and civil rights lawyers Julius Chambers and Adam Stein met with strikers and students, and they formed the Nonacademic Employees Union. Stein represented the union in negotiations held with the state attorney general's office. On the following day, March 5, black leaders and their white student supporters gathered for a meeting on the steps of Lenoir, where an audience of about five hundred heard speeches by strikers, faculty members, and organizers such as Durham activist Howard Fuller.[44]

The predicament now confronting Bill Friday was more perilous than the student challenge to the Speaker Ban law. Between the beginning of the food workers' strike and the brief but well-publicized violence at Lenoir Hall, UNC policy had been characterized, according to a historian of the strike, by "administrative circumspection." During the spring of 1969, Friday lacked regular and reliable communication with the student leadership, which was now divided and more unpredictable. With its goals less clearly defined, the student movement of 1969 was eminently more threatening and significantly more difficult to defuse.[45]

The crisis of Spring 1969 also undermined the national image of Chapel Hill liberalism. The cafeteria strike exposed the university as a paternalistic employer that paid low wages and provided what one UNC official later admitted were "lousy" working conditions. The university was vulnerable to charges of neglect and even racism toward the African American community on the Chapel Hill campus. Part of Friday's response during the strike, there-fore, was to seek to restore a reputation of enlightened management and racial liberalism. The strike in this sense, as a contemporary explained, was "almost well calculated to drive Bill Friday up the wall," and a large share of his energy was devoted to achieving favorable press coverage.[46]

Most UNC trustees, meanwhile, probably agreed with Governor Scott's hard line; they were impatient with student activism. The fact that the move-ment was led by blacks and challenged the university's traditionally paternalis-tic racial practices alarmed them and contributed to fears of black assertive-ness. But the views of trustees simply reflected public opinion in the state. "Overwhelmingly" the people of North Carolina, commented the *Raleigh News and Observer*, wanted no toleration for campus disorder. Rightly or wrongly, public opinion held that "vacillation and softness of campus admin-istrators elsewhere" were the cause of the disruptions. Yet these public atti-tudes had pushed the trustees toward an inflexible policy and left them with little "prudent choice" about how to contain the student uprising.[47]

The UNC Board of Trustees considered Scott's hard-line memorandum at its meeting on February 24. Permitting criminal offenses such as the occupa-tion of campus buildings, Scott told the board, was akin to tolerating the presence of criminals at the state art museum; "the law is law," he said. In response, Friday maintained that the UNC administration did not need greater power to contain student activism; administrators possessed a "broad delegation of authority," and there was "no need for additional or supplemen-tal action."

Just as he had during the Speaker Ban controversy, Friday sought a middle course between student impatience and trustee overreaction. He hoped to contain the situation and prevent violence and, above all, to forestall the closing of the university or the intervention of outside police forces. Working closely with Chancellor Sitterson, he steered a course of firmness and concilia-tion simultaneously. Publicly, he did not oppose Scott's position; he told the Board of Trustees on February 24 that the university would observe the laws of the state. Condemning extremists who fanned racial antagonisms, he said: "We should join men of good will who earnestly work for a society in which equal protection under the laws, constitutional guarantees, and the oppor-tunity to be productive, creative, and peaceful citizens would be accorded men of all races." Looking at the student leaders who were attending the board meeting, Friday described the "great faith" he had in students. They were, he said, "better informed, more widely travelled, and more committed to build-ing a better world than earlier generations." He advised the trustees to "listen to what they have to say." There was "a need for change in our society, but it must be achieved through the democratic process." Finding a solution would require "understanding, patience, a good measure of wisdom and abiding faith."[48]

Yet Friday knew that it was not easy to be wise and maintain an abiding faith in the polarized environment of early 1969. His main goal, he recalled five years after the event, was to protect the freedom of the university, but he realized that he was treading a thin line between accommodation and repres-sion. As UNC president, he sat astride the "two different worlds" of academics and politicians, whose views were fed by "widespread public distrust" toward campuses; even thoughtful people were convinced that events at Chapel Hill had "gotten completely out of hand." Friday was "working hard to keep the lines of communication open." In order to maintain the equilibrium of the university, he believed, it was essential to maintain academic integrity, and that was only possible by keeping the campus open. In the end, however, the trustees supported the governor. Buck Harris proposed a vote of thanks to Scott; Luther Hamilton of Morehead City praised him for sending, in his memorandum, a "courageous and inspirational message" to UNC officials.[49]

The outbreak of fighting and the closing of Lenoir Hall on March 4 posed a grave threat to university integrity and virtually ensured that the trustees would take a firm stand. The strike had now entered an explosive phase with the looming prospect of violence; Scott's intervention remained a possibility. Accordingly, Bill Friday became more directly involved. On March 5 Friday, Sitterson, and other administrators met in South Building at the chancellor's office. There, the university officials reached an important decision: to carry forward Friday's carrot-and-stick approach, they would reopen Lenoir Hall and, at the same time, speed along negotiations with the striking cafeteria workers.

Bob Scott, however, wanted more immediate action. In a Founders Day address at Elon College, he warned that police would "take whatever steps" were necessary to keep the UNC cafeteria open and to maintain the "normal operations" of the university. The governor summoned Sitterson and Friday to Raleigh for a meeting late in the afternoon of March 5. When Scott demanded that Lenoir Hall be opened immediately, Friday and Sitterson told him that opening the cafeteria in the darkness would be too risky and that they would do so after a morning negotiating session with the striking workers. Friday also asserted that sending state police and National Guard units to Chapel Hill was unnecessary. At that meeting it became obvious that one of Scott's advisers, Ben Roney, was urging the governor to order in the National Guard units waiting in Durham. Friday strenuously disagreed, contending that an invasion by troops would simply supply a "trigger" for further escalation. A "violent argument" ensued.[50] Scott insisted that the cafeteria be opened for breakfast on the following morning, March 6, despite Friday and Sitterson's preference to wait until noon. Yet both administrators left Scott's office reassured that the governor would not send in troops.

The next day, however, Scott, responding to what he described as an appeal from the Chapel Hill police, dispatched state police units to guard Lenoir Hall from further disruption; he also ordered National Guard units in Durham to move into the campus if necessary. Friday and Sitterson issued statements threatening the dismissal of professors who refused to hold classes. In a morning meeting on March 6 Sitterson told faculty members that the strike had demonstrated "injustices" among cafeteria workers and that reforms, such as immediately raising wages and improving working conditions, were under way. Faculty and students needed to exercise restraint and moderation; only then, he said, would the campus "come through this crisis." The meeting ended as 245 faculty members signed a statement asking Scott to withdraw state police from the campus.

Friday and Sitterson considered Scott's decision to send in the state police a unilateral invasion of the campus. Prior to the governor's order, there had been little direct contact between Scott and UNC administrators. Scott drafted his memorandum of February 20 without consulting anyone at UNC, and its appearance and public disclosure surprised university officials. His subsequent decision to send the state troopers was also made without extensive consultation. Both Sitterson and Friday believed that the presence of outside police on campus only aggravated the situation and heightened the potential for violence, and they resented the move. Sitterson later described Scott's decision as "astonishing." One of Friday's chief objectives throughout the cafeteria strike, remembered a close associate, was to "maintain an environment in which the incidence or opportunity for violence was minimized."

Similarly, as he explained to Chapel Hill deans on March 6, Sitterson's purpose was to "support [an] orderly, forceful and rational approach to our problems." Scott's intervention seemed to threaten the tense campus equilibrium; it was, editorialized the *Greensboro Daily News*, "unduly abrupt and abrasive." As during the long Speaker Ban controversy, Friday contended that state authorities should "leave it alone" and permit university officials to "work it out." Although Friday thought that Scott personally had little interest in "wanting to make a big display for publicity purposes," he realized that "some of the people around him would," and he knew that the governor faced a situation that was "really loaded with dynamite." Others were less charitable in their assessment. Arnold King described Scott as "a sort of loose cannon" who exploited campus unrest for "his own advancement." Sending in the state troopers, King believed, simply exacerbated a problem that Friday and Sitterson "could have settled, without any need for outside intervention." The whole affair was "grandstanding of the most egregious variety."[51]

In the meantime Sitterson and Friday continued to favor mediation. A day after the strike began, Sitterson had sent his assistant, Claiborne Jones, and the personnel director, Fred Haskell, to negotiate with the workers. Then on March 6, when Lenoir Hall, guarded by sixty-five state patrolmen and twenty Chapel Hill policemen, reopened, Sitterson instructed Jones and Joseph C. Eagles Jr., vice chancellor for business and finance, to meet with the strikers. The strikers communicated their grievances, and Jones and Eagles promised their "thorough and immediate" attention. Friday was maintaining regular contact with Sitterson; as he recalled, he "kept with that issue day by day" and was in "constant conversation" with the chancellor. During the crisis Friday, according to an aide, spent as much time at South Building as he did at UNC's offices on Franklin Street. The recollection of one contemporary that Sitterson was saying "what Bill Friday told him to say" or, of another, that Friday was a "surrogate chancellor," might be an overstatement, but there can be little doubt that the two men worked closely together. Friday felt that the intense public scrutiny accompanying the confrontation justified his intervention in campus affairs; although he was sometimes "very intrusive," he insisted on directing the course of events "to the extent that they were directible from our side." Throughout the strike, he was accordingly "very present, very apparent." Yet he also consciously avoided the limelight in order to maintain avenues of communication to all parties.[52]

While his staff bargained with the strikers, Sitterson arranged for state personnel department officials to visit the Chapel Hill campus to study the job classifications of workers and to examine the possibility of wage increases. Although the sticking point remained state-established wage levels, the negotiations, fueled by administration eagerness for a solution, moved forward. On March 11, Sitterson informed the faculty that the workers' lawyers were conferring with officials from the state attorney general's office and that the campus administration was restructuring labor-management relations in order to address grievances. Yet pressure from students, the faculty, and the governor's office continued. Earlier, on March 7, about 140 faculty members sympathetic to the strike had convened an unofficial meeting after the regular faculty meeting was canceled. When no administrators attended, about 70 faculty members and 40 graduate students sent Sitterson a resolution threatening to stop teaching unless state police were removed from the campus and the strike was settled. Friday responded firmly, warning again of dismissals. Although these threats raised the possibility of a more widespread faculty revolt, the graduate students called off their strike.[53]

As the administration and the strikers inched toward a solution, a confrontation was building between Scott's state police and student activists. The activists continued, after February 23, to occupy Manning Hall, where they operated a "Soul Food Cafeteria," and there were reports – some of them exaggerated – of unsafe and unsanitary conditions, of loudspeakers that blared music and obscenities, and of students smuggling weapons into the building. On Wednesday, March 12, Sitterson ordered the Manning Hall occupants to shut down their loudspeaker system; after demanding that the chancellor's request be delivered in writing, they acquiesced anyway. On the same day, UNC officials decided to remove the occupying students from Manning Hall two days hence – on Friday, March 14 – and they so informed the governor. Yet Scott insisted that the building be cleared a day earlier. He then ordered state police to evict the occupants on March 13 and warned UNC administrators that he would, if necessary, use National Guard units as part of a show of force. Chapel Hill chief of police William Blake, who had received a phone call from Scott that morning, walked alone and unarmed into Manning Hall, presented warrants for the arrest of seven black students and one white involved in the March 4 Lenoir Hall incident, and advised the occupants to leave the building. Durham activist Howard Fuller, a part-time social work instructor, urged the one hundred occupying students to leave in order to avoid a showdown. Speaking first to the members of the white SSOC, he told them to "split," saying that there was "no use" remaining. The white students and cafeteria workers left the building about 1:30 P.M., and, although about fifteen BSM members said that they intended to stay, they too left a few minutes later. A crowd of students congregated around Manning Hall after state troopers, just before three o'clock, secured and locked the building; after a tense confrontation there, the students moved to South Building, where speakers urged calm.[54]

Scott's further intervention united the Chapel Hill campus against him. Senior faculty on the Faculty Advisory Committee declared on March 13 that they were "profoundly shocked" at Scott's meddling in university affairs, and they believed that it would cause "lasting damage to the institution." The day after Manning Hall was cleared, Sitterson met with two thousand students in Memorial Hall. The chancellor praised the students who had shown "dignity and self-restraint" and fought back tears as he related his "deep sense of sadness" about campus "injustices" and about the presence of "outside police on campus." Pleading for patience, he told the students that "we're all in this together." At the same time, Sitterson announced that there had been progress in the negotiations with the cafeteria workers; Carolina had agreed to authorize retroactive pay raises, payment of overtime, reclassification of some of the workers to a higher wage level, rescheduling to provide for more weekends off and a five-day, forty-hour work week, and an administrative order for all supervisors to use courtesy titles when addressing cafeteria workers.[55]

The crisis had now passed, and Scott emerged from it convinced that his intervention had saved the day. Asserting that he had been in "daily contact, almost constant contact" with developments at Carolina, he criticized administrators for delay and claimed credit for forcing the situation. Despite the fact that police found no weapons inside Manning Hall, the governor maintained that "intelligence sources" – he later admitted that they were State Bureau of Investigation (SBI) informants – had led him to believe that the demonstrators were armed. As he remembered the strike, local police forces simply "didn't know how to cope with it" and lacked "the resources to cope with it." He had "no desire to operate the University," but it was his responsibility to ensure that order was reestablished. In the absence of strong leadership by UNC officials, Scott said, the situation was deteriorating, and he sent in the police at the SBI's recommendation.[56]

Scott expressed these views even more directly in a meeting of the Executive Committee on March 14. In a rambling lecture, Scott stated that he expected the university to be operated "with a minimum of disruption of the educational process" for the benefit of all students, as opposed to the "whim and caprice" of the small fraction of protesters. The time had come for a decision about who was "going to operate the University and for whom it will be operated." In an explicit criticism of UNC administrators, he claimed that "indecision, delay, and vacillation" had prevented the resolution of the crisis. The time for "positive action" had arrived; the demonstrators needed firmness. If trustees and administrators lacked resolve, disorder could spread to other campuses; the belief that further concessions could avert violence was a "forlorn hope." There would be "trouble either way," and he favored forceful action to "stamp out the work of these offenders." Bill Friday and other administrators might well be unwilling to provide such leadership, yet they would have to account for themselves before the legislature, and the governor doubted that Friday's answer would be "satisfactory" to many legislators. Although he hoped that it would be unnecessary to bypass the administrative officials of the university and act in his capacity as governor, Scott told the committee, he was willing to offer the power of his office in any way that the trustees might determine was wise.[57]

It was, in many ways, a remarkable performance. Although Bill Friday had had significant differences with governors, never had he been so directly, even savagely, criticized. Nor had he ever worked under a governor who, in effect, encouraged trustees to circumvent their own university administration. Scott had plunged himself headlong into university affairs, observed Ed Yoder, "more vigorously and openly . . . than any governor in memory." Friday, though he refrained from public comment, deeply resented the governor's intervention. Not only did it undermine his authority, but Scott's involvement also threatened to sabotage Friday's strategy of firmness and conciliation. Through persuasion and authority, the UNC president had isolated student radicals from wider university support and from the cafeteria workers, whose interests, student leaders increasingly realized, were better served through the negotiations under Sitterson's sponsorship. By mid-March Friday had orchestrated an uneasy peace, and only through diplomacy and luck was further confrontation avoided.[58]

On two other UNC campuses, meanwhile, trouble was brewing, much of it inspired by the events at Duke and Chapel Hill. At the University of North Carolina at Charlotte (UNC-Charlotte), the Black Student Union, loosely modeled after the BSM and headed by future NAACP executive director Benjamin F. Chavis, submitted a list of ten demands to Chancellor Dean W. Colvard on February 26, 1969, three days after the cafeteria strike began at Chapel Hill. These demands included the establishment of a black studies program, greater efforts to recruit black students and employ black faculty, an increase to $2.00 an hour for nonacademic employees, the abolition of grading for black students and the establishment of a pass-fail system, and the dismissal of all "racist" faculty and administrators. On March 3 Chavis and about forty black students marched to the administration building and replaced the American and North Carolina flags with a black nationalist flag. Friday and UNC vice president Henry W. Lewis maintained "close communication with the situation," and Colvard responded to the students' demands about a month later. When he offered the Friday formula of conciliation and firmness, however, no student revolt materialized.[59]

At Greensboro, the situation became more complicated. Like Chapel Hill, the University of North Carolina at Greensboro (UNCG) had integrated in 1956 under court order, and even as late as 1969 the campus was still adjusting to the growing numbers of African American students. The two students admitted in the fall of 1956 were housed in segregated facilities in Shaw Hall, with separate "Colored" bathroom facilities; when they became juniors they were given staff rooms in the residence halls. In 1964 rooms were still assigned according to race, and not until 1966 did UNCG officially adopt a non-discriminatory policy. In 1967 black students created the Neo-Black Society (NBS), which became the main forum for UNCG blacks.[60]

As was the case in Chapel Hill, student activists at Greensboro eventually focused on the conditions of the largely African American food and custodial workers. In the fall of 1968 the NBS urged students and residence hall counselors to use courtesy titles when speaking to custodians rather than addressing them by their first names. Then, on March 26, 1969, two weeks after the Chapel Hill crisis peaked, the cafeteria workers at the UNCG dining hall, which was managed by the private caterer ARA Slater, went on strike; they could accept ARA's wage offer of $1.80, but they rejected the caterer's insistence that other issues be deferred. In addition, the cafeteria workers demanded that the company not fire any of the strike leaders. The next day, NBS and sympathetic white students from the overwhelmingly women's college joined in picketing the dining hall and urging students to support the strike. That evening 750 students crowded into Cone Ballroom on campus and agreed to the boycott.[61]

The Greensboro situation grew tense that weekend. During the strike, the small number of UNCG's black students – only slightly more than a hundred in 1969 – were joined by students from the historically black North Carolina A&T State University (A&T) across town. Some A&T students were employed as cafeteria workers at UNCG, and they served as organizers of the strike; as one UNCG faculty member remembered, "what was happening here was not separate from what was happening there [at A&T]." But the alliance between the white female student government leadership and the black students and A&T sympathizers was tenuous, at best. As at Chapel Hill, the threat of police intervention, authorized either by the governor or by local authorities, was ever-present, and police armed with tear gas appeared on campus to control the demonstrations. On Saturday, March 29, a small group of students spontaneously marched on Chancellor Ferguson's residence. With students standing in his driveway shouting for him to appear, Ferguson was so angered that he refused to talk to them and insisted that they make an appointment to see him the next Monday.[62]

The crisis came to a head on the evening of Monday, March 31, 1969, when about 500 people attended another rally at Cone Ballroom; according to one observer, the mood was "tense," and about half of those present were A&T students. More students joined the crowd, which by 9:30 P.M. had grown to 1,200 people. The meeting continued into the early hours of the morning, as UNCG student government leaders struggled with participating A&T student leaders such as activist Nelson Johnson for control of the group. While Johnson pushed for a march to the chancellor's residence, white student government leaders urged restraint. With racial tensions in the open at the Cone meeting and tear gas-equipped Greensboro police lining the street outside the student union, student body president Randi Bryant realized that the situation might easily become violent. She told the audience that the chancellor, who had made it clear that he opposed a student march, would not address a mob. Saying that she had just spoken with Ferguson on the telephone – though in reality the line was busy – Bryant announced that the chancellor had agreed to a campuswide meeting the next morning. Her quick thinking forestalled what one faculty observer called a "very close call with civil disobedience that night." According to one eyewitness, Bryant's quick action "took the sting out of it" and illustrated "remarkable sensitivity on the part of the student leadership." Although Ferguson was "dog-tired" and had little to say of real substance the next day, another observer recalled, he "made the best speech he could have given the fact that things were still up in the air."[63]

It was in this tense environment that Friday became directly involved. Informed early on the morning of April 1 of the previous evening's developments, he drove to Greensboro to support Ferguson. He had, he recalled, "no specific plan in mind" but intended to provide the UNCG chancellor with "comfort" and to "help him." Friday realized that "being there" would communicate to the UNCG community that the crisis there was "important enough" to demand his presence. A faculty member who had dropped by Ferguson's office in the morning remembered seeing Friday emerge from the chancellor's office. Friday's appearance, and some conciliatory gestures from Ferguson, seemed to have quieted the storm. That day, Friday met with student government president Randi Bryant and NBS president Annie King. While he agreed that the university was officially neutral in the strike, Ferguson urged a settlement and pressed ARA to make concessions. On April 2, after the arrival of an ARA vice president, management and workers reached a settlement, and the crisis ended.[64]

Although the strike continued at Chapel Hill, the moment of confrontation had passed by early April. On March 20 the governor had endorsed legislation sponsored by his uncle, Ralph Scott, to raise the minimum wage for state workers to $1.80 per hour after Ralph arranged a meeting between striker Mary Smith – an Alamance County native who had known the Scott family – and the governor. The next day a settlement was announced, and the strikers had won what the *Greensboro Daily News* described as a "clear victory." In April six of the students arrested for violence on March 4 in Lenoir Hall were tried and convicted in district court. Each was fined $150 and placed on two years' probation; the university decided to take no separate disciplinary action.

Meanwhile, Friday arranged for the appointment of a trustee subcommittee to examine the issue of student unrest and recommend a disciplinary procedure. In May this group was reconstituted into another subcommittee, headed by Winston-Salem banker Archie Davis, to look into ways to revise the UNC *Code* to deal with student unrest. During the summer of 1969 the Davis Committee met and developed new procedures that provided for the dismissal of students and firing of faculty members involved in the "willful disruption of the educational process, destruction of property, and interference with the rights of other members of the community." Yet the rules proposed by the Davis Committee also envisioned a new disciplinary process that would respect due process by establishing a board of inquiry composed of student and faculty representatives and an attorney. These changes in the UNC *Code* were proposed to the Executive Committee and adopted unanimously with a few amendments on September 12, 1969; the full Board of Trustees endorsed the disruption policy on October 27, 1969.[65]

Like most college administrators, Bill Friday was caught off balance by the student troubles of the spring of 1969. Student radicalism, by March 1969, reflected frustration and even unreasonableness – and stood in contrast to the well-coordinated student movement against the Speaker Ban earlier in the decade. Nonetheless, the university, Friday believed, was "extremely fortunate," for no university anywhere had been prepared "to deal with the disruptive element," and the single instance of violence at the University of North Carolina was the scuffle at Lenoir Hall on March 4. After the experience of March 1969, Friday was determined to be better prepared next time, and he sought, through the new disruption policy, to create a "machinery to deal with this small segment of the school population."[66]

The Davis Committee served several purposes. The new disruption policy became a way out for the trustees and the governor. In May 1969 Scott, who in March had been sharply critical of Friday's handling of the student uprising, conceded that the district court convictions of the students had "pretty well reduced the general discussion of the issue." Moreover, he praised the trustees'

disruption policy as "a forthright and satisfactory procedure for the future."
As the *Greensboro Daily News* editorialized, the "gusty, chilly words of March"
had given way to "milder" and "more sensible" language. The disruption
policy, once it was finally adopted, gave Friday a stick to wield, in the final
resort, against student protest if it should threaten to shut down the university. Yet he was determined never to be forced to invoke that policy; his
preferred methods of resolving student unrest and confrontation remained
conciliation and mediation.[67]

Two further tests of Friday's policy toward student unrest came in 1969 and
1970. Since 1965, the dining service on the Chapel Hill campus had been
losing patronage, and UNC – like most other universities nationwide during
this period – turned administration of the dining halls over to a private
catering business in May 1969. But the cafeteria workers soon charged that the
caterer, California-based Saga Corporation, was attempting to break their
union, had sharply reduced the workforce, and had increased hours and
overtime without pay raises. On November 7, 1969, the Carolina cafeteria
workers struck again. Students rallied to their cause, and, on November 10,
they staged an "eat-in" in which students returned for multiple helpings as a
way to reduce Saga's profits. After ensuing tensions between students and the
policemen guarding the cafeteria, mediation began at the urging of Bill Friday
and Carolina officials. Friday recalled that he generally remained "two steps
back" from these negotiations; he believed, based on the experience of the
previous spring, that it was better to let Chancellor Sitterson handle the
situation. Nevertheless, at a critical juncture in early December, his intervention proved crucial. When the negotiations appeared stalled, he telephoned
the Saga president in California and asked him "point blank" what his "irre-
ducible position" was. On the heels of Friday's phone call, strikers and management reached a settlement on December 8, after a thirty-two-day strike.[68]

The events of the autumn of 1969, however, never evoked the intense,
campuswide anger of the previous March. Bob Scott's interest had passed; as
Friday explained to Harvard sociologist David Riesman, the governor had
"substantially modified his previous attitude" toward UNC. Without police
intervention, tensions throughout the Saga strike never reached the levels of
the previous spring. Even when Richard Nixon ordered the invasion of Cam-
bodia in late April 1970, thereby setting off antiwar protests and campus
closings around the country, President Friday and the Chapel Hill administration were able to contain the student explosion. Although a student strike
erupted in May, and some 387 people signed petitions in which they willfully
admitted violating the disruption policy, classes continued. Through a combination of persuasion and the threat of coercion, UNC classrooms remained

open through the spring and fall of 1970. Meanwhile, as the crisis passed at the beginning of the fall semester, Friday obtained amendments to the disruption policy that softened its impact.[69]

In the end, there was only one instance in which the disruption policy was invoked – in the case of David G. Blevins, a part-time instructor at UNC-Charlotte, who refused to hold classes during the anti–Vietnam War moratorium movement of October 1969. Yet Blevins's dismissal was irrelevant, since he had already been told by his department that he would not be rehired. After the restructuring of the entire UNC system in 1972, the UNC *Code* was again revised. Few people noticed that the disruption policy had been omitted. In May 1971 Friday was able to report to trustees that a "perceptible change" had occurred. As one student told him, he said, Chapel Hill students had "approached the precipice, viewed the abyss with alarm, and eschewed violence and unlawful confrontation."[70]

Bill Friday's response to the challenge of student activism in the 1960s provides a clear example of his leadership and administrative style. The line of consistency throughout remained Friday's commitment to protecting academic independence from political intrusion, whether in legislative restrictions over free speech or in the gubernatorial use of police force to quell campus rebellion. Friday was engaged, however, in a delicate juggling act – trying to balance an absolute right to free speech versus uncompromising anticommunism, student insistence on racial equity, and the incomprehension with which North Carolina's power structure viewed the campus rebellion.

In seeking to maintain a status quo of academic comity and civility, Friday responded to student protest defensively. Increasingly, however, he discovered that defending UNC's integrity depended on power. The rapid growth of non-UNC public colleges in the state after 1945 created new political constituencies; as in most other parts of the country, the state legislature sought greater administrative rationality. In the turbulent 1960s, as a result, the UNC system went through a major redefinition and challenge to its position within North Carolina.

CHAPTER 6 *Restructuring the University System*

FOR most of the 1960s, while the internal tranquility of the university was disrupted, Bill Friday was engaged in a battle to alter the external structure of the multicampus University of North Carolina. First came the Carlyle Commission, an attempt to rationalize public postsecondary education in the state by establishing a system of comprehensive community colleges, upgrading the teachers' colleges, and solidifying UNC's position. Then, in the mid-1960s, powerful forces upset the equilibrium attempted in the Carlyle Commission's plan and undermined UNC's political influence in the General Assembly. By the latter half of the 1960s, UNC's power was openly challenged, as higher education became a major issue in North Carolina politics.

University restructuring was the product of considerable confusion, beginning in the 1950s, in public higher education in North Carolina. Through a study commission chaired by Victor Bryant in 1955, the state's political leadership endorsed greater coordination and rationality in allocating public resources. The Bryant Commission further concluded that duplicative and unnecessary competition existed among the state's senior colleges and universities. North Carolina could not afford "several great universities," the commission's report asserted, but it certainly should "have at least one." Implicitly the "great" university would be the UNC system, while the other former teachers' colleges would be limited to basic undergraduate education. The Bryant Commission recommended the establishment of a new state agency, a State Board of Higher Education (BHE), that would coordinate, plan, and, if necessary, control the flow of resources into North Carolina's public colleges and universities.[1]

The General Assembly established the Board of Higher Education in the spring of 1955 and created what one observer described as an illusion of "peace and quiet."[2] In preventing East Carolina College and other former teachers' colleges from expanding, the BHE protected the three-campus University of North Carolina from its competitors across the state. But by the late 1950s, the BHE also began to restrain UNC expansion. Although formed to serve the interests of the UNC system by operating, as one newspaper editor remembered it, as a "board of trustees for the non-consolidated" colleges, the Board of Higher Education soon took on a life of its own. In the winter of 1957–58 a conflict erupted over the BHE's refusal to approve the construction of new married student housing at State College and Carolina, and in May 1958 the UNC trustees endorsed legislation reformulating the BHE structure in such a way as to ensure UNC autonomy. On April 21, 1959, the legislature stipulated that the BHE would become primarily a planning agency, would possess the power to "allot" rather than "determine" educational activities, and would possess only advisory power over budgets. At the same time, the board would retain complete authority over the authorization of new programs and could recommend that the legislature discontinue programs.[3]

As baby-boom children began to enter college in the 1960s and 1970s, North Carolina public colleges and universities faced a predicted explosion in enrollments. It was in this context that the Governor's Commission on Education beyond the High School – known as the Carlyle Commission – was established. The Carlyle Commission produced the most significant reorganization of the UNC system since the 1931 consolidation. According to one contemporary, it was "one of the major turning points in our educational history." To a large extent, this was a correct assessment. Laying a foundation for the stable expansion of postsecondary education in North Carolina, the Carlyle Commission broadened the mission of the University of North Carolina by providing a new mechanism for its expansion. In the wake of the Carlyle Commission, the UNC Board of Trustees sought to transform the functions of the Woman's College, which would become coeducational and offer expanded graduate programs, and of State College, which would develop an enlarged curriculum in the humanities and social sciences. These campuses, becoming full-fledged universities, would be known as the University of North Carolina at Greensboro and the University of North Carolina at Raleigh.[4]

The effort to reorganize higher education was one product of a collaborative relationship between Bill Friday and William Dallas Herring. Like Friday, Herring had unusually well-developed notions of public leadership. A native of Rose Hill, in Duplin County, Herring was graduated from Davidson College in 1938. At age twenty-three he was elected mayor of his hometown, and over the next eleven years he supervised the installation of a water and sewer system, the creation of a town fire department, and the paving of Rose Hill's streets and sidewalks. Becoming chairman of the Duplin County Board of Education in 1951, Herring served on both of the special committees chaired by state senator Tom Pearsall that were established to devise a response to the *Brown* v. *Board of Education* decision of 1954. The Pearsall Plan that emerged from these committees offered a "moderate" response through constitutional amendments that provided for local option school closings and for tuition grants to private schools in communities that faced court-imposed desegregation.[5]

Herring was no rigid segregationist, however. As school board chairman in Duplin County he had upgraded facilities for black schools, and he belonged to that category of moderates who temporarily accepted segregation but believed that the state should prepare for change. When the Pearsall Plan called for legislation and constitutional amendments to permit communities to close schools rather than integrate, Herring refused to sign the report. Only when Governor Luther Hodges personally assured him that no schools would be closed did Herring give his assent.[6]

A self-described Jeffersonian, Herring found an almost immediate kinship with Bill Friday. The two had met in 1957 through Guy Phillips, dean of the UNC School of Education, at a dinner at a steak house on New Bern Avenue in Raleigh. During that "long, leisurely evening," as Herring remembered it, he was struck by the similarity of his and Friday's educational philosophies; they shared the conviction that higher education should open a "door of opportunity" for all North Carolinians.[7]

Herring came away from such contacts with Friday persuaded that he was a kindred spirit. Friday did not "differ one bit in his philosophy from that which I espoused," Herring said. The two men subsequently "helped each other," "matured together," "planned together," and "achieved together." Convinced of a convergence of interests, Friday eventually enjoyed a relationship of total trust with Herring; they became, as he described it, "spiritual brothers." During the late 1950s, Friday and Herring agreed about the need to improve technical education for North Carolinians. Friday realized that Herring's primary concern was "to get some stability behind the community college system," and Herring endorsed Friday's desire for greater rationality in public higher education.[8]

The Friday-Herring alliance was cemented with the election of Terry Sanford as governor in 1960 and his inauguration on January 5, 1961. Sanford had plans for what he called a "New Day" in education. He relied heavily on Herring, who was a political supporter and, as he put it, his "number one" adviser on education; Sanford found Herring's ambitions to expand the community college and technical education system particularly attractive. Because he had first concentrated his energies on elementary and secondary education, however, Sanford hoped to defer the issue until the next legislative session, in 1963. But the governor's hand was forced in the spring of 1961 by the public junior colleges at Charlotte, Asheville, and Wilmington. Emboldened by the Sanford gubernatorial campaign, these institutions began lobbying for four-year, senior college status.[9]

The junior colleges' maneuver posed an immediate threat to Sanford's reputation as an education governor, and when Herring suggested that Sanford create a blue-ribbon commission to study higher education in North Carolina, Sanford endorsed the idea. Bill Friday, whom Sanford later described as his "chief ally" in higher education, played a major role in determining the membership and direction of the commission. Sanford listened to his advice on the commission; he also informed Friday that he regarded him as his "chief contact" and the "key person" who would maintain the commission's momentum. But the choice of the chairman was Sanford's. He turned to campaign supporter Irving E. Carlyle, a lawyer from Winston-Salem who had a reputation for integrity and moderate liberalism. Irving Carlyle was perhaps best known for his keynote speech at the state Democratic convention on May 20, 1954, three days after the *Brown* decision, when he defied the state's political leadership and urged North Carolinians to abide by the Supreme Court's edict. By all accounts, Carlyle's speech cost him the appointment by Governor William B. Umstead to the unexpired term of Senator Clyde R. Hoey, who had died on May 12, one week before the convention. Later, Carlyle alienated leading figures in the state by publicly opposing the Pearsall Plan. By late September 1961, with the UNC Institute of Government's John Sanders serving as secretary, the Carlyle Commission was holding its first meetings.[10]

Deliberating during the fall, spring, and summer of 1961–62, the commission delivered its report to Sanford on August 31, 1962. The report of the Carlyle Commission heralded the need to extend higher education to a greater proportion of North Carolinians. Scarcely half of the state's young people completed high school, a fifth sought schooling at the collegiate level, and a tenth received a college degree. Although higher education had become synonymous with social and economic development, the present facilities in the state were inadequate, and greater planning and coordination would be necessary to allocate public resources rationally. The commission foresaw an explosion in student enrollments as the inevitable consequence of an increased rate of college attendance and a "sudden and substantial rise" in baby-boom-age students. According to the commission's estimates, enrollments would double in the two decades after 1961. North Carolinians, the report stated, needed "a functioning *system* of public higher education and not a mere aggregation of independent institutions, each pursuing its own conception of the public interest."[11]

While commission members could readily agree on those objectives, the commission's most important decisions concerned three critical issues: the shape and financing of a new community college system, the implications of a system of higher education for the University of North Carolina, and the role of colleges at Charlotte, Asheville, and Wilmington within a new UNC structure. For both Herring and Sanford, the commission's primary goal was to increase access, partly through an expansion of the university, but particularly through the creation of a comprehensive community college system.

The new community college system became the cornerstone of Sanford's New Day in higher education. Because more than half of North Carolina's families were at or near the poverty line – a majority of them in 1962 earned less than $4,000 annually – most of the state's population simply could not afford to attend a residential college. The "preponderant need" was to make access more available during the first two years of college. The Carlyle Commission report recommended that the community colleges be "comprehensive," that is, that they offer a combination of technical-vocational courses with a general education curriculum. Along with this key feature – a central ingredient of Herring's plans from the outset – the commission report recommended that the new community college system be under the direction of the State Board of Higher Education. Because other states with community colleges had adopted this model and because federal vocational educational authorities required it, the report urged unequivocal control by the state educational system.[12]

Friday sought another objective: greater order and system in the governance of higher education. He reached this objective gradually; when the Carlyle Commission was established in 1961, he had no master plan for creating a "system" of higher education. As the commission deliberated, it inched toward this goal, and the final report called for three groups of state institutions: the University of North Carolina, concentrating on academic excellence and serving as the "primary state center" of graduate and professional programs and research; the public senior colleges (formerly the teachers' colleges for blacks, whites, and Native Americans), emphasizing undergraduate education; and the new community colleges.[13]

The position of the junior colleges at Charlotte, Wilmington, and Asheville remained unclear in this hierarchy. The commission itself had been established partly in response to their drive for four-year status, and Herring had already privately assured boosters of some form of university expansion in those cities.[14] In reality, UNC's expansion to Charlotte was inevitable. As North Carolina's largest metropolitan area, Charlotte, as Friday saw it, would have a university, and it was necessary and desirable that it should be established under the UNC umbrella. Expansion to Charlotte was no more at issue in the Carlyle Commission than was expansion of the community college system. The real question was whether – and how – Asheville and Wilmington might also be added to the system.[15]

The issue of university expansion had, in fact, placed Friday in a difficult position. Some trustees opposed expansion vigorously; Friday himself held deep-seated reservations about making Wilmington and Asheville full-fledged UNC campuses. He believed that some sort of university control was necessary, but that it would be politically impossible to expand to Charlotte without providing for the other campuses. While Asheville and Wilmington had presented a united front, boosters in those two cities feared that Charlotte might pursue a go-it-alone strategy, and they would, if necessary, sabotage its program in the legislature. Asheville and Wilmington, observed the politically astute Herring, "most certainly" possessed "the political influence to stop Charlotte, should it elect to go it alone," for a coalition of east and west would defeat the Piedmont. The reality was that Charlotte would have to "act in concert with the other two or not at all."[16]

Friday's solution was to crack open the door, ever so slightly, to expansion. On February 17, 1962, the Carlyle Commission's subcommittee on the development of a system of higher education endorsed the establishment of additional UNC campuses "according to conditions prescribed by the Board of Trustees." In March 1962, when Charlotte and Wilmington supporters brought their case directly to the UNC trustees, Friday responded by insisting that the Carlyle Commission alone consider the issue of university expansion. In June 1962 two subcommittees of the Carlyle Commission held an "extended discussion" about expansion. They recommended that Charlotte and Wilmington be converted to senior colleges by the fall of 1963 and that Asheville-Biltmore College make that transition more gradually. As for expansion, the commission decided to recommend that the way be opened for additional campuses in the university system but to leave the times and places up to the UNC trustees.[17]

The final wording of the commission's report embodied the compromise position that Friday had developed by the spring of 1962. Noting that Asheville, Wilmington, and Charlotte had all asked to become incorporated into the UNC system, the commission recommended that the legislature amend the statutes so as to permit the university to establish new campuses "under conditions prescribed by the Board [of Trustees], subject to applicable statutory procedures." Although the report stipulated that such new campuses should be created only where there was a "clear need" for graduate and professional programs – which would suggest Charlotte rather than Wilmington and Asheville – the door was left sufficiently ajar to satisfy everyone.[18]

The Carlyle Commission also considered the shape and role of the revised public higher education system. In late 1961 Lennox Polk "Major" McLendon, BHE chairman and head of the commission's subcommittee on the development of a system of higher education, endorsed changing the names of the campuses of the University of North Carolina to emphasize the existence of a single legal entity with three locations, altering State College's name and mission, and instituting coeducation at Woman's College. McLendon further proposed to define the functions of the teachers' colleges, thereby imposing "appropriate limitations and restrictions" on their expansion into graduate programs. On February 17, 1962, McLendon's subcommittee adopted a resolution that called for transforming State College and Woman's College into UNC at Raleigh and UNC at Greensboro, respectively. By June, persuaded by Friday and others, the UNC trustees accepted a new hierarchy proposed by the Carlyle Commission: the UNC campuses (with new missions for Raleigh and Greensboro), the senior colleges, and the comprehensive colleges.[19]

Still another proposal emerging from the Carlyle Commission's deliberations was an attempt to redefine the State Board of Higher Education. McLendon's subcommittee invited Harlan H. Hatcher, president of the University of Michigan, to present his opinions about statewide governance in higher education on January 5, 1962. To the Major's horror, Hatcher strongly urged that the BHE be restructured. At the February 17 joint meeting of the subcommittee on the higher education system and on community and new colleges – while McLendon was absent on a Caribbean vacation – the matter came to a head when a subcommittee was appointed to draft changes in the BHE's structure. Three days later, the subcommittee unanimously adopted changes that provided for direct representation of public colleges and universities on the board.[20]

Although McLendon disavowed the plan – which he regarded as compromising the BHE's ability to regulate higher education independently – on returning from his vacation, the commission subcommittee adopted it anyway on May 2, 1962. Considerable maneuvering followed when the proposal was forwarded to the full Carlyle Commission, which met on July 6. Despite a forty-five-minute speech from McLendon in which he claimed that the commission was about to commit "a very serious mistake on behalf of the university," the commission endorsed the subcommittee proposal by a vote of 13 to 4.[21]

The BHE reorganization plan was, as one reporter expressed it, "by far the most controversial" of the Carlyle Commission's recommendations. Immediately after the July 6 meeting, Bill Friday conferred with Governor Sanford, who assured him of his support and told him that he would not reappoint Major McLendon to the board once his term expired in June 1963. About a month later, in a telephone conversation with Friday, the governor reiterated that he would support the recommendations of the commission. Even so, Friday's supporters on the BHE were worried – with good reason, for, in the end, McLendon's persistence paid off. Although Sanford had been determined to make the Carlyle Commission report the cornerstone of his legislative package for the 1963 session, he wavered when faced with the possibility of a bloody political fight.[22]

In early November 1962 key members of the legislature, such as Speaker Clifton Blue, told the governor that a confrontation with McLendon might jeopardize the centerpiece of Sanford's program – the establishment of a comprehensive community college system. On November 11 Sanford called Friday in for a meeting at the Executive Mansion, where he delivered the bad news. He would endorse most of the recommendations of the Carlyle Commission, Sanford said, but he was scrapping the plan to reconstitute the BHE. Instead, he would seek to maintain the present structure of the board and to establish an advisory group composed of college presidents. Although Friday asked Sanford for further time to present his case, the governor's mind was made up.

Sanford tried to soften the blow in that meeting and in subsequent telephone conversations, but his reversal flew in the face of his previously firm commitments. The governor told Friday that he would not object if Friday publicly opposed him; he also promised to remove both McLendon and Winston-Salem attorney Bill Womble from the BHE. Yet Friday was unnerved by the experience. Soon after the meeting at the Executive Mansion, he drove to the Raleigh home of John R. Jordan Jr., one of his staunchest allies on the Carlyle Commission. When the doorbell rang, Jordan went to the door, "and there stood Bill Friday." Explaining that Sanford was not going to stand by his commitments, Friday was "ashen" and "shaken."[23]

On November 15, at a Founders Day speech at Methodist College in Fayetteville, Sanford made his decision public. The governor explicitly endorsed the establishment of a comprehensive community college system and the expansion of the UNC campuses, but he said nothing about reconstituting the BHE. The press quickly surmised what had happened. Sanford's decision was a humiliating reversal for Friday and his allies. Months of arduous labor and intense political conflict had ended in a disappointing conclusion. The Major was ebullient. "I can find no better way" to describe Sanford's decision, he wrote to the BHE on November 20, than to say it was "superb!" The differences between the BHE and the university would now be resolved "in the best interest of the whole State and the cause of higher education."[24]

Although the Carlyle Commission report and its implementation represented a landmark in the history of higher education in North Carolina, it aroused powerful emotions. Despite support for coeducation at Woman's College, including the backing of Virginia Lathrop and Major McLendon, the bulk of the alumnae opposed these changes. Friday recalled the icy reception that he received when he visited the Greensboro campus during the spring of 1963, shortly after the legislature had authorized coeducation.

An even stronger backlash occurred at UNC's Raleigh campus. Friday had received assurances that the name change from State College to some variation of the University of North Carolina at Raleigh would encounter little alumni opposition and would enjoy considerable support from the State faculty, which endorsed the transformation of the institution into a university in name, as it was already in fact. A trustee committee headed by Tom Pearsall, after considering thirteen suggested names, proposed a name change – North Carolina State, the University of North Carolina at Raleigh – that received the endorsement of the board of directors of the State College alumni association in late 1962. In the General Assembly's 1963 session, however, a coalition of State alumni and Republicans seeking to embarrass Governor Terry Sanford proposed another name: North Carolina State University of the University of North Carolina at Raleigh.[25]

Largely on the basis of this version of the name – which seemed to State alumni to indicate subordination to arch-rival Chapel Hill – a rebellion occurred in 1963–65. Although the legislature enacted the name change on May 10, 1963, with a compromise – North Carolina State of the University of North Carolina at Raleigh – State College alumni such as legislator Thomas D. "Buck" Bunn described the new name as "bulky" and "unwieldy." He asked legislators who were Carolina graduates how they would react to changing the name of their alma mater to "Cow College annex." For almost two years, State alumni pressed for adoption of North Carolina State University, and in the 1965 legislative session, a final name change, North Carolina State University at Raleigh (N.C. State), was adopted.[26]

The name change fight concerned seemingly trivial differences, but it exposed serious tensions within UNC. Friday characterized the controversy as "vastly overrated" and "a vehicle to unleash a lot of other emotions." At the time, he later conceded, the effort to rename State College was a mistake, but he had deferred to the wishes of Governor Sanford, who favored it. Years later, the experience still rankled with Friday. Yet once he was committed to changing State's name and mission, Friday stubbornly held his ground. Ida Friday recalled that the controversy was "devastating" to her husband; he believed that "it was a loss and it was a hard loss," chiefly because of the hostility it engendered.[27]

The implementation of the recommendations of the Carlyle Commission regarding university expansion was also controversial. Although deferring the issue, the commission had cracked the door for expansion under trustee supervision. In July 1963 the trustees authorized UNC officials to study expansion to Charlotte; after preliminary consideration in early 1964, a formal study began in March under the direction of Arnold K. King, UNC vice president for institutional development. The results of King's study, which was completed in late 1964, combined with political pressures from Charlotte and from Dan Moore, who had promised his support during his successful gubernatorial campaign that year, led to the expansion of UNC to Charlotte by legislative enactment, effective July 1, 1965.[28]

Expansion to Charlotte eventually meant expansion to Wilmington and Asheville as well. Both cities argued their cases during the Carlyle Commission deliberations; both were put off without having their hopes dashed. Wilmington and Asheville boosters believed that university expansion was only a matter of time, and they fully expected that, like Charlotte, their institutions would be admitted as full-fledged campuses conducting university-level work. In the wake of Charlotte's victory, Asheville and Wilmington launched what Friday recalled was an "enormous drive" that eventually overpowered both the political process and UNC's ability to make a decision. "The civic issue," he said, "took over the educational issue." Friday believed that university-level work was necessary and inevitable at Charlotte because of its status as a metropolitan community. But he doubted the ability of the Wilmington and Asheville campuses to become true universities. If expansion to those communities was inevitable – and political pressures indicated that it was – Friday preferred making them colleges of the University of North Carolina. His only serious disagreement with Virginia Lathrop, he said, was over this issue.[29]

The matter was referred to a trustee subcommittee in early 1968. Headed by J. A. Prevost, it recommended that the Wilmington and Asheville campuses be admitted as full-fledged campuses of the university after thoroughgoing review. Arnold King, who had earlier examined the question of UNC expansion to Charlotte, reported to the trustees on December 7, 1968. He recommended that UNC expand to Wilmington and Asheville but that these two campuses focus on undergraduate education. Nonetheless, the Executive Committee, on December 1, 1968, defeated Watts Hill Sr.'s proposal that trustees admit the two campuses as "colleges of the University." The proposal for university expansion to Wilmington and Asheville was then transmitted to the Board of Higher Education, which tried unsuccessfully to obtain assurances that the two new campuses would not offer graduate programs. The BHE approved the trustees' decision without conditions, and the General Assembly adopted expansion by enactment in April 1969.[30]

The expansion of the three-campus consolidated university to a six-campus UNC system in the 1960s profoundly altered the balance of power in higher education in North Carolina. Friday remained skeptical of expansion generally and dubious, at best, about UNC expansion to Wilmington and Asheville. He characterized this decision as "a mistake" made because of irresistible political pressure. The university's expansion threatened non-UNC rivals in the competition for state resources; non-UNC institutions were convinced that the new campuses were added to offset the political power of former teachers' colleges such as East Carolina. The fact that Charlotte – which became a four-year institution only in 1963 – was now designated to become a graduate center alarmed the former teachers' colleges. East Carolina College and its president, Leo Jenkins, struggled for two decades to improve their status. By 1965 East Carolina had the third largest enrollment in the state; according to the college's historian, ECC administration regarded the sudden elevation of Charlotte, only recently a junior college, as the "essence of condescension." To Jenkins, expansion violated the Carlyle Commission's hierarchy and undermined the rationale of the ordered, three-tiered system that it had established. Jenkins then began a campaign to elevate East Carolina's status. In 1967 he proposed that the General Assembly grant it university status independent of UNC. Although Jenkins's proposal was ultimately defeated with Governor Moore's help, the 1967 legislature transformed East Carolina and three other former state teachers' colleges – including the traditionally black A&T State College – into "regional universities." Two years later, in the 1969 session, the legislature also gave regional university status to the remaining four traditionally black colleges plus Pembroke State College, a public institution originally established for Native Americans. Moreover, legislators in 1969 granted regional universities the right, under BHE supervision, to establish doctoral programs beginning in 1972.[31]

These experiences revealed the inadequacy of North Carolina's system of coordinating higher education resources through the State Board of Higher Education. In 1965, when Governor Dan K. Moore persuaded the legislature to reorganize the BHE, he appointed Watts Hill Jr. as its chairman. Although generations of Hill's ancestors had been prominent Carolina graduates, he was determined to carve out an identity for himself by establishing, according to one observer, a "toe hold . . . to distinguish himself from his father." Hill found the BHE in "substantial disarray." It had lost most of its professional staff, including longtime director Bill Archie. Spending thirty to fifty hours a week in Raleigh, Hill pushed the board toward becoming what he called a "change agent." Under Hill's leadership, the BHE conducted numerous studies, and he was instrumental in hiring an aggressive director, Cameron West, in 1969.[32]

Hill and West believed that the emasculated role of the BHE in higher education was a root cause of the chaotic situation in the late 1960s. They pointed to the confusing impulses of university expansion and the regional institutions' drive for power as the result of a power vacuum and a lack of centralized direction. By the 1969 legislative session, the BHE, despite Hill and West's leadership, seemed incapable of rationalizing the situation. Hill and West became convinced that the only hope for order was to provide the board with greater powers, and the BHE's best prospects lay in an alliance with the impetuous young governor, Bob Scott. Scott's experience in serving as regional chairman of the Southern Regional Education Board and his membership on the Educational Commission of the States had intensified his interest in higher education. Early in 1969, Hill and West persuaded the governor to reconstitute the State Board of Higher Education. According to the terms of the legislation enacted by the 1969 General Assembly, the governor, along with the four chairmen of the appropriations and revenue committees and the two higher education committee chairmen of the two houses of the legislature, became ex officio members of the BHE, with the governor as its chairman. The BHE's reconstitution occurred without consultation with UNC officials, who probably would have opposed it. Bill Friday learned of the BHE plans in a conversation with a legislator, Clarence Leatherman; the UNC president resented it as a behind-the-scenes maneuver. To UNC partisans, the board now possessed a "completely political composition" that was too closely identified with the governor.[33]

Friday, for his part, remained troubled by the degree of legislative and gubernatorial interference. He was profoundly concerned about the politicization of higher education and about prospects of further legislative involvement in UNC affairs. Throughout most of the 1960s he had fended off political intrusions that accompanied the banning of the Dixie Classic, the Speaker Ban, and campus unrest. He realized, as he told one interviewer in 1974, that anti-UNC attacks not only had become "politically viable," but they also yielded an "exceedingly high capital value." Friday was also keenly aware of a national trend toward greater administrative rationalization of public university systems and the establishment of multicampus systems. As he later recalled, the ongoing conflict in governance between the UNC trustees and the State Board of Higher Education, combined with the emergence of politically ambitious regional universities, convinced him that some kind of change was inevitable. The critical question was the "wisest way" for that change to occur. Rather than pursuing some master plan to develop a multicampus system, however, Friday was determined to protect the university from political incursions. His primary objective in relations with the legislature in the late 1960s was to free UNC from micromanagement, either from the BHE or from the legislature.[34]

Another important ingredient in Friday's calculations was trustee opposition to major structural change. For most of the 1960s, the leadership of the UNC Board of Trustees' Executive Committee was unchanged; Victor Bryant, Virginia Lathrop, and Watts Hill Sr. were, as they had been in the 1950s, dominant figures. Those who joined the Executive Committee and remained in its inner circle, such as Tom White and Archie Davis, were part of this same leadership. These trustees saw no need to change the basic structure of the university in existence since 1931, and they resisted outside intervention. The UNC trustees were, as Dick Robinson recalled, "terribly disdainful" of the BHE, and an atmosphere of mutual recrimination prevailed. Trustees saw the BHE as an "appendage" that possessed "powers to irritate" but not to affect university decisions. On several occasions, Friday raised the matter of UNC reorganization with the Executive Committee, but he encountered "hostility and downright abrasive reaction."[35]

Despite trustee reluctance, other factors were forcing change. In 1970 North Carolina voters approved a constitutional amendment granting the governor extensive powers to reorganize state government; under the amendment, the General Assembly, with some involvement by the governor, consolidated some two hundred state agencies and boards into only twenty-five. Although the amendment was originally interpreted by Governor Scott not to include higher education, during the late autumn of 1970 he held conversations with Friday about improving state coordination of higher education. The two men remembered the details of these discussions differently, yet the governor believed that Friday endorsed structural change. As a result of their conversations, many of which occurred during brief recesses of the trustees' Executive Committee meetings, Scott thought that he enjoyed Friday's support "in principle" to reshape the UNC system. When Scott met with Friday at the governor's mansion on November 30, 1970, Friday told him that the time was ripe to move toward a single governing board, perhaps under the

UNC's umbrella. Should Scott's plans for reorganization fail, however, Friday would fight BHE interference vigorously. According to Friday, Scott "agreed with this thinking."[36]

Scott later said that the idea for restructuring originally had been Friday's, but that, because of trustee opposition, the UNC president had backed off and was not "free to speak his true feeling." The governor subsequently believed that Friday had led him "down the primrose path," and his resentment persisted throughout the restructuring battle. Yet it is unlikely that Friday provided unqualified support for restructuring, and to the extent that he favored it, his ideas remained vague. In November 1968 the BHE's long-range plan endorsed the establishment of "a single agency to plan and coordinate higher education," and afterward Watts Hill Jr. pressed Friday for his reactions to alternative structures. As Hill recalled, however, Friday was evasive, although he supported the "overall concept of a new instrument to replace the Consolidated University and the Board of Higher Education" that might be called the "University of North Carolina system."[37]

Friday later admitted that his greatest mistake was in not reaching a clear understanding with Scott, who was receiving most of his information from Cameron West, the BHE, and his political allies rather than from the UNC side. "It never dawned on me," Friday recalled, that Scott would "read it differently" and that he would be "totally misreading" Friday's intentions. While Scott conceived of higher education in political terms, Friday viewed it as an educational administrator, and he wanted a new structure to be insulated from political pressures. But Friday was ambivalent about any future university structure. Although the continuing problems with the BHE and the politicization of higher education had demonstrated the need for a new structure, he remained unwilling to abandon the trusted UNC system created in 1931 for a leap in the dark. Even had Friday sought a radical departure along the lines contemplated by Scott, he faced trustee opposition. Rather than providing Scott a blank check, Friday believed, his communications with the governor were at a preliminary stage, moving toward an undefined goal. Yet, in dealings with the voluble Scott, as one contemporary later said, Friday was probably "a little naive."[38]

The different impressions that the two men took with them about these conversations confirmed what had already become clear in the student crisis of 1969: Bob Scott and Bill Friday were polar personalities. Scott was impulsive, drawn to political conflict, spontaneous in his reactions, and willing to alienate his opponents by political overstatement. Friday, in contrast, was temperamentally cautious, eager for support from all quarters, averse to open conflict, and sensitive to public criticism. Scott believed in confrontation,

Friday in accommodation. Friday did not "willingly disagree with people," John Sanders explained, and people seldom left Bill Friday's presence "thinking they've been disagreed with." Friday's style was to discover common ground and then find areas of agreement. If Friday did not tell Scott everything he wanted to hear, still he wanted to maintain good relations with the governor, with whom he had had "more tension," he remembered, than "all the other governors put together." Slightly more than a year after the campus uprising of March 1969, Friday was seeking to repair relations with Scott, who often shot from the hip, and to reach a modus vivendi.[39]

Nonetheless, fundamental differences remained in Friday's and Scott's conceptions of restructuring. Scott, hostile toward Chapel Hill domination of state higher education, wanted to reduce the power of the old-line trustee leadership, even if that meant radically altering the 1931 structure. Friday, in contrast, only supported restructuring to the extent that it was depoliticized and preserved the existence of the UNC trustee system. He favored a model that would incorporate the state's institutions under UNC control, maintain the one-hundred-member Board of Trustees, and, as he explained to an interviewer in 1972, "go from there." As an overall objective, he sought to "keep the thing steady" so as to ensure UNC leadership in whatever new structure emerged.[40]

The fact remains that, unlike the other parties involved in planning a possible restructuring, Friday lacked a game plan. He was troubled by the current system and believed that its inadequacies had resulted in the politicization of higher education in the state to such a degree that it was beginning to threaten the future of the university. At the same time, he was unsure about which direction to follow. Friday, according to Watts Hill Jr., was reasonably secure in his belief that whatever structure emerged would necessitate his leadership. But he was not so much an earnest advocate of change as he was "resigned to its being the lesser of a number of evils." Friday's "real preference," Hill believed, was for the six units of the university to continue to influence the course of higher education behind the scenes and, in so doing, "get what they need and leave the rest for everyone else."[41]

Confident that he had reached a consensus with Friday, Scott acted swiftly. The governor convened a conference of forty trustees and BHE members – with no administrators present – for a buffet dinner at the Executive Mansion on Sunday, December 13, 1970. Appealing directly to the trustees, Scott told them that it was their responsibility to establish policy and to provide leadership. The governor favored a "new structure" different from both the university and the BHE that would require "scrambling a new batch of eggs" from which an entirely new entity would be created.[42]

By late December both the BHE and the UNC Board of Trustees agreed to cooperate with Scott. The governor then announced, in January 1971, the creation of a committee composed of one trustee from each of the nine regional universities, five trustees from UNC, and five representatives from the BHE. With the regional university and BHE members chosen on the advice of Cameron West and the UNC trustees selected after consultations with Bill Friday, the committee was headed by Lindsay C. Warren Jr., of Goldsboro, a Carolina graduate who had retired from the state senate in 1969.[43]

UNC representatives believed that the Warren Committee, which met regularly from January to April 1971, was stacked against the university. Among the five UNC trustees, there was little enthusiasm for Scott's proposals, and UNC officials, including Friday, sought to derail them. Soon after the Warren Committee first convened on January 15, UNC administrators N. Ferebee Taylor, Felix Joyner, Arnold King, and Richard Robinson had meetings, and they began to develop an alternative to the single-board model that would restore the tiered approach of the Carlyle Commission.[44]

From the beginning, UNC trustees on the Warren Committee were primarily interested in defending the university's interests, while the BHE succeeded in exploiting the fears of the regional universities' representatives about UNC domination. With these deep divisions, the Warren Committee proceeded toward a restructuring plan. On March 5 it heard testimony from the non-UNC university presidents. At Victor Bryant's insistence and over Watts Hill Jr.'s loud objections, Friday spoke for an hour and ten minutes at the Warren Committee's meeting on March 26. He had been associated with UNC since 1938, Friday told the group, and he described its unique functions and traditions of excellence. The 1931 consolidation was followed by the Carlyle Commission changes and, after 1965, by the establishment of a larger multicampus system. Aided by elaborate charts showing enrollment statistics, data on buildings, and governance structure, Friday, arguing against a single-board approach, described the university as a viable entity that should not be deconsolidated. He called for reinvigorating the Carlyle Commission's three-tiered system, removing the university from BHE supervision, and enabling the "lateral movement" of some of the regionals into the UNC system.[45]

Lindsay Warren, who wanted to complete a report for the governor sometime that spring in time for consideration by the 1971 legislative session, pushed the committee toward a decision, and he arranged for meetings between West and Friday to work out a compromise. They agreed only to identify but not to endorse a middle position: to make no changes in the status quo but to strengthen the BHE. Based on what was believed to be a

West-Friday compromise, the Warren Committee endorsed a "no-change" position on Friday, April 3, 1971. But the committee's acceptance of the status quo did not end the matter. West's enthusiasm for the "no-change" plan remained unclear; what was presented as a compromise, he later claimed, was instead a middle position that he found ultimately unacceptable. Both Hill and West believed that the vote reflected undue political influence by UNC and confusion among most of the committee members. Without Warren's knowledge, Hill, with the support of the governor, worked furiously during the next weeks to obtain a reconsideration of the committee's decision.[46]

As Hill lobbied wavering committee members, the conflict between the university forces and the rest of the committee came out in the open. To black members Maceo Sloan of Durham and the Reverend E. B. Turner of Lumberton, Hill promised greater gains for the traditionally black institutions in a new system and warned of the consequences of UNC domination. To other members who had voted with the majority, he reiterated that the governor favored structural change and that a compromise would be best left to the politicians. The vote on April 3, 1971, Hill maintained, was understood by most members to be a straw vote rather than a binding decision. The circumstances of the no-change vote had become so confused, he said, that the matter had never received full consideration. At Hill's instigation, a group of nine committee members favoring reconsideration met on April 19 at West's office, where they pledged themselves "to act as a group."[47]

Eventually, Hill's campaign bore fruit. At a meeting of the Warren Committee on April 24, Wallace Hyde proposed a reconsideration of the April 3 vote and offered a new plan for structural change. It called for the establishment of a single coordinating board, along with sixteen autonomous boards of trustees to govern the state's sixteen public institutions of higher education. With a majority favoring reconsideration, the university's position collapsed. Although it meant the deconsolidation of UNC, the Hyde Plan was endorsed by the Warren Committee by a vote of 14 to 5. The committee's two black members, Sloan and Turner, and the two Charlotte representatives, Paul Lucas and Walter Smith, had switched sides. What Victor Bryant had described to Friday the evening before the vote as a "real emergency" now existed, and the UNC forces' worst nightmare – deconsolidation and the establishment of a coordinating board – now seemed to be a likely possibility.[48]

Trustees and administrators agreed that the Hyde Plan would destroy UNC's integrity; a coordinating board having "only a modicum of academic responsibility," according to a university supporter, would destroy "the hard-earned prominence of that great institution." At the tenth and final meeting of the Warren Committee, held on May 7–8, 1971, a last-ditch effort to find a compromise failed, and the Warren Committee adopted a plan – essentially the same as the Hyde Plan – that would abolish the UNC structure and establish a single coordinating board of regents composed of forty members. This new board of regents would control new programs, budgets, and the assignment of missions to the campuses but would coexist with sixteen local boards that would govern the internal affairs of the campuses. The system head would be a "chancellor," the institutional heads, "presidents." Meanwhile, the UNC representatives on the Warren Committee delivered its minority report in which the status quo remained.[49]

Once the Warren Committee disclosed its decision on May 8, 1971, the university's minority status became public knowledge. Over the next weeks, battle lines hardened. On May 14 the Executive Committee of the UNC Board of Trustees, meeting in Scott's absence, unanimously rejected the regents plan contained in the Warren Committee's majority report. The committee reaffirmed its confidence in the UNC's current structure and requested that a minority report be written. Bill Friday, publicly and privately, criticized the majority report. In a statement denouncing the restructuring plan, he warned that it would deconsolidate the UNC system and "effectively discard the unified and highly successful" efforts of the six-campus system. To his law school classmate and state senator L. P. "Mac" McLendon Jr. (the son of Major McLendon), he wrote that the plan would "effectively dismantle the University as you and I know it." Although advocates of the majority report described their restructuring as "reconsolidation," the unified structure that McLendon's own father had "served so faithfully and well" would be abandoned. Most vulnerable of all, Friday continued, would be the UNCG campus in McLendon's hometown of Greensboro.[50]

Governor Scott, for his part, enthusiastically supported the majority report of the Warren Committee. He took his campaign directly to the university. At a brief meeting of the Executive Committee on May 24, Scott warned that the state budget would be tight in the upcoming year and that UNC would lose state funds if it opposed his restructuring plans. "I've got lots of Green Stamps over there," he declared, referring to bonus coupons that grocery stores used to give their customers, "shoe boxes full of Green Stamps." Although Friday responded by delivering a speech extolling UNC's virtues, the trustees attending probably had never experienced so direct or so blunt a threat as the one presented by Bob Scott that afternoon. Less than a year after the event, Watts Hill Sr. remembered that he was "so mad" that he said nothing. Victor Bryant had no such inhibitions. By the late spring of 1971 he had become, according to another trustee, "completely unreasonable" in his desire to preserve the status quo. After Scott's tirade, the elder trustee statesman arose from his seat "shaking and trembling." Addressing Scott directly, Bryant said: "Governor, my convictions on this subject are as strong and as deep as yours, and if it means that this great institution will have to suffer financially for the position I am taking, I think we will still be here when the fight is over. . . . You use your Green Stamps and we will use ours, and we will see who wins." The meeting of the full board on the same day then deferred action until Scott had formally presented his proposals to the legislature.[51]

The trustees did not have to wait long. On May 26, 1971, Scott conveyed most of the Warren Committee's proposals to the legislature in an address endorsing the regents plan. Scott's speech inaugurated a five-month-long political battle that became, as house speaker Phil Godwin expressed it, "the damnedest football game you ever saw." In late May, it appeared that the governor's all-out lobbying effort would overcome UNC opposition. While Scott aides roamed the halls of the legislature in search of votes, the university forces created their own political organization. On May 28, the Board of Trustees met to consider the crisis. Although he was chairman of the board, Scott did not attend, saying that he preferred to meet with legislators because "that's where the votes are." After Victor Bryant – in an "emotion-chocked voice," he told the trustees that the university would endure the crisis, "God willing" – and Friday denounced the Warren Committee's majority report, the trustees endorsed the minority report as a compromise plan for restructuring. They then appointed a special committee, headed by Archie Davis and High Point furniture executive Jake Froelich Jr., to spearhead the legislative fight. That committee would work closely with the Friends of Education, a pro-UNC lobbying organization. On May 31 Froelich established UNC headquarters in a suite of five rooms at the Raleigh Hilton Inn, a legislators' lodging place. Along with Froelich, participants in the legislative fight included house majority leader and UNC trustee Ike Andrews; significantly, Bryant played virtually no role in the effort.[52]

Bill Friday now made what he would characterize as a "willful, premeditated, deliberate decision" to withdraw from active involvement in the political fray. During most of the summer of 1971 he had no communication with Scott. Although he later conceded that Scott's generous use of hyperbole and flair for overstatement were part of his "temperament," the UNC president had taken Scott's attacks personally. Friday's partial withdrawal from the restructuring battle reflected his conviction that he should not become entangled in a personalized controversy. Moreover, he was convinced that, when it came to politics, a university president should be "in it but not of it." He relied instead on his lieutenants, principally UNC vice president Ferebee

Taylor, along with trustees Froelich and Andrews, and they reported to him "every day, on the hour, almost." Andrews and Taylor became Friday's point men; during the course of 1971 they held over two hundred meetings concerning higher education. Friday also realized that his active participation might provoke an anti-UNC backlash. He subsequently maintained that he had no direct ties with the Friends of Education lobbying effort, that he "never set foot" in its office, that he provided it no money or resources, and that he gave it no advice.[53]

Throughout the remainder of the regular legislative session of 1971, which concluded in July, both sides continued to maneuver. In early June UNC forces proposed a new plan that would strengthen the State Board of Higher Education even more than the minority report proposed but would retain the UNC system. Although university advocates offered this as a compromise, it was substantially no different from their May position. Meanwhile, the Friends of Education orchestrated an offensive by influential business leaders and campaign contributors, who called legislators and urged them to support the university. Two paid staff members, Ralph Strayhorn, a Durham lawyer and president-elect of the North Carolina Bar Association, and L. C. Bruce, a former state official, coordinated the effort.[54]

Bob Scott, despite his bravado, faced serious opposition in the legislature. In the senate on June 18, 1971, twenty-eight of fifty senators signed a statement, introduced by John Burney of New Hanover, that proposed delaying a vote on restructuring until the 1973 session and creating a legislative study commission to draft an alternative higher education bill. Burney, the powerful chairman of the Senate Finance Committee and a Scott supporter during the 1968 campaign, emerged as a leading opponent of the governor's plan. Although Scott was shocked at his defection, Burney was motivated by a conviction that the new campus at Wilmington would thrive under UNC leadership. To the surprise of many, Burney became an important UNC advocate and a leading proponent of delay, which he described as a "Molotov cocktail" thrown in the path of Scott's "blitzkrieg." Meanwhile, the next day Burney's proposal received the support of Speaker Phil Godwin, who urged a cooling-off period of study and review. Facing a legislative rebellion, Scott then demurred and endorsed, with the cooperation of the General Assembly's leadership, the calling of a special session in the autumn of 1971.[55]

Scott made another tactical change. In the latter part of June James Holshouser, Republican house minority leader and future governor, called a meeting of Bob Scott, his uncle Ralph Scott, Harold F. "Cotton" Robinson, then provost at Purdue University, and himself. At this meeting, Robinson criticized the regents plan as defective and urged instead that the governor consider a stronger governing board. After Bill Friday, N.C. State chancellor John Caldwell, and Cameron West all publicly endorsed a strong governing board, the governor announced on June 22 that he, too, favored it over the original regents plan.[56]

Yet all of this maneuvering produced no breakthrough. On June 22, the day of his dramatic announcement, Scott arranged for a late-night meeting at the Executive Mansion with Lieutenant Governor Pat Taylor, Godwin, Warren, West, and Friday; the conferees arrived at the governor's mansion at about 10:00. Friday refused to endorse the governor's plan for a stronger governing board but promised to sound out the trustees. Two days later, Friday, responding to journalists, publicly opposed the governor's proposal. The trustees had adopted a position on May 28, he said, and he was obliged to support it.[57]

With the adjournment of the General Assembly's regular session on July 21, 1971, there was a pause in the battle, as legislators returned home and Scott's and UNC's legislative managers prepared for a special-session struggle. In early September Scott held peace meetings – including a four-hour conference at the Executive Mansion on September 8 – with the UNC president and West to find a solution. Because there had been no communication with the governor since early summer, as he had explained in late August, Friday had "no clear ideas" about possible compromise. He found West and Scott wary of university intentions and chiefly concerned with the question of the presidency in the restructured system. When Scott proposed that the new system be headed by both West and Friday – West managing its internal operations, Friday its external operations – Friday found himself "surprised" and repelled by the suggestion. The meetings with Scott and West revealed the extent of personal ax grinding and how far apart the two sides remained. Friday was troubled. Not only was he convinced that a more active involvement on his part would provoke a legislative backlash, but he also harbored mixed feelings about the unfolding political battle. A year earlier he had encouraged Scott to push restructuring forward. Yet the form that restructuring had assumed had been essentially the model proposed in the BHE's 1968 planning report. Friday's concern all along was the preservation of the UNC structure and the melding of that, somehow, with restructuring. By the autumn of 1971, however, events were well beyond his control, and Scott's confrontational tactics had so alienated the UNC trustees that they remained, even in the face of almost certain defeat, hostile to compromise.[58]

Heretofore aloof from the battle over restructuring, Friday now realized that change was inevitable, and he began a behind-the-scenes lobbying campaign among the UNC trustees. A trustee negotiating committee composed of Ike Andrews, Jake Froelich, Elise Wilson, and William Johnson met with

Scott on September 22 and 24, and they endorsed a governing board for a sixteen-campus university system. The trustee representatives pressed for – and Scott supported – strong central authority, lump-sum budgets, and the explicit provision that the local boards would possess only those powers expressly delegated by the central board. Although the governor and the UNC representatives continued to disagree about the size of the board – university forces favored a 100-member board, Scott a smaller board – it appeared that a major breakthrough had occurred. After Friday and a number of UNC trustees gathered at the annual N.C. State–Carolina football game, newspaper reports suggested that key trustees were willing to compromise.[59]

With trustee support solidified, Friday appeared on October 7, 1971, before the legislature's joint higher education subcommittee, which was responsible for reporting a university restructuring bill to the legislature. Before giving his testimony that day, Friday met with an ad hoc group of trustees and UNC supporters and agreed on a position statement that would be taken to the full Board of Trustees meeting on October 18. Drawing partly on the recommendations that former governor Terry Sanford had made in September, Friday offered a radical new departure. In a move toward compromise, he informed legislators that he would ask the trustees, when they met in Chapel Hill, to endorse a "single governing structure" – a governing board, with the University of North Carolina system serving as the transitional instrument. Friday proposed that the ten non-UNC campuses be merged into the UNC system by 1973 in a phased, two-step process; half would join the university by July 1, 1972, the other half by July 1, 1973. At the same time, the existing structure of a 100-member Board of Trustees, an Executive Committee, the UNC administration, and a university *Code* would remain intact.[60]

Scott and Friday concurred in the general principle of a governing board, but they remained divided over important details. Although they agreed that the new governing board would exert virtually absolute power over budget and programs and that the local boards would have no significant powers except those specifically delegated to them, they continued to disagree about UNC's role. Scott favored a 32-member governing board with strong powers; the legislature's joint higher education committee, by a narrow margin, endorsed his proposal on October 15, 1971. UNC and the governor also disagreed about the transition to the new system and the composition of the new governing board. The joint higher education committee's bill called for the merger of all sixteen campuses on July 1, 1972, and the creation, on January 1, 1972, of a Planning Committee composed of fifteen representatives from the UNC Board of Trustees, fifteen representatives from the boards of the regional universities, and two members of the BHE (the 15–15–2 plan). This

Planning Committee would meet until July 1, 1973, when a new, permanent board would be selected.[61]

The UNC forces, including Bill Friday, sought to shape the governing board so as to retain the continuity of the UNC system. They objected to the governor's plan for several reasons. They feared that with only minority representation, UNC would have little influence over the new system; they also feared that the break in continuity would cripple the planning board's decisions and that the permanent board would likely review and perhaps disavow them. Friday visited Scott on October 11, 1971, to express these concerns, but the governor remained committed to the bill already proposed to the joint higher education committee.[62]

A week later, on October 18, the full Board of Trustees held its first formal meeting since the UNC-Scott negotiations. Although a hard-line group of trustees still favored the no-change position, the majority, realizing the inevitability of change, preferred a resolution offered by Watts Hill Sr. and the Executive Committee endorsing a central governing board under UNC leadership. The full board also sanctioned the creation of the trustee negotiating committee that had been established in September, adding a fifth member, N.C. State alumni leader Robert Jordan III, to its ranks.[63]

The special session of the legislature convened on Tuesday, October 26, 1971. Immediately preceding the session, there was a heavy traffic of telephone calls from both sides to wavering legislators; Scott was confident, however, that his forces had the necessary votes. The governor, who relied on his political advisers but also drew heavily from BHE staff members John Kennedy and Lem Stokes, was determined to mount an all-out campaign. The strategy of the UNC forces was to offer a series of amendments to Scott's bill; these amendments would provide for a Board of Governors initially consisting of all members of the UNC and regional university boards of trustees and a 30-member Executive Committee. Ultimately, the Board of Governors would decrease in size to 100 members as terms expired.[64]

University supporters had sought out fresh faces to lead the legislative fight. In the house of representatives, UNC officials persuaded Jack Stevens, a first-term legislator from Asheville, to offer the amendments. In the senate, UNC strategists agreed that Senator Gordon Allen, slated to become president pro tempore during the special session, was the best person to lead the attack. Allen had close ties with the governor, but he also had UNC connections and he needed university support to become president pro tem. Bill Friday approached him at the Carolina-State football game on October 2, 1971, and asked if Ferebee Taylor could drive to his home in Roxboro to discuss the UNC position. The next day Taylor visited Allen, who subsequently agreed to introduce the amendments provided he could maintain his political independence from the university.[65]

The state house and senate higher education committees sent identical versions of Scott's bill for debate on Wednesday, October 27. Although Scott expressed himself to Allen in "as strong a language as a governor ever uses," Allen introduced the amendments on the senate floor that day; the day before, Jack Stevens had brought them to the House Higher Education Committee. But when floor debate began, the Scott forces held firm in both houses, beating back Stevens's amendments in committee and Allen's on the senate floor.[66]

The legislative battle focused on the size and composition of the governing board and the makeup of the interim board that would supervise the transition to the new system. Regrouping after the defeat of their efforts to amend the governor's bill, the UNC forces decided to abandon their insistence on a 100-member governing board and instead concentrate on issues of representation and the interim Planning Committee. At Arnold King's suggestion, university strategists proposed that the Planning Committee specified in Scott's plan, in order to ensure continuity, become a permanent governing board after six months' time.

The political battle now took a confusing turn. Apparently uninformed of Guilford County representative McNeill Smith's intention to introduce amendments incorporating the new UNC position, John Sanders showed them to Gordon Allen on Thursday, October 28. Allen insisted that they be changed to provide for a 15–15–2 membership on the interim Planning Committee because they were otherwise identical with the joint higher education committee's bill and would more likely satisfy the governor. On the same day Allen arranged for separate meetings with Bill Friday and Representative Horton Rountree, the leader of the East Carolina University (ECU) forces in the legislature.

When Friday arrived for the meeting, according to one account, he was "tense and subdued." He had resisted attending and went to the meeting, as Friday later described it, only against his better judgment. Nonetheless, Friday, eager to find a settlement, endorsed the plan, telling the group, "I'll take whatever you pass and work with it." While Friday supported Allen's compromise, his managers in the legislature were uninformed of these negotiations and had rallied around amendments – as originally drafted by John Sanders and sponsored by McNeill Smith – that called for a 16–16 plan (sixteen UNC board representatives, sixteen representatives drawn from the boards of other institutions, and no BHE representative). After the Smith amendments passed the house, university forces prepared to introduce a similar measure in the senate. Yet Gordon Allen's 15–15–2 plan, which he was preparing to introduce in the senate, had received Friday's approval. Telephoning the UNC president, Ike Andrews, the UNC legislative leader, explained that Allen's plan disadvantaged the university. Friday admitted that he had "no business" in Raleigh, and he "dropped out of the picture entirely." In the aftermath of Friday's endorsement of Allen's amendments, however, confusion reigned.[67]

The legislative struggle apparently ended on Friday, October 29, when the house approved, by a margin of 55 to 51, the joint higher education committee bill, incorporating Allen's 15–15–2 amendments, which had already passed the senate. Scott hailed the bill's passage as landmark legislation; it meant "a victory for the taxpayers of North Carolina." In fact, however, the battle over restructuring was not yet over, as UNC partisans focused their energies on a move to reconsider the bill. Ike Andrews made an emotional appeal for UNC equality of representation. UNC, Andrews declared, was "the one thing of greatness our state has ever produced." The university was threatened, he said, because of the legislature's unwillingness to grant it an "equal voice" in the new system. Buoyed by a surge in support, Andrews moved for reconsideration. He failed on the first try, but after thirty minutes of confused attempts to round up votes on both sides, enough representatives switched sides to deadlock the house, 53 to 53, on a motion to recall the bill. According to the parliamentary rules of order, a tie killed the motion, but Speaker Phil Godwin broke the tie anyway by voting against it.[68]

Bill Friday issued a statement promising "every effort" to make the new system work and pledging that his office would cooperate fully. The bill would not become law, however, until Taylor and Godwin signed it and made the formal announcement Saturday morning that it had been ratified. University forces had one more chance, and late into Friday night both sides continued to court votes. Bob Scott spent most of the evening on the telephone, as did his aides Ben Roney and Fritz Mills, and they called up every conceivable political debt. Scott scoured the state for votes; one legislator hoping to slip away Friday afternoon had been stopped by a highway patrolman and told to return to Raleigh to see the governor. Scott offered to send a car and stretcher for Representative Charlie Phillips, of Greensboro, a Scott supporter who was hospitalized; Phillips arrived on his own locomotion. Meanwhile, some forty lawmakers who entered the Legislative Building on Saturday were greeted with handwritten notes from the governor. The previous evening, last-minute negotiations had proceeded furiously. Scott called UNC representatives about ten o'clock, rejecting Andrews's offer of additional negotiations and saying that the time had come to "count horses" in the legislature. University forces worked through the night, into Saturday morning, October 30, lobbying and calling in their own political debts. Andrews, who was up all night, turned down an offer from the ECU forces to form an alliance to defeat any restructuring. Friday received the same offer from ECU, but he rejected it because of what he believed would be its "destructive" impact on higher education.

By dismissing the ECU proposal, Friday and Andrews gambled that their position would prevail. Andrews remained confident of ultimate triumph; as he told Taylor, the UNC forces now had "the damned train back on the track." By Saturday morning, the university had converted enough house members to pass a motion to reconsider the higher education measure by a vote of 55 to 54. With reconsideration accomplished, the Scott forces caved in. A house and senate conference committee convened at about 11:30 A.M., and Sanders was dispatched to draft a new bill. Within about an hour, the conferees agreed to new legislation that provided for sixteen representatives each from UNC and the regional universities, with two nonvoting BHE representatives, on the new governing board. In another crucial concession to the UNC forces, the bill stipulated that an interim Planning Committee would be created on January 1, 1972, and the members of that committee would constitute the new Board of Governors on July 1, 1972, with staggered terms expiring in one, three, five, and seven years. Shortly before 3:00 P.M., the house passed the bill, 106 to 3; an hour later the senate approved it unanimously.[69]

In the aftermath of the legislative battle, both sides claimed victory. Scott maintained that the details of the new system did not concern him; restructuring had been accomplished. He described it as the "hardest legislative battle" of his administration; a year after the event, he told an interviewer that it had taken more time and generated more furor than any other single issue of his governorship. University partisans believed, on the other hand, that the victory on the final day of the session was critical because it ensured UNC control over implementation of the restructuring plan. Two decades later, Jack Stevens stated that the law was a "75–25 win" for the university; although not a "total win," it was a "good win." Not only did the law assure UNC supremacy in the establishment of the expanded multicampus system, it also removed the governor from governance, giving him only a brief role as chairman. For that reason, Stevens said, the university "won and won big." Ike Andrews described the battle as the most traumatic experience of his political career. "I've never seen so many people trying so damn hard in opposition to each other," he remembered. "Nobody really won this thing," but "nobody truly lost it."[70]

Bill Friday's immediate reaction was subdued. Concerned about what he called the "severe political turmoil" that came with the restructuring battle and threatened UNC's political status, he was obligated "to stay with it and straighten it out." Yet he claimed no victory. Although the ultimate result was far different from what he anticipated, Scott had accomplished restructuring largely on terms that he had favored as early as June 1971 and despite all-out opposition by UNC trustees. An expanded, multicampus system that would embrace all sixteen senior institutions in the state and a single governing board that would supersede both the State Board of Higher Education and the UNC Board of Trustees all became law in October 1971.[71]

Although Friday saw the need for restructuring, his chief concern was protecting the integrity of the UNC system. Virtually every state facing similar pressures had adopted some form of administrative rationalization of its higher education institutions, whether a coordinating board or a governing board system. Friday recognized that these national trends and the pressures inside North Carolina made change virtually inevitable. But Scott's rhetoric had solidified trustee opposition to his restructuring plans, and many Executive Committee members realized that restructuring spelled the doom of the oligarchy that had managed the University of North Carolina system for over the past four decades. Although he had encouraged Scott's interest in restructuring, Friday retreated when the governor became too closely associated with a BHE plan that created a weak coordinating board and deconsolidated UNC. Once Scott changed positions in June 1971, he had entered into territory that Friday found acceptable, but Friday faced the difficult task of persuading trustees.

In the confusing and often shifting allegiances of the political fight, most observers found it difficult to identify Friday's role. He was not, R. D. McMillan observed, "the primary mover" in the restructuring battle of 1971. A number of legislators complained that his views were a moving target, that he generally refused to commit himself. Throughout the fight, Friday publicly distanced himself from the political fray. His critics charged that he did so in order to position himself to remain president of the new system; he later insisted that he had consciously removed himself from the fray because he feared that more active involvement would damage the UNC cause. Yet the outcome of the political battle was not the result of his behind-the-scenes manipulation. Felix Joyner attributed no deviousness to Friday; Joyner believed that Scott was the only player who had a plan. In a "very mercurial political situation and a very, very odd, strange . . . cast of characters," Joyner said, Friday was "a central figure" in the struggle. It is a testament to Friday's political abilities that most people now regard the sixteen-campus system, essentially thrust upon him, as his own creation. But Friday nonetheless succeeded in later transforming a political defeat into an administrative victory by fashioning a system that bore the direct imprint of his personality and managerial style.[72]

S OMETIME in the late 1970s, a reporter for the national media traveled
to North Carolina to scrutinize the state's social, political, and educational condition. The reporter quickly discovered that there were few
people who had had more extensive contacts or influence throughout
the state than Bill Friday. "This is," he told a UNC administrator, "Bill Friday
country." The creation of a very different multicampus system after 1971
constituted a major challenge, but it also coincided with Friday's emergence as
a national statesman in American higher education. Although harboring
grave doubts about it, Friday implemented the restructuring legislation in
such a way as to create an expanded multicampus system that bore his distinctive administrative imprint. Indeed, it remains his most lasting monument to
posterity.[1]

At fifty-one years of age and at the peak of his powers when restructuring
formally occurred on July 1, 1972, Friday had developed an effective administrative style. That style embodied the qualities of Friday's personality: gre-
gariousness and sensitivity, idealism and cold-hearted efficiency, and unassuming accessibility and constant communication with the state and national
power structure. Friday had an innate interest in people and an inherent
ability to relate to them. A believer in civility, he grew up in a world, Friday
told an interviewer in 1981, "where manners made a big difference," and he
believed that there was nothing "to be gained by being rude or hard on people
because you possess the power to run over people."[2]

Part of Friday's success lay in the effortless way in which he functioned. It
was common knowledge at the consolidated university (and, subsequently, at
the UNC General Administration) offices that he treated all people, from the
staff custodian to his vice presidents, equally. Unpretentious, Friday drove

inexpensive automobiles, had little interest in a large salary, and refused many of the perquisites of his office. If a chauffeur drove him, Friday usually insisted on riding in the front seat. When the new General Administration Building was completed in 1971, he was so infuriated by a sign that read "Reserved for President" over a parking space that he refused to use it until the sign was removed. Although he continued to park in the same place near the building – and it was, according to his longtime secretary, "just understood you did not park there" – Friday shunned any trappings of the president's office.[3]

In handwritten notes to acquaintances inquiring about their families or expressing sympathy over a loss, Friday communicated human concern and reached out to people individually. Although he was a "very private person" in that he kept his own counsel and confided in few people, said a close associate, he liked people, enjoyed making new acquaintances, and gained confidences easily. A neighbor on Franklin Street described Friday as "generous, kind, and caring about people"; she cited the fact that he often brought her fresh vegetables and quietly laid them inside her door after visiting the local farmers' market early Saturday morning. This human concern was part of his style and also what Bill Aycock called a "natural" extension of his personality. Aycock saw him as an outgoing person who obviously enjoyed the company of others; friendships came naturally to him, and he radiated friendship by his very presence. Friday came across as "genuinely interested in people."[4]

Friday's interest in people translated into skills as facilitator, motivator, and conciliator. Ernest Boyer, chancellor of the State University of New York (SUNY) system during the 1970s, remembered Friday as having an informality that made him "engaging at the personal level," "direct and reassuring," and clearly uninterested in trying "to overwhelm or dominate." A close friend noted his "gentleness and modesty," combined with "caring," "duty, and obligation" – all qualities that characterized both his private and public life. Donald Anderson, the UNC provost in the 1960s, described Friday as "very democratic" in his operating style, while trustee ally George Watts Hill Sr. mentioned his "tremendous ability to get along with people and to get people working together." Friday was, Hill observed, "a master of coordinating conflicting points of view and bringing people to consensus."[5]

Friday's informal administrative style masked habits of hard work. One journalist reported that despite his relaxed appearance, a cup on his desk contained more than a dozen pencils, each sharpened to a point but most "massacred" with teeth marks and with erasers "nibbled in half." Although an efficient manager, Friday was anything but authoritarian. Zona Norwood, who joined his office as a secretary in 1967 and served as his administrative assistant for more than two decades beginning in 1972, said that Friday set high standards for his subordinates but never expected more than he was willing to do himself. By involving his subordinates, from janitors to senior staff, Friday made them all feel that they were participants; Norwood herself always felt that she was "a very important part" of Friday's team. To her, that was one of the secrets of Friday's ability to motivate: his staff felt such loyalty to him that they felt "compelled" to work hard.[6]

Few of his colleagues at General Administration worked harder than Bill Friday. In his three decades as university president, he rarely took extended vacations and was never gone from Chapel Hill for long. During summer trips with his family to Wrightsville Beach he often remained on the phone dealing with university business; frequently, he would be summoned back to Chapel Hill because of some crisis. He regularly arrived at the office at 7:00 A.M., an hour before it officially opened, and he stayed through the day, breaking only once – for lunch, which he usually had at home with Ida. On one occasion, when UNC vice president Raymond Dawson arrived early, thinking that he would beat Friday there, he found him already at his desk. Dawson concluded that the university and the state of North Carolina were Friday's "vocation and his avocation." Norwood recalled that Friday's presence at the office in the early morning was as "regular as clockwork": he was "always there first, and almost always was the last one to leave." During the busy season of preparing a UNC budget for the legislature, Friday often returned during evenings and weekends.[7]

Although he usually left the technical details to his subordinates, Friday worked constantly, whether on the telephone or at football games, to promote UNC's interests. Early in his career as a university administrator, when he became Carolina's assistant dean of students, Chancellor Robert B. House welcomed him as a new staff member. "What are the hours one is expected to be here?" Friday asked House. "William," House responded, "there are no hours in the university." Friday took House's admonition seriously. He often worked fourteen-hour days, and he was on the job every Saturday, Friday said, "almost without exception." Although he was "not one who enjoyed too much night work," Friday would often stay on the telephone well into the evening.[8]

Yet Bill Friday was also a dedicated family man. He and Ida enjoyed what one close confidant described as a "wonderful marriage" that grew into a strong partnership; according to one of their daughters, there was "always a lot of fun between themselves." In the 1950s, the Fridays built a house on White-head Circle, near the Community Church in Chapel Hill, and began a family that eventually included three daughters, Fran, Mary, and Betsy. After Bill assumed the UNC presidency in 1956, the family moved into the spacious president's residence on East Franklin Street. There the Friday girls were raised in a "very small-town atmosphere" and the Chapel Hill campus was their backyard. Mary Friday's earliest memory of the president's home was the "beauty of the place"; Fran Friday remembered it as a "great house" but "old and creaky." Growing up on East Franklin Street was a "pleasure" for all the children, and the "color and scale" of their home left a deep impression. Inside, the girls played hide-and-seek; they would drop things down the old grandfather clock in the hallway that they always assumed was bottomless. The children had a relaxed upbringing, and there was no distinction between public and private spaces in the Friday home. Friends were in and out, they often had birthday parties at home, and they rode bicycles with the numerous children who lived near them. Frequently, the three girls and their father would play basketball at the hoop outside their house.[9]

The Friday girls were about the same age as the young family of Kay and Georgia Carroll Kyser. In 1951 the Kysers moved to Chapel Hill, where Kay, at age forty-five, gave up his big-band and television career to raise their children in a large Franklin Street house that he had inherited from his uncle, Vernon Howell, former dean of the UNC Pharmacy School. Kay Kyser participated in UNC affairs as a volunteer. He campaigned for the Good Health Program and helped to establish a university educational TV system. Georgia Kyser met Ida Friday in a sculpture class at Carolina; thereafter, Bill said, they became "like sisters," with similar interests and dispositions. The Kysers and the Fridays frequently spent evenings together, sometimes at the Fridays' small apartment in Abernethy Hall, once the student infirmary but converted into apartments after the war. The Fridays had moved there from the World War II–vintage prefabricated housing at Victory Village, where they lived when Bill joined the dean of students' office.

Georgia Kyser described the Abernethy Hall flat as "bleak" and its furnishings as "pitiful," and when the Fridays eventually planned and constructed their own contemporary-style house on Whitehead Circle, she helped Ida with the move. When Bill became president, Georgia helped Ida to decorate the president's home, with the help of Greensboro decorator Otto Zenke. Completing her studies at Carolina, Georgia Kyser was graduated in 1970. Near commencement, the Fridays hosted a surprise party for her at their home; the guests wore caps and gowns, and Robert Burton House played "Pomp and Circumstance" on the piano.[10]

The Kyser-Friday friendship, which continued over the next decades, was cemented through the children; the Kyser family also included three girls. The Friday children developed unique personalities; according to Georgia Kyser, they were all "rugged individuals." Fran, born in 1951 and the oldest,

The Friday family, 1964. From left: Betsy, Bill, Frances, Mary, and Ida Friday.

was "very practical" and "very private"; she became a nurse in Chapel Hill. Mary, who was born in 1956, described herself as a typical middle child: a "little more aggressive, a little more driven, probably" than her sisters. After graduating from Carolina and the Duke Law School, Mary went on to became a corporate lawyer in London. Betsy, the youngest, was different still: at an early age she displayed a strong interest in the arts. Later she was graduated from the North Carolina School of the Arts in Winston-Salem and began a stage career in New York City. She was raised in a world, Betsy Friday remembered, that resembled a "Frank Capra family." "It really was a wonderful life," she said, and she believed everybody everywhere had similar advantages – and was surprised when she discovered that everyone did not.[11]

Despite his long hours, Bill and Ida were devoted parents. Both of them gave up cigarettes with the arrival of their children, though Bill for some years remained a cigar and pipe smoker. Their children were their chief priority, and they nurtured their development. "The idea," explained one of their daughters, "was that you were performing as best you could," without any expectations about high grades or academic performance. Except when out of town, Friday was always home for dinner. The girls were expected to be on time, well dressed, and prepared to engage in the informed dinner-table conversations moderated by their father. This ritual included a question to each daughter concerning what they had learned that day. According to Betsy, "we'd roll our eyes because we didn't want to listen to the others, but couldn't wait to talk when our turn came."[12]

Holidays were considered special, and the Fridays followed well-established routines. Christmas, said Mary Friday, was "magic." Preparing the annual fruitcake and the peanut brittle were family events that required everyone's participation. They generally sat around the fire on Christmas Eve to listen to "The Night before Christmas" and the Christmas story from the Bible; the dinner usually included fried oysters. Sometime during the night, Bill slipped out to place a telephone call posing as Santa. Each daughter took a turn talking; each was asked if she had been good that year. On Christmas morning, Ida and Bill would put the girls' stuffed animals on the winding staircase at the rear of the president's home; each girl took turns opening her presents.

According to his daughters, Friday was anything but a harsh disciplinarian. The children were permitted to watch television but its content was regulated. Although they expected parental disapproval if they misbehaved, Ida was the family disciplinarian; Bill, said Fran, "would spoil us." Mary remembered one occasion when Bill was given the responsibility of disciplining her. Friday cut switches from a bush, took his daughter into the living room, within earshot of Ida, and beat a pillow with a switch. But he could not bring himself to punish any of the girls physically, Mary said. Telling Mary not to misbehave, he warned her that if she told her mother what had happened, "I'll give you a real licking." When Fran Friday and a friend were caught smoking cigarettes at the age of eight, she received a gentle but effective reproach from her father. As Mary remembered it, their father had a "very thorough command of us." The worst thing Bill Friday could say was – after lowering his glasses – "I'm disappointed in you." His greatest influence was moral.[13]

The Fridays remained a close family despite the heavy demands of the UNC presidency. Bill was not above bringing Ida coffee in bed in the morning, and he often surprised her with presents; when she took trips without him, he would hide notes in her suitcase. On Sunday afternoons, he often took his daughters on an excursion while Ida rested; as she recalled it, he "always felt like he never had enough time for his children." The family usually took an annual two-week beach vacation, often at Wrightsville Beach or Nags Head; a "beach person," Bill enjoyed relaxation through walking and fishing. But invariably, said Georgia Kyser, he would be called back to Chapel Hill for UNC business. For years, Ida had wanted to travel abroad, but Bill was unwilling to leave Chapel Hill for any extended period of time. By the 1970s, as the children grew older, Ida began to take overseas trips on her own, often with her best friend Georgia Kyser.[14]

Bill and Ida Friday, UNC commencement, June 3, 1963.
(Courtesy of the North Carolina Collection)

A people person, Friday preferred action over ideas, a leadership characteristic that observers often misinterpreted. "I never thought of Bill as a
person with educational ideas," said John Tyler Caldwell. He rarely moved
"out in front with ideas and programs." Instead, Friday used his staff members
effectively, relying on "their thinking and their ideas" and maintaining a
"marvelous working relationship with them." Many Chapel Hillians would
agree with John Sanders's observation that Friday was "never a liberal in the
sense that Frank Graham was liberal." Some contemporaries have mistakenly
concluded that his fascination with process rather than advocacy, and with
problem solving and human relations rather than abstractions, meant that he

lacked solid beliefs. "He doesn't stake himself out so far," concluded one newspaper profile in 1981, "that he can't retreat and embrace the prevailing sentiment if his side loses." "I don't know what his personal position is on almost anything regarding higher education," declared a friend and member of the Board of Governors. Yet Ray Dawson's assessment is probably closer to the mark. He described Friday as a pragmatic idealist. In his highly developed sense of the university's obligation to the state, Friday also "had a very practical sense of what can be done under a given set of circumstances" and was "always insistent upon tailoring the agenda with what we could do."[15]

Friday's affability was misleading; sometimes those who did not know him well mistook his purpose and determination. Within what Bill Snider described as a "velvet glove" lay a "vein of iron." Soft-spoken and personable in his manner, Friday was sometimes accused of reluctance to speak out and involve himself in public controversy. Nonetheless, he was tough when vital educational principles were involved. R. D. McMillan, who worked closely with him for much of the 1970s and 1980s as UNC's representative to the legislature, described Friday as determined once he made up his mind to do something but firm "without being pushy." Zona Norwood expressed the same idea differently. Friday was "such a genuinely nice person," she observed, that it was easy to believe that he was a "softy." But persons under this misapprehension usually discovered otherwise. Inside the "soft" Friday was a "hardheaded" decision maker who could be "very firm."[16]

Friday reached decisions only after consultation with advisers and an intelligence network that Sanders described as "without equal in the state." In absorbing information and sounding out the feasibility of various alternatives, Friday spent hours on the telephone consulting this intelligence network. Dawson recalled how Friday "really worked that telephone," spending much of his day communicating "vicariously face-to-face." The only time Friday ever really got into a bad mood, Norwood stated, was when the phone stopped working. When she arrived in the morning, Norwood and Friday reviewed a "long list" of people whom he needed to reach that day, and "we'd start down the list." Lining up phone call after phone call, she maintained a running list of the status of each.[17]

In dealings with a wide array of legislators, community leaders, and UNC supporters, Friday insisted on an atmosphere of honesty, confidence, and mutual trust. Projecting integrity and distancing himself from political intrigue, he maintained a mystique of authority that he consciously encouraged at the General Assembly. Legislators "might not like him, or like what he said," observed Dawson, "but they respected him." Friday was determined to "pick his time and place," Bill Aycock said; there were few occasions when he made a proposal to trustees without some certainty of its passage.[18]

Realizing that his effectiveness as the president of a public university depended on it, Friday remained sensitive to criticism, especially in the print media. Much of this sensitivity resulted from the fact that he and the university became, as Norwood put it, "one and the same, in his mind," and when UNC received criticism "that automatically meant that it was criticism of him." On many occasions, consequently, Friday was "supersensitive," even when the faultfinding was not leveled at him personally. Yet his first reaction was to reach out to his detractors. Often, Norwood remembered, he attempted to communicate with critics and arrange a private meeting. There were not many people "who could go in that office and come out and still be mad."[19]

Friday carefully cultivated his image and that of the university. In the 1970s his office employed full-time managers of press and public relations. Reporters were well treated; most of them covering higher education issues for the state's major dailies in Durham, Raleigh, Charlotte, and Greensboro gained easy access to his office by phone and in person. In dealing with the press, Friday's approach was simple: to remain open and honest and to avoid withholding information. When he felt compelled not to reveal everything, he would often tell reporters, "I can't talk about it now, but call me later." He "worked very hard" at reinforcing the press's confidence in him; when reporters called his office, he later said, "if it could be discussed," they would "get it all" and "know the truth." This meant "good and bad, and there was plenty of bad, but I never withheld." In this way Friday sought a press relationship "that provided the university with the means of getting its story before the people."[20]

Friday regularly associated with the North Carolina Press Association (NCPA) and took time to become acquainted with the younger journalists. Jim Shumaker, as a young reporter in the 1950s, recalled that the first time he met Bill Friday was at the NCPA's annual awards banquet at the Carolina Inn in Chapel Hill. He had spotted Friday "working the crowd without really seeming to, moving easily and smoothly from group to group and lost soul to lost soul." He was "unaccountably cheerful," and when Shumaker met him, Friday "expressed warm interest in my work, my place in the world of letters and my general well-being." Shumaker was struck that Friday "really cared," that he would "share vicariously" in his triumphs and had singled him out for special attention. Later, he realized that Friday had treated many journalists similarly and had, in the process, "totally disarmed" his and UNC's critics.[21]

FRIDAY's distinctive administrative style figured prominently in the transition, during the early 1970s, to the restructured university system. Friday knew that the challenge of creating a sixteen-campus organization was daunting. In May 1972 he told an interviewer that he had consulted higher education leaders across the country and that "not one" believed that the new system would work. In the same month Friday explained to an oral history interviewer that he "did not believe in . . . [and] did not recommend" restructuring. Rather, he preferred that the state should continue to rely on the forty-two years of experience that the UNC Board of Trustees could offer. For this reason he had favored a model in which the other campuses would be gradually merged into UNC.[22]

In fact, the transition to the new system occurred more smoothly than Friday had predicted. By late November 1971 the UNC Board of Trustees had selected from its membership sixteen representatives to sit on the interim Planning Committee with the members chosen by and from the other boards. That committee, officially established on January 1, 1972, oversaw the merger of the staffs of UNC and the State Board of Higher Education. The incorporation of the BHE staff into the university structure occurred largely without incident. Although UNC trustees were unhappy with restructuring, they expended "every effort," as Victor Bryant put it, to make the new system work.[23]

The first responsibility of the planning board, which convened in early 1972 at the Quail Roost conference center near Durham, was to choose a president of the restructured UNC system. Governor Bob Scott, who served as chairman of the Planning Committee and then of the Board of Governors until November 1972, would endorse Friday only if Cameron West was named as senior vice president. On March 15, 1972, Friday met with the Personnel Committee, a subcommittee of the Planning Committee that was entrusted with the responsibility of choosing a new president. The group convened for dinner and for a subsequent evening meeting at the Executive Mansion in Raleigh. Blacks, who had been excluded from the UNC Board of Trustees, were now guaranteed representation on the Board of Governors by the 1971 restructuring legislation. Worried about the lack of African American administrators, they wanted guarantees of a black vice president, preferably Chancellor Marion Thorpe of Elizabeth City State University. Friday told the group that he had had long associations with leading black educators nationwide and had long sponsored consultations with the presidents of North Carolina's traditionally black institutions. Yet he refused to commit himself to Thorpe's appointment.

Addressing the Chapel Hill grievance that Friday, rather than the Carolina chancellor, represented UNC at the prestigious Association of American Universities (AAU) meetings (as had Frank Graham and Gordon Gray), Friday explained that the same procedure applied in the multicampus public university systems in California, Wisconsin, Missouri, and Texas. It was only proper, Friday said, that the UNC system's "chief administrative officer" represent the institution. And, realizing that Scott and others on the Personnel Committee favored requiring guarantees about West's position and transferring the new General Administration's offices away from Chapel Hill to a neutral location – a position mostly endorsed by the former regional institutions – Friday asserted that a university president should choose his own subordinates and should preserve a connection with the system's flagship campus.[24]

It was obvious to everyone concerned, as the *Raleigh News and Observer* put it, that Friday's selection as president was a "foregone conclusion." Nonetheless, as Friday later explained, he wanted this to be a "clean" decision in which the new board would voluntarily select the best person. He emphasized – just as he had to the UNC trustee selection committee in 1956 – that he would insist on the freedom to manage his own administration. "Others could do the job," he told the committee, and if the Board of Governors wanted "to pick another – inside or outside," that candidate would enjoy his full support, with no ill will. Major challenges faced the leaders of the new university system, which he said was the "most important undertaking in recent history in North Carolina." The new Board of Governors had to define its powers and exercise them intelligently.[25]

Representatives of some of the former regional universities wanted Cameron West installed as senior vice president as a counterweight to domination by former consolidated university administrators. After Friday left the meeting of the Personnel Committee that evening, Bob Scott reinforced these reservations; he had a "gut feeling," he told committee members, that West would not be appointed if the decision were left to Friday. The governor further questioned Friday's operational style, saying that Friday "didn't enjoy his full confidence," chiefly because Scott believed that the UNC president had "switched positions on him" on several occasions. Others joined in: Friday was "too much of a politician," and they could never determine where he stood on controversial issues. Yet the group could find no alternative to Friday; nor could it think of any way to pressure him into appointing West to a key position.[26]

On March 17, 1972, the Planning Committee surprised no one when it announced that it had unanimously selected Friday as president of the new system. The committee also disclosed that the UNC headquarters would remain in Chapel Hill, at least for the first three years of the new system. Friday was "grateful for the opportunity," he told reporters; the major tasks would be a "redefinition of institutional functions and putting these things together in a well-ordered system of higher education." Friday's selection, the misgivings of the regionals notwithstanding, was greeted as the inevitable decision. Friday was not "an advantage seeker, empire builder or an ambitious man who deals in favors," editorialized the *Raleigh News and Observer*. He was a "competent administrator and a fair person who appears to know more about higher education than anyone else in the state." It was only proper that Friday should choose his own team; moving UNC's headquarters away from Chapel Hill would have been an "absurd" way "to prove he will not do favors for the Chapel Hill campus."[27]

The "last thing in the world Scott ever wanted," according to a Friday associate, was for Friday to become president, yet he was resigned to that inevitability. Still resentful over what he believed was Friday's duplicity during the restructuring battle, Scott assumed that a quid pro quo of the legislation of October 1971 was that Cameron West would be awarded a significant post in the new system. Representatives of some of the regional universities supported the governor because they believed that West would defend their interests in the new structure. Although there was no commitment on Friday's part – "he never would say," according to Scott – the governor remembered pressing him on the point and asserted that he had a "feeling" that perhaps "developed into an understanding" that the position of "senior vice-president" would become available for West.[28]

Yet the perceptions of Scott and Friday were often at odds, and this case was no different. Once chosen president, despite what one reporter called "clandestine moves" by Scott and his supporters on the Planning Committee and by the black members to influence Friday's decisions on staff, Friday refused any deals. If anything, he felt obliged not to make the selections they wanted in order to avoid any appearance of deal making. Black members of the Planning Committee, caucusing among themselves to press Marion Thorpe's case, effectively torpedoed his candidacy; according to one committee member, their aggressiveness had "knocked him out." West met a similar fate, although he was eventually appointed as UNC vice president for planning. Scott continued to complain publicly about what he considered to be Friday's double-dealing, but the governor was frustrated. In the end, Friday did not make West senior vice president, and by late 1972 West had left the state to become commissioner of higher education in Illinois.[29]

By the autumn of 1972, the new multicampus system was in place. Although the transition to the new system was smooth, the new board faced major issues, not the least important of which was the means by which it would achieve consensus. Great uncertainty prevailed at many of the campuses. The traditionally black institutions feared that they might become submerged in the new system. In contrast, a common complaint at Chapel Hill was that restructuring would dilute the quality of and diminish state support for the flagship campus. For about a decade before restructuring, the Carolina campus and the consolidated university experienced an ambivalent relationship. Frank Porter Graham, as UNC president, had routinely – and with the cooperation of his chancellor, Robert House – intervened in campus affairs at Chapel Hill. The location of both the local administration and the consolidated UNC office in South Building made jurisdictional confusion virtually inevitable, but even after Friday moved his offices to Franklin Street and then, in 1971, to the more spacious Raleigh Road quarters, strains persisted between the Carolina administration and Friday's office.

The physical presence of the president created at least some tension with most of the Carolina chancellors after House. The fact that Friday continued to have direct contact with Carolina students and faculty members often irritated the chancellors. When the president and the chancellor met at social or ceremonial occasions, chancellors sometimes felt uncomfortably reminded of the preeminence of the president in Chapel Hill. It was the UNC president, rather than the Chapel Hill chancellor, who occupied the big white house on the campus; nationally, according to one Carolina chancellor, "the appearance of educational leadership" radiated toward Friday. The essence of the problem, according to Carlyle Sitterson, was that with the president and chancellor in the same small town, "you can't have two number ones in the same place, and that's essentially the position of the chancellor in this system."[30]

Although relations with the Carolina chancellors required tact and diplomacy, the ambitions of the university campuses recently merged into one multicampus system posed a far more serious challenge. To coordinate the operations of this complex new organization, Friday chose Raymond H. Dawson, an Arkansas native who had received a Ph.D. in political science from Chapel Hill in 1958, taught briefly at Ohio State University and then returned to the Carolina campus in 1960. Eight years later he became dean of the College of Arts and Sciences. Sometime in the winter of 1972, Dawson received a telephone call from Zona Norwood asking him to come to the president's office. There, Friday asked Dawson to take the position of vice president for academic affairs. Dawson, requesting time to think about his response, consulted with Ferebee Taylor, who by then had left Friday's office to become chancellor at Chapel Hill. Despite some misgivings about leaving the Carolina campus, Dawson accepted the job.[31]

The creation of a new multicampus system became a consuming challenge for Bill Friday and Ray Dawson. Although the consolidated university had existed since 1931, restructuring meant, as Dawson recalled, "something very new and different": the university was venturing into "uncharted territory," with minefields of troubling issues. What would the policy of the new system be, for example, toward private institutions, which were beginning a campaign, successful in 1971, to win state support for financial aid? How much power would the new local boards of trustees actually exercise? How could the desegregation of traditionally white and traditionally black institutions best be accomplished?[32]

The general parameters of the new structure closely resembled the consolidated university system. The *Code* developed by a Board of Governors subcommittee headed by Victor Bryant and adopted in 1972 was closely modeled on the *Code* that the UNC Board of Trustees had approved during Gordon Gray's administration. As he had since 1956, Friday insisted on a small staff at General Administration; not only was he personally averse to top-heavy bureaucracy, but he also sought to preserve the operating responsibilities of the local campus administrations. As one of his vice presidents later remarked, in leading the university he struck a "remarkably good balance" between centralization and decentralization, and that was "conscious on his part."[33]

From the beginning, the Board of Governors functioned as a distinct entity. Elected by the legislature, the new board was more representative, more inclusive, but also more difficult to manage than the old UNC Board of Trustees. Gone was the Executive Committee, the intimate and consensual group that made most of the important decisions and provided a power base for Friday. Under the new system, there was no comparable entity: the Board of Governors functioned as its own Executive Committee. The Board of Governors, Friday privately concluded in December 1973, was not yet a "melded, functioning entity," and there was "as much politics within it as there is between it and Raleigh." Indeed, it was already split into factions. As Ray Dawson would later observe, the early history of the new system required a "fleshing out of the structure itself."[34]

The most important facet of melding diverse allegiances into a single system was the assignment of missions for the sixteen UNC campuses. Under the restructuring legislation of October 1971, the General Assembly had rescinded its decision of 1969 to extend doctoral programs to all of the state's public universities; the Board of Governors would determine campus missions. As Dawson recalled, UNC General Administration knew little about ten of the sixteen campuses; determining institutional missions, although essential, was a "tall order." Friday, during the first year of the new system, dispatched a delegation of UNC administrators and Board of Governors members to visit multicampus systems in California and Illinois; Eugene C. Lee, a political scientist and expert on the subject, spoke with board members in Chapel Hill in September 1972. General Administration's first decision was to impose a moratorium on all new programs and begin, within a year, an inventory of existing graduate programs across the state. Four years later, in 1976, a long-range plan was completed, and it served as a guide for the next two decades.[35]

By awarding doctoral-granting status to only three institutions – Chapel Hill, Raleigh, and Greensboro (all of which already had that authority) – the long-range plan dampened the ambitions of UNC-Charlotte and East Carolina University to become graduate centers. The long-range plan also provided a rationale for allocating state support to law schools. East Carolina, Appalachian State, and Charlotte all harbored ambitions in this regard, yet General Administration announced that there would be no further state-supported law schools beyond those already in existence at Chapel Hill and North Carolina Central. Similarly, the Board of Governors, based on the long-range plan, restricted offerings in engineering to N.C. State, UNC-Charlotte, and A&T, while it limited nursing programs to nine of the sixteen campuses. The long-range plan further assigned institutional classifications to the sixteen campuses, employing the Carnegie designations of Research, Comprehensive, or Baccalaureate institution, classifications that remained for many years.

The long-range plan of 1976 provided a blueprint for implementing restructuring. In 1971 the legislature, in enacting a self-denying ordinance, had bequeathed the management of public higher education to the Board of Governors. The board possessed the power to request new funds in a single lump sum, without reference to institutions, and to distribute new funds according to its own priorities, a power that Dawson described as a "radical departure." The cornerstone of the Board of Governor's blueprint for the exercise of these sweeping powers became established with the long-range plan. Most of it stuck, concluded Dawson, despite subsequent tinkering and fine-tuning.[36]

Friday played an instrumental part in this process of melding. Although he was no longer as close to the chancellors as he had been before the 1971–72 restructuring, he worked hard to establish effective relationships with the nonconsolidated university chancellors. Restructuring had brought an enormous change for all of them: no longer able to take their cases directly to the legislature, they were told to relinquish much of their previous autonomy over programs and budget. "It took a rare and unusual kind of leadership to bring this confederation together and make it work," remarked Dawson. Much of the success in restructuring, he believed, hinged on the relationship between Friday and the chancellors and local boards of trustees. The large extent to which he won their respect, trust, and confidence became Friday's "unique contribution."[37]

Friday and John F. Kennedy, UNC Founders Day, Kenan Stadium, October 12, 1961.

The successful establishment of UNC's expanded, sixteen-campus system during the 1970s propelled Friday into the limelight in national higher education circles. By the early 1980s, American Council of Education president Robert H. Atwell would describe Friday and Notre Dame University president Father Theodore Hesburgh as "the two towering giants among the leaders of higher education in this country." The University of North Carolina without Friday, Atwell said, was like UCLA basketball without Coach John Wooden; functioning without Friday would be "an impossible task." Others agreed with the assessment that Friday had become a figure of influence and stature among American university presidents.[38]

BILL Friday had been well known nationally for much of the 1960s, and he exercised considerable influence in the presidential administrations of Lyndon B. Johnson and Jimmy Carter. Two days before Christmas 1963, historian Eric F. Goldman, on leave from Princeton University as an aide to President Johnson, telephoned Friday, who was stripping furniture in the basement of the president's home in Chapel Hill. Goldman had contacted other educators, journalists, and writers around the country for their suggestions on what the president should include in his State of the Union address on January 8, 1964, and Princeton president Robert F. Goheen, an old friend of Friday's since they both had become university presidents in the 1950s, had recommended that Goldman speak with Friday. Days after his thirty-minute conversation with Goldman, Friday, along with other members of this informal "brain trust," drafted a response under complete secrecy. In a letter to Goldman sometime in the autumn of 1964, Friday pointed out that Johnson's opponent in the election, Arizona senator Barry M. Goldwater, was attracting large numbers of college-age Americans to his cause. Friday argued that Johnson should seek to solidify his support among young Americans by inviting a representative group of college students to the White House.

Meanwhile, Goldman had received a proposal from John W. Gardner, president of the Carnegie Corporation, for the establishment of a national service plan whereby one hundred able young men and women would serve in a fifteen-month training program in the federal government. Gardner's Presidential Corps could offer a substitute for military service, but its chief purpose would be to attract top-flight young talent to public service. Although Goldman was attracted to the notion, he was "not much taken" with yet another government internship program like others that had been proliferating in the Great Society. Instead, he decided to combine the Friday and Gardner proposals into a different program. In a memorandum to Johnson, he urged a convening of college leaders to announce a new White House Fellows program.[39]

When the president enthusiastically approved the idea, Goldman organized support for the new program; it was launched on October 3, 1964. Subsequently, the UNC president played a major role in establishing the White House Fellows program. In meetings with other college and university leaders, Goldman, Dean Rusk, Robert McNamara, and Johnson, the Commission on White House Fellows was created. Friday served as chairman of the commission's executive committee in its formative years. By late 1964 the executive committee had developed an expanded statement of purpose, criteria for selecting the fellows, a list of organizations from which to solicit nominations, and a statement describing the assignments of the fellows.[40]

During the first years of the program Friday participated in the selection of the White House Fellows. Johnson had insisted that the fellows should serve only in the "highest level" of government; one was assigned to the vice president, four to the White House staff, and one each to the ten cabinet members. In the program's first year, competition was intense, with over three thousand applications for only fifteen fellows. Supported primarily by outside philanthropy, the program was a spectacular success. Its graduates included future Colorado senator Timothy Wirth, presidential aide to Lyndon Johnson and later CNN president Tom Johnson, and national security adviser and chairman of the Joint Chiefs of Staff Colin H. Powell. By the late 1960s, after the program had become financed by federal funds, Friday had little more to do with it. Nonetheless, he considered the establishment of the White House Fellows to be among his most significant national achievements.[41]

Friday developed close connections with other members of the Johnson White House. John W. Gardner, whom Friday had known when Gardner was president of the Carnegie Corporation, became secretary of the Department of Health, Education, and Welfare (HEW) in the summer of 1965. When Francis Keppel resigned as assistant secretary for education, Gardner telephoned the UNC president on May 12, 1966, to offer him the job. Friday was sorely tempted, yet he felt a strong obligation to remain in his post at a time when the Speaker Ban controversy and political interference by the legislature threatened UNC. Six days after Gardner's offer, Friday informed the HEW secretary that there were "pressing reasons involving the future of the University that would not permit me to leave Chapel Hill just now." Some twenty years later, Friday reflected that this was the one major career decision he might have made differently.[42]

Friday became associated with presidential adviser Bill Moyers through his involvement with the White House Fellows program. Moyers once told him, in a meeting in the East Room, that he should "come on up and help us out." In late 1965 Moyers urged – unsuccessfully – that Friday be appointed U.S. commissioner of education. Later, Friday's name appeared prominently on a short list of possible ambassadorial appointments, and he was considered for undersecretary of HEW in January 1968.[43]

Friday's relationship with members of the Johnson administration led to his chairmanship of a special White House Task Force on Education that was organized, met, and drafted conclusions in 1966–67. While in office, Lyndon Johnson made use of some 135 presidential task forces; their chief purpose was to jump-start policy making and, as one historian has written, "to short-circuit" normal bureaucratic channels. Johnson's task forces employed an unusual array of talent, much of it from universities, but their reports were kept secret and available only to White House advisers. In 1964 John Gardner chaired a task force on education that provided a blueprint for the Elementary and Secondary Education Act and the Higher Education Act, both of which were enacted into law in 1965 and became centerpieces of the Great Society's educational program. In 1966 Johnson and his advisers organized a second task force to consider further legislation covering elementary, secondary, and higher education. When he first suggested the second task force on education to Johnson, presidential aide Joseph A. Califano Jr. had forwarded the recommendations of Gardner, who was now HEW secretary, and speechwriter and adviser Douglass Cater, for its membership. Although they had initially proposed that Pittsburgh superintendent of schools Sidney Marland head the task force, the president eventually settled on Bill Friday, apparently in an attempt to achieve regional balance. William B. Cannon, a leading official with the Bureau of the Budget and executive secretary of the Gardner task force, became executive secretary of Friday's group.[44]

Friday first heard about the task force from Gardner, who urged him to accept the assignment. Califano formally approached him about heading the group during a telephone call in October 1966. The Gardner task force of 1964 should serve as a model, Califano said, but he urged Friday to go further. "We were to look at his recommendations . . . and chart whatever was necessary beyond there," Friday recalled. Califano imposed few limitations. Friday's mission was "extremely broad": to review formal education in the United States and "to determine future directions for American education, with particular emphasis on the role which the Federal Government should play in the field of education." As "starting conditions," he told Friday not to concern himself about the costs of new programs; the task force should focus instead on "ideas and vitality."[45]

The fifteen-member task force was composed of a "first-rate group of people," Friday noted. Vice chairman Marland, who had served on the Gardner task force, advocated expanded federal support for elementary and secondary education. Most of the other members were anything but shrinking violets. They included leaders from higher education such as Lee A. DuBridge, president of the California Institute of Technology; John Fischer, president of Columbia Teachers' College; Alexander Heard, chancellor of Vanderbilt University; Fred Harrington, president of the University of Wisconsin; and Edward H. Levi, provost of the University of Chicago and subsequently U.S. attorney general. Thomas Pettigrew, a Harvard educational psychologist, and Samuel M. Brownell, a professor of urban educational administration, also advanced strong views.[46]

After an initial White House conference with Califano on November 14, 1966, the task force held its first meeting on November 22 in the Executive Office Building. Welcoming the group, Friday described the task force's "great opportunity . . . to render a great and essential service" to the nation. He then turned the floor over to U.S. commissioner of education Harold "Doc" Howe II, who raised the central issues confronting the group: the differences between categorical aid and broad federal grants, the role of two-year colleges, the relationship of the federal government to students, student aid, and the role of federal officials in planning.[47]

Further discussion, according to Friday, "roamed the pasture," after which the task force members agreed to submit memoranda outlining their views. They decided to hold a total of six meetings, each convening on the second weekend of every month during the first half of 1967. Between the second meeting on January 13–14 and submission of the final report in June, the group worked furiously. Assigned Room 446 in the Executive Office Building, the members divided themselves into two subcommittees, one addressing elementary and secondary education and the other higher education. On Saturday morning of their weekend meetings they held, Friday said, a "scramble session" to present ideas, which would be indiscriminately recorded on a flip chart. Executive director Bill Cannon then digested and analyzed these ideas and, after additional research by Bureau of the Budget staff, prepared a report for the next meeting.[48]

By June 1967, the task force had drafted a 149-page secret report. Its focus, Friday explained in a cover letter to President Johnson, was the "uneducated citizen who, for reasons of poverty and consequent lack of motivation, has never had a chance." The federal government should guarantee every citizen access to education. The members of the task force were convinced that "major steps" were necessary "to extend the equality of opportunity for learning and to advance the quality of American education at all levels." Their report urged that the United States undertake a "moon shot" approach in curriculum and instruction in order to avoid a "national calamity" in public education. It recommended a doubling of the funding in the Elementary and Secondary Education Act of 1965 and more specific targeting of federal support for public schools. The states should seek to correct the imbalance in public school financing, which tended to discriminate against cities. In one of its most controversial recommendations, the report proposed that Congress appropriate $1.25 billion to begin experimentation in "educational parks" located between white suburbs and black inner cities that would seek to attract a biracial school population in the nation's fifty largest metropolitan areas.[49]

The task force's recommendations for higher education were also bold. The report proposed that all existing support for colleges and universities be increased, but that the federal government should initiate a program of general aid to all institutions that would provide 10 percent of instructional costs plus one hundred dollars per student. It also suggested the use of experimental projects, including the creation of a National Social Science Foundation that would support inquiry in social science disciplines and experiment with federal financing of a student's freshman year. Moreover, the report urged the establishment of additional remedial services for minority students and the encouragement of further integration of historically white and historically black campuses through the development of cooperative programs as well as the sharing of programs and faculties.

This was an ambitious agenda, but unfortunately its presentation to Johnson coincided with a new set of realities. By the summer of 1967 the Vietnam War was absorbing most of the president's time and energy; little remained for domestic affairs, despite the frenetic creation of new task forces and policy initiatives. The war had cost Johnson his overwhelming political majority in Congress, and Republican opposition to the Great Society was solidifying. Even more important, the financial costs of the war made new "moon shot" initiatives such as those proposed by the Friday task force virtually impossible.

On May 20, 1967, Friday received a telephone call from Califano at 11:00 A.M. during a meeting of the task force at the Executive Office Building. The president, Califano said, wanted to see the task force immediately. Friday led the members to the Cabinet Room of the White House, where Johnson kept them waiting. When he finally arrived, the president, whom Friday remembered as a "great tall fellow," turned to Friday. "Well," he said, "what have you got to say?" "Mr. President," Friday responded, "we have some things we want to share with you." Each task force member was to present part of the group's report; Lee DuBridge went first. After DuBridge's five-minute presentation, Friday was about to call on another colleague when Johnson interrupted him. "I want to talk to you all a bit," he said, and began a long harangue on the Vietnam War. An hour later, in characteristic fashion, Johnson was still talking when he abruptly rose and left the room. Friday felt "deeply frustrated" at the end of that meeting. While sympathizing with the troubled president, he realized that six months' work was likely down the drain. Friday experienced "a sense of futility."[50]

Although a historian would describe the Friday task force's recommendations as "far-reaching," they were politically dead as soon as they were presented to Johnson. In the summer of 1967, Califano appointed twenty-four interagency task forces to help construct a new legislative agenda for the Ninetieth Congress in 1968. Doc Howe, who headed the education interagency task force, delivered his report to Califano on October 23, 1967. Although he supported a "bold, new" initiative on education, Howe rejected the central recommendations of the Friday group. Like other members of the Office of Education, Howe worried about education programs that had been established but were underfunded, and he feared that the task force's recommendations would meet a similar fate. He believed that "educational parks" would be "highly controversial and probably not politically viable," and he was dubious about general aid to higher education. Most important, implementation of the group's proposals would be "enormously expensive" in a

Friday and Lyndon B. Johnson at the White House, 1968. Also in photograph:
William Hastie.

stringent budgetary period. Howe's recommendations to table the report of
Friday's task force and Johnson's decision not to seek reelection in March 1968
precluded any further dramatic new initiatives in education.[51]

IN the 1960s and 1970s, Friday participated in all national organizations and
commissions relating to higher education. Soon after his inauguration as
UNC president, he became active in the American Council on Education
(ACE), a large umbrella organization including most American colleges and
universities; Friday served as its chairman in 1964–65. He was also a regular
participant in the Association of American Universities, a smaller organization that represented the elite research universities in the nation. Friday recalled the first AAU meeting he attended, in 1957. Sitting at a table in the
University Club in New York, he was introduced to a formidable array of
university presidents: Nathan M. Pusey of Harvard, Wallace Sterling of Stanford, Grayson Kirk of Columbia, David Henry of Illinois, Whitney Griswold
of Yale, and Barnaby Keeney of Brown. For a thirty-six-year-old, this was
"quite an exposure." When another young university administrator took a

vacant seat beside him, Friday introduced himself to Princeton president Robert F. Goheen, and that was the beginning of a lifelong friendship.[52]

Clark Kerr, president of the University of California (UC) system, had a similar experience at the AAU meeting a year later. His predecessor at California, Robert Gordon Straub, had not attended AAU meetings, and that, according to Kerr, was "much resented." In 1958, at Kerr's first meeting, Pusey asked whether the new UC president would "neglect his obligations to American higher education as the previous one did." Friday, who was sitting next to Kerr, leaned over and said, "I, at least, am happy to see you here." Kerr was struck with how "friendly, supportive, and . . . sensitive" Friday was. That encounter was "a good beginning" for a friendship, and over the next nine years of Kerr's presidency, he and Friday regularly associated at the semiannual AAU meetings.[53]

Slightly intimidated by that august body, Friday kept his "mouth shut for a good long while." But eventually he took an active part in the proceedings, and in 1971–72 he served as president of the AAU. He also participated in the American Association of State Universities and Land-Grant Colleges – although the N.C. State chancellors usually attended its meetings. In all of these national associations concerned with higher education Friday was acknowledged as a leading figure.[54]

The UNC president also left his imprint on at least two major commissions established to examine the future of American higher education: the Carnegie Commission on the Future of Higher Education (1967–71) and the Sloan Commission on Higher Education (1977–80). The Carnegie Commission had an ambitious agenda. Financed by a grant from the Carnegie Corporation, the commission was an elite group of major leaders in education such as former UC system head Clark Kerr, who chaired the commission, Notre Dame University president Theodore Hesburgh, former Harvard University president Nathan Pusey, Princeton's Institute for Advanced Study director Carl Kaysen, University of Illinois president David Henry, and Harvard sociologist David Riesman. The commission met thirty-three times at twenty-six locations around the country, for a total of seventy-seven days. It issued twenty-one special reports and sponsored special studies appearing in some eighty publications; these examined virtually every aspect of American higher education, including studies of predominantly black institutions, the financing of medical education, the economics of higher education, the role of alumni in colleges and universities, and the impact of technology.

The Carnegie Commission came into existence because of a perceived political, demographic, and economic crisis – what University of Illinois president David Henry called a "crossroads on a good many issues" – in

Carnegie Commission on the Future of Higher Education, Faculty Lounge, Morehead building, Chapel Hill, November 1968. Seated, from left to right: Father Theodore Hesburgh, William Scranton, Joseph P. Cosand, Alan Pifer, Ralph Besse, David Henry, Clark Kerr, Luther Hodges, William Friday, Stanley Heywood, Clifton Phalen, David Riesman, Norton Simon, Carl Kaysen, Nathan M. Pusey, and Alden Dunham.

American higher education. The student revolts nationwide, as Friday wrote, had partially obscured the fact that the American university was "in a state of deterioration." American higher education, members of the commission speculated, might go the way of the railroad industry. Burdened by "old mentalities, old practices, old and rigid operating rules, an older and aging labor force, and restrictive government controls," railroads had experienced steady decline for most of the twentieth century. A similar decline was conceivable – but not inevitable – for American colleges and universities. Although higher education faced an era of self-doubt, the commission remained confident of its "continued vitality" and its "essential value to American society."[55]

The Carnegie Commission attempted to establish itself as an independent voice in higher education, and many of its recommendations were translated into policy. The commission endorsed the establishment of Area Health Education Centers (AHECs) as a means of extending health care from university medical centers to underserved rural areas. A number of states dabbled in the AHEC concept, but as Chairman Clark Kerr said, "the only state that really picked it up was North Carolina under Bill Friday."[56]

Other recommendations had to do with the financing of college costs, and it was on this issue that significant divisions within the commission arose. Some members of the Carnegie Commission, especially Kerr, Kaysen, and Riesman, favored federal support through subsidized students loans. Most of the national organizations of higher education, including the ACE, advocated greater institutional support through lump-sum grants based on a head count of students, a position represented on the Carnegie Commission. At a meeting of the commission held at Chapel Hill in November 1968, the group seemed deadlocked on the issue of federal aid, and it appeared likely that there might be an open breach. On the first night of the meeting, Riesman recalled, he went to bed convinced that no consensus would emerge. But, to his astonishment the next day, Bill Friday succeeded in swinging David Henry – and, eventually, the rest of the commission – behind the idea of student loans. Friday's support for Riesman took "extraordinary courage" because it ran contrary to the position on federal aid on the part of most public university presidents. The commission thus endorsed federal aid through subsidized student loans – what became the Basic (Pell) Grant program. Administered on the basis of need, subsidized loans sought to equalize access and opportunity. Commission members were also convinced that, as Kerr put it, "if the money goes through students, you're less likely to have the federal government come in with controls."[57]

In the end, the consensus of the Carnegie Commission on federal aid prevailed. Despite, as Kerr described it, "a very bad feeling" among many university leaders that "we were conducting treason against higher education," Congress in 1972 established the Pell system of federally subsidized, low-interest loans. Soon Pell grants were helping to finance over three million students at a cost of $4 billion a year. The development of the Pell system was undoubtedly the Carnegie Commission's most enduring legacy. Theodore Hesburgh was not engaging in hyperbole when he characterized the group as "probably the most important educational commission in the history of the country, if not the world."[58]

The Sloan Commission, organized on November 28, 1977, the day of its first meeting, was financed by the Alfred P. Sloan Foundation. With twenty-two members and a research staff of eight, its purpose was to examine the relationship between American colleges and universities and the federal government and to accomplish a "creative reconciliation" between them. In meetings that continued until June 1979, the commission considered the proper form of federal aid to higher education, the needs of elite versus large public institutions, and the role of federal regulation and intervention in college and university affairs. Headed by Louis W. Cabot and with Carl Kaysen, who had by then joined the MIT faculty, serving as vice chairman, the commission was composed of a diverse membership that included business leaders, lawyers, physicians, journalists, and public servants. The mission of the Sloan Commission was to examine the impact of higher education's "growing dependence on and interaction with government, especially the Federal Government."[59]

After eleven meetings, the Sloan Commission issued its report, *A Program for Renewed Partnership*, in early 1980. Much of it concentrated on federal regulation of higher education. Particularly in the 1970s, the report asserted, college and university administrators spent an increasing portion of their time on federal regulations. This "tension" came, however, during a period when American higher education was suffering from "the pangs of entering a new age, one of uncertainty and growing pessimism," as the end of the baby boom portended a surplus capacity and financial pressures. Government, in the 1950s and 1960s, had been a "powerful and generous ally"; now, it seemed, "the entire camel" was "bumping and thumping around inside the higher education tent." Although federal regulation was necessary, the report urged that universities be permitted their traditional autonomy and freedom from outside intervention.[60]

Among its recommendations, the report called for an increase in federal aid to improve facilities for the handicapped and minorities at colleges and universities. In order to coordinate desegregation efforts, it proposed the creation of a Council for Equal Opportunity in Higher Education. It also suggested that higher education governing or coordinating boards include more lay members, that minimum standards of quality be initiated, that a mechanism for periodic qualitative reviews be established, and that a National Educational Loan Bank and merit scholarship system be created.

With a diverse membership and a broad agenda, the Sloan Commission was unable to achieve unity, and its report was published with dissents by four members. Friday dissented from the commission's recommendations regarding periodic review of educational programs at public institutions. These reviews, the report stated, should be conducted by scholars rather than regulators, whose intervention would cause "profound uneasiness" among academics. The commission report also argued that while states should "invite" private colleges to participate, it should not require them to do so.

It was on this point that Friday vigorously disagreed. Private colleges and universities, in the past decade, had become "major claimants" for state funds, and in many states – including North Carolina – legislatures had established formulas for providing virtually unrestricted aid to private institutions and their students. With federal aid tied to enrollment, public aid was necessary for the survival of many smaller colleges. Because they had become recipients of public funds, Friday suggested, private colleges should also receive closer governmental scrutiny. Otherwise, "public policy requirements regarding the use of public funds and avoidance of costly duplication and wastefulness would be applied to one segment of higher education and not to the other while both are being funded from federal and state sources."[61]

FRIDAY had emerged as a leader of considerable national stature by the late 1970s; he also became one of North Carolina's most prominent public figures.

Part of the reason for his widespread influence, especially among opinion shapers in the state, lay in his two decades of service as UNC president. But his statewide prestige – and the almost impregnable position that he occupied in the state – reflected his considerable involvement in North Carolina affairs. In the mid-1950s Gordon Gray helped to plan the new Research Triangle Park (RTP), an industrial complex that drew on three research universities – Duke University, Carolina, and N.C. State. As Gray's assistant, Friday was involved in early discussions of RTP, and he played a larger role when he became UNC president. In September 1956 he first met with the Research Triangle Committee, which had been organized by Governor Luther Hodges and was composed of business representatives such as Wachovia Bank president Robert M. Hanes and university leaders such as Duke University president Hollis Edens. When Hanes asked Friday to nominate an executive director of the committee from the university, Friday selected George Lee Simpson Jr., a protégé of Howard Odum at the UNC Institute for Research in Social Science.[62]

There were significant differences among the creators of the Research Triangle Park about its mission. Romeo Guest, a builder of industrial plants from Greensboro, was an early advocate of the park because he saw it as a source of construction business for his company. Hodges believed that economic development should remain the primary objective; RTP should attract new, higher-wage industries to complement the older Piedmont industries of tobacco, textiles, and furniture. In contrast, UNC sociologist Howard W. Odum had long wanted a major research institute that would pool the resources of the three universities in the Triangle area, but Odum's institute would have little to do with economic development.[63]

Friday's skill in mediating these divergent views was decisive. In 1958 the Research Triangle Committee, considering how it might organize a research institute within RTP, examined nine similar research institutes that were loosely affiliated with universities around the country, such as Stanford's Stanford Research Institute and Carnegie-Mellon's Mellon Institute; these institutes provided contract services to governmental agencies and to industry. George Herbert, a Naval Academy graduate who formerly worked for the Stanford Research Institute, visited North Carolina and first met Friday in the summer of 1958. As Herbert recalled, Friday and others persuaded him that a Research Triangle Institute (RTI), which would function as a contract research operation within RTP, was a viable enterprise – this at a time when there was considerable uncertainty about the future of such enterprises nationwide. Friday and the others were "truly committed" to the RTI idea.[64]

The establishment of the Research Triangle Institute occurred only after a major debate that exposed the internal differences among the founders of the

Research Triangle Park. Most of the other institutes in the country were created with organizational independence, although they retained some form of affiliation with universities. The business leaders on the Research Triangle Committee, such as Archie Davis, who joined it in 1958 when Hanes became terminally ill with cancer, had been avid fund-raisers and supporters of the project, but they wanted the RTI to be under the direct control of the Research Triangle Park, which in turn would be controlled by a business- and industry-dominated board and would be engaged in land development. George Herbert strongly opposed Davis's conception. Friday made a vigorous case, Herbert recalled, at a crucial meeting of the Research Triangle Committee in the autumn of 1958, for securing the support of the universities for the proposed institute. Carolina, N.C. State, and Duke were vital to the development of the park itself, Friday said, and responsibility for any research institute should lie with them. Grant the institute start-up funds, he said, and then let it develop separately from the private sector–oriented Research Triangle Park Foundation. In the end, Friday's view prevailed.

According to Herbert, Friday was "a very key individual in getting the Triangle headed in the right direction." But once the institute was established, Friday maintained a low profile; for the most part he delegated day-to-day involvement to senior UNC administrators William Whyburn and, later, Ray Dawson. Although an ex officio member of the boards of both organizations, he rarely involved himself in their affairs unless he was needed. "You always knew that Bill was there in a supportive role," remembered Herbert. "If you had a problem and wanted to go talk with Bill about it, you knew that you would have a receptive ear." Citing Friday's "innate positive attitude and enthusiasm," Herbert noted that he always knew that he had "the full support and backing of the guy who was the University of North Carolina," and this was "terribly important as the years went by."[65]

Almost twenty years after the founding of RTP, Friday helped to locate the National Humanities Center (NHC) at the park. In 1975 the Research Triangle Park established a Triangle Universities Consortium (TUCASI). Designed to attract additional research enterprises and directly responsible to the three universities, the consortium was given a 120-acre tract of land in the developed northern portion of the park. Coinciding with TUCASI's establishment was a campaign led by the American Academy of Arts and Sciences and scholars elsewhere to create a National Humanities Center somewhere in the country. Morton W. Bloomfield, a vice president of the academy and a professor of English literature at Harvard, who headed the NHC effort, spent the summer of 1975 as a visiting professor at Chapel Hill. Academy officials

A moment of relaxation, Lake Toxaway, N.C., 1975.
(Courtesy of the North Carolina Collection)

had broached the prospect of locating the National Humanities Center in the Research Triangle area earlier, but when they asked for a $5 million donation from local authorities, they were turned down. Sometime during the summer of 1975, the idea of locating the NHC in North Carolina was revived when Hugh Holman of UNC's English Department telephoned Bill Friday one evening at his home. "We've got a chance to become the site of the National

Humanities Center," he said. In late summer, contacts were established between TUCASI and Bloomfield and John Voss of the American Academy.[66]

Bloomfield and Voss had been searching for a site for two years when they heard from the TUCASI group. Bloomfield was joined by two other academy representatives who traveled to Chapel Hill for a meeting hosted by Friday in late August 1975 at the Carolina Inn. Archie Davis attended at Friday's invitation; so did Carolina's William Little, Duke's Juanita Kreps, and N.C. State's Claude McKinney. As Davis subsequently recalled, the academy representatives made "a right interesting proposition." Summarizing the work of academy officials, Bloomfield described offers from the University of Michigan and the University of Texas to house a humanities center; Texas had promised $10 million in support. Would it be possible, Bloomfield asked, for RTP to make land and resources available to establish and maintain a humanities center?[67]

Friday and Davis left the four-and-a-half-hour dinner meeting fascinated by what they had heard. Davis had asked academy officials how much space they would need, and they had made some quick calculations: the proposed building, at 30,000 square feet, would cost about $1.5 million to construct, while overhead costs would be about $225,000 a year. Davis believed that he could raise the funds to construct the building, but only if the three Research Triangle universities could pledge $75,000 a year each to maintain the building. After promising their support at the meeting, the university representatives had secured the required pledge from Carolina, Duke, and N.C. State within forty-eight hours. At the same time, Davis left the meeting having told the academy representatives that he would do everything in his power to get the land grant approved and to raise the money for the construction of a building.

Friday and Davis swung into action. The academy committee would decide the location of the humanities center in November 1975. This gave the Friday-Davis team only sixty days to obtain financial support. Time was pressing; raising that large a sum of money in so short a time was, Friday said, "a pretty nervy thing for Mr. Davis and me to think we could pull off." Soon after the Carolina Inn meeting, Friday went to the Executive Committee of the Research Triangle Park Foundation and told the members that locating the humanities center at the park would "advance higher education in this state by fifteen, twenty years, or more." Having secured the foundation's support, Friday and Davis assured the American Academy delegation that the necessary funds could be raised. If the humanities center would locate in the Research Triangle Park, TUCASI would donate fifteen acres from its tract, and Davis would raise the money for a building and for an initial endowment.[68]

Archie Davis raised $1.5 million dollars in just thirty-two days. On October 1, 1975, he and Hugh Holman flew to Boston to present the RTP offer formally, and by the end of the month the academy site committee had chosen the Research Triangle Park over the other finalists. In the location of the National Humanities Center in North Carolina, Friday was, as one NHC officer put it, a "towering figure." William J. Bennett, who later became NHC director, maintained that Friday did an "excellent selling job." The site committee members, Bennett said, were "overwhelmed" by the Friday-Davis proposal, and they were "just terribly impressed with the intellectual depth and range of the people with whom they were talking."[69]

Just as Friday served as a sort of guardian angel for the Research Triangle Park, he acted as a protector of the National Humanities Center during its infancy. By the spring of 1976, the center had organized a board of directors and appointed Bennett as associate director. Finding a permanent director proved more difficult. When Morton Bloomfield, in the spring of 1976, asked Friday, he unequivocally refused. The NHC's executive committee then appointed a search committee headed by McGraw-Hill executive Dan Lacy. Lacy, who was graduated Phi Beta Kappa from Carolina in 1933, had worked as the supervisor of North Carolina's Historical Records Survey, a WPA project, in the late 1930s. After holding positions at the National Archives and the Library of Congress, he went to work for McGraw-Hill in 1966; by the 1970s he was a senior vice president and executive assistant to publishing tycoon Harold McGraw. Lacy joined the NHC's executive committee after it had already been established; he was chosen because of his friendship with Charles Frankel, a distinguished philosopher at Columbia University who had been involved with the American Academy's site committee. As Lacy remembered it, he was tapped to head the search committee primarily because "everybody agreed from the beginning" that the NHC director should be Frankel.[70]

The selection of the NHC's first permanent director was critical, for the choice signified the seriousness of the new enterprise to the academic world. The director needed an unusual combination of skills: prestige among humanists, fund-raising abilities, and the skills to manage a new operation. Soon after the search committee was organized, Lacy urged the members to recruit Frankel, and in late January 1977 Frankel agreed to become president and director of the NHC. The "only way to persuade him to do it," according to Bennett, was for the center to accept Frankel's terms. He would remain in New York and travel to North Carolina only twice a month. Moreover, Frankel agreed to stay on as director only until September 1978, though he was subsequently persuaded to assume the position permanently. Bennett, and to a certain extent Elizabeth Aycock, continued to manage the day-to-day operations of the center, and construction began on a new building in the spring of 1979. It was named, appropriately, for Archie Davis, and preparations began for the center's first class of fellows in the following autumn.[71]

After the NHC's establishment, Friday, aside from serving on the board, had little to do with it, and he participated only minimally in the search for Frankel. Bennett, as the center's operational director, compared his relationship with Friday to the relationship between the cabinet and the president of the United States. Bennett would call him when a problem arose among the three sponsoring universities or when any other "serious matter" deserved his attention. Friday usually offered "sage advice," Bennett said; on some occasions, he told Bennett that he would personally handle the matter.[72]

Friday served as a buffer, according to Dan Lacy, between the NHC and the "North Carolina power and academic structure" into the 1980s. Only when crises occurred would he involve himself. There was such a crisis in May 1979, when Frankel and his wife were murdered by burglars in their home in Westchester County, New York. Frankel's death produced a "real crisis for the center," Lacy recalled, because it had been "uniquely built" around Frankel. His appointment had provided national credibility and standing, and a large portion of the NHC board favored choosing someone of similar stature to replace him. Another view, to which Friday subscribed, held that William Bennett, who was deeply immersed in the operations of the center, should become director. After a year of indecision by the NHC leadership, Bennett, who was seen as a man of "extremely high intelligence and tremendous energy and a good deal of charm" and who was "enormously popular" with the fellows, became permanent director. In this effort Friday "cast the mantle of his support around Bennett," according to Lacy, and provided him "protection and strength." Even after the succession crisis following Frankel's death had passed, Friday remained a "benign presence" in NHC affairs.[73]

In other respects, Friday maintained an involvement in state affairs that extended beyond the UNC presidency. In the early 1970s Smith Richardson, one of the heirs to the Richardson-Vick pharmaceutical fortune, telephoned Friday and asked him to collaborate with Duke president Terry Sanford and Davidson College president Samuel R. Spencer in the creation of a leadership institute near Greensboro. As chairman of the first board of the Center for Creative Leadership, Friday helped to establish it as one of the nation's leading corporate and military leadership training institutes, with offices in Greensboro, Colorado Springs, San Diego, and Brussels. The CEOs of most major corporations, along with every brigadier general in the U.S. Army, received leadership training at the center. Friday later described the Center for Creative Leadership as a "laboratory" where the strengths of university and industry intersected.[74]

Nothing gave Bill Friday greater personal pleasure or more exposure state-wide than his television interview show, *North Carolina People*. Broadcast by WUNC-TV, the state's public television network, the program first aired in 1971, while UNC was making the transition from a six-campus to a sixteen-campus system. In that year, John Young, director of WUNC-TV, approached Friday about moderating a conversation between the five living North Carolina governors. Although Friday first responded that he knew nothing about television, he eventually agreed to do the project. About a month after the show aired, Young called suggesting that Friday try a one-on-one interview show. The first guest was Robert Burton House, former Chapel Hill chancellor. Friday came prepared with thirty-six questions written on a yellow pad, but ten minutes into the interview he realized that he had already used two-thirds of the questions. To Friday's close-ended questions, House simply answered "yes" or "no"; Friday was both "out of business" and "terrified." Finally, he asked House about his World War I experience, and House "just took off" in his answer. Although Friday remembered the interview as "absolutely awful," Young incorporated the show into North Carolina public television's regular programming.[75]

The first episodes of *North Carolina People* were run on a shoestring. Maurice Talbot produced the show, and his secretary, Ruth Ann Ford, did the scheduling. In the 1970s Friday's public relations aide, former *Charlotte Observer* reporter Jay Jenkins, wrote a list of questions that Friday usually followed. By 1980, when Dick Snavely became producer, Friday had gained more confidence and generally developed his own questions. Over the years, the guests included a variety of people in the state. Some were native North Carolinians who had achieved national reputations: TV personalities David Brinkley and Charles Kuralt, *New York Times* columnist Tom Wicker, Duke University professor and secretary of commerce Juanita Kreps, and band leader and Friday's old friend Kay Kyser.

All of the post-1954 governors – Luther Hodges, Terry Sanford, Dan Moore, Bob Scott, and James Holshouser – appeared separately on the show. With the election of Jim Hunt to the governorship in 1976, Friday regularly hosted sitting governors; Hunt appeared on the program ten times, whereas his successor, Jim Martin, was a guest every year that he was governor. In March 1984 Friday and the production crew traveled to Washington, D.C., to interview Senator Jesse Helms; Snavely described it as one of the best interviews Friday had ever done. Other guests on *North Carolina People* were ordinary North Carolinians with occupations that viewers found interesting.[76]

After his retirement from the UNC presidency in 1986, *North Carolina People* remained a part of Friday's public persona. He enjoyed the attention

With Tom Wicker on *North Carolina People*. (Courtesy of the North Carolina Collection)

that he received on the show, Snavely said; Friday had an ego that was "becoming to him." He appreciated being stopped by people across the state and told that they enjoyed the show. On the set, Friday communicated ease, both to the guests and to the production crew. One guest said that he was "never threatening"; he succeeded in doing "everything possible to pull out what you want to say and what you're interested in." A columnist for the *Salisbury Post* remembered being so scared of appearing on television that she was certain that "those drums in my chest would drown out our voices." But she quickly found Friday's smile "comforting." He was "so relaxed – even if he didn't fall for my try at turning the questions on him." As she left the set, she realized that he had been a great university president because "you trust him immediately and totally."[77]

There was a "mutual admiration" between Friday and the WUNC-TV crew that worked with him. Friday regarded the production of the show as a "laboratory for young people." The television crews knew him lovingly as "Uncle Bill," in large part because of his effort to relate personally to each of them and his ability to remember their names and details about them. "The newest student on the crew, and the professional, he treats all alike," regarding them all as part of a team, Snavely said. Even people who joined the *North Carolina People* production crew after he retired from the UNC presidency respected him and quickly understood his stature in the state. "They quickly catch that," said Snavely. "Just his general aura will give that to you."[78]

By the 1970s Friday's "general aura" was well established not only in North Carolina, but also within higher education circles and among national opinion shapers. Much of his effectiveness as UNC president depended on the preservation of that aura, and through the 1970s and 1980s Friday carefully cultivated his image, realizing that his most effective weapon as a leader was his reputation and mystique. Yet at the peak of his power and as he neared the end of a long and distinguished career, Friday would face grave challenges to his leadership. For just as the new, sixteen-campus system was in place, it would experience, in the proposed organization of a medical school at East Carolina, a serious test of its coherence and validity as a system.

CHAPTER 8 *The East Carolina Challenge*

ALMOST immediately after its establishment, the expanded multi-campus UNC system faced a serious test: the effort to create a second state-supported medical school at East Carolina University in Greenville. Since the 1950s, ECU had been seeking to transform itself from a modest teachers' college into a major university; in the 1960s, under President (and, after 1972, Chancellor) Leo W. Jenkins, ECU attracted support in the legislature for its cause. Bill Friday viewed East Carolina's campaign for a greater share of state resources with increasing alarm. Although he had, in the 1950s and 1960s, sought to expand access to higher education, Friday believed that the democratization of North Carolina's colleges and universities, at least as it appeared in East Carolina's educational populism, posed great dangers. Increased access in the post-1945 era meant rapid, and virtually unregulated, expansion, particularly of politically powerful regional universities such as Western Carolina, Appalachian State, and, above all, East Carolina. Although state resources were spread more widely during the post-1945 expansion in North Carolina higher education, in the late 1960s such expansion appeared to threaten the quality of education. The system of allocating public resources seemed out of control; nothing typified this more than the legislature's decision in 1969 to authorize the State Board of Higher Education to award doctoral-granting status to all of the regional universities.

Restructuring in 1971–72 represented an attempt by the political structure to resolve the conflict between increased access and the need for planning in order to allocate public resources for higher education more rationally. But among institutions like ECU, old habits of dealing directly with the General Assembly died slowly. Many of the new UNC campuses had developed strong political followings in the 1960s, and although legislators accepted a self-denying ordinance in 1971, there was, as Ray Dawson described it, some "chipping away." The most serious challenge to the new system came from East Carolina's continuing drive for elevated status, a drive that focused on the establishment of a medical school.[1]

The idea of making medical services more available to the far reaches of North Carolina had long been popular. In 1944–45 the North Carolina Hospital and Medical Care Commission, which was appointed by Governor J. Melville Broughton, recommended major changes. In 1947, during the administration of Governor R. Gregg Cherry, the General Assembly enacted legislation extending public health and hospital services by expanding the University of North Carolina Medical School in Chapel Hill; over the next five years, $68 million was spent and 5,000 new hospital beds were added. Under the leadership of Dean W. Reece Berryhill, Chapel Hill became a center of these new health services. Yet the expansion of hospitals and medical resources occurred unevenly, in North Carolina as in all other states, with a greater proportion of physicians practicing in the urban Piedmont than in the rural areas of eastern and western North Carolina. Sometime in 1964, Leo Jenkins, seizing upon that unmet need, began a campaign to elevate East Carolina's status through the establishment of a new medical school.[2]

After the East Carolina College Board of Trustees approved his proposal on October 1, 1964, Jenkins lobbied the General Assembly. A bill was presented to the legislature under the sponsorship of state senator Robert Morgan, chairman of the ECC Board of Trustees. The bill enjoyed the support of some North Carolina physicians, including J. W. R. Norton, who was the state health director, and Lenox D. Baker, professor of orthopedic surgery at the Duke University Medical School and president of the North Carolina State Board of Health. In July 1965 the General Assembly appropriated $250,000 to plan a two-year medical school, despite the objections of Governor Dan K. Moore, the State Board of Higher Education, and the deans of the state's three existing medical schools (UNC at Chapel Hill, Duke, and the Bowman Gray School of Medicine at Wake Forest University). At the last minute, however, legislators added what an ECU official later called a "little thorn." If East Carolina could not obtain accreditation by January 1967, the BHE would assume direct oversight of the effort.[3]

This schedule, given the college's inadequate science curriculum and research facilities and the lack of a major hospital in Greenville, was impossible. Two representatives from the Liaison Committee on Medical Education (LCME) – the accrediting body representing the American Medical Association's Council on Medical Education and the Association of American Medical Colleges – visited the Greenville campus in the summer of 1965; they reported deficiencies in the basic sciences and clinical facilities at East Carolina. The LCME recommended the use of consultants to study the prospects for an ECU medical school, and in January 1966 the consultants' report proposed that East Carolina expand its health sciences offerings rather than establish a medical school. Unfazed, East Carolina continued to enjoy solid support from legislators representing rural counties of both the east and the west. When the General Assembly transformed the state's teachers' colleges into regional universities in 1967, it left out the provision that the Board of Higher Education should oversee the ECU medical school program; the BHE's control was never restored. Meanwhile, in 1966 East Carolina had established a School of Applied Health and Social Professions as an administrative umbrella to inaugurate a new medical school. A year later the legislature renewed authorization for the medical school, establishing a Health Sciences Institute when it made East Carolina a regional university. In November 1967 ECU hired Edwin Monroe, a Greenville internist, to head the institute. The first members of a medical school faculty – including Wallace R. Wooles, director of the Division of Medical Services – were appointed in 1970.[4]

In the campaign for a medical school, East Carolina fused eastern North Carolina jingoism, resentment by the east and west of Piedmont dominance, and anti–Chapel Hill sentiment. The proposed institution, Monroe told legislators in the spring of 1969, "would not attempt to duplicate complex medical centers such as those now present in Chapel Hill or Durham." Instead, by producing greater numbers of primary care physicians rather than the more specialized physicians graduated at Duke and Chapel Hill, it would make primary-care physicians more available in the region and improve the quality of health care. The *Charlotte Observer* offered a different interpretation. There was nothing to explain ECU's bid for a medical school, it editorialized in December 1970, that made any sense except that school's "great ambition" and the "great hopes" it had inspired in eastern North Carolina. The issue had become primarily a political rather than an educational question.[5]

The ECU campaign faced strong opposition from the Chapel Hill medical school and from legislators reluctant to pay the daunting costs – estimated in the hundreds of millions of dollars – that a new medical school entailed. ECU boosters consistently underestimated these costs, while they also made the case that federal funds would pay a large portion of the expense. When East Carolina proposed a $2.4 million appropriation in 1969 to establish a two-year program, the General Assembly backed off, providing only $375,000 for planning. Another LCME accreditation visit in October 1970 also stalled the ECU campaign. The curriculum, the LCME reported in January 1971, was "very tentative and subject to change"; there was a shortage of faculty, and instruction in the basic sciences and clinical facilities remained inadequate. The committee cited another "major concern": whether graduates of East Carolina's proposed two-year program would be accepted into four-year programs in an era in which two-year programs seemed obsolete.[6]

Despite these setbacks and continued opposition, the East Carolina forces pushed on. But when ECU brought its renewal request before the 1971 legislature, the Board of Higher Education, in a report on medical education released on February 19, 1971, contended that the physician shortage would best be eased by expanding enrollments at existing medical schools. The BHE proposed that enrollment at the UNC School of Medicine be doubled, along with that of in-state medical students at Duke and Bowman Gray; in order to encourage greater numbers of black physicians to practice in North Carolina, the all-black Meharry Medical College in Nashville, Tennessee, should receive substantial state subsidies. Further, the board rejected, as costly and unnecessary, the establishment of either a two-year medical school or a four-year state-supported medical school in Greenville. Instead, it proposed creating a one-year program, modeled on a similar program in Indiana, that would permit students to complete one year of medical school at East Carolina before transferring to Chapel Hill.[7]

The BHE's report received the enthusiastic support of Governor Bob Scott, then in the midst of the restructuring battle. In a news conference on February 19, 1971, he cast the Chapel Hill medical school and the consolidated university as villains and charged that UNC was doing all it possibly could to block the approval of medical education at East Carolina University. The BHE plan required Chapel Hill to accept ECU medical students, Scott noted; it would be necessary to require their transfer by law because "they are not going to do it" without a legislative edict, and "we are going to have to tell them to do it." Personally, Scott said, he favored the establishment of a second state medical school at Greenville. He warned that the university was "maneuvering [in] every way possible," in "almost frantic and sometimes comic" attempts, to create a medical school at Charlotte and to establish a one-year program at N.C. State; these efforts, he asserted, had begun only after UNC officials perceived a threat from ECU. In this struggle, Scott declared, the "blue bloods" of UNC would not prevail.[8]

Before 1971, Bill Friday had been only marginally involved in the controversy. During the late 1960s he monitored Jenkins's campaign carefully, attempting to protect the UNC School of Medicine and to encourage alternatives to a medical school in Greenville. Most of his dealings with ECU were cordial, and he maintained an effective working relationship with Leo Jenkins. When he could, Friday worked through subordinates and avoided assuming an uncompromising public position on what was becoming, by the early 1970s, a highly charged political issue. But as political support for a larger ECU program clearly emerged – and as UNC restructuring loomed near – Friday found direct involvement unavoidable.

On February 26, 1971, ECU and UNC officials met to develop plans for a joint program. Although Friday, in a meeting with Jenkins in Chapel Hill on February 10, had refused ECU's request to accept large numbers of transfers from a future two-year program, the BHE report and Scott's loud intervention seemed to cast new light on the matter. At the hour-long meeting on the twenty-sixth, called at the request of state attorney general and ECU trustee Robert Morgan, Friday brought East Carolina's Wallace Wooles and Ed Monroe together with UNC School of Medicine administrators Arden Miller and Cecil Sheps, along with Carolina chancellor Carlyle Sitterson. The Chapel Hill and ECU representatives agreed to form a parent committee to oversee the ECU-UNC relationship and to report to Jenkins, Sitterson, and Friday on a joint budget request. In April 1971 this joint committee arranged to establish a transfer program providing for a first year at Greenville and the final three years at Chapel Hill. A month later the ECU Board of Trustees and Governor Scott endorsed the one-year arrangement as a way station toward a full four-year program, and legislative approval followed in July 1971.[9]

In the proposed one-year arrangement, Friday was buying time, as he sought to delay expansion of the Greenville program and to deflect the possibility of a second full-fledged state-supported medical school. Friday wanted not only to limit the ECU program but also to contain it by bringing it under stricter UNC control, and these objectives were bolstered by the intervention of the LCME and outside accreditors. In November 1971, about two weeks after the General Assembly enacted restructuring, the LCME again visited North Carolina to evaluate the ECU one-year program and the transfer arrangement. In the ECU-UNC transfer program, the committee concluded, real administrative authority remained uncertain. As a precondition to accreditation, the LCME required that the UNC School of Medicine assume complete control over the ECU program. Because of the uncertainty of administrative authority, the LCME renewed accreditation of Chapel Hill's medical school for two rather than the usual seven years.[10]

This, then, was the situation confronting Friday when the new, sixteen-campus system was inaugurated in July 1972. East Carolina had obtained legislative support for planning a medical school as early as 1965, and despite the virtually unanimous opposition of the Board of Higher Education, outside consultants, and the medical school establishment at Chapel Hill, ECU's hopes for a new medical school remained alive. In a one-year program affiliated with Chapel Hill, ECU supporters saw the opening to a full four-year program. Future calls for the expansion of this program were very likely, Friday realized, but launching a public counterattack to the ECU campaign would almost certainly create a backlash. In a purely political battle, Friday believed, East Carolina would probably prevail; containing this powerful political issue was possible only if the issues were defined educationally. Public counterattack was not part of Friday's style anyway; conciliation and settlement were. Only months into the new, sixteen-campus UNC system, Friday faced a major challenge: how to limit East Carolina's ambitions within the new system, satisfy the vocal ECU supporters on the Board of Governors, and address the strong political mandate for Leo Jenkins's campaign to establish a medical school at Greensboro.

After the 1972 restructuring, Jenkins reported to Friday and the UNC Board of Governors; Jenkins, now a chancellor in the new UNC system, proceeded cautiously. According to Monroe, Jenkins got off to a "kind of quiet" beginning. All chancellors were now required to stay out of legislative politics except as directed by the UNC president, and Jenkins, who had been conspicuous politically, stopped lobbying the General Assembly on what Monroe believed were "pretty direct orders." Ray Dawson viewed the matter differently. Even in pushing for the new medical school, Jenkins wanted to act as "a team player," but he faced strong pressures from ECU supporters. Jenkins balanced the desires of UNC officials and his Greenville constituency, and when he operated outside the limits of the system, "he never let himself get caught at it."[11]

Both Friday and Jenkins insulated themselves from the medical school conflict through subordinates such as Dawson and Monroe. If a harsh speech had to be made, a Jenkins aide would make it; Jenkins could deny involvement. After 1972, the direct political lobbying fell primarily to Ed Monroe. According to a member of the UNC medical faculty who knew him, Monroe "really canvassed this state," working through a network of local medical societies and legislators in open defiance of the purposes, he believed, of the newly restructured system. Similarly, although he remained fully informed about ECU's campaign, Friday continued to manage UNC strategy from a distance. Even after events in the early 1970s forced him to take a more active role, Friday continued to work through, in Monroe's words, his "point" men, Felix Joyner and Ray Dawson.[12]

Yet the major participants – ECU and UNC medical school officials alike – were dissatisfied with Friday's attempts to contain ECU educational populism. At Chapel Hill, the medical school faculty believed that he was doing too little, and efforts to run a joint program with ECU were frustrating. According to one faculty member, the medical school faculty was "stretched" because of the expanding enrollment at Chapel Hill, along with its responsibilities, under the one-year program, for teaching in Greenville. The faculty members further worried that an expensive new medical school would drain off resources from the Chapel Hill program, and many of them favored a more visible anti-ECU campaign.[13]

In contrast, East Carolina supporters believed that Friday was doing too much. Accreditation pressures from the LCME, Jenkins wrote in January 1972, meant that no agency would recognize the ECU program as anything but a "satellite of the University of North Carolina." As a result, neither side in the controversy was happy with ECU's one-year program. In late February 1972 the new dean of the UNC School of Medicine, Christopher C. Fordham III, reported dissatisfaction within his faculty with the current joint arrangement. Greenville resisted outside control over the admission and promotion of students, curriculum development, and the recruitment of faculty. Other administrators, such as UNC-Chapel Hill vice chancellor for health affairs Cecil Sheps, feared that the relationship with East Carolina might affect the status and perhaps even the accreditation of the Chapel Hill program.[14]

In June 1972, as part of the restructured UNC system's first biennial budget (for 1973–75), Jenkins proposed the development of a two-year program as a first step toward establishing a four-year, degree-granting school. Bob Scott responded, as chairman of the Board of Governors, by appointing a board committee to make recommendations. Headed by Robert B. Jordan III, that committee deliberated through the summer and fall of 1972. Here, the role of Friday and his staff was crucial. Ray Dawson worked closely with the committee; he attended most of the meetings and provided support and advice. Friday met with the Jordan Committee on November 10 and presented a detailed proposal. While he avoided bluntly opposing a second state-supported medical school at Greenville, his position was clear. He told the Jordan Committee that although there was a recognized shortage of physicians in North Carolina and that "better delivery" of health care was necessary in rural areas, establishing a new freestanding program was not the answer. Friday instead recommended expanding the number of entering medical students at Chapel Hill, reaching agreements to increase the enrollment of North Carolina students at Duke and Bowman Gray, and retaining the present one-year program at Greenville until the accreditation problems were resolved. The last and most novel of Friday's proposals was that the Jordan Committee defer the controversial issue of creating a new medical school by appointing a blue-ribbon group of outside experts to conduct a comprehensive study. Only by depoliticizing the issue of medical education, Friday believed, could a second state-supported medical school be avoided.[15]

The Jordan Committee endorsed all of Friday's recommendations. It proposed greater state support for enrolling more North Carolinians at Chapel Hill and in-state private medical schools, preserving the one-year program at ECU and its relationship with the medical school at Chapel Hill, and establishing a panel of consultants to examine the need for another four-year state-supported medical school. The committee also strongly advised that a standing committee on health affairs be established in the Board of Governors and that a UNC staff person be designated to coordinate it.[16]

Bob Jordan presented the committee's report to the Board of Governors on January 2, 1973. Noting that his group faced a "difficult and exacting task" when it was appointed six months earlier, Jordan urged the board to adopt its report, which agreed on the need for more physicians produced by North Carolina medical schools. The Jordan Committee offered no solution to the vexatious issue of an ECU medical school; indeed, in his statement Jordan ignored the question. The board, equally eager to defer the matter to a nonpolitical, neutral body, adopted the report unanimously. Efforts then began to organize the panel of consultants who would report to the board in the autumn of 1973. In February and March, William A. Dees Jr., who had replaced Governor Scott as chairman of the board in December 1972, received twenty-seven nominations. After consulting with the Jordan Committee and with medical education leaders, he appointed in April 1973 a panel of five outside experts headed by the distinguished medical educator Ivan L. Bennett Jr., a Wilmington, North Carolina, native and dean of the medical school of New York University.[17]

Meanwhile, the problems of ECU's one-year program continued. In late January 1973 another LCME survey team visited Greenville and Chapel Hill. The survey team's report, kept secret until it became public in April, had more bad news for ECU boosters. The Chapel Hill medical school deserved "full and complete accreditation," but the ECU program was "seriously lacking in acceptable quality in its present form." The LCME investigators cited the inferior quality of the faculty, a weak science support base, and inadequate clinical training. They also criticized Chapel Hill for its ineffective control over the Greenville program.[18]

The LCME reported its findings unofficially to UNC administrators at the end of January but did not make its formal report until April 9, 1973. In late April, UNC officials circulated the LCME report to board members, but the public exposure of the substance of the report on April 26 and its full contents the day after forced the matter.[19] Jenkins and Friday conferred at the General Administration Building on April 27, and they agreed in principle that the LCME report required, as Friday informed the Board of Governors, that the one-year program should be the "direct responsibility" of the dean of the UNC School of Medicine. Jenkins, who told reporters that he had "no choice" but to accept Chapel Hill control, also met with Fordham, who assured the ECU chancellor of his "full cooperation . . . to make this thing work." "It will be this way or there will be no program," Jenkins said; he hoped that the new arrangement would "clear the air."[20]

ECU partisans, however, ceded control of their program to Chapel Hill only as a holding action. Temporarily accepting this compromise, Jenkins complained that his opponents had used "every trick in the book . . . to discredit, sabotage and destroy the effort that we have undertaken." Before the LCME's report could be considered by the Board of Governors, "misleading headlines and critical interpretation" had distorted its meaning. The "real victims," he said, were North Carolinians, who suffered from "insufficient health care." Monroe went further. The LCME's report was unfair, he claimed in a press statement, because it evaluated the ECU medical curriculum according to the standards of a full four-year program rather than as an adjunct to the Chapel Hill program. Compared to one-year offerings elsewhere, ECU's medical program stood up well. The operating budget and resources allocated by the state were far less than ECU needed to maintain a good program, and fractious relations with Chapel Hill had further hampered its ability to operate. "We have fought for eight years now to establish a medical school to meet the needs of the people of North Carolina," declared Monroe; ECU partisans would continue the fight until "the people's needs are met." But until a four-year program was established at Greenville, "we can continue to expect this kind of prejudicial treatment from the medical school establishment and from some newspapers in the state."[21]

Both the advocates of a freestanding program at Greenville and the Chapel Hill medical school supporters, who were increasingly alienated by the heavy-handed political tactics emanating from ECU, awaited the actions of the Bennett Panel, which met during the summer and autumn of 1973. Visiting North Carolina one long weekend a month, the panel interviewed politicians, administrators, and educators. It worked for almost six months and spent, according to the panel's executive secretary, Jules Levine, a "tremendous amount of time" in the state, collecting data from publications, conducting interviews, reviewing scores of documents, visiting facilities and faculties at Greenville and Chapel Hill, and consulting with political leaders and medical professionals in Raleigh.[22]

Throughout its investigations, the consultants and Bill Friday shared a similar point of view. Friday remained confident that the Bennett Panel would endorse the UNC position, though he had little contact with the panel. Although the outside experts met with him occasionally, those contacts did not occur, as Levine put it, "constantly and excessively." Rather, Friday's role was "more of a facilitator to help us get it done." The UNC president was careful about dictating any result and insisted only on "a clean, objective look" to resolve the issue. Friday had insulated himself from the political controversy by delegating much of the responsibility to his subordinates, primarily UNC secretary John Kennedy, a former BHE official who handled most of the day-to-day management of the case. Although Friday avoided public opposition, few people close to him doubted that he believed that the establishment of the ECU medical school was unsound educationally and would threaten the fragile new restructured system. For Friday, the Bennett Panel members offered an alternative to costly and probably unsuccessful political combat. As outside experts, they would probably support his position and might defuse the political issue.[23]

Although ECU partisans also realized that the Bennett Panel was unfavorably disposed toward their cause, they remained confident. As one legislator told the consultants, the General Assembly had "repeatedly, whether wisely or unwisely," indicated its intention to establish a medical school at ECU. Greenville administrators were openly resentful of the panel, which they viewed as a smokescreen for a Chapel Hill power play. According to Ed Monroe, ECU had participated minimally in the panel's selection, and its membership "stacked" the case. Another ECU official later described the Bennett Panel as a "put-up job." Monroe believed that Ivan Bennett would be strongly disposed against another medical school in the state. Kenneth Crispell, another panel member, was dean of the University of Virginia's medical school and had opposed state support for the Eastern Virginia Medical School in Norfolk. There was "no way anybody with his background was going to favor developing another medical school," Monroe asserted. The fact that Crispell's colleague at Virginia, Jules Levine, served as executive secretary of the panel, Monroe said, further prejudiced the case.[24]

While the panel deliberated, ECU officials complained that Greenville was not receiving fair consideration. In September 1973, only days before the Bennett Panel delivered its final report, ECU dean Wallace R. Wooles wrote to Levine complaining that the panel had visited Greenville only twice, once to interview Monroe and himself and then to see Jenkins. At no time, wrote Wooles, did the panel request materials describing their plans for a degree-granting medical school at ECU. That suggested that the Bennett Panel had prejudged the matter. Ivan Bennett responded aggressively. There was "no purpose for your letter save one," he asserted, and that was an attempt to put on record "a deliberately misleading and erroneous" rendition of the panel's actions with regard to ECU. By his count, the consultants had visited Greenville three times, and one of the meetings took up an entire day. Rather than refusing to review any ECU plans on paper, the panel had made a determined effort to obtain as much information as possible.[25]

ECU officials nevertheless were confident that, whatever the consultants recommended, the General Assembly would eventually decide in their favor. Levine recalled that Leo Jenkins expressed "adversarial" attitudes toward the Bennett Panel. Although "very pleasant and a gentleman," Levine characterized Jenkins as knowing "what he wanted" and "vigorously pursuing it." Jenkins was not "too concerned" about the panel; he followed "his own agenda." Although Monroe and other ECU officials were "not pleased," Levine was struck by Jenkins's obvious belief in the probability of success. The ECU medical school decision was no longer an issue about the objective need for medical education. Levine realized that, by the end of the panel's deliberations, Jenkins desperately wanted a new medical school, eastern North Carolina favored it, and the political outcome was a foregone conclusion.[26]

The Bennett Panel report was sent to the Board of Governors on September 14, 1973, for examination. Noting the "pervasive public worry and anxiety" about the lack of physician care, the report maintained that this was a national problem. In North Carolina, public policy consideration of the matter had narrowed to a "single-minded intensity" that had become "acrimonious, partisan, and regional." But the politicization of the issue had obscured possible alternatives to a new medical school. Acknowledging a physician shortage, the Bennett Report asserted that the chief problem lay in attracting and retaining physicians. Along with attendance at medical school, the chief factors influencing physicians' location in a community were medical resources and access to professional education. State resources, the report argued, should support postgraduate residency training rather than undergraduate medical education.[27]

The Bennett Report confronted two thorny questions: first, did North Carolina need another medical school, and, second, was East Carolina the appropriate location? To both of these questions, the panel responded unequivocally. Establishing another medical school, it argued, would not alleviate the primary care physician shortage. Nor was Greenville the best location. Pronouncing its "substantial agreement" with the findings of the LCME survey team, the panel urged that, if the one-year program were continued, "complete authority and responsibility" for managing it should be assigned to the Chapel Hill medical school. The result of a political compromise in 1971, the one-year program had reduced the academic autonomy of East Carolina and was bitterly resented in Greenville; as for Chapel Hill, administering the program "placed it in the awkward position of being responsible for a pedestrian program which it had had no hand in planning and about which it had been not only unenthusiastic but highly critical." The Bennett Panel strongly opposed the creation of a four-year, degree-granting program at East Carolina. Establishing a new medical school was not only "premature" but also based on "a lack of understanding of what the establishment of such a school would involve."[28]

Instead of a new medical school, the Bennett Report proposed full-fledged state support for Area Health Education Centers (AHECs). Beginning in 1967, the UNC School of Medicine had begun a community medicine program at several state hospitals; in 1971 Chapel Hill sent sixteen full-time medical school faculty members to seven North Carolina hospitals and rotated medical students and residents through these facilities. Bill Friday became better acquainted with AHECs through his participation in the Carnegie Commission on the Future of Higher Education, which endorsed AHECs as an effective way to distribute resources of university medical centers to rural areas. In 1971 UNC received a federal grant under the terms of the Comprehensive Health Manpower Training Act and formally established AHECs in Charlotte, Wilmington, Raleigh, and Asheville. The AHECs provided clinical training for medical students, interns, and residents; continuing education for primary care physicians; regional training of family nurse practitioners; and health manpower to smaller regional hospitals. The Bennett Panel had consulted closely with I. Glenn Wilson, who as associate dean of the UNC School of Medicine had promoted the community medicine program; he brought the program to the panel's attention and provided written materials. In the final report, the panel seized on the idea and proposed an ambitious program of state support.[29]

The Bennett Report disrupted the calm that had characterized the Board of Governors' consideration of East Carolina's medical school campaign. The board met on September 27, 1973, to discuss the panel's proposals. Bob Jordan began by moving, with Jake Froelich's second, that the board adopt the recommendations of the Bennett Report and that it direct Bill Friday to implement them. The ECU forces rallied in opposition behind a substitute motion offered by Reginald F. McCoy, a former ECU trustee, that the Bennett Report be referred to a reconstituted Jordan Committee that included greater East Carolina representation. In the final ballot, however, Jordan's motion carried by a vote of 22 to 8.[30]

The Bennett Report was endorsed over the vehement objections of ECU partisans. African American board members provided some support for East Carolina's position out of a belief that a second state-supported medical school would increase the number of black physicians in North Carolina. E. B. Turner, a black minister from Lumberton, criticized the Bennett Report because it said little about minorities. But most of the eight votes against adopting the report came from ECU boosters. Former ECU trustee W. W. Taylor Jr., from Raleigh, described the report as an "obvious and studied effort" to torpedo a freestanding four-year medical school at Greenville. Despite the Bennett Report, he said, the establishment of a new medical school at ECU was as certain as the sun rising in the east each morning.

The ECU officials fought on. Eight dissenting members of the Board of Governors signed a minority report claiming that North Carolina's health crisis could be eased only through the production of larger numbers of physicians. They believed that the best means to alleviate this shortage was to expand East Carolina's medical curriculum to a full four-year program.[31] The Bennett Report, Jenkins publicly suggested soon after the Board of Governors meeting, foresaw no physician crisis, but "the people" would want to "know why the Board of Governors voted as they did." Robert L. Jones, chairman of the ECU Board of Trustees, argued the case even more strenuously. Nothing could be gained by "procrastination" or by "putting off the inevitable," he wrote in a letter to the Board of Governors. The Bennett Report contained "discrepancies and irrationalities." Jones challenged its findings, claiming that panel members had inadequately investigated the ECU medical program and had exaggerated the costs of expanding it.[32]

After the board voted on September 27, Friday and his staff provided cost estimates for implementing the Bennett Report. In a meeting of the Board of Governors on November 16, 1973, the UNC president proposed the expenditure of $30 million to expand the AHEC program; although the plan would provide for 250–300 new primary care residencies in nine hospitals statewide, the bulk of the costs – some $25 million – would go toward enlarging existing community hospital facilities in order to operate the AHECs. Friday urged the board to continue the one-year program at Greenville under the direction of William Cromartie, a professor of medicine and associate dean for clinical sciences at Chapel Hill. Under Cromartie's supervision, the one-year program at ECU would work toward the goal of "full integration" with the UNC School of Medicine of admissions, curriculum, student examinations, faculty recruitment and promotion, and budget.[33]

In response to the unveiling of Friday's proposal, rancor broke out in the board. After Earl Britt moved approval, David Whichard, a Greenville newspaper editor and ECU loyalist, offered a long amendment that would establish a degree-granting program at East Carolina. After Whichard's motion was defeated, 21 to 8, another board member moved to expand ECU's program in some undefined fashion once the accreditation issue was resolved. But the compromise motion also failed, though by a narrower margin of 15 to 12. The original Britt motion then carried, and the meeting adjourned with open differences within the Board of Governors. In early December 1973 eight board members then took the extraordinary step of sending a minority report to the General Assembly. Describing the "lack of sufficient manpower" as "the major constraint to the provision of adequate health care to North Carolinians," the minority report called for the establishment of a four-year medical school at ECU.[34]

The game was far from over, however. While the Bennett Panel deliberated, the Medical Manpower Commission, appointed by the legislature in the spring of 1973, examined the physician shortage. Cochaired by Assemblyman Jay Huskins of Statesville and state senator Billy Mills, the commission released its report on December 13, 1973, three months after the Bennett Report. The Medical Manpower Commission recommended that a second year be added to the ECU medical curriculum, that the entering class be doubled, that a new building be constructed, and that ECU's operating budget be increased to bolster faculty and staff support. There was "little doubt," the commission asserted, that public opinion was "ahead of the medical profession in its willingness to underwrite whatever it costs to improve access to medical care." The commission further urged that an AHEC system be established "concurrently" with an expanded ECU medical curriculum.[35]

By encouraging the Board of Governors to appoint an independent panel of experts, Bill Friday had hoped to defuse and depoliticize the issue of medical education. Although the Bennett Report confirmed Friday's doubts about the ECU medical school and offered an alternative in the AHEC program, the report had little direct political effect. The two differing positions represented in the Bennett Report and the Medical Manpower Commission Report seemed to cancel out each other. When the legislature convened in early 1974, the stage was set for a conflict in which UNC General Administration was at a decided disadvantage, for the political coalition in favor of expanding medical education to ECU at whatever cost remained intact. In early 1974, after the legislature convened, forty-two members of the North Carolina House of Representatives signed a statement sponsored by Jay Huskins and Senator James Garrison of Stanly County calling for the immediate expansion of the ECU medical program. When the legislature convened in February 1974, newspapers were reporting that the General Assembly was about "equally divided" between opposing UNC and ECU forces; while UNC maintained an edge in the house, ECU was ahead in the senate.[36]

The East Carolina program not only enjoyed strong legislative support, it also commanded the backing of the Democratic Party. In early 1974, for example, fifty-eight of the sixty-four supporters of the ECU expansion in the house were Democrats, while thirty-four of fifty Republicans supported the UNC position. In 1972 Jim Holshouser had become the first Republican governor of North Carolina elected since 1896, making Jim Hunt, elected lieutenant governor in 1972, the leader of the Democratic Party as well as a powerful force in state government. As a longtime ECU supporter, Hunt made health care part of his political agenda; health care, he said, was a "pressing concern" that transcended the needs of the new, restructured UNC system. In 1973 he warned that if the Board of Governors did not establish a four-year medical school at Greenville, then the legislature would do so anyway. The need for more physicians in eastern North Carolina and in other rural areas of the state had given the ECU proposal "a very strong position" in the legislature; the "great force" behind it did not come from East Carolina University but from the people of the state, who saw a "pressing need" for more doctors.[37]

While most legislators wanted to satisfy an impatient political constituency, Friday sought to hold the line against ECU expansionism. After consulting with Friday and other UNC officials, state senator Ralph Scott and representative Carl Stewart, of Gastonia, circulated on February 5, 1974, a so-called compromise. Like the Huskins-Garrison proposal, it would expand the ECU program to two years "as soon as practical" but would do so under the control of the UNC Board of Governors. Friday did not endorse the proposal; Stewart and Scott left meetings with UNC officials aware that Chapel Hill opposed the attempt by some legislators to establish specific timetables for ECU expansion. While representative Herbert L. Hyde floated another compromise, still other lawmakers were attracted to the position of Edgecombe County representative Larry Eagles, who had proposed in 1973 that the matter of establishing a new medical school be submitted as a bond package that could be decided by public referendum. House speaker James Ramsey embraced the Eagles plan; house majority leader Billy Watkins of Granville County described it as "a possible solution to what had appeared a stalemated situation." But neither the UNC General Administration nor ECU officials accepted any of these proposals, and the referendum proposal was defeated in committee on February 7, 1974. Both sides were prepared to settle the matter in the legislature.[38]

At a Board of Governors meeting on February 8, Chairman Bill Dees warned that any attempt by the General Assembly to overrule the board could "turn the clock back, plunging higher education in North Carolina once again into the arena of political log rolling and regional rivalry." At stake was the "integrity and credibility" of the Board of Governors system. The UNC proposal, adopted from the Bennett Report, called for expanded medical education and an invigorated AHEC system that was "far-reaching" and "imaginative" and would provide physicians for neglected rural areas of the state. Any discussion of compromise at this point, he said, was impossible, for this was not "an area in which you talk about taking more or less of something you are trying to achieve." Dees remained assured of support and the "greater reservoir of confidence" that existed for UNC in the legislature.[39]

With Friday insulated from involvement, last-minute negotiations took place in early February 1974. After an unsuccessful attempt to reach a compromise by convening a larger group of thirty-five pro-UNC and pro-ECU legislators, four UNC representatives, four state senators, and four state representatives met for seven hours at a Greensboro motel on Sunday morning, February 10, at the invitation of Lieutenant Governor Hunt and Speaker Ramsey.[40] The results of the Greensboro conference were encouraging enough to delay hearings by the Joint Appropriations Committee, which were originally scheduled for the next day to consider the proposal to expand the ECU medical program immediately. On February 12 the twelve-member group of legislators reconvened at N.C. State for twelve hours. But the impasse persisted. ECU supporters wanted specific guarantees about when expansion would occur, while UNC supporters resisted giving those guarantees. Both sides, however, remained confident that they possessed sufficient legislative support to prevail. "Nobody was in a mood to compromise," commented Ralph Scott, and both sides remained convinced that they had "the horses to win."[41]

The ECU medical school issue dominated the 1974 legislative session. It intruded on the appropriations and budget-making process; a new medical school required a major state budgetary commitment. According to one lawmaker, the controversy "hovered over us." It was "on the mind of everyone here," said Representative Horton Rountree of Greenville. The Joint Appropriations Committee opened hearings on the proposed ECU medical school on February 19, 1974, and heard testimony from twenty-two persons. Endorsements for the new school came from such diverse groups as the Western Carolina University faculty and the Christian Action League, a statewide organization that had come into existence to lobby against adoption of a new liquor-by-the-drink law. Meanwhile, both Jim Hunt and former governor Bob Scott supported a "sane and reasonable compromise" that would establish the medical school and still preserve the restructured UNC system.[42]

Far more injurious to the UNC cause, however, was the erosion of support among Republicans, who had heretofore formed a solid pro-UNC block. Party unity was seriously strained in late February, as moderates allied with Holshouser and conservatives allied with U.S. senator Jesse Helms were in open conflict. When former state representative and Republican moderate William E. Stevens of Caldwell County entered the U.S. Senate race and prompted the withdrawal of state senator Hamilton C. Horton Jr., conservative Republicans vowed to seek revenge against Holshouser on the ECU issue. One Republican commented on February 25 that "ECU has gained a lot of votes in the last couple of days" as a result of the factional infighting; another Republican promised that he would not let the governor and his allies "get away with this."[43]

The Republican split played a major role in the events of February 26, 1974, when the Joint Appropriations Committee met to consider proposals regarding the status of the ECU medical school. In a preliminary vote, ECU partisans succeeded, by a narrow 40–39 vote, in ensuring that the medical school measure would be included as part of the main appropriations bill rather than considered separately on the floor of the legislature. Then, by a vote of 49 to 28, the committee endorsed the Scott-Stewart "compromise" measure that called for increasing the enrollment of medical school students at ECU, the addition of a second year, and an appropriation of $15 million to construct a basic sciences building. But the key provision of the Scott-Stewart measure was that the Board of Governors would determine the pace of ECU's expansion. With the twenty Republican members of the committee split evenly, ECU partisans, in a last-minute decision, threw their support behind the Scott-Stewart proposal. Their strategy succeeded. The vote was a "real setback," said UNC floor leader Jack Stevens; UNC General Administration would now reassess its strength.[44]

After the Joint Appropriations Committee vote, the UNC opposition effectively crumbled. On February 27 Stewart told reporters that the battle had ended and that "troubled waters" had stilled. With the appropriations process under the control of Scott and Stewart – they were the respective chairmen of the senate and house appropriations committees – the *Raleigh News and Observer* reported by early March that passage of the Scott-Stewart provision was "almost certain." Even Stevens admitted that the UNC forces were completely routed in the senate and severely weakened in the house. Republican leaders meanwhile announced that their party, and Governor Holshouser, would not oppose the Scott-Stewart measure. Soon after the UNC defeat, Chairman Dees and President Friday issued statements announcing their willingness to abide by the legislature's mandate. On March 8, in a meeting of the Board of Governors, UNC General Administration formally surrendered. Dees announced immediately after the meeting that the board would implement "in good faith" any legislation enacted, and he promised to cease any further lobbying efforts in the General Assembly. In the first week of April, the legislature adopted the General Appropriations Act; Section 46 of that act incorporated the Scott-Stewart proposals for expanding ECU's medical school program.[45]

The legislature's actions during the 1974 session marked a turning point in the East Carolina medical school struggle. Although the legislature fully funded the AHEC program, it also stipulated that the ECU program be expanded; ECU boosters were convinced that this meant degree-granting status. UNC officials had always assumed that the state could afford either the AHEC program or the ECU medical school, but not both. The legislature thought otherwise. In Section 46, which was officially enacted on April 8, 1974, the legislature directed the UNC Board of Governors to formulate "comprehensive plans" for the further development of medical education at Greenville by adding a second year to its one-year program.[46]

The legislative mandate, running contrary to the Bennett Report's recommendations, was not only profoundly frustrating but also difficult for UNC administrators to implement. The Liaison Committee on Medical Education had concluded that the one-year program suffered from profound problems, not the least of which was its unwillingness to continue under Chapel Hill's direction. How would the addition of a second year at Greenville help to address the accreditation issue? If the second year was added and the program expanded, what form would the future cooperative relationship between the Chapel Hill medical school and ECU officials take?

To Chancellor Leo Jenkins at least, the answer was simple: the legislature, in enacting Section 46, had provided for the "ultimate development of a degree-granting school," a medical school that, pursuing a "somewhat different mission" than that of Chapel Hill, would focus on producing primary care physicians. Jenkins believed that the task of UNC leaders was to ensure the "orderly expansion" of the ECU program to four-year status. Friday viewed the matter differently. As he told the Board of Governors on May 10, 1974, the legislature had only provided for a two-year program – without any clear intent that this meant necessarily a four-year program – but it could be accredited only if a "clear pathway" for medical students existed between ECU and Chapel Hill.[47]

In fact, an important issue remained: whether control over the two-year program would lie in Greenville or in Chapel Hill. Friday, convinced of the inevitable, agreed with Jenkins that ECU should be granted primary responsibility, and the UNC president so informed the Board of Governors on May 10. The board then unanimously authorized Friday to assign to Jenkins the task of planning a two-year program. But LCME officials again intruded. On June 14 they rejected a freestanding two-year program and, as a precondition of accreditation, insisted on joint planning controlled by Chapel Hill. Friday's immediate reaction was cautious, and he sought to assure ECU supporters that he was not seeking to impede legislative intent. The LCME's ruling, he said in a statement on the fourteenth, was not "going to deter us." The General Assembly's mandate was clear, and he intended to carry it out.[48]

Intense negotiations followed. On July 11 Friday met with Jenkins, David Whichard, and Chapel Hill medical school dean Chris Fordham. Although Friday and Jenkins promised their cooperation, Fordham, according to Friday, was "candid, not negative" in his assessment. On July 16 Friday issued a memorandum stipulating that the ECU program be administered as a "component" of the UNC School of Medicine. Fordham was granted sole responsibility to implement Section 46, and Friday instructed him to appoint a full-time director of the ECU medical school who would hold a faculty position at Chapel Hill.[49]

As was true throughout the ECU medical school fight, Bill Friday occupied a difficult position. Attempting to implement Section 46 through the July 16 memorandum, he temporarily succeeded in finding a workable compromise with Jenkins. Yet ECU-Chapel Hill tensions soon undermined good relations. The LCME's intervention and Friday's July 16 memorandum enraged ECU boosters; local board of trustees leaders Robert Jones and Robert Morgan and other trustees pressured Jenkins to resist Chapel Hill control. When William Cromartie, associate dean of the Chapel Hill medical school and recently appointed by Fordham as director of the ECU program, requested the resignation of Dean Wallace Wooles, who had led the drive for ECU independence, East Carolina boosters rallied. On July 25 Jenkins telephoned to warn Friday that the settlement was about to unravel.[50]

Although, according to Fordham, Jenkins had concurred earlier in Wooles's resignation, the ECU chancellor reversed his position in late July. The situation was so serious that Fordham, with Friday's encouragement, flew to Greenville for a conference with Jenkins on July 26, 1974. Although he realized that Fordham and Cromartie needed to have their own team to carry out the planning effort, Jenkins said, he was personally reluctant "to proceed in the face of these counter pressures." Other ECU officials, including Edwin Monroe, Vice Chancellor Robert Holt, and Wooles, joined the meeting; they displayed "continued truculence." Fordham, believing that Monroe and Wooles were unwilling to "set the past aside . . . and to help us in moving ahead," returned to

Chapel Hill convinced that he faced an impasse. He communicated these impressions at a meeting with Bill Friday, Ray Dawson, and Felix Joyner on July 29.[51]

News of the UNC-ECU stalemate eventually leaked to the press. On July 30 state representative Horton Rountree reported a "shakeup" at Greenville. He warned of a backlash among legislators who feared that Chapel Hill was attempting to sabotage the General Assembly's mandate. Rountree was unconcerned with accreditation; his concern was increasing the supply of primary care physicians in North Carolina. "I don't care what the AMA and the AAMC says," he declared. "We're trying to get doctors, and we're trying to be different from Chapel Hill."[52]

Jenkins, caught between his obligation to fulfill Friday's July 16 memorandum and intense ECU trustee pressure, remained paralyzed. On July 30, despite a third meeting with Fordham in ten days, the ECU chancellor refused to permit Wooles's ouster. Frustrated at the stalemate, Fordham composed a press release in which he maintained that UNC-ECU planning could not proceed unless Jenkins and his friends endorsed "the effort in good faith." Fordham was "deeply disturbed" by the "regional polarization" that had taken place in planning so far, and he wanted to "move ahead on a basis of cooperation" with ECU. Having made his statement, the medical school dean left Chapel Hill on vacation.[53]

Meanwhile, Leo Jenkins continued behind-the-scenes contacts with Friday. In a telephone conversation on July 30, he criticized the July 16 memorandum and accused the UNC president of acting dictatorial. After this outburst, Jenkins calmed down, and he and Friday agreed to try to appease Wooles with another appointment at the ECU medical school. Nonetheless, the East Carolina campaign begun by Jenkins nine years earlier was now moving toward a resolution that neither he nor Friday wanted. The years of conflict had embittered the small ECU medical faculty, which was convinced that the Chapel Hill medical school establishment and the UNC General Administration were determined to maintain ECU's second-class status. Similarly, the ECU trustees and supporters would accept nothing less than total independence. The situation offered alternatives no more attractive for Friday. Through his subordinates, he had opposed the establishment of an ECU medical school. Once the legislature expressed its intent in Section 46, Friday sought to accommodate East Carolina and had even been willing to cede nearly total autonomy to Greenville. But the LCME had made that impossible, and both he and Jenkins faced limited choices.[54]

Friday was well aware of the continued pressures on Jenkins. On the morning of July 31, 1974, the ECU chancellor telephoned Friday to report an uprising in his board of trustees. Chairman Robert Jones had written to the state attorney general and ECU booster Robert Morgan to complain about the LCME intervention and Friday's July 16 edict; Jenkins had tried unsuccessfully to mollify Jones. Meanwhile, ECU booster David Whichard, a member of the Board of Governors, telephoned Jenkins. In a thirty-minute conversation, he was "exceedingly abusive and profane," charging the ECU chancellor with "selling out" to the Chapel Hill authorities. Now Jenkins, expressing "a great deal of weariness" about the matter, insisted that Wooles be kept on as dean and that the July 16 memorandum be reconsidered. Urging calm to Jenkins, Friday then called Fordham to stress the need for reconciliation.[55]

The impasse ended the next day, August 1, when Jenkins issued a statement denying any obstruction on the part of ECU and pledging full cooperation and "complete good faith." ECU administrators were doing "everything possible to carry out the wishes of the General Assembly and the people of North Carolina," he told reporters in a press conference. In a spirit of teamwork, Wooles had "unselfishly" offered his resignation and accepted reassignment. There would be a "first-rate medical program" at ECU, Jenkins promised. "We in North Carolina have the need, the money, the ability and the desire to accomplish this." "Any detractors," he added, might as well "pack their bags."[56]

Despite Wooles's resignation, mutual suspicion between Greenville and Chapel Hill persisted. In early August, Fordham asserted privately that Jenkins was guilty of "frank treachery" and that "an open, man to man dialogue with him" was "idealistic and unrealistic." Ed Monroe and other ECU officials, Fordham believed, continued to sabotage efforts to establish Chapel Hill's control. In a meeting with Dawson and Friday, Fordham complained about Monroe's "continuing efforts to undermine the whole process."[57]

Bill Friday, like Leo Jenkins, faced unrelenting political pressure. In early August 1974 Lieutenant Governor Jim Hunt wrote to Friday strongly urging the establishment of an autonomous program at Greenville. The General Assembly, Hunt claimed, had intended to lay the foundations of a four-year program when it enacted Section 46; he complained about UNC foot-dragging and the exclusion of East Carolina from the planning process. Friday remained firm. Meeting with Hunt on August 5, he revealed correspondence from Carl Stewart and Ralph Scott specifying that Section 46 did not require a four-year medical school. The UNC president also reassured Hunt of progress at Greenville. Following a meeting in mid-August with Ray Dawson, UNC counsel Richard R. Robinson, and assistant attorney general Andrew Vanore, ECU trustee chairman Robert Jones became persuaded that a lawsuit would be fruitless. But other ECU supporters continued to apply pressure, insisting on the inevitability of an independent ECU medical school.[58]

As Fordham's planning efforts dragged into Autumn 1974, the prospects for compromise appeared increasingly unlikely. In September, Fordham proposed a two-year ECU program that called for medical students to split their residency by attending Chapel Hill during their second and third years and then completing the fourth-year rotation at Pitt County Memorial Hospital in Greenville. But the ECU faculty and Pitt County hospital physicians strongly favored a more traditional curriculum of academic study during the first two years at Greenville, followed by the final two years at Chapel Hill. The conflict between the Chapel Hill planning group, composed of Fordham and Cromartie, and ECU faculty and administrators further poisoned Chapel Hill–Greenville relations. The Chapel Hill medical school faculty members believed that they were serious about creating a viable program and that the ECU faculty was not. From their point of view, as Fordham remembered, the situation was "intolerable." Among the ECU faculty, as Monroe explained to Jenkins, there was a "pervasive atmosphere of dismay, increasing frustration, and extremely low morale." When University of Texas physician Robert Tuttle visited Greenville as an outside consultant, he encountered "an almost overwhelming sense of distrust and rejection" toward Chapel Hill administrators. The prospects for a "real rapprochement," he said, were "truly dismal." Chapel Hill authorities faced a "virtually impossible" task.[59]

By October 1974 ECU officials, including Jenkins, were openly defying the planning structure established by Friday in his July 16 memorandum. When a search committee for a permanent dean of the ECU organization met on October 4, 1974, Jenkins said that he favored a freestanding program and that any new dean should have a "primary institutional loyalty" to Greenville. Predicting that the legislature might soon "change the ground rules" and establish a four-year program, he urged the committee to defy the administrative hierarchy created by Fordham and Friday. Five days later, in an article appearing in the *Raleigh News and Observer*, Jenkins announced a breach with Fordham and said that East Carolina would reject Chapel Hill's dominance. In particular, he claimed, UNC curricular proposals violated the intent of Section 46.[60]

Chris Fordham faced the likely prospect of continued resistance at Greenville. It was a "virtual certainty," he reported on October 7, that the "Greenville people will not accept leadership, ideas, innovation, [and] direction from the UNC-CH campus." This was obvious "to everyone who has visited thus far," he wrote, and this "level of hostility" would become evident to any visiting LCME accrediting team. In these circumstances, Fordham expressed "serious doubts" about a joint ECU-UNC program under Chapel Hill's control. Fordham had become so frustrated with the situation that he wondered whether it was inevitable that an independent, four-year program would be established at East Carolina. As Associate Dean I. Glenn Wilson later observed, the leaders of the Chapel Hill medical school were convinced that the General Assembly "wanted to hold us hostages until they could wear the issue out."[61]

The failure of Fordham's planning effort left Friday with few choices. Having exhausted efforts to deflect the ECU medical school drive, he realized that the state's political leadership had spoken. Friday made a long presentation to the Board of Governors' Planning Committee on November 8, 1974. Recounting the history of the ECU medical school initiative, he pointed out that his original preference, with the enactment of Section 46, was to assign full control of the program to Jenkins, but the Liaison Committee on Medical Education had rejected that alternative. The failed efforts at joint UNC-ECU planning demonstrated that the LCME's required administrative model – a two-year program with administrative authority in Chapel Hill – was impossible to achieve. The implementation of Section 46, if it was to have a "meaningful impact," necessitated establishing a four-year program at East Carolina.[62]

Although the Planning Committee was strongly inclined to agree with Friday, there was grumbling nonetheless, especially among former UNC trustees. George Watts Hill Sr. described Section 46 as "crazier than hell," though he supported Friday. Nearing the end of a long career as a UNC trustee and a member of the first Board of Governors, Victor S. Bryant asserted that a four-year program at Greenville might well "cripple" the Chapel Hill medical school. If adding a second year was not possible, he asked Friday, should the ECU program be expanded at all? "If we do not move forward on the lines we suggest or something like them," Friday replied, "I don't really believe we would be carrying out the legislature's intent." In the end, the Planning Committee overwhelmingly endorsed Friday's recommendation that a four-year medical program be established at Greenville, with Bryant casting the only dissenting vote. A week later the full Board of Governors met and approved the program, which the General Assembly fully funded in the spring of 1975. By 1981 the East Carolina University School of Medicine had obtained full accreditation and was graduating its first class of physicians.[63]

Years later, Bill Friday expressed frustration about the establishment of the East Carolina medical school. The state's political leadership, through the legislature, had acted decisively, and "there was only one thing to do," and that was to make the ECU medical school "as fine a school as you can make it." By late 1974 a four-year medical school at East Carolina had become inevitable; the issue "had its own momentum" and was beyond the control even of Chancellor Jenkins. The simple fact, said Friday, was that "there was no point fighting it any longer." At some point that fall, the UNC president visited Senator Monk Harrington, a legislative leader of the ECU forces whom Friday had known for a long time. Harrington fully realized Friday's opposition and the reasons for it; although the General Assembly insisted on a new medical school anyway, Friday told Harrington, the same standards prevailing at Chapel Hill would also apply to Greenville, "if I've got anything to do with it." That meant "a lot of money, and you've got to leave it alone and let its credibility to be built on the basis of merit." Although this was not "the right decision," Friday would seek to implement it nonetheless. With this conversation, Harrington promised no further political intervention.[64]

For Friday, the decision to establish a second state-supported medical school was made for political rather than educational reasons. He acquiesced in it only with the assurance that the school would be organized under the tight supervision of the UNC structure and with the full financial support of the General Assembly. A key figure in bringing the political movement under "this tent," according to Friday, was William Laupus, appointed dean of the ECU program. After the legislature appropriated the money for the new medical school in June 1975, Laupus met at a Raleigh restaurant with Leo Jenkins, Robert Holt, and Ed Monroe on one side, and Ray Dawson, Felix Joyner, and Bill Friday on the other; Laupus remembered a "very tense" atmosphere. But he also recalled that Friday made a determined effort to ease tensions and to draw together the battle-hardened officials. Over the years the UNC-ECU reconciliation became complete, as university administrators worked through Laupus – and developed new bonds of trust and confidence – to establish the ECU program. Laupus was instrumental in melding the new medical school into the UNC structure.[65]

Almost twenty years later, most UNC officials described the ECU medical school as unnecessary and expensive, but they conceded its development into a respectable program. Most of them remained impressed by the power of the political moment: over the objections of the educational and medical establishments, the legislature established the program anyway. The "political encumbrances," observed Glenn Wilson, were "such that the information was not received." Despite persuasive data that a second state-supported medical school would not improve primary health care, the political leadership "didn't want to hear the facts." But purely political battles are rarely resolved on facts alone. Instead, concluded Wilson, it was the "signs and symbols and emotions" that persuaded public opinion and the North Carolina General Assembly.[66]

The North Carolina legislature financed a costly expansion at Chapel Hill, the most ambitious AHEC program in the nation, and a system of tuition subsidy grants to Bowman Gray and Duke for in-state students – all, in part, so that it could also establish a new medical school at Greenville. The extraordinary costs of a second state-supported medical school constituted, Felix Joyner said, money that was not "transferable to anything else." By the time the legislature had financed the enterprise, the political forces involved were so powerful that the General Assembly was "willing to spend the money for that purpose, and it wasn't something that detracted from the rest of the higher education enterprise." In the end, the organization of the East Carolina medical school, though challenging the viability of the restructured university, had little to do with higher education. Its establishment, UNC lobbyist R. D. McMillan later reflected, was a "foregone conclusion."[67]

It is a common perception among Chapel Hill medical school administrators that the outcome of this long and, for them, frustrating episode reflected a failure of Bill Friday's leadership style. Many of them believed that, had he launched what one administrator called a "public education campaign" to convert public opinion, the battle might have been won. Yet the decade-long ECU medical school controversy, if anything, demonstrated the resiliency of the restructured UNC system and Friday's ability to adapt to new circumstances.[68]

Because of a highly politicized environment, Friday's options were severely limited. Two decades' experience in academic administration convinced him that university presidents – and the institutions that they represent – should remain in but not of the political system; an all-out campaign on behalf of a cause that was perhaps already lost would be not only futile but also politically suicidal. He also felt that such an offensive against the ECU medical school would have been "wasted time and energy." In characteristic fashion, Friday preferred behind-the-scenes management rather than outright confrontation, and he wanted to head off further fissures within the Board of Governors. He tried "very hard" – and succeeded, except in the case of the Bennett Report – in preventing the issue from ever coming to a vote. Friday, realizing "what the vote was going to be in the legislature," sought to avoid an issue that would "tear up" the board. Open debate, he believed, would not "serve any purpose."[69]

As had been true for most of the 1960s and early 1970s, events thrust Friday into a position where he had to defend the status quo. While protecting traditional academic freedoms enjoyed by the university community in the Speaker Ban controversy, he defended assaults on the consolidated UNC structure in the restructuring battle. Protecting the status quo also meant restricting access of an upstart institution such as East Carolina University to a greater share of state resources; although a proponent of democratized access to higher education, Friday opposed unbridled expansion that ignored the usual procedures of educational planning and program development embodied in the post-1931 UNC system.

While defending UNC's traditional privileges, Friday exhibited a unique skill: transforming apparent defeats to his, and the university's, advantage. The Speaker Ban controversy provoked political intervention and trustee betrayal, but it ultimately resulted in a court decision that secured academic freedom at UNC. Student unrest seriously challenged the tranquility of the Chapel Hill campus, yet Friday weathered the storm as well as any major university president in the country. Restructuring occurred by means of a political process over which Friday had little control, yet the melding of sixteen diverse campuses into a new university system became one of his most important legacies. And though the legislature established a second state-supported medical school in Greenville over Friday's objections, he succeeded in incorporating it into the UNC system and in finally ending a long era of aggressive ECU expansionism.

If the East Carolina challenge tested the mettle of the sixteen-campus university system and Friday's ability to lead it, both were even more sorely tried by the difficulties of incorporating the five traditionally black institutions into the new UNC structure. Those campuses, neglected examples of Jim Crow higher education, had long been isolated from the state and national mainstreams. Despite decades of meager support and de jure segregation, the formerly all-black campuses had enjoyed considerable autonomy. Restructuring changed all of this, and, after 1972, these five campuses came under the direction of UNC General Administration. Friday faced the most formidable challenge of his career, for UNC's special purpose in North Carolina – providing dynamic and creative leadership for the state's uplift and development – was now besieged.

The Dilemmas of Power

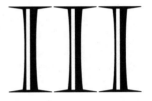

O F the issues that Bill Friday confronted as head of the post-1972 multicampus UNC system, none was more personally confounding and more threatening institutionally than the question of desegregation. In 1972 five traditionally black institutions came under the UNC umbrella, campuses that simultaneously remained proud symbols of African American autonomy and vestiges of a long history of inequitable state support. Melding these institutions into the UNC system, in the face of their desire for continued independence and greater state support, became an obvious task of restructuring.

Friday's challenge was compounded by sociological and historical complexities. African Americans had been excluded from the University of North Carolina for most of its history; not until the federal courts required race-blind admissions in the 1950s did Carolina and other UNC campuses admit black students. During the nineteenth and early twentieth centuries, black North Carolinians seeking a college education in the state could attend only all-black institutions; by the 1920s the legislature created what became the most extensive Jim Crow higher education system in the South. The traditionally black institutions (TBIs), products of neglect and underfunding, were part of a larger institutional inequality whereby the greater share of public resources flowed toward traditionally white institutions (TWIs).

Southern public higher education was integrated by court order in the 1950s and early 1960s; in North Carolina, the ruling in 1955 of the three-judge panel in *Frasier* v. *Board of Trustees of the University of North Carolina* desegregated UNC without incident. But during the next fifteen years, only a small number of black students were admitted to Carolina, State, and Woman's College. Although the state's public universities observed race-blind admissions policies in the late 1960s, formerly all-white colleges remained overwhelmingly white and formerly all-black colleges continued to be overwhelming black. In 1968, 1.7 percent of the student body at North Carolina's eleven traditionally white institutions was black; at the five traditionally black institutions, white enrollment was about 1 percent. Significant, qualitative differences in facilities, curricula, and faculties also persisted among white and black institutions.[1]

Although in the 1940s and 1950s Friday did not take a public stand on behalf of integration, in private he strongly believed in racial justice. In the late 1940s Bill and Ida had left a local Baptist church over its exclusion of blacks and had taken part in the formation of the integrated Community Church. Despite the need to persuade an often reluctant and sometimes segregationist Board of Trustees, Friday supported an end to exclusion and improved access for African Americans in North Carolina higher education. In the 1960s and until restructuring, he expanded contacts with TBI presidents, holding regular meetings with them about upgrading faculties, developing support from philanthropic foundations, and fostering student and faculty exchanges.[2]

Meanwhile, in 1959 the State Board of Higher Education began a decade-long effort to upgrade the black campuses. In 1963 and 1964 outside consultants hired by the board to evaluate TBI programs, students, administrations, and faculties found severe problems in leadership and academic standards. The BHE sponsored a conference on traditionally black institutions in March 1965; it subsequently dispatched another team of consultants to visit the black campuses. In 1966 the board began negotiating with TBI officials about raising standards and upgrading facilities and faculties, and in May 1967 it issued a report that called for higher admission standards at the campuses and expanded facilities for black students at North Carolina community colleges. Yet so strong was the opposition, particularly among TBI administrators, to these recommendations – which meant, effectively, excluding a large proportion of black students from entering TBIs – that the plan was eventually abandoned.[3]

In a report entitled *Planning for Higher Education in North Carolina*, issued in November 1968, the BHE became the state's earliest advocate of a new model for college and university desegregation. The document included a detailed study of TBIs and provided new data on enrollment, faculty, and curriculum. While rejecting closings and mergers as instruments of desegregation, *Planning for Higher Education* maintained that the state's five predominantly black public universities "should be continued in a form and with a spirit quite different from anything they have known in the past." By expanding educational opportunities to African Americans who might not otherwise attend college, the TBIs were performing a "real service," yet they were starved for state support. The BHE recommended an infusion of public money over a period of ten to fifteen years to transform these institutions "radically."[4]

Both the BHE and Bill Friday were largely frustrated in any efforts to transform the TBIs immediately, as political deadlock prevailed until UNC restructuring in 1971–72. The formerly all-black institutions remained suspicious of the white power structure; their leaders were determined to preserve traditional rights. UNC trustees expressed little interest in upgrading institutions outside of the orbit of the University of North Carolina and possessed no authority to do so. The leadership of the General Assembly, which the UNC leadership largely represented, did little to improve the TBIs, partly out of indifference and partly because of its preoccupation with issues such as campus unrest, UNC restructuring, and the politics of medical education. Not until outside pressures intruded, in the form of scrutiny by federal courts and federal bureaucrats, did the logjam end.

The passage of the Civil Rights Act of 1964 completely altered the terms of desegregation in public education, including higher education. The act's Title VI, which prohibited the use of any federal funds by agencies that discriminated, placed a powerful new tool in the hands of those seeking to eradicate the vestiges of the South's Jim Crow education. In elementary and secondary public education, the mandate of the Civil Rights Act and a new judicial activism would ultimately bring "comprehensive" desegregation – the mixing of white and black students in ratios that approximated racial demographics and the use of "forced" busing. Federal officials, armed with Title VI's threat to end federal funding, began to develop a new model of federal involvement in public education.[5]

In contrast, there was no such clear legal or policy solution for higher education. Not until 1992 did the Supreme Court issue a general ruling about ending the vestiges of segregated postsecondary education, though the lower courts in the 1950s integrated southern public universities on the basis of the *Brown* decision. Once the Civil Rights Act transformed elementary and secondary school desegregation, no clear guidelines, either from courts or federal officials, existed for higher education. The early school desegregation cases were initiated by the Department of Health, Education, and Welfare, yet there was no separate enforcement agency until President Lyndon B. Johnson, late in his administration, established by executive order the Office for Civil Rights (OCR) to deal with the thorny issues of desegregating northern public schools and public hospitals. Yet so absorbed was that office with the complex variety of cases emerging across the South that it paid virtually no attention to higher education.[6]

That situation changed in the early months of the Nixon administration. Between January 1969 and February 1970, Leon Panetta, the director of OCR, sent letters to ten states with historically segregated public higher education facilities. To satisfy the requirements of the Civil Rights Act, Panetta wrote, it was insufficient to follow a nondiscriminatory admissions policy if enrollments reflected a de jure "racial identification." Panetta applied the now-familiar tools of elementary and secondary desegregation: he asked state higher education authorities to prepare a desegregation plan within 120 days after receipt of his letter that would be subject to review and comments by federal authorities. The states' final plans were due 90 days after receiving OCR's comments.[7]

Panetta's letters were written amid considerable bureaucratic confusion. A liberal on racial policies in an administration that was seeking the white backlash vote, Panetta resigned under fire on February 17, 1970. His successor, Stanley Pottinger, who became OCR director in March 1970, avoided activism on school desegregation and pursued what a later OCR director called a "play-it-out-over-a-long-period-of-time approach." Richard M. Nixon, who had been elected in 1968 on a law-and-order plank, offered voters a respite from the civil rights activism of the Kennedy-Johnson years. Despite appointing a liberal HEW secretary, Robert Finch, in 1970, the Nixon White House began to send signals that it would not enforce the Civil Rights Act of 1964. Attorney General John Mitchell confirmed this as official policy, and Pottinger deliberately slowed OCR intervention. Whereas HEW had initiated about six hundred administrative proceedings between 1964 and March 1970, it did not take any such action from March 1970 to February 1971. And whereas federal funding for forty-four public school districts was terminated in 1968–69, only two cutoffs occurred in 1970 and none in 1971.[8]

Eloise Severinson, who headed OCR's Region III, based in Charlottesville, Virginia, was responsible for securing compliance in North Carolina. She had been investigating segregation in North Carolina public higher education as early as 1969, and Panetta's letter to state authorities was originally drafted in her office, in consultation with the Board of Higher Education. In September 1969 Severinson dispatched an OCR investigating team to North Carolina, where it visited five UNC campuses; another team arrived in February 1970. Based on the teams' findings, Severinson urged that Friday and UNC accept an "affirmative duty to adopt measures necessary to overcome the effects of past segregation." Going beyond race-blind admissions, she suggested, these policies should require that minority students be aggressively recruited, a greater number of blacks participate in intercollegiate athletics, more black faculty be added, firms doing business with the university abide by non-discriminatory hiring practices, and fraternities and other student organizations not discriminate on the basis of race.[9]

Although Panetta's letter was addressed to Governor Bob Scott, no one from his office ever officially responded.[10] Friday, replying on April 13, 1970, accepted most of Severinson's recommendations. But OCR officials continued to press UNC; Severinson, who did not respond to Friday until July 9, urged more consultations. On August 11 and 12, Friday met with officials at OCR's Region IV headquarters in Atlanta for further negotiations, and out of these meetings he agreed to a memorandum of understanding in which UNC promised to institute the measures suggested by Severinson.[11]

Ultimately, this early round of UNC-HEW negotiations proved fruitless. Friday committed UNC only to vague and probably meaningless guarantees, but they were as much as HEW had obtained from any other southern state system of higher education. Along with North Carolina, Florida, Louisiana, Mississippi, and Oklahoma did not meet Panetta's deadline. Five other states – Arkansas, Georgia, Maryland, Pennsylvania, and Virginia – had submitted plans that OCR judged unacceptable. Despite the fact that OCR considered all ten states to be in violation of the Civil Rights Act, HEW made no move to invoke Title VI and begin administrative proceedings to cut off federal funds.

In response to the apparent stalemate in federal efforts to effect school desegregation, the NAACP Legal Defense and Educational Fund, Inc. (LDF) forced the issue. It filed suit, on October 19, 1970, asking that a Washington, D.C., federal district court require HEW to enforce Title VI of the Civil Rights Act and impose judicial control upon the department. Although HEW's record in elementary and secondary school desegregation during the Nixon administration became a major component of the case, the LDF contended that the ten southern states receiving Panetta's letters in 1969–70 were in noncompliance with the Civil Rights Act. While asking that the court compel HEW to require public school desegregation or terminate federal funds, the LDF also argued that HEW was legally obliged to seek the integration of southern public universities. The case became known as *Adams* v. *Richardson*, so named because Kenneth Adams, a black parent, appeared first in the alphabetical list of plaintiffs and Elliot Richardson, the secretary of HEW, was the defendant.[12]

Washington federal judge John H. Pratt issued a landmark decision in the *Adams* case in November 1972. A native of New Hampshire, Harvard graduate, and former Marine Corps captain who had lost an arm in combat, Pratt had been appointed to the bench by Lyndon Johnson four years earlier. HEW lawyers argued that the law gave them the necessary discretion to achieve voluntary compliance on the part of the states in both segregated school districts and de facto segregated public university systems. Citing recent Supreme Court rulings in public school desegregation cases, Pratt rejected that reasoning and followed the high court's decision in *Alexander* v. *Holmes County*, which, in October 1969, directed that desegregation should occur "at once." Because efforts to achieve voluntary compliance had failed, Pratt maintained, HEW's "limited discretion" had ended; the Civil Rights Act required the department to invoke Title VI and terminate federal funding. HEW possessed "no discretion to negate the purpose and intent of the statute," wrote Pratt, "by a policy described in another context as one of 'benign neglect.'" On the contrary, it had "the duty" to pursue desegregation actively. Pratt then ordered HEW and the LDF to come to terms on the details. Relying on a plan drafted by the LDF, Pratt issued a declaratory judgment and injunction on February 16, 1973. Reiterating that the time permitted by the Civil Rights Act for the desegregation of public education had long since passed, Pratt asserted that HEW was obliged to begin enforcement proceedings. He ordered the agency to do so within 120 days of his order and to verify subsequent progress every six months.[13]

HEW appealed the *Adams* decision, arguing before the U.S. Court of Appeals for the District of Columbia, which met en banc in Washington on April 16, 1973, to hear the case. The decision of the court, which was issued on June 12, 1973, affirmed the most important elements of Pratt's order. The court of appeals agreed with Pratt that HEW, in elementary, secondary, and higher education, had "expressly adopted a general policy which is in effect an abdication of its statutory duty." Like Pratt, the appeals court rejected HEW's claim of "prosecutorial discretion" and "absolute agency discretion" in enforcing Title VI. Accordingly, the court affirmed that HEW was obliged to proceed toward elementary and secondary school desegregation "at once." But the court of appeals acknowledged that the desegregation of higher education would proceed differently. Lacking experience in dealing with colleges and universities, HEW officials possessed no clear guidelines on the subject. The "stark truth" was that HEW would have to assess carefully "the significance of a variety of new factors as it moves into an unaccustomed area," and it would need more time to define and enforce desegregation. Rather than the 120-day deadline imposed by Pratt, the court of appeals ruled that HEW should provide the ten *Adams* states 120 days to respond, after which they might negotiate changes over an additional 180-day period. Instead of Pratt's four-month framework, in other words, the court of appeals granted the *Adams* states ten months to devise an acceptable formula for desegregation.

The appeals court modified the *Adams* decision in another significant respect. Judge Pratt had adopted the school desegregation model developed in *Green* v. *New Kent County* (1968), *Alexander* v. *Holmes County* (1969), and *Swann* v. *Charlotte-Mecklenburg* (1971). The *Green* decision established that henceforth there should be neither black schools nor white schools, but "just schools"; the *Alexander* decision, that desegregation should occur "at once"; and the *Swann* case, that radical measures should be employed to ensure racial mixing. Yet the *Swann* model directly imperiled the traditionally black institutions, for the process of public school desegregation had resulted in mass closings of all-black schools and the busing of African American students to formerly all-white schools. Recognizing that TBIs might bear the brunt of desegregation, the appeals court ruled that they fulfilled a "crucial need" and would "continue to play an important role in Black higher education."[14]

While HEW was appealing Pratt's decision in the winter and spring of 1973, Stanley Pottinger left the Office for Civil Rights to become assistant attorney general for civil rights and was replaced by Peter E. Holmes. After serving as a legislative assistant to Senator Robert P. Griffin of Michigan, Holmes had joined Leon Panetta at OCR to coordinate congressional relations. As OCR director, Holmes was forced to begin preparations to comply with Pratt's order of February 16, 1973, which he later characterized as "an unfortunate development" that imposed a "very inflexible" schedule and "very burdensome" reporting requirements upon OCR. In late March 1973 Holmes telephoned Friday to inform him that OCR had "no alternative" but to enforce Pratt's order, pending appeal. Holmes requested further information about the remaining vestiges of segregation in the state's system of higher education. Reviewing data on faculty and enrollment, which revealed extensive de facto segregation, Holmes in May 1973 instructed Friday to submit a plan by June 11 – the day before the appeals court issued its opinion – to end racial duality in state-supported schools.[15]

Holmes's efforts in the spring of 1973 were, in fact, halfhearted. Though he sought out and received plans from eight of the ten *Adams* states, the OCR director offered little direction, nor possessed much conception himself, of what those plans should contain. All that Holmes provided to UNC officials was the admonition that each part of their desegregation plan should describe specific proposals to accomplish desegregation and estimate when they would be implemented. As Ray Dawson later observed, Holmes's guidance was "very vague." Aside from stating that a greater number of black students should be enrolled in traditionally white institutions, Holmes "didn't go much beyond that in laying out any specifics or guidelines as to the nature or composition of the plan."[16]

Yet the district court's decision in the *Adams* case meant that UNC's desegregation plan – entitled *A State Program to Enlarge Educational Opportunity in North Carolina* and submitted in June 1973 – was unacceptable. On November 10, 1973, Holmes rejected it on the grounds that it lacked specific numerical goals for increasing minority faculty and students at both TWIs and TBIs and established a deadline for revising the plan of April 8, 1974. In response, Friday directed John Sanders, who had become vice president for planning on November 1, and Richard Robinson to assemble a new plan. In mid-December 1973 Friday led a team of UNC officials to meet with Holmes at the OCR regional office in Atlanta. While the UNC representatives sought more specifics from the Office for Civil Rights, they also explained the practical problems and what Sanders characterized as the "infeasibility" of some of Holmes's directives.[17]

To Friday, the Atlanta meeting pointed up a basic confusion in HEW's approach. While emphasizing that UNC should be race blind in admissions and employment, Holmes also insisted, as did the court of appeals, on preserving the "racial identifiability" of TBIs. Friday left Atlanta thoroughly alarmed. Holmes had cross-examined him, he said, and there was no doubt in his mind that the federal government was seeking "substantial changes" in southern public universities. Friday was struck by how little OCR officials seemed to understand higher education. He cited Holmes's "absurd" contention that UNC could shift faculty from TBIs to TWIs, one that ignored the "contractual relationship" between campus administrations and their faculties. Nonetheless, because it could terminate federal funds, the OCR possessed a "powerful weapon" that threatened university autonomy.[18]

Over the next months, UNC staff redrafted the desegregation plan. Admitting a history of discrimination, the new plan announced systemwide desegregation, with or without federal pressure, and contested the notion that inequities persisted in public funding. On the key question of numerical goals – and how OCR would measure UNC's success at desegregation – the plan urged HEW to abandon an "exclusive reference" to numbers. Rather, UNC would pursue three objectives: a higher participation rate by all students in postsecondary education, especially a higher "going-rate" among blacks; greater quality and equality of educational opportunity for all races; and greater opportunities for "multi-racial experiences within the post-secondary education context."[19]

On February 8, 1974, the Board of Governors approved the UNC desegregation plan, but with what one reporter called "little optimism" about its acceptance, and two days later a UNC delegation led by John Sanders delivered the plan in Washington. Receiving the UNC plan was OCR's chief specialist in higher education, Burton Taylor. There had been a succession of heads of the higher education division, yet Taylor, who served as both deputy head and acting head, outlasted them all. A brother of William Taylor, one of the nation's leading civil rights lawyers, Burt Taylor was a Great Society appointee who was committed to desegregation. Because OCR had devoted most of its resources to elementary and secondary school desegregation, only a small cadre of specialists was working on higher education; Taylor, said Holmes, had the "closest handle" on the issues and enjoyed considerable authority. Meeting with Taylor, Sanders argued for the UNC plan's adoption. While OCR officials awaited the arrival of plans from the other *Adams* states, Holmes took an extended leave of absence for one of several back operations, and in this crucial period Burt Taylor and his associate Mary Lepper were, according to Sanders, "running the shop."[20]

With Taylor and Lepper both assuming an adversarial position toward UNC, the auguries seemed unfavorable for the North Carolina plan. Black activists, including the LDF, were unhappy with it. They argued that the plan went no further than Friday's agreement with OCR in August 1970 or the rejected plan of June 1973. The LDF encouraged the formation of an in-state lobbying organization composed of TBI alumni; it was established in late 1973 as the North Carolina Alumni and Friends Coalition (NCAFC). In January 1974 the NCAFC obtained a hearing from a biracial committee that was advising Sanders and in the next month offered its own desegregation plan. The coalition proposed that the membership of the Board of Governors, the State Board of Education, and the UNC General Administration be at least 25 percent black, that the membership of the boards of trustees of the TBIs be at least 60 percent black and the TWIs at least 25 percent black, that the faculty at TWIs be at least 15 percent black, that duplicative programs at adjoining TBIs and TWIs be eliminated, that North Carolina A&T State University and North Carolina Central share all of the state's extension activities, and that the law schools at Central and Chapel Hill each offer different specialties.[21]

Black members of the Board of Governors expressed a similar disquiet. One of them was Julius L. Chambers. Chambers had attended segregated schools in Mount Gilead in Montgomery County, was graduated from the all-black North Carolina College for Negroes (later North Carolina Central University) in 1958, and received an M.A. degree in history at the University of Michigan. In the autumn of 1959 he joined a handful of other African Americans at the UNC Law School. Although he was the top student in his class and editor of the *North Carolina Law Review*, the indignity of segregation deeply humiliated him; like other black students on campus, he was not permitted to mix socially with whites or to participate in student life. Black and white students at Carolina in the late 1950s, he recalled vividly, "didn't associate, and there was sort of a defined role, unwritten, that black students served in one place, or participated in one place and white students in another." Upon graduation from law school, Chambers worked with the LDF for a year before establishing a law practice in Charlotte in 1964. In 1970 he argued the landmark *Swann* case before the U.S. Supreme Court.[22]

Chambers, as a distinguished North Carolina Central alumnus, had been elected to the interim Planning Committee and then to the Board of Governors in 1972. Because of a busy schedule and frequent absences, according to one account, he had only a "limited" effect at board meetings. But HEW and OCR intervention in university affairs kindled his interest, and at several points he joined the discussion. Chambers was elected president of the LDF in 1974, and, throughout his tenure on the UNC Board of Governors, he maintained contacts with the LDF field representative, Jean Fairfax. Impatient with what he perceived as university foot-dragging, and as a veteran of the LDF struggle to achieve elementary and secondary desegregation, he sought to apply that model to higher education. By his own account, Chambers was a person who had lived "with all deliberate speed for fifteen or twenty years" and believed that public education could be desegregated at a much faster pace "once the courts said it had to be done."[23]

When the UNC desegregation plan was presented to the Board of Governors on February 8, 1974, Chambers voiced strong objections. He saw little difference between that plan and the rejected plan submitted in June 1973. Explaining that he was concerned about the impact of the UNC plan, which he said would drain black faculty from TBIs but do little to attract qualified white faculty to them, he argued that its guarantees were too weak. "I am a victim of discrimination myself," Chambers added, noting that he had attended both North Carolina College for Negroes and the law school in Chapel Hill, and he made his "own comparisons." The UNC plan, he warned, represented a marked failure on the part of the state to enhance the TBIs. "Without more concern by the Board for the black institutions," he observed later, "the black institutions would end up basically as unequal educational programs."[24]

The Office for Civil Rights responded to the North Carolina plan in a memorandum presented to Friday, UNC administrators, and North Carolina community college system president Ben Fountain at a meeting in Washington on April 15, 1974. The memorandum, which bore Taylor's imprint, criticized the North Carolina plan for insufficient commitment to "definite, reviewable intermediate steps or milestones by which progress in developing the final action may be measured." Such "milestones" would provide measures of "whether or not the plan is satisfactorily fostering state-wide desegregation." Where it was impossible for the plan to be specific, it should include "a commitment to meet the requirement in question, a description of the process by which it will be met, and a time schedule for meeting the schedule within the life of the plan." OCR also wanted a firm commitment that North Carolina would pay the cost of desegregation. If the legislature was unwilling to commit those resources, then UNC should take "alternative action" to achieve desegregation. Moreover, OCR wanted a reporting procedure that provided regular data, and it insisted that UNC supply a semiannual flow of information by which its movement toward "milestones" could be measured.[25]

Nor was that all. The federal officials, believing that existing measures of inequity were inadequate, desired a more comprehensive study of existing academic programs, facilities, and admissions standards at the traditionally black institutions. As part of the long-range planning process, this study would identify deficiencies at the TBIs and how the state proposed to remedy them. OCR further sought assurances that future resources and programs would flow equally to TWIs and TBIs, and it urged that "desegregation impact determinations" – that is, an assessment of the impact of all policy decisions on desegregation – be applied to any new academic programs, facilities, and admission policies contemplated by the UNC system. The Office for Civil Rights also insisted that TBIs and TWIs receive the same level of state funding by 1976.

What would eventually become the most controversial component of the OCR program – the identification and elimination of duplicating curricula that fostered segregation at TWIs and TBIs – was also covered in the OCR comments of April 1974. The state plan submitted in February had raised this issue, but only in the context of the uncompleted long-range plan's efforts to identify systemwide duplication. North Carolina's five TBIs had been established during segregation, as the *North Carolina State Plan* expressed it, when black North Carolinians "had no other access to such opportunities under the legally segregated system of education." As a result, the TBIs were created "expressly to duplicate programs already in existence in the State." The *Plan* suggested that long-range planning would identify and eliminate "instances of unnecessary and costly duplication of programs within the University" and would determine whether program duplication was "racially motivated or sustained."[26]

The OCR seized upon the *Plan's* discussion of unnecessary program duplication but pressed for firmer guarantees. It urged that the plan be revised to ensure that UNC could not add new curricula that would "perpetuate competition based upon duplication of offerings among predominantly black and white institutions." The OCR made a distinction between "basic" offerings, mostly undergraduate courses duplicated at TWIs, and "specialized" courses that tended to appear at the graduate level. The office suggested that the program duplication might not just involve, as indicated in the *Plan*, A&T, UNCG, Elizabeth City State University, and College of the Albemarle, but also nearby institutions such as UNC–Chapel Hill and North Carolina Central. As long as North Carolina responded "promptly, effectively, and in good faith" in carrying out the new commitments sought in the memorandum, the implementation of the revised plan would be "deemed acceptable."[27]

OCR's criticisms of the *Plan* struck at the heart of the differences about the meaning of desegregation. Bill Friday saw it as incremental, unknown, and impossible to define; he was disturbed by a basic contradiction in OCR's simultaneous insistence on desegregation and the maintenance of the historically black character of the TBIs. Although willing to acknowledge most of Taylor's criticisms and incorporate them into the revised plan, Friday refused, until the completion of a more thorough study of the matter, to supply assurances that state resources could be equalized between TBIs and TWIs by 1976. OCR representatives, and especially staffers such as Burt Taylor, regarded Friday's response as evasive and as a smokescreen for resistance to meaningful desegregation. They preferred a model that would be as reliable as pupil assignment and compulsory busing had been in public school desegregation. As it had in negotiations with elementary and secondary school districts in the South, OCR wanted clear guarantees, measurable goals, and timetables.

UNC participants recognized another dimension to the OCR negotiations. At the staff level, which was occupied by Great Society appointees, OCR tended to identify with the LDF agenda, but at the higher levels of the agency, including the office of Director Holmes, and especially at the HEW secretary level there was markedly less enthusiasm for root-and-branch desegregation. Although the severity of Taylor's critique led some UNC officials such as John Sanders to conclude that the university "had better prepare for litigation at an early stage," further negotiations with OCR officials made it clear that Holmes and OCR moderates held the upper hand. On May 6, 1974, Friday agreed to "some modification" of the February 8 plan that addressed Taylor's critique, including greater specificity about implementation and timing; although these changes, he said, contained "some enlargement" of commitments, they did not involve "basic changes" in the plan or any new commitments. Accordingly, a modified UNC proposal, known as *The Revised North Carolina State Plan for the Further Elimination of Racial Duality in the Public Post-Secondary Education Systems*, was sent to OCR in early June 1974.[28]

Friday was confident of the eventual acceptance of this plan by Peter Holmes, who, he realized, had pursued the case under duress. Friday also knew that there was little White House enthusiasm for the controversy. Both Holmes and senior university officials remembered the OCR-UNC relationship as far from adversarial. Ray Dawson described Holmes as a "very reasonable person" and their communications as a "very amicable exchange." Holmes, he believed, was "a person with whom we felt we could work." The feelings were mutual. The UNC team sought to "work cooperatively, and negotiate cooperatively with the department in all respects," Holmes said. Twenty years after the event, Holmes had "nothing but fond memories" of Friday. The UNC president interpreted HEW's effort to comply with *Adams* more candidly. "There really was not a high degree of commitment there," he would later say. Rather, HEW policy was "more a perfunctory chore to be carried out," and the department was "willing to let you define the rudimentary kind of things that you were willing to do."[29]

On June 14 Holmes telephoned Governor Holshouser, requesting a general statement summarizing the commitments that the state was offering. In a letter four days later, Friday responded. The *Revised North Carolina State Plan* of June 1974 pledged UNC to provide a regular, semiannual accounting of progress, to supply a "racial impact" study of any new programs, to avoid any policies that would impede desegregation, to introduce new, attractive programs to TBIs while eliminating any unnecessary duplication between "proximate pairs" of TBIs and TWIs, and to inaugurate a new faculty applicant listing service in order to publicize job openings and to encourage the application of minority candidates. Friday emphasized that the revised plan committed the university to a study that would identify disparities between TBIs and TWIs and serve as the basis for future policies. He also stressed that resources could not be equalized by 1976 but assured Holmes that equalization would be possible by 1980.[30]

North Carolina's revised plan, and the summary provided by Friday, satisfied Peter Holmes and other OCR officials. Two other states, Louisiana and Mississippi, refused to submit plans, and Holmes referred them to the Department of Justice for litigation. The seven remaining states – Arkansas, Florida, Georgia, Maryland, Oklahoma, Pennsylvania, and Virginia – filed acceptable plans in the summer of 1974. Holmes telegraphed his acceptance of the North Carolina plan on June 21, noting that the details of monitoring would assume a specific form only as the means of measurement became more refined. Nevertheless, he warned that HEW would keep a close eye on future developments. "It is our intention," Holmes said, "to closely monitor the implementation of the plan, particularly in the first two years of its life."

Should there be a "failure to achieve results," it might be necessary to modify the plan "at the time any such failure becomes apparent."[31]

THE suspicions of OCR hard-liners and LDF activists about UNC's intentions were confirmed in late 1974 with UNC's decision to locate a new state-supported school of veterinary medicine (SVM) at N.C. State. Despite the reluctance of UNC officials to support a vet school, which they believed was unnecessary and expensive, powerful political interests, including the state's agribusiness forces and former governor Bob Scott, wanted one. Since 1949, the state had paid tuition subsidies for North Carolina students educated at out-of-state SVMs. By the late 1960s, however, demand had outstripped the supply of new veterinarians, and in 1970 the Board of Higher Education commissioned a consultant, Calvin W. Schwabe of the University of California at Davis, to study the feasibility of organizing a vet school in the state. Subsequently, the Schwabe Report recommended that an SVM be situated at the Research Triangle Park and jointly sponsored by N.C. State and Carolina.

Following restructuring of the UNC system, political pressure for the vet school continued, and the General Assembly in 1974 instructed the Board of Governors to consider the issue and to report to the legislature in 1975. The board then appointed a committee, chaired by John Sanders, which met during the summer and autumn of 1974. The SVM issue took on a new meaning in August and September 1974, when Sanders and his committee met with the dean of the School of Agriculture at North Carolina A&T State University in Greensboro. According to the A&T dean, the new vet school, or at least a major component of it, should be located at A&T.[32]

Earlier that year, the Board of Governors had hired two consultants, Clarence R. Cole and LaVerne D. Knezek, both of Ohio State University's SVM, to recommend a site for the proposed school. Cole's report, presented to UNC administrators on October 29, 1974, concluded that A&T had only recently expressed interest; that its site was too small (only twenty-five acres); that its library facilities were inadequate; that it lacked supporting schools of medicine, dentistry, and pharmacology; and that few North Carolina veterinarians endorsed a Greensboro location. Cole unequivocally recommended locating the new veterinary school at N.C. State. Using a numerical scale, he awarded N.C. State a score of 1,051, A&T a score of 499.[33]

The Cole Report was presented to the board at its meeting of November 15, 1974. Statements by various groups and individuals followed. Lewis Dowdy, chancellor of A&T, maintained that the omission of a racial impact study flawed the decision-making process. In determining the location of the new vet school, he said, the board had forsaken a "golden opportunity to make a giant step forward toward greater desegregation of higher education." John Caldwell, State's chancellor, asserted that although the university was properly committed to desegregating, "absolutely nothing" in the *Revised North Carolina State Plan* required that issue to become the "dominating consideration" in every UNC decision.[34]

After accepting the revised plan, Holmes had assigned monitoring responsibility to OCR's Atlanta regional office, then headed by William Thomas. Sometime in the autumn of 1974, Thomas learned through LDF contacts of the Board of Governors' veterinary school deliberations. Fearing that the Board of Governors would reach a final decision, he traveled unannounced to Chapel Hill to appear at the board meeting of November 15. Obtaining the floor, Thomas presented his case. The vet school issue, he explained, had become a major test of the credibility of North Carolina's revised plan. Although UNC had promised not to institute any new programs that would impede the progress of desegregation, the Board of Governors was now considering awarding a new vet school to a traditionally white institution, even though locating it at a traditionally black institution would attract white students and enhance state support. OCR and HEW, Thomas said, were not insisting that the location of the new vet school at Raleigh would necessarily impede the elimination of racial duality. Rather, the chief problem was the lack of any effort on the part of UNC to determine the racial impact of this major new program.

University officials and board members were taken aback. Lacking any warning of Thomas's arrival, they resented his intrusion into university affairs. UNC officials considered the vet school issue as predating the revised plan's framework for new programs, and they wondered why OCR had suddenly injected itself into this issue. "Can we ever make a judgment without first clearing it with HEW?" asked Victor Bryant. Why, Friday asked Thomas, had the OCR expressed interest in the vet school but no interest in the proposed medical school at East Carolina? Why should a new medical school not also be located at a TBI? The question struck at a basic contradiction in OCR's program, for it was unwilling to question the location of a fantastically expensive medical school at a TWI that presumably also might have been located at a TBI. Thomas's response was evasive. Although he had not fully considered the comparison, the new medical school in Greenville had in fact been established as a result of an alliance between state black leaders and ECU boosters. The ECU program was "in place," Thomas said, a "done deal." When Friday reminded him that the ECU facility was then still only a one-year program while a Department of Veterinary Science had existed at N.C. State for some time, Thomas backed off.

According to Ray Dawson, OCR officials avoided the comparison – and any involvement in the ECU medical school fight – because they realized that they "would get the hell beat out of them." OCR officials "weren't about to lie down in front of a locomotive" that had "left the station long ago." Thomas's intervention confirmed the suspicions of UNC administrators such as Dawson, who believed that OCR had seized on the vet school issue to "see if they could derail that." The "hook" that OCR had fastened on was, Dawson explained, the Board of Governors' commitment in the revised plan to conduct a racial impact study prior to the development of any new program. After some discussion, the Board of Governors agreed that John Sanders should perform such a study and present his findings at its meeting on December 18, 1974.[35]

Although the results of Sanders's racial impact study were a foregone conclusion, Thomas continued to lobby hard. In late November, he wrote to Friday insisting that he see the study before its presentation to the board; Thomas also threatened to make an appearance at that meeting. Friday responded by admitting that there might be instances when "informal consultation" with OCR would be "appropriate and helpful," but he refused to permit Thomas any right of prior approval. Thomas accepted this only grudgingly, complaining that the circumstances of the location of the new vet school were "considered by this office to be unusual." Resigning himself to the inevitable, he declared that, in the future, such racial impact studies should be built into the process and conducted well before the board had reached a decision.[36]

The Board of Governors, to no one's surprise, approved the location of the new veterinary school at N.C. State at its December 18 meeting. Sanders's racial impact study predicted that a vet school located at State would enroll 18 percent blacks and 6 percent other minorities, while one at A&T would enroll 20 percent whites. State's ability to establish an SVM, said Sanders, was clearly superior to A&T's, while the racial impact was "about the same." Yet the issue was by no means closed. In a statement to the board, the North Carolina Alumni and Friends Coalition urged that the school be located at A&T. Julius Chambers then offered a last-minute motion to delay a decision until a role could be created for A&T. When the board voted to establish an unspecified "related activity" at A&T, Chambers called the concession a "crumb," the "same kind of discrimination that has taken place historically." The board's decision was "symptomatic" of a pattern of weak state support for TBIs, he said.[37]

Few people were completely satisfied with the decision. Deeply offended, A&T administrators and alumni agreed with Chambers. Working with A&T officials were the *Adams* plaintiffs (members of the NAACP Legal Defense and Educational Fund), who believed that the affair provided concrete evidence of UNC's unwillingness to seek meaningful desegregation. UNC officials had had an opportunity to locate a major program at a TBI, one that would attract a significant number of white students and provide solid assurance of the state's willingness to upgrade a long-neglected institution. That UNC refused to locate the vet school at A&T confirmed their belief that, at root, the allocation of resources in favor of TWIs and to the disadvantage of TBIs had changed but little.

Friday and his UNC team saw the matter differently. The UNC officials admitted that initially the decision to establish a vet school had been a political decision generated from outside the UNC system – mostly at the insistence of Bob Scott and the state's agricultural interests – and that locating a vet school at N.C. State, which was tightly connected to these interests, was a political necessity. To a lesser degree than was true in the ECU medical school controversy, the vet school case was an example of powerful political interest groups bringing irresistible force to bear on the university. Facing these realities, as Felix Joyner observed, board members may have been "unenthusiastic" about a new vet school, but they had already "pretty successfully" removed themselves from it. Yet, to Friday and his advisers, the OCR's last-minute intervention further muddied the waters; A&T administrators and alumni became interested only after urging by OCR and activist groups.[38]

The wide divergence of perspectives that separated UNC administrators and HEW officials was based on clashing conceptions of the *Revised North Carolina State Plan*. HEW authorities believed that the plan should serve as both a road map to the desegregation of a de jure segregated system and a statement of the university's contractual obligations. They were convinced that the revised plan could be enforced only through constant supervision and pressure, and that its success hinged on either good faith or outright coercion. Although the HEW bureaucracy was split between the proponents of a zealous prosecution and those in favor of compromise and voluntary compliance, most officials subscribed to the need for supervision of and intervention in university affairs. Friday vigorously resisted the notion that the revised plan was the only path to desegregation. He continued to believe that restructuring itself had opened a new chapter in the state's educational history and had begun an irreversible process of equalization of state resources. Most of his career as a university president had been spent defending UNC against the intrusion of state political forces. With the intervention of OCR, Friday had employed his characteristic skill in mediation and compromise to compose an acceptable plan, but he would continue to resist interference by outside forces in the autonomous university.

These differences were further amplified in March 1975, when, in a letter to Friday, William Thomas renewed his petition. Asking the Board of Governors to suspend its decision, the letter had an ominous tone. The vet school case, Thomas said, raised "serious questions" about the *Revised North Carolina State Plan* and "the manner in which it is being implemented." He cited the fact that a new program had been established with scarcely any attention to its racial impact; Sanders's efforts in December 1974 only raised "fundamental differences" between OCR and UNC. The decision to locate the vet school at Raleigh rather than Greensboro relied on conditions that were themselves the product of past discrimination – the low quality of A&T's facilities – and the Cole Report was therefore "tainted." The report had criticized A&T for having little interest in establishing a vet school during the early 1970s, yet these were years, Thomas pointed out, before UNC restructuring. In sum, the very process that the university had used to make this decision was flawed, and the way in which it was made raised basic questions about "future decisions of this nature." Thomas proposed a more serious racial impact study, presumably conducted with OCR participation; if that study also resulted in a decision favorable to N.C. State, UNC should locate a program of "similar stature and attractiveness" at A&T. The head of OCR's Atlanta office demanded a response from UNC within thirty days.[39]

Thomas's formal complaint escalated OCR's intervention considerably, and Friday's response, sent in late April, restated the UNC position. Thomas had no doubt been steeled by a significant tilt within OCR's Washington headquarters toward greater pressure and arm twisting. In the spring of 1975, OCR director Holmes took a leave of absence for back surgery and remained away from his office for most of the summer. Replacing him was the deputy director, Martin Gerry, who became acting director in Holmes's absence. Gerry, a lawyer in Richard M. Nixon's Wall Street firm, was an early recruit of the Nixon administration. He had had long experience in OCR, having served as Leon Panetta's executive assistant in 1969; when Panetta was fired, Gerry became the executive assistant for HEW secretaries Elliot Richardson and Caspar W. Weinberger. In 1974 he was appointed OCR's deputy director. In his work with Panetta, Gerry recalled that he had been "somewhat involved" in higher education desegregation, but most of his projects then and later at HEW had to do with discrimination against Hispanics, the elimination of language barriers in public schools, and the famous Boston school desegregation case.[40]

Later described by an OCR official as "sort of a Ripon Society" and a "very liberal" Republican, Gerry advocated a stronger federal role in higher education desegregation. When he became acting director and first learned of the vet school case, he considered it a flagrant violation of the spirit and intent of the *Revised North Carolina State Plan*. After a time, however, he "didn't particularly like the approach we took to the higher education desegregation." Gerry believed that "significantly greater pressure" was necessary to obtain substantive results, even if it meant closing institutions or instituting mandatory student assignments. He became convinced that the University of North Carolina was not "doing very much." To Gerry, locating an attractive and high-profile new program such as a veterinary school at a TBI was an "obvious example" of how to avert mandatory student assignments.[41]

In the spring and summer of 1975, control over the vet school case shifted from Thomas and the Atlanta OCR regional office to Gerry and OCR headquarters in Washington. Washington officials sensed that the matter had evolved into such a high-level controversy that regional bureaucrats were in over their heads. R. Claire Guthrie, who joined OCR as a fresh law school graduate in 1974, recalled that Thomas's handling of the issue was inept; most OCR people perceived it "as being not terribly well-grounded in the realities of life." In contrast to Virginia, where OCR regional staff continued to monitor desegregation, Washington OCR officials "lost confidence" in Atlanta's ability to deal with North Carolina.[42]

UNC officials had little inkling that Gerry's attitudes were any different from those of Holmes. When Gerry became acting director, John Sanders wrote to Friday hopefully. Sanders had sent Gerry a note of congratulation, adding that one from Friday "might help," though for public purposes Gerry might find it "more convenient if we yelled in protest." Yet by the summer of 1975, Friday and UNC officials discovered that Gerry's attitude toward desegregation differed starkly from Holmes's rather passive approach. Gerry was interested in drawing a line in the sand; if necessary, he wanted to take North Carolina to court. "I wanted either to negotiate out a plan that we thought was good and then go defend it," he remembered, or "if we didn't think we could get that, cite them and have a hearing." If OCR could win an administrative hearing, it would have a "much stronger legal hand."[43]

In fact, Gerry wanted a test case. He believed, as he later put it, that it was time to "fish or cut bait." The issue of desegregation might well become a "festering wound," and, with the presidential election of 1976 looming, endless rounds of negotiations could lead to a high political price. Accordingly, he sent out letters to eight states, criticizing the implementation of the *Adams* plans and laying the basis for a noncompliance declaration and administrative hearings. Gerry focused particularly on Maryland and North Carolina. He later said that he had decided Maryland was "the place to start." Like North Carolina, Maryland had submitted a desegregation plan that Holmes accepted in late June 1974. On August 7, 1975, the OCR regional director in Philadelphia, Dewey Dodds, sent that state a seven-page letter later described by a special assistant to the HEW secretary as "totally inappropriate." When the governor of Maryland, Marvin Mandel, rejected Dodds's letter, subsequent negotiations seemed to lead out of the impasse. Then, on December 15, 1975, another letter arrived, this time from Gerry, who had by now become permanent OCR director; Gerry also called a news conference in which he denounced the "consistent failure" of Maryland's higher education system to comply with its own desegregation plan. Faced with Title VI administrative proceedings, Maryland sued in federal district court. Reaching a decision in March 1976, the court held that HEW had performed in an "arbitrary" way and refused to seek compliance either through good faith or voluntary means. OCR policy had been implemented "arbitrarily and whimsically" because HEW had provided excessively vague guidance about how to effect desegregation. The court enjoined HEW from holding administrative hearings.[44]

In the spring and summer of 1975, the resolution of the *Mandel* case lay in the future, but Gerry's more zealous approach to enforcement in North Carolina must be seen in the context of the Maryland case. As in Maryland, Gerry sought to force the issue in North Carolina. In a fifty-one-page letter sent on July 31, Gerry charged that UNC had delayed in reporting data on enrollments and hiring. (Before the 1970s, there had been no reliable statistical measure of the racial composition of the student body – nor did federal officials permit UNC officials to ask for information by race; inaugurating a new system was further delayed by restructuring.) Gerry also criticized the university's delay in completing its long-range plan and its promised TBI study, and he contended that the location of the vet school at N.C. State rendered UNC in noncompliance with Title VI of the Civil Rights Act. Though UNC had implemented "some of the less significant commitments made in the plan," it had failed "to fulfill the most critical commitments contained in the document." He therefore would seek administrative proceedings to terminate federal funds. As an HEW official later admitted, North Carolina, because its problems were perceived as "more serious" than other states, had been singled out for high-pressure tactics.[45]

The primary impact of Gerry's letter was to stiffen UNC resolve. Some members of the Board of Governors favored litigation. Tom White, the only open opponent of desegregation on the board, described Gerry's letter as an "interesting study in intellectual dishonesty, callousness, calumny and caprice." He believed that it was a "waste of time and effort" dealing with the OCR, and he preferred litigation. Even Friday's old adversary U.S. senator Jesse Helms, in a letter to the UNC president, had earlier endorsed his position and promised to lend support in freeing the state "from the harassment of outside intervention by HEW."[46]

The reactions of White and Helms were predictable. Both had consistently opposed desegregation, and Friday disagreed with their line of reasoning. Though desiring university desegregation, he opposed the clumsy and, he believed, counterproductive OCR threats. Those threats had succeeded, in fact, in alienating opinion beyond rock-ribbed segregationists, and there was sentiment among board members otherwise sympathetic to racial equity to reject conciliation in favor of open conflict with the federal government. Philip Carson, an Asheville board member since 1973, objected to Gerry's July 31 letter on the grounds that it was "not only unfair and unreasonable but untenable." The most disturbing implication of Gerry's threat, he wrote to Friday, was that HEW assumed that UNC's decisions were "racially motivated" and that it was "incapable of acting in a non-discriminatory manner without the OCR overlooking and approving every detail of the operation of the University." Carson believed that it was time to take a firm stand with OCR and, if necessary, to litigate.[47]

Before 1975, Friday had delegated day-to-day management of the conflict with OCR to John Sanders and, by 1975, to Ray Dawson, Felix Joyner, and Cleon Thompson. After receiving Gerry's letter of July 31, Friday joined the issue forcefully. At a news conference on August 6, he declared that the Board of Governors, in locating the vet school at N.C. State, had made the "right decision." "I support that decision," he added. He also criticized OCR for acting before it had received UNC's compliance report, sent on July 31, which he believed would have demonstrated genuine progress. Had Gerry waited, "at least two-thirds" of his criticisms would have been answered. At a Board of Governors meeting on August 19, Friday elaborated. The basic issue, he said, was simple: would HEW permit the board "to make a judgment as to the location of a major educational program on the basis of the Board's evaluation of *all* the relevant considerations"? Or should the board make such a decision based only on race? The university, Friday argued, had "no choice" but to reject OCR's insistence on locating the program at A&T or on establishing a program there of "similar stature."[48]

Responding to more than forty questions raised in Gerry's letter, Friday asserted that UNC was in "substantial compliance" with the *Revised North Carolina State Plan*; all sixteen campuses had exceeded the plan's goals for integration. He admitted that the long-range plan had been delayed, but it was "not part of a scheme to avoid compliance." The crux of the dispute with OCR lay in the vet school decision. He would continue "to stand for the right and authority" of the board to reach decisions "free of imposed restrictions."

Submitting to OCR's demands on the vet school would not only limit that autonomy, but it would also "amount to a duplication dictated by race" – an objective contrary to the spirit of genuine desegregation. The vet school decision did not necessarily mean that traditionally black institutions would always suffer from a competitive disadvantage; new programs, Friday promised, would be forthcoming based on "compelling needs and opportunities." The university would reject any policies that had "no clear relationship to the need for the program or the resources of the institution to sustain it."[49]

Although Friday had pleaded his case on the grounds of university autonomy, not all quarters were convinced. Three days after his statement to the Board of Governors, the *Charlotte Observer* commented that the issue was not so simple; the controversy confirmed the adage that "Them that has, gets." The UNC system, in deciding not to close A&T, was obligated to make it a "stronger, fully integrated institution." The location of the vet school was "based not upon educational considerations but upon power considerations." As had been true for East Carolina University, N.C. State would receive an expensive new program "because it has power and influence – even though such a school is not needed in North Carolina."[50]

In late August 1975 OCR increased its pressure. On the twenty-second, Burton Taylor complained to a Raleigh reporter that UNC officials had made it "very clear what they're going to do and what they're not going to do." The vet school decision, he declared, was only one example of a larger neglect. TBIs faced the prospect of "being second," and for the immediate future, they would remain inferior; the "net effect" of locating the vet school at N.C. State was to "perpetuate the strength of the predominantly white institutions." OCR and UNC had reached an impasse.[51]

In response, Friday, in typical fashion, sought conciliation and behind-the-scenes influence. As he often did with hostile editorials, he wrote directly to the *Charlotte Observer*'s editor, C. A. "Pete" McKnight, explaining that the UNC vet school decision was based on educational rather than political factors. When Burt Taylor went public with his criticisms, Friday used his contacts with F. David Mathews, recently appointed HEW secretary, whom he had known when Mathews was president of the University of Alabama. Sending Mathews a copy of Taylor's comments, Friday asserted that it was "a wiser policy to refrain from arguing one's case in the newspapers." Meanwhile, he telephoned Roy McKinney, head of OCR's higher education division, who agreed to disavow Taylor's comments as "not in any way the official views" of OCR. McKinney further promised that OCR officials would be prohibited from making statements to the press and that only authorized representatives would, because of the "sensitive nature" of the negotiations, grant media interviews.[52]

For a good part of his tenure as secretary, Mathews was unable to exert much control over the Office for Civil Rights, which occupied a unique position in the federal bureaucracy. Martin Gerry had strong connections with the Ford White House and reported to its Domestic Policy Council, then under the influence of Vice President Nelson Rockefeller's staff; Rockefeller's staff was liberal on civil rights policy and exerted influence over OCR affairs in the Ford administration. Gerry's crackdown on Maryland and North Carolina had the administration's encouragement, and the OCR acting director could thus bypass Mathews, whom Gerry later described as a "figurehead secretary." Few major decisions on civil rights policy, recalled one OCR staffer, were not made directly out of the White House. Gerry, sharing a liberal Republican tradition with Rockefeller and his staff, received high-level support.[53]

Nonetheless, Mathews attempted to exert more direct control in the late summer of 1975. His involvement became possible with the return of Peter Holmes from his convalescence in September 1975. Although Holmes agreed with the OCR position on the vet school case, he was not much interested in the particulars of the case and was willing to seek conciliation with UNC. Holmes and Gerry differed significantly, according to OCR staff attorney R. Claire Guthrie. Whereas Holmes was "more political and less substantive," she said, Gerry seemed "more substantive and less political." Gerry "tried harder to put forth an image of really caring about the mission of the agency . . . [by being] more committed." Holmes was less tied to that mission and more prepared for compromise. Gerry was concerned with his image with the LDF and the advocacy groups; as Guthrie recalled, "I don't think Peter [Holmes] cared." The vet school question was a "symbolic" issue, Holmes later acknowledged, but he believed that the matter "was not our decision to make." And so long as that decision did not involve overt racial motivations, he said, "I didn't think we could differ with it, as a matter of law and policy."[54]

Holmes and Mathews converged in their views, and during late August and September 1975, in three separate telephone conversations, Friday made UNC's case to the HEW secretary. On September 23, 1975, Roy McKinney called Friday and invited him to visit Washington in early October for a peace conference with Holmes to settle the vet school case. The meeting with Holmes brought a quick resolution. Friday arrived in Holmes's office on October 2 with a team of UNC staff members. Guthrie, who was present, remembered that Friday dominated the negotiations. The meeting took place in a large conference room with long tables; the setup was "terrible," she noted, because of the uncertainty of "who gets arranged and how you decide what the head of the table is." Walking into the room, Friday scrutinized the layout and placed himself at the head of the table, with his staff situated so that the UNC end of the table became the "working part of the room." Psychologically, Friday took command. This became "his meeting," Guthrie said, "in large part because of the way he'd gotten us to sit down." She was "just astounded" at his performance.[55]

When the meeting ended, Friday announced that the OCR-UNC conflict was "now history." A "new understanding" had been reached with the Office for Civil Rights, he said, and the issue was "behind us." Reiterating his earlier commitment to study the traditionally black institutions, Friday promised to accelerate efforts in long-range planning. Peter Holmes left the meeting satisfied that an acceptable compromise had been reached. The essential issue, he told reporters, was not where the vet school would be located but how the state had reached the decision and whether the TBIs could compete for new programs. Despite UNC's decision in this instance, future resources might flow toward the TBIs. "It's not a question of where the school would be specifically located, in and of itself," he explained, "but the ability of the predominantly black institutions to compete with other campuses in attracting new programs, students and faculty." Regardless of the written statements of William Thomas and Martin Gerry to the contrary, Holmes asserted that OCR had never insisted that the "vet school should be located at one campus or another."[56]

The Friday-Holmes meeting seemed to vindicate the UNC president's style of conciliation and face-to-face contact. The resolution of the controversy, he wrote to Holmes, meant that the university and OCR enjoyed "an improved mutual appreciation of the many problems that we must resolve" in order to accomplish desegregation. Holmes had accepted his explanations "of the several exigencies which have precluded more rapid progress on some of the commitments contained in the North Carolina State Plan." Friday assured Holmes of "our determination to move forward, as promptly as possible, to complete those essential tasks on which work remains to be done"; the future of TBIs continued to be bright and future planning, including the long-range plan and the promised TBI study, would result in significant progress.[57]

The outcome of the vet school case in October 1975 became, for others, the last straw. At A&T there was acute disappointment. Chancellor Lewis Dowdy complained to Friday that HEW had "missed a golden opportunity to achieve its own announced objective of assuring wider opportunities and integration for the predominately black colleges and universities." To those who had looked to HEW for leadership, this was "distressing" news indeed. A&T leaders wanted "to destroy, once and for all, the myth that a historically black institution could not establish and maintain a highly qualified professional program." The day after the Board of Governors authorized locating the vet school at N.C. State, on December 19, 1974, A&T supporters had filed a motion amending a desegregation suit launched by an African American Winston-Salem resident, J. Alston Atkins, in 1970. The *Atkins* suit, initiated in the Greensboro federal district court, asked that the sixteen-campus system be required to adopt an open admissions policy and that each campus be required to accept a 25 percent black enrollment. Because the *Adams* case superseded it, however, the *Atkins* suit had lain dormant until lawyers representing A&T and the North Carolina Alumni and Friends Coalition revived it.[58]

The district court heard the case on December 7, 1976, and issued its opinion on June 28, 1977. The plaintiffs, Atkins and the NCAFC, contended that the decision to locate the vet school at State was ipso facto unconstitutional, and they requested an interim injunction to stay the Board of Governors' decision pending a full consideration of the case by the court. Judge Eugene Gordon ruled against them, saying that the harm that would be imposed on the defendants was greater than the harm inflicted on the plaintiffs. Moreover, Gordon held that the board's decision was not unconstitutional. Two years later, a three-judge panel of the Fourth Circuit Court of Appeals upheld Gordon's decision in *Atkins* v. *Scott*.[59]

The conclusion of the vet school controversy began a longer and considerably more intensified conflict. The experience opened wounds among UNC administrators, OCR officials, TBI leaders, and civil rights advocacy groups, and after late 1975 an atmosphere of mutual suspicion prevailed. Ray Dawson was convinced that OCR and HEW had come under the domination of the LDF and was no longer a neutral party. HEW, he later said, "just folded" and accepted the LDF's contention that the desegregation plans of the *Adams* decision were untenable. The conflict with HEW had expanded, in Friday's eyes and those of his aides, from a secondary matter to, in Dawson's words, "an overriding issue." It dominated "virtually everything that we were doing." By the end of 1975 the proper means of desegregating UNC had become of "very great and real concern" to Friday, who was frustrated in his inability to reach a permanent accommodation. "We were not looking for a fight," said Dawson; the university was seeking a settlement. Yet it was becoming "harder and harder to communicate" with federal officials.[60]

Officials at OCR, meanwhile, viewed UNC's unwillingness to develop acceptable policies as all the more disheartening because the University of North Carolina was the preeminent public university system in the South and Bill Friday was an educator of regional and national prominence. Moreover, the UNC staff was always well prepared in negotiations. Paradoxically, UNC became a target because it had offered, as Guthrie later described it, "the most sophisticated plan" of all the *Adams* states. Compared to Virginia's desegregation proposal of 1974, which Guthrie called "an overstatement" to describe as a plan, North Carolina "really had taken its responsibilities more seriously." The university was "further ahead in terms of sophistication of analysis and, arguably, responsiveness"; it had a significant investment in "really trying to accomplish something."[61]

According to Guthrie, while other *Adams* states remained vague about their intentions and objectives, Friday was specific about goals and the limits to which UNC could accommodate OCR. Other states provided material yet refused to draw a line "either on process or substance"; as OCR perceived it, as long as the *Adams* states responded, they were "being cooperative." Friday's approach was to be completely forthcoming in submissions to OCR. Yet on occasion – and the vet school controversy was one such occasion – he and his staff would "sit down in the road" and "draw a line" on issues of "process or substance." OCR, as a result, came to perceive UNC not only as a formidable adversary, but also as uncooperative and provocative.

By 1975 many OCR officials viewed the vet school battle as exemplifying UNC's lack of candor and good faith. Although UNC officials always appeared well prepared and "very much in charge," OCR harbored suspicions that university administrators, including Friday, were obstructing meaningful desegregation. Claire Guthrie had a different view. She never accepted the accusation that UNC's modus operandi showed a "lack of candor"; if anything, the opposite was true. In her dealings with them, she found university officials "straightforward." If they disagreed, they said so, explained the basis for their disagreement, and willingly put "whoever in the room with you that you wanted to see." After Guthrie left OCR in 1976 to become assistant general counsel at Princeton University, she had frequent dealings with federal officials. She maintained that UNC's approach was the most effective. "The way to deal with any enforcement official," she said, was "to give them everything they want." In most instances, those officials were given too much information to digest; that usually meant that they would "go away for a long time" and perhaps "never come back." Guthrie always believed that the UNC staff had the right "feel." They were helpful and open, yet they kept their own counsel; they were, in her assessment, "well coached."[62]

The experience of the vet school had also confirmed the suspicions of the LDF litigants in the *Adams* case and NCAFC that UNC's *Revised North Carolina State Plan* was deficient. According to Julius Chambers, Friday assumed the "rather strong position that the university had done all that it needed to do." That position, he thought, was "somewhere along the middle, or somewhere right in the middle" of opinion on the Board of Governors.

Chambers believed that UNC restructuring had imposed a new campus hierarchy in which the TWIs remained on top, the TBIs on the bottom. Friday lacked the firm commitment "to bring the black institutions up to par, even in the tiered structure that they came up with to compete with the white institutions." For Chambers and other civil rights activists, this meant that the university was avoiding meaningful change; "simply following this limited path that the university administration was advocating was not going to do any more than what it had [done]" in the past.[63]

The resolution of the vet school controversy had reinforced another reality: the conflict over desegregation had become a battle largely involving Bill Friday's leadership. Highly sensitive about image, Friday tended to personalize UNC issues, and he was particularly attuned to any impression that he was seeking to forestall racial progress. UNC counsel Dick Robinson later said that Friday was "deeply aggrieved personally" by the controversy with HEW, "personally offended by the suggestion that the university was not doing right." In short, Friday viewed the controversy in "very personal terms." The UNC president had long prided himself on a record of accomplishment in race relations, yet he found himself caught in a situation in which none of the alternatives would satisfy all sides. Racial inequities in higher education were the product of a long history of discrimination, yet policy solutions were not immediately apparent. Friday, no matter how personally committed he was to racial justice, was responsible to a Board of Governors and a legislature whose interest in desegregating higher education remained unclear. The charge that the university was violating the Civil Rights Act, and that it was not treating black citizens properly, "really hurt him deeply," but it reflected deeply embedded attitudes and conditions existing in North Carolina.[64]

Once the conflict with OCR in 1975 threatened to produce Title VI administrative hearings, Friday made management of the controversy a top priority. Temperamentally uncomfortable with public conflict, he had always operated as a face-to-face mediator, and he brought those skills to bear in full force after 1975. Although Friday did not involve himself in the details of negotiations, he operated with a formidable UNC staff, anchored by Vice Presidents Joyner, Dawson, Sanders, and Thompson, and this inner circle came to provide much of the UNC president's advice. By the end of the vet school controversy, Dawson had assumed a general-in-chief status in the conflict, while other senior staff, including counsel Dick Robinson, spent an increasing amount of their time on the matter. At the same time, Friday employed what Robinson later called the "Friday treatment" of mediation and behind-the-scenes consultation.[65]

To Friday's adversaries in OCR, he remained enigmatic. Martin Gerry remembered him as having "a good deal of personal charm" and an acute political instinct. Gerry was also deeply impressed by the UNC operation, which he judged the most imposing of any of the southern university systems with which he dealt. Yet the sophistication of UNC's legal, political, and public relations machine was also a source of frustration for OCR officials such as Gerry, who never understood Friday's political constraints, or, as Gerry expressed it, "the moccasins he was in." In the end, Gerry admitted that Friday must have faced some "extraordinarily difficult challenges to even do what he did."[66]

By 1975 there was a convergence of views about North Carolina among some HEW bureaucrats and career civil rights lawyers in the LDF. Lacking clear and specific standards, HEW officials had fumbled their way toward a policy. In what Peter Holmes called a legal and policy "vacuum," a "bunch of bureaucrats" attempted the mammoth task of disassembling the remnants of a far-flung segregated system of higher education. Their principal experience had been with what then appeared to be a successful model of elementary and secondary schools; in higher education, they found, according to Holmes, "complete frustration." Those who had had the closest contact with and knowledge of the UNC case continued to believe that the university needed to be disciplined. "There was a lot of sympathy in the department" when Gerry's July 31 letter was sent, Claire Guthrie recalled, "for just hard-lining it." For the time being, the balance of power, both in terms of the Republican aversion to civil rights activism and the status of the *Adams* case, restrained them from intervening more actively in North Carolina.[67]

Although they had lost in the vet school case, advocates of a more radical approach to the desegregation of higher education would, under different circumstances, return for renewed battle. UNC desegregation and the conflict with HEW had already occupied a large share of Bill Friday's attention, but after 1975 it came to absorb even more of his and his staff's energy. The charge of racial injustice fundamentally undermined UNC's claim to moral and educational leadership in North Carolina and the South, yet defining a just solution, and implementing it in concert with the state's political leadership, constituted the most difficult challenge of Friday's career.

CHAPTER 10 *Queen Elizabeth in the*
Baltimore Orioles Dugout

R AY Dawson in 1981 observed that most of UNC's "tribulations" of the past decade had resulted from its refusal to "bend to an intolerant orthodoxy" and its unwillingness to accept the dictates of a civil rights establishment. Wielding powerful influence over national opinion shapers, the civil rights orthodoxy operated through a system of interlocking directorates that abided by a uniformity of rhetoric. Because the civil rights orthodoxy insisted on uniformity of thought and action, according to Dawson, UNC's struggle with HEW was comparable to earlier efforts to protect academic freedom during the era of Joseph R. McCarthy.[1]

Dawson's observations betrayed a frustration typical of Bill Friday and other UNC administrators. Dedicating the better part of a decade to resisting federal intervention, they believed that an "intolerant orthodoxy" was determined to restrict the university's freedom. The attitudes of UNC administrators exemplified a wide gulf in perceptions between federal policymakers and university officials. Eventually, these two well-intentioned sides would reach an impasse out of basic confusion about the application of traditional tools of desegregation to higher education. The UNC case was "the most difficult civil rights problem of my tenure as Secretary," HEW secretary Joseph A. Califano Jr. later wrote; no other area of policy making created "as much agony within the civil rights movement." Blacks remained deeply divided; the federal court's mandate in the *Adams* decision placed Califano "in the middle of issues as complex and subtle as any I faced in this arena." This was an instance in which Lyndon Johnson's adage that "it was harder to know what was right than to do what was right" certainly applied.[2]

Managing the desegregation controversy became the greatest challenge of Bill Friday's leadership and certainly one of the gravest tests the University of

North Carolina had encountered in its two centuries of existence. Only a few years after restructuring into a sixteen-campus system – and as a direct result of restructuring – UNC was forced to seek new and more radical measures to achieve racial equity. Yet genuine desegregation took on different meanings. For many North Carolinians, desegregation had already occurred in the 1950s when the university adopted a race-blind admissions procedure. On the other hand, the view of the NAACP Legal Defense and Educational Fund was that, because the university system contained vestiges of segregation, more radical measures were needed.

In keeping with his leadership style, Friday selected a middle path. That meant consultation with all sides and, if possible, conciliation and compromise rather than public confrontation. In the confusing arena of university desegregation – where black activists sought both desegregation and the maintenance of historically black institutions – that also meant attempting to preserve North Carolina's five historically black campuses. Although Friday would face endless frustration in attempting conciliation, he saw an amicable solution to the dilemma of desegregation as a necessary prerequisite to maintaining racial harmony in the state and to continued public support, from both whites and blacks, for the University of North Carolina.

By 1975, despite HEW's acceptance of UNC's *Revised North Carolina State Plan*, it was becoming increasingly difficult to produce standards that were both realistic to university administrators and satisfactory to federal regulators. The plaintiffs in the *Adams* case regarded the Office for Civil Rights's approval of the state plans as another example of the Nixon-Ford administration's determination to obstruct the Civil Rights Act, and they applied additional legal pressure. But what decisively changed OCR policy, and the agency's relations with UNC, was the election of Jimmy Carter to the presidency in November 1976 and the appointment, in the spring of 1977, of a new team of HEW officials.

ALL of these developments remained in the future in late 1975. In the six months following the resolution of the vet school controversy, a period of brief calm ensued. As Dawson recalled, the HEW-UNC relationship remained "quite cordial" and "quite constructive," and OCR sent clearly positive signals to UNC officials about the implementation of the *Revised North Carolina State Plan*. During this honeymoon period, UNC completed both its long-range plan and the promised companion study of the traditionally black campuses. After self-study by the TBIs and, as Friday put it, "extensive and frank discussions" with their chancellors, *A Comparative Study of the Five Historically Black Constituent Institutions of the University of North Carolina* was released on June 11, 1976.[3]

Raymond H. Dawson

The *Comparative Study* concluded that there was no disparity in state support for white and black institutions; if anything, it asserted, per capita funding of enrolled students remained consistently higher at TBIs. The rate of increase in funding was similar between historically white and historically black campuses, although it was significantly higher at historically black general baccalaureate institutions. The study also maintained that a rough parity existed at traditionally black and white campuses in state financial support of library and academic programs. There was "no discrimination" in the pattern of state budgetary support for traditionally black institutions, and there existed a "basic comparability" among similar white and black institutions in terms of funding.[4]

While asserting that the state was currently financing higher education without discriminating by race, the study also provided a basis for TBI enhancement. Although the historically black campuses were among the fastest-growing institutions in the sixteen-campus system, only about 7 percent of their enrollments were white; at historically white campuses, the figure for minority enrollment was 5 percent. Entering SAT scores were "significantly higher" at TWIs. Physical facilities were older and in greater need of improvement at the historically black institutions, though they had a greater percentage of buildings undergoing renovation than did the white campuses. The proportion of faculty members with Ph.D.'s was "consistently lower" at TBIs, and the professional programs at historically black institutions, such as Central's law school or A&T's nursing school, had "major program deficiencies" that demanded correction.[5]

The *Comparative Study* served as a basis for further upgrading and enhancement, but it did not satisfy UNC's critics. The LDF believed that real change would come only as the result of heightened legal pressure, and in August 1975 it filed a new motion in Judge John H. Pratt's court. Claiming that the 1974 state desegregation plans were inadequate, the LDF asked that the court impose new standards on southern public universities. None of the state plans, the motion declared, constituted "a genuine desegregation plan" that satisfied either *Adams* or HEW standards; OCR had accepted these plans in a "blatant regression from its own specific desegregation criteria." As a result, "no substantial change" had occurred in the segregated pattern of southern public higher education.[6]

The LDF motion focused much of its attention on North Carolina. Reviewing the 1973–74 negotiations between OCR director Peter E. Holmes and UNC officials, the LDF characterized the university as exhibiting "intransigence," "denial," and "defiance." The *Revised North Carolina State Plan* was nothing more than another means of noncompliance, and an "argumentative tone" pervaded the document. Once accepted, the UNC plan, the LDF asserted after only a year's experience, had achieved little progress toward its limited objectives; continued problems at the North Carolina Central Law School and the vet school controversy served as concrete examples of failure.

In the autumn of 1975, soon after the LDF filed its motion, the UNC Board of Governors considered intervening in the *Adams* case. But after conferring with attorneys in Washington, a special board committee recommended against intervention because it would bring UNC under court jurisdiction.[7] Although the LDF motion remained dormant in Pratt's court through much of 1976, new developments had occurred by the end of that year that would transform the *Adams* case. Ray Dawson noticed a decided change in UNC relations with the Office for Civil Rights in the autumn of 1976. That summer, the university had forwarded a copy of its *Comparative Study* to OCR but had received no response. Dawson remembered worrying that the signs from Washington appeared to be unfavorable. His fears were soon realized. After the election of Jimmy Carter, Martin Gerry, who had been installed as permanent OCR director a year before and who was emboldened by the new political environment, resurrected his critique of the 1974 desegregation plans. At a meeting of the Southern Education Foundation in Atlanta in early November, he told the participants, including Jean Fairfax and other LDF representatives, that the *Adams* plans were "deficient in major areas," including enhancement, admissions and retention, compensatory programs, and faculty hiring. Gerry repeated these points in private meetings with a group of southern higher education officials on December 7 at the OCR regional office in Atlanta.[8]

The time was now ripe, Gerry declared on the seventh, for a settlement of the *Adams* case, and OCR was prepared to broker more specific standards. Consensus between the *Adams* states and the LDF could provide a way out for OCR, which the Pratt court had ruled was doing too little and the *Mandel* court had said was doing too much. The question of specific standards was crucial. "If we don't resolve the question of standards," Gerry said, "judges will." The LDF was willing to move from abstractions to specific standards; Gerry believed that the states should do the same. Yet southern higher education officials viewed Gerry's appeal skeptically. This was a "revolutionary proposal," according to a UNC representative, advanced by a lame-duck bureaucrat, when desegregation plans had already been accepted and were being administered by the states. Not surprisingly, the group summarily rejected Gerry's initiative.[9]

Friday was troubled by what Gerry's fishing expedition implied for federal desegregation policy. After long and sometimes excruciating negotiations,

UNC and OCR had agreed that the *Revised North Carolina State Plan* would serve as a blueprint for desegregation. Now Gerry was suddenly proposing that this plan be scrapped in favor of a leap in the dark – a new process of developing and defining specific standards by which progress could be measured. Writing to Gerry on December 17, Friday elaborated. When would states that had not received letters from Leon Panetta in the 1969–70 period and that were not involved in the *Adams* litigation become subject to federal scrutiny? When would private institutions be included? As for writing new criteria, UNC would neither accept nor participate in such a process. Friday wanted "no misunderstanding on this subject": if the Board of Governors were asked to develop a new state plan or to modify the existing one, he added, it would very likely refuse to do so.[10]

Frustrated by the adverse reaction of North Carolina and the other *Adams* states, Gerry took another step during his last days in office. Based on his remarks to the Southern Education Foundation in early November 1976, LDF lawyers, the plaintiffs in *Adams* v. *Richardson*, asked Gerry, who was a defendant, to restate his comments to the foundation for the court record. On January 13, 1977, when Gerry made a deposition to the LDF lawyers in Washington, the renewed proceedings of the *Adams* case took a bizarre turn, for his written testimony clearly indicated that he had become a friendly witness. In the deposition Gerry said that the plans of the remaining six *Adams* states, which had been accepted by OCR in 1974, were failing to achieve desegregation. His preferred course of action followed the outline of his proposals of December 7. HEW should seek, either through amendment or clarification, substantially changed state plans, and their revision should focus on three crucial areas: the admission of minority students, TBI enhancement, and increased minority faculty. Gerry supported the idea of reevaluating all of the state plans against more precise standards.[11]

Gerry's deposition was a bombshell. Friday realized that the admission by an OCR official that the Office for Civil Rights had failed to live up to the standards of *Adams* meant real trouble. On obtaining a transcript of Gerry's testimony, Ray Dawson immediately confirmed that the news was not good. A new order from Judge Pratt soon followed. Four days after Gerry made the deposition, Pratt instructed OCR to develop by March 1, in consultation with LDF lawyers, a joint timetable and format for renegotiating the state desegregation plans. Based on this new framework, they should then come to an agreement on a more clearly defined set of standards for evaluating university desegregation. Gerry's admissions about the state plans had left Pratt little choice. As an LDF official observed, the Gerry deposition was a "major factor" in persuading the judge to order new state plans. Peter Holmes, who had made a deposition for the LDF in October 1975, had already conceded that the general pattern of desegregation had remained unaffected by the state higher education plans. Yet Gerry's testimony was far more damaging. He not only indicted the *Adams* plans but agreed with the LDF's call for their re-negotiation. Gerry's parting shot as OCR director – he left the post when Jimmy Carter was inaugurated on January 20 – signaled a new turn in HEW's attitude toward the *Adams* case.[12]

Expanding on his preliminary order of January 17, Judge Pratt issued a second supplemental order on April 1, 1977. Based on the LDF motion of August 1975, Pratt now ruled that the 1974 plans of six states had "failed to achieve significant progress toward higher education desegregation." Those plans were flawed from the outset because they did not meet the standards that Holmes had imposed during the negotiations of 1973–74. Citing the Holmes and Gerry depositions, Pratt pointed out that OCR had acknowledged that the state plans "haven't worked." Those plans were now invalid, and OCR should so inform the *Adams* states. By early July 1977 HEW should transmit specific standards for "acceptable" desegregation plans; the states should respond with revised plans by early September, and HEW should either accept or reject the revised plans by early January 1978. Pratt provided no specific counsel on what the new criteria should contain; rather, he encouraged consultation with the LDF.[13]

The only substantive guidance Pratt offered concerned the historically black campuses. Fearing that the *Adams* case might require the closing of TBIs, the National Association for Equal Opportunity in Higher Education (NAFEO), which represented 107 TBIs, had filed an amicus curiae brief on March 21, 1976, in Pratt's court, arguing against the LDF motion of August 1975. Rather than equal opportunity, NAFEO maintained, equality of educational attainment should become the goal of desegregation. TBIs played a special role as a bridge between inferior segregated black public schools and American society; there should be a "transitory period in which remedial type activity must be instituted in order to rectify past inequality."[14]

Once it became clear, in January 1977, that Pratt would rule in the plaintiffs' favor, the NAFEO assumed a different approach. In a brief filed on March 3, 1977, the association contended that the historical mission of the formerly all-black campuses was to increase access to higher education. The brief warned that closings of TBIs could diminish educational opportunities for blacks. The revised state plans should focus on African American educational needs rather than on "mechanical, numerical schemes" that ignored the "end results to be accomplished." TBIs had been and would continue to remain "primary producers" of black graduates; protecting black colleges should form the "corner-stone" of desegregation. The NAFEO brief went further. The revised state plans, it maintained, should explicitly recognize the TBIs as having already conformed to "both the letter and spirit of Title VI" and should place no further burdens on them by requiring "arbitrary quotas" of white students or staff.[15]

Pratt accepted this line of reasoning. "The process of desegregation," he wrote in his second supplemental order of April 1, "must not place a greater burden on Black institutions or Black students' opportunity to receive a quality public higher education." Recognizing the "unequal status" of historically black campuses and the "real danger" that desegregation might actually diminish opportunities for African American students, he affirmed that new HEW criteria should seek the contradictory goals of desegregation and the preservation of the "racial identifiability" of the TBIs.[16]

On April 8, 1977, a week after Pratt's second supplemental order, Bill Friday reported on the *Adams* case to the Board of Governors, meeting at Fayetteville. Reviewing the history of *Adams* and UNC's efforts to desegregate, Friday reminded board members that, since no state was a party to the litigation, the order could not be appealed. The case, he continued, had failed to consider the extent to which Title VI requirements affected TBIs. If, as the Pratt court suggested, federal policy protected their "racial identifiability," how could the UNC system pursue both this goal and the "mutually exclusive" objective of desegregation?

Until this contradiction was resolved, Friday said, it was impossible for the university and the state of North Carolina to determine a desegregation policy that would satisfy federal officials. Judge Pratt had rejected the *Revised North Carolina State Plan* but had refused to give North Carolina clear guidance for the future. "In the absence of such definitive and reliable guidance," Friday declared, "we would engage in a trial and error process at the peril of discovering, after making great additional efforts, that such efforts were legally insufficient." North Carolina should respond to HEW court-mandated efforts to draft new standards by obtaining specifics of what the state was required to do in order to desegregate; in the future it would ignore "vague, confused, and unexplained directives from HEW."[17]

Pratt's order of April 1 had come in the midst of a presidential transition. Elected in November 1976, Jimmy Carter in early 1977 appointed Joseph A. Califano Jr. as secretary of HEW. A skilled lawyer who had served on Lyndon Johnson's White House staff, Califano was an impatient man who enjoyed wielding power. The new secretary wanted to make a difference in HEW, particularly in civil rights enforcement. He was more concerned about reinvigorating civil rights policy than about any other task he faced, he later wrote. Growing up in Brooklyn, New York, Califano was raised in a family that did not tolerate racism and never used racial epithets. While serving in the navy's Judge Advocate Corps in the mid-1950s, he was "stunned" to discover that Arlington, Virginia, still maintained segregated movie theaters, and his wife picketed a segregated theater on Glebe Road. In 1962 and 1963 Califano was a special assistant to Secretary of the Army Cyrus Vance when troops were sent to quell violence at the University of Mississippi, and he visited Oxford with legendary Justice Department official John Doar. Later he was involved, from Washington, in the desegregation of the University of Alabama. Califano believed that the Office for Civil Rights had suffered a "savage toll" during the Nixon-Ford years, a victim of the Republican Party's southern strategy. As a Johnson adviser, he had witnessed OCR's creation. Johnson told him that the Office for Civil Rights should be free from and independent of other agencies; the office should be "at the Secretary's throat," forcing him to pay attention to civil rights.[18]

OCR, Califano was convinced, was thoroughly demoralized when he took office. "Slashing mindlessly from issue to issue," it possessed neither a sense of purpose nor a strong loyalty to the White House. A good number of Johnson appointees had survived the Nixon-Ford years, but the agency had become a "dumping ground for scores of unqualified bureaucrats" who damaged civil rights policy by "inept negotiating" or by identifying the wrong issues. Operating with a White House that was "openly hostile to its mission," OCR had "lost its bearings." In the transition to the new administration, David Mathews, the outgoing HEW secretary, told Califano that OCR had become a "law unto itself." It would take actions without informing him and even engaged in public attacks on the secretary. F. Peter Libassi, former special assistant for civil rights under Johnson's HEW secretary John Gardner and acting director of OCR from January to May 1977, remembered that OCR staffers "looked like prisoners of war who had just been released from a prison camp." "Shell-shocked" and "terribly depressed" over the lack of progress during the previous eight years, OCR staff were also "excited about what could happen again."[19]

The senior OCR team that Califano appointed reflected his ties to the civil rights community. As the general counsel of HEW, who would be responsible for writing the new criteria for state plans, he appointed Libassi. As OCR deputy director he chose Cynthia Brown, who had worked with the Leadership Conference on Civil Rights and the Lawyers' Conference for Civil Rights under Law. And as OCR director he selected David S. Tatel, an attorney with impeccable civil rights credentials. Tatel, who was legally blind, had a sharp mind and, observed Califano, an "extraordinary command of the facts." Aiding Califano in the search for an OCR director was HEW deputy general counsel Richard Beattie.[20]

Califano had only been in office a few weeks when he received Pratt's order of April 1 requiring HEW to draft new criteria on which to base new revised state plans for higher education desegregation. Because Tatel was not appointed until early May, the responsibility for drafting the criteria fell to an informal task force consisting of Libassi, HEW deputy assistant secretary David Breneman, then on leave from the Brookings Institution, and HEW official Michael O'Keefe. At various times this task force drew in other members of HEW, including Commissioner of Education Ernest L. Boyer, Assistant Secretary for Education Mary Frances Berry, Assistant Secretary for Policy and Evaluation Henry Aaron, Califano's special assistant Richard Cotton, and career bureaucrats such as Burton Taylor and HEW staff lawyer Arline Mendelson.[21]

The HEW task force operated with serious handicaps. Under the court's schedule, it had only three months to complete its work, and it functioned with little expertise. Although Breneman, Boyer, and Berry all had experience in higher education, those drafting the criteria made only token efforts to consult university leaders, especially those in the South. That spring Libassi formed a blue-ribbon panel of twelve experts from the higher education community, yet it played a minimal role, meeting only once for a few hours to offer its advice. When later questioned, one panel member, Harold "Doc" Howe II, former commissioner of education under Lyndon Johnson, could not even remember serving. Nor could anyone else show that this group ever had much to do with fashioning the *Adams* criteria. According to David Breneman, the blue-ribbon panel was "a good faith effort to try to get some additional parties involved." It served the "political agenda" of fostering "legitimacy" or exerting "clout." In the absence of "a major substantive role," however, the panel quickly became "window dressing."[22]

The task force's deliberations during the spring of 1977 exposed differences within HEW. Mary Frances Berry was then waging a losing battle with Ernest Boyer for primacy in educational policy. Both of them served on the HEW task force, yet they were unable to present a united front. In addition, there were major differences within the department about how to deal with Bill Friday and North Carolina. Divisions between Tatel and Libassi surfaced almost as soon as Tatel took over. Libassi had joined the Carter administration first as Califano's consultant in dealing with OCR, then as acting OCR director, then as HEW general counsel. As a result, the writing of the new criteria was, as Breneman recalled, "his baby." With Tatel's arrival early in May, the balance of power changed. Although Tatel later maintained that he sought to mediate a conflict between HEW moderates and OCR radicals, as a civil rights lawyer he was inclined toward a hard-line policy. Tatel soon questioned the task force's direction. The new OCR director wanted a vigorous policy; he believed that confrontation and eventually litigation would accomplish desegregation. Breneman noted that Tatel expressed strong opinions and had "definite interests" in the case; he favored injecting OCR "into it in a much more significant way than they had been into it." Rather quickly Tatel concluded that *Adams* enforcement had not succeeded "because OCR had failed to bite the bullet." He and his colleagues at OCR would change that, he believed. They would resolve the case themselves or take it to court; either way, there would be a solution. "It wasn't in anybody's interest," Tatel later reflected, "to have this issue fester for another two decades." A "very genuine conflict" between Tatel's immediatist approach and Libassi's incrementalism ensued, and Tatel's arrival marked a significant shift in attitude toward the *Adams* states.[23]

In April 1977 the LDF had supplied the earliest draft of the new *Adams* criteria. This draft relied on the elimination of so-called program duplication to achieve desegregation, and the fund lobbied hard for its adoption. LDF field representative Jean Fairfax sponsored meetings with representatives of southern advocacy groups, including black alumni associations such as the North Carolina Alumni and Friends Coalition (NCAFC). The LDF's position also enjoyed strong support within OCR. Burt Taylor, according to Mary Frances Berry, "thought strongly" that the elimination of program duplication should become a centerpiece of the criteria; OCR staffers who had worked for the LDF, such as director of policy Melvin Leventhal and his deputy Norman Chachkin, supported Taylor. Berry favored eliminating program duplication only as leverage for TBI enhancement. In contrast, Breneman, Boyer, and, to a large extent, Libassi feared that HEW emphasis on program duplication would lead to excessive intervention in and micromanagement of university affairs.[24]

Boyer said that one of the earliest meetings he attended after he took office as U.S. commissioner of education concerned the LDF's early draft of the criteria. Boyer considered the matter of higher education desegregation as "not inconsequential," and his interest was "far more than casual," given his own experience as chancellor of the State University of New York system. He found the draft criteria, especially the emphasis on the forced shifting of faculty and programs, "really startling," an intervention that went "far beyond" anything he might have "remotely dreamed of" as a university leader. There was considerable internal tension between moderates such as himself and those within HEW who wanted to "go for broke." At the time he expressed his strong objections, contending that these measures were both self-defeating and not "politically . . . doable."[25]

In May and June 1977, Libassi's go-slow, voluntaristic approach and Tatel's more aggressive strategy were in open conflict. In part, this clash was bureaucratic; Libassi recalled that while the OCR director's job was "to make new law," the general counsel's was "to say what the law is now." But there was also an ideological fissure. Tatel, arriving just as the criteria task force was beginning its work, found the Office for Civil Rights in disarray, with a backlog of cases and, in his view, an untrained and inefficient staff. Productivity was "low" and management was "poor." Tatel, trained in civil rights law and long associated with litigation, naturally gravitated toward the confrontational strategy of Burt Taylor and the LDF. As OCR director, he was in regular contact with LDF representatives; in more than two and a half years in office, for example, Tatel conducted over twenty conversations with Jean Fairfax. He also had frequent exchanges with LDF attorneys Joseph Rauh Jr., Elliott Lichtman, John Silard, and other *Adams* litigators.[26]

Tatel relied on the flow of information from Fairfax and the black alumni groups with whom she communicated. These groups, including the NCAFC, served as watchdogs, seeking to increase state support for TBIs while preserving their traditional racial character. In meetings with such groups and the LDF, Tatel acknowledged that black elementary and secondary schools had suffered the greatest burden during desegregation and indicated that this was an experience that he did not intend to repeat in the area of higher education.[27]

The criteria task force had few formal contacts with UNC officials during its deliberations. On April 14, 1977, Libassi convened a meeting of chancellors and presidents of universities from the *Adams* states, including Bill Friday. But the general counsel used the occasion to explain HEW procedures in drafting the criteria, and he offered the university administrators little opportunity to express themselves. Libassi subsequently claimed that there were "numerous contacts" between HEW officials and UNC administrators during April and May, and that these exchanges occurred in an atmosphere of "candor and directness," including telephone conversations with Friday that dealt with the criteria's specifics. In such contacts, Libassi found Friday to be an "able, capable, and astute" leader with whom he felt "very comfortable in seeking his advice and calling him on the phone." He later said that he had "lots of phone conversations" with Friday, in which the two men would "talk out the problems and what they meant," what Friday was seeking, what his political problems were, and how he was trying to manage the process. Yet Friday could not recall these conversations, and Ray Dawson, who by the spring of 1977 was coordinating UNC's response to federal pressure, remembered a virtual blackout of information concerning the task force's activities.[28]

UNC's first inkling of HEW intentions came in early June, when Peter Libassi, David Breneman, and Michael O'Keefe arrived in Chapel Hill to discuss an early version of the new criteria. On the afternoon of June 6 and the morning of June 7 at the General Administration Building, the HEW officials conferred with Bill Friday, UNC vice presidents Ray Dawson, John Sanders, Cleon Thompson, and Felix Joyner, and Jeffrey H. Orleans, a former OCR staff attorney who had joined the UNC administration as a lawyer under UNC counsel Dick Robinson in 1975 and had become deeply involved in the case. Friday also brought along William A. Johnson, a judge from Lillington, North Carolina, and chairman of the Board of Governors. Libassi, remaining mysterious about the actual contents of the criteria, spoke from a spiral notebook on his lap that contained the working draft. No written version of this draft was ever distributed to university administrators, who were eager to know more about HEW's thinking and who were expecting a give-and-take session in which they could present their views.[29]

In fact, the basic shape of the criteria had already been determined. By the end of the conference, recalled Orleans, there was "a clear sense" that HEW's mind was already made up. These meetings provided some new and disturbing "signaling" from HEW about its intentions, Dawson said. Lacking anything in writing, UNC officials had no effective means of responding, and most of the discussion concentrated on obtaining more specific information for the Libassi team. Over the course of the two-day conference, Libassi consulted with the president of the community college system, Ben Fountain; with UNC officials, the HEW delegation discussed new standards of employment and reviewed the university's history and system of governance. Also covered was the racial composition of the governing boards of the UNC system and of the community college system.[30]

The main topic, however, was student enrollments. Libassi wanted more specific data on the proportion of in-state black high school graduates entering traditionally white institutions and of in-state white high school graduates entering traditionally black institutions. He explained the concept of "parity" in student enrollments, whereby equal proportions of white and black high school graduates would attend the sixteen-campus university. As UNC officials discovered, parity translated into a 480 percent increase over five years in black in-state enrollment at TWIs. When Libassi asked for UNC's response to these goals, Dawson told him that even half of parity – a 240 percent increase in black enrollments – would be "a demanding task." University representatives then pressed Libassi about increasing white enrollments at TBIs, but they encountered a disturbing silence. The UNC officials were skeptical and even alarmed.

Libassi would later describe the June 6–7 meeting as an exercise in testing out the emerging HEW criteria against campus realities. He had hoped that there would be a mutually beneficial exchange of information: HEW officials would brief UNC about the drafting of the new *Adams* criteria, the university would furnish HEW officials with greater details about the unique conditions in North Carolina. On matters of enrollment, faculty hiring, enhancement, and reporting and compliance methods, he recalled, the information provided by North Carolina officials led to modifications in the criteria. This meeting, he said, supplied vital facts concerning what UNC officials thought "would work in North Carolina, what they could do and what they could not do." His "definite impression" was that the UNC representatives believed that the draft criteria were "feasible and workable," and that they exhibited a "positive attitude" toward him in their negotiations.[31]

David Breneman was more candid. Within HEW, there was "a real sense of political sensitivity" regarding North Carolina; it was well known that Bill Friday possessed influential contacts in the White House, a trump card in any negotiation. The HEW task force wanted to avoid alienating Friday, and it treated him and North Carolina differently than it did the other *Adams* states. Task force members had visited other states for consultations during May and June, but only in North Carolina did a full HEW team arrive. The HEW team was seeking to smooth things over, as well as to "try the ideas out," "to convey information," and to elicit UNC's reaction.[32]

The actual impact of these meetings, Breneman said, was startling. The HEW officials expected to face "a more astute group of people in North Carolina," yet soon after their arrival they realized that they were outclassed by a formidable array of UNC expertise. Although Friday's staff was "utterly cordial," it was also "adversarial." With superior data at their disposal, the UNC representatives were able to expose the vagueness of the new HEW standards, and they quickly shot down the ideas that the task force members tested out in Chapel Hill. Friday's team, according to Breneman, demonstrated that the standards HEW proposed were "preposterous, undoable, unmeasurable, or already accomplished." The net result, according to Breneman, was that "we were sort of chewed up and spit out."

Even David Tatel would later acknowledge a clash of perceptions. UNC senior staff members, he said, were as personally invested in this as OCR hardliners. Both sides were "all dug-in"; the stakes were high. UNC officials "weren't about to compromise." Consequently, Tatel found that UNC was "much more adversarial" than any of the other *Adams* states with which he dealt. In the end, UNC people differed little from OCR people; both sides were suffering from "battle fatigue."[33]

According to UNC attorney Jeffrey Orleans, the psychology of the meeting – and of the HEW-UNC relationship – was crucial. Libassi, Breneman, and O'Keefe arrived on the scene in the spring of 1977; although they represented the most sympathetic HEW faction – and the most informed about higher education – they had little comprehension of the attitudes of Friday and his staff. Senior UNC administrators believed that they had made an agreement with the U.S. government in 1974; now it was reneging, with the way smoothed by the arrival of Breneman, an academic, and Libassi, a "smooth-talking lawyer." Orleans was struck by how neither side really understood the other; it was "like Queen Elizabeth in the Baltimore Orioles dugout." UNC officials left the June 6–7 meeting with feelings that ranged from "suspicion to despair."[34]

Ray Dawson, who had become immersed in the issue of desegregation by June 1977, was deeply troubled. He regretted that the *Revised North Carolina State Plan* had not been given a chance; he believed that if "we could have taken stock in another year of where we were," the revised plan could have been updated. Instead, it was scrapped, and UNC was asked to take a leap in the dark. Most disquieting of all was the full impact of HEW's new approach. Dawson did not like what he saw. There now appeared to be a "shift in emphasis" on the department's part; desegregation would create a radically new role for the historically white campuses, with little attention paid to minority presence at historically black campuses. The latter subject was "just not on their minds." According to Dawson, HEW was now seeking some very demanding standards that would almost certainly be impossible to meet. It was obvious to him that the federal officials were marching under "two flags" – the integration of the university and the preservation of the racial identifiability of the TBIs – even though those objectives were at odds.[35]

The likely prospect of renewed conflict was disheartening to Dawson and Friday. The new posture contained in the *Adams* criteria demonstrated, Dawson noted, "how difficult our predicament was." In the Nixon-Ford years, ambivalent and halfhearted enforcement policies masked a divergence of views with the LDF and the civil rights establishment. Now federal officials were, for the most part, themselves members of the civil rights establishment. Everyone in UNC administration sympathized with the objectives of the civil rights movement and favored the integration of the university. Dawson himself, as a Carolina dean, had taken an active role in increasing black enrollment at Chapel Hill. But the likelihood seemed great that the university would oppose civil rights activists and perhaps even HEW; the prospect, he said, was painful. The clash between accepted civil rights solutions and UNC's own interests was particularly difficult for Bill Friday, as it became increasingly clear that the federal government would ask for new policies that university administrators thought were unreasonable and antithetical to de-segregation.[36]

The fears of Bill Friday and Ray Dawson were realized on July 2, 1977, when David Tatel officially transmitted the new *Adams* criteria to Governor Jim Hunt; they arrived at Friday's home in Chapel Hill the following day by special delivery. Friday dispatched a copy to the members of the Board of Governors and immediately convened his top advisers over the Fourth of July weekend. In late June Peter Libassi had telephoned to inform Friday that he, with Califano's full support, had modified the proposed 240 percent increase in in-state black enrollments at the traditionally white institutions.[37] Libassi remained vague about what the new standard would be. On July 5, however, Friday learned that Criterion II-B-2 specified an increase of 150 percent over five years, which became known as the "150 percent rule." Friday doubted whether this standard could be met, but he was understandably relieved. "I thought its achievement," he said later, "was certainly more likely" than a 240 percent (50 percent of "parity") or a 480 percent (parity) increase. It was "less objectionable . . . but still probably unattainable." UNC officials found other parts of the *Adams* criteria equally disturbing. Most offensive was Criterion I-F, which required that UNC obtain prior approval from OCR before it implemented any "major change in the operations" of the university that might affect the elimination of racial duality.[38]

The day that the criteria arrived in Chapel Hill, Friday received a telephone call from Califano. The secretary was in a cordial mood; he and Friday had worked together closely on Lyndon B. Johnson's White House Task Force on Education, and Friday supported Califano's bid to become HEW secretary. Califano, certain that two old associates could work together, wanted to know his reaction. He had read the criteria, Friday said, but he had done so "very hastily" and was unprepared to offer a complete and studied response. Draw-ing Califano's attention to Criterion I-F, he strongly objected to the provision for prior restraint by the OCR. That provision, he said, was "unfortunate," should never have been included in the criteria, and needed to be changed immediately. He also urged that significant modifications be made in the enrollment standards embodied in Criterion II-B-2 and elsewhere. Although he expressed some concern about Criterion II-C, which called for the elimina-tion of unnecessary program duplication and would later become a central issue in negotiations, at the time he considered the provision of secondary importance.[39]

Friday's public response to the *Adams* criteria, on July 5, was measured. Although he had resisted – and would continue to resist – any attempt to impose OCR's prior approval of UNC programs, other aspects of the criteria were "not unreasonable." Strong recruitment efforts and additional money from the legislature, he told reporters, would move the university toward HEW goals and timetables without a drastic overhaul of the UNC system. HEW officials also showed some willingness to compromise; in the days after the public release of the criteria, HEW agreed to withdraw Criterion I-F.[40]

Privately, however, Friday and his top staff were worried, and out of a hurriedly called meeting on July 4 emerged a consensus that the criteria had made the future of desegregation even more perilous for UNC. Friday and his aides felt certain that the enrollment goals for undergraduates were unreachable, while others, especially those dealing with graduate enrollment, were "somewhat artificial." At a considerable expenditure of time and energy, the university had prepared the *Revised North Carolina State Plan* in 1974; now it appeared that HEW would act "as if nothing had happened since 1974, and that it was all just starting in 1977." Despite Libassi's assurances during the June 6–7 meeting that the revised plan would serve as the foundation of any new plans, the *Adams* criteria, according to Dawson, "stood in a vacuum," and it remained unclear what was unacceptable or acceptable in the revised plan, what changes needed to made, and at what point UNC might reach a "unitary" condition of desegregation. No wonder that Dawson would later describe himself and his associates as "perplexed" about how to proceed on that July Fourth weekend.[41]

Friday faced a demanding schedule; UNC, based on Judge Pratt's timetable, had only sixty days to respond. Almost immediately he established a process for drafting a new desegregation plan. During the first two weeks of July, he met with the sixteen UNC chancellors and held day-long conferences with each of them and their chief academic officers and admissions directors. Since the Planning Committee of the Board of Governors, the full board, and then the governor were required to approve any new plan, the UNC staff needed something in hand by early August.[42]

While Dawson and other senior staff furiously drafted a new plan, Friday presented the matter to the Board of Governors at its meeting on July 15. Most of the four black members approved HEW's proposals. "I thank the Lord every night for HEW and . . . [what] they have done to help the South," said Joseph J. Sansom Jr. of Raleigh. Without federal supervision, he believed, disparities between black and white universities would "go back in the same place it's been in the past." Reaction among white board members was decidedly negative; a reporter who polled half of the board found "strong opposition." "Any time you start establishing quotas in regard to educational systems," said T. Worth Coltrane of Asheboro, "you're fixing to destroy the system."[43]

Friday assured the racially polarized Board of Governors that he would defend the university while seeking meaningful desegregation. UNC officials had not wanted a confrontation with HEW, he said; the matter was thrust upon them. Desegregation remained a primary goal, but "considerations of race and considerations of historic institutional racial identity" should not be the "dominant and compelling factors in making educational decisions." HEW policy remained ambiguous, Friday went on. Not only were the criteria being applied unevenly to public institutions, but also private colleges and universities were exempt from federal pressure. He reiterated the fact that HEW was pursuing the contradictory objectives of desegregating traditionally white institutions while maintaining the racial character of historically black campuses. HEW's mixed signals reaffirmed Friday's own conviction that UNC should "determine independently what is and what is not required of us" in desegregation.[44]

It was, Friday stated, nearly impossible to implement the *Adams* criteria. The UNC president repeated his earlier assertion that it was reasonable to attempt a doubling of black enrollment at TWIs within five years. But other objectives, such as increasing black faculty and enhancing black campuses, were more difficult. The most basic distinction between the desegregation of elementary and secondary schools and the desegregation of colleges and universities was the element of choice. Public schools had compulsory attendance and pupil assignment; no such rules operated in colleges and universities. University administrators could not dictate what institutions students should attend. The UNC system did not have the power, and should not have the power, to move faculties between campuses in order to achieve desegregation; each appointment was to the faculty of a specific institution, not the university at large. Academic programs were not "simply packages or pieces of furniture that can be put in a moving van and transported to another campus with ease and composure."

The *Adams* criteria, Friday continued, had raised fundamental issues "of tremendous importance to the future development of public higher education in North Carolina and to all of the institutions of our University." These issues were so important that he could not yet discuss the specifics of UNC's response. Friday had originally hoped that the *Revised North Carolina State Plan* could become the framework for "an atmosphere of mutual interest and cooperation," and he had intended that it undergo a four-year review beginning in 1978. The arrival of the new HEW criteria made that impossible, and UNC was now "in a markedly different situation." Scrapping the revised plan, the OCR had placed the university in limbo between compliance and noncompliance. At the end of his speech, black members of the board sat quietly while Friday received an enthusiastic reception from the white members.

Less than a week later, on July 20, Friday met with Tatel for the first time in Washington. (At a series of meetings held earlier in July, when the new OCR director had conferred with representatives from each of the *Adams* states, authority over negotiations had been transferred from Libassi to Tatel.) Accompanying Friday was the Ray Dawson-Cleon Thompson team, along with community college president Ben Fountain. On the other side were Libassi, Tatel, and Burt Taylor, who was in charge of OCR's evaluation of the revised state plans. Friday opened the two-hour meeting with a statement of UNC's position: UNC would carry forward and extend the commitments and general plan of action described in the 1974 *Revised North Carolina State Plan.* Any revisions would be based on "our best assessment of the successes and shortcomings of the approved plan of 1974." Friday urged OCR officials to abandon the micromanagement of their predecessors. "Tell us what you want us to do," he told the HEW officials. "Tell us the goal. Tell us what you want these systems to look like, and then let us get there."[45]

Libassi, who later described his own approach as conciliatory, attempted to convince the UNC team that the *Adams* criteria would protect the university from such micromanagement. He also announced that HEW was withdrawing the prior approval provision, Criterion I-F. That section was "just wrong," he later said at a press conference; it had been the product of a "midnight drafting session" when "something got by." But the discussion was dominated by Tatel and, to a certain extent, Taylor, both of whom were eager to proceed with the desegregation. Tatel later asserted that he wanted to avoid micromanagement; OCR's enforcement strategy, which would establish goals but permit university administrators to devise the means to reach them, was "in response to what mainly Bill Friday had told us." On leaving the meeting, Friday told reporters that the conference was "good," "profitable," and included a "frank kind of discussion"; HEW and UNC agreed on the "basic objective" of encouraging more blacks to attend the TWIs. Yet, citing the examples of prior approval by HEW and the need to eliminate unnecessary duplication, Friday reasserted that UNC would not relinquish its autonomy. It therefore "could not and would not" accept all of the criteria. "Educational judgment ought to be exercised by the University," he said. "There can be no exception to that."[46]

After numerous late-night drafting sessions involving Ray Dawson, John Sanders, and others, Bill Friday presented UNC's new desegregation plan to the Planning Committee of the Board of Governors on August 14, 1977. In July Friday had indicated, both to the Board of Governors and to OCR, that he considered the 1974 *Revised North Carolina State Plan* still workable. He was willing to make minor modifications to achieve greater black enrollment at traditionally white institutions, but he would not compromise the university's control over decision making. The plan submitted on August 14 became known as the *Revised North Carolina State Plan . . . Phase II*. Reaffirming the main commitments of the 1974 revised plan – to increase the proportion of North Carolina's black population in the public university system, to encourage the integration of student bodies at the sixteen UNC campuses, and to ensure that the quality of instruction for both blacks and whites would be "equally high" – *Phase II* stated what it would and would not accept from the criteria. Rejecting one of HEW's major premises – that enrollment patterns demonstrated the existence of racial segregation – the new desegregation plan distinguished between racial duality and racial segregation. Because of "racial consciousness," blacks were voluntarily attracted to TBIs, whites to TWIs. If the chief problem was racial duality, then the criteria did not "provide consistently appropriate or correct guidance." UNC accordingly felt free to accept some HEW directives while rejecting others when they were "legally unnecessary or educationally impracticable or defective."[47]

The greatest bone of contention between HEW and UNC was the question of undergraduate enrollments. Criterion II-B-2 called for, by 1983, either the enrollment of black entering freshmen and transfer students at half the rate of whites or a 150 percent increase in black enrollment at TWIs.[48] *Phase II*, describing this formula as "mechanistic and arbitrary," warned that excessively zealous application of this standard could drain off students from TBIs. There was already strong competition for the ablest black students in North Carolina high schools among in-state and out-of-state private institutions, which were offering attractive financial incentives. The criteria were less specific about increasing white enrollment at traditionally black institutions. Indeed, Criterion II-D specified that the establishment of numerical goals for white enrollment in TBIs should be preceded by greater black enrollment in the entire UNC system and in TWIs, by efforts to enhance TBIs, and by the elimination of program duplication and the location of new programs at black institutions. Criterion II-D further stated that no numerical goals for minority enrollment should be established until 1979.[49]

Phase II strongly rejected this approach. The integration of student populations should occur at all campuses, traditionally white and black alike. The UNC system reaffirmed its goals for white enrollment at historically black campuses; the university believed that it would be "detrimental and legally wrong" to alter the projection incorporated in the 1974 revised plan. Increasing white enrollment at TBIs was necessary as larger numbers of black students were attracted to TWIs. To abandon efforts to integrate the TBIs would mean announcing that "they are to remain for an indefinite period 'black' institutions," and this would contribute to "the perpetuation of racial duality, not its elimination."

Impressively argued, *Phase II* was a forceful challenge to the *Adams* criteria and the HEW-OCR team that had written them. UNC's new plan reaffirmed the basic elements of the 1974 revised plan and offered an often biting, sometimes devastating critique of the criteria's sweeping abstractions. In presenting it to the Planning Committee on August 14, Friday realized that UNC was throwing down the gauntlet. "We are cast in the role, by force of circumstances," he told the Planning Committee, "of responding to a set of criteria . . . that say to us how we should proceed to 'desegregate' our institutions." No one wanted segregation; if the matter were "that simple and that straightforward, there could be no possible basis for any adversarial relationships except on means and details." He deplored having the university placed in the position of defending itself against assertions that "depict us wrongly as racially segregated." It seemed likely that "racial identifiability" might become the overriding consideration in all educational decisions, and this would force UNC to seek goals that combined "qualities of arbitrariness with unreasonableness." Friday described the 150 percent rule as neither "realistic [n]or feasible, however desirable [it] may be." "We have no intention of backing away from this," he said. "We aren't entering into this with the idea these fundamental decisions are negotiable. They're not."[50]

With the unanimous support of the Planning Committee, *Phase II* now awaited approval by the full Board of Governors on August 22. Five days before that meeting, David Tatel, who was touring the *Adams* states on the eve of Judge Pratt's deadline, traveled to Chapel Hill and conferred with Bill Friday, Ray Dawson, and Cleon Thompson in Friday's office. Although Tatel would later characterize the discussions as "quite positive," the UNC president disclosed no details of *Phase II*. Tatel left Chapel Hill believing that an "acceptable plan" would be forthcoming.[51]

The truth was that *Phase II* only thinly masked a deep frustration and anger among UNC officials with the *Adams* process; the university had drawn a line in the sand. *Phase II* made it clear that UNC resented the arbitrariness and unreasonableness of the criteria and that it would not relinquish control over basic educational decisions. Nor was that all. UNC had now adopted a tone that HEW officials could easily construe as defiant. Soon after *Phase II* was written, Friday sent it off to Harold Howe, then head of the Ford Foundation. Howe asked an associate at the foundation, Jim Jordan, to analyze the plan. Jordan characterized the UNC plan as a "total commitment to the intent and spirit of the Civil Rights Act," but as "resistant and slightly defiant with respect to some of the specifics of the *Adams* criteria," resentful of the implication that the university remained segregated, and insistent that racial duality could not be "removed by fiat." Although *Phase II* was "laborious and repetitive at times," it was also "reasoned and quite convincing." Jordan predicted that it would face a "tough gauntlet" in HEW.[52]

The nature of the emerging conflict came into clearer focus at the Board of Governors meeting on August 22. After Hugh C. Daniel, chairman of the Planning Committee, presented the new desegregation plan, divisions within the board became apparent. William Johnson, elected chairman of the Board of Governors in July 1976, had become the board's most vocal critic of federal intervention. He described *Phase II* as "perhaps the most important single document presented to this Board since it came into being." The criteria, he believed, contained much that was "unrealistic, unwarranted, unreasonable and unworkable." They violated UNC's integrity and constituted "an unjustified infringement" of its autonomy. Fully accepting them would mean endorsing principles that were "educationally unsound." The criteria threatened the university's excellence and impaired "its capacity properly to meet and serve the higher education needs of all citizens of our State." Johnson strenuously opposed ceding "a vital portion of the affairs and operation" of UNC to "outside, even non-resident, forces and agencies." The university did not "belong to the Department of Health, Education and Welfare, nor to Judge Pratt and the District Court over which he presides." It belonged to the people of North Carolina.[53]

A majority of the five black board members did not support *Phase II*. While two black members were in favor of the plan, Joseph Sansom voted against it, claiming that North Carolina had been "negligent" in fulfilling its obligations to desegregate since the *Brown* decision in 1954. Another black member, Louis T. Randolph, of Washington, North Carolina, abstained. The fiercest opponent of *Phase II* was Julius Chambers, who resigned on the day that the board met. The UNC desegregation plan, he said, was not a "sincere commitment" to bring greater numbers of blacks into the UNC system. Blacks were unable "to get a fair shake in the University." Chambers was disturbed by the "manner and tenor" of the functioning of the Board of Governors. He did not believe that the UNC administration was "committed to equal treatment and opportunities for minorities." Finally, in relinquishing his seat, Chambers asserted that he could better serve the interests of the state off the board than on it.[54]

Approved by the board on August 22, *Phase II* was sent to Governor Hunt, who formally submitted it to OCR on September 2. Yet well before the formal transmittal, negotiations were already under way in the form of telephone conversations on August 24 and 25 between OCR's Burton Taylor and Arline Mendelson and UNC attorney Jeffrey Orleans. These back-channel discussions had Friday's full support. Yet no communication followed until OCR staff had completed its analysis of the UNC plan in mid-October, when Mendelson called Orleans to arrange a meeting with UNC officials. Although wary of any high-level conference that did not include a written response from OCR, Friday dispatched Orleans to meet with Mendelson face-to-face on October 28. Orleans and Mendelson reviewed existing differences, but at Friday's insistence the meeting only produced "an exchange of information." Friday further instructed Orleans to delay higher-level negotiations until UNC had received OCR's written critique.[55]

When it finally arrived on November 7, 1977, the OCR analysis was a detailed, line-by-line examination of the UNC plan that filled some sixteen typewritten pages. With regard to the traditionally black institutions, OCR criticized the absence of specifics on enhancement, pressed for more details about program duplication, and sought a commitment by UNC to establish new programs at those institutions. Although Peter Libassi had disavowed it in July 1977, the OCR's comments revived Criterion I-F, which required advance notification of any major changes in university programs. OCR rejected UNC's commitments on undergraduate enrollments, found fault with its insistence on using the number of high school graduates in 1976 rather than projections for 1982 as the basis for its calculations, and dismissed its enrollment goals for black students at traditionally white institutions. Most remarkable of all, the OCR analysis asked UNC to withdraw its goals for white attendance at traditionally black institutions, which it described as "inappropriate as well as insufficient."[56]

The negotiations over the next two months concentrated almost entirely on enrollment goals for black students at TWIs. *Phase II* rejected the criteria's 150 percent rule as a mechanistic formula that threatened to siphon off black students from the TBIs; it substituted in its place a systemwide goal to increase the percentage of all black students attending TWIs from 25 to 33 percent. The OCR, on the other hand, required a 150 percent increase over 1976 levels by 1982.

When Friday met with the Board of Governors on November 11 to report on the OCR response, he concentrated on the enrollment issue. The OCR analysis, he said, had made racial identifiability at UNC institutions of paramount importance, an approach that the board had found unacceptable. The issue was nothing less than "control over the educational future of all the institutions." Such control, Friday emphasized, lay with the board rather than with HEW. The clash with federal officials was rooted in OCR's "apparent insistence" on a "literal acceptance" of the criteria as a "binding definition" of UNC's course of action.[57]

Friday made this case when he and Ray Dawson met with Tatel and Burt Taylor in Tatel's office in Washington on November 16, 1977. Lasting most of the morning, the meeting focused primarily on TBI enhancement and increasing black enrollment at the TWIs. When Taylor asserted that UNC had little regard for black institutions, both Dawson and Friday disagreed strenuously; it was "an incredible comment," Dawson recalled. Both he and Friday pointed to the genuine progress experienced by the historically black campuses since they had become part of the UNC system in 1972. (Dawson subsequently described this encounter with Taylor – this was only the second time that they had met – as "troublesome" and "disturbing" because it revealed an "astonishingly naive and uninformed view of the historically black institutions.")[58]

Friday and Dawson then elaborated on the relationship of the TBIs to the UNC system. Friday reminded Tatel that the black institutions had only been under UNC supervision for five years and that the university was only beginning to make progress in upgrading them. The Board of Governors, though theoretically possessing arbitrary powers, in reality relied on campus initiative. The traditionally black campuses, Friday said, had "major physical facility needs"; Dawson added that the academic quality of the TBIs was low and that upgrading and enhancement would be a long-term process. The meeting ended with general agreement that the differences between HEW-OCR and UNC, focusing primarily on Criteria II-B-2 and I-F, could be narrowed.[59]

Although the Board of Governors approved a response to the Office for Civil Rights on December 5 that restated the university's position, there was already some evidence that Tatel was seeking a compromise. On November 30 he had met with the North Carolina congressional delegation about the UNC case. Then, in a letter to North Carolina congressman L. H. Fountain on December 5, the day the board adopted its response to the OCR critique, Tatel indicated the need for a "supplemental statement" that would establish the terms of a possible settlement. The UNC staff quickly drafted the supplemental statement so that the Planning Committee and full board could review it before the new year, and on December 30, the Board of Governors approved it.[60]

Friday hoped that the supplemental statement, which was immediately forwarded to Tatel, would resolve UNC's outstanding differences with OCR. Although the UNC president had some basis for optimism, continuing disagreements between the two sides, and a gulf in perceptions and objectives, became obvious when Tatel conveyed OCR's response to the supplemental statement at a meeting attended by Cleon Thompson, Ray Dawson, and Arline Mendelson at the OCR regional office in Atlanta on January 19, 1978. The attention of the UNC representatives was "forcefully called" to, in Dawson's words, a "radical departure": Tatel's draft analysis now focused attention on Criterion II-C, which called for the elimination of "unnecessary" program duplication at TBIs and TWIs.[61]

Tatel later asserted that duplication had always been a major issue. The duplication of course offerings at TWIs and TBIs – especially at institutions that were in close geographic proximity – remained a prominent vestige of de jure segregation; for that reason, he believed that it had to be identified and eliminated. To Tatel, ending racial duality in higher education meant ending program duplication, and the issue could become, for colleges and universities, what pupil assignment and busing had been for elementary and secondary schools – a "strong desegregation device." Criterion I-B had required TBI enhancement; Pratt's second supplemental order had specified that the burden of desegregation should not fall on historically black institutions. The best way to accomplish TBI enhancement and to satisfy Pratt's order, Tatel had come to believe, was through the elimination of program duplication, which was "at heart part of the enhancement effort."[62]

Tatel had always intended to make duplication the centerpiece of the OCR campaign; the question was when. In drafting the criteria, a "fundamental difference of opinion," as Libassi remembered it, had already arisen between HEW moderates and radicals; the radicals tended to embrace the issue of program duplication enthusiastically. OCR hard-liners, David Breneman later said, were "intensely hostile" to higher education. "Exceptionally cynical" about UNC, they viewed Friday and people like him as "pretty bad guys" who were determined to subvert meaningful desegregation. Their view was that HEW needed to control UNC "every way you can." The advocacy groups were also strong supporters of using the elimination of program duplication as a tool of desegregation. On the eve of the Pratt deadline for accepting or rejecting the North Carolina plan, Tatel now embraced the view of the NAACP Legal Defense and Educational Fund and the North Carolina Alumni and Friends Coalition, a sudden shift that, to some UNC partisans, suggested that he had intended to reject the plan all along.[63]

Meanwhile, Tatel's forceful injection of the duplication issue into the negotiations took UNC administrators aback. Friday and his staff had already raised their concerns about Criterion II-C regarding program duplication with HEW on several occasions. Little had been said about it in these discussions, and, although the issue remained an "ominous cloud hanging back there," according to Dawson, UNC "just kind of set that one aside." At meetings with Libassi and Tatel during the summer and autumn of 1977, OCR representatives had said little about Criterion II-C; as Dawson recalled, it "never really came into the foreground as a major issue of division." During the negotiations of the previous November and December, Tatel had informed UNC officials that time was pressing. Now, with the emergence of the duplication issue, that sense of urgency disappeared; UNC was told to "start all over again and do another plan." The "burning, central, foremost issue" was the elimination of unnecessary duplication. Coming at a meeting that Dawson and Thompson had fully expected would result in a settlement, Tatel's message about II-C was "surprising" and "startling."[64]

Dawson and Thompson left the meeting with Tatel on January 19 in a glum mood. The UNC vice presidents were scheduled to leave Atlanta on a late afternoon flight, but sleet delayed their departure for two and a half hours. They landed at Raleigh-Durham to find the Triangle area paralyzed by a winter storm and Dawson's car covered with ice. As he drove west on Highway 54 into Chapel Hill late that evening, Dawson saw trees felled by the ice and "total pitch darkness"; there was not a light on anywhere. The power at his home was off and remained so for three days, adding to the gloom and feeling that life was in "shambles."[65]

Tatel's bombshell had an equally discouraging impact on Friday. Like Dawson, he believed that a literal interpretation of Criterion II-C meant that UNC had "no place else to turn" and that a settlement was remote. Friday and Dawson both desperately wanted an accommodation. Although the university was "not prepared to settle at any price," remembered Dawson, Friday preferred a settlement. The longer the matter remained unresolved, the more divisive and disruptive it would become. "It was a source of contention within the state and within the University," said Dawson. He and Friday believed that they were seeking the same objectives as OCR – racial integration, educational equity, and greater opportunity for black North Carolinians. But UNC officials were unwilling to "just give in and let them do it any way they wanted to." Although Friday wanted a solution, he realized that the new emphasis on II-C created conditions that a majority of the Board of Governors would find unacceptable. Four days after the Atlanta meeting with Tatel, Friday, after consulting with Bill Johnson and Governor Hunt, wrote to the OCR director. Based on his negotiations with Tatel during December, Friday stated, he had thought that a settlement was at hand. Now the OCR director wanted "very substantial changes" that Friday would have to advise the Board of Governors were "not acceptable."[66]

In a last-minute attempt to find a solution, Friday traveled to Washington on January 30 to meet with Tatel, but he found the OCR director unwavering.

On February 1 Joe Califano telephoned Friday and said that he would reject the UNC plan. Again trying to avert a confrontation, Friday briefly outlined his objections to Tatel's January 19 comments and asked for a delay. But Califano, like Tatel, was determined to press the matter. Throughout the spring and autumn of 1977, though remaining out of public view on the UNC desegregation case, the HEW secretary had kept a close watch over the matter. Listening to the internal debate within HEW that raged over the writing and implementation of the *Adams* criteria, Califano by the spring of 1978 had tilted toward Tatel and the OCR radicals. He believed, Libassi recalled, that the time was ripe to become more aggressive toward UNC. On February 4, 1978, while he officially accepted the higher education desegregation plans submitted by Arkansas, Florida, and Oklahoma, he rejected the plans of North Carolina, Virginia, and Georgia. Battle lines were drawn by mid-February 1978, and a war mentality prevailed among the UNC and HEW forces. David Tatel, who enjoyed strong support from Califano, was determined to wear down what he regarded as UNC intransigence. The university, meanwhile, felt boxed in, unable to resolve a difficult situation and the victim of an apparent campaign by OCR to single it out. Califano's decision to reject *Phase II* was disappointing, Friday told the Board of Governors on February 10, but he refused to make concessions on the duplication issue. HEW was now intent on forcing UNC to begin an "educational experiment that would seriously disrupt" academic programs and that could inflict "long-lasting damage." This experiment was based on an "unproven assumption that it might, or might not, result in major changes in the racial composition of student populations." The "basic disagreement" lay in the university's refusal to abdicate some of its "key responsibilities for higher education."[67]

Friday's fears were soon confirmed. At HEW he had developed the greatest rapport with general counsel Peter Libassi, who had coordinated the writing of the desegregation criteria but had attempted to moderate the hard line of the OCR radicals. On one occasion that spring, according to Friday, Libassi took him aside. He sympathized with the UNC position, he said, explaining that OCR hard-liners now held the upper hand in the North Carolina case. "You know why they're doing this?" Libassi asked Friday. "They think if they can break UNC, they can break anybody."[68] The HEW attorney explained OCR's thinking in a subsequent interview. "You can't go and pick on states where it's easy," he said, and avoid dealing with a "leader" like UNC. "If you don't get them to move, the other states are going to be very difficult to move." David Breneman noted that after the negotiations of 1974–75, OCR radicals became "probably more hostile to North Carolina than almost any other state." To the radicals, UNC was the "most obstreperous" and the "toughest adversary" they faced. They were determined to discipline UNC.[69]

Tatel later asserted that it was "very clear" from the outset of his tenure at OCR that North Carolina was "the most important" of the *Adams* states. It possessed the best public university system in the South; unlike some of the other states, he reflected, North Carolina had several "really fine" institutions. But what gave the UNC case even greater visibility was Bill Friday. Because of his stature within the state and nationally, he "raised the level of North Carolina." He had great political assets in Washington and "great access to the media." Dealing with Friday was "very different" from dealing with any other leader in higher education; a decade later, Tatel could not remember the names of the other *Adams* chancellors and presidents. But, he declared, he would "never forget Bill Friday's name."[70]

UNC officials were certain, as one administrator put it, that the university had become an "ideal target" for OCR, and agency negotiators "drove their hardest bargain" with North Carolina because they realized that the case was "precedent-setting." Others were convinced that the university received special treatment for another reason: North Carolina had long enjoyed a reputation as the most progressive southern state, especially in race relations, and whatever path it took in desegregation would deeply influence other states in the region. An attorney who subsequently represented UNC expressed it this way: if "this most progressive of systems" followed the OCR's model of desegregation, then others would fall in line, for "who among the southern states could profess to be better than North Carolina, in terms of moderation, and liberalism, and higher education?"[71]

Whether or not HEW singled out North Carolina is debatable: Joe Califano, maintaining that North Carolina received no special treatment, stated that every other *Adams* state was under precisely the same pressure. Others, including the LDF's Julius Chambers, agreed. Notwithstanding those assertions, UNC had become a linchpin in the entire *Adams* process. Califano, who until early 1978 had played a minor role in the UNC case, regarded North Carolina as an important test. Ed Yoder, a UNC graduate who had worked for the *Greensboro Daily News* and became editorial page editor for the *Washington Star* in June 1975, later described Califano as "the most shameless and . . . nakedly, unashamedly, political administrator I know anything about." Most of what Califano did, he recalled, was political, much of it "half-cocked." The fact that he was "at the bottom of the woodpile" in the UNC case made Yoder suspicious. Once, when he was preparing to compose a hostile editorial, he telephoned Califano. Why, he asked Califano, did he focus so much attention on North Carolina? The HEW secretary responded that North Carolina was the "bellwether." It had long enjoyed a reputation as a progressive state. By forcing North Carolina to do certain things, HEW could establish a "benchmark" against which to measure other states. On several other occasions, he told Yoder that this was HEW's basic political strategy.[72]

By February 1978 litigation with HEW, an acrimonious conflict that could seriously affect the university's national reputation, seemed increasingly likely. For much of the previous decade, the issue of desegregation had come to occupy more and more of Bill Friday's time and energy; by the winter and spring of 1978, it was all-consuming for him and his staff. In the past, he had brought all of his great skills to bear on the problem. He had sought accommodation with three OCR directors and four HEW secretaries, only to find that the agreements could be repudiated. By 1978 the "Friday treatment" of compromise and consensus building no longer seemed to work. Friday's access to the pinnacles of power appeared equally ineffective; indeed, he found himself almost powerless, despite contacts with the Carter White House.

By 1978 the issue of desegregation had become the supreme test of Friday's university presidency; the UNC president, according to one account, was "obsessed with it."[73] UNC desegregation was an exceedingly complex story that defies any easy characterization as a conflict between integrationists and southern segregationists. Although Friday was now fully involved in an effort to upgrade the traditionally black institutions and to achieve greater racial balance in enrollments, by resisting complete federal control he was susceptible to outside criticism. Not only did the controversy test Friday's skills at accommodation and compromise, but it also challenged his abilities to hold together the precarious Board of Governors system, the political unity and support that had long backed the University of North Carolina, and the high esteem that he had always enjoyed from editorialists in the state.

The unequal conditions at traditionally white and traditionally black institutions remained, and Friday's challenge was to move toward change without disrupting the delicate equilibrium of the UNC system. Despite the assertions of the 1976 *Comparative Study*, there were obvious differences in the quality of programs, faculties, and physical plant at TBIs and TWIs in North Carolina. Yet there was no clear or easy path toward ending those inequities. UNC's policies of the early 1970s were insufficient, and the gradualism and indifference characterizing the pre-1974 era would likely maintain unequal education. After 1974 the UNC Board of Governors adopted aggressive desegregation policies only in response to outside pressure. But more radical measures, such as the LDF model of program mergers and closings, had no more clearly beneficial effect. In a delicate balancing act, Friday juggled the historically black campuses' fears of merger with conservatives' unwillingness to grant federal authorities any right of supervision. The increasingly intrusive OCR challenge threatened to upend Friday's hold, and perhaps UNC's as well, and the coming years would sorely test his leadership.

CHAPTER 11 *The Chasm May Be Narrow,*
but It Also Runs Deep

W HEN HEW secretary Joseph Califano rejected the revised UNC desegregation plan in February 1978, Bill Friday faced a forty-day deadline to settle the case, after which administrative proceedings to terminate federal funding under Title VI would begin. Friday pursued a two-track strategy. While continuing to encourage negotiations with HEW in hopes of a compromise, he also sought the help of political contacts in the Carter White House. Friday's ties to Carter were the closest that he had ever had with any president. During the campaign, Friday had served on a task force to define Carter's policy positions on education, and he had supplied the president-elect with advice about appointments during the transition in late 1976 and early 1977. Friday's closest associations in the White House were with Juanita Kreps, secretary of commerce and on leave as a Duke University professor, and Stuart Eizenstat, Carter's domestic policy adviser. A Carolina graduate, Eizenstat had been a student in one of Ray Dawson's political science courses at Chapel Hill; he and Friday were well acquainted by the time of Carter's inauguration.

As the conflict with the Office for Civil Rights headed toward a disastrous conclusion in 1977–78, Friday appealed directly to the White House. Elected officials from North Carolina, such as Governor Jim Hunt and Senator Robert Morgan, informed Carter that the HEW-UNC dispute could hurt him politically. Friday maintained close touch with the White House through Eizenstat; through that pipeline, the UNC president, according to Califano, supplied a "running version" of events. Friday also pressed his case through Kreps, who argued for the university at a cabinet meeting on February 6, 1978, and, a week later, during a private meeting with Carter. But Carter remained ambivalent about the controversy. Although he wanted it settled, he was also determined not to alienate civil rights groups. As a result, he straddled the fence, publicly remaining an unqualified supporter of desegregation, privately urging Califano to seek a solution.[1]

Yet no breakthrough resulted from White House involvement. On February 20, 1978, Dawson traveled to Washington to meet with HEW officials. But because David Tatel, who was ill, was absent, the discussions led nowhere. A more serious attempt at accommodation occurred two weeks later, on March 7, when Friday led a UNC delegation composed of Dawson, Felix Joyner, Cleon Thompson, Bill Johnson, Dick Robinson, and Jeffrey Orleans to Washington. On the HEW side was an equally formidable team: Tatel, Peter Libassi, Califano special assistant Richard Beattie, Edward Rutledge from the U.S. Commission on Civil Rights, and Libassi special assistant June Zeitline, along with OCR staffers Jeff Champagne, Arline Mendelson, and William Thomas. The UNC representatives began the meeting by presenting a new proposal responding to the OCR's January 1978 critique. Then the group adjourned for a half hour while the HEW-OCR team caucused.

When the two sides reassembled, Libassi, the meeting's moderator, urged accommodation. He reviewed the case by remarking that there were major and minor issues dividing the university and OCR; once the major concerns had been resolved, the minor ones would follow. Libassi then asked Tatel to identify the major problems to be settled. According to the OCR director, three issues remained: the elimination of program duplication, the 150 percent rule, and graduate and professional enrollment. Of these, he considered program duplication the most fundamental. Dawson entered the discussion, arguing that, rather than the elimination of unnecessary program duplication, the real issue was expanding opportunities for black students. Libassi, faced with these two well-established positions, favored compromise. He suggested that each side preserve its approach but "agree to disagree" on the matter of program duplication. Was it not possible to focus on results instead of means? Could HEW, rather than insisting on the elimination of program duplication, agree that it was a "means to an end," one that might be otherwise achieved?[2]

Neither side, however, was interested in compromise. When the HEW general counsel asked UNC to conduct a duplication study of undergraduate business offerings at Chapel Hill and North Carolina Central University, both Friday and Thompson strenuously objected. Tatel also maintained his position that the basic deficiencies to which OCR had earlier objected persisted. While Libassi agreed to promote conciliation through meetings with OCR staff, Friday was convinced that there was no further point in talking. Tatel remembered that the meeting ended on a decidedly "cold" tone. Friday left again discouraged. "Having spent the last month in almost daily involvement with OCR," he wrote on March 13, he feared that there was "no reasonable way of accommodation." Litigation, he believed, had become inevitable.

Despite the apparent failure of negotiations, Joe Califano was sending different signals. At a cabinet meeting on March 13, he told President Carter that he wanted an agreement with UNC before the March 22 deadline of Judge John H. Pratt's court. Carter requested a memorandum outlining HEW's position and promised that he would take the matter up with Governor Hunt; the HEW secretary realized that the White House now considered the resolution of the case a major priority. Although previously uninvolved in the details of the HEW-UNC negotiations, Califano plunged forward with a thirty-minute telephone conversation with Friday on March 21, 1978. Identifying the main issues as program duplication, the 150 percent rule, increased enrollment of black graduate students, and greater proportions of black faculty, Califano sought concessions. But Friday remained firm. As Califano recalled, he sensed that Friday was "bridling" at his high-pressure tactics. The conversation, which at times became heated, ended inconclusively.[3]

Facing a court-mandated deadline, Califano announced on March 22, 1978, that "unconstitutional vestiges" of segregation and a "separate and unequal system of higher education" remained and that Title VI administrative proceedings would begin to cut off UNC's federal funding. Responding immediately, Friday, at a press conference in Chapel Hill, described Califano's announcement as "deeply disappointing" and "wrong." Rather than opposing HEW pressure because of any "attitude of defiance," the university was refusing to commit itself to "educationally unwise" actions and "unreasonable requirements" that would strip UNC of its autonomy. Although he doubted whether negotiations could continue, Friday called for a "new relationship" between HEW and UNC.[4]

HEW's assertions, which were contained in a seventy-five-page document announcing the onset of Title VI enforcement proceedings, deeply offended the UNC president. One senior UNC official, commenting anonymously in the *Raleigh News and Observer*, said that the HEW statement described university administrators as "racial bigots" and swept aside their efforts over the past decade to desegregate. Friday questioned HEW's good faith in previous negotiations; the talks in early 1978, he feared, were "for the record, and nothing more." UNC had offered an "honest facing" of its prospects for desegregation; there was no "good purpose to be served by offering assurances that we can do things we do not believe are attainable."[5]

Commencing administrative proceedings on March 22, Califano told reporters that he hoped that negotiations would continue. Two days later, he telephoned Hunt and Friday and indicated that he was willing to negotiate.

Although many of the members of the Board of Governors were in no mood to negotiate, an ad hoc lawyers' committee – organized in the autumn of 1975 when litigation first seemed a possibility – convened a three-hour meeting with Friday and attorneys Andy Vanore and Carl Vogt, whom the university had hired from the law firm of Watergate special prosecutor Leon Jaworski, to consider Califano's overture. The committee recommended preparing a defense for administrative proceedings and considering "independent legal proceedings" – a countersuit – that would be based in North Carolina. In the meantime, the university's legal counselors would also examine the new Califano initiative.[6]

Califano was, in fact, torn between two alternative approaches. Although he leaned toward the position of Tatel and the OCR radicals, he faced "overriding" orders from the White House to settle the case in order to avoid additional political damage. In late April 1978, with negotiations stalled, the president warned Califano that if he could not resolve the matter Carter would talk directly to Governor Hunt. Califano insisted that Carter delay this move, fearing, he later explained, that the president "would settle for too little and be embarrassed if the federal court rejected the agreement." Califano then requested a two-week delay while OCR negotiators met with UNC representatives.[7]

Friday was aware of White House pressure on the HEW secretary; much of it had resulted from his own exertions. Opinion among the white members of the Board of Governors had hardened, and Chairman Bill Johnson had become the leading hard-liner. Meanwhile, by April and May 1978, Carl Vogt was playing a significant role in negotiations and laying the groundwork for a possible UNC countersuit. Serious negotiations did not occur, however, until the latter part of April, when Dick Beattie, who had become HEW's lead negotiator, conducted a new round of shuttle diplomacy.[8]

Beattie, a native New Yorker, Dartmouth graduate, former marine, graduate of the University of Pennsylvania law school, and member of Cyrus Vance's law firm in New York City, had written to Califano expressing interest in working in HEW in early 1977. After Beattie spent an afternoon with Califano, the HEW secretary offered him a job as deputy general counsel. Beattie's negotiations with UNC culminated in his visit to Chapel Hill on April 27, 1978. After negotiating sessions during the morning and afternoon brought little progress, U.S. commissioner of education Ernest L. Boyer joined the meeting in the midafternoon. Without the knowledge of Tatel and the OCR staff, Califano had summoned Boyer to his office. "Get on a plane," he told Boyer, "we've got to work something out." Boyer had enjoyed a close professional and personal relationship with Friday since Boyer's days as head of New York's SUNY system, and he stayed with the Fridays during his Chapel Hill visit. "I just knew if I could talk to anybody on the planet Earth honestly," Boyer recalled, "it would be with Bill Friday," whom he believed wanted a reasonable solution and would understand both sides of the issue.[9]

On the crucial issue of program duplication, Boyer offered a new perspective. As Beattie and Dawson debated the question of which "core" curricula should be considered duplicative at traditionally white institutions and traditionally black institutions – and which "non-core" curricula should not be – Boyer proposed that there be no a priori definition of what constituted core curricula. OCR and UNC negotiators had focused on a list of eight "core" subject areas identified in the OCR analysis of January 19, 1978; Boyer suggested that HEW abandon this as a basis for negotiation. He could not conceive, Boyer told Beattie and Dawson, of HEW attempting to "write the master plan" for the University of North Carolina. Instead, he recommended that the two sides set aside any prior definitions and embark on an objective study of program duplication. If courses and curricula were found to be duplicative, then the Board of Governors would consider appropriate remedies. On the other hand, he said, it was entirely possible that such a study might not find unnecessary program duplication.[10]

Boyer's proposal came like a bolt out of the blue. To Friday and Dawson, it constituted a "major change" in HEW's approach by which the department would abandon the narrow, literalist demands of Tatel and OCR radicals. According to Dawson, UNC officials found it "heartening." Boyer's suggestion, which Beattie seized upon as a possible solution, relinquished the "going-in proposition" that there would be a "fixed and common definition of core curricula." UNC officials were convinced that Boyer, one of the few HEW officials with any background in higher education, had cut through the bureaucratic confusion and offered an approach rooted in the realities of a university.[11]

Over the next two weeks, Beattie and the UNC team, which included counsel Carl Vogt and Andy Vanore, hammered out a document, known as *Supplemental Statement II*, that defined UNC's obligations. But David Tatel, uninvolved in negotiations since early March, interjected his influence by insisting that strict standards be included against which the UNC duplication study would be measured. In fact, Tatel remained suspicious of Beattie and Boyer's peace plan, and when Beattie returned from another trip to Chapel Hill on May 7, Tatel openly challenged the agreement. Tatel would endorse it, he wrote in a memorandum to Beattie on May 8, only if a written guarantee of OCR approval of "standards" were included. In other memoranda, Tatel argued that the proposed December 1978 deadline for the university was too generous.[12]

Not until Califano overruled Tatel did the outlines of an agreement emerge. Califano received a handwritten note from President Carter on May 11. "Contact me re N.C. desegregation suit," it read. "Your two weeks are up." That afternoon, Califano reached Friday by telephone in Chapel Hill, and they spoke for thirty to forty minutes. In three additional phone conversations that afternoon and evening, the two men sought a settlement, and the matter so occupied Friday that he canceled the taping of *North Carolina People*. At 10:45 on the evening of May 11, the two men reached agreement on the language of the proposed *Supplemental Statement II*.[13]

Although *Supplemental Statement II* dealt with a range of outstanding differences between OCR and UNC, its focus was on program duplication and enhancement of the five historically black campuses. It described the unique educational missions of the TBIs: North Carolina A&T State and North Carolina Central would develop graduate programs; Winston-Salem State, Elizabeth City State, and Fayetteville State would remain general baccalaureate institutions. UNC promised to provide OCR with a detailed program review of the TBIs and, in the future, to suggest new programs that were consistent with their missions. During the summer 1978 session of the General Assembly, UNC would seek an additional $10.3 million for new construction at the traditionally black institutions. *Supplemental Statement II* also agreed to conduct a detailed study of physical plant and plant maintenance at the TBIs.

By far the most controversial provision of *Supplemental Statement II*, however, was its commitment to eliminate unnecessary program duplication. To accomplish this goal, UNC would conduct a special study of degree offerings at TWIs and TBIs located in "geographically proximate" areas; these included Winston-Salem State, A&T, and UNCG in the Triad area, and Chapel Hill, N.C. State, and North Carolina Central in the Triangle area. The study would also scrutinize offerings in engineering at two traditionally white institutions, N.C. State and UNC-Charlotte, as well as at one traditionally black institution, A&T. The duplication study would be presented to the Board of Governors and then to OCR.

Supplemental Statement II, however, also included reservations about how far the university would go in the matter of program duplication. Although UNC accepted responsibility, it asserted that the desegregation of TBIs and TWIs was "not solely dependent on the identification of some distinctive, specialized mission" for geographically proximate institutions. Nor was desegregation dependent on enrollments in unduplicated programs. In a state with one black campus, such an approach might make sense; in North Carolina, it did not. OCR had already acknowledged the existence of North Carolina

Central's law school; it was only one example of the need for a "heavy burden of proof" before resorting to mergers or closings of programs.[14]

Friday took *Supplemental Statement II* to the regularly scheduled meeting of the Board of Governors on May 12, 1978. He and Ray Dawson both argued hard for board support of the agreement, which they presented as a genuine compromise. Title VI proceedings had been avoided, Friday asserted, and it was now unnecessary "to protect our interests and defend the integrity of the university." Califano had personally assured him that the agreement embodied in *Supplemental Statement II* would lead to HEW acceptance. Although by 5:00 P.M. the board had endorsed the agreement, dissension remained. Some board members unsuccessfully attempted to prevent consideration of the agreement; discussion lasted more than four hours – the longest closed session to that date in the history of the Board of Governors. Among the members of the ad hoc lawyers' committee, only Worth Coltrane, William Dees, and John Jordan supported the compromise unconditionally. Dees, who had become the board's strongest advocate of conciliation, maintained that North Carolina faced a genuine opportunity: it could settle with HEW and preserve university autonomy with only minimal concessions.[15]

Among board hard-liners, Philip Carson favored compromise only if HEW unequivocally accepted the agreement that day. But *Supplemental Statement II*'s most vocal critic was Bill Johnson. Although he later said that opposing Friday was "the toughest thing" he had ever been involved in, the former superior court judge rejected any compromise that legitimized federal intervention. UNC had already made too many concessions to outside interference; the state should take a stand and litigate. The agreement, he said, would "ultimately come back to haunt us with dire consequences and results." If HEW subsequently became unhappy with any aspect of the compromise, it might again threaten the university. "In due course," Johnson predicted, "we will again have to face the question of whether the actions we may have taken . . . will meet the requirements of various bodies and agencies." Although the meeting concluded with support for Friday, three board members – Johnson, Jake Froelich Jr., and Laurence A. Cobb of Charlotte – voted against him.[16]

On the same day, Califano convened a news conference in Washington to announce HEW's approval of *Supplemental Statement II*. It was an "excellent plan," Califano said, which he intended to support with all the resources at his disposal. Canceling the Title VI proceedings to cut off $89 million in federal funds to UNC – 17 percent of its operating budget – Califano told reporters that a settlement was "far preferable" to a legal battle. Califano's statement made the best of a bad situation as far as he was personally concerned – the best in view of the heavy pressure from the White House. "I am confident that the plan recently agreed to by HEW and UNC," Stuart Eizenstat wrote to North Carolina senator Sam J. Ervin Jr. on July 24, would "foster equal educational opportunity" and also protect the "high standards of excellence" at UNC. As a 1964 Carolina graduate, Eizenstat was "particularly pleased" by the settlement. Jimmy Carter had personally lobbied Califano, and in the summer of 1978 the president telephoned Bill Friday while the UNC president was vacationing at Kill Devil Hills. Suffering from a painful tooth infection, Friday was awakened by the call about 2:00 P.M. on July 20. Carter asked if any problems remained with HEW, and Friday replied that there were none. Carter said that he wanted to be "helpful" to the UNC cause. After Friday expressed his good wishes to Carter, telling him that "we thought of him often," Carter ended the conversation by saying that sometimes his job was "almost as difficult" as being a university president.[17]

No sooner had the ink dried on the UNC-HEW agreement, however, than ominous signs appeared. David Tatel, excluded from the April and May negotiations, considered White House intervention as inappropriate and "not constructive" because it repeated what he termed the "UNC line." Rather than attempting to learn more about the issue, he later explained, Carter's advisers wanted the UNC case settled because it was not "good for the president." Not surprisingly, Tatel refused to acquiesce. "I had my doubts about . . . whether it would ever lead to an acceptable plan," he subsequently maintained. There were "simply too many contingencies." Almost immediately, he questioned the legitimacy of the settlement and felt no allegiance to Ernest Boyer's new formula for compromise.[18]

Although Judge Pratt's second supplemental order of April 1, 1977, granted the NAACP Legal Defense and Educational Fund the right to review any new desegregation plans prior to their acceptance by HEW, the LDF was excluded from the spring 1978 negotiations. In March 1978 Califano had negotiated and accepted plans from Georgia and Virginia without LDF participation, and the fund shot off protest telegrams in both instances. When no response came from HEW and word leaked from the Office for Civil Rights that a settlement with North Carolina was imminent, LDF attorney John Silard, on May 8, threatened to bring the matter to Pratt. HEW negotiator Dick Beattie then telephoned Silard and promised to permit him to review the proposed settlement, but no further communication followed until after Califano had already endorsed the May 12 agreement. In response, Silard filed a motion seeking to return the matter to court.[19]

In the summer of 1978, under persistent LDF pressure, Tatel delayed endorsing the UNC-HEW agreement, and on June 12 he agreed only to support it provisionally. Even more serious as far as UNC was concerned, Tatel, in late June and July, wrote to Friday questioning the October 1975 agreement with Peter Holmes regarding the location of the new school of veterinary medicine at N.C. State. Califano again intervened, stating that the location of the vet school was no longer an issue. Although Califano, in a letter to Governor Hunt on July 11, blocked Tatel's resurrection of the vet school controversy, he acquiesced in the OCR director's interpretation of the settlement as a *provisional* agreement. Boyer later maintained that, for Califano, Boyer's negotiations "got him out of the box," but that the HEW secretary was presented with "an ultimatum internally," in the opposition of Tatel and OCR, "that he couldn't live with, and so he had to back off." As a result of this internal uprising, "the deal that we struck never was pulled off." UNC officials, though initially elated at the prospect of settlement, were by midsummer 1978 convinced that OCR hostility would continue. Ray Dawson described Tatel's revival of the vet school issue as "deeply troubling." It suggested an "ephemeral quality" to the HEW-UNC negotiations; Tatel was suggesting, he believed, that no continuity existed between OCR directors. The episode had even wider implications, for UNC officials remained concerned about "who was making the decisions" in Washington and how "binding" and how "durable" any agreements with HEW – including the May 1978 agreement – might be in the future.[20]

Tatel's saber rattling seemed to confirm the predictions of critics of Friday's policy of conciliation, including not only Bill Johnson but also the *Raleigh News and Observer*. Soon after the UNC-HEW agreement was approved, an editorial in that newspaper described the settlement as the "best this state could hope for," but far from "an absolute Tar Heel win, or even . . . the end of the game." The university, it believed, had appeased Washington mainly by pledging to "do certain things without specifying how." The agreement, it predicted, had not ended the matter. The LDF could challenge the settlement; HEW might subsequently abandon it. In any event, the "real crunch" would come when UNC offered specifics, and in the meantime OCR had placed its foot "in the door of university operation."[21]

Preoccupied with the legislative session of that summer, UNC officials did not begin the duplication study promised in *Supplemental Statement II* until the fall. The study aroused fears, especially on the Greensboro and Winston-Salem campuses, about possible program mergers or closings, and in September the *Greensboro Daily News* described the UNC-HEW agreement as a "tenuous peace which could erupt into open controversy again." At the two Greensboro campuses there was apprehension that they might become convenient targets. Located on either side of Greensboro's downtown, UNCG and

A&T had both been established in 1891, and, as a women's college and a prominent black land-grant college, respectively, they had developed in a de jure segregated environment with separate constituencies. In the late 1970s, parallel programs existed at both institutions. UNCG had created a School of Nursing, for example, out of an associate nursing B.A. degree program established in 1956; both A&T and Winston-Salem State organized nursing programs in 1953, as the North Carolina legislature, on the eve of the *Brown* decision, attempted to equalize programs. By 1977, however, there were major gaps between the nursing programs: whereas 89 percent of UNCG students passed the nursing exam, the proportion was only 20 percent at A&T and 26 percent at Winston-Salem State.[22]

On September 27, 1978, Tatel and Beattie met with Friday and Dawson in Washington. OCR felt pressure from the *Adams* litigants, Tatel explained; they believed that HEW was giving the states too much time to revise their plans. But the chief topic of the meeting was the UNC duplication study. Reviewing developments in other states, Tatel told the UNC officials about efforts in Georgia, Florida, Virginia, and Oklahoma to speed desegregation by eliminating program duplication. Friday and Dawson argued that any attempt to institute significant curriculum changes at Chapel Hill, perhaps by moving programs to North Carolina Central, was unrealistic, and that there was "not even a remote possibility" that the Board of Governors would approve them. It was "educational nonsense" anyway, they said; the same would be true in applying such a model to A&T and UNCG.[23]

The reluctance of the two UNC administrators to embrace a program duplication model shocked Tatel; according to Dawson, he was "very disturbed." Tatel feared that UNC's unwillingness to adopt program shifts might well lead to "another major conflict" between UNC and HEW. His main concern was achieving quick enrollment changes. If the numbers could show a decided improvement, he said, perhaps the need for focusing on program duplication could be shunted aside, even if that meant that OCR might become open to renewed legal pressure from the LDF. Tatel concluded the meeting by offering OCR's help in preparing the duplication study, but Friday and Dawson offered no reply. Repeating the experience of the spring of 1978 was "out of the question," they said; the duplication study, once approved by the Board of Governors, would be its "definitive statement" on the subject.

The prospects for the success of the May 1978 agreement, which depended on the duplication study, were therefore not auspicious. While UNC remained unwilling to accept any part of the program duplication model, Tatel was veering into OCR's radical camp. The primacy of the radicals became apparent in November, when Georgia and Virginia submitted revised plans that accepted the program duplication model. In Virginia, the historically black Norfolk State and the geographically proximate historically white Old Dominion University had agreed to consolidate twenty-six duplicative programs. But OCR rejected the Virginia plan because it regarded these changes as insufficient. A confrontation seemed likely.[24]

Pessimistic about the prospects of settlement, Ray Dawson took charge of writing the duplication study and imposed an information blackout until it was presented to the Planning Committee of the Board of Governors in early December. UNC staff attorney Jeff Orleans later observed that Dawson, in preparing the duplication study, was "going to write what he felt was right," and the probability that Dawson would present a study that would satisfy Tatel and OCR was "zero." Not surprisingly, the duplication study presented to the Planning Committee on December 1 and the full board a week later found no "educationally unnecessary" program duplication at geographically proximate campuses in the Triangle and Triad areas. It argued instead that UNC campuses served limited geographic regions and that the curricula offered there were consistent with those of comprehensive universities nationally.[25]

At the Board of Governors meeting, Friday emphasized that the duplication study reaffirmed UNC's policy of providing increased access to white and black North Carolinians. The legacy of segregation, he asserted, could not be erased through coercive measures that damaged morale and the institutional structure. He described the study's recommendations as "significant, historic milestones in the evolution of the board." Although he expected trouble from OCR about the matter, he reassured board members that UNC had done the right thing. "We've done the best we know how to do, and, in the doing, demonstrated a good faith effort." If the decision were made on educational grounds alone, HEW would approve the study.[26]

Officially submitted to OCR on December 15, 1978, the UNC duplication study made another round of conflict inevitable. Georgia and Virginia moved closer to a settlement with HEW, and their desegregation plans were accepted in early 1979. Although these plans were substantially less ambitious than that of UNC, they accepted OCR's emphasis on the elimination of program duplication. Both states embraced program transfers between adjoining campuses – Georgia at the traditionally white Armstrong State College and the traditionally black Savannah State College and Virginia at the traditionally white Old Dominion University and the traditionally black Norfolk State.[27]

In the early spring of 1979, UNC officials became convinced, as John Sanders wrote, that federal officials were "making deals with all states except

North Carolina." In fact, according to Califano, Tatel was "infuriated" by the UNC duplication study and believed that Friday was acting in bad faith. "For the first time," Califano wrote in his memoirs, "I had real doubts about our ability to settle North Carolina." He also feared that the state's political climate, combined with Friday's "hurt and anger" about the unfavorable national exposure, would make future conciliation impossible. Nonetheless, with Carter pressing him for a settlement, the HEW secretary felt obliged to "pursue every possibility," and he ordered Tatel to "walk the last mile."[28]

Tatel, however, encountered pressure from all sides. On January 12, LDF attorney and longtime civil rights litigator Joseph Rauh Jr. denounced the UNC plan as "massive resistance to desegregation in higher education." The university's assertion that no unnecessary duplication existed was "an incredible defiance of the law of the land." Rauh, along with prominent organizations such as the Leadership Conference on Civil Rights, demanded that Joe Califano and the HEW immediately terminate UNC's federal funding. Despite arm-twisting from Califano, Tatel had already reaffirmed his strong commitment to the program duplication model. He employed Kenneth Clark, a black educational psychologist who had testified in the *Brown* case two decades earlier, as a consultant to report on the UNC duplication study. Clark's analysis, and that of the OCR staff, was unfavorable; Mary Berry, who favored a stronger program of TBI enhancement, also reviewed the duplication study. On January 18, 1979, Tatel sent an OCR working paper on the UNC plan to Bill Friday. It concluded that "extensive duplication" persisted, despite UNC claims. Tatel was convinced, he later explained, that UNC had reneged on its commitments in the May 12 agreement, and he rejected the validity of the duplication study. At the same time, he opened the door for further negotiations, even offering to meet with Friday.[29]

Bill Friday was in no mood for negotiation, however. On January 22, three days after receiving Tatel's telephone call that communicated OCR's rejection of the duplication study, Friday met with the UNCG faculty and promised to avoid "cosmetic" changes like those embraced by Virginia in order to reach a settlement with HEW. Quoting an LDF characterization, Friday asserted that he would rather be a "redneck hero" than sacrifice university autonomy. On January 25 the UNC president formally and testily responded to Tatel. Complaining that UNC submissions to OCR had never received any response, he discounted the office's January 18 working paper as a basis of negotiation. The OCR analysis contradicted "the letter and spirit" of the May 1978 agreement and was a "summary rejection" of UNC's findings. Friday emphatically took issue with OCR's conclusions, and he resented its "pervasive . . . unwillingness" to "acknowledge the legitimacy or effectiveness of our efforts and achievements." The UNC plan, he maintained, was perfectly adequate, whereas the program duplication model that OCR was promoting had no legal basis.[30]

Wary of White House reaction, HEW officials sought to portray themselves as the more reasonable party in the dispute. Friday's strong letter to Tatel was "obviously not helpful," Beattie explained to Eizenstat, "but we are still trying to open up the lines of communication." Speaking to Friday by telephone near the end of January, Tatel urged negotiations. The official HEW deadline, he said, was not until March 11; that left more than a month to negotiate, and if any progress could be achieved, HEW would more than likely postpone the official filing of administrative proceedings. Tatel concluded the conversation by expressing the hope that litigation could be avoided. He reaffirmed his position in a letter to Friday on February 16. Only differences about program duplication posed a "truly serious" obstacle to settlement, Tatel wrote. He fully expected that negotiation could resolve those differences.[31]

Tatel's stand on program duplication, combined with his offer of negotiation, received Califano's full support. On February 9 the HEW secretary called a press conference in Washington, where he again rejected the UNC desegregation plan. Califano hoped that North Carolina would propose changes as acceptable as those of Georgia, whose plan federal officials had recently approved. Various combinations of program shifts and the location of new programs at historically black UNC campuses were all "opportunities available to the North Carolina system." The details of the program shifts did not concern Califano; he was not "in the business of crossing t's and dotting i's." Nonetheless, the implicit message of his press conference was that HEW would continue to insist that the program duplication model form a central part of the UNC desegregation plan.[32]

Meanwhile, HEW officials adopted a new tactic. On February 6, 1979, North Carolina's five TBI chancellors visited Tatel; also present were Governor Hunt's assistant John A. Williams Jr., Cleon Thompson, Mary Berry, and Roger Sharpe, a former North Carolina state senator who was serving a year-long internship in Tatel's office. The chancellors had requested the meeting out of a concern about possible program mergers or closings; they were, according to Califano, "increasingly worried that their institutions might be merged out of existence." The visit had been arranged by Hunt's office – the governor and his staff believed that it would bring additional pressure on OCR – and the TBI delegation had been flown to Washington on Hunt's jet. Suspecting that Friday was deliberately inflaming TBI fears, Tatel and Berry took pains to reassure the chancellors. Each was given the opportunity to make a five-minute presentation explaining the ambitions of their institutions. When the chancellors told Tatel that they wanted enhancement rather than program closings, he surprised them by saying that HEW officials were also seeking this goal. "I tried to make them understand that instead of coming up here and telling us to lay off," Tatel recalled, "they ought to be coming up here and telling us to be as tough as we can to protect the black institutions." One observer noted that Tatel's sympathetic attitude made a "tremendous difference" in altering the climate of the meeting. At its conclusion, the chancellors thought that the HEW officials should "come down to see what's going on." A few days later, one of the TBI chancellors renewed the invitation.[33]

When Tatel communicated the invitation to Califano, the HEW secretary saw it as a "terrific opportunity." Tatel should travel with a "large press entourage," he said, and "show everybody what those institutions were really like." If they were as bad as HEW officials believed they were, Califano told Tatel, then North Carolinians, once informed, would rally behind an effort to enhance them. According to Califano, pressure came from the White House, where both Friday and Hunt placed calls urging that the trip be called off. Nevertheless, he remained convinced that the trip would have a "tremendous impact." "If we could get North Carolina citizens to see the dramatic difference in quality," Califano later wrote, then "we might be able to get a little support from them."[34]

Eventually, Tatel also endorsed an HEW tour of the state. The North Carolina press, he believed, was inaccurately portraying the conflict over desegregation as primarily a Chapel Hill matter; UNC desegregation, Tatel intended to show, involved other campuses at least as much, perhaps even more. Tatel wanted a "first-hand" opportunity for federal officials to see the historically black campuses. A secondary motivation was a feeling in OCR and HEW that the people of North Carolina "had not been accurately told the story of these five black institutions" and that, with the appropriate press exposure, in-state public opinion would turn against UNC's position. Many North Carolinians were ignorant of the deficiencies at TBIs, Berry would explain; with proper exposure, they could "be moved to do something." A well-publicized visit to North Carolina could provide a "better first-hand look" at the differences between the traditionally black and traditionally white institutions.[35]

Even before the trip began, however, major differences were emerging between Mary Berry and David Tatel. While Tatel had dominated the negotiations with UNC after he took office in 1977, Berry had played a minor role, through her brief and inconclusive participation with the *Adams* criteria task force. Berry was eager to have some influence, however, at least partly for bureaucratic reasons – her office, as yet, remained ill-defined and powerless. She enjoyed the limelight and was willing to use it to her maximum advantage. Berry, a historian and a graduate of historically black Howard University, shared Tatel's view of the federal government's enforcement responsibility. Unlike Tatel, however, she strongly believed that TBI enhancement should become HEW's primary objective. Policy and bureaucratic tensions thus punctuated the Berry-Tatel relationship.[36]

Delayed by a snowstorm that dumped two feet of snow and closed the airports in the Washington area, the HEW team arrived in North Carolina a day late, on Tuesday, February 20, 1979. Traveling with Tatel and Berry were OCR officials Al Hamlin and Roger Sharpe, as well as Colleen O'Connor, who was in charge of HEW public relations. The federal officials were eager for press exposure, and at all times there were reporters with them. UNC vice president Cleon Thompson and associate vice president Vic Hackley accompanied the group during its three-day trip by chartered aircraft to the five TBIs – A&T, Elizabeth City State, Fayetteville State, North Carolina Central, and Winston-Salem State – and to three TWIs – N.C. State, Carolina, and UNCG.[37]

Tatel, Berry, and their entourage began with a visit to North Carolina Central, Fayetteville State, and Winston-Salem State on Wednesday, February 21. The visits there confirmed their preconceptions about underequipment; Tatel described the "reality of it" as "overwhelming." At Central, they toured a physical education building with dank classrooms and a leaky roof; the swimming pool in the gymnasium was considered too unclean to swim in. At Fayetteville, one faculty member told Tatel that if he wanted his students to conduct serious science experiments, he sent them to local high schools where the equipment was superior. Spending the evening in Greensboro, the Tatel-Berry team encountered strong feelings from the African American community. In a ninety-minute meeting with the North Carolina Alumni and Friends Coalition at their hotel, the Greensboro Hilton, the visitors were grilled, according to a press account, about their intentions with regard to desegregation. Walter Marshall, a Winston-Salem State graduate and High Point teacher, described Bill Friday as a "dictator"; the political power structure would "cater to anything he says." Marshall feared that Joe Califano, out of concern for adverse political fallout from his antismoking campaign, would "sell-out," and that the TBIs would become "lost in the shuffle." Repeating his earlier assurances to the TBI chancellors, Tatel told coalition members that his chief objective was to strengthen the historically black institutions.[38]

The next day, Thursday, February 22, Tatel and Berry were able to compare historically white UNCG with historically black A&T. They first visited

UNCG, where Berry asked Chancellor James S. Ferguson to show them some of the institution's worst problems. He replied that he would present "neither our worst, nor our best," but a true sampling. Visiting the library, laboratories, and classrooms, the delegation noted that at 9:00 A.M. these facilities seemed empty. Apparently ignoring the Tuesday-Thursday class schedule – in which classes began at 9:30 rather than at 9:00 – Berry concluded that there was an "underutilization" of facilities at UNCG. At A&T, she and her associates were met by a group of some twenty-five chanting black protesters, who feared that federal pressure would lead to merger. Although Tatel concluded that A&T was the "nicest black campus we've seen so far," Berry asserted that the facilities there did not compare with those of UNCG.[39]

By the end of the tour UNC officials had concluded that the HEW officials were pursuing a predetermined agenda. Facilities were obviously inadequate at the historically black campuses; the chief purpose of the Tatel-Berry team was to expose them. At most of the campuses, Berry was said to have checked library catalogues to see if they listed a copy of her book, a study of the failure to use the Fourteenth Amendment to protect the legal rights of African Americans. Berry measured facilities for research science by counting autoclaves – costly sterilization equipment – while she took inventory of how many computer terminals were available. The UNC representatives Thompson and Hackley complained that she was more interested in sensationalization than in the truth. Thompson later reflected that Berry's chief concern was "getting her headlines" and that "she was always looking for a reporter." On the last day of the tour, when she was asked if the group wanted to see Elizabeth City State's new industrial arts building, Berry reportedly was uninterested, preferring to inspect the campus's "old buildings."[40]

By the time the trip ended with a luncheon hosted by Bill Friday in Chapel Hill, university officials were convinced that the chief purpose of the visit was to sensationalize the UNC-HEW controversy. Although Mary Berry told reporters that the final meeting was a "nice friendly chat that aided the digestive juices," in fact the luncheon was tense. Aside from UNC's resentment of its public pillorying by the HEW officials, Friday realized that David Tatel was uneasy. Berry had sought headlines, even at the expense of alienating UNC officials; she also wanted greater influence over the negotiations, from which she had been all but excluded. Berry and Tatel were, according to Friday, self-evidently "abrasive to each other and constantly moving for a position of primacy." At the luncheon, Friday had so much trouble finding time alone with Tatel that he had to resort to taking him to the rest room adjacent to his office for a few moments of privacy. There, the OCR director confided that he was "very frustrated" and regretted the excessive newspaper stories that had appeared in the North Carolina press; this was not his doing, he assured Friday. Earlier, Tatel had received a phone call from Califano ordering him to stop personal attacks; Tatel told the HEW secretary to confront Berry. Meanwhile, both Tatel and Berry sought to persuade Califano to remove each other from the North Carolina case. By now, Friday was persuaded that the Office for Civil Rights was in disarray, that it was dominated by intrigue and inefficiency. Califano, while permitting and perhaps even encouraging the infighting, had tilted toward Tatel.[41]

In public, Tatel remained restrained, maintaining that the TWIs and TBIs were "clearly unequal" and required corrective action by the state. Berry was jubilant about the results of the trip, which had enlightened federal officials about local conditions and educated North Carolinians about the problem of undersupported TBIs. The state's historically black schools had "very poor resources available to them," she told a reporter who interviewed her during an automobile ride from Greensboro to Raleigh; but what was striking was the existence of "pockets of interested, concerned, hustling people who are working to get private and federal funds to offset their lack of state money." In a memorandum of February 27 to Joe Califano, Berry declared that the University of North Carolina had a "long way to go" before state resources at traditionally black institutions could be considered adequate. In contrast, the traditionally white institutions had "more than adequate resources for the educational programs they offer." At the historically black campuses, laboratories and libraries were deficient, physical education facilities were a "disgrace," and other facilities were "shockingly below the quality and variety" of those at nearby TWIs.[42]

HEW officials felt that the North Carolina tour had produced a decided shift in public opinion in their favor. Tatel later described it as a turning point, primarily because it quieted criticism of OCR policies, not only among the state's editorialists but also at the White House and within North Carolina's congressional delegation. It was, Dick Beattie suggested, a "very helpful, very effective trip in . . . moving things along." On the second day of the trip, Governor Hunt had been moved to issue a statement describing how his heart "just ached" about the "old worn-out" TBI facilities; the HEW tour, he noted, had "made us more aware" of the problem. The *Greensboro Daily News*, normally a stalwart UNC supporter, admitted that there were "marked" contrasts between the TBIs and TWIs and that "nobody in his right mind" would contend otherwise. The *Charlotte Observer* agreed that facilities at the state's traditionally black institutions fell "far short of adequacy" and that upgrading had not "come near making up years of neglect." Even Ray Dawson would later concede that the Tatel-Berry tour was "not altogether unsuccessful" in swaying the attitude of the North Carolina press.[43]

The Tatel-Berry visit primarily concerned public images, and it aggravated tensions. One reporter, who detected "some hard feeling and bruised egos," was understating the matter. In the future, university officials would blur the different styles and objectives of David Tatel and Mary Berry; as a result of their visit, according to Jeff Orleans, senior UNC staff had "a lot less" confidence in the possibility of accommodation. Moreover, the harsh criticisms of the TBIs narrowed UNC's freedom of movement, because Friday and his aides did not want to seem to be conceding anything to federal officials. "We not only didn't have a back door," said Orleans, "but we felt like we were in a trash compactor." Despite his public stand on the Tatel-Berry tour – and HEW's belief that it could obtain a better deal from the governor than from Friday – Jim Hunt was deeply aggrieved by what he considered to be unwarranted federal interference in state affairs. Immediately before Tatel and Berry's arrival in North Carolina, Hunt had telephoned the White House to complain.[44]

UNC officials perceived the Tatel-Berry tour as a "premeditated and planned assault" that was intended to discredit the university; many of them, recalled UNC vice president Roy Carroll, were "terribly insulted" by the HEW intervention. Friday took most of the criticism offered by Tatel and Berry personally, and he feared that their visit had damaged UNC's national image.[45] UNC-HEW relations had deteriorated despite the efforts of White House officials, who were unable to overcome Califano's personal support for the trip. When Carter aides such as Jack Watson and Stuart Eizenstat urged him to cancel it, Califano retorted, according to one account, that "he was going to run his office his way and if they didn't like it they could have it." Although Califano believed that the trip had yielded significant public relations benefits, White House officials knew better. Just when it appeared that "some progress" was possible, Eizenstat wrote in a memorandum to President Carter on March 5, the HEW secretary had dispatched a team to North Carolina. That visit had been "highly publicized," despite Califano's explicit assurances to Watson that "he would insure *minimum* publicity." During the Tatel-Berry tour, "several caustic and personal indictments" were made of Bill Friday, Eizenstat observed, and the visit had "set back the course of negotiations." Hunt had informed the White House of his "extreme displeasure," and he described the Tatel-Berry tour as another instance of the administration "wounding itself unnecessarily in North Carolina." Carter would carry North Carolina in 1980, Hunt predicted, only if federal officials were barred from the state in the future.

Eizenstat had received most of his information from Ray Dawson, his former teacher, who had sent him a lengthy memorandum on the HEW visit on March 2. If there had ever been any doubt about where Eizenstat's sympathies lay, he now made himself clear. The outstanding issue in the HEW-UNC controversy, Eizenstat explained, was program duplication. UNC's opposition, he believed with considerable reason, was based on its conviction that program shifts would hurt black schools and not accomplish significant desegregation. Despairing of further influence with HEW, Eizenstat advised President Carter to intervene directly. "I am concerned that unless *you* communicate with Secretary Califano and urge him in the strongest terms to settle this matter," he wrote, the administration would enter a "confrontation mode" that would "do neither the cause of integration nor the cause of the Administration any good."[46]

Eizenstat had no doubt that Califano's policy would result in a legal confrontation that would injure the cause of desegregation and become "a disaster of the first magnitude politically." That message had already filtered through to Califano; as he recalled in his memoirs, Hunt and Friday had a "sympathetic ear" in Eizenstat, who informed Califano that the controversy with UNC was hurting both Carter and the university. But the "greatest pressure" from above came from "an unexpected quarter" – Vice President Walter F. Mondale, who called Califano on March 8. Just before he boarded a jet en route to the Middle East, Carter asked Mondale to tell Califano that he did not want the HEW secretary to bring suit against North Carolina. Califano, feeling betrayed by such a committed civil rights supporter as Mondale, told the vice president that he would be legally obliged to proceed with an administrative proceeding if negotiations failed. Mondale encouraged Califano to settle the case on two other occasions.[47]

White House pressure stimulated further negotiations. On March 6 and 8, 1979, an HEW official leaked a suggestion that the Office for Civil Rights would drop its demand for ending program duplication in exchange for a TBI enhancement program. Yet Friday remained cautious. "Whatever we do," he told a reporter, needed to be consistent "with the freedom of the university to order its own academic future." That would remain a "basic requirement."[48] With Friday noticeably absent, a UNC delegation consisting of Ray Dawson, Felix Joyner, and Cleon Thompson traveled to Washington for yet another round of negotiations. Facing a deadline of March 14 by which to accept or reject the UNC plan, HEW had invited university officials to a meeting hosted by HEW general counsel Peter Hamilton. Opening the three-hour conference on March 8 by calling for compromise, Hamilton reminded the participants – including OCR representatives Paula Kuebler, Arline Mendelson Pacht, Roger Sharpe, and Jeffrey Champagne – of the impending March 14 deadline. HEW and UNC disagreed primarily about the elimination of program duplication as a tool of desegregation. The elimination of duplication was simply one such tool; the real issue, he believed, was TBI enhancement, and this meeting would provide an opportunity for OCR to present a general conception of an enhancement package that HEW might accept.

Hamilton then left the room, and Pacht, using transparencies projected on an overhead screen (she provided no written copies), revealed the OCR proposal. The Office for Civil Rights was recommending that the university shift the master's program in engineering at UNC-Charlotte to A&T, phase out the bachelor's program in nursing at UNCG, transfer an existing clothing and textile program from A&T to UNCG, shift the food and nutrition program from UNCG to A&T, and transfer commerce and distributive education from UNCG to A&T. Pacht suggested, as well, that UNC establish baccalaureate programs in podiatry, optometry, and pharmacy at Winston-Salem State. The UNC delegation was appalled. After Joyner and Thompson cautiously asked how many of the recommendations were binding, Dawson, whom one observer described as "quite upset," joined the fray.[49]

Although his first impulse was to tell HEW officials to "stuff it and walk out" because the OCR proposal was "demeaning to the university and to the state," Dawson composed himself for a reply. It was difficult to see any connection, he said, between what Pacht had presented on the overhead transparencies and the "entire history of our relationship with the OCR." Less than a year ago, on May 12, 1978, Secretary Califano had accepted the provisions set forth in *Supplemental Statement II*. In that document, UNC agreed to conduct a duplication study, the details of which had been determined in negotiations with Dick Beattie and Pacht. Now, the OCR proposal of March 8, 1979, effectively set aside the acceptance of the May 12 plan and laid down "an entirely different set of rules, however ill-defined." Once again, the Office for Civil Rights was asking the university to "start all over again." In Dawson's opinion, there was nothing more to talk about. Although the participants were able to compose a statement for waiting television cameras and reporters that described the meeting as "informative," the gap between HEW and the university remained formidable.[50]

If anything, the March 8 meeting reaffirmed a gap in perceptions. UNC asked for more specifics; OCR officials believed that it was providing them. The OCR proposal was not made available in writing in order to avoid leaks to the press, Tatel later claimed, and because the recommendations were hypothetical. This represented an attempt on OCR's part "to be helpful and to give the state some guidance on the type and approach of the plan that would be acceptable to us." Roger Sharpe described Arline Pacht's presentation, in providing the specifics of an acceptable settlement, as part of a "concil-iatory" approach by OCR. Since OCR had "really exhausted" efforts to elicit a North Carolina proposal that would "accommodate the [*Adams*] criteria," remembered Pacht, "finally the time had come" for HEW to offer more specific guidance.[51]

Ray Dawson, for his part, left Washington gravely concerned. Not only did he return to Chapel Hill with "an empty bucket, as always," but also the university still had "a sword over its head" with the threatened cutoff of federal funds. Although UNC officials desperately wanted a settlement, Dawson had reached the limit of his patience. He personally resented HEW's attitude. He objected to traveling to Washington "to be seated around a table like little schoolboys and made to take notes." Moreover, he regarded OCR's sugges-tions as unworkable nonsense, and he found that they contributed little to the negotiations.[52]

Meanwhile, UNC played its remaining card – further backchannel White House communications. Four days after the abortive Washington meeting, Dawson again telephoned Eizenstat to remind him of the March 14 deadline. The next day, Friday relayed the same message to Joanne Hurley, Eizenstat's subordinate, adding that he believed Al Hamlin, rather than David Tatel, "clearly" perceived "what the situation is in N.C." Eizenstat subsequently urged Califano to make a greater effort to settle the dispute; after numerous subsequent telephone conversations, the HEW secretary agreed to another round of negotiations. On March 12, Eizenstat also asked Friday to make concessions on the program duplication issue. When Friday responded that any concessions were "out of the question," Eizenstat told him that he should do "everything humanly possible to get this issue out of the way."[53]

Further impetus for negotiations came from Governor Hunt. In a tele-phone conversation with Hunt on March 12, Califano explained that he feared further litigation from the LDF if he delayed proceeding against UNC. Hunt countered that OCR had "dumped everything they had on my folks," despite legitimate UNC efforts to negotiate a settlement. Softening his tone, Califano then told Hunt that he agreed that Mary Berry's stridency had been counterproductive; he had removed her from the case. Moreover, he was willing to retreat on the program duplication issue if the university would renew negotiations. Hunt, however, said that UNC officials were in no mood to return to Washington. Attitudes had "hardened . . . because of the treat-ment received," and UNC was leaning toward litigation. But Califano, plead-ing for further talks, offered to send a delegation to Chapel Hill. Hunt re-sponded that "nothing could be lost by doing so."[54]

Bill Friday was less enthusiastic. When Hunt telephoned on the evening of

March 12 to report his conversation with Califano, Friday wondered whether the governor had made any concessions. Although Hunt assured him on this point, Friday worried about a division in North Carolina's ranks. When he called Bill Johnson, the Board of Governors chairman's response to the last-minute negotiating effort was "strenuous, direct and wholly negative." Friday pointed out that it was risky for the university to become the "terminal force" in negotiations. After further discussion Johnson finally relented; even then, he said that he would not object only if Friday and Hunt insisted, but he continued to oppose fruitless talks.[55]

On this flimsy basis, on March 13, less than a week after the disastrous meeting in Washington, Califano sent Tatel and Hamlin to meet for several hours with Friday, Joyner, Dawson, and Thompson at the president's home in Chapel Hill, outside the reach of the press. Thanking Tatel and Hamlin for coming, Friday reviewed the March 8 discussions, which he described as a "great disappointment." The university, he said, wanted a settlement; timing, because of the Board of Governors meeting scheduled for March 16, was critical. Reminding OCR officials that the board was already developing new programs on historically black campuses, Friday – for the first time in the history of the HEW-UNC negotiations – came forward with a specific commitment of resources and programs. Planning had begun for a new program in mechanical engineering and a new master's degree in applied mathematics at A&T. In addition, there would be new baccalaureate degrees in accounting, economics, and recreation education, along with new graduate centers, at Winston-Salem State, Fayetteville State, and Elizabeth City State, as well as improvements in North Carolina Central's law school. He also supported further TBI enhancement, including a $1 million, onetime appropriation for instructional supplies and equipment and $20 million for capital improvements. Friday was willing to propose all of this to the Board of Governors in March, but before he did so he wanted an "unequivocal answer" from OCR officials that this would mean acceptance of the UNC plan.[56]

Tatel's response was tepid. He would inform Califano of the UNC proposal, he said, and he expected that the HEW secretary would reply by the March 14 deadline. But he was not optimistic. The proposal was interesting but contained nothing new; the additional $20 million would only repair existing structures, while $1 million for new equipment and supplies was insufficient. The graduate centers at Fayetteville, Winston-Salem, and Elizabeth City were "both too amorphous and unspecific for us to deal with," and, in any event, they simply continued to duplicate existing programs at TWIs. The basic problem remained: how to achieve desegregation rapidly. Friday's plan might well lead to the upgrading of black campuses, but it would not necessarily result in greater enrollment of white students at black campuses. To Tatel, acceptance of the OCR recommendations presented at the March 8 meeting – to which UNC officials had responded so negatively – remained essential to any settlement. Tatel was then asked if HEW was requiring other *Adams* states writing higher education plans – as OCR was suggesting for North Carolina – to commit to establishing new professional schools at TBIs. When Tatel replied in the negative, Friday expressed his "great disappointment." If the UNC proposal were rejected, he said, the university would "fight with every resource at its disposal to maintain its integrity and to see that it is given proper and fair treatment for the . . . accomplishments it has made." He was dismayed that a settlement hinged on the "one factor" of closing and moving programs.[57]

Despite Tatel's hard line, Califano, under White House pressure, leaned toward settlement. Accused by the LDF of "contemptuous conduct" for ignoring the March 14 deadline, Califano sent out peace feelers. Through intermediaries with UNC contacts, Califano let it be known that he would not press the program duplication issue if UNC would commit greater funds for TBI enhancement. He made the same point in another telephone conversation with Jim Hunt on March 15. On the same day, Califano appealed for a face-to-face meeting with Friday. Fresh from Tatel's latest rejection, Friday flew to Washington that afternoon. The UNC president looked tired, Califano later wrote, "years older than just a year before." According to Califano's account, Friday began the meeting by reviewing his commitment to desegregation. Califano interrupted him. "Bill, I've known you for years," he said. "You don't need any credentials with me." Desegregation as dictated by the federal government, Friday continued, might lead to the exclusion of greater numbers of black students. "If we don't keep places like Elizabeth City open," he said, "where will the blacks go?" "Exhausted and in despair," Friday then described the political circumstances limiting his freedom of movement; he could make only so many concessions. Opinion on the Board of Governors had hardened; it was a "matter of principle" for them. When the two-hour meeting ended, Friday and Califano were unable to agree.[58]

Friday's chronicle of the discussion, written that day, tells a different story. The meeting, also attended by Dick Beattie and a woman taking notes, began with Califano complaining about pressure from LDF and providing Friday with a copy of its recent attempt to have the HEW secretary cited for contempt. Continuing, Califano said that he lacked a "clear understanding" of Friday's position; he wanted an exchange of ideas that would "sharpen the issues that might divide us." Over the next hour – uninterrupted, by Friday's account – the UNC president made his case. Since the 1972 restructuring,

UNC had sought to increase integration, enhance the TBIs, and expand access to educational opportunity at all levels. Up to now, the university had been engaged in Phase I – the identification and removal of TWI-TBI inequities; Phase II would involve a more comprehensive implementation. Friday then summarized the package that he had presented to Tatel on March 13.

Following this long presentation, Califano pressed for additional UNC concessions. Friday's proposal was deficient, he said, because it did not provide for enough new construction or unique programs at the traditionally black institutions. To Friday, this reaction demonstrated that Califano "did not understand our program planning procedures," and he explained them to him. As for an infusion of new funds, Califano remained vague, although information leaked to the *Charlotte Observer* the next day indicated that HEW was seeking between $90 million and $120 million in new funds for TBIs. Ignorant of this figure, Friday pointed out that North Carolina did not have surplus revenues and that a large appropriation could only be financed through a bond referendum, but that would require an assessment of the building needs of the entire sixteen-campus system. Although the meeting ended inconclusively, according to Friday's account, there seemed no certainty of an impasse.[59]

In a comparison of Califano's and Friday's versions of the crucial March 15 meeting, two significant differences emerge. First, Friday's portrayal asserts – and later evidence verifies it – that negotiations continued. Immediately after the meeting the UNC president told reporters that the conference had been beneficial, that Califano wanted to continue talking, and that he was personally involved in the negotiations. Second, Califano acknowledged that an infusion of state funds into the TBIs might overcome the program duplication impasse, and subsequent HEW overtures bore this out. Within days of the Califano-Friday meeting, it became public knowledge that Califano had backed away from Tatel's position and that he supported the idea of granting UNC a specific period in which to find alternatives to achieve desegregation other than the elimination of program duplication. Over the weekend of March 18–19, Roger Sharpe reaffirmed this new approach in a telephone call to state senator James Edwards of Hickory. Sharpe suggested that a settlement could be reached if the TBI enhancement package were increased to the $60 million to $80 million range.[60]

Friday, however, bridled at further concessions. At the Board of Governors meeting on March 16, he gave a full accounting of the failed negotiations, including the recent attempts by HEW to shift from duplication to a massive infusion of state funds into the TBIs as the price of a settlement. Fully expecting HEW's ultimate rejection of this or any other alternative, Friday announced that the board had retained the services of the Washington law firm of Charles Morgan Jr. to represent the university and to replace attorney Carl Vogt. The selection of Chuck Morgan, a flamboyant and often abrasive Alabama civil rights lawyer who had headed the southern regional offices and the Washington offices of the American Civil Liberties Union (ACLU), was made at Bill Johnson's insistence. Morgan was known to have a close connection with Attorney General Griffin Bell; he also maintained an impeccable civil rights record and, by the late 1970s, had a growing reputation for opposing federal intervention. As a civil rights lawyer in Birmingham during the 1960s, Morgan reportedly kept flood lights shining in order to protect his family from Klansmen bombers. As an antiestablishment gadfly, he defended Vietnam War resisters Howard Levy and Muhammad Ali. After leaving the ACLU, he formed a law firm, Morgan and Associates, and among his first clients in 1979 was Sears, Roebuck, and Company, which he defended against federal charges of discrimination in employment. To many of his civil rights colleagues, Morgan was guilty of what one journalist called a "classic sellout."[61]

Bill Johnson was eager to jettison Vogt's conciliatory style. Morgan offered perfect credentials: he hardly could be described as a segregationist, yet he also agreed with Chairman Johnson's view of the dangers of federal intervention. He was someone, according to Jeff Orleans, "who didn't have to apologize to the South for not having southern credentials, and didn't have to apologize to liberals for not having liberal credentials." Morgan's opinion on the role of the federal government coincided with that of Johnson, "a person of very deep feelings," according to John R. Jordan Jr. Johnson believed that "the federal government's position was wrong, he resented it, and he just wanted to fight." For him, it had become "a matter of principle, the hell with the rest of it." For the moment, the choice of Morgan suggested that Friday himself was leaning toward Johnson's position, and the board, on the motion of George Watts Hill Sr., seconded by Jake Froelich, rewarded the UNC president with a standing ovation.[62]

Nonetheless, over the next weeks, negotiations continued between attorneys from HEW's general counsel office and Morgan's firm. Joseph J. Levin Jr., another Alabaman who had coordinated the Justice Department transition for the Carter White House in 1977 and had served as chief counsel for the National Highway Traffic Safety Administration in the late 1970s, supervised the case for Morgan. Levin had just joined the firm, and because Morgan was overwhelmed with the Sears problem, Levin was assigned primary responsibility for the day-to-day handling of the UNC-HEW dispute. In late March, as the threat of an HEW funding cutoff loomed, Friday took "himself out of it," according to an HEW source, "while the lawyers talk[ed]." Yet the negotiations, primarily between Levin and HEW counsel Peter Hamilton, went nowhere. Hamilton offered to settle if UNC would commit itself to establish "new and unique" programs at TBIs beyond those identified in previous negotiations, to expand capital construction projects beyond the $20 million previously promised by Friday, to freeze any "overtly duplicative" programs, and to adopt a program duplication model if admissions goals were not met within five years. But when Levin insisted that the proposal be delivered in writing, Hamilton, citing "bureaucratic difficulties," refused.[63]

Joe Califano, facing an LDF effort to cite him for contempt, could hold off no longer, and on March 26 he announced that he was rejecting the UNC desegregation plan and instructing the HEW general counsel's office to begin administrative proceedings. Rather than cutting off the nearly $90 million in total federal aid to UNC, however, Califano selected $10–$20 million in program aid for termination. HEW had met UNC "more than half way," he said in a news conference, reiterating the latest terms. The university should provide the historically black campuses with "unique missions" through "new and unduplicated programs," along with new funds for upgrading and enhancement. Califano was willing to suspend, for a five-year period, the *Adams* criterion that program duplication be eliminated if the university could demonstrate that that requirement was not necessary to accomplish desegregation. Califano had obtained Tatel's support for the latter measure, and the OCR director so informed Governor Hunt in writing. Califano was certain that a settlement that included no reference to ending program duplication would not withstand court scrutiny, while Tatel remained "quite skeptical" that an enhancement program could work. Tatel had insisted that the guarantee to eliminate program duplication in five years was crucial to any settlement, but he hoped that North Carolina would accept it as a viable compromise. At several points, according to one reporter, Califano was "almost apologetic" in announcing a termination of funding, which he described as a "last resort" undertaken "with enormous reluctance." The cutoff of funds would not take effect for thirty days, and, in the meantime, Califano urged that negotiations continue.[64]

Friday believed that HEW's terms – its insistence on the expenditure of nearly $100 million for TBIs and on a commitment to make program shifts should other desegregation measures fail by the end of five years – represented an unreasonable interference in university autonomy. The distance between HEW and UNC, as the *Greensboro Daily News* editorialized, was "at once so great and so small." "The chasm may be narrow, but it also runs deep." Although Jim Hunt, on March 29, promised to make up any terminated federal funds, the battle lines had hardened. Friday, personally averse to litigation, continued to encourage negotiations between Morgan and Hamilton during the first two weeks of April. Yet there was little likelihood that the Morgan team, which was itself strongly aligned with Johnson and board hardliners, would reach a settlement, and its proposals were the same as those rejected by Tatel in mid-March. Meanwhile, on March 30 HEW gave the university twenty days to request a hearing or forfeit all federal funding.[65]

Hunt, for his part, was desperately seeking to avoid litigation. Because he was a strong supporter of the Carter administration, his inability to settle the case favorably could be easily portrayed as a political failure. As Tatel subsequently observed, the governor faced a difficult dilemma. Hunt wanted to be helpful and had his heart "really in the right place"; Tatel left with a "very, very positive reaction of him, as someone who wanted to see this resolved and wanted to see it resolved in the right way." At the same time, Tatel maintained that Hunt "wasn't willing to take on the people in North Carolina whose view was that nobody should touch the UNC system." To Tatel, Hunt faced the same problem that confronted a university president who was forced to fire "a very successful football coach": "he couldn't touch it."[66]

In effect, Hunt straddled the issue, and both sides believed that he sympathized with their position. Yet his main objective was to reach a settlement and to avoid litigation. Hunt "asked us not to sue," according to John Jordan, and even "begged" the board to avoid litigation; the governor's views were in tune with Friday's and those of the pro-conciliation faction on the Board of Governors. Friday and Hunt each believed that negotiations could succeed, recalled Joe Levin, because of a personal relationship with Califano. Yet neither Friday nor Hunt realized that his efforts made little difference: Califano had, Levin said, "a dogmatic approach to civil rights," as did Tatel, and "there was no true negotiation."[67]

Hunt's efforts to encourage conciliation encountered Johnson's determined opposition, and what Levin would call a "real dispute internally" raged within the Board of Governors, UNC administration, and the governor's office about how to proceed. Jordan recalled a meeting, sometime in April 1979, when Johnson led a delegation to Hunt's office to discuss the possibility of a lawsuit. "Nobody got to say a damned word except Bill Johnson," recalled Jordan. During the meeting Johnson became agitated and flushed; he rose out of his chair and walked all around the room. By the spring of 1979, the internal divisions on the North Carolina side had become so intense that Hunt "bowed out of it," Levin remembered; he "just picked up his marbles and went home."[68]

With a funding cutoff deadline of April 20 – the same day as a scheduled

Board of Governors meeting – the negotiations shifted to backchannel communications. White House officials were becoming increasingly uneasy about litigation. On April 9, 1979, White House aide Jack Watson telephoned Califano to inquire how negotiations between the attorneys were proceeding; he also asked whether a telephone call from Carter to Hunt would help. Resisting White House pressure, Califano appealed to the president to defer any intervention until "we have had a chance to press the issue further with counsel for UNC." Nonetheless, Stuart Eizenstat was unwilling to wait. "Although we tentatively defer to Joe's judgment on the matter because he is so much closer to the negotiations than we are," he wrote to Carter, he and Watson were both concerned "about waiting too late for you to ask Jim Hunt for his help in resolving this dispute." Eizenstat urged Carter to call Califano.[69]

Carter pressed Califano to break the logjam, asking him in a brief note on April 12 to "do everything possible to work an [sic] N.C. settlement" and again offering to telephone Hunt. Instead, Califano himself spoke with Hunt twice over the next two days. The Board of Governors, led by Johnson, had "dug in their heels," the governor reported, and though he was willing to support a $40 million program of TBI enhancement and upgrading, he could do nothing to alter board opinion on eliminating program duplication. Califano countered by insisting, once again, that UNC would have to take some measures to reduce program duplication in order to avert court intervention, but the most that Hunt was willing to support was the creation of a blue-ribbon state panel to examine the question.[70]

Califano, abandoning contacts through the attorneys, moved backchannel communications into high gear. For whatever reason – including perhaps his conviction, as Orleans expressed it, that Tatel "was not someone who could get a deal" – Califano focused his hopes for settlement on HEW negotiator Dick Beattie. A former Marine Corps aviator, Beattie was described by Orleans, who spent considerable time with him during the negotiations, as "bright, confident, hard working." To Orleans, it was clear that Beattie opposed litigation. "He didn't think it was good for the government to be suing the state of North Carolina," and he "didn't think it was good for the state of North Carolina." Of all the federal officials, Beattie, Orleans believed, possessed the "best understanding" of the political pressures that Friday and UNC officials were under.[71]

On April 16, Easter Monday, Califano sent Beattie to meet with Jim Hunt at his family farm in Rock Ridge, North Carolina. Hunt, agreeing to the meeting, asked Friday to gather key documents beforehand. On the sixteenth Beattie told Hunt that the university's March 13 proposal was insufficient but did not indicate what would be acceptable; continuing differences remained over program duplication. Nonetheless, Hunt emerged from the discussion hopeful. The day after he met with Friday, Dawson, Joyner, Thompson, and Johnson and strongly advised them to continue talking to Beattie, who had promised to return shortly. The governor suggested that he might sweeten the deal by endorsing additional state appropriations in the upcoming legislative session.

Beattie did indeed return, this time with Tatel, and on April 18 the HEW team conferred with Hunt, Friday, and Dawson at the General Administration Building. There, Hunt offered to press the legislature to forego a promised tax reduction in order to appropriate an additional $40 million for new buildings at TBIs – this would be in addition to the $20 million already promised by Friday and another $9 million committed, totaling nearly $70 million. Friday pledged to conduct a comprehensive study at the end of a five-year period; if that study did not reveal "significant achievement" in desegregation, the board would examine other, unspecified steps.[72]

Hunt's offer was, by far, the most ambitious commitment ever made by a North Carolina political leader to rectify past ills in public higher education. The crisis with HEW ended the North Carolina power structure's inaction, and it now offered a major commitment toward TBI enhancement. Not only did Governor Hunt propose to abandon a politically popular tax relief measure, but he also committed himself to propose major expenditures toward TBI enhancement. But Tatel rejected this proposal, insisting that it would not produce significant desegregation. When UNC negotiators asked for a specific figure for TBI enhancement, one that would satisfy federal officials, neither Tatel nor Beattie – after a forty-minute recess – was willing to commit to a dollar amount in writing. "Our concern," Tatel was reported to have said, "is in moving people."[73]

On April 19, after the HEW negotiating team had returned to Washington, Califano telephoned Hunt. Califano's recollection of the conversation was that they agreed on a four-point program: the investment of over $40 million of new state funds in the TBIs, the establishment of some twenty-two new programs at the historically black campuses, a university promise that no new programs would be established at TWIs that would impede desegregation, and a pledge that if the latter three measures failed to accomplish desegregation after four years, UNC would take additional steps, including the elimination of program duplication. At some point, wrote Califano, Friday was included in the negotiations, and he and Beattie drafted specific language to present at the Board of Governors meeting on April 20. Even with an agreement in hand, according to Califano, the absolute opposition of Bill Johnson doomed the settlement, and the board chose litigation instead.[74]

When Califano's rendition of the latter stage of these negotiations was published in 1981 in his memoirs, *Governing America: An Insider's Report from the White House and the Cabinet*, Jim Hunt and UNC officials vehemently rejected it. Hunt denied ever having reached an agreement with Califano; John Jordan described Califano's account as "absolutely untrue."[75] If there was any sabotage of a potential agreement that occurred, Dick Beattie later asserted, it was by hard-liners within OCR, who were determined to take the UNC case to litigation. More than a decade later, Ray Dawson asserted that there was never a moment in the spring of 1979 when the two sides were close to settlement, primarily because Joe Califano refused to compromise on the most important issues. "If Califano wanted a settlement," said Dawson, "he kept it pretty carefully in the background." Most of what the HEW secretary had to offer was "just a rehash of the old position." UNC vice president Roy Carroll, another member of Friday's inner circle, agreed. "If there was ever any kind of tentative agreement," he later stated, "I never saw it."[76]

There is evidence to substantiate Califano's contention that any agreement faced sabotage from Bill Johnson and other hard-liners on the Board of Governors. Jimmy Carter himself, scribbling a note on an Eizenstat memorandum, wrote, "Joe & Jim had [an] agreement worked out . . . [that] sounded quite reasonable to me," but the "Bd of Gov's would not agree."[77] Nonetheless, with the fading of memories and absence of clear documentation, it is impossible to determine the precise extent to which any detailed settlement was reached. The university's acceptance of the fourth condition – that the university would commit itself to eliminating program duplication if all other measures failed to achieve desegregation at the end of four years (rather than the five years previously proposed by Califano) – would mean that Bill Friday had caved in on the crucial issue of university autonomy. Such a concession, on which the entire agreement hinged, was highly unlikely.[78]

It is more probable that Friday and Beattie found some thin thread on which to base future negotiations. Subsequent testimony from David Tatel, who repeated an account told to him by Beattie, is revealing. Tatel recalled that, on the morning of the Board of Governors meeting, Friday and Beattie had worked out a formula for continuing future negotiations – "some suggestions for possible future avenues of discussion" – but that Bill Johnson, with the strong backing of Morgan, "absolutely refused" to permit it to appear before the board. Friday, Tatel said, was "as upset as we were." Even so, Tatel admitted that he would have considered the formula for future negotiations as "entirely unacceptable." Subsequently, Carroll and Dawson both partly confirmed this account. Carroll described last-minute negotiations that were conducted in only general terms – without any draft documents – but the talks went no further because of strong opposition from Johnson, who insisted on litigation. According to Dawson, Beattie dictated a proposal for a settlement over the telephone on the morning of April 20, but there was "no clear direction" from HEW about "what would have been acceptable." Conflicting signals regarding HEW's intentions were appearing everywhere, as Califano communicated with Hunt, Beattie negotiated through other channels, and Tatel was involved at still another level. "It was very difficult to know with whom we were dealing," remembered Dawson, who characterized this period as a "very confusing time."[79]

If his heart told him to persist in the search for conciliation, Friday's head, appearing in the guise of Johnson's stubborn insistence on litigation, instructed him otherwise. In the minutes of the Board of Governors meeting on April 20 and in newspaper accounts, there is no mention, as Califano suggested, that Friday brought a four-point settlement to the full board. Instead, the minutes reveal that Friday reviewed the failed negotiations of mid-April in an effort to show board members that every effort had been made to reach a settlement. He spoke of the UNC offer of March 13, of the March 15 meeting with Califano, of the failed negotiations between Morgan and Peter Hamilton, and of the last-minute attempts by Califano to reach a settlement. After telephone conversations with both Califano and Beattie on the evening of April 19, Friday told the board members, he believed that they "had come to the point where agreement could be reached, because the issue of duplication – of control over UNC's educational programs – appeared to have been resolved as we have insisted." But later that evening, HEW's insistence on preserving program duplication as a mandatory recourse after a specified period reemerged, "with proposals we could not agree to." As a result, Friday concluded, "we have no agreement, no end to this ordeal, to bring to you today, despite all that we have done to try to bring it to resolution."[80]

In fact, serious differences, primarily over the program duplication model of desegregation, still separated the university from HEW, and, Califano's assertions to the contrary, no settlement resulted from the Beattie-Friday negotiations prior to the April 20 deadline. Friday instead was searching for a way to keep talking in order to avoid litigation. On April 20 litigation became inevitable, and the theme of the board meeting, as Jeff Orleans later described it, was "Bill Johnson in a huff." Despite a motion by Bill Dees seeking one more opportunity to negotiate with Califano, hard-liners now ruled the day. Friday granted the floor to Chuck Morgan, who outlined recent developments, strongly urged litigation, and even circulated a draft complaint and brief that would be submitted in court. The board, frustrated by the fruitless negotiations, then passed Phil Carson's motion that the university, in the eastern district federal court in Raleigh, challenge HEW's right to terminate federal support for UNC.[81]

The initiation of the lawsuit was a repudiation of Friday's style of conciliation and compromise; indeed, the board resolution specifically stated that all future negotiations were to be conducted only with the knowledge and participation of Bill Johnson, as board chairman, and Chuck Morgan, as UNC counsel.[82] Bill Friday, trained as a lawyer, fully realized that litigation might be divisive, tortuous, and perhaps even disastrous for black-white relations as well as for the continuing viability of the multicampus UNC system. But by the spring of 1979 he had no other option. He had pressed the power structure, not only the UNC Board of Governors but also the governor and the legislature, for an unprecedented commitment of new resources for TBIs, and he was willing to accept ambitious goals for increasing minority enrollments at TWIs and TBIs. What Friday could not accept – either personally or as the UNC president – was HEW's control of educational decision making. At loggerheads over these vital questions, HEW and Bill Friday moved into an unknown and perilous future.

L ITIGATION with HEW revealed two sometimes conflicting dimensions of Bill Friday's leadership. As had been true during the two decades of his university presidency, Friday was convinced that his primary obligation was to insulate the campuses from interference from outside agencies, whether they be state politicians, governors, or, in this instance, the federal government. As early as the vet school negotiations of 1974–75, he identified a principle of university autonomy and refused to abandon it. On the other hand, Friday was temperamentally inclined toward conciliation. Since childhood he had been averse to conflict, personal and professional, and had always believed that reasonable people could arrive at a reasonable compromise. Highly sensitive to UNC's national image, Friday regarded a costly and contentious legal battle as unnecessary, wasteful, and potentially disruptive.

Although the university's conflict with HEW in the spring of 1979 represented a failure of Friday's facility for compromise, paradoxically it was also his finest hour. Maintaining his position despite a cross fire between federal officials and hard-line Board of Governors members took "real courage" and "singleminded determination," UNC vice president Roy Carroll recalled. This was, as Ray Dawson later reflected, "a major crisis in the history of the university" and "a very important turning point in the life of the university that required some exceptional leadership that he was in a unique position to give." Not only was there a great danger of political intervention that would seek, as other *Adams* states had done, to reach agreement with federal officials at whatever cost to the university, but there was also the "most dangerous" potential in the conflict – racial polarization. Friday's primary accomplishments were that he maintained a focus on educational issues, preserved the integrity of UNC, and retained the confidence of the black community and the TBI chancellors in his leadership. In a sense, observed Dawson, it was almost as if his whole career as UNC president was but a preparation for the HEW struggle.[1]

ON April 24, 1979, at 2:30 P.M., the University of North Carolina – represented by Washington attorneys Joe Levin and Ed Ashworth, and, from the North Carolina state attorney general's office, by Andy Vanore – filed suit in Raleigh in the U.S. district court for the eastern district of North Carolina.[2] The next day UNC asked the General Assembly to appropriate $40 million to enhance the state's five traditionally black campuses; despite some grumbling, the legislature subsequently passed the package virtually intact.[3]

University lawyers had selected the site for their legal battle carefully. Although HEW resisted the transfer of jurisdiction from Washington to Raleigh – it unsuccessfully contested the move in Judge John H. Pratt's court on May 1 – UNC's legal team believed that the university would receive a more sympathetic hearing in a North Carolina court. Filing the case in the eastern district was, according to one UNC administrator, "a matter of, in blunt language, . . . shopping for a judge." UNC attorneys had rejected the state's middle district, in Greensboro, because they believed that the judges' workload was too heavy; they avoided the western district because they were uncertain in which direction one of its two judges, James McMillan – who had issued a sweeping order requiring crosstown busing in *Swann*, the Charlotte-Mecklenburg busing case – might lean. In the eastern district, the sole active judge was Franklin T. Dupree Jr., a Carolina graduate and an alumnus of the UNC Law School, who had a reputation for hard work and clear legal thinking. On April 27, three days after UNC began legal action, Dupree issued a temporary restraining order deferring the cutoff of federal funds until the case could be heard.[4]

In late May and early June 1979, Dupree made two additional rulings. The first, issued on May 23, was that the case could not be transferred to Pratt's court. Because UNC had not been a party to the *Adams* dispute, he reasoned, there was "no identity of parties" in the present suit. And whereas *Adams* considered the problem of "non-action" by HEW, UNC's claim involved "actual or threatened action." "Judicial economy and litigation convenience," Dupree asserted, were better served by keeping the proceedings in North Carolina. The plaintiffs were North Carolinians, and most of the documentary and testimonial evidence was located in the state. Most important, the substantive issues of the case went to "the heart of this state's ability to exercise its discretion in developing higher education."[5]

Two weeks later, after hearing arguments, Dupree ruled on the central question before his court – whether HEW could cut off funds to the university. The judge's decree offered hope for both sides. HEW could claim success in Dupree's rejection of UNC's three major objectives – to prohibit HEW from holding administrative hearings to terminate funds, to invalidate the *Adams* criteria, and to declare that the university had met the constitutional requirements for desegregation. On the other hand, Dupree's judgment contained two glimmers of hope for the UNC cause. First, he extended the jurisdiction of his court over HEW's Title VI administrative proceedings and reserved the right to review their outcome (in October 1979, Pratt affirmed this jurisdictional issue). Second, Dupree ordered that no cutoff of federal funds could occur until the administrative proceedings had been concluded, thus temporarily removing the sword hanging over UNC. "No litigant should have to battle a Kafkaesque bureaucracy," he wrote, "while being pressured into compliance through the threat of 'deferrals' which are part and parcel of the original controversy." While Joe Califano called the ruling a "significant victory," Bill Friday told reporters that he welcomed the decision because it ended the immediate threat of the termination of federal funds and offered UNC an opportunity to present its case.[6]

Dupree's finding was, in fact, a legal masterstroke – what the *Raleigh News and Observer* called a "shrewdly balanced ruling." His opinion was "wise," observed the *Greensboro Daily News* in an editorial entitled "A Call to Reason." The university had launched the case "in a state of desperation, not to mention defiance," while HEW was bound in "a strait of a different sort" – the mandate of Pratt's court order in the *Adams* case to accelerate higher education desegregation. His ruling offered incentives for both sides. HEW won the right to conduct administrative hearings; Dupree agreed that UNC's constitutional challenge was premature before the outcome of that hearing became known. The university, meanwhile, succeeded in delaying the termination of federal funding. Ultimately, however, the *Greensboro Daily News* suggested, UNC would be the winner. Dupree's court, it believed, had established a new standard of reason and understanding.[7]

Subsequent legal maneuvering and delaying tactics ensured that the administrative proceedings would not begin until the summer of 1980, more than a year later.[8] In the meantime, Friday shored up his position. Although the North Carolina press generally supported him – the *Greensboro Daily News* asserted, for example, that the UNC countersuit was "fully justified" – newspapers outside the state often viewed the matter differently.[9] Their portrayal confirmed Friday's worst fears about national exposure: observers outside North Carolina too easily concluded that UNC was resisting desegregation.

In an April 1979 editorial entitled "Still Separate in North Carolina," the *New York Times* asserted that the dispute had "dragged on far too long." Why had North Carolina, supposedly the South's most progressive state, been unable to come to terms, while Georgia and Virginia had reached agreement? The answer, the newspaper asserted, was that desegregation of the university system had failed, and that the cause of that failure was UNC's refusal to adopt measures such as the elimination of program duplication. UNC's responses so far had been unpersuasive.[10]

Friday was shaken by the *Times* editorial. Georgia and Virginia had reached a settlement with HEW, UNC officials believed, not because of the superiority of their plans, which, in their projected enrollment increases and new state resources, were less ambitious than the UNC plan. Rather, the Office for Civil Rights accepted the Georgia and Virginia proposals because they acquiesced in the program duplication model of desegregation. Upset by what he considered to be a distortion of the case, Friday telephoned *Times* editor Max Frankel and arranged a meeting between Frankel's editorial staff and a senior UNC delegation. Meanwhile, Friday also promoted the UNC point of view by calling and sending material to national leaders of higher education.[11]

On another front, Friday reassured the TBIs and the state's black community by endorsing an enhancement package that gave the historically black campuses all that he had promised Califano in the April negotiations. On May 9 Friday appeared before the legislature's joint appropriations committee and requested that it set aside an additional $40 million for the TBIs. To other groups, on the other hand, he remained steadfast on the issue of UNC autonomy. Although he wanted to end racial duality, Friday told a UNC alumni group in May, he disputed HEW's efforts to "mold" the university "according to its notions." There was "not a shred of evidence" that the program duplication model would speed desegregation, he assured Greensboro Kiwanians later that summer. Although the university did not favor defying the federal government, Friday said, "I do not believe UNC should ever yield to the federal or state government on who will teach and what will be taught."[12]

Yet Friday had not given up hope of a negotiated settlement. In the early months of litigation, there were tensions between the UNC president, who was never completely reconciled to a court battle, and Board of Governors hard-liners and Chuck Morgan. Morgan, whom Joe Levin later described as a "deeply suspicious human being," trusted few people in North Carolina. He was "hostile" to Andy Vanore, the lead attorney from the state attorney general's office, because he perceived him as "a threat to his control over the case." Morgan resented Bill Friday because of his preference for negotiations, and he "went through the roof" about the last-minute, backchannel negotiations that Friday conducted during late April 1979 with David Tatel and Joe Califano. This was an unhappy beginning to Levin's participation in the case, and much of Levin's energy was devoted to mending fences. Morgan's dominant personality alienated a number of UNC administrators, and tensions did not ease until Morgan took himself off the case.[13]

Predictably, Friday had bristled at the April 20, 1979, board resolution, which one UNC official later described as "clearly a slap in the face to Bill." Friday was disturbed by the board's sweeping delegation of powers to Chuck Morgan and other lawyers. When HEW sent a consultant, William Fuller, to visit the UNC campuses in July 1979, university attorneys directed Friday to order that no UNC officials should accompany Fuller on university time and that no documents should be provided unless they were in the public domain. Friday, though yielding to the advice of counsel, privately observed that this was "the wrong policy for this or any other University."[14]

Despite the board's designation of Morgan and Levin as the sole representatives in any negotiations with HEW, Friday continued to seek a settlement. On April 23, 1979, only three days after the board voted to litigate and a day before its lawyers filed suit, Friday telephoned Joanne Hurley in Stuart Eizenstat's office. On the heels of their conversation, Eizenstat called Dick Beattie that evening and urged him to communicate directly with Friday. Beattie contacted the UNC president the next morning to offer further negotiations. When Friday relayed Beattie's invitation to Bill Johnson, the Board of Governors chairman responded that the board resolution of April 20 prohibited him from engaging in more talks. But Friday persisted, proposing that Johnson and Morgan visit with HEW officials. When Johnson insisted that the matter be postponed, Friday privately noted that it would be "a profound mistake" to reject conciliation.[15]

Friday communicated Johnson's opposition when Eizenstat telephoned on the evening of April 24. Along with the recent hostility toward HEW by board members such as Johnson, Friday explained, there were remaining "difficulties in and around this matter"; they included the "abiding obstinance" of David Tatel and the "shifting positions" of Joe Califano. Eizenstat proposed to break the logjam. Whenever Friday believed the timing would be appropriate, Jimmy Carter could telephone Johnson "to urge him to reach some kind of settlement." Friday, thanking him, said that should he need "to exercise that option he had given me, I would," but he would seek to resume negotiations without presidential intervention.[16]

Stuart Eizenstat and other White House officials were growing uneasy at the prospect of a long, bitter controversy in a state whose political support was crucial for Carter's reelection. In early May Eizenstat and Jack Watson made contact with Califano and strongly advised accommodation. On May 14, 1979, Carter telephoned Jim Hunt with a similar message; the two men agreed that Califano should communicate directly with Bill Johnson. When Califano called him later that week, Johnson said that he opposed further negotiations and would meet with HEW officials in Washington only if Morgan accompanied him. Meanwhile, Friday continued to express his misgivings about his exclusion from the negotiating process, which, he believed, prevented him from performing his duties as UNC president.[17]

Califano and Beattie pressed on, asking Johnson to attend a negotiating session in Washington. HEW officials insisted, however, that he go without Morgan, maintaining that Califano could not be as candid with counsel present. But Johnson remained unenthusiastic about further talks, and after one meeting had been scheduled, he managed to cancel it. Jim Hunt, informed of Johnson's footdragging, summoned the Board of Governors chairman to the Executive Mansion, where he urged him to reschedule the visit and to become "very aggressive" in presenting the UNC position. The differences between Johnson's desire for continued litigation and Friday's support for negotiation were never starker, and the tensions between the two men became acute.[18]

Throughout the summer of 1979, Johnson and the board hard-liners held the upper hand. The proposed Johnson-Califano negotiations were stalled because Morgan imposed four preconditions: that the talks could not require future action by UNC, that there would be no further discussion of the program duplication model, that any written amendment to the UNC plan could include no reference to the *Adams* case, and that the university would admit no liability. Morgan's preconditions, at least for the time being, effectively torpedoed a conference in Washington that was to have included Friday, Johnson, and Vanore. These preconditions were devised without Friday's knowledge. Because of his exclusion from HEW negotiations, he feared that any hope of compromise was slipping away.[19]

While the UNC-HEW negotiations stalled, the Carter administration did not enjoy a peaceful summer.[20] The Iranian Revolution threw world petroleum markets into chaos, causing an oil shortage and long lines to buy gasoline in the United States, while the president's standing in public opinion polls plummeted. In July 1979 Carter appeared on national television to describe a national crisis; he reshuffled the cabinet, taking the opportunity to rid himself of Califano, who had become a political liability in North Carolina and elsewhere. As Califano's replacement, Carter chose Patricia Roberts Harris, a selection that gave Friday renewed hope of a breakthrough. Friday had served with Harris on the Carnegie Commission on the Future of Higher Education, and he considered her an ally. No sooner had Harris been confirmed as the new HEW secretary than she sent word, in a meeting with Senator Jesse Helms in late July, that both she and Carter wanted a settlement.[21]

Friday soon established contact with Harris's office and arranged a high-level meeting for October 3, 1979. Despite Johnson's opposition, the meeting took place, with Johnson, Ray Dawson, Felix Joyner, and Cleon Thompson accompanying Friday. If, however, Bill Friday was expecting a breakthrough during the one-hour session, he was sorely disappointed. After an exchange of greetings, Secretary Harris asked Friday and the UNC delegation to present their case. Friday came, as usual, thoroughly prepared. As he began the detailed argument that he hoped would lead to a settlement, Harris, according to Dawson, interrupted him to interject criticisms. When Friday described the obvious duplication between the law schools at North Carolina Central and Chapel Hill – a duplication that OCR had previously approved – Harris ignored his remarks. Friday had made only part of his presentation when Harris casually closed her notebook, signifying that the meeting was over. She told Friday to mail the rest of his comments to her. Dawson subsequently called the encounter "frankly embarrassing" and Harris's behavior "arrogant and rude, almost studiedly so."[22]

The October 3 meeting proved a disaster for HEW-UNC relations. Friday was insulted by Harris's reception, which seemed inexplicable given his earlier association with her. Dawson and other university officials were furious. It may have been, as Friday initially suspected, that "her views of duplication and duplication's impact on the racial mix in higher education" were the same as David Tatel's, yet the fact remains that, by the end of October, Harris had driven Tatel from office. Intent on installing her own people, she was, according to Dick Beattie, "terrible" to the OCR director. Soon after her arrival at HEW, Tatel met with Harris to brief her on the UNC case; he later described the meeting as "unpleasant." Not only did she "belittle" him in front of HEW staff for being "politically insensitive" – referring to the White House's desire to settle the dispute with UNC – but she also lashed out at Tatel for presenting his written briefing without tabs or an executive summary. Tatel later said that the executive summary was immediately before her. It seemed to him that she had found a pretext for knuckling under to "the crowd at the White House" that was seeking "to tone down this Office for Civil Rights that was causing all this trouble." Tatel complained about the incident to Califano, who leaked it to the press; Harris wrongfully blamed the leak on Tatel, who vehemently denied being responsible.[23]

Joe Levin interpreted Harris's behavior differently. It mattered little whether she were white or black, he said, for "she behaved . . . in that way towards just about everybody that she came into contact with." She was, Levin believed, the "perfect successor to Joe Califano, because her sense of human touch was probably just about as sharp as his." Tatel observed that Harris was an "incredibly smart" person who was always better prepared for a briefing than Califano had been. But she also had a "toughness" and an edge to her personality that "just undermined her."[24]

Yet the most tenable explanation of Harris's dressing-down of Friday can be found in the challenges confronting all the HEW and Education secretaries during the Carter administration: the mandates of the *Adams* decision, the imperatives of litigation, and, above all, the pressing responsibilities they felt toward the civil rights community. As an African American woman, Harris did not need to prove her credentials; attacking Friday and the university, however, would clearly demonstrate that she stood with civil rights activists. Having undermined the position of David Tatel, no doubt at the White House's urging, Harris faced the accusation that she was acquiescing in a watering down of meaningful desegregation. She believed, as she subsequently informed reporters, that North Carolina had "an excellent dual" system of higher education that was "constitutionally impermissible." Despite a personal association with Bill Friday of some thirteen years, she said, "we haven't had the answer that the Constitution requires." As Friday later reflected, Harris had to "prove herself" as HEW secretary.[25]

Whatever Harris's motivations, the October 3, 1979, encounter was a chastening experience for Friday. Responding angrily to the personal attack, he recognized the futility of continuing high-level negotiations. "I see no need to pursue any further discussion with the Department just now," he wrote on the day of the meeting. "There is no willingness and certainly no open mind to hear proposals by us or anyone else on the way peaceful compliance might be achieved." Friday reported the substance of the meeting – and his feelings about it – to Jim Hunt and, in Washington, to the sympathetic ears of Secretary of Commerce Juanita Kreps and Stuart Eizenstat. Others at HEW also understood Friday's position. Weeks after the episode, Friday received a telephone call from an HEW official who said that he had been "unfairly treated." "You deserved much better than you got from Secretary Harris," the official declared, indicating that he was deeply embarrassed over the matter and had had a "troubled conscience" since the meeting.[26]

When Friday told Hunt what had happened, the governor telephoned the White House to complain about Harris's behavior. But the White House did little about the matter until after the Board of Governors meeting on October

12, when Friday reported the status of negotiations. Hunt, fearing that the story might be leaked and seeking to distance himself politically from the sinking White House ship, released an account of the October 3 meeting to the press on October 12. Privately, Hunt informed the Carter administration that unless the UNC-HEW case was "settled satisfactorily," it would become "absolutely impossible" for him to support the president.[27]

Newspaper accounts of the story about the October 3 meeting brought consequences. Eizenstat telephoned Friday the day the story appeared, on Saturday, October 13, and explained the White House's dilemma: backchannel support for the UNC position had, for the time being at least, been exhausted. Nonetheless, he promised to speak to Carter on the following Monday. So informed, Carter called Hunt on October 19, and he observed that this was not the first time that Harris had "lost control." The president instructed Eizenstat to investigate, and his inquiry vindicated Friday's account. Nonetheless, there is little evidence that the White House ever put any pressure on Harris.[28]

Infuriated by the press reports on October 13, Harris called Friday. Hunt had released the story, she said, only because of Friday's angry response; he was "no longer a growing boy or a shrinking violet," and Harris expected him to deal directly with her. When she tried to blame him for the story, Friday responded that she had made similar, and he believed unfounded, charges about UNC's use of the press on October 3. Harris's accusation was unfair, he said, and she should not hold him responsible. Friday then attempted to assure Harris that he had supported her appointment as secretary and still had confidence in her. By the end of the conversation, according to Friday, the confrontation had "cooled," and he told Harris that further communication would come through university counsel.[29]

Friday expressed himself more candidly to others. Immediately after speaking with Harris, he telephoned the chairman of the Board of Governors to report the conversation, confirming Johnson's suspicion about the futility of negotiations. He was tired of "being used," Friday told Johnson, who appreciated Friday's ordeal and denounced Harris's "misuse" of her position. Friday then called John A. Williams Jr., a top Hunt adviser; from now on, Friday said, he would resist any future attempts by HEW officials to abuse him.[30]

The disastrous October 3 meeting had a decidedly chilling effect on Friday's efforts to conciliate. For the next few months, at least as long as Harris retained jurisdiction over the case, Friday despaired of exerting any cabinet-level influence. By the end of 1979, the Carter White House, absorbed in the Iran hostage crisis and in the declining prospects for reelection, was in disarray. In early December 1979, Jesse Helms, repeating a report from someone on the White House staff, told Friday that the Carter administration was dissatisfied with Harris, who had become a "burden" to the president. According to a black leader with White House contacts, Marian Wright Edelman, "chaos reigned in Washington." With little control over the situation, Friday permitted Chuck Morgan and Joe Levin to submit a draft consent decree that restated UNC's position since April 1979 to HEW attorneys in late October 1979, just as Tatel was leaving office. He was replaced by Roma Stewart, who became the OCR director on December 1. Stewart, a black woman and Washington civil rights attorney, was not well disposed toward the UNC proposal; as she told reporters in mid-November, "my impression is that I didn't like it." The new head of OCR believed that the law "ought to be obeyed – yesterday," and she was "not that interested" in compromise. "If all the right is on one side, the side that is right ought to get all the remedy; and I don't think you can compromise civil rights." Not surprisingly, by December 1979 Harris had rejected the UNC proposal.[31]

With backchannel negotiations in limbo, the focus of the case during late 1979 and 1980 was on the administrative hearings.[32] The proceedings were divided into two parts, beginning with HEW's presentation of its case and concluding, after a lengthy recess, with UNC's rebuttal. The trial began on July 22, 1980, when both sides made opening statements. Richard Foster, an HEW staff attorney, argued that UNC had done little to end de jure segregation since 1954, and, as a result of this historical pattern, blacks, who made up 22 percent of the state's population, were attending effectively segregated schools. Instead of attempting to enhance the traditionally black institutions, Foster contended, the state had established new, virtually all-white campuses at Charlotte, Asheville, and Wilmington. At present, most blacks attended overwhelmingly black schools, most whites overwhelmingly white schools. For students, faculty, and administrators there remained a "complete and utter racial duality."[33]

Joe Levin then countered with a lengthy opening statement. The UNC case, he said, differed significantly from the relatively simple efforts to desegregate all-white public schools in the 1950s and 1960s; it was "not about provincial defiance, recalcitrance or resistance," but about the "earnest efforts of a major national university system to broaden the participation of black students in higher education." The university's defense would show, he said, that federal officials knew little about higher education generally and even less about UNC. HEW officials had pursued a disastrously intrusive policy that eventually, in the guise of the program duplication model, became "fixated on the concept of body count." "What they insist upon will not work," said Levin, and it would "turn the UNC institutions into educational oddities in

American higher education." The program duplication model was a "quick fix" and an "untried theoretical mechanism" that reflected a "complete and utter disregard for the predictable destructive educational consequences for the entire system." Federal officials were walking "backwards into the eighties, their eyes upon the relatively simple and mechanical approach to integrating elementary and high schools during the 1950s and 1960s." But the reality was that, in higher education, the simple had become simplistic, and a mechanical approach was "as inappropriate and as destructive as employing an axe in order to sculpt fine crystal."[34]

Government attorneys called a procession of witnesses during the last week of July and the first half of August in order to demonstrate the continued existence of segregation in higher education at UNC.[35] After a recess of several weeks, the government resumed its case in September 1980, calling its most important witnesses. David Tatel testified for two days, on September 22 and 23. He reviewed the progress of the case from May 1977, when he became OCR director, to October 1979, when he resigned. Julius Chambers was called to the stand on September 25; he described his own efforts to desegregate the university. In October HEW concluded by summoning two additional experts on higher education desegregation, Robert Dentler and Dora Catherine Baltzell, of Abt Associates, a Cambridge, Massachusetts, educational consulting firm. Both witnesses presented data demonstrating inequities between the TBIs and TWIs, while Dentler testified in favor of the program duplication model as an effective method of desegregation. By October 31, 1980, after the NAACP Legal Defense and Educational Fund called its own witnesses, the government rested its case. In the meantime, UNC prepared its rebuttal, which did not begin until February 1981.[36]

THE onset of administrative hearings was a rebuke to Friday's conciliatory style. The conflict with HEW was a running sore, and his inability to contain it – and the apparent damage to UNC's image as a leader in the New South – deeply wounded him. When the *Raleigh News and Observer* published an editorial on May 2, 1980, citing recent evidence of financial disarray and mismanagement at the state's TBIs as confirmation of Friday and the university's "malignant neglect," he could scarcely contain his displeasure. In a private letter to Claude Sitton, the paper's editor, Friday declared that there had never been "a more serious charge" leveled at the university. The situation was frustrating, he said, and he could grasp that frustration "better than the writer of the editorial could ever grasp" it. Friday admitted that mismanagement at historically black campuses was a systemic problem, but this was, he believed, the product of their long-standing isolation from the mainstream of

American higher education. The improvements at the mostly black campuses, rather than the result of "heavy pressure" from HEW, came out of the Board of Governors's comparative study of 1976 and its review of physical plants completed in 1978. UNC had made real progress with the TBIs, Friday wrote, despite, not because of, HEW's "adversarial role" and its insistence on "unsound educational decisions."[37]

Even while administrative hearings ground on, the backchannel communications that had ended a year earlier were revived. In late 1979 the White House announced the reorganization of HEW into two new cabinet-level departments, Health and Human Services (HHS) and Education, effective May 28, 1980. After a power struggle in which Patricia Harris attempted to maintain jurisdiction over OCR, the assistant secretary for civil rights was transferred to the new Department of Education under Secretary Shirley M. Hufstedler, a former federal judge from southern California. The White House's decision to remove OCR from Harris's control was related in part to its unhappiness about the UNC case, yet Hufstedler, who had been appointed to the bench by Lyndon Johnson, brought with her the reputation of a bright and capable jurist who was firmly committed to the civil rights agenda. As Griffin Bell informed Friday at a meeting in Atlanta, Hufstedler would likely "create more pressure on us than that received from the last two Secretaries."[38]

The early contacts with Hufstedler were, in fact, discouraging. Soon after she took office, Friday sent out feelers to see if negotiations with the new secretary were possible. Douglass Cater, a former special assistant to Lyndon Johnson and an acquaintance of Friday's, had just returned to the nation's capital after a sojourn in Europe. In Washington, Cater and his wife shared their townhouse with Liz Carpenter, former press secretary of Lady Bird Johnson, who had recently arrived to become Hufstedler's assistant secretary for public affairs. Cater arranged a dinner with Hufstedler and Friday, who flew to Washington for the occasion. Although Cater's hope had been that "two reasonable human beings could get together and talk their way out of this impasse," the get-together yielded little progress. Cater described it as a "totally unsuccessful dinner," but he remained uncertain why Hufstedler, who was "unprepared to discuss the thing at all," had agreed to attend. When the UNC case was raised, she seemed uninterested in negotiations, and Friday quickly sensed that there was little point in pursuing the matter.[39]

Hufstedler brushed off Friday's overtures apparently for two reasons. The first was pressure from the LDF; soon after her swearing-in, she had participated in an LDF meeting in Warrenton, Virginia, where civil rights activists made a strong case against UNC. In early contacts with UNC counsel, moreover, Hufstedler was irritated by Chuck Morgan's attempts to have her deposed. As a result, in mid-June 1980 Dick Beattie called Friday to say that any further negotiations through the secretary's office would be suspended.[40]

Friday found Beattie's news "terribly disappointing," and he believed that Hufstedler had made a "very bad decision." Ten days later, he renewed his campaign through Stuart Eizenstat. In a letter to Eizenstat, Friday suggested that the case could cost Carter North Carolina in the fall election. Friday's dire warning evidently had some effect, for on July 11, 1980, Gene Eidenburg, a White House aide, telephoned to say that Hufstedler was now willing to consider negotiation. Eidenburg advised Friday to call the education secretary the following day, on Saturday, July 12, but Friday, after consulting with Ray Dawson and John R. Jordan Jr., who had just become chairman of the Board of Governors, refused. Also on July 11, Beattie telephoned Dawson, asserting that "movement was taking place." In a subsequent conversation with Friday, Beattie "strenuously urged" him to talk to Hufstedler. Finally, after additional consultations with Dawson and Jordan, Friday agreed to make the call.[41]

In a conversation the next morning at 9:00, Friday found Hufstedler significantly more forthcoming. She endorsed negotiations, she said, but only if they could remain completely confidential. That Monday, July 14, Hufstedler dispatched her aide Gilbert Kujovich to negotiate with UNC without the knowledge of the OCR bureaucracy.[42] Dawson described Kujovich as a "nice young man" who was a heavy smoker of True cigarettes and "a lean fellow, sort of a bean-pole." Kujovich, who had been a law clerk for Hufstedler, arrived in Chapel Hill on the morning of July 14 and remained until about 2:30 in the afternoon. The meeting with Kujovich was a "review session," as Friday characterized it, but it also soon became apparent that the Hufstedler aide was a sympathetic listener, and his visit revived Friday's optimism. "I genuinely believe that he wishes to settle the case if at all possible, and soon," he wrote.[43]

Kujovich's attitude seemed different from that of previous HEW representatives. The *Adams* criteria, Kujovich said, lacked the force of a court order and were not binding, and he did not necessarily agree with Tatel's interpretation of Criterion II-C, which required the elimination of unnecessary program duplication. Kujovich envisioned a settlement that would include three components: first, a description of UNC's accomplishments in desegregation; second, a statement of the goals and objectives already laid out in earlier plans and submissions; and, third, a declaration of additional goals and objectives for the future. Friday, Dawson, and their guest were joined for lunch by UNC vice presidents Roy Carroll, Felix Joyner, and Cleon Thompson; Dawson then drove Kujovich to the airport. On the way, Dawson, citing the 1974 *Revised North Carolina State Plan* and vet school issue, reminded Kujovich of the HEW's track record of not keeping commitments; the university would insist that any agreement include ironclad guarantees that future administrations or secretaries could not disavow.[44]

Kujovich's visit to Chapel Hill on July 14 began a new, and to Friday, promising, negotiating channel. The UNC president had never abandoned hope that the controversy could be settled outside of litigation, and the election of John R. Jordan Jr. as Board of Governors chairman meant a board leadership that jibed with his own. Friday "really wanted to settle," Dawson remembered. He believed that litigation with HEW was "highly wasteful of time and resources, that it was senseless, useless," and he was "delighted" at Hufstedler's initiative, which offered the possibility of a breakthrough. Kujovich also elevated hopes in Washington, where Gene Eidenburg was briefed on the progress of the initiative. Subsequently, Eidenburg telephoned Friday on July 21, and the two men agreed that Kujovich would return to Chapel Hill three days later, on July 24.[45]

UNC officials were eager to test Kujovich's willingness to negotiate, and they questioned him closely during his second visit. Kujovich came with specifics. He concurred that the program duplication model was "perhaps the most disruptive way to integrate." He also assented to a consent decree in Judge Dupree's court, although he noted that the Department of Education would still need to defend any agreement in the *Adams* court. The particulars of that consent decree, however, remained vague. Soon after the July 24, 1980, conference with Kujovich, Friday convened a meeting of the Board of Governors' ad hoc lawyers' committee. Reviewing developments through the Kujovich channel, Friday told the committee that he expected to hear again, probably the next week, from Education officials, and he asked it to consider whether he should proceed further. Two hours of debate then ensued between hard-liners and supporters of conciliation over not only whether to take the talks seriously, but also whether and when to include university counsel, which had so far been excluded from negotiations. The ad hoc committee agreed that Friday should receive Kujovich's telephone call and then notify Levin of the latest developments.[46]

Less than a month later, at a meeting in Friday's home, the UNC president again reviewed developments, this time with the university legal team of Joe Levin, Andy Vanore, and Dick Robinson, along with Roy Carroll, Cleon Thompson, Ray Dawson, and John R. Jordan Jr. Friday, after pointing out that the negotiations had been so secret that they heretofore had excluded university counsel, explained how "cautious and confidential" their discussions should remain; nothing from this meeting should be used in the administrative proceedings. Kujovich, he told the group, did not object to a settlement based on a consent decree; he was also willing to abandon HEW's long-standing insistence on ending program duplication. On both issues, Friday considered Kujovich's positions to be "major concessions." But Kujovich had also introduced a new element into the talks – a so-called doctrine of comparability that would set a new standard for measuring TWI-TBI equity and could, Friday believed, become a "rather serious arena for debate." Nonetheless, he was convinced that Kujovich sought to "move ahead, that he wanted to reach a settlement." Levin, who had a good working relationship with UNC administrators, was not threatened by backchannel negotiations. He agreed to oversee whatever proposals Kujovich presented. By the end of the meeting, the UNC lawyers all strongly endorsed further discussions.[47]

Negotiations continued with Kujovich through the months immediately preceding the election, as the Carter White House considered a resolution of the UNC situation an urgent political priority. The president supported an "amiable settlement of this dispute," Eizenstat wrote in September. Eizenstat had spoken directly with Secretary Hufstedler and hoped that the impasse could be broken. After November 4, 1980, when Carter went down to defeat by Ronald Reagan, who carried North Carolina, negotiations continued. In addition to his two trips to Chapel Hill that summer, Gilbert Kujovich visited Friday and his staff on four occasions before the election. When he again flew to Chapel Hill on November 6 and 7, an agreement appeared to be in hand. On November 7 Friday approved the tentative understanding and, while he visited Jim Hunt on November 9 to be sure of his support, awaited reactions from Washington. Hunt telephoned Hufstedler, who said that she had not yet reviewed the details of the agreement but "enthusiastically endorsed" continued efforts to reach an accommodation. Soon after the election, Carter called Hunt; the president promised that he would push for negotiations and asked the North Carolina governor to keep him abreast of developments in the case.[48]

Throughout much of November 1980, it seemed that the two sides were on the verge of a settlement. Kujovich had proposed an agreement that would call for a comparative study of the differences between TBIs and TWIs at the end of a five-year period, in 1985. He also favored firm goals on enrollments and employment that were similar to those required in the *Adams* criteria. There remained significant differences about the role of OCR and its ability to evaluate UNC desegregation in the future; Kujovich had proposed a monitoring committee to which UNC officials took immediate exception. Nonetheless, the HEW negotiator had so far seemed amiable, reasonable, and trustworthy. Above all, he had omitted from discussion the most difficult issue of all – the question of the extent to which UNC would, in the future, commit itself to using a program duplication model of desegregation.[49]

Friday's high hopes for a settlement arising out of the Kujovich negotiations were dashed on December 2, 1980, when Kujovich again traveled to Chapel Hill with what UNC officials immediately recognized was a radically different set of proposals. They believed that the enrollment goals transmitted on December 2 – an increase to 12 percent black enrollment at TWIs by 1986 and a requirement that the retention rates of black students should not be greater than 25 percent less than that of whites – were unrealistic. These more demanding enrollment goals became threatening in light of another provision inserted in the agreement: Education's insistence on a future role in monitoring desegregation. UNC particularly objected to a new requirement that additional measures would have to be taken if the university failed to reach its enrollment goals. Friday feared that this new provision would become an opening wedge to further OCR intervention. Rather than a self-contained consent decree, Kujovich's new plan would have the university back in the familiar and frustrating cycle of OCR supervision.

Friday had no doubt that these last-minute additions to the settlement agreement were an act of sabotage by OCR hard-liners. The new proposals, he wrote, were "not the wishes of Mr. Kujovich; far from it." Rather, they represented the views of OCR staffers, who now reentered the negotiations. "I can only conclude that the staff of the Office for Civil Rights has again imposed its will," Friday wrote. As a result, he concluded, it was very likely that UNC and the Carter administration would be frustrated in their efforts to reach an "honorable agreement" about "the greatest social issue we have faced in generations."[50]

Other UNC officials offered a different interpretation. Ray Dawson, skeptical about the negotiations from the beginning, later described Hufstedler's response as a "flat, clear, unequivocal turndown." University administrators were pawns, he believed, in nothing more than an "election ploy." In an act of political cynicism, White House officials "wanted to pass the word that they were trying to reach a settlement" primarily because "they needed some Democratic votes down South." Although Kujovich had dealt with UNC in good faith, Dawson thought that Hufstedler had not. To him, this was the only possible explanation for the rapidly changing events in the autumn of 1980.[51]

Bill Friday was deeply disappointed. Until December 2, Kujovich had assured UNC officials that any settlement would come in the form of a consent decree to be supervised by Dupree's court, not by OCR. He further asserted that the standards of the *Adams* criteria would not be controlling. University officials had objected in August when Kujovich had suggested reintroducing language about the program duplication model, and in subsequent talks he had withdrawn it. By November, the proposed consent decree called for specific measures of "comparability" between TWIs and TBIs; a five-year development plan for each TBI; new, five-year enrollment projections for the university system and detailed measures to meet them; and new proposals to increase the number of black faculty and employees. At that time Friday was confident that the two sides were close to an agreement. But Kujovich's proposals of December 2 "departed significantly" from the "laboriously developed" understandings worked out over the course of eight separate meetings.[52]

With this setback, Friday was in no mood to negotiate. At the December 2 meeting, he informed Kujovich that the groundwork for talks had been so "fundamentally altered" that further discussion was impossible. Shirley Hufstedler telephoned Governor Hunt on December 11 to urge that the new proposals become the basis for negotiations. When Hufstedler called Friday the next day, he again told her that HEW's game plan was unacceptable and that the upcoming administrative proceedings, scheduled to reconvene on February 16, would have to be postponed if negotiations were to continue. Nonetheless, Friday agreed to travel to Washington for a face-to-face conference with Hufstedler.[53]

That meeting, which took place on December 17, proved fruitless. Hufstedler informed Friday that any consent decree should include two features of the Education Department's December 2 proposals. First, there should be some "mechanism of evaluation" to monitor the agreement that would go beyond mere court supervision. This mechanism would measure enrollment and retention rates and how well they measured up to UNC's goals; it might involve representatives of the university, public schools, foundations, the business community, and the governor's office. Second, Hufstedler demanded that there be an "equivalency" in the expenditure of future capital funds for TBIs and TWIs in North Carolina. After consulting with UNC senior staff and attorney Joe Levin, Friday responded coolly. Indicating that he had abandoned hope for the Kujovich channel, he insisted that further negotiations take place through counsel. It was absolutely necessary, Friday added, to delay the administrative proceedings until May 1. On December 18 Gilbert Kujovich told Friday, now back in Chapel Hill, that further negotiations had been suspended. Thus ended the last attempts to resolve the matter during the Carter administration.[54]

Facing the uncertainty of the administrative proceedings, Friday and his staff felt that the risks of an injurious settlement were too great to take. The latest proposals from the Department of Education, Dawson wrote in a memorandum on January 22, 1981, suggested that federal officials continued to insist on unacceptable concessions. Submitting to Education would almost certainly mean future demands that would become "virtually irresistible after we have acknowledged the legitimacy of their position." But the closing and merger of programs – the prospect of which was already causing acute anxiety at the historically black campuses – would likely lead to strong objections by faculty and students and a succession of lawsuits. Meanwhile, commitments by UNC to TBI enhancement could bring further frustration; "what we seek and obtain is dismissed as not enough." In any event, as Dawson saw it, the choice between settlement and continued litigation was "dismal" because of the "unreasonable and arbitrary and still undefined nature of the requirements we are still to try to meet." The current situation could be best described as "heads they win and tails we lose."[55]

An air of inevitability characterized the conflict in the winter of 1981, as the administrative proceedings continued. "Like a long-running movie with a surreal plot," editorialized the *Greensboro Daily News*, the desegregation controversy had entered its second decade and fourth presidential administration, "with no end in sight." It seemed as if too much had been invested "in this arduous process to stop now." After the appearance of some thirty government witnesses from July to October 1980, the university presented its case beginning on February 23, 1981. Speaking on behalf of UNC were experts such as conservative black economist Thomas Sowell, who testified on March 5 that UNC was not segregated and that program shifts would be self-defeating. But the most dramatic testimony came from UNC officials like Felix Joyner and, especially, Ray Dawson, who documented the previous four years' frustrating negotiations with HEW. By May 1981 UNC had completed its argument, and the hearings were adjourned until June 22, when the government planned to call rebuttal witnesses.[56]

Even as UNC presented its case, however, negotiations with HEW resumed during the early days of the Reagan administration. After the Republican sweep in November 1980, speculation immediately began about its impact on the UNC-HEW controversy. Jesse Helms reportedly said on election night that the resolution of the dispute was now just a phone call away. Julius Chambers similarly predicted that Ronald Reagan's election would imperil the administrative hearings, although he warned that the LDF would take action quickly if the new administration terminated them. Friday was more cautious, telling reporters that he knew nothing about how the election results would effect the desegregation case.[57]

In fact, although Helms's comment was an exaggeration, the senator used his influence with the new administration to settle the case favorably for the university. On January 14, less than a week before Reagan's inauguration, Friday and Dawson met with Helms and his aides, Clint Fuller and Sam

Currin, for two hours. After the UNC officials reviewed the chronology of events, Helms offered his help. In the meantime, Friday also spoke with Republican senator-elect John East, a former ECU professor. Although both Helms and East represented constituencies that had been hostile to Friday and the university – either overtly or behind the scenes – the UNC president did not reject their assistance. "The door is always open," he told a North Carolina legislative committee on February 3, and he was hoping that "the burden will soon be lifted, so that we can indeed devote ourselves to constructive efforts rather than litigation." The case was not about desegregation, he said; if that were true "there would be no controversy." Rather, the real issue was university autonomy – "whether it will determine for itself what shall be taught, where and by who[m] it shall be taught, or whether a regulatory agency in Washington will make those decisions."[58]

Publicly, Helms urged conciliation; privately, he sought to influence the new Reagan administration. "Suffice it to say," Helms announced to the press, he would do everything that he could "to get the federal government off the back of the University of North Carolina," and now was the "time to do it." Helms made the matter a high priority. At his confirmation hearings as the new secretary of education, Terrell H. Bell had already announced that there would be a "dramatic change" in the way the case was pursued and that he would sit down with UNC officials to "listen and learn." Although the Reagan White House brought him in to fulfill a campaign promise to abolish the Department of Education, Bell was an experienced educator, having served as superintendent of public instruction and as commissioner of higher education in Utah, as well as U.S. commissioner of education from 1974 to 1976.[59]

On January 16, 1981, Currin informed Friday that Helms's office had established contact with Bell's aide, Elam Hertzler, and that a meeting would soon occur. That meeting, which originally was to assemble representatives of the *Adams* states, took place on the morning of February 4 in Bell's office. Among those present were Bell, Friday, Dawson, Levin, and the two North Carolina senators. The conference was an introductory session, lasting ninety minutes, in which the participants discussed the background of the desegregation controversy, what UNC's position was, and on what issues the two sides disagreed. "It was a visit to discuss the history of this relationship more than anything else," Friday told reporters, "but whether or not there will be any more meetings is clearly at their option." The university was "willing at any time and all times to work toward a reasonable settlement," and he wanted the new administration to become informed of that position. Yet he was not optimistic; this was the sixth cabinet secretary with whom he had dealt, and UNC had "made this effort before."[60]

Friday emerged from the meeting with a strong personal rapport with Bell. According to Dawson, the two men "hit it off very well." As a cabinet officer with experience in higher education, Bell quickly trusted Friday and told him that he wanted cooperation rather than conflict. The new education secretary believed, as he recalled, that the case needed a "fresh start" in order to obtain a settlement. Friday immediately made it clear that he would cooperate. When Bell expressed some interest in obtaining the perspectives of North Carolina's traditionally black campuses, Friday helped to arrange a meeting with the five TBI chancellors. Nonetheless, although UNC and Education had improved relations during the winter of 1981, they realized that it would be impossible to reach a settlement before the administrative hearings resumed on February 24. As a result, both sides prepared for a new round of highly complex negotiations.[61]

Meanwhile, Helms's pressure and the Reagan administration's desire to resolve the UNC controversy were moving matters to a head. On February 27 Helms and Currin met with Bell, who said that he and the White House both wanted to settle the case, but to do so in such a way as to withstand court scrutiny. Accordingly, Bell inaugurated substantive negotiations that would result in a consent decree signed by Bell and Friday, subject to Judge Dupree's approval. Bell's determination to settle was crucial, Friday remembered, and the education secretary initiated "extensive conversations" with Board of Governors chairman Jordan. The White House also became directly involved; during the transition Helms had met with Reagan at Blair House in Washington and encouraged him to find a solution. "We've got to get that thing straightened out," he reportedly said. The president-elect assured the senator that he would appoint a secretary of education who would settle the case amicably. As an indication of its importance to the White House, Bell, at the February 27 meeting with Helms, appointed Douglas Bennett as his lead negotiator. Bennett, who had no previous experience at either Education or HEW, was primarily a political operative. A West Point graduate and former infantry captain in the Vietnam War, he had served as Gerald Ford's White House personnel director; by the time of Reagan's inauguration, he was a Georgetown tax attorney and Republican loyalist. Another round of negotiations thus began with Bennett's arrival in Chapel Hill for an initial meeting on March 6, 1981.[62]

Over the next four months, negotiations proceeded through the Bennett channel. Along with six visits to Chapel Hill, Bennett met with UNC representatives in Washington; between March and June 1981, there were about twenty bargaining sessions. The talks, held during the administrative hearings and without the knowledge of OCR staffers, took place either in Bennett's or

Levin's office in Washington or at the Carolina Inn in Chapel Hill.[63] UNC officials emphasized that they would no longer involve themselves in meaningless discussions. The university would no longer be used as a "cat's paw for somebody's purposes," Dawson told Bennett, but if they were "really interested in a settlement" UNC would negotiate, on two conditions. First, no settlement should be framed in such a way as to make subsequent repudiation by a new presidential administration or cabinet officer possible. "We've been that road twice," Dawson declared, and "we're not going that way again"; the settlement must be in the form of a consent decree that would be under the supervision of the Dupree court, so that the university could respond to attacks before any administrative decisions were made. Second, there must be no reference to the program duplication model.[64]

Bennett had received his marching orders, which were, Levin said, "to figure out some way to settle this case." Accordingly, he quickly accepted Dawson's conditions but insisted on an arrangement that would stand the test of court scrutiny. By April 24, 1981, Bennett and UNC agreed to incorporate a settlement in a detailed consent decree, and Dawson spent much of May preparing a draft of the document. While serving on the Morehead Scholars selection committee that year, Dawson, with the concurrence of its director, Mebane Pritchett, spread out his materials and wrote the draft in one of the Morehead building's interview rooms. At the end of each day, he reviewed the completed portions with Friday and Dick Robinson before sending them off to Joe Levin.[65]

Although the bargaining continued on a formal level, Bennett frequently telephoned Friday, often late at night at his home. Levin was irritated by this parallel track of negotiations, but he realized that "you couldn't get Bill not to talk to these people" and he "just couldn't stand the prospect . . . of something not being received or listened to, or dealt with." Talks at the ground level, with Bennett, were conducted by Joyner, Dawson, and Levin. Although veteran HEW and Education attorney Richard Foster was involved, the day-to-day representative accompanying Bennett was another attorney from Education, Antonia "Tony" Califa. Califa represented the Education bureaucracy, which was, according to Levin, "very hostile" to a settlement. Although his role was to serve as a kind of "damage control" over the talks, Califa had no direct experience in the case and exerted little influence.[66]

Califa's limited authority reflected the dominance of Douglas Bennett, who, based on one account, managed the negotiations "in a very military fashion." The White House operative had a formidable ego. Bennett advertised himself as having educational expertise because of his appointment to the West Point Board of Trustees. Rather than referring to the vice president as "Vice President Bush," he called him "George"; at one point, he told a university negotiator that the president was "following what I do very closely." Califa, a burly bureaucrat who was allied with the OCR radicals, was an unlikely sidekick, but he and Bennett worked hard toward hammering out an acceptable consent decree.[67]

By late March, rumors had surfaced in the press of a breakthrough in the negotiations, which up to then were shrouded in secrecy. On March 26, 1981, LDF attorney Joe Rauh, somehow learning of the talks, denounced a possible settlement. An announcement was "imminent," he told reporters before attending a session of the administrative hearings, and it was "underhanded and sleazy" that Bill Friday was settling the case without consulting the LDF or the North Carolina black community. This was an attempt by Friday to "win from the Reagan administration what he cannot win in court." Friday, however, remained silent about the negotiations, refusing Rauh's bait. Rauh had made "major contributions to our country during his long career," Friday said, and he "genuinely" regretted that Rauh had resorted to "such vindictiveness at the close of his career." But the story of secret negotiations broke when Dawson was testifying, and the LDF sought to embarrass UNC by raising the matter while he was on the stand. On cross-examination, the LDF, which was an intervener in the case, asked Dawson what he knew about the negotiations. According to one reporter, it was "like a bomb exploded in that room." Simultaneously, both Levin and Vanore sprang to their feet, shouting "Don't answer" to Dawson. Judge John Mathias then ordered a conference in which he instructed LDF attorneys that "if a settlement can be negotiated then I think we ought to welcome that." When the attorneys emerged, Mathias ordered that the question be withdrawn. But the LDF lawyer who was present at the conference stated that that day's events had left no doubt in his mind that the backchannel negotiations were actually taking place. The next day Dawson denied that any "settlement" had been reached, that a "new proposal" had been drafted, or that an "exchange of paper" had occurred. He said nothing, however, about new negotiations.[68]

Actually, the two sides were far from a final agreement, and the negotiations dragged on. In late April, whereas one Education official later described the talks as "going full blast," Friday reported to the ad hoc committee that they were proceeding smoothly but that differences remained. The small working group of Bennett, Califa, Dawson, Joyner, and Levin divided the talks into areas of substantive disagreement – TBI enhancement, budgets, and recruiting – and here serious negotiations proceeded. Having abandoned any discussion of the duplication model as a means of eliminating curricular duplication, Education officials raised the issue of faculty employment. In that area

UNC General Administration agreed to assume greater responsibility, specifying, for example, that faculty could not be employed at a TBI without a terminal degree unless the UNC president approved the appointment. The university pledged that the student-faculty ratio at TBIs would remain at least as favorable as at counterpart TWIs; it also promised new capital construction projects at the TBIs.

The most significant gaps continued to concern enrollment goals for black students at TWIs and white students at TBIs. Senator Helms subsequently told reporters that the talks became "sticky" on this issue, with the two sides disagreeing primarily on numerical goals. The UNC negotiators proposed that enrollments be measured by the entire system rather than by individual campuses; Education officials concurred but insisted that UNC provide more specific enrollment projections. The "toughest point," Dawson recalled, remained the enrollment issue, and federal officials "hung very tough on that."[69]

Differences persisted among the UNC forces about how much power to concede to federal officials. Although Bill Johnson had left the chairmanship, he remained on the Board of Governors and, with other hard-liners, was unwilling to accept anything but unconditional victory. Joe Levin sympathized with Johnson's position – and later believed that his stance had been correct – and he had doubts in the spring of 1981 about Friday's willingness to offer too many concessions. In fact, so apparent were these differences between Levin and the hard-liners and the university administration and its board supporters that, Levin remembered, "hard feelings resulted." There was even a time when he and Felix Joyner, with whom Levin had struck up a friendship, were no longer on speaking terms.[70]

Not until June 1981 did UNC and the Education Department come to terms. On Thursday, June 11, Tony Califa went to Levin's Washington office, and the two attorneys worked until the early hours of the following morning. At 4:30 A.M. on June 12, Califa called Douglas Bennett at home with the news that a tentative settlement had been reached. Only a few key details remained. On the weekend of June 12–14, Bill Friday received an evening telephone call at his home from Jesse Helms, who was attending the outdoor drama at Manteo on Roanoke Island to give a eulogy to the late playwright Paul Green. Negotiations were then stalled on enrollment goals. Federal officials had asked UNC to commit itself to increase black enrollment at TWIs over five years; UNC would not go beyond 10.6 percent. Would Friday call Attorney General William French Smith? the senator asked. When Friday contacted Smith, who was a "very late comer into this thing," he found additional evidence of the willingness of the Reagan White House to settle the case, and Smith agreed to the 10.6 percent goal. It was at this point that Helms "really believed that something was going to be worked out and very quickly."[71]

Over the weekend, a settlement emerged. On Monday, June 15, the ad hoc lawyers' committee of the Board of Governors met and unanimously approved the agreement, while on the same day Bell and Helms met with Attorney General Smith to arrange for Justice Department attorneys to file the consent decree in the Raleigh federal district court. Two days later, press reports began appearing about a possible settlement that UNC officials would present to the Board of Governors for approval at a special meeting on Saturday, June 20. At that meeting, with Bell's approval in hand, the Board of Governors gave its strong support to the consent decree, which was submitted to Judge Franklin Dupree; he issued an eight-page-memorandum opinion on July 17, 1981, that approved the consent decree as "fair, reasonable, and adequate." The document, ruled Dupree, complied "substantially" with the 1977 *Adams* criteria; UNC's refusal to endorse the program duplication model reflected a consensus among higher education experts that this approach was "educationally unsound and likely to lead to further desegregation."[72]

The consent decree represented a major victory for UNC. The university agreed to implement a wide-ranging program that included better publicity, recruitment efforts, and scholarships in order to attract a larger number of minority students to its sixteen-campus system. UNC would seek a goal of 10.6 percent black enrollment at TWIs and a 15.0 percent white enrollment at TBIs. It also would establish new programs, construct new facilities, and continue to enhance the existing programs of the state's five traditionally black institutions. The university made all of these commitments to the Dupree court rather than to OCR, and progress would be measured by a good-faith standard. Finally, the consent decree provided for UNC commitments over five years; court supervision would end on December 31, 1988.[73]

Along with the end of OCR supervision, the major accomplishment of the consent decree was the federal government's abandonment of the program duplication model of desegregation. Bennett, early in the most recent round of negotiations, made this concession; what was at issue was the extent to which the university would remain bound by enrollment and employment goals. The agreement affirmed UNC's position, which was that the decree should include only nonbinding goals. At long last, from the viewpoint of UNC officials, the university would no longer be under the eye of the federal bureaucracy. Associate vice president for planning Gary Barnes, who joined the General Administration in 1979, had taken charge of assembling statistical data for the administrative hearings. For Barnes, who had often worked seventy or eighty hours a week on the case, the signing of the consent decree meant that an "incredible weight" was lifted. Still, the cumulative stress of the dispute was "slow to dissipate" for everyone at General Administration.[74]

Friday took no great delight in the settlement. Eight years of on-again, off-again conflict had been bruising, both personally and professionally, and the seemingly kafkaesque nightmare had taken a heavy psychic toll. The case had placed both him and the university under a grueling national spotlight. Ironically, within weeks of the announcement of the consent decree, Joe Califano published his *Governing America*. "I hope that you will take the time to read the book," Califano wrote to Friday in June 1981, for he believed that his account of the case was a "fair rendition of a difficult situation." Uncharacteristically, he did not answer Califano's letter for two months – Friday always responded promptly to correspondents – because, he said, he first wanted to read the book. His reply in August made it clear that he did not agree with the former secretary's version of events; although he expressed himself briefly and obliquely, he told Califano that it served "no useful purpose to argue or quarrel further, so let the matter be closed."[75]

For Friday's adversaries, however, the matter remained open. Joe Rauh immediately condemned the agreement, which he described as a "sellout of civil rights by the Reagan administration." Frank Porter Graham, he said, was "whirling . . . in his grave," for what the government had accepted from UNC was worse than what Califano had rejected two years earlier.[76] Julius Chambers agreed with this assessment; the settlement was a "sellout" that relied unnecessarily on voluntary compliance to accomplish desegregation. The LDF immediately attempted to prevent the signing of the consent decree, and, failing that, challenged its legality. When, on June 25, 1981, Judge John Pratt, who was not unhappy to be relieved from that portion of the quagmire of *Adams*, refused to intervene, the LDF petitioned the U.S. Court of Appeals for the D.C. circuit. That court, which ruled en banc on June 10, 1983, also affirmed the consent decree and Dupree's supervision of it. When the Supreme Court refused to hear the case, the UNC desegregation dispute was over.[77]

Bill Friday's reluctance to say much about the case – then or later – reflected a harsh reality: journalists, especially members of the national press, tended to portray UNC's side of the controversy negatively. On July 11, 1981, a *New York Times* editorial sharply criticized the consent decree. But as Levin's subsequent letter to the editor maintained, the editorial made "misleading assumptions and factual errors." The *Times* had incorrectly contended that the LDF had launched the suit in 1970 against the university; Levin pointed out that UNC was not a party to the *Adams* litigation. The paper further claimed that the program duplication model was a universally accepted formula for successful desegregation, an assertion that Levin said demonstrated that the editorialists had "no appreciation of the evidence presented during the trial." The university also received hostile treatment in a segment on the case aired in September 1981 on the popular CBS *Sunday Morning* program, hosted by UNC-Chapel Hill graduate Charles Kuralt. In the piece, CBS reporter Ed Rabel suggested that the UNC settlement would turn back the clock for civil rights activists. UNC officials and other observers in North Carolina were horrified. Ray Dawson called the segment "appalling" and "unbelievable," while Friday characterized it as "inadequate, if not unfair." The *Raleigh News and Observer's* Claude Sitton, who was not always sympathetic to the UNC position, said that the CBS presentation was a "mugging" of the university. Indeed, it was filled with images of George Wallace's attempts in the early 1960s to block the integration of the University of Alabama. After a storm of protests, including communications from both Jim Hunt and Bill Friday, CBS aired a seven-minute follow-up report that presented UNC's perspective and provided five minutes of interview footage with Friday. Nonetheless, the damage was done: as Dawson observed, if you deal with "simple generalizations," as television tends to do, the original CBS presentation was "all you need to know."[78]

University desegregation remained, for the remainder of Friday's presidency, a central concern. During the 1980s efforts to desegregate through merger or the program duplication model encountered significant problems in Virginia, Tennessee, and Georgia. In Georgia, for example, a federal district judge in 1981 described the program shifts at Savannah State and Armstrong State – Savannah gave up instruction in teacher education and Armstrong relinquished business education – as having "comparatively little effect" on desegregating enrollments. HEW had projected that 500 black students and 500 white students would follow the transfer of the business administration and teacher education programs. In fact, only 114 whites and 85 blacks transferred; 80 percent simply went elsewhere. The failure of the program duplication model in the 1980s seemed to vindicate Friday's steady adherence to principle.[79]

In the mid-1980s an OCR task force conducted a follow-up study of the ten *Adams* states. After visiting most of the public institutions in those states, the task force made its findings public in 1988. The results were illuminating. Six of the *Adams* states were judged as falling short of compliance with desegregation plans drafted and approved in the late 1970s, whereas four others, including North Carolina, were found to be in compliance. Significantly, the desegregation plans of four states that settled with OCR in 1978–79 rather than contest the program duplication model – Florida, Georgia, Oklahoma, and Virginia – were found to be ineffective.[80]

The UNC desegregation program, embodied in the 1981 settlement, helped to increase state funding for traditionally black institutions. As a result of the consent decree, twenty-nine new degree programs were established at the TBIs and five other new programs were begun. By the late 1980s, UNC's historically black campuses were receiving as much or more state funding per student as comparable historically white campuses, while budgeted average teaching salaries were identical for TBIs and TWIs at comprehensive and baccalaureate universities. Greater state funding transformed facilities at traditionally black institutions. In the 1980s the General Assembly appropriated over $95 million – an amount greater than that allowed by any other southern state – for new construction and renovation of the TBI campuses. At Fayetteville State, where over $18 million was spent on facilities, new library and school of business administration buildings were constructed; at A&T, the infusion of state funds brought new library and new engineering school buildings.

Even more dramatic progress could be seen in the composition of the faculties and students on UNC campuses. Between 1972 and 1991, largely as a result of a pre-consent decree program that encouraged faculty to complete the Ph.D., the percentage of faculty members holding the doctorate increased from 27 percent to 77 percent at Elizabeth City State, from 32 percent to 76 percent at Fayetteville State, and from 34 percent to 67 percent at Winston-Salem State. While faculty qualifications improved, UNC programs begun under the consent decree, such as the minority presence student grants program (which expended $9.4 million for minority scholarships during the 1980s), stimulated significant changes in student enrollment. Black enrollment at historically white institutions grew from slightly more than 3 percent in 1972 to over 8 percent twenty years later. Although this fell short of the consent decree goal of 10.6 percent, UNC ranked first nationally in the increase in black enrollment at TWIs between 1976 and 1986. Meanwhile, white enrollment at TBIs increased from 5 percent in 1972 to almost 19 percent twenty years later and exceeded the consent decree goal of 15 percent.[81]

The resolution of the North Carolina case did not end *Adams*-related litigation. Joe Levin was involved in disputes in Louisiana in the early 1980s and in Alabama in the early 1990s. Although, unlike the controversy at UNC, these cases primarily related to governance, Levin later said that his legal strategy in Louisiana and Alabama did not differ "one iota" from the strategy that he used in North Carolina. Both sides used many of the same witnesses; many of the same issues, including the viability of the program duplication model, continued to occupy center stage. Government lawyers, Levin maintained, had not "learned a thing" about higher education since the UNC settlement.[82]

Since the UNC consent decree of 1981, the issue of the desegregation of higher education has remained murky. After almost two decades of litigation, the *Adams* case was formally closed in 1990. The outcome was favorable to Levin in the Louisiana case, but, in the summer of 1991, a federal judge in Birmingham, Alabama, in *Knight* v. *State of Alabama*, required Alabama colleges and universities to make more strenuous efforts to desegregate. Even more important was a higher education desegregation conflict involving Mississippi, *United States* v. *Fordice*, that reached the U.S. Supreme Court and was decided in June 1992. In an eight-to-one decision, the Court overturned the ruling court of appeals, which had concluded that the adoption of race-neutral policies fulfilled the "affirmative duty" to desegregate. In an opinion written by Justice Byron White, the Court held that Mississippi's attempt to desegregate had been insufficient, and it suggested that closings and institutional mergers could be adopted. In contrast to the general tenor of the *Adams* rulings, moreover, the Court urged that "racial identifiability" of institutions be eliminated.[83]

The *Fordice* decision, the first time since *Brown* v. *Board of Education* that the U.S. Supreme Court had attempted a substantive ruling on the desegregation of higher education, threatened to confuse state policies considerably. Abandoning the long-standing court protection of the "racial identifiability" of TBIs, *Fordice* now laid open the possibility of new and more drastic measures, including the closing of TBIs, as a new model for desegregation. In a concurring opinion, Justice Clarence Thomas stated that although "a state is not constitutionally required to maintain its historically black institutions as such, I do not understand our opinion to hold that a state is forbidden from doing so." Justice White's opinion provided no clear guideposts for appropriate means of enforcement – either through the courts or the federal bureaucracy – or for the creation of normative standards to determine if and when universities had truly desegregated. As the lone dissenter, Antonin Scalia, put it, the majority opinion "has no proper application in the context of higher education, provides no genuine guidance to states and lower courts, and is as likely to subvert as to promote the interests of those citizens on whose behalf the present suit was brought." He predicted "a number of years of litigation-driven confusion and destabilization in the university systems of all the formerly de jure states, that will benefit neither blacks nor whites, neither predominantly black institutions nor predominantly white ones." "Nothing good will come of this judicially ordained turmoil," Scalia wrote, "except the public recognition that any Court that would knowingly impose it must hate segregation."[84]

Although the *Fordice* decision brought into question the security of the UNC settlement eleven years earlier, Bill Friday's legacy remained clear. Friday had consistently endorsed methods very much in accord with his own political and administrative style: voluntarism and face-to-face persuasion combined with the eventual conversion of the power structure to the goal of desegregation. The Office for Civil Rights, in contrast, wanted immediate results and drastic methods, including program closings and mergers. It also sought continuing control over educational policy, which would have amounted to unprecedented federal intervention in higher education and might have damaged UNC's carefully constructed multicampus system.

In the end, President Friday prevailed. Despite an educational system in which vestiges of racial segregation remained, Friday obtained major commitments toward more integrated enrollments and boosted state support for TBIs. The University of North Carolina adopted a program rooted in the planning and decision-making process developed as part of the UNC system rather the more radical measures demanded by OCR. Even as his program obtained significant results in terms of enrollment integration and TBI enhancement, Friday succeeded further in removing the arena of debate from the federal bureaucracy to the courts and in ending the threat of OCR supervision. His handling of the long battle with HEW and then the Department of Education was the greatest challenge to and the most significant triumph of his presidency.

I N 1986, as he began his sixty-sixth year, Friday faced retirement from university leadership and the beginning of a new period in his life. In the early and mid-1980s, many members of the Board of Governors sensed that an important transition was taking place. Some believed that the board should exercise more control over the UNC budget, despite the fact that budget making was a presidential responsibility. Others thought that Friday should have dealt more severely with some of the TBI chancellors and taken a firmer stand with HEW. Still other board members wanted a change from the Friday style. All of them were aware that Friday would soon retire and that his departure would create a leadership vacuum.[1]

Although UNC administrators were aware of increased tensions on the Board of Governors during the long siege over desegregation, they probably did not appreciate the degree of frustration that existed. Arnold K. King subsequently observed that although Friday had been UNC president "a long time" and had "done practically everything right," some board members, overwhelmed by the responsibilities of the massive UNC system, believed that they had become "rubber stamps" for his administration. Friday later admitted that he did not fully recognize this sense of frustration and that he "should have seen it more clearly." His failure to identify board sentiment was his "mistake," he said.[2]

In fact, Friday would step down as a result of a policy he himself had implemented soon after he took office in 1956: mandatory retirement at sixty-five for all UNC chancellors, senior administrators, and faculty. Friday enforced that rule without exception; more than twenty chancellors and scores of other senior administrators had retired under his watch. But because retirement had never been forced on the UNC president, uncertainty remained about Friday's future. At a meeting with the Board of Trustees at UNC-Asheville in 1983, Friday announced that he would abide by the university's retirement policy for chancellors. Later, at a Board of Governors meeting in Cullowhee, he said that he would leave effective July 1, 1985. He also suggested a procedure for selecting his successor. Nonetheless, by the summer of 1984 no decision had been formally announced.[3]

Against this backdrop, the UNC Board of Governors proceeded during the summer of 1984 to elect a chairman to succeed John R. Jordan Jr. For the first time in the board's history, the election was contested; Chairmen Dees, Johnson, and Jordan had all been elected by acclamation. By 1984 the board was badly divided. Jordan's anointed successor was Wayne Corpening, a board member since 1975 and mayor of Winston-Salem; Jordan had suggested him because he was an N.C. State graduate who would follow three consecutive Carolina graduates and because he enjoyed the blessing of Friday's strongest supporters on the board. Opposition to Corpening rallied around Phil Carson, an Asheville attorney and board member since 1973, who had been aligned with hard-liners on the HEW/Education imbroglio. During June and July 1984, a heated campaign took place. Carson traveled the state, calling on every member of the board. He succeeded in persuading Walter Royal Davis, a recent addition to the board, to break a pledge of support for Corpening. Davis, a wealthy Texan, believed that under Friday's heavy hand the Board of Governors had not exercised its proper authority. "Bill Friday was running everything," as Jordan described Davis's position, and board members had become "rubber stamps." Carson seized on Davis's criticisms, Jordan said, telling members that the board would be revitalized if he were elected. Carson also claimed that Chairman Jordan had acquiesced in Friday's domination.[4]

When the board met on July 27, 1984, Davis immediately nominated Carson. Before the meeting, four candidates had emerged: Corpening, Carson, Jake Froelich, and Greenville newspaper publisher, Chapel Hill alumnus, and ECU stalwart David J. Whichard II. But on the morning of the twenty-seventh, when it became apparent that Corpening would win a plurality of the vote, Whichard and Froelich swung their support behind Carson. By a margin of only one vote, Carson carried the election, and Froelich was elected vice chair. According to Jordan, Carson's surprise victory resulted from all-out lobbying by Davis to influence undecided votes on the board. Thereafter, Carson, Davis, and Froelich privately conferred at the Governors Inn in the Research Triangle Park before board meetings to determine their position on issues. Davis, Jordan maintained, was "the man behind the chairmanship."[5]

Friday formally announced his decision to retire on September 14, 1984, when he told board members that he would leave office in 1986. During the next eighteen months, Chairman Carson directed the search for a new UNC president. After the board met privately at Southern Pines in late November 1984, the search was formally organized in January 1985.[6] The selection committee, headed by Carson, held meetings across the state to sound out public opinion and then solicited advice from prominent educators around the nation. By Fall 1985, the committee had received 103 nominations and applications for the UNC presidency; 16 candidates were eventually interviewed. In December, reports appeared in the press that the committee was divided into two factions. One, a majority of seven, wanted a new president from outside the UNC system; Fred Davison, president of the University of Georgia, was their leading candidate. The other faction, composed of the remaining four committee members, favored continuity of leadership; its choice was UNC vice president Raymond H. Dawson. Prospective candidates were told by some members of the selection committee that the Board of Governors wished to depart from Friday's leadership style. Yet a clear consensus never materialized in the search committee. By January 1986 the deadlocked committee, now a year in existence, was looking for an acceptable alternative. On January 10 Carson reported to the Board of Governors on the status of the search, denying that any discord existed. Then, during the next week, C. Dixon Spangler Jr., a Charlotte construction executive and chairman of the State Board of Education, emerged as the consensus candidate. Spangler had earned a reputation on the State Board of Education as an advocate of decisive decision making, businesslike management, and strong board involvement. After meeting with the selection committee on January 22 and 24 and speaking with committee members by telephone on January 30, he accepted the UNC presidency. The story was disclosed in the *Raleigh News and Observer* after an enterprising reporter noticed that Spangler was registered at Chapel Hill's Hotel Europa; a source on the selection committee confirmed the reporter's suspicions.[7]

In what the *Charlotte Observer* called a "brief, unemotional farewell" at the Board of Governors meeting on February 14, 1986, Friday proposed that Spangler assume the presidency on March 1. Friday left office abruptly, he later explained, in order to ensure that Spangler would be in place during the coming session of the General Assembly and so that he, Friday, could help to ease the transition. At the February meeting, the board members greeted Friday's departure with tributes and a standing ovation. They also made him an emeritus professor at Carolina but refused, in a gesture bitterly resented by his partisans, to permit Friday to vacate his post early with a leave of absence.[8]

Over the next few weeks local and national journalists reflected on Friday's unprecedented tenure as UNC president. Friday was "widely regarded as one of academe's most competent and knowledgeable leaders," commented the *Chronicle of Higher Education*. A person of "warm, crinkly, intense manner," the *New York Times* told its readers, he had during his three decades in office become "one of the most respected leaders of American higher education." But perhaps the warmest tribute appearing in a national newspaper came from Jonathan Yardley, a Carolina graduate, former *Greensboro Daily News* writer, and by then book critic for the *Washington Post*. Friday, wrote Yardley, was "one of the most prominent and respected citizens" of North Carolina and "one of the three or four most influential figures in postwar American higher education." As the "best friend the scholarly community could have asked for," he had contributed a lifetime of "genuine, selfless public service." Rather than operating as a self-promoter, Friday had "worked quietly, patiently, devotedly – and, when the occasion called for it, forcefully – to give the people of North Carolina the best public university their resources" could support. At his retirement, Friday had bequeathed a university better than they could have "reasonably hoped for."[9]

Equally grateful praise came from the editorial pages of most local newspapers. How could the citizens of North Carolina appropriately express their appreciation to "the likes of an educational giant like Bill Friday"? asked the *Durham Herald*. Friday had been a strong leader, unflinching in the face of difficult decisions, willing to stir controversy or soothe ruffled feathers when necessary and to champion causes for the university and the state. Friday's retirement, added the *Wilmington Morning Star*, meant that the odds were "heavy" that his "presence, style, and grace" would leave with him.[10]

Friday observed his last day in office, February 28, 1986, in a somber mood. One aide called it the "end of an era" of "great accomplishment and great leadership." Another longtime lieutenant, Arnold King, compared Friday's departure to George Washington's farewell to his officers. "They felt sad, and we feel sad, and we'll miss him." King believed that there "certainly" would not be another UNC leader "who comes along anytime soon who has his skills in managing institutional affairs." Sorting through his desk that morning – a desk and an office that no one but Friday had occupied – he showed the assembled reporters a beach photograph of his granddaughter, Miranda. With his vice presidents behind him "soaking up every last drop of his presence," according to one reporter, he convened his final press conference as UNC president at 11:00 A.M. "Thirty years was really too long to stay," he told the journalists assembled. No two days in three decades had ever been exactly the same, but this day was different. "I know I won't feel this way anymore, ever again," Friday said, and the hardest part would be relinquishing "the opportunity to work on a daily basis with the wonderful people who are all around

At the inauguration of C. D. Spangler, 1986.

me." Asked if he would involve himself in any causes in the future, Friday, with a mischievous look, said, "I'm not going to tell you, because I don't know." What he would begin the next morning, he said, was his own business. After the press conference, Friday went home for lunch, returned to the General Administration Building for a 3:30 farewell party, and then left his office for the last time.[11]

FRIDAY'S retirement from the presidency was traumatic, for both him and UNC. He spent Spring 1986 in an office on the top floor of Davis Library on the Chapel Hill campus gathering his papers. UNC's institutional character had for three decades been synonymous with his leadership and personality, and Friday's absence was felt. When developments involving the university occurred, remembered Zona Norwood, who served on Spangler's staff for several months to help with the presidential transition, the press, which had been accustomed to Friday's accessibility, sought him out. But Friday forced himself to remain detached, though his first impulse was to respond as UNC's chief representative. The "most important thing," he later said, "was cutting myself off from that world." Despite the impulse to pick up the phone and intervene, "you have to restrain yourself" and "go out and work in the yard and get over it."[12]

Although retirement was disorienting to Friday on one level, it was liberating on another. He was free to devote more time to the construction of a new home that he and Ida had spent years planning one block from the Chapel Hill campus. No longer subject to a grueling schedule and heavy responsibilities, Friday enjoyed a less stressful routine. Georgia Kyser often shared dinner with the Fridays, and on days when she and Ida were out together late into the afternoon, they would sometimes return to find that Bill had already cheerfully prepared dinner for them. Despite his more relaxed pace, Friday observed lifetime habits. He remained an early riser; Kyser recalled that their dinners together usually ended by eight o'clock, when both Fridays began to tire. During Bill and Ida's more frequent trips abroad, Bill usually arose before anyone and had already explored his surroundings before Ida awakened. Friday also spent more time with his daughter Fran and his two grandchildren, who lived in Chapel Hill. He kept in regular touch by telephone with his other daughters, Betsy, an actress and dancer in New York City, and Mary, an attorney in London.

Retirement did not mean inactivity, however; Friday had no intention of withdrawing entirely from public affairs. During the last decade of his UNC presidency, his name had surfaced periodically in speculations about candidates for the U.S. Senate or the governorship. According to Ida, Bill Friday had always been drawn to public life. If he had remained a lawyer, she was "positive" that he would have entered politics. Another observer, state commissioner of agriculture Jim Graham, called Friday a "master politician." That attraction to public life, a keen fascination with politics, and an impressive information network all made speculation about Friday's political ambitions, as he faced retirement, virtually inevitable.[13]

Although he rejected suggestions that he enter the race for the U.S. Senate in 1980 and the governorship in 1984, Friday had seriously considered a political career in 1985, when Democratic leaders such as Lieutenant Governor Robert Jordan III advised him to stand for John East's Senate seat the following year. On September 28, 1985, former governor Terry Sanford took Friday aside after the inauguration of Duke University president H. Keith Brodie and urged him to run. Earlier, Chris Scott, an official with the state AFL-CIO, had commissioned a poll that showed Friday leading the field. The North Carolinians most attracted to a Friday candidacy, the poll suggested, were ticket-splitting whites who had abandoned the Democratic party during the 1970s and 1980s.[14]

Friday wrestled with the possibility of a Senate campaign for most of October 1985. He asked pollster Louis Harris, a Carolina graduate and long-time friend, to critique Scott's sampling. Harris did not doubt the poll's accuracy, but he predicted an all-out negative campaign by the Republicans. Was Friday willing to endure the scrutiny, as well as the financial cost and the price that his family would have to pay? When Friday said that he did not know, Harris asked him: "Can you get up every morning and look in the mirror and say, 'I am the man who ought to be elected,' and smile when you say it?"[15]

Friday weighed his alternatives. In the first week of October, he told John R. Jordan that he was "not removing himself" as a candidate, but that he would not resign the UNC presidency early in order to enter the campaign. During the last week of that month, he twice spoke by telephone with Bob Jordan, who, as the highest-ranking Democratic leader in the state, was leading the search for a strong opponent to Senator East. Then, in a public statement issued on October 24, 1985, Friday withdrew himself from consideration. He appreciated "the need for action to be taken," but he was convinced that his own responsibilities and obligations precluded any contemplation by him of a candidacy.[16]

Friday later described his withdrawal from consideration as one of two decisions – the other being his refusal to join HEW under John Gardner in 1966 – about which he had second thoughts. "Whether it was the right choice or not," he said, "one can never know." Friday decided against a Senate campaign for several reasons. Lacking an organization, he would need to raise a considerable amount of money and recruit a staff from scratch. Moreover, he remained obligated to UNC during the period of transition to a new president. But perhaps the chief factor in Friday's decision was his belief that the university might become an issue in the political campaign. He remembered the painful experience of Frank Graham during the senatorial primary of 1950, when ugly personal attacks on Graham and his role at UNC resulted, Friday believed, in adverse political consequences for the university for the next two decades. Sources from within the organization of Senator Jesse Helms confirmed that preparation had already begun for a highly negative campaign against Friday. "The university didn't need that," Friday later observed. In refusing to enter the race, he told John R. Jordan, one of many people who had urged him to run, he was protecting his family and UNC. "Why John, you know what they'll do?" he said. "They'll do everything in the world to win. It doesn't matter to them."[17]

Although declining to enter politics, Friday remained prominent in public affairs by accepting the presidency of the William R. Kenan Jr. Fund. The

Kenan family, benefactors of the University of North Carolina since its founding in 1789, had amassed a significant fortune in the twentieth century. William R. Kenan's oldest sister, Mary Lily Kenan, married Henry M. Flagler, an early partner of John D. Rockefeller and later a Florida real estate developer. The couple had no children, so when Flagler died in 1913, much of his wealth passed to Mary Lily; after her death in 1917, a large part of her estate was left to her sister and to her brother and executor, William R. Kenan Jr. In 1915 Mrs. Flagler established the Kenan professorships at Carolina. Subsequently, Kenan money set up professorships at leading southern research campuses and then across the country; by the 1990s there were over ninety-two William R. Kenan Jr. professorships at fifty-six colleges and universities nationwide. William R. Kenan Jr. also gave the money for the construction of Kenan Stadium and Field House in 1926 as a memorial to his parents.[18]

Almost from the beginning of his UNC presidency, Friday worked closely with the Kenan family. William R. Kenan Jr., who died in 1965, bequeathed his dairy farm, Randleigh Farm, and a herd of cattle to the UNC system; eventually the cattle and the proceeds from the farm went to N.C. State University at Raleigh. The Randleigh Farm and the Randleigh herd were not an ordinary bequest. Rather, they were a major addition to N.C. State's program in agriculture. Bill Friday supervised the transfer of the herd and the purchase of 400 acres east of Raleigh to establish an operating dairy farm for N.C. State. Later, he proposed that the Kenan Trust provide $10 million to establish twenty-five additional Kenan professorships and to endow the chemistry program at Chapel Hill. In 1971, at Friday's urging, the Kenans dispersed grants, through the Southern Regional Education Board, to traditionally black institutions around the country. Through all of these activities, Friday became an influential adviser to the Kenan family.[19]

As the Kenan Trust became more involved with private secondary schools in the 1970s, Friday had less to do with the philanthropy, but he developed a friendship with the cousin of William R. Kenan Jr., Frank H. Kenan, and with Frank's son, Thomas S. Kenan III, both of whom were loyal UNC supporters. Just before Friday retired from UNC, Frank Kenan approached him about becoming president of the W. R. Kenan Jr. Fund in Chapel Hill (and, two years later, about taking on the executive directorship of the parent philanthropy, the W. R. Kenan Jr. Charitable Trust, which eventually moved from New York to Chapel Hill). Kenan assured Friday that he could spend most of his time "helping the state" and continuing his public service activities. After some thought, Friday accepted the appointment. In the autumn of 1986, as president of the Kenan Fund, Friday moved into a penthouse office in the new Kenan Center, located on the south side of the Carolina campus near the new Dean Smith Center, the basketball arena known as the "Dean Dome." The Kenan Center eventually housed the offices of the William R. Kenan Jr. Fund, the William R. Kenan Jr. Charitable Trust, the executive program of UNC's Kenan-Flagler Business School, and the Frank Hawkins Kenan Institute of Private Enterprise.[20]

Under Friday's leadership, Kenan philanthropy ventured into new directions. The Kenan Trust expanded its efforts to seek out national liberal arts colleges with fine educational traditions but small endowments, such as Skidmore College, Guilford College, and Gettysburg College. A bequest under the trust's four-year private liberal arts college challenge grants program was preceded by a careful screening process. The Kenan Trust sent candidates a long questionnaire; at a later stage, Friday and members of the Kenan board visited each institution to interview administrators and faculty in order to determine faculty and library strengths. Then, the trust offered a large, matching bequest toward expanding the endowment.[21]

Even more ambitious was the Kenan foray into literacy. Appointed chairman of Governor Jim Martin's commission on literacy in 1985, Bill Friday subsequently urged the Kenans to support a large-scale effort to reduce illiteracy in the United States. Not long after Tom Kenan joined the Kenan Trust as a trustee, Friday arranged a meeting with Secretary of Education William J. Bennett in 1987, and Friday and Tom Kenan traveled to Washington to learn more about literacy projects around the nation. Who was carrying on the "most imaginative, innovative, and creative work" in literacy in the country? they asked Bennett. "I don't know who the best is," Bennett responded, "but I think Sharon Darling is very impressive." In 1985 Darling, who was director of Kentucky's Adult Education Program, began to combat adult illiteracy; the next year, the Kentucky state legislature expanded what was then known as the Parent and Child Education (PACE) program into six rural counties. By the time that Friday and Kenan first visited Darling in Taylorsville, Kentucky, in 1987, the program had spread to eight rural counties.[22]

After what Friday called "one of the most interesting days I've spent" – with Darling in Taylorsville – he and Kenan were both convinced that Darling's approach offered a workable model. In December 1987 the trustees of the Kenan Charitable Trust promised to fund a literacy program supervised by the Southern Regional Education Board and coordinated by Secretary of Education Bennett. In February 1988 the Kenan Trust fully supported Darling's PACE program in Kentucky, which was transformed into the Kenan Family Literacy Program; the Kenan project was then established at three sites in Louisville and in four counties – Granville, Cumberland, New Hanover, and Madison – in North Carolina. By the early 1990s the Kenan Trust had made the literacy project one of its most important philanthropic initiatives.[23]

Rather than attempting to address illiteracy among individuals, the Kenan program treated the problem as one rooted in the family. Parents went to school with their children in the school bus and ate breakfast in the school cafeteria. Then, attending separate adult education classes, they learned the basic skills of reading, mathematics, and written and oral communication and were counseled in their job searches and in prevocational skills. Later in the day, parents and children were united for a forty-five-minute session, and they ate lunch together. By the end of the school day, parents had also taken part in volunteer activities and received forty-five minutes of instruction in parenting.

Not only did the great majority of participating parents increase their academic aptitude scores at the end of the one-year program, but also their children improved their developmental skills. According to teachers, parents learned faster than other adults in the literacy programs because they were motivated to learn in order to be able to read to their children. These "disappeared" parents – people who had been locked in a family cycle of illiteracy and poverty – discovered a new "taste of accomplishment" and a new sense of self-esteem.[24]

The Kenan program was so successful under Darling's leadership that the Kenan Trust established a National Center for Family Literacy in Louisville in April 1989. Its purposes were to provide information and help to family literacy initiatives across the country, to promote public awareness of the program to eradicate illiteracy, and to finance new model demonstration efforts. At the same time, the Kenan model of literacy education was expanded to twenty-nine sites in eleven states.

THE Kenan Trust's literacy program coincided with what Friday described in 1989 as the "second education of William Friday." This "second education" was not, Friday later explained, part of any "premeditated design." Rather, it grew out of an exposure to conditions of underdevelopment, undereducation, and poverty that prevailed among as many as 2 million North Carolinians. Two important experiences during Friday's last years as UNC president figured prominently in his second education. The first was his chairmanship of the North Carolina 2000 Commission, the Commission on the Future of North Carolina. Governor Jim Hunt formally organized the 2000 Commission in June 1981, with Friday and UNC playing a major role. The commission's report, issued in 1984, identified poverty, illiteracy, undereducation, and ill health among a large portion of North Carolinians as the state's most important problems. Although widely hailed, the report was effectively buried when Republican Jim Martin was elected governor in 1984. But for Friday, the experience on the 2000 Commission exposed "a whole world out there" of poor and marginal people.[25]

The second influence on Friday's second education was his participation on the Southern Growth Policies Board (SGPB), an interstate compact organization based in the Research Triangle Park. The year that Friday retired from UNC, the SGPB convened the Commission on the Future of the South. Every six years, the commission analyzed the region's condition and made recommendations for the next six years. Organized by Arkansas governor and future U.S. president Bill Clinton, who served as SGPB chairman in 1986, the Commission on the Future of the South was headed by former governor William Winter of Mississippi and included nineteen other members. One result of the commission's work was a startling report, *Halfway Home and a Long Way to Go*, written by novelist and UNC faculty member Doris Betts. Although the New South had seemingly come of age, the report asserted that new policies should focus on the marginal people of the region.[26]

In the late 1980s and early 1990s, Friday spent much of his retirement describing the "hidden" dangers of illiteracy, poverty, poor health, and economic underdevelopment to leaders across North Carolina. His main objective was to increase public awareness about the rural and urban underclass in the state, the portion of North Carolina's population that was generally forgotten in the glitz of the developing urban centers of Charlotte, the Research Triangle, and the Piedmont Triad (Greensboro-High Point-Winston Salem area). As a child of the Great Depression, he told one audience, he had seen "how hard and even brutal poverty, illiteracy, and deprivation could be." Now he wanted to address that deprivation. Poverty and ignorance "do not wear a Republican or Democrat label," he said in 1991; instead, doing something to improve social and economic conditions displayed a nation's sense of economic justice, its moral accountability, and its standard of compassion. North Carolina's marginal population had been "hidden from us for all too long a time."[27]

After the *Greensboro News and Record* ran a prize-winning, seven-part series on poverty in 1986, entitled "The Poor Among Us," J. Gordon Chamberlin, a retired professor who had been active in the newly organized Human Services Institute in Greensboro, approached Friday. "I want to ask you to preside at a meeting," he said. "I want to get fifteen North Carolinians together and just ask them the fundamental question, 'What does the word "poverty" mean to you?'" Armed with statistics of poverty and human suffering, Chamberlin succeeded in attracting Friday's interest. Poverty, it seemed, was part of a larger social cycle of illiteracy, poor health, and underdevelopment, and Friday was, as one intimate put it, "outraged."[28]

Together, Chamberlin and Friday established the North Carolina Poverty Project. Based in Greensboro, it educated different sectors of public opinion –

the press, schools, and churches – about the existence of poverty and challenged them to consider it as a social problem. Chamberlin and Friday, with an expanded committee of fifteen formed in the spring of 1986, agreed on an "education for action" approach, which, over a five-year period, would attempt to shape public opinion. At the same time, Friday spoke to numerous civic groups about poverty. When he traveled into communities, he immediately attracted the attention of local elites; as one associate put it, Bill Friday softened their hearts and made them think.[29]

Another example of Friday's concern about the "hidden danger" of underdevelopment in the state was his contribution to the Rural Economic Development Center (REDC). After Jim Hunt's departure from the Executive Mansion in 1985, Lieutenant Governor Jordan sponsored a legislative study commission on economic development and the creation of new jobs. Formed on July 15, 1985, the Jobs Commission issued a report in November 1986. It recommended that North Carolina adopt a "growth-from-within" strategy of economic development through new partnerships between state and local governments, educational institutions, and the private sector. Rural development offered one prominent illustration of the commission's growth-from-within strategy, and among its thirty-seven recommendations was a call for the creation of a new Rural Economic Development Center.[30]

During the late summer of 1986, Bob Jordan and future REDC director Billy Ray Hall asked Bill Friday to lead the REDC's steering committee. Accepting in early October 1986, Friday steered the fledgling center toward creation with the selection of George Autry to draft a mission statement. Autry had already become an important figure in Friday's second education. Friday was familiar with Autry's report, *Shadows on the Sunbelt* (1985) – which strongly influenced the Southern Growth Policies Board's *Halfway Home* report – and Friday and Autry became acquainted through their mutual association with William Winter. Autry had first met Friday when he went to North Carolina as an advance man for Hubert Humphrey, who visited the state in February 1967. Seven months later, Autry founded MDC, Inc., an antipoverty organization in Chapel Hill jointly sponsored by the Great Society's Office of Economic Opportunity and the National Association of Manufacturers. MDC was an offshoot of another antipoverty organization, the North Carolina Fund. A national organization with special emphasis on the South, MDC promoted workforce economics for the bottom half of the population. It studied the social transformations of rural outmigration, the transition from an agricultural to a manufacturing workforce, and the creation of a racially integrated workforce.

After Friday's departure from UNC, Autry and MDC began a close association with him. Lacking staff at the Kenan Trust, Friday often turned to Autry, an elegant writer and clear thinker, as a speechwriter and wordsmith. Autry and MDC helped to prepare the staff work early in the Kenan family literacy program, writing a report underpinning it. When the Rural Economic Development Center was first established, MDC played a major role. After drafting the REDC mission statement, Autry composed several position papers that further defined the center and its purposes. When the center's board was formed, MDC staff interviewed all of the board members and compiled a report outlining their views on rural development. If the REDC was to become "a new force for change and progress," as Autry recalled, it would require a "very diverse board coming together." MDC's job was to "pull them together as closely as possible into one vision."[31]

Friday supervised the new center's establishment at Raleigh in the winter and spring of 1987. Focusing on human, business, agricultural, and natural resources, as well as on rural infrastructure, the REDC tested possible policy or entrepreneurial solutions. The center established new projects and publicized them if they were successful. In the late 1980s, for example, the REDC commissioned a rural capital markets analysis; it concluded in December 1987 that there was a dire credit shortage in rural North Carolina. The next year, the REDC helped to establish the North Carolina Enterprise Corporation to finance rural entrepreneurs; the board of the corporation held its first meeting in May 1989. Thereafter, however, the center discontinued any formal connection with that project. In another instance, the REDC in 1988 persuaded the General Assembly to appropriate $500,000, along with a $150,000 grant from the Mott Foundation, to create a micro-enterprise loan fund. In a trial demonstration, the loan fund encouraged lending to small businesses in rural North Carolina. Other REDC projects included a rural leadership training program, operated through the UNC Institute of Government, and a minority economic development program. In January 1990 the center sponsored a Rural Summit in which thirty-eight North Carolina rural leaders participated. "Our motto," REDC director Billy Ray Hall said, was "to study the issue, find the best way to solve it, and then get it set up for rural North Carolina."[32]

When Friday retired as REDC board chairman in 1991 after a five-year stint, his impact was clear. "We'll always have his presence in our midst," Hall said; Friday had "aimed the ship," and the REDC headed in a clear direction. Friday would remain an "invisible force." He continued on the REDC board, albeit in a smaller role, but the center, Hall explained in 1991, had now reached a stage where it possessed an institutional identity. There would be "no other Bill Friday," but the philosophy and the operation of the center was well established. Friday helped to raise "us as a child." The REDC, by the 1990s, had matured into institutional adolescence.[33]

In the late 1980s Friday became the state's leading spokesman on the problems of poverty and the marginalization of a large portion of North Carolinians. As an unassailable icon of public service in the state, Friday carried his message to North Carolina's main corridors of power. In March 1988 he told a meeting of the North Carolina Citizens for Business and Industry (NCCBI), representing the state's business leadership, about the urgent needs of poor North Carolinians. The NCCBI had served the state well over the years; its "spirit of entrepreneurship, of private enterprise as we know it, led to the emergence of North Carolina as an industrial and agricultural leader among states." Business leaders of the state – many of whom Friday had known as trustees – possessed "enormous personal power," but they wielded it "through an uncommon sense of public service, freely and gladly given to advance the state." Through their wise leadership, North Carolina had provided for the Good Health Program, the Research Triangle Park, the community college system, an expanded university, and the building of a superior roads system.[34]

Now Friday was calling those same North Carolina entrepreneurs to return to a similar conception of leadership. New issues lay on the horizon: pollution, nuclear power, the absence of moral and personal standards, and the pervasiveness of greed. But the primary issue before North Carolinians was education, on which the future depended. Describing his own "personal journey," Friday told how he had discovered the problems of illiteracy, economic underdevelopment, and poverty, all of which were "sobering and disturbing." High rates of illiteracy and poverty had created a large displaced class of citizens; the latter included children who constituted the future of the state.

The speech before the North Carolina Citizens for Business and Industry had a major impact. Not only did it receive widespread press coverage, but it also made an impression on the state's business leaders. The head of "some big company" usually spoke to the NCCBI about subjects such as opportunities for international trade, reflected one observer. Friday's speech "sort of caught everybody off guard" and "really raised awareness." Casting his text in a way that directly affected those present – through a message that poverty and illiteracy not only were morally wrong but also imperiled the state's future work force – Friday exhibited the skills of the salesman and the politician. His forthright call elicited loud applause, and in future meetings the NCCBI extended its discussion to issues of poverty and undereducation.[35]

Friday's involvement with poverty, literacy, and rural development expanded into another area affecting the lives of marginalized North Carolinians – access to health care. In early 1991 representatives of the North Carolina Institute of Medicine, a group funded by the Kate B. Reynolds Trust, conducted a study of health care in the state. Friday agreed to head a wider study group, the Health Access Forum, a forty-member committee composed of physicians and other health care professionals, local and state government officials, and representatives of the health insurance industry and of private business. In late November 1992 the Health Access Forum released a press statement describing a program that would extend minimum health coverage to the nearly 1 million uninsured North Carolinians through a state-run, managed care system. The forum presented its findings to the legislature in early December 1992, and it helped to form the basis for the General Assembly's consideration of the matter in its 1993 session.[36]

MUCH of Bill Friday's time after "retirement" was consumed by his involvement in efforts to study and control intercollegiate sports. Throughout most of his adulthood, Friday had been interested in the role of spectator sports in college and university life, but during his last years as UNC president, in the early and mid-1980s, he had focused on the commercialization of intercollegiate athletics. When television networks began broadcasting basketball games at noon – before the church hour had ended – Friday objected vehemently and even persuaded the Atlantic Coast Conference to prohibit broadcasts before 1:00 in the afternoon. Beginning in the summer of 1982, he combined forces with Harvard president Derek Bok and American Council on Education (ACE) president Jack Peltason. With the support of other college presidents, they formed an ad hoc ACE group of college and university presidents to lobby the NCAA for reforms in intercollegiate athletics.[37]

Their reform program during the next two years sought to reassert the control of college and university presidents over intercollegiate athletics in the NCAA. The fruits of their labors were the organization, in 1984, of the Presidents' Commission, which asserted presidential control within the NCAA, and the passage of Proposition 48, which established minimum SAT scores for entering student athletes. A year later, the reform movement culminated with the NCAA's enactment of the "death penalty." Under its provisions, institutions consistently violating the rules could be severely disciplined, and colleges and universities were encouraged to conduct, every five years, a self-study of their management of intercollegiate sports.[38]

When the NCAA Presidents' Commission announced in early October 1986 that it would not adopt the recommendations of another ACE-sponsored committee led by UCLA chancellor Charles E. Young, Friday – now retired –

told reporters that he was "disappointed but certainly not shocked," for he was "past the point of being shocked by anything the NCAA does." The Presidents' Commission reflected the opinion of American higher education generally, and it would require considerable courage to adopt the ACE proposals. The NCAA, he believed, was too connected to the status quo; the time had come "for action and action must be taken."[39]

Through much of 1987, there seemed little likelihood that reform would be forthcoming from within the NCAA. At meetings in San Diego in January and Dallas in June, a group of athletic directors succeeded in blocking even the minimal reforms that the Presidents' Commission was endorsing. By the summer of 1987, as athletic directors succeeded in blocking reforms in the NCAA, Friday concluded that the Presidents' Commission, created to spearhead reform within the NCAA, was in "deep trouble." Despairing of the possibility of significant change from within the NCAA, Friday favored the establishment of a national commission that could diagnose the problems of intercollegiate athletics and then propose and advocate specific solutions. For much of 1987 he explored the possibility of obtaining the support of philanthropic foundations, "poking around," as Ernest Boyer recalled, "at how to get something going." By late 1989, after almost a year of his lobbying, the Knight Foundation – organized out of the Knight-Ridder media empire – agreed to support a national commission.[40]

The Knight Commission report, *Keeping Faith with the Student-Athlete: A New Model for Intercollegiate Athletics*, was released to the public in January 1991. Both Friday and retired Notre Dame University president Father Theodore Hesburgh, cochairs of the commission, appeared on ABC's morning television show, *Good Morning America*, to promote the report, which was unveiled in a PBS special produced by journalist Bill Moyers and underwritten by the Knight Commission. Moyers's special was followed by a roundtable discussion with Friday, Hesburgh, other commission members, NCAA executive director Richard Schultz, and outside experts.[41]

Keeping Faith sought to address the chief issues of intercollegiate sports. Intercollegiate sports had reached a "critical juncture," and higher education faced three possible futures. College and university leaders might reform themselves, Congress might impose a regulatory system, or continued abuses might destroy the "intrinsic value" of sports and higher education's claim to a "high moral ground." Clearly the commission preferred the first alternative, and it proposed a new model for intercollegiate sports. The current system emphasized the student athlete as an athlete, whereas the Knight Commission urged that the student athlete be considered primarily as a student. In most institutions, athletes were recruited first and admitted later; the NCAA's reg-

In "retirement."

ulations imposed few academic constraints. The system should return to "first principles": the system should exist, first and foremost, for the student athletes participating in intercollegiate sports.[42]

This basic reform would become possible through Hesburgh's "One-Plus-Three" formula, in which academic administrators, rather than athletic directors, would exercise direct control over athletics. Under strong presidential leadership, academic integrity, financial integrity, and accountability through certification would become possible. Presidents should seek and receive unqualified power to supervise athletics from their trustees, presidents should control the athletics conferences and the NCAA, and presidents should control their institutions' involvement with television. In keeping with the principle of academic integrity, student athletes should meet minimum academic requirements and complete the institution's course of study. To establish financial integrity, athletics costs should be reduced by cutting both coaching staffs and scholarships, while booster clubs should be strictly controlled. Finally, the NCAA, and the institutions themselves, should develop a certification procedure that would examine the progress of big-time programs.

Although the Knight Commission had no power to impose its reforms, it did have, Friday asserted, a "very positive" effect. Over the next two years, the commission continued to function, chiefly to advocate the NCAA's adoption of its proposed reforms. At its meeting in January 1992, the NCAA, according to a subsequent Knight Commission report, made "substantial progress" toward enacting ten of twenty major recommendations of the commission. More than 25,000 copies of *Keeping Faith* were circulated, and a number of colleges and universities adopted many of its recommendations. Further, public opinion polls revealed a significant change in public attitudes: whereas a Louis Harris poll in 1989 suggested that 78 percent of Americans believed that big-time intercollegiate sports were out of control, only 47 percent held that view in 1992.[43]

Friday and the other commission leaders proposed two major changes in the structure and organization of intercollegiate sports. The first was that the Presidents' Commission, which had been created in the mid-1980s to assert presidential power and control within the NCAA, should become a permanent, codified part of the organization. The second key reform advocated by the Knight Commission was athletic certification. The commission proposed that the NCAA require periodic certification of all athletics programs by some outside group that would examine admissions policies, as well as graduation rates, grade performance, and curricular requirements of all athletes. Outside auditors would also determine the extent of presidential control and accountability.[44]

As he neared the middle of his seventh decade, friends and acquaintances marveled at how Bill Friday in his retirement kept busier than most people still in mid-career. He no longer worked the eighty-hour week that began with the apprenticeship to Gordon Gray, but he remained deeply committed to public affairs. In his new commitment to battling illiteracy and poverty and improving health care in North Carolina, he found a pace of life that was more diverse, had a "little less intensity," and over which he was more his

Friday and Bill Clinton, UNC Founders Day, Kenan Stadium, October 12, 1993.

"own master." Although he would tell acquaintances of his intention to reduce his engagements, his closest associates doubted whether he would ever withdraw from public responsibilities.[45]

Friday's dedication to North Carolina affairs, his extraordinary need for public involvement, his skill in the supervision of policy making, and his ability to traverse a variety of bureaucratic mazes while maintaining direct, human-to-human contact all made it likely that Bill Friday would continue to play a major role in the life of North Carolina. In many ways, his own life had become synonymous with the life of the Tar Heel state. Born in the heart of the industrialized southern Piedmont, he had developed unusually effective human relations skills while in college, skills that found important challenges in a tumultuous period of change in the Chapel Hill of the 1940s and 1950s.

Friday's thirty-year presidency of the University of North Carolina marked a major transition in the history of the university and of American higher education. Refining what had been almost instinctive skills of human relations and personnel management, Friday constructed a greatly elaborated version of the multicampus university established in 1931. As that system evolved during the 1950s, 1960s, and 1970s, he both shaped and was shaped by it. But indisputably the sixteen-campus UNC system bore the mark of his personality and style, a style unlike that of his predecessor Frank Porter Graham. Whereas Graham attacked issues publicly, with inspirational appeals, Friday approached them behind-the-scenes, usually by attempting to construct a consensus that avoided public confrontation.

At times, these distinctive qualities of leadership and administration obviously failed Friday. During the Speaker Ban crisis, compromise and conciliation left unresolved the conflict between uncompromising anticommunism and uncompromising academic freedom. Similarly, Friday's style of consensus building reached a dead end in the spring of 1979 with the collapse of the negotiations with HEW over university desegregation.

Nonetheless, Friday's leadership abilities enabled him, and the University of North Carolina, to survive three decades of a polarized climate inside and outside the academy. No other public university president of the post-1945 era faced greater challenges in highly politicized attempts to establish a governance system for higher education, anticommunism and political intrusions in the 1960s, the centrifugal and sometimes nihilistic impact of campus unrest, the politics of medical education, and the federal government's attempt to dominate the character and pace of desegregation. But Friday's career, during this tumultuous period of university growth and expansion, did not just involve survival. Building on a twentieth-century tradition of UNC presidents Edward Kidder Graham, Harry Woodburn Chase, and Frank Porter Graham, in which the university functioned as a dynamic center for the purposeful development of the state of North Carolina, Friday expanded the reach of the university into the public affairs of the state. In the process, he grew into the most enduring of recent North Carolina leaders, a builder of a new university structure, and a dominant figure in post–World War II American higher education.

Notes

ABBREVIATIONS

BHER   North Carolina State Board of Higher Education Records, NCDAH
COHC   Centennial Oral History Collection, UNCG Library, Greensboro
DNCB   *Dictionary of North Carolina Biography*, edited by William S. Powell
GA   UNC General Administration, Chapel Hill
IG   Institute of Government Records, University Archives, UNC–Chapel Hill
IHF   Ida Howell Friday
JCPL   Jimmy Carter Presidential Library, Atlanta
Kenan   William C. Friday Correspondence, William R. Kenan Jr. Center, Chapel Hill
LBJPL   Lyndon Baines Johnson Presidential Library, Austin, Tex.
NCBHC   North Carolina Baptist Historical Collection, Wake Forest University,
            Winston-Salem
NCDAH   North Carolina Division of Archives and History, Raleigh
RAC   Rockefeller Archive Center, North Tarrytown, N.Y.
SBC   North Carolina Speaker Ban Collection, UNCG Library, Greensboro
SBSCR   North Carolina Speaker Ban Study Commission Records, NCDAH
SCUA/UNCG   Special Collections and University Archives, UNCG Library, Greensboro
SHC   Southern Historical Collection, UNC–Chapel Hill
SOHP   Southern Oral History Program Collection, UNC–Chapel Hill
UA/UNC   University Archives, UNC–Chapel Hill
WCF   William C. Friday

If no repository is indicated, interviews are by the author and are currently available as part of
SOHP, UNC–Chapel Hill.

INTRODUCTION

1. Quoted in Ravitch, *Troubled Crusade*, p. 15.

2. These figures are from Mohr, "National Forces in Regional Perspective"; Conkin, "Bleak Outlook for Academic History Jobs," p. 1; Ravitch, *Troubled Crusade*, pp. 183–84; Kerr, *Great Transformation*, chart 1, pp. xiv–xv. For two important studies of another university presidency, see Ashmore, *Unseasonable Truths*, and Hershberg, *Conant*.

3. Kerr, *Great Transformation*, p. xii.

4. Snider, *Light on the Hill.*

5. Luebke, *Tar Heel Politics.*

6. Link, *The Paradox of Southern Progressivism.*

CHAPTER 1

1. Interviews with WCF, October 3, 1990, March 13, 1991, January 30, 1992; interview with John R. Friday, November 8, 1993; marriage records, Rockbridge County Courthouse, Lex-

ington, Va. Bill was the only one of the five Friday children to be born in Dallas. For brief mention of Linwood College, see Cope and Wellman, *The County of Gaston*, p. 164; for a fuller account, see Davenport, "History of Linwood College." Bill Friday's father was christened David Lathan Friday but eventually went by David Latham Friday. His younger friends and business acquaintances called him "Dave," his older friends and family "Lath." I go by the latter.

2. Goodridge Wilson, "Boyhood Days of Goodridge Wilson Spent Near Raphine, Va.," *Lexington News-Gazette*, March 26, 1969; Rawlings, "Early History of Raphine," p. 35; interview with WCF, November 24, 1992; interview with John R. Friday, November 8, 1993.

3. I am indebted to William Walker Rowan III for this genealogical information. See Rowan to WCF, January 21, 1992, in author's possession. Maggie Strain sold hats and met William Rowan while he and his brothers were maintaining a store in Russellville, Ark. Her father, originally from Ohio, was a Union army physician, during the Civil War. He later retired to Raphine. Interview with John R. Friday, November 8, 1993.

4. Interviews with WCF, March 13, 1991, January 30, 1992; interview with John R. Friday, November 8, 1993.

5. Interview with John R. Friday, November 8, 1993. One of the best known of the South Fork Fridays was William Grier Friday, a distant cousin. "Skipper," as he became known, pitched the 1923 season with the Washington Senators; he appeared in seven games and recorded a 6.90 earned run average. Interviews with WCF, March 13, 1991, November 24, 1992.

6. Interviews with WCF, October 3, 1990, March 13, 1991, January 30, 1992; interview with John R. Friday, November 8, 1993. For genealogical information on the Fridays, see *The Genealogy of Peter Heyl*.

7. Interview with WCF, January 30, 1992; interview with John R. Friday, November 8, 1993. Once, when asked about his ancestry, Lath described a family that had lived in Gaston County for over five generations, yet he admitted that it was a "past that I don't know." Bill Friday recalled years later that his father talked "once in a while" about his family's history, "but not a lot." Dave Baity, "D. L. Friday: He Works Every Day of the Week," *Gastonia Gazette*, November 26, 1967; interviews with WCF, March 13, 1991, November 24, 1992.

8. Interviews with WCF, March 13, 1991, January 30, 1992; Baity, "D. L. Friday."

9. As his only full brother, Lath had the closest feelings of affection for William Clyde; even two years after his death, he still mourned him.

10. Interviews with WCF, October 3, 1990, January 30, 1992; interview with John R. Friday, November 8, 1993; interview with Mary Friday, October 4, 1992; interview with Fran Friday, April 27, 1994.

11. Interviews with WCF, October 3, 1990, January 30, 1992; interview with IHF, September 16, 1992; interview with John R. Friday, November 8, 1993; interview with Mary Friday, October 4, 1992; interview with Robert Pomerantz, March 21, 1990; interview with John L. Morgan Jr., February 26, 1990.

12. Interview with WCF, January 30, 1992; Johnson and Smith, *Men of Achievement*, p. 81. Dalton Stowe, a contemporary of Bill Friday in Dallas, remembered that D. L. was "always making trips" and "did a lot of selling." Interview with Stowe, February 12, 1990.

13. Interview with Wilma Thornburg, February 12, 1990; interview with WCF, January 30, 1992.

14. Baity, "D. L. Friday"; interviews with WCF, March 13, 1991, January 30, 1992.

15. Interviews with WCF, October 3, 1990, March 13, 1991, January 30, 1992; interview with John R. Friday, November 8, 1993.

16. Cope and Wellman, *The County of Gaston*, pp. 1–2, 68–69, 107; Pope, *Millhands and Preachers*.

17. Pope, *Millhands and Preachers*, table VI, p. 52; interview with John R. Friday, November 8, 1993; interviews with WCF, October 3, 1990, January 30, 1992; Geoffrey Mock, "Bill Friday Leaving Legacy at UNC," clipping from *Gastonia Gazette*, June 2, 1985, in subgroup 1, ser. 1, Subject Files, WCF Papers, UA/UNC.

18. Interview with Dalton Stowe, February 12, 1990; interview with Robert F. Summey, November 20, 1992; interview with John R. Friday, November 8, 1993; interview with WCF, January 30, 1992.

19. Interviews with WCF, October 3, 1990, January 30, 1992.

20. Interview with John R. Friday, November 8, 1993; interview with WCF, October 3, 1990. Friday remembered that the great aunt of James Worthy, later a Carolina and Los Angeles Lakers basketball star, worked for the Fridays for a number of years.

21. Interview with WCF, January 30, 1992; interview with John R. Friday, November 8, 1993; interview with Fran Friday, April 27, 1994.

22. Interview with Thornburg, February 12, 1990; interview with Stowe, February 12, 1990; interview with WCF, January 30, 1992; interview with John R. Friday, November 8, 1993.

23. Interview with WCF, October 3, 1990; interview with Robert F. Summey, November 20, 1992; interview with John R. Friday, November 8, 1993. See Charles Babington, portrait of WCF, *Greensboro Daily News*, October 25, 1981, but compare with interview with John R. Friday, November 8, 1993. According to John Friday, so strict was the observance of the Sabbath that family members were not even permitted to read the newspaper on Sunday, but this was the practice in Raphine rather than Dallas (although not clear from the newspaper story). When asked directly about whether he was prohibited from reading at home on the Sabbath, Bill Friday responded that "Grandpapa's shadow didn't reach that far." Interview with WCF, January 30, 1992.

24. Interview with Thornburg, February 12, 1990; interviews with WCF, October 3, 1990, January 30, 1992; interview with Robert F. Summey, November 20, 1992; interview with John R. Friday, November 8, 1993. Active in the women's club, Beth Friday led an effort to place a boulder in the square as a war memorial marker.

25. Interviews with WCF, October 3, 1990, March 13, 1991, January 30, 1992.

26. Ibid.; Joe Parker, "Best Wishes Bill Friday," *Hertford County News-Herald*, February 26, 1986.

27. Interviews with WCF, October 3, 1990, March 13, 1991, January 30, 1992.

28. Ibid.

29. Interview with Stowe, February 12, 1990; interview with Thornburg, February 12, 1990.

30. Interview with John R. Friday, November 8, 1993; interviews with WCF, October 3, 1990, March 13, 1991, January 30, 1992; "Friday Discusses Education and His 30 Years as UNC Chief," *Fayetteville Times*, February 24, 1986; interview with Robert F. Summey, November 20, 1992; interview with Dalton Stowe, February 12, 1990; Charles Babington feature, *Greensboro Daily News*, October 25, 1981.

31. Interview with John R. Friday, November 8, 1993; interviews with WCF, October 3, 1990, March 13, 1991, January 30, 1992. According to Friday's sister, Betty, Lath required that Bill, Rudd, and John participate in declamation contests but did not push Dave into it. Interview with Betty Friday Harris, February 12, 1990.

32. Interview with WCF, January 30, 1992; interview with John R. Friday, November 8, 1993.

33. Interviews with WCF, October 3, 1990, March 13, 1991, January 30, February 13, 1992; interview with Robert F. Summey, November 20, 1992.

34. Charles Babington, feature, *Greensboro Daily News*, October 25, 1981; interview with WCF, January 30, 1992; interview with Robert F. Summey, November 20, 1992.

35. Interviews with WCF, October 3, November 28, 1990, January 30, 1992; interview with John R. Friday, November 8, 1993; interview with Wilma Thornburg, February 12, 1990; Mock, "Bill Friday Leaving Legacy at UNC."

36. Interviews with WCF, March 13, 1991, January 30, 1992.

37. Interviews with WCF, October 3, 1990, March 13, 1991, January 30, 1992.

38. Interviews with WCF, October 3, 1990, March 13, 1991; interview with Dalton Stowe, February 12, 1990; interview with Summey, November 20, 1992.

39. Interview with Stowe, February 12, 1990; interview with WCF, January 30, 1992; interview with Robert F. Summey, November 20, 1992.

40. Interviews with WCF, October 3, 1990, March 13, 1991, January 30, 1992. But compare these views with the memories of his brother, who recalled that "it just happened that my father had a pretty good job, and we never suffered for hunger, or clothing, or anything on that order." John Friday did not feel that he did without "at all." Interview with John R. Friday, November 8, 1993.

41. Interviews with WCF, October 3, 1990, March 13, 1991, January 30, 1992; Santford Martin, "William Clyde Friday, '41," *North Carolina State College News*, December 1956.

42. Interview with WCF, March 13, 1991.

43. Interview with WCF, January 30, 1992; interview with John R. Friday, November 8, 1993; interview with A. Douglass Allison, May 14, 1991; interview with Mary Friday, October 4, 1992.

44. Interviews with WCF, March 13, 1991, January 30, 1992.

45. Ibid.

46. Interviews with WCF, October 3, 24, 1990, January 30, 1992; interview with WCF, by Bill Williams, for the *Gastonia Gazette*, June 4, 1971, in subgroup 1, ser. 1, Subject Files, WCF Papers, UA/UNC. According to John Friday, a sixth-grade teacher, a Mr. Souther, also a Wake Forest graduate, urged Lath to send his sons to the Baptist college. Interview with John R. Friday, November 8, 1993.

47. Interviews with WCF, October 3, 1990, January 30, 1992; *Bulletin of Wake Forest College*, pp. 38–39.

48. Interviews with WCF, October 3, 1990, March 13, 1991, January 30, 1992.

49. Interviews with WCF, October 3, 24, 1990, March 13, 1991, February 13, 1992.

50. Hazing had been outlawed, but other traditions remained. During his first month of school, Friday and other freshmen were required to buy ribbons displaying the student colors, gold and black, and wear them during the first month and at all sports events, where freshmen attendance was mandatory. Freshmen were prohibited from visiting the town after 9:00 P.M. except on weekends. They were expected to display proper school spirit and were required to memorize the college song. Tradition also held that they should speak to any schoolmates they passed on campus. As one student publication expressed it, friendly greetings were the college's "oldest tradition, . . . a tradition that many visitors somehow do not understand." Interview with WCF, February 13, 1992; *Official Handbook of . . . Wake Forest College*, pp. 12, 14; "Life in the Day of a Wake Forest Student," *Wake Forest Howler, 1938* (yearbook). The account in the *Howler* described a typical student, Herman Hadley, in the 1937–38 school year; Hadley was a twenty-year-old junior transfer from East Carolina Teachers' College.

51. Paschal, *History of Wake Forest College*, 3:36, 139; interviews with WCF, October 3, 24, 1990, February 13, 1992.

52. Interviews with WCF, October 3, 24, 1990, January 30, February 13, 1992.

53. *Bulletin of Wake Forest College*, p. 41ff.; "1938–39 Leaders Chosen," *Old Gold and Black*, April 15, 1938; interviews with WCF, October 24, 1990, February 13, 1992.

54. "Mr. Friday," p. 3; interview with Charles Romeo Lefort, January 26, 1990; interviews with WCF, October 3, 24, 1990, February 13, 1992; interview with John R. Friday, November 8, 1993.

55. Interviews with WCF, October 3, 24, 1990, February 13, 1992.

56. Reagan, *North Carolina State University*, pp. 18–19, 110; Carpenter and Colvard, *Knowledge Is Power*, "Fiftieth Registration Largest in History of College," *The Technician*, September 15, 1939; interview with William B. Aycock, February 6, 1990, SOHP; *State College Record* 39, no. 8 (1939–40): 21–22. The *State College Record* (38, no. 8 [1938–39]: 277) listed a total enrollment of 2,254 students.

57. Interview with WCF, October 26, 1990.

58. "Lack of Rooms Curtails Rise in Enrollment," *The Technician*, September 23, 1938; interviews with WCF, October 24, 1990, February 13, 1992; interview with Allison, May 14, 1991.

59. Interview with WCF, October 24, 1990; interview with A. Douglass Allison, May 14, 1991.

60. Interview with Allison, May 14, 1991; interview with WCF, February 13, 1992.

61. "Welcome, Freshmen!," *The Technician*, September 16, 1938; Hart, *School of Textiles*, p. 12; interview with WCF, October 24, 1990. The name of the Textile School was changed to the School of Textiles in 1943. Hart, *School of Textiles*, p. 28.

62. Hart, *School of Textiles*, p. 24; *State College Record* 39, no. 8 (1939–40): 139; interview with WCF, October 24, 1990; interview with A. Douglass Allison, May 14, 1991.

63. *State College Record* 38, no. 8 (1938–39): 278; Hart, *School of Textiles*, p. 28; *State College Record* 39, no. 8 (1939–40): 139; interviews with WCF, October 24, 1990, February 13, 1992. For the textile curriculum, see *State College Record* 39, no. 8 (1939–40): 142.

64. "Mr. Friday," pp. 3–4; interviews with WCF, October 24, 1990, February 13, 1992.

65. Interview with IHF, October 1, 1990, SOHP; interview with Robert Pomerantz, March 21, 1990; interview with A. Douglass Allison, May 14, 1991; interview with C. R. Lefort, January 26, 1990; interviews with WCF, October 24, 26, 1990, February 17, 1992; interview with Arnold Krochmal, July 24, 1991; "Lefort Campus Leader during College Career," *The Technician*, September 29, 1939; interview with Paul Lehman, May 10, 1990.

66. Interview with WCF, October 26, 1990; interview with C. R. Lefort, January 26, 1990.

67. Martin, "William Clyde Friday, '41"; interviews with WCF, October 24, November 28, 1990, January 14, 1991, February 13, 17, 1992.

68. *The Technician*, September 29, November 17, 1939; WCF, "Sports Comments," ibid., February 16, 1940, April 26, 1940; interview with Krochmal, July 24, 1991.

69. "Sports Comments," *The Technician*, February 16, 1940.

70. Ibid., September 13, 1940; Mickey May, "Gleanings," ibid., November 8, 1940; interview with Robert Pomerantz, March 21, 1990.

71. "Reams in Selected Golden Chain Head" (May 17, 1940), "College 'Who's Who' Picks Nineteen Men from State College" (September 27, 1940), "Leading Students Picked by Blue Key" (November 8, 1940), and "Young Democrats Plan Organization for Campus Club" (February 9, 1940), *The Technician*; interview with Paul Lehman, May 10, 1990; Reece Sedberry,

"Senior of the Week: Bill Friday," *The Technician*, January 10, 1941; interviews with WCF, January 14, 1991, February 17, 1992.

72. "Friday Elected Senior Leader in Close Race," *The Technician*, May 10, 1940; interview with Paul Lehman, May 10, 1990.

73. Interview with Lehman, May 10, 1990; interviews with WCF, October 24, 26, 1990, February 17, 1992.

74. "Mr. Friday," p. 5; interview with WCF, February 13, 1992.

75. "To the Royal Order of the Rail We Dedicate This Gruesome Tale," *The Technician*, November 22, 1940.

76. Luke Thomason appeared to have been a member of the group, but he did not so indicate in the yearbook. There may well have been others who belonged to this loose group but neglected to note their membership in *The Agromeck*. Interview with WCF, October 26, 1990; see also *The Agromeck* for 1941, in which the seniors listed their membership in the Royal Order of the Rail.

77. Interview with Paul Lehman, May 10, 1990; interview with James Graham, November 18, 1991; interview with WCF, October 24, 1990; "Mr. Friday," p. 5.

78. Bruce C. Halsted to William A. Link, February 10, 1990, in author's possession; "Mr. Friday," p. 5; interview with C. R. Lefort, January 26, 1990; Henry Rowe, "Gleanings," *The Technician*, February 14, 1941; "Gleanings," *The Technician*, May 16, 1941; interview with WCF, February 17, 1992.

79. Interview with Lehman, May 10, 1990; interview with Allison, May 14, 1991.

80. Interview with Lehman, May 10, 1990; interview with WCF, February 17, 1992; "Lecture Committee Will Seek Speakers in Nation's Capital," *The Technician*, January 10, 1941.

81. Interview with John L. Morgan, February 26, 1990; interview with C. R. Lefort, January 26, 1990.

82. Interview with Lefort, January 26, 1990; interview with Paul Lehman, May 10, 1990.

83. Interview with WCF, February 17, 1992; "Friday Attending Student Meeting in New Orleans" (April 5, 1940), and WCF to the Editor (April 19, 1940), *The Technician*; Martin, "William Clyde Friday, '41"; Sedberry, "Senior of the Week"; "Bill Friday Will Preside at State-wide Convention," *The Technician*, March 28, 1941. On Friday's involvement with the NYA board, see interview with WCF, February 13, 1992.

84. Interview with Paul Lehman, May 10, 1990.

85. "Appropriations Issue Faces Committee Soon," *The Technician*, February 8, 1941; interview with WCF, April 17, 1974, subgroup 1, ser. 1, WCF Papers, UA/UNC; interview with WCF, October 24, 1990.

86. Stephen Sailer, "Gleanings," *The Technician*, March 7, 1941; Sedberry, "Senior of the Week"; interview with A. Douglass Allison, May 14, 1991; Halsted to Link, February 10, 1990; interview with Katherine Stinson, April 16, 1990. When Henry Rowe wrote satirical predictions about the future of some leading State College students as they neared graduation in 1941, he forecast that "Willie" Friday would enjoy a "long and successful career as president of one of the foremost female institutes in the State." Enrollment at this school, predicted Rowe, would triple; Friday would pause long enough from his administrative responsibilities to teach a course in marriage problems. Rowe, "Gleanings," *The Technician*, May 23, 1941.

87. Interviews with WCF, October 24, 1990, February 13, 1992.

88. "Mr. Friday," p. 3; interview with WCF, February 17, 1992.

89. Interviews with WCF, October 24, 1990, February 17, 1992; "Mr. Friday," p. 3; "Com-

mencement Exercises Will Be Final Ceremony for 312 Class Graduates," *The Technician*, May 30, 1941; WCF, "A Memo to the Class of '91," speech at North Carolina State University commencement, May 11, 1991, Kenan.

90. Interview with WCF, October 24, 1990; Martin, "William Clyde Friday, '41"; interview with Paul Lehman, May 10, 1990.

91. Interview with WCF, October 26, 1990.

CHAPTER 2

1. Interview with John L. Morgan Jr., February 26, 1990; interviews with WCF, October 24, 1990, February 17, 1992.

2. Interviews with WCF, October 24, 1990, March 13, 1991, February 17, 1992; interview with Paul Lehman, May 10, 1990.

3. Interviews with WCF, October 24, 1990, February 17, 1992.

4. Interviews with WCF, October 24, 26, 1990, March 13, 1991; interview with Paul Lehman, May 10, 1990; Santford Martin, "William Clyde Friday, '41," *North Carolina State College News*, December 1956; interview with C. R. Lefort, January 26, 1990; interview with WCF, June 21, 1979, subgroup 1, ser. 1, Subject Files, WCF Papers, UA/UNC.

5. Interview with Lefort, January 26, 1990; interviews with WCF, October 26, 1990, February 17, 1992; "Mr. Friday"; *State College Record* 41, no. 4 (March 1942): 15.

6. Interviews with WCF, October 24, 26, 1990, February 17, 1992.

7. Interviews with WCF, October 24, 1990, March 13, 1991, February 17, 1992; interview with Lehman, May 10, 1990; interview with IHF, October 1, 1990, SOHP.

8. Interviews with IHF, October 1, 1990 (SOHP), September 16, 1992; interviews with WCF, October 26, 1990, March 13, 1991; interview with Lehman, May 10, 1990.

9. Interview with Lehman, May 10, 1990.

10. Interview with IHF, September 16, 1992; interview with Mary Friday, October 4, 1992.

11. Interviews with IHF, October 1, 1990 (SOHP), September 16, 1992; interview with WCF, February 17, 1992.

12. Interviews with IHF, October 1, 1990 (SOHP), September 16, 1992.

13. Interviews with IHF, October 1, 4, 1990, SOHP.

14. Interview with IHF, October 1, 1990, SOHP; interview with Mary Friday, October 4, 1992.

15. Interviews with IHF, October 1, 4, 1990, SOHP; "Ida Friday," *Chapel Hill Weekly*, December 16, 1962.

16. Interview with IHF, October 1, 1990, SOHP.

17. Interview with IHF, October 4, 1990 (SOHP), September 16, 1992.

18. Interviews with IHF, October 1, 1990 (SOHP), September 16, 1992; "Ida Friday," *Chapel Hill Weekly*.

19. Interviews with IHF, October 1, 1990 (SOHP), September 16, 1992.

20. Ibid.

21. Ibid.; interviews with WCF, October 24, 1990, March 13, 1991, February 17, November 24, 1992.

22. Interviews with WCF, October 24, 1990, March 2, 1992.

23. Interviews with WCF, October 24, 1990, February 17, March 2, 1992; interview with IHF, October 1, 1990, SOHP; interview with Edward A. Smith, November 27, 1992.

24. Interview with Lefort, January 26, 1990; interview with IHF, October 1, 1990, SOHP; interviews with WCF, October 24, 1990, February 17, March 2, December 1, 1992.

25. Interview with Smith, November 27, 1992.

26. Interview with WCF, October 24, 1990; interview with IHF, September 16, 1992.

27. Interviews with IHF, October 1, 1990 (SOHP), September 16, 1992; interviews with WCF, March 2, December 1, 1992.

28. Interviews with IHF, October 1, 1990 (SOHP), September 16, 1992; interviews with WCF, October 24, 26, 1990, February 17, March 2, December 1, 1992; Geoffrey Mock, "Bill Friday Leaving Legacy at UNC," clipping from *Gastonia Gazette*, June 2, 1985, in subgroup 1, ser. 1, subject files, WCF Papers, UA/UNC; "Ida Friday."

29. U. G. Lee, *Employment of Negro Troops*, pp. 22, 51; Reddick, "The Negro in the United States Navy," pp. 202–4; Polenberg, *War and Society*, p. 125. Also on segregation in the armed forces, see Blum, *V Was for Victory*, pp. 122–40, and Nalty, *Strength for the Fight*, pp. 184–204.

30. Interview with WCF, October 26, 1990; interview with Edward A. Smith, November 27, 1992.

31. Allen, *The Port Chicago Mutiny*, pp. 41–42, 64.

32. According to the best account of the African American wartime experience in the navy, naval ammunition depots became "dumping grounds" for unskilled and often disgruntled black workers. Many of them were illiterate; disciplined persons were commonly shipped to ammunition depots. Nelson, *The Integration of the Negro*, pp. 80–81.

33. Interview with Edward A. Smith, November 27, 1992; interviews with WCF, December 14, 1973 (SOHP), October 26, 1990, March 2, December 1, 1992; interview with IHF, September 16, 1992.

34. Interviews with WCF, October 26, 1990, March 2, December 1, 1992; interview with IHF, September 16, 1992.

35. *Building the Navy's Bases*, 1:339–43; interviews with WCF, October 24, 26, 1990, March 2, 1992.

36. Interview with Smith, November 27, 1992; interview with WCF, December 14, 1973, SOHP.

37. Interview with WCF, October 26, 1990; David Perkins, "Conflict, Growth: A UNC Era Ends as Friday Retires," *Raleigh News and Observer*, March 2, 1986.

38. Interviews with WCF, October 26, 1990, March 2, 1992.

39. Interviews with IHF, October 1, 1990 (SOHP), September 16, 1992; interviews with WCF, October 24, 1990, January 14, 1991, March 2, 1992.

40. Interviews with WCF, October 24, 1990, March 2, 1992; interview with IHF, October 1, 1990, SOHP; Martin, "William Clyde Friday, '41"; interview with WCF, by Bill Williams for the *Gastonia Gazette*, June 4, 1971, in subgroup 1, ser. 1, Subject Files, WCF Papers, UA/UNC. On Wettach, see "UNC Law Dean to Retire," *Raleigh News and Observer*, March 28, 1949.

41. "Friday Says Thank You," *Carolina Alumni Review* 74, no. 2 (Winter 1986): 36; interview with WCF, October 24, 1990; interviews with IHF, October 1, 1990 (SOHP), September 16, 1992.

42. Interviews with WCF, October 24, 1990, March 2, 1992; interviews with IHF, October 1, 1990 (SOHP), September 16, 1992; "Ida Friday," *Chapel Hill Weekly*. Georgia Kyser recalled that for years, the woman, who remained in Chapel Hill, would encounter the Fridays and be "too embarrassed" to speak to them. Interview with Georgia Kyser, October 15, 1991.

43. Interview with Terry Sanford, April 17, 1991; *Yackety Yack*, 1946, p. 104; interview with

William Aycock, April 11, 1990; "UNC Law Dean to Retire," *Raleigh News and Observer*, March 28, 1949; Pete Ivey, "Last of the Law School's 'Great 7' Calls It a Day," *Chapel Hill Weekly*, June 25, 1972.

44. Interviews with WCF, October 26, November 19, 1990.

45. Interview with WCF, October 26, 1990.

46. "Friday Says Thank You," p. 36; interviews with WCF, October 24, 26, 1990; interview with IHF, October 1, 1990, SOHP. The wife of Bill's brother, Dave, was a Raleigh native; her mother knew Davis's wife and was able to secure the apartment for Bill and Ida. The Fridays lived at North Street as long as Bill was in law school. The building housed four apartments, two in the basement and two on the ground floor. Alongside them were Don Henderson, who later became Senator J. William Fulbright's chief foreign policy aide, and his wife. Directly above the Hendersons was Orville Campbell, who would serve as a publicist for the Woman's College in Greensboro and then own and publish the *Chapel Hill Weekly*. Above the Fridays was a recent graduate of the UNC Law School, future governor, senator, and Duke University president Terry Sanford, and his wife, Margaret Rose Sanford. Residence at North Street was a pleasant experience; although a basement apartment, Ida remembered it as "a nice place to live." Interview with WCF, October 24, 1990; interviews with IHF, October 1, 1990 (SOHP), September 16, 1992; "Tar Heel of the Week: Orville Campbell," *Raleigh News and Observer*, March 6, 1955.

47. Interview with Richard Jenrette, May 8, 1990; Wilson, *The University of North Carolina*; Snider, *Light on the Hill*, pp. 155–68.

48. Interview with WCF, October 24, 1990.

49. Interview with John R. Jordan Jr., November 18, 1991; Ivey, "Last of the Law School's 'Great 7' Calls It a Day."

50. WCF, "What Albert Coates Has Meant to the University," *Southern Pines Pilot*, March 25, 1970. Coates was able to obtain significant benefactions from Greensboro industrialist Ben Cone, Greensboro insurance magnate Julian Price, and Winston-Salem business leaders James G. Hanes, Bowman Gray, and Gordon Gray. "Coates Words and Music: How He Built the Institute," *Greensboro Daily News*, September 2, 1962; Snider, *Light on the Hill*, pp. 226–27.

51. Interview with William Cochrane, April 19, 1991; Coates, *What the University of North Carolina Meant to Me*, pp. 91–92; interviews with WCF, October 26, 1990, March 2, 1992; interview with Gladys Coates, June 10, 1991.

52. Interview with Sanford, April 17, 1991; interview with Aycock, April 11, 1990; Herbert O'Keefe, "Tar Heel of the Week: W. B. Aycock," *Raleigh News and Observer*, July 22, 1956; interviews with WCF, October 24, 1990, December 14, 1973 (SOHP); interview with Dees, April 30, 1990.

53. Interview with Aycock, April 11, 1990; interview with Dees, April 30, 1990.

54. Interview with William Aycock, April 11, 1990; interview with Terry Sanford, April 17, 1991; interview with IHF, October 1, 1990, SOHP; interview with John R. Jordan Jr., November 18, 1991.

55. Interview with Dees, April 30, 1990; interview with Aycock, April 11, 1990.

56. Interview with WCF, March 2, 1992; interview with Aycock, April 11, 1990.

57. Interview with William Cochrane, April 19, 1991; interviews with WCF, October 26, 1990, March 2, 1992; interview with Aycock, April 11, 1990; interview with John R. Jordan Jr., November 18, 1991. The *Yackety Yack*, 1948, p. 236, listed Friday as president of the student association.

58. Interview with IHF, October 1, 1990, SOHP; fellowship card, IHF, Fellowship Recorder Cards, GEB; Korstad, *Dreaming of a Time*, pp. 40–43. Ida Friday described Morgan as the "most wonderful teacher I ever had." She taught her "an appreciation of basic psychology on social issues of our life – especially of race, human dignity, and appreciation of each person for their own worth."

59. Isabella Davis, "Lucy Morgan of UNC Doesn't Show Any Scars, but Her Battle for Public Health Is Grim," *Durham Morning Herald*, August 7, 1961; interview with Lucy Morgan, May 24, 1987, SOHP; interview with Lucy Morgan and Eunice Tyler, July 24, 1991; interview with IHF, October 1, 1990, SOHP; interview with WCF, March 2, 1992.

60. Interview with IHF, October 1, 1990, SOHP.

61. Interview with IHF, October 1, 4, 1990, SOHP.

62. Interview with William Aycock, April 11, 1990; interviews with WCF, October 3, 26, 1990, March 2, 1992; Sherry Johnson, "Friday Ready to Shed Limelight at UNC," *Raleigh News and Observer*, November 1, 1981; interview with WCF, by Bill Williams for the *Gastonia Gazette*.

63. Interview with IHF, October 4, 1990, SOHP.

64. Interview with C. R. Lefort, January 26, 1990; interview with Arnold K. King, February 7, 1990.

65. Interview with WCF, by Bill Williams for the *Gastonia Gazette*; interviews with WCF, October 24, 26, 1990; interview with IHF, October 4, 1990, SOHP; Martin, "William Clyde Friday, '41"; Johnson, "Friday Ready to Shed Limelight at UNC."

CHAPTER 3

1. Interview with WCF, October 24, 1990; interview with Richard Jenrette, May 8, 1990; interview with Anne and Donald Anderson, March 19, 1990; "UNC Instructor Given New Post," *Raleigh News and Observer*, July 21, 1946; "Weaver Is New Dean Replacing E. L. Mackie," *Daily Tar Heel*, September 24, 1948; "UNC Names Assistant Dean," *Raleigh News and Observer*, September 24, 1948. Jenrette pointedly stated that Weaver was not "egotistical."

2. Interview with Richard Jenrette, May 8, 1990; interview with Gay Currie Fox, August 10, 1992; "Weaver Is New Dean Replacing E. L. Mackie" (September 24, 1948) and "School Gives Dean Weaver Study Leave" (April 2, 1949), *Daily Tar Heel*; interview with IHF, October 4, 1990, SOHP.

3. Emman Frances Baber, "Chapel Hill Folks Like Their Police Chief," *Raleigh News and Observer*, July 22, 1951; interview with WCF, October 26, 1990; interview with IHF, October 4, 1990, SOHP.

4. Hard feelings often resulted. Friday recalled that, thirty years after the fact, he was awakened by a phone call in the middle of the night from a former student whom he had expelled. "Do you remember me?" he asked Friday, who replied that he did not. "Well, I'm not coming up there to kill you, but you were the fellow that threw me out of the University for what I did. And you said you'd never let me back in, and I haven't been back in. And I'm still angry, but I just wanted to wake you up one time and make you get up out of bed." "Well, I'm sorry that you still carry the anger," Friday replied, but "I hope that life has been good to you." Interviews with WCF, October 26, 1990, March 18, 1992.

5. Interviews with WCF, October 26, 1990, March 18, 1992; interview with Gay Currie Fox, August 10, 1992.

6. "John Gates Denied University Building," *Daily Tar Heel*, January 13, 1949; interview with

WCF, March 18, 1992. On Graham and anticommunism, see Pleasants, "A Question of Loyalty" (for brief mention of the Gates episode, see especially p. 422). On anticommunism on campus generally, see Schrecker, *No Ivory Tower*. A similar potential for disruption lay in the visit of evangelist Billy Graham to the Chapel Hill campus on February 8, 1951. Gay Currie, then director of the campus YMCA and part of a group, along with Friday, who frequently ate and socialized at the Carolina Inn, had initially suggested the visit. She was the daughter of Presbyterian missionaries to China and a childhood friend of Ruth Bell Graham, wife of Billy Graham and daughter of another China missionary, Nelson Bell. Currie encouraged students to invite Graham, then beginning a long career as his generation's best-known evangelist. He would present, she argued, "another point of view" before a campus that had long tolerated diverse opinions. Currie also persuaded Friday, saying that Graham had spoken on other campuses but never at Chapel Hill. Although Weaver opposed the idea – once the invitation had been made and accepted – on the grounds that Graham was not sufficiently intellectual, Currie and Friday held their ground, and they were supported by student leaders, including the editors of the *Daily Tar Heel*. The visit was a great success, attracting a packed house of 2,69 people in Memorial Auditorium. Interview with Gay Currie Fox, August 10, 1992; Chuck Hauser, "2,77 Pack Memorial to Hear Billy Graham," *Daily Tar Heel*, February 9, 1951.

7. Interview with Elizabeth Lindsay, August 17, 1992; interviews with WCF, October 26, 1990, March 18, 1992.

8. Interview with WCF, October 26, 1990; interview with Jenrette, May 8, 1990.

9. Interview with King, February 7, 1990; interview with Gay Currie Fox, August 10, 1992; *Yackety Yack*, 1949, 1950; "UNC Dean Gets Fellowship," *Raleigh News and Observer*, January 10, 1956; interview with WCF, March 18, 1992.

10. WCF, speech at Dallas High School Commencement, June 1949, subgroup 1, ser. 1, file entitled "Speeches (typescript): Pre-Presidency, 1949–1951, 1954–1955," WCF Papers, UA/UNC.

11. WCF, speech to the New Bern, N.C., Junior Chamber of Commerce, subgroup 1, ser. 1, file entitled "Speeches (typescript): Pre-Presidency, 1956," WCF Papers, UA/UNC.

12. Interviews with WCF, October 26, November 19, 1990; entry on Robert Burton House, *DNCB*, 3:210; interview with Arnold K. King, February 7, 1990.

13. Coates, "William Donald Carmichael, Jr."

14. Interviews with WCF, October 26, November 19, 1990, March 2, 1992.

15. Interview with IHF, October 4, 1990, SOHP; interview with Dean W. Colvard, January 29, 1990; interview with Anne and Donald Anderson, March 19, 1990; interview with WCF, November 19, 1990; interview with William D. Snider, May 2, 1990.

16. Interviews with WCF, November 19, 1990, March 18, 1992.

17. Lockmiller, *Consolidation of the University of North Carolina*; Wilson, *University of North Carolina under Consolidation*, pp. 1–47.

18. Ashby, *Frank Porter Graham*; entry on Graham, *DNCB*, 2:332–33; Pleasants and Burns, *Frank Porter Graham*, pp. 19–22; Snider, *Light on the Hill*, pp. 202–12; Ehle, *Dr. Frank*.

19. Interview with King, February 7, 1990; interviews with WCF, November 19, 1990, March 6, 1991; interview with Dean W. Colvard, January 29, 1990.

20. Interview with Anne and Donald Anderson, March 19, 1990; interview with John R. Jordan Jr., November 18, 1991; interviews with King, June 10–11, 1985 (SOHP), February 7, 1990; King, remarks to the Board of Governors, BOG minutes, September 12, 1980, subgroup 2, ser. 2, subser. 3, WCF Papers, UA/UNC.

21. Interviews with WCF, April 17, 1974 and June 21, 1979 (WCF Papers, UA/UNC), November 19, 1990.

22. Interviews with WCF, October 24, November 19, 1990, March 18, 1992.

23. WCF, *Graham and Human Rights*, pp. 3–4.

24. Interviews with WCF, April 17, 1974 (WCF Papers, UA/UNC), November 19, 1990; interview with Anne and Donald Anderson, March 19, 1990; interview with Dean W. Colvard, January 29, 1990; interview with IHF, October 4, 1990, SOHP. For other accounts of the Gardner Award dinner, see Ashby, *Frank Porter Graham*, p. 244, and Pleasants and Burns, *Frank Porter Graham*, pp. 5–18.

25. Interview with WCF, April 17, 1974 (WCF Papers, UA/UNC), October 24, 1990; Sherry Johnson, "Friday Ready to Shed Limelight at UNC," *Raleigh News and Observer*, November 1, 1981; interview with IHF, October 4, 1990, SOHP; Ashby, *Frank Porter Graham*, pp. 102–3; Pleasants and Burns, *Frank Porter Graham*, p. 42.

26. Interview with WCF, October 24, 1990; Pleasants and Burns, *Frank Porter Graham*, pp. 145–246; Ehle, *Dr. Frank*, pp. 161–85.

27. Interview with WCF, April 17, 1974 (WCF Papers, UA/UNC), March 18, 1992; interview with IHF, October 4, 1990, SOHP; Pleasants and Burns, *Frank Porter Graham*, pp. 244–46; WCF, *Graham and Human Rights*, p. 11.

28. Interview with WCF, November 19, 1990.

29. Stern, *The Oppenheimer Case*, p. 259.

30. Entry on Gordon Gray, *DNCB*, 2:350–51.

31. Interview with WCF, November 19, 1990.

32. Interview with WCF, October 24, 1990, March 6, 1991.

33. Interview with John R. Jordan Jr., November 18, 1991; interview with WCF, November 19, 1990; Snider, *Light on the Hill*, p. 238; interview with Arnold K. King, June 10–11, 1985, SOHP.

34. Interview with Edwin M. Yoder, April 19, 1991.

35. Interview with King, February 7, 1990; interviews with WCF, November 19, 1990, March 6, 1991, March 18, 1992; "New Position Is Announced," *Raleigh News and Observer*, April 10, 1951.

36. Interview with William Aycock, April 11, 1990; Santford Martin, "William Clyde Friday, '41," *North Carolina State College News*, December 1956; Geoffrey Mock, "Bill Friday Leaving Legacy at UNC," clipping from *Gastonia Gazette*, June 2, 1985, in subgroup 1, ser. 1, Subject Files, WCF Papers, UA/UNC; interview with IHF, October 4, 1990, SOHP.

37. Interview with Bostian, March 11, 1991; interview with Dean W. Colvard, January 29, 1990; interview with King, February 7, 1990.

38. Interviews with WCF, November 19, 1990, March 6, 1991, March 18, 1992; Martin, "William Clyde Friday, '41"; "Tar Heel of the Week: William C. Friday," *Raleigh News and Observer*, December 5, 1954; interview with WCF, October 24, 1990; WCF to Gray, March 20, 1952, ser. 1, subser. 1, file entitled "Correspondence: Friday, William Clyde, 1952–1957," WCF Papers, UA/UNC; Wilson, *University of North Carolina under Consolidation*, p. 369.

39. Interview with Jordan, November 18, 1991; interview with Edwin M. Yoder, April 19, 1991.

40. Interview with WCF, October 24, 1990; interview with Colvard, January 29, 1990. Gay Currie Fox recalled that Friday arranged a dinner for Eleanor Roosevelt – and "had the courage" to do so – with faculty and state political leaders. Interview with Fox, August 10, 1992.

41. Interview with WCF, October 24, 1990.

42. Wilson, *University of North Carolina under Consolidation*, pp. 366–67; interview with WCF, March 6, 1991.

43. Interview with WCF, March 6, 1991; Cresap, McCormick, and Paget, "Survey of Administrative Management, University of North Carolina," MS in SCUA/UNCG Library; Wilson, *University of North Carolina under Consolidation*, p. 370; interview with Carey T. Bostian, March 11, 1991.

44. Interviews with WCF, March 6, 1991, March 18, 1992; Wilson, *University of North Carolina under Consolidation*, pp. 370–73.

45. Wilson, *University of North Carolina under Consolidation*, chap. XV, pp. 381–82, 390–91.

46. Ibid., pp. 396–97; *Findings and Recommendations . . . in the Case of Dr. J. Robert Oppenheimer*, interviews with WCF, November 19, 1990, March 6, 1991. Interview with WCF, April 9, 1992.

47. Interview with King, February 7, 1990; interview with Edwin M. Yoder, April 19, 1991; interview with WCF, March 6, 1991.

48. Interview with Carey T. Bostian, March 11, 1991; "From University to Cuckoo-Land?," editorial, *Daily Tar Heel*, January 10, 1956. After the editorial, students circulated petitions seeking the recall of the newspaper's editors, Louis Kraar and Ed Yoder. David Cooper, "Chancellor Voices Views," *Raleigh News and Observer*, January 25, 1956.

49. Interviews with WCF, November 19, 1990, March 6, 1991, March 2, April 9, 1992.

50. Wilson, *University of North Carolina under Consolidation*, pp. 388–89; interviews with WCF, November 19, 1990, March 6, 1991.

51. Interviews with WCF, November 19, 1990, March 6, 1991, March 18, 1992; interview with IHF, October 4, 1990, SOHP; interview with Bostian, March 11, 1991.

52. Interview with Jordan, November 18, 1991; interviews with WCF, October 24, November 19, 1990, March 2, April 9, 1992.

53. Interview with WCF, March 6, 1991; "Friday Has Come Up Ranks," *Daily Tar Heel*, January 5, 1956.

54. Interview with WCF, October 24, 1990; interview with King, February 7, 1990; "Purks Stepped Up; Friday Gets UNC Job," *Asheville Citizen*, January 5, 1956.

55. *Rocky Mount Evening Telegram*, January 1956, enclosed in Hiden Ramsey to L. P. McLendon, January 25, 1956, McLendon Papers, SHC; "The Overlapping of Consolidations," *Chapel Hill Weekly*, December 13, 1955.

56. Interviews with WCF, November 19, 1990, April 9, 1992; *Epps et al.* v. *Carmichael*, *McKissick* v. *Carmichael*.

57. Wilson, *University of North Carolina under Consolidation*, pp. 383–86; Snider, *Light on the Hill*, pp. 246–47; "Court Overrules UNC Policy against Admission of Negroes," *Raleigh News and Observer*, September 11, 1955; *Greensboro Daily News*, September 11, 1955; interview with William Aycock, March 8, 1990, SOHP. NAACP lawyers first brought suit against Chapel Hill's School of Pharmacy in 1933; the case was dismissed. Tushnet, *The NAACP's Legal Strategy*, pp. 52–53; Cheek, "An Historical Study"; Burns, "Graduate Education for Blacks," pp. 195–218.

58. Interview with King, March 4, 1991; "UNC Trustees Hoist Bars to Negro Undergraduates," *Raleigh News and Observer*, May 24, 1955; Vaughn, "Integration of Negroes in the Law School," pp. 67–71. For brief mention of the *Frasier* case, see Crow, Escott, and Hatley, *History of African Americans*, p. 173. On the UNC attempts to evade integration, see Gordon Gray to Carey T. Bostian, Edward K. Graham Jr., and Robert B. House, May 24, June 3, 21, July 8, 1955; Graham to Gray, June 2, 16, 1955, Graham Papers, SCUA/UNCG.

59. Robert Burton House to James R. Walker, October 12, 1951, and Walker to House, October 1951, subgroup 1, ser. 1, subser. 1, Carmichael Papers, UA/UNC; Vaughan, "Integration of

Negroes in the Law School," pp. 67–71; memorandum entitled "Present Difficulties Arising from the Admission of Negro Students," summer 1955, Graham Papers, SCUA/UNCG. In the law school, one of the earliest black students was barred from attending Carolina sporting events.

60. *Frasier* v. *Board of Trustees; Greensboro Daily News*, September 11, 1955; *Raleigh News and Observer*, September 15, 1955, March 6, 1956. Even before the judges reached their decision, it was perfectly clear to Friday how they would rule. "Now, we have presented our view honestly on this," he told trustees and administrators, but "I suspect we're going to lose on this decision when we go back in and if we do, I advise you people at the University to go right back to Chapel Hill and process these applications in good faith." Interview with J. Carlyle Sitterson, March 6, 1991.

61. Interview with IHF, October 15, 1990, SOHP; interview with WCF, October 3, 1990. See also WCF to McLendon, April 5, 1951, box 1, McLendon Papers, SHC. In 1962, for example, there were sixty-three blacks enrolled in all programs at Carolina; of these, only twelve were undergraduates. Even in law, the numbers of black students actually decreased between 1951, when five blacks were enrolled, and 1961, when two blacks enrolled. See Robert B. Watson Diary, November 26, 1963, p. 389, Rockefeller Foundation Archives, RG 2 (General Correspondence, 1963), box GC 462 (unprocessed), RAC.

62. Chafe, *Civilities and Civil Rights;* Francis Simmons McConnell to William D. Carmichael Jr., February 21, 1957, subgroup 1, ser. 1, WCF Papers, UA/UNC; interview with J. Carlyle Sitterson, November 6, 1987, SOHP; Administrative Council minutes, President's Cabinet, December 10, 1957, subgroup 1, ser. 1, WCF Papers.

63. Interview with Arnold K. King, February 7, 1990; interview with WCF, March 6, 1991; King, *Multicampus University of North Carolina*, pp. 3–4.

64. *Chapel Hill Weekly*, January 20, 1956; interview with King, February 7, 1990; interview with IHF, October 4, 1990, SOHP; *Rocky Mount Evening Telegram*, January 1956.

65. Interview with Terry Sanford, April 17, 1991; interview with William Aycock, April 11, 1990; interview with Dean W. Colvard, January 29, 1990; Burke Davis, "Unpretentious Bill Friday Esteemed Highly at UNC," *Greensboro Daily News*, January 15, 1956; "People Think Friday Is the Man for the Job," *Chapel Hill Weekly*, January 20, 1956.

66. Mock, "Bill Friday Leaving Legacy at UNC"; interview with Betty Friday Harris, February 12, 1990; Harris Purks to L. P. McLendon, August 1, 1958, box 1, McLendon Papers, SHC; Wilson, *University of North Carolina under Consolidation*, p. 400; interview with Arnold K. King, February 7, 1990.

67. On the Woman's College generally, see Strobel, "Ideology and Women's Higher Education," pp. 156–88; Junk, "The Waiting Task," and Kearney, "All Out for Victory."

68. Magnhilde Gullander, statement before investigating committee, March 9, 1956, subgroup 4, ser. 1, Carmichael Papers, UA/UNC; interview with Richard Bardolph, May 14, 1991, COHC; Hieb, "General Education, . . . Graham, and the Woman's College"; Magnhilde Gullander to William D. Carmichael, March 1954, Carmichael Papers.

69. Interview with Betty Brown Jester, March 22, 1990, COHC; Elizabeth Hathaway to Robert M. Hanes, October 29, 1955, subgroup 4, ser. 1, Carmichael Papers, UA/UNC; George W. Dickieson to Hanes, March 3, 1956, ibid.

70. Gladys Tillett to WCF, March 6, 1956, subgroup 4, ser. 1, Carmichael Papers, UA/UNC; interviews with WCF, October 3, 1990, March 6, 1991; interview with Arnold K. King, March 4, 1991.

71. Edward K. Graham to Barbara Parrish, March 1, 1956, subgroup 4, ser. 1, Carmichael

Papers, UA/UNC; interview with King, March 4, 1991; "Woman's College Probe Will Begin Next Week," *Winston-Salem Journal*, March 3, 1956; "Probe Begins at Woman's College," *High Point Enterprise*, March 8, 1956; interview with WCF, March 6, 1991; interview with Betty Brown Jester, March 20, 1990, COHC; interview with Anne and Donald Anderson, March 19, 1990.

72. Interview with Arnold K. King, February 7, 1990; interview with IHF, October 4, 1990, SOHP; Lane Kerr, "Graham to Resign from Woman's College," *Greensboro Daily News*, May 28, 1956; John A. McLeod Jr., "Trustees Accept Resignation of Graham," *Greensboro Record*, May 28, 1956; Kerr, "Resignation of Graham Accepted," *Greensboro Daily News*, May 29, 1956; interviews with WCF, October 24, 1990, March 6, 1991.

73. WCF, speech to Woman's College faculty, May 31, 1956, subgroup 1, ser. 1, WCF Papers, UA/UNC; interview with Anne Anderson, March 19, 1990. "Some faculty members have been caught in the harsh crossfire and suffered unjustifiably; others have stood courageously on the firing line, reluctantly and fully cognizant that if their cause had failed, they would have been victims of their own outspokenness; still others have used the existing unrest as a vehicle for self-aggrandizement and for vindicative retaliation; still others, of course, have remained aloof from the seething caldron." "New Era at Woman's College," editorial, *Greensboro Daily News*, May 30, 1956.

75. "Friday's Administration," editorial, *Greensboro Daily News*, May 31, 1956; interview with IHF, October 4, 1990, SOHP.

75. "Information on Candidates for [the] Presidency of the University of North Carolina, Submitted by [the] Combined Faculty Committee from the Three Institutions," March 27, 1956, subgroup 3, Board of Trustees Records, UA/UNC; "Friday Is Due to Become Next President of UNC," *Asheville Citizen*, October 19, 1956.

76. Interviews with WCF, October 24, November 19, 1990, March 13, 1991, March 2, 1992. The same story is told in Jay Jenkins, "The Friday Years" (MS in Kenan), although Jenkins dates it to the later selection of Friday for the permanent job of UNC president.

77. "Candidates for Presidency," March 29, 1956, subgroup 3, Board of Trustees Records, UA/UNC; interview with IHF, October 15, 1990, SOHP. For biographical material on De Vane, see *Who's Who in America*, 1956–57 ed. (Chicago: Marquis Who's Who, 1957), 29:666.

78. Interviews with WCF, October 24, 1990, April 9, 1992; interview with IHF, October 15, 1990, SOHP.

79. Wilson, *University of North Carolina under Consolidation*, p. 399; King, *Multicampus University of North Carolina*, pp. 8–9; Snider, *Light on the Hill*, pp. 255–56; Woodrow Price, "With Plans for University, New President Takes Over," *Raleigh News and Observer*, October 28, 1956; interview with WCF, March 2, 1992; interview with IHF, October 15, 1990, SOHP; interview with Jordan, November 18, 1991; Snider, "Twenty-Nine Tumultuous Years," p. 15; WCF, *Graham and Human Rights*, p. 2.

CHAPTER 4

1. Bob Brooks, "Bill Friday Inaugurated as University President," and "Heaven's Blessings Attend Him," editorial, *Raleigh News and Observer*, May 9, 1957; Arthur Johnsey, "Good Faculty Pledge Is Made by Friday at Inauguration," and Burke Davis, "Raleigh Notebook" (May 9, 1957), *Greensboro Daily News*; interview with WCF, April 9, 1992. For the text of Friday's speech, see *North Carolina State College News* 29 (June 1957): 4–9.

2. "Heaven's Blessings Attend Him"; King, *Multicampus University of North Carolina*, pp. 6–7.

3. Stone, "The Graham Plan of 1935"; Ashby, *Frank Porter Graham*, pp. 131–36; Snider, *Light on the Hill*, pp. 220–22; interview with William Aycock, February 6, 1990, SOHP.

4. Board of Trustees minutes, January 25, 1954, subgroup 2, ser. 1, subser. 3, WCF Papers, UA/UNC.

5. "NCAA Puts State on Probation for Four Years" (November 14, 1956), and Bob Brooks, "No Rules Violated, Frosh Cager States" (November 15, 1956), *Raleigh News and Observer*.

6. Dick Herbert, in a *Raleigh News and Observer* column on November 15, 1956, as well as Carey Bostian, in his interview of March 11, 1991, both contended that Kentucky was behind the NCAA investigation.

7. "NCAA Puts State on Probation"; "No Rules Violated"; Smith Barrier, "State College Placed on Four-Year Probation by NCAA," *Greensboro Daily News*, November 14, 1956.

8. William A. Shires, "Friday to Probe Ban against State," *Charlotte Observer*, November 15, 1956; interviews with WCF, November 28, 1990, March 18, April 9, 1992.

9. Interview with WCF, November 28, 1990; "UNC President's Statement," *Raleigh News and Observer*, November 14, 1956; interview with Carey T. Bostian, March 11, 1991.

10. "Big Four, Clemson Set Up Own Grants-in-Aid System" (December 8, 1956), "State College Asks Another Probe; Weaver Calls ACC Meeting" (December 16, 1956), and "ACC Accepts State's Bid for Full Probe of Charges" (December 23, 1956), *Raleigh News and Observer*; "Bostian Says 'No Decision' Yet on Probe," *Greensboro Daily News*, December 9, 1956; Carey T. Bostian, "Report to President Friday on the Moreland Case," December 21, 1956, subgroup 1, ser. 1, Subject Files, WCF Papers, UA/UNC.

11. Executive Committee minutes, February 25, 1957, subgroup 2, ser. 1, subser. 3, WCF Papers, UA/UNC; interviews with WCF, November 28, 1990, April 9, 1992; WCF to Bostian, March 5, 1957, subgroup 1, ser. 1, WCF Papers.

12. Interview with WCF, April 9, 1992.

13. See extracts of confidential report no. 27, by NCAA Committee on Infractions, December 23, 1960, and H. J. Dorricott to Aycock, January 10, 1961, telegram, box 10, Aycock Papers, UA/UNC. Aycock took charge of the UNC investigation of the NCAA charges and decided not to appeal the probation. In the course of the inquiry, he got to know McGuire's assistant, Dean Smith, so well that he concluded, "if it was ever my opportunity to hire a basketball coach" then Smith would be "the one that I would want to head our basketball program." Interview with William Aycock, March 6, 1990, SOHP.

14. Joe Tiede, "Local Cage Front Silent on Scandal," *Raleigh News and Observer*, March 23, 1961; "Lid Clamped on Cage Scandal until April 4," *Charlotte Observer*, March 23, 1961; "Cage Scandal Evidence to Be Given in April," *Greensboro Daily News*, March 23, 1961; interview with William Aycock, March 6, 1990, SOHP. The North Carolina press reported that Brown had been permitted to leave the university under "less than honorable" conditions. According to Aycock, however, Brown left of his own accord. "Doug Moe Kicked Out of Carolina," *Raleigh News and Observer*, May 4, 1961; "Aycock Suspends Doug Moe for Not Admitting $75 Gift," *Charlotte Observer*, May 4, 1961; Executive Committee minutes, May 22, 1961, subgroup 2, ser. 1, subser. 3, WCF Papers, UA/UNC; interview with Aycock, March 6, 1990, SOHP.

15. Interview with Aycock, March 6, 1990, SOHP. A delegation of students marched on the chancellor's residence that evening, and Aycock hastily set up a meeting at Gerrard Hall to explain his apparent overruling of the student government. By the end of the meeting, he was

given a standing ovation. "Doug Moe Kicked Out of Carolina"; interview with Aycock, March 6, 1990, SOHP. Since Brown had not been convicted of any honor offense, had been permitted to leave the university honorably, and had "co-operated completely" with campus officials, the Men's Honor Council found him not guilty. Report of honor trial of Doug Moe, May 2, 1961, box 9, file entitled "Athletics, 1961," Aycock Papers, UA/UNC.

16. Interview with WCF, November 28, 1990; interview with Jay Jenkins, May 30, 1991.

17. Dick Herbert, "Three N.C. State Players Charged with Cage Fixing," Joe Tiede, "Litchfield Admits Intent but Didn't Shave Points," "State's Games with Duke, UNC Among 4 Included in Disclosure," and Herbert, "The Sports Observer," column, all in *Raleigh News and Observer*, May 14, 1961; Phil Grose, "Bribers Also Sought Better Performances," and Jay Jenkins, "Case's Suspicions Started Probe," *Charlotte Observer*, May 14, 1961; "Basketball Scandals Hit Wolfpack Team" and Smith Barrier, "Muehlbauer, Litchfield Admit Part in Fix," *Greensboro Daily News*, May 14, 1961.

18. WCF, report to Board of Trustees, May 22, 1961, file entitled "Athletics, 1953, 1963–1964," subgroup 1, ser. 1, WCF Papers, UA/UNC; interview with Caldwell, January 26, 1990; interview with WCF, May 5, 1992.

19. Interview with John T. Caldwell, January 26, 1990; interview with WCF, May 5, 1992; Irwin Smallwood, "Dixie Classic Dead – But Is It Really?," *Greensboro Daily News*, May 23, 1961; Davis Merritt, "Classic Was Big Part of State's Budgeting," *Charlotte Observer*, May 23, 1961.

20. Caldwell, statement to Board of Trustees, May 22, 1961, in file entitled "Athletics, General, 1953, 1963–1964," subgroup 1, ser. 1, WCF Papers, UA/UNC; interview with William Aycock, April 11, 1990.

21. Friday report, "Intercollegiate Athletics," in Executive Committee minutes, May 22, 1961, subgroup 2, ser. 1, subser. 3, WCF Papers, UA/UNC; Dick Herbert, "Basketball De-Emphasis Gets Okay of Trustees," *Raleigh News and Observer*, May 23, 1961; Smith Barrier, column, *Greensboro Daily News*, May 23, 1961; Jay Jenkins, "UNC, State Cut Emphasis on Athletics," and Davis Merritt, "UNC, NC State Deflate Basketball," *Charlotte Observer*, May 23, 1961.

22. Interviews with WCF, November 28, 1990, May 5, 1992.

23. WCF, in Board of Trustees minutes, May 22, 1961, in file entitled "Athletics, General, 1963–1964," subgroup 1, ser. 1, WCF Papers, UA/UNC; Smith Barrier, "Dixie Classic Killed in Cage De-Emphasis," *Greensboro Daily News*, May 23, 1961; Jay Jenkins, "Some Trustees Opposed Move," *Charlotte Observer*, May 23, 1961.

24. Caldwell, comments in Board of Trustees minutes, May 22, 1961, in file entitled "Athletics, General, 1953, 1963–1964," subgroup 1, ser. 1, WCF Papers, UA/UNC.

25. Aycock made it clear in April 1961 that the decision to rehire McGuire, made by 1962, would "rest largely on the unfolding events during the next twelve months," when the NCAA would inspect the program. William Aycock to Frank McGuire, April 28, 1961, box 9, file entitled "Athletics, 1961," Aycock Papers, UA/UNC; Jack Horner, "McGuire to Philly as Coach-VP," *Durham Morning Herald*, August 3, 1961.

26. "Friday Lays Heavy Hands upon the Sacred 'System,' " editorial, *Charlotte Observer*, May 24, 1961; "Good Belated Step," editorial, *Raleigh News and Observer*, May 23, 1961; interview with R. D. McMillan, May 14, 1991; interview with William D. Snider, May 2, 1990.

27. Selby D. Kornegay to WCF, December 7, 1961, subgroup 1, ser. 1, WCF Papers, UA/UNC; interviews with WCF, December 5, 1974 (SOHP), March 18, May 5, 1992; Graham to John T. Caldwell, copy to WCF (May 30, 1961), and Mark Davis to WCF (May 31, 1961), file entitled "Athletics: Dixie Classic Controversy, 1961," subgroup 1, ser. 1, WCF Papers.

28. Interview with John T. Caldwell, January 26, 1990; Byron Ray Jackson to WCF (March 25, 1963), Roger R. Jackson Jr. to WCF (December 2, 1963), Raleigh Merchants' Bureau, Board of Directors, telegram to WCF (December 27, 1963), and WCF, statement to Board of Trustees (May 25, 1964), subgroup 1, ser. 1, WCF Papers, UA/UNC; Irving E. Carlyle to WCF, January 24, 1964, file 64, box 1, Carlyle Papers, NCBHC. Friday himself believed that the political consequences had been overestimated. Interview with WCF, May 5, 1992.

29. D. B. Stallings to WCF, May 27, 1964, subgroup 1, ser. 1, WCF Papers, UA/UNC; Jesse Helms, WRAL Viewpoint Editorial #780, subgroup 1, ser. 8, WCF Papers; Jake Morrow to WCF, August 1961, subgroup 1, ser. 1, WCF Papers.

30. Spearman, senior honors' thesis, pp. II/6–10; William B. Aycock to I. M. O'Hanlon, December 26, 1963, subgroup 1, ser. 1, WCF Papers, UA/UNC.

31. Helms, WRAL Viewpoint Editorial #264, subgroup 1, ser. 8, file entitled "WRAL Television: Editorials, 1961–1971," WCF Papers, UA/UNC.

32. Helms, WRAL Viewpoint Editorials #275, 502, 582, ibid.

33. William B. Aycock to I. M. O'Hanlon (December 26, 1963), Lambeth to WCF (September 27, 1963, file entitled "Speaker Ban: General, August 1963"), WCF to William D. Carmichael Jr. (October 29, 1958), Aycock to WCF (December 1, 19, 31, 1958), WCF to Aycock (December 2, 28, 1958), Carmichael to WCF (January 5, 1959), and Carmichael, report entitled "Two Loyalty Oaths Required," subgroup 1, ser. 1, WCF Papers, UA/UNC.

34. Spearman, senior honors' thesis, p. III/1; "80 Arrested in Protests at Raleigh," *Greensboro Daily News*, May 9, 1963; "Raleigh Finds Silence No Solution to Race Problem," editorial, *Charlotte Observer*, May 14, 1963; Chafe, *Never Stop Running*, pp. 178–79.

35. Bob Lynch, "92 Negroes Arrested Here," *Raleigh News and Observer*, May 9, 1963; Johanna Adler, "Special Race Relations Group Is Proposed Here," and Lawrence Maddry, "Holiday May Delay Trials of Negroes until Monday," *Raleigh Times*, May 9, 1963; "New Arrests Overflow Wake Jail" (May 10, 1963), and "New Protests Are Staged by Negroes" (May 12, 1963), *Greensboro Daily News*; Chafe, *Never Stop Running*, p. 179.

36. Spearman, senior honors' thesis, pp. III/4–5; interview with William Aycock, April 11, 1990; Johanna Adler, "Negro Students Leave Jail" (May 10, 1963), Allen Paul, "City Is Quiet after Intense Day of Strife" (May 11, 1963), and Adler, "Protests Postponed as Bi-Racial Group Set Meet Tonight" (May 13, 1963), *Raleigh Times*; Jonathan Friendly, "76 Business Firms Here Integrating," *Raleigh News and Observer*, June 6, 1963. As the uprising continued into June 1963, inevitably, indeed purposefully, the demonstrators made themselves known to the governor and legislature. Earlier, on the evening of May 10, demonstrators marched to the Executive Mansion to confront Governor Sanford and boo him. Sanford had been participating in the North Carolina Symphony ball; the hymn singing by protesters at times drowned out the music inside. Bob Lynch and Roy Parker Jr., "Negroes Boo Gov. at Mansion," *Raleigh News and Observer*, May 11, 1963; Bette Elliott, "Negroes Visit Governor," *Raleigh Times*, May 11, 1963.

37. Bob Smith, "What's Wrong at UNC? (1)," unidentified clipping, June 15, 1965, box 2, file entitled "Speaker Ban – Clippings," Sharp Papers, UA/UNC.

38. Spearman, senior honors' thesis, pp. III/4–10; Roy Parker Jr., "Marchers' Footsteps Echoed in Assembly," *Raleigh News and Observer*, June 29, 1963; interview with WCF, May 5, 1992.

39. Interview with Robert Morgan, March 24, 1987, SBC; Helms, WRAL Viewpoint Editorial #631, subgroup 1, ser. 8, WCF Papers, UA/UNC.

40. Interview with WCF, November 28, 1990; Spearman, senior honors' thesis, chap. V;

testimony of Phil Godwin, August 11, 1965, "Hearing before Speaker Ban Study Commission," subgroup 1, ser. 1, WCF Papers, UA/UNC.

41. Interview with WCF, November 28, 1990; James Ross, "Bill to Ban Speakers Passed," *Greensboro Daily News*, June 26, 1963; Jay Jenkins, "Senate Chief Kills Opposition to Bill," *Charlotte Observer*, June 26, 1963; interview with David M. Britt, June 4, 1991. For accounts of the Speaker Ban controversy, see King, *Multicampus University of North Carolina*, chap. 4; Timothy Gunther, "No Reds in Blue Heaven"; Spearman, senior honors' thesis, pp. I/4–8, VII/6; Stewart, "Speaker Ban Law Episode," p. 61; Snider, *Light on the Hill*, pp. 271–79; Jenkins, "The Friday Years." Clarence Stone provided a rendition of the bill's passage in Stone to William T. Graves, March 8, 1965, in which he claimed that it was "passed like any other Bill." Stone Papers, box 6, SHC.

42. Smith, "What's Wrong at UNC? (1)"; Ralph Scott to James L. Godfrey (October 11, 1963), Scott to William B. Aycock (October 11, 1963), Scott to Gary Blanchard (October 23, 1963), and Louis R. Wilson to Isaac Wright (July 3, 1963), subgroup 1, ser. 1, WCF Papers, UA/UNC. Friday later wrote, "I believe the legislation resulted more from participation by faculty members from our Raleigh and Chapel Hill campuses in racial demonstrations in Raleigh during the legislative session." WCF to C. W. Tilson, November 6, 1963, ibid.

43. Smith, "What's Wrong at UNC? (1)"; interview with Aycock, March 8, 1990, SOHP; interview with WCF, May 5, 1992.

44. Interview with Aycock, April 11, 1990; WCF, notes for Executive Committee meeting, July 8, 1963, subgroup 1, ser. 1, WCF Papers, UA/UNC.

45. Interview with Aycock, April 11, 1990; WCF, notes for Executive Committee meeting, July 8, 1963, and "Statement of President Friday to the Board of Trustees, October 28, 1963," subgroup 1, series 1, WCF Papers, UA/UNC; Allen Paul, "Senate Refuses to Recall Bill Banning Red Speakers," *Raleigh Times*, June 26, 1963; interview with David M. Britt, June 4, 1991; interviews with WCF, February 23, 1987 (SBC), November 28, 1990, May 5, 1992.

46. Interview with Jordan, November 18, 1991; Spearman, senior honors' thesis, pp. I/8–9; interview with WCF, February 23, 1987, SBC.

47. Paul, "Senate Refuses to Recall Bill Banning Red Speakers"; WCF, notes for Executive Committee meeting, July 8, 1963; Spearman, senior honors' thesis, pp. I/9–10; interview with Terry Sanford, April 17, 1991; interview with John R. Jordan Jr., November 18, 1991. A similar resolution was signed by fourteen members of the house.

48. Interviews with Sanford, December 18, 1986 (SOHP), April 17, 1991.

49. Interview with John R. Jordan Jr., November 18, 1991; interview with David M. Britt, June 4, 1991. Others seemed to concur in this view. See interview with J. Carlyle Sitterson, March 6, 1991. According to Arnold King, Sanford "filibustered on the Speaker Ban law, and didn't do much about it." Interview with King, February 7, 1990.

50. Philip P. Godwin to WCF (June 29, 1963) and WCF to Godwin (July 2, 1963), subgroup 1, ser. 1, WCF Papers, UA/UNC; William Wise Smith to T. Clarence Stone, June 28, 1963, Stone Papers, box 3, SHC; WCF to William P. Fidler, July 4, 1963, subgroup 1, ser. 1, WCF Papers, UA/UNC; interview with WCF, November 28, 1990; "This Last-Minute Law Surely Is Not Worthy of N.C. Senate," editorial, *Raleigh Times*, June 26, 1963. See also "Speech-Ban Bill Unworthy of N.C. General Assembly," editorial, *Charlotte Observer*, June 27, 1963.

51. "Mr. Bruton and the Campus Speakers," editorial, *Greensboro Daily News*, June 29, 1963.

52. J. C. Peele to WCF (June 21, 28, 1963), WCF to Peele (June 24, July 2, 1963), and Isaac C. Wright to WCF (July 1, 1963), subgroup 1, ser. 1, WCF Papers, UA/UNC; Helms, WRAL

Viewpoint Editorial #640, June 27, 1963, subgroup 1, ser. 8, ibid. UNC officials were "in no position to demand public confidence," said Helms; "they must earn it." They were "public servants, paid with tax funds, and therefore answerable to the public. . . . This is what the law passed by the legislature is all about." A few days later he said, "So we see what happens when so-called 'liberalism' receives a setback." The free speech issue was simply a "smokescreen" that obscured the "basic issues involved." Helms, WRAL Viewpoint Editorial #642, July 1, 1963, ibid.

53. Interview with R. D. McMillan, May 14, 1991; Robert F. Campbell to WCF (July 24, 1963), and WCF to Campbell (August 5, 1963), subgroup 1, ser. 1, WCF Papers, UA/UNC.

54. Interview with Sitterson, March 6, 1991; interview with Aycock, April 11, 1990.

55. Administrative Council minutes, July 2, 1963, subgroup 1, ser. 1, WCF Papers, UA/UNC.

56. WCF, handwritten notes for Executive Committee meeting (July 8, 1963), and "Draft of a Resolution Implementing House Bill 1395" (July 8, 1963, attached to Executive Committee minutes, July 8, 1963), ser. 1, subser. 3, ibid.

57. WCF, statement (September 12, 1963), and H. F. Robinson to WCF (September 20, 1963), subgroup 1, ser. 1, ibid.; interview with William Aycock, April 11, 1990; Administrative Council minutes, August 29, 1963, subgroup 1, ser. 1, WCF Papers, UA/UNC.

58. Bryant to WCF (October 3, 1963, subgroup 1, ser. 1), and Executive Committee minutes (October 18, 1963, subgroup 1, ser. 1, subser. 3), WCF Papers, UA/UNC.

59. Aycock, statement to the Board of Trustees, October 28, 1963, in *Speeches and Statements of William Brantley Aycock*, pp. 157–61.

60. Interview with Aycock, April 11, 1990; Godwin to WCF (November 1, 1963) and WCF to Godwin (November 6, 1963), subgroup 1, ser. 1, WCF Papers, UA/UNC. See a similarly conciliatory tone in WCF to Gordon Hanes, December 10, 1963, subgroup 1, ser. 1, WCF Papers.

61. Stewart, "Speaker Ban Law Episode," p. 80; Fred H. Weaver to Medford Committee (January 15, 1965), and "Report of the Special Committee in Connection with H.B. 1395 of the 1963 General Assembly" (enclosed in William Medford to Dan K. Moore, April 24, 1965), subgroup 1, ser. 1, WCF Papers, UA/UNC.

62. Interview with King, February 7, 1990; interview with WCF, May 5, 1992; Medford to Moore (January 27, 1965) and Jennings G. King to WCF (April 6, 1965), subgroup 1, ser. 1, WCF Papers, UA/UNC.

63. "Report of the Special Committee"; interview with WCF, May 5, 1992; Stewart, "Speaker Ban Law Episode," pp. 83–84.

64. Fields to WCF (May 20, 1965), WCF to Dan K. Moore (May 22, 1965), and testimony of Fields, "Hearing before Speaker Ban Study Commission" (August 11, 1965), subgroup 1, ser. 1, WCF Papers, UA/UNC.

65. Thomas J. White to Derwood B. Bray, May 25, 1965, file 129, White Papers, SHC; interview with David M. Britt, June 4, 1991; Russell Clay, "Resolution Offered on Gag Study" (June 3, 1965), "Retreat from Duty," editorial (June 3, 1965), and Clay, "Moore Defends 'Study' Approach" (June 4, 1965), *Raleigh News and Observer*; Jay Jenkins, "Speaker Ban Changes Are Unlikely Now," *Charlotte Observer*, May 29, 1965; T. Clarence Stone, undated speech, ca. 1965, box 6, Stone Papers, SHC.

Hard-line opposition to repeal or amendment was bolstered by FBI director J. Edgar Hoover, who wrote to Hoover Adams, conservative editor of the *Dunn Daily Record*, on April 2 that a "danger" existed in permitting Communists to speak on campuses because they "have made and are making recruits in our schools and colleges and universities." "FBI Chief Supports Speaker Ban," *Charlotte Observer*, May 31, 1965.

66. Laurie Holder Jr., "Moore Urges Legislators to Leave Gag Law Alone," *Raleigh News and Observer*, June 2, 1965; "Moore Moves to Forestall Action on Speaker Ban," *Greensboro Daily News*, June 2, 1965; Stewart, "Speaker Ban Law Episode," p. 82. The *Charlotte Observer* ("What's with This Position Ban?," June 3, 1965) called this a "weaseling approach" that reflected Moore's "finger-in-the-wind philosophy."

67. Moore appointed conservative Democrats such as Colonel William Joyner, a Raleigh attorney who had supported Willis Smith against Frank Graham in the senatorial primary of 1950; Charles Myers, president of Burlington Industries; and Gordon Hanes, state senator and member of the wealthy Winston-Salem family. Wilson newspaper publisher Elizabeth Swindell, leading Baptist Rev. Ben C. Fisher, state senator Russell Kirby, and state representatives A. A. Zollicoffer and Lacy Thornburg rounded out the membership. Clay, "Eight Men, Woman Named to Study Gag"; Britt to William T. Joyner (June 25, 1965) and Jane P. Ryder to Britt (June 29, 1965), box 2a, SBSCR.

68. Russell Clay, "Gag Law Threatens Grants" (August 12, 1965), Kate Erwin, "Gag Law Called 'Political Interference' with Schools" (August 12, 1965), Clay, "Legion Prefers Ban Even If Profs Leave" (August 13, 1965), and "Tortuous Way Out," editorial (August 14, 1965), *Raleigh News and Observer*; Jay Jenkins, "Speaker Ban Group Hears Law Debated" (August 12, 1965), and Jenkins, "Speaker Ban Upheld by Legion Speakers" (August 13, 1965), *Charlotte Observer*; testimony of Fields, in "Hearing before Speaker Ban Study Commission," subgroup 1, series 1, WCF Papers, UA/UNC.

69. Adrian King, "Controversy Surprises Speaker Ban Sponsor" (August 12, 1965), Clay, "Legion Prefers Ban Even If Profs Leave," and "Tortuous Way Out," editorial (August 14, 1965), *Raleigh News and Observer*; testimony of Godwin, Morgan, and White, August 12, 1965, in "Hearing before Speaker Ban Study Commission," subgroup 1, series 1, WCF Papers, UA/UNC.

70. Interview with Britt, June 4, 1991.

71. Hanes to WCF, July 26, 1965, subgroup 1, ser. 1, WCF Papers, UA/UNC.

72. WCF, memorandum of record, September 3, 1965, subgroup 1, ser. 1, file entitled "Speaker Ban: General, Sept. 1–9, 1965," WCF Papers, UA/UNC.

73. Executive Committee minutes, September 3, 1965, ser. 1, subser. 3, WCF Papers, UA/UNC. The trustees reaffirmed that the university would not permit the advocacy of the violent overthrow of government but also restated its support of the "long-established tradition of free and open discussion in the search for truth and knowledge."

74. Russell Clay, "UNC Hits at Root of Ban Controversy," and Laurie Holder Jr., "Presidents: Ban Law Is Not Needed," *Raleigh News and Observer*, September 9, 1965; "Leftist-Grade Charge Labeled 'All Rubbish,'" *Greensboro Daily News*, September 9, 1965; Joe Doster, "UNC Officials Ask Repeal of Speaker Ban," *Charlotte Observer*, September 9, 1965; interview with William Aycock, April 11, 1990.

75. Testimony of WCF, September 8, 1965, "Hearing before the Speaker Ban Study Commission," subgroup 1, ser. 1, WCF Papers, UA/UNC. The text of Friday's statement is reprinted in *Charlotte Observer*, September 11, 1965.

76. Jonathan Yardley, "UNC's Compelling Counterattack," signed editorial, *Greensboro Daily News*, September 10, 1965.

77. ECC resolution, quoted in Russell Clay, "UNC Offers Alternate to Ban Law," *Raleigh News and Observer*, September 9, 1965.

78. Russell Clay, "UNC Offers Alternate to Ban Law," *Raleigh News and Observer*, September 9, 1965; Joseph Knox, "Ban Law Repeal Linked to Trustees' Stand," *Greensboro Daily News*, September 9, 1965; Joe Doster, "Speaker Ban Law Amendment Likely," *Charlotte Observer*, September 10, 1965; testimony of WCF, "Hearing before Speaker Ban Study Commission," subgroup 1, ser. 1, WCF Papers, UA/UNC; interview with David M. Britt, June 4, 1991. Britt noted that Morgan supported the change, but when it came before the special session of the legislature in November 1965, he voted against the compromise. This may have reflected his belief, expressed as early as September 12, that the UNC proposal fell far short of what he thought were the necessary restrictions. "Bob Morgan Says UNC Proposal Is Not Acceptable to Legislature," *Greensboro Daily News*, September 13, 1965.

79. Interview with Britt, June 4, 1991; interview with WCF, May 5, 1992; James Gordon Hanes to Louis C. Allen, September 10, 1965, box 2, file 21, Hanes Papers, SHC; WCF to Britt, October 19, 1965, box 3, SBSCR; Report of the Britt Commission, November 1965, subgroup 1, ser. 1, WCF Papers, UA/UNC; Laurie Holder Jr., "Governor Calls Special Session to Amend the Speaker Ban Law," *Raleigh News and Observer*, November 6, 1965. Britt, in October 1965, told commission members that "strict secrecy" was "essential for us to accomplish our purpose." Britt to members of the commission, October 1, 1965, box 3, SBSCR.

80. Jay Jenkins, "New Speaker Policy Hurtles toward Law as UNC Oks It," *Charlotte Observer*, November 13, 1965; Russell Clay, "UNC to Set Stage Today for Session" (November 12, 1965), and Laurie Holder Jr., "University Adopts New Campus Speaker Policy" (November 13, 1965), *Raleigh News and Observer*; Arthur Johnsey, "Assembly Called to Amend Ban Law," *Greensboro Daily News*, November 6, 1965. Jesse Helms called the Britt Commission report "almost artistic in its doubletalk." The reality of the compromise was that the trustees would be able "to do only what they choose to do." Helms, WRAL Viewpoint Editorial #1224, November 10, 1965, subgroup 1, ser. 8, WCF Papers, UA/UNC.

81. Jay Jenkins, "Quick Action Seen at Special Session," *Charlotte Observer*, November 9, 1965; Russell Clay, "Commission's Report Gets Nod in Legislative Session" (November 14, 1965), "Assembly Convenes Today to Consider Ban Change" (November 15, 1965), Clay, "Voting May Begin Today on Speaker Ban Changes" (November 16, 1965), Laurie Holder Jr., "Britt Pleads Strongly for Change" (November 16, 1965), Holder, "House Approves Ban Overhaul" (November 17, 1965), and Holder, "Teeth Extracted from State's Troublesome Speaker Ban Law" (November 18, 1965), *Raleigh News and Observer*; James Ross, "Legislator-Legion Group Planning Fight to Keep Speaker Ban Teeth" (November 10, 1965), "Amendments to the Amendment?" (November 10, 1965), John Garcia, "Ban Supporter Vows to Fight Amending Law" (November 11, 1965), Arthur Johnsey, "Hard-Fought Victory Seen for Ban Change" (November 15, 1965), and Johnsey, "Legislators Confident of Amendment" (November 16, 1965), *Greensboro Daily News*; Joe Doster, "House OKs Change in Speaker Ban Law" (November 17, 1965), and Jay Jenkins, "Assembly Yanks Ban Law Teeth" (November 18, 1965), *Charlotte Observer*; Stewart, "Speaker Ban Law Episode," pp. 106–7.

82. "North Carolina's Time of Testing," editorial, *Greensboro Daily News*, November 15, 1965; Jay Jenkins, "Ban Session Will Be Test for Moore" (November 15, 1965), and "Amendment Will Not Open Red Flood Gate – Britt" (November 16, 1965), *Charlotte Observer*; "Scraps to the Lions," editorial, *Raleigh News and Observer*, November 6, 1965. Arnold King later described the new speaker policy as "almost taking an oath not to hurt your mother." Quoted in Stewart, "Speaker Ban Law Episode," p. 105.

83. Interview with WCF, November 28, 1990.

84. Interviews with WCF, November 28, 1990, May 5, 1992.

1. Russell Clay, "Invited Speakers Causing Concern," *Raleigh News and Observer*, January 29, 1966; C. O. Cathey, memorandum to file, February 2, 1966, box 2, Sharp Papers, UA/UNC; Joe Doster, "UNC May Not Have Power to Ban Controversial Figure" (February 4, 1966), and James K. Batten, "Aptheker Called Bore, Not Threat" (February 7, 1966), *Charlotte Observer*. Actually, Wilkinson was neither an admitted Communist nor had he taken the Fifth Amendment. When questioned about Communist Party membership by a HUAC subcommittee in Atlanta in 1958, Wilkinson responded, "As a matter of conscience and personal responsibility, I refuse to answer any questions of this committee." The distinction made little difference, as events would show. Wilkinson was to speak March 2, Aptheker March 9. J. Carlyle Sitterson recalled that Aptheker had spoken at Chapel Hill immediately before World War II and that he had appeared on a panel with him. Interview with Sitterson, November 4, 1987, SOHP.

2. King, *Multicampus University of North Carolina*, pp. 62–63; regulations about speakers, enclosed in A. K. King to Paul F. Sharp, January 14, 1966, box 2, Sharp Papers, UA/UNC; Executive Committee minutes, January 14, 1966, ser. 1, subser. 3, WCF Papers, UA/UNC.

3. A. J. Beaumont to C. O. Cathey, February 4, 1966, box 2, file entitled "Speaker Ban, 1965–1966," Sharp Papers, UA/UNC.

4. Paul F. Sharp to WCF, January 27, 1966, subgroup 1, ser. 1, file entitled "Speaker Ban: Board of Trustees, 1963–1968," WCF Papers, UA/UNC; Clay, "Invited Speakers Causing Concern"; A. J. Beaumont to C. O. Cathey, February 4, 1966. Sitterson remembered that he and Sharp "were of one mind" about their approach. Interview with J. Carlyle Sitterson, March 6, 1991.

5. Executive Committee minutes, January 28, 1966, ser. 1, subser. 3, WCF Papers, UA/UNC.

6. Interview with Sitterson, March 6, 1991; Clay, "Invited Speakers Causing Concern"; Executive Committee minutes, January 28, 1966; J. Carlyle Sitterson deposition, October 5, 1966, SBC.

7. "The Big Little Boo," *Greensboro Daily News*, February 7, 1966; Gordon Hanes to WCF (January 1966, February 2, 1966), Britt to WCF (January 29, 1966), and Zollicoffer to WCF (February 1, 1966), subgroup 1, ser. 1, file entitled "Visiting Speakers: General, 1966," WCF Papers, UA/UNC. See also Mrs. M. A. Bolt to WCF, February 5, 1966, subgroup 1, ser. 1, file entitled "Visiting Speakers: Aptheker-Wilkinson Appearance, Feb. 1966," WCF Papers; Joe Doster, "Speaker Bids Put University on the Spot," *Charlotte Observer*, February 3, 1966; Russell Clay, "Moore Says He's Opposed to Speakers," *Raleigh News and Observer*, February 3, 1966.

8. Arthur Johnsey, "Moore Stand on Speech Hit" (February 3, 1966), Johnsey, "Students Split on Barring Red" (February 3, 1966), and James Ross, "Red Speaker Issue Uniting UNC Faculty and Students" (February 6, 1966), *Greensboro Daily News*. The *Daily Tar Heel* conducted a poll that found that 80 percent of the students supported Aptheker's right to speak. Pat Stith, "UNC Campus Leaders Join Bid for Red's Appearance," *Daily Tar Heel*, February 5, 1966. According to the paper's editor, student groups endorsed the invitations "to remove this complicating factor from the decision facing the executive committee of the board of trustees because we wish the decision to be made solely on the grounds of academic freedom, not emotional opposition to the inviting organization. . . . We are united in our opposition to Dr. Aptheker's views and actions, but we are also united in our belief that he has the right to speak." Ernie McCary, press statement, February 4, 1966, subgroup 1, ser. 1, file entitled "Visiting Speakers: General, 1966," WCF Papers, UA/UNC.

9. Interview with WCF, May 5, 1992; Joe Doster, "UNC May Not Have Power to Ban Controversial Figure," *Charlotte Observer*, February 4, 1966; Russell Clay, "Controversial Speakers Denied Forum on Campus," *Raleigh News and Observer*, February 8, 1966; Spruill to J. Carlyle Sitterson, February 18, 1966, box 5, Sitterson Papers, UA/UNC; Spruill to Sharp (February 6, 1966), Corydon Spruill to Sharp (February 6, 1966), and Paul Green to WCF (February 12, 1966), subgroup 1, ser. 1, files entitled "Visiting Speakers: General, 1966" and "Visiting Speakers: Aptheker-Wilkinson Appearance, Feb. 1966," WCF Papers, UA/UNC.

A group of Chapel Hill's chaplains and religious workers issued a "statement of concern" announcing that they were "deeply concerned over the present atmosphere of mistrust and dismay" prevailing on campus. They urged trustees to "re-affirm now a policy of genuine freedom of inquiry at this university." Refusing that freedom, the statement said, meant they would "refuse to be a university." "A Statement of Concern from the Chaplains and Religious Workers at the University of North Carolina in Chapel Hill, February 3rd, 1966," subgroup 1, ser. 1, file entitled "Visiting Speakers: General, 1966," WCF Papers, UA/UNC.

10. Russell Clay, "Controversial Speakers Denied Forum on Campus," *Raleigh News and Observer*, February 8, 1966; statement of Faculty Advisory Committee, February 6, 1966, in Executive Committee minutes, ser. 1, subser. 3, WCF Papers, UA/UNC.

11. Ambrose B. Dudley, "The Students Must Know What They Are Fighting," *Durham Sun*, March 10, 1966; statement by Paul Dickson III, in Executive Committee minutes, ser. 1, subser. 3, WCF Papers, UA/UNC.

12. Friday, notes of Executive Committee meeting, February 7, 1966, subgroup 1, ser. 1, file entitled "Visiting Speakers: General, 1966," WCF Papers, UA/UNC.

13. "Under the Dome" (*Raleigh News and Observer*, February 3, 1966) commented that Moore's public opposition "could turn the tide in what apparently was a delicate balance of opinion among members of the executive committee of the Consolidated University board of trustees." See also Grady Jefferys, "Speaker Ban Drama Ready for Curtain," and "Collision Course," editorial, ibid., February 7, 1966.

14. Executive Committee minutes, February 7, 1966; Charles Hauser, "Trustee Committee Compromised in Its Speaker Ban Deliberations," *Greensboro Daily News*, February 9, 1966; Joe Doster, "Trustee Committee Bars Red Speaker from UNC," *Charlotte Observer*, February 8, 1966. "People like Watts Hill stood with me," Friday recalled. Interview with WCF, November 26, 1990.

15. Clay, "Controversial Speakers Denied Forum"; Luther Hamilton to WCF, February 8, 1966, subgroup 1, ser. 1, file entitled "Visiting Speakers: Aptheker-Wilkinson Appearance, Feb. 1966," WCF Papers, UA/UNC; "The Aptheker Decision," editorial, *Greensboro Daily News*, February 9, 1966.

16. Interviews with WCF, November 26, 1990, May 5, 1992; James S. Ferguson to WCF, February 8, 1966, subgroup 1, ser. 1, file entitled "Visiting Speakers: General, 1966," WCF Papers, UA/UNC. Ferguson was responding to David M. Britt to WCF, January 29, 1966, ibid. Friday commented that he "could not reduce my initial reactions to Britt's letter to paper because I fear I was more explosive than you." WCF to Ferguson, February 14, 1966, ibid.

17. Donald B. Anderson to UNC chancellors, February 9, 1966, box 2, file entitled "Speaker Ban, 1965–1966," Sharp Papers, UA/UNC; Russell Clay, "Trustees to Tackle Speaker Rules," *Raleigh News and Observer*, February 28, 1966.

18. William D. Snider to William B. Aycock, February 21, 1966, subgroup 1, ser. 1, file entitled "Visiting Speakers: General, 1966," WCF Papers, UA/UNC.

19. Interviews with WCF, November 26, 1990, May 5, 1992.

20. David Perkins, "Conflict, Growth: A UNC Era Ends as Friday Retires," *Raleigh News and Observer*, March 2, 1986 (WCF quotations); interviews with WCF, November 26, 1990, May 5, 1992. Although Dickson died prematurely and could not be interviewed, a fellow student leader, Jim Medford, remembered him "clearly indicating" that he was in communication with Friday. Interview with James Medford, January 27, 1988, SBC.

21. Arthur Johnsey, "Students Split on Barring Red," *Greensboro Daily News*, February 3, 1966; Perry Young, "Students Invite Moore to Speak," *Raleigh News and Observer*, February 9, 1966; interview with William Aycock, April 11, 1990; Pat Stith, "UNC Students to Delay Action," *Greensboro Daily News*, February 9, 1966. The student group adopted the name "Committee for Free Inquiry" after it was decided that suggestions to name it the "Committee for Free Speech" would confuse it with the Berkeley Free Speech Movement. "For us to take the same name as the Berkeley movement," said one student, "would be a prostitution of our purpose." Stith, "UNC Students to Delay Action."

22. Pat Stith, "UNC Students Draft Letter to Governor," *Greensboro Daily News*, February 12, 1966; Paul Dickson III to WCF, February 11, 1966, subgroup 1, ser. 1, file entitled "Speaker Ban: Board of Trustees, 1963–1968," WCF Papers, UA/UNC; *Dickson v. Sitterson*, at 492; Sitterson deposition, October 5, 1966, SBC; Robert F. Kepner to C. O. Cathey, February 21, 1966, box 5, Sitterson Papers, UA/UNC.

23. Sitterson to Frank Porter Graham, April 5, 1966, box 5, Sitterson Papers, UA/UNC; Arthur Johnsey, "Trustees Give Chancellors Decision on Red Speakers" (March 1, 1966), and William D. Snider, "Tar Heel Talk" (March 2, 1966), *Greensboro Daily News*; Russell Clay, "Chancellors Get Speaker Control," *Raleigh News and Observer*, March 1, 1966; Jay Jenkins, "Authority over Speakers Returned to UNC Heads," *Charlotte Observer*, March 1, 1966.

24. "UNC Ponders Wilkinson Talk," *Raleigh News and Observer*, March 2, 1966; Ed Freakley, "Students to Hear Wilkinson Talks," *Greensboro Daily News*, March 2, 1966.

25. "Motion of the American Association of University Professors and The University of North Carolina Conference for Leave to File a Brief as *Amicus Curiae*," in SBC; Sitterson to Victor S. Bryant (March 4, 1966) and Sitterson to Michael Simpson (March 22, 1966), box 5, Sitterson Papers, UA/UNC.

26. *Dickson v. Sitterson*, at 493; interviews with Sitterson, November 4, 1987 (SOHP), March 6, 1991; Sitterson to Bryant, March 4, 1966, box 5, Sitterson Papers, UA/UNC.

27. "Down to the Pinfeathers," editorial (March 4, 1966), and "Chancellor Bans Aptheker, but Approves Other Reds" (March 5, 1966), *Greensboro Daily News*.

28. Interview with James Medford, January 27, 1988, SBC; Perry Young, "Wilkinson Barred from UNC," *Raleigh News and Observer*, March 3, 1966; Pat Stith, "Wilkinson Speaks from Off Campus," and "Students Plan Wilkinson Ban Test in Court," *Greensboro Daily News*, March 3, 1966; King, *Multicampus University of North Carolina*, p. 66; "Motion of the American Association of University Professors"; Sitterson deposition, October 5, 1966, SBC; Sitterson, press release (March 1, 1966), and Sitterson to Dickson (March 4, 1966), box 5, Sitterson Papers, UA/UNC. A. J. Beaumont was informed ahead of time about the schedules of Wilkinson's and Aptheker's visits. Interview with Medford, January 27, 1988, SBC.

29. Pat Stith, "UNC Group to Picket Sitterson" (March 4, 1966), and Stith, "Students Seek Ban-Test Funds" (March 5, 1966), *Greensboro Daily News*; interview with James Medford, January 27, 1988, SBC.

30. "Aptheker Speaks at Chapel Hill" and "Freedom Dodger," editorial, *Raleigh News and*

Observer, March 10, 1966; "Motion of the American Association of University Professors"; Joseph Knox, "Aptheker Speaks in Chapel Hill after Banishment from Campus," *Greensboro Daily News*, March 10, 1966; Jay Jenkins, "TV Camera Spots Aptheker Anguish," *Charlotte Observer*, March 10, 1966.

31. Corydon Spruill to Sitterson, March 28, 1966, and J. Carlyle Sitterson to Paul Dickson III, March 31, 1966, box 5, Sitterson Papers, UA/UNC; *Dickson v. Sitterson*, at 495–96; Sitterson deposition, October 5, 1966, SBC.

32. *Dickson v. Sitterson*, at 497–99; "Federal Court Rule Puts End to Speaker Ban," *Raleigh News and Observer*, February 20, 1968.

33. Smith to Albert Coates, extracted, 1975, and Smith to Vermont Royster, February 2, 1979, SBC.

34. "UNC Officials Hope Issue Is Dead," *Raleigh News and Observer*, February 20, 1968; David S. Greene, "State's Speaker Ban Law Nullified by Federal Court," *Greensboro Daily News*, February 20, 1968; Jay Jenkins, "There Will Be Shouting and Hollering, but Speaker Ban Revival Is Doubtful," *Charlotte Observer*, February 21, 1968; King, *Multicampus University of North Carolina*, pp. 67–68; Executive Committee minutes, March 8, May 13, 1968, ser. 1, subser. 3, WCF Papers, UA/UNC.

35. Interview with J. Carlyle Sitterson, March 6, 1991; Smith to William D. Snider, January 25, 1979, SBC.

36. King, *Multicampus University of North Carolina*, pp. 73–75; Snider, *Light on the Hill*, pp. 281–83; Williams, " 'It Wasn't Slavery Time Anymore,' " pp. 43–48; interview with Preston Dobbins, December 4, 1974, SOHP; "Demands of the Black Student Movement," December 11, 1968, box 1, file entitled "Black Student Movement," Sitterson Papers, UA/UNC; "Negro Demands to Be Studied by UNC," *Durham Morning Herald*, December 13, 1968; Raymond H. Dawson to Sitterson, January 16, 1969, box 1, Sitterson Papers; Rick Gray, "Blacks, Sitterson: Both against the Wall," *Greensboro Daily News*, February 23, 1969; Sitterson reply, January 24, 1969, box 1, Sitterson Papers.

37. Wayne Hurder, "UNC Whites March in Support of BSM," *Daily Tar Heel*, February 8, 1969; "Chapel Hill Student Stage Sympathy Rally," *Greensboro Daily News*, February 8, 1969; Williams, " 'It Wasn't Slavery Time Anymore,' " pp. 59–60, 81–85; "Students 'Occupy' College Building," *Charlotte Observer*, February 6, 1969; Rod Cockshutt, "1,000 Duke Students Clash with Police," *Raleigh News and Observer*, February 14, 1969; Sitterson, reply to demands of BSM, January 24, 1969, subgroup 1, ser. 7, file entitled "Campus Disruption (Student Unrest): Black Student Movement: Statements, 1968–1969," WCF Papers, UA/UNC.

38. "UNC Meet to Air Black Demands" (February 18, 1969) and "Students Are Restless on Chapel Hill Campus" (February 20, 1969), *Raleigh News and Observer*; "North Carolina U. Answers Negroes," *New York Times*, January 26, 1969; Steve Knowlton, "UNC Official Agrees to Discuss Student Movement Demands," *Charlotte Observer*, February 18, 1969.

39. " 'Revolutionary' Tactics Promised by UNC Blacks," *Raleigh News and Observer*, February 19, 1969; Gray, "Blacks, Sitterson: Both against the Wall"; Jerry Adams, "Blacks Press UNC to Act This Week," *Charlotte Observer*, February 19, 1969; "Students Are Restless on Chapel Hill Campus," *Raleigh News and Observer*, February 20, 1969; "Blacks at UNC-CH Set Friday Deadline," *Greensboro Daily News*, February 19, 1969.

40. "UNC Officials to Enforce the Law" and "Not 'Revolution,' " editorial, *Raleigh News and Observer*, February 20, 1969; Ross Scott, "Friday Vows Quick Move against Any Group Trying to Occupy UNC Building," *Durham Morning Herald*, February 20, 1969; Rick Gray, "UNC

President Warns Students against Disruption" (February 20, 1969), and "Threats in Chapel Hill," editorial (February 21, 1969), *Greensboro Daily News*.

41. Crabtree, *North Carolina Governors*, pp. 140–42.

42. Robert W. Scott to WCF, February 20, 1969, subgroup 1, ser. 7, file entitled "Campus Disruption (Student Unrest): Black Student Movement: Statements, 1968–1969," WCF Papers, UA/UNC; Russell Clay, "Scott Orders Law Enforcement on State Campuses," *Raleigh News and Observer*, February 22, 1969; James Ross, "Scott's Campus Memorandum Less Than Confidence Vote," *Greensboro Daily News*, February 22, 1969.

43. Rod Cockshutt, "UNC Campus Quiet, Relaxed," *Raleigh News and Observer*, February 22, 1969; Robert Stephens, "Negroes Meet, Stay Mum in Chapel Hill," *Greensboro Daily News*, February 22, 1969; Williams, " 'It Wasn't Slavery Time Anymore,' " pp. 2–3; Buck Goldstein and Joe Shedd, SAGA Strike and Boycott Daily Log, 1969, box 8, file entitled "Saga Food Service: Strike and Boycott Daily Log of Events, 1969," Office of the Vice Chancellor, Records of the UNC-CH Vice-Chancellor for Student Affairs, UA/UNC; Robert Stephens, "UNC Workers Walkout Forces Grievance Talk" (February 24, 1969), and Rick Gray, "Food Handlers Strike Widens at University" (February 26, 1969), *Greensboro Daily News*; "UNC Students Able to Eat Despite Employees' Strike," *Durham Morning Herald*, February 25, 1969; Steve Knowlton, "UNC Cafeteria Workers Call Boycott," *Charlotte Observer*, February 25, 1969; King, *Multicampus University of North Carolina*, pp. 76–77; John B. Graham, "An Account of the Events Surrounding the Development of Regulations on 'Disruption,' " box 2, Sitterson Papers, UA/UNC.

44. Goldstein and Shedd, SAGA Strike and Boycott Daily Log; King, *Multicampus University of North Carolina*, p. 77; Bob Lynch, "Fight Erupts at UNC in Dining Hall," *Raleigh News and Observer*, March 5, 1969; Rick Gray, "SSOC Slows Down UNC-CH Cafeteria," *Greensboro Daily News*, March 4, 1969; Steve Knowlton, "Violence Erupts Briefly at UNC," *Charlotte Observer*, March 5, 1969; Graham, "An Account of the Events Surrounding the Development of Regulations on 'Disruption' "; statement, March 11, 1969, box 6, file entitled "Strike – Non-Academic Workers, 1968–1970," Sitterson Papers, UA/UNC; Williams, " 'It Wasn't Slavery Time Anymore,' " pp. 115–17. Fuller told the audience that workers should "fight any way they need to bring about their demands." Students, he said, were the "real niggers" and "white Uncle Tom's" if they accepted all that "the man" laid down. He urged their support but said that "we can always bring some folks over here if it comes to that." Quoted in Fred W. Schroeder Jr. to C. O. Cathey, March 5, 1969, box 6, file entitled "Strike – Non-Academic Workers, 1968–1970," Sitterson Papers.

45. Williams, " 'It Wasn't Slavery Time Anymore,' " p. 256.

46. Interview with Richard H. Robinson, June 3, 1991.

47. "No Prudent Choice," editorial, *Raleigh News and Observer*, February 26, 1969.

48. Russell Clay, "University Board Endorses Scott's 'Disorders' Memo," *Raleigh News and Observer*, February 25, 1969; Arthur Johnsey, "Trustees Back Scott, Friday," *Greensboro Daily News*, February 25, 1969; "Scott Denies Lack of Confidence in N.C. College Administrators," *Charlotte Observer*, February 25, 1969; Arthur Johnsey, "Trustees Back Scott, Friday," *Greensboro Daily News*, February 25, 1969; Friday, excerpt from statement to the Board of Trustees, February 24, 1969, subgroup 1, ser. 7, file entitled "Campus Disruption (Student Unrest): Black Student Movement: Statements, 1968–1969," WCF Papers, UA/UNC.

49. Interview with WCF, December 5, 1974, SOHP; Clay, "University Board Endorses Scott's 'Disorders' Memo."

50. Robert Stephens and Jack Betts, "Scott Alerts Guard, Orders UNC Dining Hall Reopened," *Greensboro Daily News*, March 6, 1969; King, *Multicampus University of North Carolina*, p. 78; "Campus Testing," editorial, *Raleigh News and Observer*, March 7, 1969; "Slowdown in Chapel Hill," editorial, *Greensboro Daily News*, March 7, 1969; interviews with WCF, December 14, 1973, and December 5, 1974 (SOHP), November 26, 1990, May 5, 1992; interview with Ralph Scott, April 22, 1974, SOHP; interview with Bob Scott, April 4, 1990.

51. Interview with Richard H. Robinson, June 3, 1991; Sitterson, notes of meeting with deans, department chairmen, and directors, March 6, 1969, box 6, file entitled "Strike – Non-Academic Workers, 1968–1970," Sitterson Papers, UA/UNC; interview with WCF, December 5, 1974, SOHP; interview with King, February 7, 1990; Williams, " 'It Wasn't Slavery Time Anymore,' " p. 126; "Showdown in Chapel Hill," editorial, *Greensboro Daily News*, March 7, 1969; Steve Knowlton, "Cafeteria Opened; Police on Guard," *Charlotte Observer*, March 7, 1969.

52. Bob Lynch and Jack Childs, "Police Guard UNC Cafeteria," and Childs, "UNC Workers Struggle to Unite," *Raleigh News and Observer*, March 7, 1969; Robert Stephens, "Lenoir Hall Dining Hall Remains Open as Police Enforce Scott's Order," *Greensboro Daily News*, March 7, 1969; Goldstein and Shedd, SAGA Strike and Boycott Daily Log; interview with WCF, December 5, 1974, SOHP; interview with Richard H. Robinson, June 3, 1991; interview with Ralph Scott, April 22, 1974, SOHP; Williams, " 'It Wasn't Slavery Time Anymore,' " pp. 196–98.

53. "UNC Strikers to Get Job Review" (March 8, 1969), "Chapel Hill Campus Quiet Saturday" (March 9, 1969), "UNC Instructors May Be Dismissed" (March 10, 1969), and "UNC Takes Action on Grievances" (March 12, 1969), *Raleigh News and Observer*; Steve Knowlton, "70 Faculty Members Seek UNC Walkout," *Charlotte Observer*, March 8, 1969; "Class 'Rescheduling' Urged until Police Leave UNC-CH" (March 9, 1969) and "Teachers Must Meet Classes" (March 10, 1969), *Greensboro Daily News*; notes of a conversation with Professor Lind, March 1969, subgroup 1, ser. 7, file entitled "Campus Disruption (Student Unrest): Black Student Movement: General, Feb. 1969," WCF Papers, UA/UNC; Weldon Thornton to J. Carlyle Sitterson (March 8, 1969) and UNC Chancellors, statement (March 9, 1969), box 6, file entitled "Strike – Non-Academic Workers, 1968–1970," Sitterson Papers, UA/UNC.

54. Williams, " 'It Wasn't Slavery Time Anymore,' " pp. 168–70, 207–15; Jack Childs and Bob Lynch, "UNC Blacks Vacate Building," *Raleigh News and Observer*, March 14, 1969; Tony Lentz, "Carolina Building Evacuated; 7 Students Give Up to Police," *Durham Morning Herald*, March 14, 1969; Goldstein and Shedd, SAGA Strike and Boycott Daily Log; James L. Godfrey to Sitterson (March 12, 1969), Claiborne S. Jones, memorandum to the file (March 13, 1969), and Sitterson to A. S. Waters (March 13, 1969), box 6, file entitled "Strike – Non-Academic Workers, 1968–1970," Sitterson Papers, UA/UNC. Although Friday never met Fuller, he later conceded that Fuller "did something very important" by withdrawing the students from a potentially violent situation. Interviews with WCF, March 19, 1975 (SOHP), May 5, 1992. Fuller had "a sense of judgment about the situation," and he deserved considerable credit for defusing the crisis. Interview with WCF, November 26, 1990.

55. Statement, Faculty Advisory Committee, March 13, 1969, box 6, file entitled "Strike – Non-Academic Workers, 1968–1970," Sitterson Papers, UA/UNC; "UNC Admits 'Injustices'; Workers Get Back Wages," *Raleigh News and Observer*, March 15, 1969; Goldstein and Shedd, SAGA Strike and Boycott Daily Log.

56. Russell Clay, "UNC 'Delays' Drew Police Call – Scott," *Raleigh News and Observer*, March 18, 1969; Arthur Johnsey, "Scott Hopes Direct Action Strengthened Administrators,"

Greensboro Daily News, March 18, 1969; interview with Ralph Scott, April 22, 1974, SOHP; interview with Bob Scott, April 4, 1990. Bob Scott recalled that one of the men who later worked on his security detail, Mike Frye, was then an SBI agent. Frye looked young enough to be a student, but the students discovered him and named him "Agent of the Week."

57. "Remarks by Governor Bob Scott, Executive Committee, University of North Carolina," in Executive Committee minutes, March 14, 1969, ser. 1, subser. 3, WCF Papers, UA/UNC.

58. Edwin M. Yoder, "Forum: Bob Scott & the University," *The Carolinian*, March 25, 1969.

59. Colvard to Chavis, March 20, 1969, copy in box 48, file entitled "General Correspondence, R, 1969," Ferguson Papers, SCUA/UNCG; Lewis to the Executive Committee, February 27, 1969, box 1, file entitled "Black Student Movement," Sitterson Papers, UA/UNC; Susan Jetton, "UNC-C Black Students Fail to Get Okay for New Group" (February 25, 1969), Edward Cody, "Blacks Pull Down Flags at UNC-C" (March 4, 1969), and "Black Students Doing Selves a Disservice as Automatons," editorial (March 5, 1969), *Charlotte Observer*.

60. "Report of the Ad Hoc Committee on University Racial Policies," in box 48, file entitled "General Correspondence, R, 1969," Ferguson Papers, SCUA/UNCG.

61. "Slater Workers Strike" and editorial, *The Carolinian*, March 28, 1969; Joe Knox, "Partial Walkout Fails to End Food Service," *Greensboro Daily News*, March 28, 1969; "Students Support Workers, Boycott Slater Services," *The Carolinian*, March 29, 1969; "Cafeteria Workers' Strike, U.N.C.-G., March 26–April 2, 1969," in box 48, Ferguson Papers, SCUA/UNCG.

62. Interview with M. Elaine Burgess (November 8, 1990) and interview with Robert M. Calhoon (February 1, 1990), COHC.

63. Interview with James Allen, September 11, 1990; interview with Robert M. Calhoon, February 1, 1990, COHC.

64. Interview with WCF, November 26, 1990; "Cafeteria Workers' Strike, U.N.C.-G., March 26–April 2, 1969"; Robert M. Calhoon to M. Elaine Burgess, ca. 1969, box 48, Ferguson Papers, SCUA/UNCG; interview with Calhoon, February 1, 1990, COHC.

65. "UNC Pay Hike Conditionally OK'd," *Raleigh News and Observer*, March 19, 1969; King, *Multicampus University of North Carolina*, pp. 80–81; interview with Ralph Scott, April 22, 1974, SOHP; "Gov. Scott Approves Pay Hikes for 5,000" (March 22, 1969) and "Settlement for Chapel Hill," editorial (March 25, 1969), *Greensboro Daily News*; Executive Committee minutes, May 9, 14, 26, July 7, September 12, October 26, 1969, ser. 1, subser. 3, WCF Papers, UA/UNC; WCF to Bob Scott (October 7, 1969), Henry Lewis to Archie K. Davis (October 21, 1969), WCF to Davis (October 27, 1969), and Davis to WCF (October 29, 1969), subgroup 2, ser. 1, subser. 2, file entitled "Student Disruption: Executive Committee Special Committee on, 1969," WCF Papers.

66. Executive Committee minutes, May 9, 1969, ser. 1, subser. 3, WCF Papers, UA/UNC.

67. Ibid.; "The Governor and UNC," editorial, *Greensboro Daily News*, April 15, 1969.

68. "UNC Food Workers Strike; Say They Want a Union" (November 8, 1969), "Striking UNC Food Workers Hear Student Proposal for Union Vote" (November 10, 1969), "UNC Students Stage Eat-In to Support Food Strikers" (November 11, 1969), "Mediation Follows Fights in UNC Worker Strike" (November 13, 1969), and "University Food Strike at End" (December 9, 1969), *Raleigh News and Observer*; Bob Lock and Steve Enfield, "Cafeteria Staff Out Again at Chapel Hill," *Charlotte Observer*, November 8, 1969; Robert Stephens and Rick Gray, "Cafeteria Closed as Workers Strike at UNC-CH Again" (November 8, 1969), and Gray, "Mediation Offer Is Accepted in Cafeteria Strike at UNC" (November 12, 1969), *Greensboro Daily News*; interview with WCF, March 19, 1975, SOHP; Elizabeth Brooks and Mary Smith,

"Employee Grievances of Saga Food Service Workers at UNC," in Graham, "An Account of the Events Surrounding the Development of Regulations on 'Disruption'"; UNC Non-Academic Employees Union to Sitterson, November 10, 1969, box 6, file entitled "Strike – Non-Academic Workers, 1968–1970," Sitterson Papers, UA/UNC.

69. WCF to David Riesman, June 25, 1969, subgroup 1, ser. 8, file entitled "Carnegie Foundation: Comm. on the Future of H.E.," WCF Papers, UA/UNC; WCF to the UNC chancellors (June 25, 1970), Victor Bryant to WCF (July 10, 1970), "Statement Regarding Petition Signers and University Disruption Policy to the Executive Committee" (July 10, 1970), William A. Dees Jr. to President's Consultative Committee (July 17, 1970), and WCF to Hall A. Thompson (July 30, 1970), subgroup 2, ser. 1, subser. 2, file entitled "Student Disruption: Executive Committee Special Committee on, 1970," WCF Papers. Mary Friday recalled that the sense of encirclement was such in those days that the family went over possible escape routes from the president's home should any demonstration threaten violence. Interview with Mary Friday, October 4, 1992.

70. "UNC-C Instructor's Case Tests New Disruption Policy," *Charlotte Observer,* November 10, 1969; King, *Multicampus University of North Carolina,* pp. 90–91.

CHAPTER 6

1. Bratton, *East Carolina University,* pp. 290–94; *State Supported Higher Education in North Carolina,* p. 54 (quotation).

2. According to the terms of the act, the BHE would "promote the development and performance of a sound, vigorous, progressive, and co-ordinated" system of higher education in the state. The new board, composed of nine members, no more than one of which could be a graduate of the same institution, was granted the authority to determine the major functions and activities of each college and university, including the power to approve new degree programs and to recommend budgets. The law also specifically provided for overlapping jurisdictions. The boards of trustees of the teachers' colleges and the university, it stated, "shall continue to exercise such control over the institutions as is provided by law." In a provision that UNC trustees later regarded as an exemption, the act provided that the establishment of the new agency would not deprive the university of any "powers or initiative" that it then possessed. See House Bill 201, chap. 1186, in *Session Laws and Resolutions,* 1955, pp. 1183–86. For the UNC view of this provision, see George Watts Hill to WCF, August 22, 1957, subgroup 1, ser. 8, WCF Papers, UA/UNC.

3. Interviews with Arnold K. King, February 7, 1990, March 4, 1991; interview with John Sanders, January 25, 1991; interview with William D. Snider, May 2, 1990; Pearsall to Bryant, Barber, Mintz, and Taylor (December 19, 1958), McLendon to Pearsall (January 6, 1959), and Mintz to Pearsall (January 8, 1959), subgroup 1, ser. 8, WCF Papers, UA/UNC; Executive Committee minutes, January 12, 1959, ser. 1, subser. 3, WCF Papers; Jonathan Friendly, "Higher Board Right, but Lost" (April 22, 1962), and "Lesson in History," editorial (April 25, 1962), *Raleigh News and Observer.* For the new law governing the powers of the BHE, see *Session Laws and Resolutions,* 1959, pp. 275–76.

4. William Dallas Herring to Terry Sanford, April 23, 1963, reel 33, frame 180, Herring Papers, NCDAH.

5. The two Pearsall committees included the Pearsall Commission appointed by Governor William Umstead and the Pearsall Commission appointed by Luther Hodges. Batchelor, "Save Our Schools."

6. Interview with William Dallas Herring, February 2, 1990.

7. Ibid.; interview with WCF, April 28, 1992.

8. Interview with William Dallas Herring, February 2, 1990; interviews with WCF, January 7, 1991, April 28, 1992.

9. Text of inaugural address, *Raleigh News and Observer*, January 6, 1961, and *Greensboro Daily News*, January 6, 1961; interview with Terry Sanford, April 17, 1991.

10. Interview with William Dallas Herring, February 2, 1990; interview with Sanford, April 17, 1991; interview with WCF, April 28, 1992; Herring to WCF, July 13, 1961, reel 20, frame 642, Herring Papers, NCDAH; entry on Irving Edward Carlyle, *DNCB*, 1:324–25; King, *Multicampus University of North Carolina*, pp. 44–45; McLendon to John P. Kennedy, August 5, 1961, subgroup 1, ser. 8, file entitled "Carlyle Commission: General, 1961," WCF Papers, UA/UNC; McLendon to Herring, September 25, 1961, reel 20, frame 704, Herring Papers. For a general view of the Carlyle Commission, see Snider, *Light on the Hill*, pp. 266–68.

11. *Report of the Governor's Commission on Education*, pp. 17, 27.

12. Ibid., pp. 65–76.

13. Ibid., pp. 49–76.

14. Addison Hewlett, for example, was added to the commission to represent Wilmington. Herring to WCF (November 6, 1961) and WCF to Herring (November 7, 1961), reel 20, frame 784, Herring Papers, NCDAH; interview with WCF, April 28, 1992. On the Carlyle Commission and UNC expansion, see King, *Multicampus University of North Carolina*, pp. 45–50.

15. Reynolds to Herring, November 10, 1961, reel 20, frame 797, Herring Papers, NCDAH; interview with WCF, April 28, 1992.

16. Herring to WCF, January 24, 1962, reel 23, frame 625, Herring Papers, NCDAH (also in subgroup 1, ser. 8, file entitled "Carlyle Commission: General, Jan.–May, 1962," WCF Papers, UA/UNC). On UNC's thinking regarding expansion and the Carlyle Commission, see John Sanders, "Proposals with Respect to Two-Year Institutions," February 1, 1962, subgroup 1, ser. 8, file entitled "Carlyle Commission: General, Jan.–May, 1962," WCF Papers.

17. Resolution, Committee on Development of a System of Higher Education, February 17, 1962, reel 24, frame 122, Herring Papers, NCDAH; Herring to Fred B. Graham, June 16, 1962, reel 24, frame 1055, ibid. (also in subgroup 1, ser. 8, file entitled "Carlyle Commission: Special Committee, 1962," WCF Papers, UA/UNC); minutes, Committee on Development of a System of Higher Education and Committee on Community Colleges and New Colleges, June 11, 1962, reel 24, frames 1000–1004, Herring Papers; WCF, "Presentation by President Friday to the Executive Committee of the Board of Trustees on Friday, June 15, 1962," subgroup 1, ser. 8, file entitled "Carlyle Commission: General, June–Dec. 1962," WCF Papers.

18. *Report of the Governor's Commission on Education*, pp. 51–52.

19. McLendon to WCF, December 12, 1961, reel 20, frame 921, Herring Papers, NCDAH; resolution, Committee on Development of a System of Higher Education, February 17, 1962, reel 24, frame 122, ibid.; WCF, "Presentation by President Friday to the Executive Committee of the Board of Trustees on Friday, June 15, 1962," subgroup 1, ser. 8, file entitled "Carlyle Commission: General, June–Dec. 1962," WCF Papers, UA/UNC.

20. McLendon to WCF (November 13, 1961) and Sanders to WCF (November 17, 1961), subgroup 1, ser. 8, file entitled "Carlyle Commission: Committees: #2, 1961–1962," WCF Papers, UA/UNC. The UNC president would become an ex officio member of the board, along with one chancellor from a UNC campus, two presidents of senior colleges (who would be elected from their ranks), one president of a state junior college (also elected from the ranks),

two presidents of private institutions (appointed by the governor), the chairman of the State Board of Education, and four lay members (appointed by the governor). Herring to William C. Archie, February 24, 1962 (reel 24, frames 129, 148), Herring to Irving Carlyle, February 26, 1962 (reel 23, frame 1014), and "Outline, Development of Recommendations RE Board of Higher Education," February 1962 (reel 24, frame 129), Herring Papers, NCDAH; minutes, Committee on Development of a System of Higher Education, February 17, 1962, reel 23, frame 988, Herring Papers; Archie to Arthur M. Bannerman, March 14, 1962, Governor's Commission on Education beyond the High School Series, BHER.

21. *Raleigh News and Observer*, July 1, 1962; Herring, notes of the meeting of the Carlyle Commission, June 22, 1962, reel 24, frames 1074–76, Herring Papers, NCDAH; *Charlotte Observer*, June 23, 1962; James Ross, "Board Reorganization Settlement Proposed," *Greensboro Daily News*, July 1, 1962; Glenn Keever, "Board Reorganization Proposal Wins Support of Commission," *Raleigh Times*, July 7, 1962; James Ross, "New Setup for Board Approved," *Greensboro Daily News*, July 7, 1962; Jack Claiborne, "Education Reshuffle Voted," *Charlotte Observer*, July 7, 1962; Claude E. Teague to Frank Porter Graham, July 11, 1962, ser. 1.2, file 55, Graham Papers, SHC; Carlyle Commission minutes, July 5, 1962, reel 25, frames 140–43, Herring Papers.

22. Glenn Keever, "Reorganization of the Ed. Board Was Hottest Recommendation," *Raleigh Times*, July 11, 1962; WCF to Carlyle, July 9, 1962, subgroup 1, ser. 8, file entitled "Carlyle Commission: General, June–Dec. 1962," WCF Papers, UA/UNC (also in reel 25, frame 152, Herring Papers, NCDAH); WCF to Carlyle (August 3, 1962) and Sanders to WCF (August 7, 1962), subgroup 1, ser. 8, file entitled "Carlyle Commission: General, June–Dec. 1962," WCF Papers. In early September Friday spoke with the governor "at length" about the commission's report, and Sanford assured Friday that he would "stand firm." WCF to Herring, September 12, 1962, reel 33, frame 216, Herring Papers (also in subgroup 1, ser. 8, file entitled "Carlyle Commission: General, June–Dec. 1962," WCF Papers).

23. Herring, notes of phone conversations with WCF, November 11, 16, 1962, reel 33, frame 242, Herring Papers, NCDAH; interview with Herring, February 2, 1990; interview with John R. Jordan Jr., November 18, 1991.

24. Jay Jenkins, "Sanford Is Abandoning Plan to Revamp Education Board," *Charlotte Observer*, November 16, 1962; Roy Parker Jr., "Gov. Backs Broad Plan for Colleges," *Raleigh News and Observer*, November 16, 1962; Arthur Johnsey, "UNC Plans of Growth Outlined," *Greensboro Daily News*, November 16, 1962; McLendon, memo to BHE members and staff, November 20, 1962, reel 33, frame 201, Herring Papers, NCDAH.

25. King, *Multicampus University of North Carolina*, pp. 50–51; WCF to R. Walker Martin, November 14, 1962 (subgroup 2, ser. 1, subser. 2, file entitled "North Carolina State University Name Change, Sub-Committee on: General, 1962"), and "Report of the Special Committee of the Board of Trustees," January 25, 1963 (subgroup 1, ser. 1), WCF Papers, UA/UNC; Pearsall, supplemental statement to the Board of Trustees meeting, January 25, 1963, ser. 1.2, file 80, Graham Papers, SHC. The senate version had originally been "North Carolina State, the University of North Carolina at Raleigh," but the house reversed this. David Cooper, "College Name Amended," *Raleigh News and Observer*, April 24, 1963; Jay Jenkins, "What's in a Name" (April 24, 1963), and Jenkins, "College Bill Okd in House" (April 25, 1963), *Charlotte Observer*; Arthur Johnsey, "House Revolts in Renaming N.C. State" (April 24, 1963), and Johnsey, "Education Bill Gets Approval" (April 25, 1963), *Greensboro Daily News*. Terry Sanford recalled that he pushed for the name change in 1963. He said that it "wasn't a very satisfactory name"

and he believed that it was "rather stupid, but the power of the governor's office put it through." Interview with Sanford, December 18, 1986, SOHP. For a brief account of the name change controversy, see King, *Multicampus University of North Carolina*, pp. 50–51.

26. Cooper, "College Name Amended"; "Assembly Oks Name" (May 11, 1963) and "Master Step for Education Taken by General Assembly," editorial (May 13, 1963), *Charlotte Observer*; interview with WCF, January 28, 1991; resolution of the North Carolina State College Alumni Association (December 14, 1963), M. Edmund Aycock, "A Statement Made before the Executive Committee of the Board of Trustees of the University of North Carolina" (March 13, 1964), and Executive Committee minutes (April 26, May 8, September 13, 1964), subgroup 2, ser. 1, subser. 3, WCF Papers, UA/UNC.

27. Interviews with WCF, January 28, 1991, May 2, 1972 (IG); David Perkins, "Conflict, Growth: A UNC Era Ends as Friday Retires," *Raleigh News and Observer*, March 2, 1986; interview with IHF, October 30, 1990, SOHP.

28. King, *Multicampus University of North Carolina*, pp. 92–98; interview with Donald Anderson, March 19, 1990; interview with Arnold K. King, February 7, 1990; interview with John Sanders, January 25, 1991; Watts Hill Jr., testimony, UNC-HEW Case File, GA.

29. Interviews with WCF, January 28, 1991, June 17, 1992; interview with John Sanders, January 25, 1991.

30. King, *Multicampus University of North Carolina*, pp. 101–5; Executive Committee minutes, December 1, 1968, February 24, 1969, subgroup 2, ser. 1, subser. 3, WCF Papers, UA/UNC; interview with Watts Hill Jr., March 13, 1972, IG; Arthur Johnsey, "Board of Higher Education Approves UNC Expansion," *Greensboro Daily News*, March 8, 1969.

31. Interview with WCF, May 2, 1972, IG; interview with Watts Hill, Sr., February 29, 1972, IG; interview with Winfred Godwin, April 23, 1990; interview with Dean W. Colvard, January 29, 1990; Bratton, *East Carolina University*, pp. 377, 386–400.

32. Interview with Winfred Godwin, April 23, 1990; Watts Hill Jr., testimony, UNC-HEW Case File, GA.

33. Watts Hill Jr. to Dan K. Moore, December 8, 1966, subgroup 1, ser. 8, file entitled "Board of Higher Education, July–Dec. 1966," WCF Papers, UA/UNC; interview with Watts Hill Jr., March 13, 1972, IG; interview with Elise Wilson, May 3, 1972, IG; interviews with WCF, December 14, 1973 (SOHP), May 2, 1972 (IG), January 28, 1991; interview with Watts Hill Sr., February 29, 1972, IG; King, *Multicampus University of North Carolina*, pp. 105–6, 108; Snider, *Light on the Hill*, p. 289.

34. Interviews with WCF, May 2, 1972 (IG), December 5, 1974 (SOHP), January 28, 1991. When the BHE attempted to exert greater control over UNC's budget in August 1969, for example, Friday resisted vigorously. WCF, memorandum of record, August 19, 1969, subgroup 1, ser. 8, file entitled "Board of Higher Education, Aug.–Dec. 1969," WCF Papers, UA/UNC; interview with Watts Hill Sr., February 29, 1972, IG.

35. Interview with Richard H. Robinson, June 3, 1991; interviews with WCF, May 2, 1972 (IG), June 17, 1992.

36. "Single College-University Agency Pondered by State," *Greensboro Daily News*, February 6, 1970; "Legislator Switches Stand, Opposes State Reorganization," *Winston-Salem Journal*, October 6, 1970; "Reorganization Stalled," editorial, *Greensboro Daily News*, October 7, 1970; King, *Multicampus University of North Carolina*, p. 111; WCF to Scott (September 21, 1970) and Victor S. Bryant to Scott (October 13, 1970), subgroup II, ser. 2, file entitled "Executive Reorganization Amendment, 1969–1971," IG; interview with Dean W. Colvard, January 29,

1990; interview with Scott, November 1, 1972, IG; interview with WCF, June 17, 1992; WCF, memoranda of record, November 30, 1970, July 29, 1971.

37. Roy Parker Jr., "Sen. Scott Cites Education Peril," *Raleigh News and Observer*, July 25, 1971; WCF, memorandum of record, July 29, 1971; interview with Scott, November 1, 1972, IG; North Carolina Board of Higher Education, *Planning for Higher Education*, p. 360; interview with Hill Jr., March 13, 1972, IG; Hill Jr., "More Effective Governance of Higher Education, President William C. Friday's Viewpoint," enclosure in Hill Jr. to Cameron West, December 16, 1970, in subgroup II, ser. 2, file entitled "Meeting of the Board of Higher Education at Whispering Pines, November 19–20, 1970," IG.

38. Interviews with WCF, May 2, 1972 (IG), June 17, 1992; interview with Robert B. Jordan III, April 13, 1972, IG. Colvard recalled a meeting of the Administrative Council, composed of the UNC chancellors, at which Friday reported the conversations with Scott; most of the chancellors agreed on the need for change. But any forward motion on these conversations, Colvard noted, "died" after trustee opposition arose against it; the result was a "hiatus" that caused even greater confusion. Interview with Dean W. Colvard, January 29, 1990.

39. Interview with John Sanders, January 25, 1991; interview with WCF, December 14, 1973, SOHP.

40. Interview with WCF, May 2, 1972, IG.

41. Hill Jr., "More Effective Governance of Higher Education, President William C. Friday's Viewpoint," enclosed in Hill Jr. to Cameron West, December 16, 1970, subgroup II, ser. 2, file entitled "Meeting of the Board of Higher Education at Whispering Pines, November 19–20, 1970," IG.

42. Interview with Watts Hill Jr., March 13, 1972, IG; interview with Watts Hill Sr., February 29, 1972, IG; Paul Jablow, "Scott Looks to New Ways to Run 9 Campuses," *Charlotte Observer*, December 16, 1970; transcript of Scott's comments, December 14, 1970, subgroup II, ser. 2, file entitled "Governor's Meeting with Trustees, December 13, 1970," IG; interview with Watts Hill Jr., March 13, 1972. For an account of the meeting, see King, *Multicampus University of North Carolina*, pp. 111–13.

43. Arthur Johnsey, "Higher Education Unit Supports Scott's Call to Reorganize System" (December 19, 1970), and Johnsey, "UNC Trustees Back Scott on Reorganizing" (December 30, 1970), *Greensboro Daily News*; Gene Marlowe, "University Unit Backs Scott Move," *Raleigh News and Observer*, December 30, 1970; Arthur Johnsey, "Lindsay Warren Heads Education Study Group," *Greensboro Daily News*, January 9, 1971; Gene Marlowe, "Warren Will Head Study of Schools' Organization," *Raleigh News and Observer*, January 9, 1971; interview with Watts Hill Jr., March 13, 1972, IG.

44. Interview with Watts Hill Sr., February 29, 1972, IG; N. Ferebee Taylor to WCF, memorandum, January 20, 1971, subgroup II, ser. 2, file entitled "Warren Commission's Initial Meeting, January 15, 1971," IG.

45. Interview with Paul Lucas, March 29, 1972, IG; Lindsay Warren to members of the Warren Committee (February 24, 1971), Ferebee Taylor to Victor Bryant (March 3, 1971), Taylor to WCF (March 10, 1971), and Richard H. Robinson to WCF (March 17, 1971), subgroup II, ser. 2, file entitled "Fifth Meeting of the Warren Commission, March 5–6, 1971," IG; WCF to Warren, March 9, 1971, subgroup I, ser. 8, file entitled "Higher Education, Study Committee (Warren Comm.), General, Jan.–Apr. 1971," WCF Papers, UA/UNC. Wallace Hyde, a Western Carolina University trustee, feared that the Warren Committee masked an effort by UNC to "close the door" on the regionals' expansion. Interview with Hyde, March 16, 1972, IG.

46. WCF, memorandum of record (April 5, 1971), interview with Warren (June 19, 1971), interview with WCF (May 2, 1972), interview with Hyde (March 16, 1972), Watts Hill Jr., notes of meeting (April 3, 1971), Hill Jr., "Outline Reasons for Reconsideration of the Present Plan" (April 4, 1971), and Hill Jr. to Warren, draft memorandum (April 5, 1971), subgroup II, ser. 2, file entitled "Eighth Meeting of Warren Commission, April 3, 1971," IG; Victor S. Bryant to WCF, May 26, 1971, subgroup 1, ser. 8, file entitled "Higher Education, Study Committee (Warren Comm.), General, May 1971," WCF Papers, UA/UNC. According to some members of the committee, the governor subsequently intervened to obtain an endorsement of the single-board approach. Scott himself later admitted that he telephoned several of the black members of the Warren Committee to urge them to be present and to support restructuring, but this, he claimed, had nothing to do with the question of reconsideration. Interview with J. P. Huskins (March 15, 1972), interview with Ike Andrews (July 3, 1972), interview with Robert B. Jordan III (April 13, 1972), Watts Hill Jr. to Warren, draft of memorandum (April 5, 1971), and Warren to Hill (April 7, 1971), subgroup II, ser. 2, file entitled "Attempts at Reconsideration, April 4–24, 1971," IG; interview with Lucas, March 29, 1972, IG; interview with Warren, June 19, 1971, IG. Hill apparently met with Scott on April 7 to discuss the matter, and the governor was noncommittal. Hill Jr. to Doris Horton et al., April 6, 15, 1971, subgroup II, ser. 2, file entitled "Attempts at Reconsideration, April 4–24, 1971," IG. Scott claimed that he "did not have anything to do at all" with the move for reconsideration. The distinction he made was that he urged those absent at the April 3–4 meetings to attend the subsequent meetings. Interview with Scott, November 1, 1972, IG.

47. Hill Jr. to Doris Horton et al., April 15, 1971; interview with Maceo Sloan, May 3, 1972, IG.

48. WCF, memorandum of record, April 26, 1971, subgroup II, ser. 2, file entitled "Ninth Meeting of the Warren Commission, April 23–24, 1971," IG; Roy Parker Jr., "Votes Switched on Restructuring," *Raleigh News and Observer*, May 26, 1971; King, *Multicampus University of North Carolina*, pp. 115–16.

49. "Comments on the Hyde Plan," April 28, 1971, subgroup II, ser. 2, file entitled "Ninth Meeting of the Warren Commission, April 23–24, 1971," IG; Watts Hill Jr., notes of meeting, May 7, 1971, subgroup II, ser. 2, file entitled "Tenth Meeting of Warren Commission, May 7, 1971," IG.

50. Interview with Andrews, July 3, 1972, IG; Ned Cline, "Warren Panel Votes to Split UNC System," and Cline, "Plan's Future Is in Doubt," *Greensboro Daily News*, May 9, 1971; Gene Marlowe, "Study of Education Backs Regents Plan" (May 9, 1971), and "Warren Study: Challenge of Change," editorial (May 10, 1971), *Raleigh News and Observer*; Executive Committee minutes, May 14, 1971, subgroup 2, ser. 1, subser. 3, WCF Papers, UA/UNC; Arthur Johnsey, "Trustees Oppose Regents Plan," *Greensboro Daily News*, May 14, 1971; Gene Marlowe, "UNC Unit Pledges Fight on Regents," *Raleigh News and Observer*, May 15, 1971; WCF to McLendon, May 17, 1971, subgroup 1, ser. 8, file entitled "Higher Education, Study Committee (Warren Comm.), General, May 1971," WCF Papers.

51. Roy Parker Jr., "Godwin Says It's Too Late to Study Education Issue" (May 11, 1971), Parker, "Scott: Assembly Has Time to Act" (May 18, 1971), and "Regents Bid Set by Scott" (May 21, 1971), *Raleigh News and Observer*; interview with Dean W. Colvard, January 29, 1990; Arthur Johnsey, "Don't Fight Revision, Scott Tells Trustees," *Greensboro Daily News*, May 25, 1971; Gene Marlowe, "Governor Said Holding Budget Ax over UNC," and Roy Parker Jr., "Battle Lines Are Drawn on Universities," *Raleigh News and Observer*, May 25, 1971; interview with Hill Sr., February 29, 1972, IG; interview with Robert B. Jordan III, April 13, 1972; Albert Coates's

account, in subgroup II, ser. 2, file entitled "Board of Trustees Meeting, May 24, 28, 1971," IG; King, *Multicampus University of North Carolina*, p. 118.

52. Roy Parker Jr., "Rivalries Deplored by Scott," Gene Marlowe, "Central Control Proposed," and text of Scott speech, *Raleigh News and Observer*, May 26, 1971; Arthur Johnsey, "Scott Urges Approval of Board of Regents," *Greensboro Daily News*, May 26, 1971; Leonard, "Reorganization of Public Senior Higher Education," p. 13; Ned Cline, "Governor Shifts to Soft Sell on Revision Plan," *Greensboro Daily News*, May 27, 1971; Roy Parker Jr., "Committee Support Seen for Education Changes" (May 27, 1971), Gene Marlowe and Jack Aulis, "State Board Backs Scott's Regents Plan" (May 28, 1971), and Gene Marlowe, "UNC Trustees Vote to Fight Scott Plan" (May 29, 1971), *Raleigh News and Observer*; Ned Cline, " 'We're in a Struggle Like Never Before' – UNC Trustee," *Greensboro Daily News*, May 29, 1971; Gene Marlowe, "UNC Offers Its Plan" (June 1, 1961), and Roy Parker Jr., "Two Compromises Studied" (June 2, 1971), *Raleigh News and Observer*; interview with Bryant, May 1, 1972, IG. For an overview of the political battle, see King, *Multicampus University of North Carolina*, pp. 113–40.

53. Interviews with WCF, May 2, 1972 (IG), January 28, 1991, June 17, 1992; interview with Dean W. Colvard, January 29, 1990; interview with Ike Andrews, July 3, 1972, IG.

54. Gene Marlowe, "UNC Forces to Compromise" (June 9, 1971), Marlowe, "Restructuring Bills Clog Hoppers" (June 13, 1971), and Marlowe, "Regents Plan Foes Busy at 'Home' " (June 14, 1971), *Raleigh News and Observer*; "Strayhorn Leads Deconsolidation Fight," *Charlotte Observer*, June 3, 1971.

55. Ned Cline, "5 Senators May Hold Key to Restructuring," *Greensboro Daily News*, June 2, 1971; Roy Parker Jr., "Most Senators Ask Delay on Regents Plan Till '73," *Raleigh News and Observer*, June 19, 1971; Ned Cline, "Scott's Hopes on UNC Plan May Be Dead" (June 19, 1971), and Cline, "Sen. John Burney the Big Obstacle" (June 23, 1971), *Greensboro Daily News*; "Godwin Endorses Postponement Bill," *Raleigh News and Observer*, June 20, 1971; Ned Cline and Arthur Johnsey, "Scott Forces Appear Set to Health Education Efforts for Session," *Greensboro Daily News*, June 22, 1971; Gene Marlowe, "Regents Fight Showdown Delayed until This Fall," *Raleigh News and Observer*, June 23, 1971; Ned Cline, "Scott Accepts Fall Education Session," *Greensboro Daily News*, June 23, 1971; Bob Boyd, "Scott Postpones Higher Education Reorganization" (June 23, 1971), and "Scott Could Redeem Self, If Not His Green Stamps," editorial (June 24, 1971), *Charlotte Observer*.

56. Leonard, "Reorganization of Public Senior Higher Education," p. 15; "NCSU's Caldwell Favors Governing Regents Board" (June 17, 1971), Roy Parker Jr., "Stands Shifting on Regents" (June 22, 1971), and Gene Marlowe, "West Pro Central Board" (June 22, 1971), *Raleigh News and Observer*; Ned Cline, "Scott Accepts Fall Education Session" (June 23, 1971), and "The Governor De-escalates," editorial (June 25, 1971), *Greensboro Daily News*.

57. Leonard, "Reorganization of Public Senior Higher Education," p. 16; Roberts, *The Governor*, pp. 81–87; interview with WCF, June 17, 1992; Gene Marlowe, "Friday Reaffirms UNC Anti-Regents Stand" (June 25, 1971), and "Educators Will Move or Be Shoved," editorial (June 29, 1971), *Raleigh News and Observer*.

58. Roy Parker Jr., "Burney Maps New University Setup," *Raleigh News and Observer*, September 9, 1971; Ned Cline, "UNC Compromise in the Works," *Greensboro Daily News*, September 9, 1971; Gene Marlowe, "Restructuring Foes Offer Compromise" (September 18, 1971), and Marlowe, "Trustees Unit Backs Burney" (September 20, 1971), *Raleigh News and Observer*; interview with WCF, May 2, 1972, IG; Leonard, "Reorganization of Public Senior Higher Education," pp. 17–19; WCF to Warren, August 31, 1971, subgroup 1, ser. 8, file entitled

"Higher Education, Study Committee (Warren Comm.), General, Aug. 1971," WCF Papers, UA/UNC; Ferebee Taylor, notes of conference with Scott, September 22, 1971, file entitled "Higher Education Act: Discussion, Aug.–Sept. 1971," WCF Papers; Gene Marlowe, "Education Battle Shifting in Focus," *Raleigh News and Observer*, September 12, 1971; David E. Gillespie, "Scott Begins Talks about UNC Plan," *Charlotte Observer*, September 11, 1971.

59. Interview with WCF, May 2, 1972, IG; "Under the Dome," *Raleigh News and Observer*, October 3, 1971; Leonard, "Reorganization of Public Senior Higher Education," pp. 20–22; summary of conference, September 22, 1971, and Ike F. Andrews to WCF, September 29, 1971, IG.

60. William D. Snider, "A Middle Way for Restructuring" (October 3, 1971), Ned Cline, "Friday Says He'll Accept Single Board Plan" (October 8, 1971), and text of position statement (October 8, 1971), *Greensboro Daily News*; Gene Marlowe, "Friday Backs Central Board" (October 8, 1971), and Marlowe, "Trustees Support Friday" (October 12, 1971), *Raleigh News and Observer*.

61. Gene Marlowe, "New Powers Written into Higher Education Measure" (October 14, 1971), and Marlowe, "Strong Board Wins Subcommittee's OK" (October 15, 1971), *Raleigh News and Observer*; Arthur Johnsey, "Joint Committee Backs Strong Central Board," *Greensboro Daily News*, October 16, 1971; Leonard, "Reorganization of Public Senior Higher Education," pp. 22–23.

62. Leonard, "Reorganization of Public Senior Higher Education," p. 24.

63. Executive Committee minutes, October 11, 1971; "Restructuring of Higher Education in North Carolina," October 7, 1971, IG; Marlowe, "UNC Board Backs Friday's Plan and Opposes Restructuring Bill," *Raleigh News and Observer*, October 19, 1971; Ned Cline, "UNC Trustees Drop Opposition to Board," *Greensboro Daily News*, October 19, 1971; Leonard, "Reorganization of Public Senior Higher Education," pp. 24–25.

64. Roy Parker Jr., "General Assembly Reconvening Today," *Raleigh News and Observer*, October 26, 1971; interview with Scott, November 1, 1972, IG.

65. Leonard, "Reorganization of Public Senior Higher Education," pp. 25–27; interview with Ike Andrews, July 3, 1972, IG.

66. Roy Parker Jr. and Jack Aulis, "Passage Is Urged by Scott," *Raleigh News and Observer*, October 27, 1971; Larry Tarleton and Bob Boyd, "Education Bill Appears Headed toward Enactment," *Charlotte Observer*, October 28, 1971; "Scott Urges Passage of Restructuring Bill" (October 27, 1971), Ned Cline, "Committees to Send Bill Unchanged to Floor" (October 27, 1971), and Arthur Johnsey and Cline, "Restructuring Passes Two Biggest Hurdles" (October 28, 1971), *Greensboro Daily News*; Leonard, "Reorganization of Public Senior Higher Education," pp. 27–29; interview with Ike Andrews, July 3, 1972, IG.

67. Larry Tarleton, "Legislators OK Strong Central Board for UNC," *Charlotte Observer*, October 29, 1971; Leonard, "Reorganization of Public Senior Higher Education," pp. 30–39; John Sanders, "The Evolution of the Idea of Making the Initial Board of Governors a Permanent Body," August 15, 1972, MS in author's possession; interview with Andrews, July 3, 1972, IG; interview with Robert B. Jordan III, April 13, 1972, IG; Gene Marlowe and Roy Parker Jr., "University Control Bill Nears Assembly Passage," *Raleigh News and Observer*, October 29, 1971; interview with WCF, May 2, 1972 (IG), June 17, 1992.

68. Gene Marlowe, "Assembly Passes Governing Board Bill," *Raleigh News and Observer*, October 30, 1971; Ned Cline, "Restructuring Passed but Faces New Test," *Greensboro Daily News*, October 30, 1971; Larry Tarleton, "Education Bill Triggers Full-Scale Political War,"

Charlotte Observer, October 30, 1971; Leonard, "Reorganization of Public Senior Higher Education," pp. 45–51; interview with Andrews, July 3, 1972, IG.

69. Leonard, "Reorganization of Public Senior Higher Education," pp. 51–60; Sanders, "Evolution"; interview with WCF (May 2, 1972), interview with L. P. McLendon Jr. (April 24, 1972), interview with Andrews (July 3, 1972), and interview with Robert B. Jordan III (April 13, 1972), IG. The law also provided that each biennial session of the legislature would elect eight new members for eight-year terms and that a minimum of four blacks, four women, and four members of the minority political party – the Republicans – would be elected. Gene Marlowe, "UNC Forces Win 'Balance of Power,'" and Roy Parker Jr., "It Was Like a Horse Race and Rep. Ike Andrews Won," *Raleigh News and Observer*, October 31, 1971. Jack Stevens said that he voted with the majority, and against UNC, to enable him subsequently to make a motion to reconsider, yet this seems somewhat improbable given the fact that his vote would have carried the house for the university. Interview with John S. Stevens, July 23, 1991. For another brief account of the restructuring battle, see Snider, *Light on the Hill*, pp. 292–93.

70. Interview with Scott, November 1, 1972, IG; interview with John S. Stevens, July 23, 1991; interview with Ike Andrews, July 3, 1972, IG. Scott discounted the significance of the legislative battle in an interview almost two decades later; the passage of time no doubt altered his perspective. Interview with Scott, April 4, 1990.

71. Interview with WCF, December 5, 1974, SOHP. Since 1972 the sixteen-campus UNC system has included the following institutions: Appalachian State University (Boone), East Carolina University (Greenville), Elizabeth City State University, Fayetteville State University, North Carolina A&T State University (Greensboro), North Carolina Central University (Durham), North Carolina School of the Arts (Winston-Salem), North Carolina State University (Raleigh), Pembroke State University, the University of North Carolina at Asheville, the University of North Carolina at Chapel Hill, the University of North Carolina at Charlotte, the University of North Carolina at Greensboro, the University of North Carolina at Wilmington, Western Carolina University (Cullowhee), and Winston-Salem State University.

72. Interview with McMillan, May 14, 1991; interview with Joyner, January 18, 1991; interview with John Sanders, January 25, 1991.

CHAPTER 7

1. Interview with Raymond Dawson, quoting Cleon Thompson, August 1, 1991.

2. Sherry Johnson, "Friday Ready to Shed Limelight at UNC," *Raleigh News and Observer*, November 1, 1981.

3. Jay Jenkins, "The Friday Years," MS in Kenan; interview with Zona Norwood, April 3, 1991; interview with Cleon Thompson, January 30, 1991. His daughter described his ability to deal with people from all walks of life equally his "great hallmark." Interview with Mary Friday, October 4, 1992.

4. Interview with Raymond Dawson, January 30, 1990; interview with Mary Friday, October 4, 1992; interview with Georgia Kyser, October 15, 1991; interview with Aycock, April 11, 1990. "He has the ability to confer with just about anybody," observed his brother. Interview with John R. Friday, November 8, 1993.

5. Interview with Ernest Boyer, May 9, 1990; interview with Georgia Kyser, October 15, 1991; interview with Donald Anderson, March 19, 1990; interview with Watts Hill Sr., February 29, 1972, IG.

6. Geoffrey Mock, "Bill Friday Leaving Legacy at UNC," clipping from *Gastonia Gazette*, June 2, 1985, in subgroup 1, ser. 1, Subject Files, WCF Papers, UA/UNC; interview with Zona Norwood, April 3, 1991.

7. David Perkins, "Conflict, Growth: A UNC Era Ends as Friday Retires," *Raleigh News and Observer*, March 2, 1986; Mock, "Bill Friday Leaving Legacy at UNC"; interview with Fran Friday, April 27, 1994; interview with Dawson, January 30, 1990; interview with Norwood, April 3, 1991.

8. Interview with Dawson, January 30, 1990; interview with WCF, April 1, 1991.

9. Interview with Georgia Kyser, October 15, 1991; interview with Mary Friday, October 4, 1992; interview with Fran Friday, April 27, 1994.

10. Interview with Georgia Kyser, October 15, 1991; interview with IHF, October 4, 1990, SOHP; interview with WCF, November 24, 1992; entry on James Kern Kyser, *DNCB*, 3:384.

11. Interview with Kyser, October 15, 1991; interview with Mary Friday, October 4, 1992; Waldorf, "It Was a Wonderful Life."

12. Interview with WCF, April 1, 1991; interview with Fran Friday, April 27, 1994; interview with Mary Friday, October 4, 1992; Waldorf, "It Was a Wonderful Life."

13. Waldorf, "It Was a Wonderful Life"; interview with Mary Friday, October 4, 1992; interview with WCF, April 1, 1991.

14. Interview with Kyser, October 15, 1991; interview with Mary Friday, October 4, 1992; interview with IHF, October 15, 1990, SOHP. When asked by a reporter whether her father spent enough time with his children, Mary Friday responded, "My goodness, if he had more time we couldn't have stood it." Interview with IHF, October 15, 1990, SOHP.

15. Interview with Caldwell, January 26, 1990; Charles Babington, profile of WCF, *Greensboro Daily News*, October 25, 1981; interview with Dawson, January 30, 1990.

16. Snider, "Twenty-Nine Tumultuous Years"; interview with McMillan, May 14, 1991; interview with Norwood, April 3, 1991.

17. Babington, feature, *Greensboro Daily News*; interview with Dawson, January 30, 1990; interview with Norwood, April 3, 1991.

18. Interview with Dawson, January 30, 1990; interview with Aycock, April 11, 1990.

19. Johnson, "Friday Ready to Shed Limelight at UNC"; interview with Norwood, April 3, 1991.

20. Interview with WCF, April 1, 1991. Friday hired State College classmate Rudy Pate and, later, former *Charlotte Observer* reporter Jay Jenkins. Immediately before and especially after restructuring, another staff person, former Robeson County legislator R. D. McMillan, handled the university's day-to-day lobbying efforts. Rudy Pate to WCF, October 9, 1967, subgroup 1, ser. 1, WCF Papers, UA/UNC.

21. Shumaker, "Let Me Share This with You."

22. Interview with WCF, May 2, 1972, IG.

23. King, *Multicampus University of North Carolina*, chap. 9; Executive Committee minutes, November 12, 1971, subgroup 1, ser. 1, subser. 3, WCF Papers, UA/UNC; Robert W. Scott to WCF and Cameron West, November 15, 1971, and John Sanders, "Analysis of an Act to Consolidate the Institutions of Higher Learning in North Carolina," November 24, 1971, subgroup 1, ser. 2, subser. 4, file entitled "Planning Committee: General, 1971," WCF Papers; Gene Marlowe, "UNC Partisans Win Seats," *Raleigh News and Observer*, November 23, 1971; interview with Felix Joyner, January 18, 1991; Bryant to WCF, November 29, 1971, subgroup 2, ser. 1, subser. 4, file entitled "Planning Committee: General, 1971," WCF Papers.

24. WCF, memorandum of record, March 7, 1972, IG; "Closed-Door Meeting Unwise Move," editorial, *Raleigh News and Observer*, January 9, 1972; WCF, notes in meeting with Personnel Committee, March 15, 1972, subgroup 2, ser. 1, subser. 4, file entitled "Planning Committee: Jan.–June 1972," WCF Papers, UA/UNC; WCF, memorandum of record, March 16, 1972, IG; interview with WCF, June 17, 1992. The notion that Friday's office should be moved had been discussed for several years. See Thomas B. Bunn to WCF, March 16, 1965, and "Get the Consolidated University Office Out of Chapel Hill?," Spring 1967, subgroup 1, ser. 8, file entitled "General Administration (location), 1965–1967," WCF Papers. In 1966 Luther Hodges chaired a trustee committee examining the process by which trustees were selected, and in the course of its proceedings he endorsed moving Friday's office to the Research Triangle Park. In July 1966 the Executive Committee formally supported keeping the Consolidated Office in Chapel Hill. Executive Committee minutes, July 12, 1966, subgroup 2, ser. 1, subser. 3, WCF Papers.

25. Gene Marlowe, "Friday Likely to Head New System," *Raleigh News and Observer*, January 6, 1972; interview with WCF, June 17, 1992; WCF, notes in meeting with Personnel Committee, March 15, 1972, subgroup 2, ser. 1, subser. 4, file entitled "Planning Committee: Jan.–June 1972," WCF Papers, UA/UNC.

26. Gene Marlowe, "Grumbling Breaks Out on Bill Friday's Moves," *Raleigh News and Observer*, March 18, 1972.

27. Gene Marlowe, "Friday Gets Top Post in Universities" (March 18, 1972), and "Friday Will Prove His Fairness," editorial (March 21, 1972), *Raleigh News and Observer*.

28. Interview with Felix Joyner, January 18, 1991; interview with Robert Scott, November 1, 1972, IG.

29. Ned Cline, "It's Clear Friday Will Call Staff Selection Shots," *Greensboro Daily News*, March 18, 1972; Gene Marlowe, "Grumbling Breaks Out on Dr. Friday's Moves," *Raleigh News and Observer*, March 18, 1972.

30. Interview with William Aycock, April 11, 1990; interview with WCF (December 5, 1974) and interview with Sitterson (November 6, 1987), SOHP.

31. Interview with Dawson, January 30, 1990; interview with Felix Joyner, January 18, 1991.

32. Interview with Dawson, January 30, 1990. Most of the issues were addressed in Arnold K. King to WCF, memorandum, February 26, 1973, subgroup 1, ser. 1, file entitled "General, 1970–1974," WCF Papers, UA/UNC.

33. Interview with Dawson, November 20, 1991; interview with Roy Carroll, August 8, 1991; King, *Multicampus University of North Carolina*, pp. 173–76.

34. Interview with WCF, December 14, 1973, SOHP; interview with Dawson, January 30, 1990. Most of the board's melding, according to Philip Carson, was because of Bill Friday. Interview with Carson, July 18, 1991.

35. Interview with Dawson, January 30, 1990.

36. Interview with Dawson, November 20, 1991; interview with WCF, February 25, 1991.

37. Interview with Dawson, November 20, 1991.

38. Atwell to WCF (September 25, 1984) and Alexander Heard to WCF (September 26, 1984), subgroup 1, ser. 1, file entitled "Friday, William Clyde: Retirement, 1984–1986," WCF Papers, UA/UNC.

39. Goldman, *The Tragedy of Lyndon Johnson*, pp. 35–37, 238–41; interview with WCF, December 3, 1990.

40. WCF to Goldman, October 5, 1964, subgroup 1, ser. 8, file entitled "President, Office of:

White House Fellows, Commission on, 1964," WCF Papers, UA/UNC; interview with WCF, December 3, 1990; minutes, meeting of the Commission on White House Fellows (November 10, 1964), and Eli Evans to WCF (December 1964), subgroup 1, ser. 8, file entitled "President, Office of: White House Fellows, Commission on, 1964," WCF Papers.

41. Minutes, meeting of the Commission on White House Fellows, November 10, 1964.

42. WCF, memorandum of record, May 21, 1966, subgroup 1, ser. 1, file entitled "Friday, William Clyde: Education, U.S. Department, Friday Position With, 1966," WCF Papers, UA/UNC.

43. Interview with WCF, July 10, 1987, LBJPL.

44. Graham, *Uncertain Triumph*, pp. 62, 168.

45. Ibid., p. xxi; Califano to WCF, November 1, 1966, subgroup 1, ser. 8, file entitled "President, Office of: Education, Task Force on, 1966," WCF Papers, UA/UNC; interview with WCF, July 10, 1987, LBJPL.

46. Interview with WCF, July 10, 1987, LBJPL. Brownell was added after Marland complained about "the lack of public school men" on the task force. Marland to William B. Cannon, November 23, 1966, subgroup 1, ser. 8, file entitled "President, Office of: Education, Task Force on, 1966," WCF Papers, UA/UNC.

47. WCF, notes on meeting (November 22, 1966), and minutes, task force meeting (November 22, 1966), subgroup 1, ser. 8, file entitled "President, Office of: Education, Task Force on, 1966," WCF Papers, UA/UNC.

48. Interview with WCF, July 10, 1987, LBJPL; Califano to WCF (November 1, 1966) and WCF to John Gardner (November 23, 1966), subgroup 1, ser. 8, file entitled "President, Office of: Education, Task Force on, 1966," WCF Papers, UA/UNC. The task force subsequently met on February 10–11, March 17–18, April 14–15, May 19–20, and June 16–17.

49. WCF to Lyndon B. Johnson, June 1967, subgroup 1, ser. 8, file entitled "President, Office of: Education, Task Force on, 1967," WCF Papers, UA/UNC; interview with WCF, July 10, 1987, LBJPL; Graham, *Uncertain Triumph*, pp. 169–74; "Report of the [Friday] Task Force on Education," June 30, 1967, Kenan.

50. Interviews with WCF, July 10, 1987 (LBJPL), December 3, 1990.

51. Graham, *Uncertain Triumph*, pp. 175–77, 183–84; interview with WCF, July 10, 1987, LBJPL; Goheen to WCF (October 30, 1967), WCF to task force members (January 31, 1968), and Howe to WCF (February 5, 1968), subgroup 1, ser. 8, files entitled "President, Office of: Education, Task Force on, 1967" and "President, Office of: Education, Task Force on, 1968, 1976, 1987," WCF Papers, UA/UNC.

52. Interview with WCF, November 24, 1992. Friday also twice turned down the chance to become ACE president. Ibid.

53. Interview with WCF, December 3, 1990; interview with Clark Kerr, April 6, 1990. For more on the AAU, see interview with Edgar Shannon, February 22, 1991.

54. Interviews with WCF, December 3, 1990, November 24, 1992; interview with David Henry, February 9, 1990.

55. Interview with Henry, February 9, 1990; WCF to Riesman, March 17, 1969, subgroup 1, ser. 8, file entitled "Carnegie Foundation: Comm. on the Future of H.E., 1969," WCF Papers, UA/UNC; interview with WCF, December 3, 1990; Carnegie Commission on the Future of Higher Education, *Priorities for Action*, pp. 1–9.

56. Interview with WCF, November 24, 1992; interview with Kerr, April 6, 1990.

57. Henry to Kerr, draft (February 1969), and WCF to Henry (February 3, 1969), subgroup 1,

ser. 8, file entitled "Carnegie Foundation: Comm. on the Future of H.E., 1969," WCF Papers, UA/UNC; interview with Henry, February 9, 1990; interview with WCF, November 24, 1992; Kerr, *Great Transformation*, p. xviii; interview with Kerr, April 6, 1990; Riesman to William A. Link, July 13, August 27, 1993, in author's possession.

58. Interview with Kerr, April 6, 1990; Kerr to members of Carnegie Commission (January 31, 1967), Alan Pifer to WCF (March 30, 1967), Kerr to WCF (May 9, 1967), WCF to Kerr (May 16, October 2, 1967), Kerr to members of commission, with attachment (January 31, 1968), and David Henry to WCF (January 27, 1969), subgroup 1, ser. 8, file entitled "Carnegie Foundation: Comm. on the Future of H.E.," WCF Papers, UA/UNC; WCF, memoranda of record, January 18, March 4, 1971; interview with Hesburgh, June 7, 1990. Friday described the Carnegie Commission as "by far the most massive study of higher education this country's ever had." Interview with WCF, November 24, 1992. Clark Kerr described it as "the most respected and prestigious group in higher education in the United States, perhaps not only at that time, but also almost in American history." "There was no other group that carried as much weight as we did." Interview with Kerr, April 6, 1990.

59. Sloan Commission minutes, November 28, 1977 (file entitled "Sloan Commission: Minutes, 1977–1979"), and Louis W. Cabot to WCF, September 27, 1977 (file entitled "Sloan Commission: General, 1977"), subgroup 1, ser. 8, WCF Papers, UA/UNC. The commission also met on January 23, March 13, May 2, June 27, September 12–13, December 14–15, 1978, February 5–6, March 19–20, May 1–2, and June 25–27, 1979.

60. Report of the Sloan Commission, in subgroup 1, ser. 8, file entitled "Sloan Commission: General, 1980," WCF Papers, UA/UNC.

61. Ibid.

62. Interview with WCF, January 7, 1991.

63. Interview with George Herbert, May 13, 1991; interview with Elizabeth Aycock, June 13, 1991.

64. Interview with Herbert, May 13, 1991; interview with WCF, November 24, 1992.

65. Interview with Herbert, May 13, 1991; Larrabee, *Many Missions*; interviews with WCF, January 14, 1991, November 24, 1992.

66. William K. Lehmkuhl to Archie K. Davis, June 20, 1975, subgroup 1, ser. 8, file entitled "National Humanities Center, 1975," WCF Papers, UA/UNC; interview with Elizabeth Aycock, June 13, 1991; interview with Dan Lacy, May 8, 1990; interview with Archie K. Davis, January 17, 1990; interviews with WCF, January 7, 14, 1991.

67. Interviews with Archie K. Davis, May 19, 1986 (SOHP), January 17, 1990; interview with William J. Bennett, April 24, 1991; interview with WCF, January 14, 1991.

68. Interview with WCF, January 14, 1991; interview with Elizabeth Aycock, June 13, 1991.

69. Davis to William L. Bondurant (September 15, 1975), Davis to WCF (October 23, 1975), John Voss to WCF (October 28, 1975), and WCF to Davis (November 4, 1975), subgroup 1, ser. 8, file entitled "National Humanities Center, 1975," WCF Papers, UA/UNC; interview with Elizabeth Aycock, June 13, 1991; interview with Davis, January 17, 1990; interview with Lacy, May 8, 1990; interview with Bennett, April 24, 1991.

70. Interview with Bennett, April 24, 1991; WCF to Charles Frankel (April 1, 1976), Bloomfield to WCF (April 5, 1976), and NHC executive committee minutes (November 11, 1976), subgroup 1, ser. 8, file entitled "National Humanities Center, 1976," WCF Papers, UA/UNC; interview with Elizabeth Aycock, June 13, 1991; entry on Lacy in *Who's Who in America*, 43d ed. (New York: Marquis Who's Who, Inc., 1984), 2:1871–72.

71. Interview with Lacy, May 8, 1990; interview with Bennett, April 24, 1991; Lacy to members of the NHC directorship search committee (January 21, April 20, 1977), and NHC executive committee minutes (January 29, 1977), subgroup 1, ser. 8, file entitled "National Humanities Center, 1977," WCF Papers, UA/UNC.

72. Interview with Bennett, April 24, 1991.

73. John Voss to WCF (May 15, June 6, 1979) and Lacy to Edward Levi (August 30, 1979), subgroup 1, ser. 8, file entitled "National Humanities Center, 1979," WCF Papers, UA/UNC; interview with Lacy, May 8, 1990.

74. Interview with WCF, January 7, 1991.

75. Interview with WCF, November 24, 1992.

76. Interview with Dick Snavely, May 28, 1991. I am grateful to Mr. Snavely for sharing his lists of interviews for *North Carolina People*, 1971–91, and for his willingness to lend me a number of tapes of past interviews.

77. Interviews with Mary Turner Lane, September 9, 16, 1986, May 21, October 1, 28, 1987, SOHP; Rose Post, "It's Over before You Know It," *Salisbury Post*, March 2, 1986; interview with WCF, November 24, 1992.

78. Interview with Snavely, May 28, 1991; Rose Post, "Friday Loves Television Job," *Salisbury Post*, March 2, 1986. Snavely retired in 1991. Interview with WCF, November 24, 1992.

CHAPTER 8

1. Interview with Raymond H. Dawson, January 30, 1990.

2. On the expansion of the UNC Medical School, see the report of the North Carolina Hospital and Medical Care Commission (1944–45), Clarence H. Poe, ed., "Hospital and Medical Care for All Our People," photocopy in possession of William J. Cromartie; Lefler and Newsome, *North Carolina*, pp. 625–26, 678. I am indebted to Dr. Cromartie for sharing this document with me.

In the spring of 1964 a physician from Plymouth, N.C., Ernest W. Furgurson, urged Jenkins to establish a new medical school at East Carolina in order to ease the shortage of doctors in the area. In June 1964 the retired dean of the Duke University Medical School, Wilbert C. Davison, endorsed the organization of a two-year program at ECU. Bratton, *East Carolina University*, pp. 361, 367; interview with Edwin Monroe, June 11, 1991; interview with WCF, February 25, 1991.

3. Interview with Edwin Monroe, June 11, 1991.

4. Bratton, *East Carolina University*, pp. 363–68; Jay Jenkins, "Assembly Units OK ECC Med School" (June 5, 1965), "Med-School Lobby Rolling Over State's Best Interests," editorial (June 6, 1965), and Jenkins, "Senate OKs ECC Med School Bill" (June 9, 1965), *Charlotte Observer*; Jay Jenkins, "ECC's New Approach Will Delay Medical-School Plan," *Charlotte Observer*, February 18, 1966; interview with Monroe, June 11, 1991; Cameron West to Watts Hill Jr. (October 7, 1970) and Hill to West (October 12, 1970), file entitled "Medical Education, 1963, 1968–1970," Marjorie P. Wilson to Leo W. Jenkins, January 29, 1971, file entitled "Medical Education, Jan–Feb 1971," and "History of the East Carolina Program in Medical Education," July 1974, file entitled "Medical Education, June–Aug 1974," subgroup 1, ser. 1, WCF Papers, UA/UNC.

5. "2-Year Med School Bid Made by ECU," *Raleigh News and Observer*, March 19, 1969; interview with R. D. McMillan, May 14, 1991; "Bid for ECU Medical School Flies in Face of Evidence," editorial, *Charlotte Observer*, December 28, 1970.

6. Marjorie P. Wilson to Leo W. Jenkins, January 29, 1971.

7. "Gov. Scott Backs ECU Med School," *Charlotte Observer*, March 14, 1969; Jack Childs, "Scott Skirts Stand on ECU, Office," *Raleigh News and Observer*, February 11, 1971; interviews with Edwin Monroe, June 11, 18, 1991; Jack Claiborne, "ECU Med School Might Nip One Here," *Charlotte Observer*, January 6, 1971; "Report of Educational Programs Committee [of the BHE] . . . Concerning the Request of East Carolina University for a Master of Medical Science Degree," February 1971, subgroup 1, ser. 1, file entitled "Medical Education, Jan–Feb 1971," WCF Papers, UA/UNC.

8. Robert Scott, transcript of comments before BHE, February 19, 1971, subgroup 1, ser. 1, file entitled "Medical Education, Jan–Feb 1971," WCF Papers, UA/UNC; Gene Marlowe, "1-Year Med Unit Backed for ECU" (February 20, 1971), and "Under the Dome" (February 26, 1971), *Raleigh News and Observer*.

9. Gene Marlowe, "ECU, UNC Discuss Medical Unit," *Raleigh News and Observer*, February 27, 1971; WCF to Jenkins, February 11, 1971 (subgroup 1, ser. 1, file entitled "Medical Education, Jan–Feb 1971"), Executive Committee minutes, February 12, 1971 (subgroup 2, ser. 1, subser. 3), WCF, memorandum of record, February 26, 1971, Sitterson to Isaac Taylor, Cecil Sheps, C. Arden Miller, and Merrell Flair, March 1, 1971, WCF Papers, UA/UNC; Report of the Joint Committee (April 15, 1971) and BHE minutes (May 1971, fragment), subgroup 1, ser. 1, file entitled "Medical Education, Mar–Sept 1971," WCF Papers; Ned Cline, "Scott Backs One-Year Med School for ECU," *Greensboro Daily News*, May 12, 1971; Howard Covington, "ECU Med School Backed," *Charlotte Observer*, May 12, 1971; Ned Cline, "ECU Trustees Will Settle for One-Year Medical School," *Greensboro Daily News*, May 13, 1971.

10. Glen R. Leymaster to Christopher C. Fordham III, November 23, 1971, subgroup 1, ser. 1, file entitled "Medical Education, Mar–Sept 1971," WCF Papers, UA/UNC.

11. Interview with William Laupus, December 3, 1991; interviews with Dawson, January 30, 1990, November 20, 1991; interview with Monroe, June 11, 1991.

12. Interview with William Cromartie, May 23, 1991. Monroe became ECU's chief advocate, and he described relations with UNC officials as tense. Dawson and Joyner saw him, he believed, as mainly responsible for the East Carolina campaign; Monroe viewed Dawson as his chief adversary in whom he "never saw anything warm." "If you're looking for a hard-nosed, cold-blooded, point man, hatchet man," he commented, "I can't think of anybody better to fill the bill than Ray Dawson." Interview with Dawson, November 20, 1991; interview with Monroe, June 18, 1991.

13. Interview with Cecil Sheps, May 15, 1991; interview with I. Glenn Wilson, May 6, 1991.

14. Jenkins to Bob Scott, January 6, 1972 (subgroup 1, ser. 1, file entitled "Medical Education, Jan–June 1972"), and Executive Committee minutes, February 28, 1972 (subgroup 2, ser. 1, subser. 3), WCF Papers, UA/UNC.

15. Edwin W. Monroe to WCF, June 20, 1972 (subgroup 1, ser. 1, file entitled "Medical Education, Jan–June 1972"), and Board of Governors minutes, August 14, 1972 (subgroup 2, ser. 1, subser. 3), WCF Papers, UA/UNC; interview with Dawson, January 30, 1990; WCF, remarks to the Jordan Committee, November 10, 1972, subgroup 1, ser. 1, file entitled "Medical Education, Aug–Nov 1972," WCF Papers, UA/UNC.

16. "Report of the Committee to Study the Request of East Carolina for a Second Year of Medical Education," subgroup 1, ser. 1, file entitled "Medical Education, Dec 1972," WCF Papers, UA/UNC.

17. Statement of Robert B. Jordan III, January 2, 1973, in Board of Governors minutes,

January 2, 1973 (subgroup 2, ser. 1, subser. 3), and Board of Governors minutes, February 9, March 15, April 15, May 11, 1973, subgroup 2, ser. 1, subser. 3, WCF Papers, UA/UNC. The other members of the panel were Kenneth Crispell of the University of Virginia Medical School; Kurt Deuschle, professor of community medicine at Mt. Sinai Medical School; Lloyd C. Elam, president of Meharry Medical College; F. Carter Pannill, vice president for health sciences at SUNY-Buffalo; and Robert S. Stone, vice president for medical affairs at the University of New Mexico. Stone resigned from the panel in May 1973 to become director of the National Institutes of Health.

18. Raymond Dawson, memorandum for the record, January 31, 1973 (subgroup 1, ser. 2, file entitled "Health Affairs Program: Medical Education: ECU Medical School, 1973–1976"), and Dawson to WCF, January 31, 1973 (subgroup 1, ser. 1, file entitled "Medical Education, Jan–Mar 1973"), WCF Papers, UA/UNC.

19. Monroe complained about the "unfair and prejudicial" way in which the press covered the story. Edwin Monroe to William A. Dees Jr., April 30, 1973, subgroup 1, ser. 1, file entitled "Medical Education, Apr–June 1973," ibid.

20. "Accrediting Unit Hits UNC-ECU Med Plan" (April 26, 1973), "ECU School of Medicine Found Weak" (April 27, 1973), and Ferrel Guillory, "Med School Accord Set by UNC, ECU" (April 28, 1973), *Raleigh News and Observer*, WCF to the Board of Governors, April 30, 1973, subgroup 1, ser. 1, file entitled "Apr–June 1973," WCF Papers, UA/UNC.

21. Statements by Jenkins and Monroe, in *Raleigh News and Observer*, April 28, 1973.

22. Interview with Levine, February 23, 1991.

23. Ibid.

24. Hamilton C. Horton Jr., statement before Bennett Panel, July 16, 1973, subgroup 1, ser. 1, file entitled "Medical Education, July–Sept 1973," WCF Papers, UA/UNC; interview with Edwin Monroe, June 18, 1991; interview with William Laupus, December 3, 1991. WCF, hearing of Horton's statement, commented that he would "talk with him right away because he obviously is creating profound difficulty for us." WCF to Archie K. Davis, July 17, 1973, subgroup 1, ser. 1, file entitled "Medical Education, July–Sept 1973," WCF Papers.

25. Wallace R. Wooles to Levine (September 4, 1973), Ivan L. Bennett Jr. to Wooles (September 13, 1973), subgroup 1, ser. 1, file entitled "Medical Education, July–Sept 1973," WCF Papers, UA/UNC.

26. Interview with Levine, February 23, 1991.

27. "A Statewide Plan for Medical Education in North Carolina," September 1973, subgroup 1, ser. 1, file entitled "Medical Education, July–Sept 1973," WCF Papers, UA/UNC.

28. "A Statewide Plan for Medical Education in North Carolina"; Board of Governors minutes, September 14, 1973, subgroup 2, ser. 2, subser. 3, file entitled "Planning Committee: General, 1971," WCF Papers, UA/UNC; interview with Levine, February 23, 1991.

29. Interview with Laupus, December 3, 1991; interview with Clark Kerr, April 6, 1990; interview with WCF, February 25, 1991; "A Statewide Plan for Medical Education in North Carolina"; interview with I. Glenn Wilson, May 6, 1991.

30. Board of Governors minutes, September 27, 1973, subgroup 2, ser. 2, WCF Papers, UA/UNC.

31. "A Minority Report from the Board of Governors to the Members of the General Assembly," December 7, 1973, subgroup 1, ser. 1, file entitled "Medical Education, Dec 1973," ibid.

32. Angela Davis, "UNC Panel OK's Medical Report," and Ferrel Guillory, "ECU Board Head Challenges Report," *Raleigh News and Observer*, September 28, 1973.

33. "Recommended Actions Consistent with the Report of the Panel of Medical Consultants," November 16, 1973, subgroup 1, ser. 1, file entitled "Medical Education, November 1973," WCF Papers, UA/UNC.

34. Board of Governors minutes, November 16, 1973, subgroup 2, ser. 2, subser. 3, ibid; "A Minority Report from the Board of Governors to the Members of the General Assembly," December 7, 1973, subgroup 1, ser. 1, file entitled "Medical Education, Dec 1973," ibid.

35. King, *Multicampus University of North Carolina*, pp. 184–85; interview with Monroe, June 18, 1991; Fordham, "A Report to President Friday on Planning for the Implementation of Section 46," subgroup 1, ser. 1, file entitled "Medical Education, Nov 1974," WCF Papers, UA/UNC; Ferrel Guillory, "Unit Urges ECU Med Expansion," *Raleigh News and Observer*, December 13, 1973.

36. On February 3, 1974, the *Raleigh News and Observer* reported that 69 legislators in the house opposed expansion of the one-year program, 64 favored it, and 35 were undecided. In the senate, 21 favored the ECU position and 17 the university position, while 12 were undecided. "Assembly Tally Close on ECU," ibid. See also Jack Scism, "Med School Compromise Is Unlikely," *Greensboro Daily News*, February 3, 1974.

37. Ferrel Guillory, "Governor's UNC Stand Low Key" (February 17, 1974), and Leslie Wayne, "ECU Med Plan Backing Seen" (April 17, 1973), *Raleigh News and Observer*.

38. Leslie Wayne, "ECU Referendum Pushed in House" (February 6, 1974), Ferrel Guillory, "Ramsey Role Weighed in ECU Med Dispute" (February 7, 1974), Wayne, "ECU Referendum Stymied by Panel" (February 7, 1974), Claude Sitton, "ECU Issue Getting Too Hot to Handle" (February 10, 1974), and Wayne and Guillory, "Powerful ECU Proponents Lead Med School Drive" (March 3, 1974), *Raleigh News and Observer*; Jack Scism, "Ramsey Revives ECU Bond Idea" (February 6, 1974), and Scism, "UNC Forces Win Med School Test" (February 8, 1974), *Greensboro Daily News*. Ramsey and Watkins were apparently prepared to announce, had they not suffered the setback in committee, that a two-year program at ECU had been authorized and that a $50 million bond referendum would implement this decision. Scism, "ECU Med School a Question of How Much and When?," *Greensboro Daily News*, February 8, 1974.

39. Leslie Wayne, "UNC Unit Reaffirms Med Stand," *Raleigh News and Observer*, February 9, 1974; Jack Scism, "Legislators May Have Begun to Untangle ECU 'Thicket,'" *Greensboro Daily News*, February 9, 1974.

40. Leslie Wayne, "Accord on ECU Pursued," *Raleigh News and Observer*, February 11, 1974; Jack Scism, "Meeting Fails to Resolve ECU Issue," *Greensboro Daily News*, February 11, 1974. The participants in the February 10 meeting were UNC Board of Governors members Robert Jordan, William Johnson, Reginald McCoy, and David Whichard; Senators Eddie Knox of Mecklenburg County, Gordon Allen of Person County, Kenneth Royall of Durham, and Thomas E. Strickland of Wayne County; and Representatives Jay Huskins of Iredell County, John Gamble of Lincoln County, Larry Cobb of Mecklenburg County, and George Miller of Durham. Scism, "Legislators May Have Begun to Untangle ECU 'Thicket,'" *Greensboro Daily News*, February 9, 1974.

41. Leslie Wayne, "Joint Panel Delays Hearings on ECU," *Raleigh News and Observer*, February 12, 1974; Jack Scism, "Final Try at ECU Compromise Slated," *Greensboro Daily News*, February 13, 1974; Wayne, "ECU Compromise Efforts Abandoned," *Raleigh News and Observer*, February 15, 1974; Scism, "Medical School Issue Coming to Showdown," *Greensboro Daily News*, February 15, 1974.

42. Jack Aulis, "Med School Issue Dominates, Colors 1974 Assembly" (February 15, 1974), Leslie Wayne, "Hearings Begin on ECU" (February 20, 1974), Wayne, "Both Sides Air Views at Hearings on ECU" (February 21, 1974), Wayne, "Joint Panel Puts Off Vote on Med School" (February 22, 1974), "CAL May Back ECU Med Plan" (February 14, 1974), "God Unlikely to Settle ECU Issue," editorial (February 16, 1974), Ernie Wood, "Wake President Supports UNC Board" (February 19, 1974), and "WCU Teachers Back ECU Medical School" (February 21, 1974), *Raleigh News and Observer*; Harvey Harris, "CAL Stand Resurrects Tax Issue," *Greensboro Daily News*, February 25, 1974; "Scott Urges Flexibility on Issue" (February 22, 1974), "Hunt and Scott Just Pretending" (February 26, 1974), and "Scott Hits Board's Stand" (February 26, 1974), *Raleigh News and Observer*.

43. "Under the Dome," *Raleigh News and Observer*, February 26, 1974.

44. Jack Scism, "Legislators Introduce Another Bill on ECU," *Greensboro Daily News*, February 7, 1974; Leslie Wayne, "ECU Expansion OKd by Panel" (February 27, 1974), "ECU Vote Disappoints Governor" (February 27, 1974), and "Time for Med School Reflection," editorial (March 1, 1974), *Raleigh News and Observer*; Jack Scism, "ECU Med School Compromise Bill May Win Favor" (February 26, 1974), Scism, "Joint Committee Gives ECU Key Victory on Med School" (February 27, 1974), and Scism, "ECU Conflict May be Over" (March 3, 1974), *Greensboro Daily News*.

45. Leslie Wayne, "Quiet Prevails on ECU Front" (February 28, 1974), Wayne and Ferrel Guillory, "Powerful ECU Proponents Lead Med School Drive" (March 3, 1974), "Bennett: ECU Med Plans Not Opposed by Governor" (February 28, 1974), and Wayne, "UNC Quits Fight on Med School" (March 9, 1974), *Raleigh News and Observer*; Jack Scism, "UNC Board Reconciled to Decision," *Greensboro Daily News*, March 9, 1974; Leslie Wayne, "State Budget Adopted," *Raleigh News and Observer*, April 6, 1974.

46. Interview with Raymond Dawson, January 30, 1990; WCF to Jenkins, April 30, 1974, subgroup 1, ser. 1, file entitled "Medical Education, Mar–May 1974," WCF Papers, UA/UNC.

47. Jenkins to WCF, May 22, 1974 (subgroup 1, ser. 1, file entitled "Medical Education, Mar–May 1974"), and Board of Governors minutes, May 10, 1974 (subgroup 2, ser. 2, subser. 3), WCF Papers, UA/UNC. Friday wrote to the sponsors of the act, Ralph H. Scott and Carl J. Stewart Jr., asking specifically if the legislature's intent was to establish a four-year program, and they responded that it was not. Scott and Stewart to WCF, May 23, 1974, subgroup 1, ser. 1, file entitled "Medical Education, Mar–May 1974," ibid.

48. "ECU Is Told to Plan for Second Med Year" (May 11, 1974), and "UNC, ECU Told to Plan Med Expansion Jointly" (June 15, 1974), *Raleigh News and Observer*.

49. Board of Governors minutes, July 12, 1974, subgroup 2, series 2, subser. 3, WCF Papers, UA/UNC; Jenkins to WCF (July 8, 12, 1974), WCF to Jenkins (July 16, 1974), Fordham to WCF (July 15, 1974), and WCF to Jenkins, Fordham, and Taylor (July 16, 1974), subgroup 1, ser. 1, file entitled "Medical Education, June–Aug 1974," ibid.

50. WCF, memorandum of record, July 25, 1974, subgroup 1, ser. 1, file entitled "Medical Education, June–Aug 1974," ibid.

51. Fordham, "Dean's Log on the Planning Effort for the Implementation of Section 46, July 17, 1974–November 7, 1974," entry for July 28, 1974, subgroup 1, ser. 1, file entitled "Medical Education, Nov 1974," ibid.

52. "ECU Med Director Bypass Is Alleged," *Raleigh News and Observer*, July 30, 1974.

53. Steve Adams, "ECU Accord Remains Elusive," *Raleigh News and Observer*, July 31, 1974; Fordham log, July 30–31, 1974, subgroup 1, ser. 1, file entitled "Medical Education, Nov 1974,"

WCF Papers, UA/UNC; "Jenkins Chided on ECU Med School Role," *Raleigh News and Observer*, August 1, 1974.

54. "Jenkins Chided on ECU Med School Role"; WCF, memorandum of record, July 30, 1974, subgroup 1, ser. 1, file entitled "Medical Education, June–Aug 1974," WCF Papers, UA/UNC.

55. WCF, memorandum of record, July 31, 1974; Fordham log, August 1–2, 1974, subgroup 1, ser. 1, file entitled "Medical Education, Nov 1974," WCF Papers, UA/UNC; "Jenkins Chided on ECU Med School Role"; Steve Adams, "ECU Med Dean Quits," *Raleigh News and Observer*, August 2, 1974.

56. Adams, "ECU Med Dean Quits."

57. Jenkins, statement, August 1, 1974 (file entitled "Medical Education, June–Aug 1974"), and Fordham log, July 28, 30, 31, August 1, 2, 21, September 16, 1974 (file entitled "Medical Education, Nov 1974"), subgroup 1, ser. 1, WCF Papers, UA/UNC; Fordham, "A Report to President Friday on Planning for the Implementation of Section 46"; Steve Adams, "Hospital Is Reluctant to Give Space to ECU" (October 1, 1974), and "Reluctance Slows Med School Plan" (October 6, 1974), *Raleigh News and Observer*.

58. Hunt to WCF (August 2, 1974), WCF to Hunt (August 9, 1974), and WCF to William A. Dees Jr. (August 19, 1974), subgroup 1, ser. 1, file entitled "Medical Education, June–Aug 1974," WCF Papers, UA/UNC.

59. Interview with William Cromartie, May 23, 1991; interview with Cecil Sheps, May 15, 1991; interview with Fordham, January 25, 1991; Monroe to Jenkins (August 30, 1974) and unsigned memorandum of meeting (September 10, 1974), subgroup 1, ser. 1, file entitled "Medical Education, Sept–Oct 1974," WCF Papers, UA/UNC.

60. Daniel T. Young to Fordham, October 4, 1974, subgroup 1, ser. 1, file entitled "Medical Education, Sept–Oct 1974," WCF Papers, UA/UNC; King, *Multicampus University of North Carolina*, p. 188; Leo W. Jenkins, "Mandate on ECU Medical School Must Be Carried Out," *Raleigh News and Observer*, October 9, 1974.

61. Fordham log, October 7, 1974, subgroup 1, ser. 1, file entitled "Medical Education, Nov 1974," WCF Papers, UA/UNC; interview with Wilson, May 6, 1991.

62. WCF, "The Expansion of the East Carolina University School of Medicine: Recommendations of the President to the Committee on Educational Planning, Policies, and Programs and the Committee on Budget and Finance," subgroup 1, ser. 1, file entitled "Medical Education, Nov 1974," WCF Papers, UA/UNC.

63. Steve Adams, "UNC Panels Approve 4-Year ECU Med Unit," *Raleigh News and Observer*, November 9, 1974; Board of Governors minutes, November 15, 1974, subgroup 2, ser. 2, subser. 3, WCF Papers, UA/UNC; King, *Multicampus University of North Carolina*, p. 192; Steve Adams, "ECU Medical School Okd as Price Tag Soars," *Raleigh News and Observer*, November 16, 1974.

64. Interviews with WCF, February 25, 1991, November 24, 1992.

65. Interview with William Laupus, December 3, 1991; interview with WCF, November 24, 1992.

66. Interview with Wilson, May 6, 1991.

67. Interview with Joyner, January 18, 1991; interview with R. D. McMillan, May 14, 1991.

68. Interview with Sheps, May 15, 1991; interview with Wilson, May 6, 1991; interview with Cromartie, May 23, 1991; interview with Fordham, January 25, 1991.

69. Interviews with WCF, February 25, 1991, November 24, 1992.

1. North Carolina State Board of Higher Education, *Planning for Higher Education*, p. 202. The five TBIs were Elizabeth City State University, Fayetteville State University, North Carolina A&T State University (Greensboro), North Carolina Central University (Durham), and Winston-Salem State University.

2. Robert B. Watson Diary, November 25, 1963, Rockefeller Foundation Archives RG 2 (General Correspondence, 1963), box GC 462, file entitled "University of North Carolina – Friday," RAC; WCF to Kenneth R. Williams, April 17, 1964, and "Summary of a Conference between Officials of the University of North Carolina and the Presidents of the Five North Carolina State-Supported Colleges That Are Predominately Negro in Enrollment and Faculty, May 13, 1964," subgroup 1, ser. 1, file entitled "Black Institutions: Relations with, 1964," WCF Papers, UA/UNC. Ida moved her church membership, while Bill did not. Interview with IHF, October 15, 1990, SOHP; interview with WCF, February 20, 1991.

3. North Carolina State BHE, *State Supported Traditionally Negro Colleges in North Carolina*.

4. North Carolina State BHE, *Planning for Higher Education*, pp. 206–7.

5. Orfield, *Must We Bus?*

6. Crystal C. Lloyd, "Adams v. Califano: A Case Study in the Politics of Education," p. 50, working paper for the Sloan Commission on Government and Higher Education, January 1978, subgroup 1, ser. 1, file entitled "Sloan Commission: General, Jan. 1978," WCF Papers, UA/UNC; interview with F. Peter Libassi, May 16, 1991.

7. King, *Multicampus University of North Carolina*, pp. 204–5; Lloyd, "Adams v. Califano," pp. 50–52; Jack Childs, "Scott Gets Integration Order," *Raleigh News and Observer*, February 20, 1970. Panetta sent letters to Arkansas, Florida, Georgia, Louisiana, Maryland, Mississippi, North Carolina, Oklahoma, Pennsylvania, and Virginia. For Panetta's account of his stormy tenure as OCR director, see Panetta and Gall, *Bring Us Together*.

8. "Panetta Resignation Described as Forced," *Raleigh News and Observer*, February 20, 1970; Robert Novak and Rowland Evans, "HEW's Panetta Hounded Out of Office," *Greensboro Daily News*, February 21, 1970; interview with Martin Gerry, August 28, 1991; *Adams* v. *Richardson*, 351 F. Supp. 636 (1972).

9. Severinson wrote a separate letter regarding each campus. Severinson to WCF, January 26, 28, March 11, 17, 25, 1970, UNC-HEW Case File, GA; Susan Jetton, "HEW: Recruit More Blacks," *Charlotte Observer*, February 6, 1970. Watts Hill Jr. subsequently claimed a major role in Severinson's intervention. Hill, testimony and deposition, UNC-HEW Case File.

10. Actually, Scott possessed no direct authority over the state's system of public higher education, then on the verge of major change. By the fall of 1970, no one in the governor's office or in the BHE had composed a reply to Panetta, and his letter went unanswered. OCR regional officials, meanwhile, lacked adequate staff or bureaucratic resolve to pursue the case. Scott to Eloise Severinson, June 10, 1970, and J. Stanley Pottinger, affidavit, UNC-HEW Case File, GA.

11. WCF to Severinson (April 13, 1970) and Severinson to WCF (July 9, 1970), UNC-HEW Case File, GA; Executive Committee minutes, March 13, July 10, September 11, 1970, subgroup 2, ser. 1, WCF Papers, UA/UNC; WCF to Horace Bohannon, August 13, 1970, UNC-HEW Case File.

12. Lloyd, "Adams v. Califano," pp. ii, 50–52, 57–58; Crow, Escott, and Hatley, *History of African Americans*, pp. 174–75.

13. *Adams* v. *Richardson*, 351 F. Supp. 636 (1972) and 356 F. Supp. 92 (1973).

14. Ibid., 480 F.2d 1150 (1973); interview with John H. Pratt, April 18, 1991.

15. Interview with Holmes, April 18, 1991; Holmes to WCF, March 27, May 21, 1973, UNC-HEW Case File, GA.

16. Holmes to WCF, May 21, 1973, and Dawson, testimony, UNC-HEW Case File, GA.

17. Peter E. Holmes to James E. Holshouser, November 10, 1973, UNC-HEW Case File, GA; Jack Scism, "UNC Integration Plan Too Narrow" (November 14, 1973), and Don Hill, "N.C. Told to Revise Desegregation Plan" (November 14, 1973), *Greensboro Daily News*; Board of Governors minutes, November 16, 1973, subgroup 2, ser. 2, subser. 3, WCF Papers, UA/UNC; Sanders, "Questions Put to Mr. Holmes, Atlanta, 12–13 December 1973," subgroup 1, ser. 5, file entitled "HEW: Desegregation: UNC System: General, 1973–1980," WCF Papers.

18. King, *Multicampus University of North Carolina*, p. 209; interview with WCF, December 14, 1973, SOHP.

19. Citing recent efforts, which included "special assistance" appropriations to the TBIs by the General Assembly in the 1967–69 and 1969–71 bienniums, the plan also noted that North Carolina had appropriated $4 million for library improvement, $500,000 to strengthen administrative staffing, and $750,000 to help to equalize faculty salaries. The result was that the "popularly presumed disparity" in operating funds between TWIs and TBIs was "not so readily perceivable as has been supposed." *North Carolina State Plan*, pp. 77–78.

20. Angela Davis, "UNC Board Adopts New Racial Plan," *Raleigh News and Observer*, February 9, 1974; Jack Scism, "University Integration Plan Voted," *Greensboro Daily News*, February 9, 1974; interview with Martin Gerry, August 28, 1991; Sanders to WCF, January 19, February 28, 1974, subgroup 1, ser. 5, file entitled "HEW: Desegregation: UNC System: General, 1973–1980," WCF Papers, UA/UNC; interview with Holmes, April 18, 1991.

21. Lawrence Cooper to WCF (January 7, February 12, 1974), WCF to Cooper (January 11, 1974), Cooper to Holshouser (February 11, 1974), and "A Statement on Dismantling of Higher Education (Black Perspective) by North Carolina Alumni and Friends Coalition" (February 1974), UNC-HEW Case File, GA; Sanders to WCF, February 28, 1974, subgroup 1, ser. 5, file entitled "HEW: Desegregation: UNC System: General, 1973–1980," WCF Papers, UA/UNC.

22. Chambers, deposition, UNC-HEW Case File, GA. On Chambers and the *Swann* case, see Douglas, "Changing Times."

23. Interview with Philip Carson, July 18, 1991; Chambers, deposition, UNC-HEW Case File, GA.

24. Board of Governors minutes, February 8, 1974, subgroup 2, ser. 2, subser. 3, WCF Papers, UA/UNC; Chambers deposition, July 3, 1980, UNC-HEW Case File, GA; Davis, "UNC Board Adopts New Racial Plan"; interview with Julius L. Chambers, June 18, 1990. For another black critique, see Kelly Alexander Jr. to WCF, April 26, 1974, WCF Correspondence, GA.

25. "Office for Civil Rights Response to the *North Carolina Plan for the Further Elimination of Racial Duality in the Public Postsecondary Education Systems*, February 8, 1974," enclosed in Peter E. Holmes to James E. Holshouser Jr., April 24, 1974, UNC-HEW Case File, GA.

26. *North Carolina State Plan*, pp. 201–2.

27. "Office for Civil Rights Response to the *North Carolina Plan*"; Angela Davis, "UNC Anti-Bias Plan Rejected," *Raleigh News and Observer*, April 27, 1974.

28. Sanders to WCF (April 18, 1974) and WCF to the UNC chancellors (May 6, 1974), subgroup 1, ser. 5, file entitled "HEW: Desegregation: UNC System: General, 1973–1980," WCF Papers, UA/UNC; Ben E. Fountain Jr. to James E. Holshouser Jr., June 10, 1974, UNC-HEW Case File, GA.

29. Interview with Dawson, February 4, 1991; interview with Holmes, April 18, 1991; interview with WCF, February 20, 1991.

30. WCF to Holmes, June 18, 1974, enclosed in Holshouser to Holmes, June 18, 1974, UNC-HEW Case File, GA; Don Hill, "College Integration Plans OK in Eight States – HEW," *Greensboro Daily News,* June 22, 1974.

31. Holmes to Holshouser, July 19, 1974, UNC-HEW Case File, GA; Angela Davis, "HEW Approves UNC Plan," *Raleigh News and Observer,* June 22, 1974.

32. King, *Multicampus University of North Carolina,* pp. 198–99; *Atkins* v. *Scott,* at 874–75.

33. Cole, "Analysis of Alternate Locations for a School of Veterinary Medicine in North Carolina," October 29, 1974, subgroup 1, ser. 5, file entitled "Veterinary School: Cole Report, 1974," WCF Papers, UA/UNC.

34. Interview with Dawson, February 4, 1991; Thomas to WCF, March 25, 1975, subgroup 1, ser. 5, file entitled "Veterinary School: HEW Involvement, 1974–1975," WCF Papers, UA/UNC; King, *Multicampus University of North Carolina,* pp. 199–200.

35. Interview with Dawson, February 4, 1991; Board of Governors minutes, November 15, 1974, subgroup 2, ser. 2, subser. 3, WCF Papers, UA/UNC; William H. Thomas to WCF (October 18, November 14, 1974) and Dawson, testimony, UNC-HEW Case File, GA; Steve Adams, "Vet School Is Approved; No Site Yet," *Raleigh News and Observer,* November 16, 1974; Ned Cline, "UNC Board Delays Action on Vet School," *Greensboro Daily News,* November 16, 1974.

36. Thomas to WCF (December 16, 1974), WCF to Thomas (December 6, 1974), and Thomas to WCF (December 16, 1974), UNC-HEW Case File, GA.

37. Steve Adams, "UNC Board Approves Vet School for NCSU," *Raleigh News and Observer,* December 19, 1974; *Atkins* v. *Scott,* at 876; King, *Multicampus University of North Carolina,* p. 201.

38. Lloyd, "Adams v. Califano," pp. 70–76; interview with Cleon Thompson, January 30, 1991; interview with Joyner, January 18, 1991.

39. Thomas to WCF, March 25, 1975, subgroup 1, ser. 5, file entitled "Veterinary School: HEW Involvement, 1974–1975," WCF Papers, UA/UNC.

40. Interviews with Gerry, August 6, 28, 1991.

41. Interview with R. Claire Guthrie, August 5, 1991; interview with Gerry, August 6, 1991.

42. Interview with Guthrie, August 5, 1991.

43. Sanders to WCF, April 29, 1975, subgroup 1, ser. 5, file entitled "HEW: Desegregation: UNC System: General, 1973–1980," WCF Papers, UA/UNC; interview with Gerry, August 28, 1991.

44. Interview with Gerry, August 28, 1991; *Mandel* v. *U.S. Department of Health, Education, and Welfare.*

45. Daniel C. Hoover, "UNC Special Target for HEW" (August 7, 1975), and Steve Adams, "UNC Denies Reluctance to Integrate" (August 20, 1975), *Raleigh News and Observer;* Rick Gray, "HEW Plans to Sue UNC," *Greensboro Daily News,* August 6, 1975; interview with Dawson, February 4, 1991.

46. "UNC Is Threatened with Cutoff of Aid," *Raleigh News and Observer,* August 6, 1975; Thomas J. White to WCF, August 6, 1975, WCF Correspondence, GA; Helms to WCF, May 2, 1975, subgroup 1, ser. 5, file entitled "Veterinary School: HEW Involvement, 1974–1975," WCF Papers, UA/UNC.

47. Carson to WCF, August 7, 1975, WCF Correspondence, GA.

48. Hoover, "UNC Special Target for HEW"; "Remarks by President William Friday on The Report of the University of North Carolina to Governor Holshouser in Response to the July 31, 1975 Letter from Martin Gerry, Acting Director of the Office of Civil Rights of the Department of Health, Education, and Welfare, to the Governor," August 19, 1975, subgroup 1, ser. 5, file entitled "Veterinary School: HEW Involvement, 1974–1975," WCF Papers, UA/UNC.

49. Steve Adams, "UNC Denies Reluctance to Integrate," *Raleigh News and Observer*, August 20, 1975; Paul Bernish, "U.S., UNC Clash over Vet School," *Charlotte Observer*, August 20, 1975.

50. "Call It Power: UNC Knows the Word," editorial, *Charlotte Observer*, August 22, 1975.

51. Steve Adams, "HEW Position on UNC Is Unchanged," *Raleigh News and Observer*, August 22, 1975.

52. WCF to McKnight (August 22, 1975) and WCF to Mathews (August 22, 1975), WCF Correspondence, GA; WCF, memorandum of record (August 22, 1975), and McKinney to WCF (September 12, 1975), subgroup 1, ser. 5, file entitled "Veterinary School: HEW Involvement, 1974–1975," WCF Papers, UA/UNC. On Friday's relations with Mathews, see Ned Cline, "Shorter Route Beckons in UNC-HEW Dispute," *Greensboro Daily News*, August 20, 1975.

53. Interview with Gerry, August 28, 1991. Gerry described three people with whom he had the most contact: Jim Cannon, chairman of the Domestic Policy Council; Dick Parsons, White House general counsel; and Paul O'Neill, deputy director of OMB.

54. Interview with Gerry, August 28, 1991; interview with Guthrie, August 5, 1991; interview with Holmes, April 18, 1991; Holmes, letter to the editor, *Washington Star*, September 23, 1975. Holmes was responding to an editorial by Ed Yoder, "The Lash of the Law," *Washington Star*, September 5, 1975. See also Yoder to WCF, September 24, 1975, subgroup 1, ser. 5, file entitled "HEW: Desegregation: UNC System: General, 1973–1980," WCF Papers, UA/UNC.

55. Board of Governors minutes, September 26, 1975, subgroup 2, ser. 2, subser. 3, WCF Papers, UA/UNC; WCF, memorandum of record, September 22, 1975, WCF Correspondence, GA; interview with Guthrie, August 5, 1991.

56. Jack Betts, "HEW Quits Vet School Fight," *Greensboro Daily News*, October 3, 1975; Shirley Elder, "HEW Backs Off on Vet School," *Raleigh News and Observer*, October 3, 1975; interview with Guthrie, August 5, 1991. Holmes took the same position in Holmes to James T. Broyhill, November 3, 1975, UNC-HEW Case File, GA.

57. WCF to Holmes, October 3, 1975, WCF Correspondence, GA.

58. Dowdy statement, October 6, 1975, enclosed in Dowdy to WCF, October 10, 1975, subgroup 1, ser. 5, file entitled "Veterinary School: NC A&T University Proposal, 1974–1975," WCF Papers, UA/UNC; Steve Adams, "Motion Is Filed to Block Vet School Plan," *Raleigh News and Observer*, December 20, 1974.

59. *Atkins v. Scott*. Justice Harrison L. Winter, it should be noted, wrote a strong dissenting opinion.

60. Interview with Dawson, February 4, 1991.

61. Interview with Guthrie, August 5, 1991.

62. Ibid.

63. Interview with Julius L. Chambers, June 18, 1990.

64. Interview with Richard H. Robinson, June 3, 1991.

65. Ibid.; interview with Roy Carroll, August 8, 1991.

66. Interview with Gerry, August 28, 1991.

67. Interview with Holmes, April 18, 1991; interview with Guthrie, August 5, 1991.

1. Dawson, speech at University Day, University of North Carolina at Chapel Hill, October 12, 1981, North Carolina Collection, UNC–Chapel Hill.

2. Califano, *Governing America*, p. 244.

3. According to Cleon Thompson, UNC was "still number ONE" with Gerry. Dawson, deposition and testimony, UNC-HEW Case File, GA; WCF to Mathews (November 5, 1975) and Sanders to "all hands" (October 30, 1975), WCF Correspondence, GA; interview with Guthrie, August 5, 1991; Cleon Thompson to WCF, Dawson, Joyner, and Sanders (February 3, 1976) and Peyton R. Neal Jr. to WCF (February 10, 1976), WCF Correspondence (Neal was an N.C. State and UNC law school graduate); WCF, "Remarks by President William Friday to the Board of Governors on *A Comparative Study of the Five Historically Black Constituent Institutions of the University of North Carolina*," subgroup 1, ser. 1, file entitled "Black Institutions: Traditionally Black Institutions, 1973–1976," WCF Papers, UA/UNC. In November 1975 Martin Gerry, accompanied by OCR lawyers Claire Guthrie and Colquitt Meachum, visited North Carolina for a site visit that Friday, writing to David Mathews, characterized as "most constructive" and "most helpful." Under the direction of Ray Coble, who was serving as John Sanders's statistical expert at UNC's planning division, the university developed a regular, and apparently acceptable, system of reporting desegregation data to OCR. Following their presentation of a semiannual report to OCR officials in Washington on January 30, 1976, Gerry informed UNC that the university's performance was so good that it would be unnecessary for OCR to prepare a written evaluation. Its method of data collection, he stated, would serve as a model for other states. Gerry went so far as to say that Maryland higher education officials, then embroiled in the *Mandel* case, should consult with Bill Friday about "possible improvement" in their relationship with HEW. In early February 1976 Colquitt Meachum described UNC as having "the best" administrative system that she had encountered during her tenure at OCR.

4. *A Comparative Study of the Five Historically Black Constituent Institutions of the University of North Carolina*, June 11, 1976, copy in SCUA/UNCG.

5. Ibid.

6. "Motion for Further Relief and Points and Authorities in Support Thereof," August 1, 1975, UNC-HEW Case File, GA.

7. On September 26, 1975, a special board committee composed of John R. Jordan Jr., Thomas J. White, and William Johnson recommended intervention and the hiring of private counsel. UNC officials then sought the assistance of Williams and Jensen, a Washington law firm that had litigated suits by school districts fighting federally mandated public school desegregation. On November 5 a delegation composed of board chairman Bill Dees, Johnson, Dick Robinson, and Assistant Attorney General Andrew Vanore conferred with attorneys J. D. Williams and Robert E. Jensen for three hours in their Washington offices. Jensen argued strongly against intervention. North Carolina was not then under Judge Pratt's supervision; should UNC enter the case, the court might issue a binding order. Based on that advice, the Board of Governors decided against litigation, at least for the time being. Board of Governors minutes, September 26, October 24, November 14, 1975, subgroup 2, ser. 2, subser. 3, WCF Papers, UA/UNC; Richard H. Robinson to Special Board of Governors Committee on HEW Litigation (November 12, 1975) and Jensen to Vanore (November 11, 1975), WCF Correspondence, GA.

8. Dawson, testimony, UNC-HEW Case File, GA; Jean Fairfax to participants in Southern Education Foundation Consultation, January 18, 1977, WCF Correspondence, GA. According

to UNC administrator Ray Coble, who attended the meeting, Gerry told of recent discussions with LDF representatives. As litigants in the *Adams* case, LDF attorneys had become familiar figures to Gerry and Holmes; Gerry told Coble that he had spent "more time dealing with" Julius Chambers "than any other single person I know." Ray Coble to WCF, December 16, 1976, WCF Correspondence, GA.

9. Ray Coble to Cleon Thompson, December 16, 1976, WCF Correspondence, GA.

10. WCF to Gerry, December 17, 1976, ibid.

11. Gerry, deposition, UNC-HEW Case File, GA.

12. Dawson, deposition, ibid.; Richard H. Robinson to WCF, January 17, 1977, WCF Correspondence, GA; interview with Pratt, April 18, 1991; Jean Fairfax to participants in Southern Education Foundation Consultation, November 1976, January 8, 1977, WCF Correspondence; Lloyd, "Adams v. Califano," pp. 77–80.

13. Pratt, second supplemental order, *Adams v. Califano.*

14. "Brief of the National Association for Equal Opportunity in Higher Education," March 21, 1976, enclosed in Charles Lyons to WCF, March 24, 1976, WCF Correspondence, GA.

15. "Statement by the National Association for Equal Opportunity in Higher Education," March 3, 1977, UNC-HEW Case File, GA.

16. Pratt, second supplemental order, *Adams v. Califano*; Lloyd, "Adams v. Califano," p. 84; Ferrel Guillory, "Desegregation Plan of UNC 'Not Adequate,'" *Raleigh News and Observer*, April 2, 1977; Rick Gray, "Judge Rules UNC Still Discriminates," *Greensboro Daily News*, April 2, 1977; Ned Cline, "Judge Rules UNC Plan Hurts Blacks," *Charlotte Observer*, April 2, 1977.

17. WCF, remarks to the Board of Governors, April 8, 1977, WCF Correspondence, GA.

18. Califano, *Governing America*, pp. 212–19.

19. Ibid.; interview with Libassi, May 16, 1991. Richard Beattie later said that OCR during the Nixon-Ford years was always represented to him as a "very demoralized place" because "they just did not do anything." Interview with Beattie, June 26, 1991.

20. Interview with Beattie, June 26, 1991.

21. Arline Burstein Mendelson Pacht, deposition, and Libassi, affidavit, UNC-HEW Case File, GA.

22. Mary Frances Berry, deposition, Harold Howe, deposition, Pacht, deposition, and F. Peter Libassi, affidavit, ibid.; interview with Breneman, May 10, 1991.

23. Interview with Breneman, May 10, 1991; interview with Libassi, May 16, 1991; interview with Tatel, August 7, 1991.

24. Pacht, deposition, Berry, deposition, and Tatel, deposition, UNC-HEW Case File, GA.

25. Interview with Boyer, May 9, 1990.

26. Interview with Libassi, May 16, 1991.

27. Tatel, deposition, UNC-HEW Case File, GA; Lloyd, "Adams v. Califano," pp. 49–50; Lee E. Monroe, "A Profile of North Carolina Alumni and Friends Coalition," attached to John T. Caldwell to WCF, March 25, 1977, WCF Correspondence, GA; Tatel, testimony, UNC-HEW Case File.

28. Libassi to WCF (April 7, 1977) and WCF to Libassi (April 12, 1977), WCF Correspondence, GA; Libassi, affidavit, UNC-HEW Case File, GA; interview with Libassi, May 16, 1991.

29. Orleans, deposition, and Dawson, deposition and testimony, UNC-HEW Case File, GA; interview with Dawson, February 4, 1991.

30. Interview with Orleans, May 17, 1991; Dawson, deposition, UNC-HEW Case File, GA.

31. Libassi, affidavit, UNC-HEW Case File, GA.

32. Interview with Breneman, May 10, 1991.

33. Interview with Tatel, August 7, 1991.

34. Interview with Orleans, May 17, 1991.

35. Dawson, testimony, UNC-HEW Case File, GA; interview with Dawson, February 4, 1991.

36. Interview with Dawson, February 4, 1991. The dilemma, according to Friday's daughter, "cut right to the core." Interview with Mary Friday, October 4, 1992.

37. This would have been 50 percent of "parity" – that is, a situation in which black and white freshmen attended TWIs at the same proportion. Parity would have meant a 480 percent increase in black entering freshmen and transfers at TWIs by 1983.

38. "HEW to Tell UNC Racial Plan Today," *Raleigh News and Observer*, July 5, 1977; Pacht, deposition, UNC-HEW Case File, GA; Califano, *Governing America*, pp. 246–50; Dawson, deposition, and WCF, affidavit, UNC-HEW Case File.

39. Interview with WCF, February 20, 1991; Ferrel Guillory, "Adopt Race Plan, HEW Tells UNC," *Raleigh News and Observer*, July 6, 1977; Ned Cline, "UNC Given Guidelines on Blacks," *Charlotte Observer*, July 6, 1977; Dawson, deposition and testimony, UNC-HEW Case File, GA.

40. Steve Adams, "Black Recruitment Seen as Necessary" (July 6, 1977), and Adams, "Friday Ready to Fight Rules Despite Shift" (July 7, 1977), *Raleigh News and Observer*.

41. Dawson, testimony, UNC-HEW Case File, GA.

42. "Statement of President Friday to the Planning Committee, 14 August 1977," subgroup 1, ser. 1, file entitled "Black Institutions: Traditionally Black Institutions, 1977–1979," WCF Papers, UA/UNC; Dawson, testimony, UNC-HEW Case File, GA; Lloyd, "Adams v. Califano," p. 91.

43. Steve Adams, "UNC Board Members Criticize HEW's Plans," *Raleigh News and Observer*, July 8, 1977.

44. WCF, statement, Board of Governors minutes, July 15, 1977, subgroup 2, ser. 2, subser. 3, WCF Papers, UA/UNC; Rob Christiansen, "Friday: Race Can't Control UNC's Goals," and Ferrel Guillory, "UNC School Plan May Apply Elsewhere," *Raleigh News and Observer*, July 16, 1977; Jack Betts, "Friday Calls HEW Rules Double Standard for N.C.," *Greensboro Daily News*, July 16, 1977.

45. Tatel to WCF (July 7, 1977) and "General Outline, Meeting with HEW Officials" (July 20, 1977), WCF Correspondence, GA; Dawson, deposition, UNC-HEW Case File, GA; Lloyd, "Adams v. Califano," pp. 7–11; interview with Tatel, August 7, 1991.

46. Interview with Libassi, May 16, 1991; interview with Tatel, August 7, 1991; Ferrel Guillory, "HEW, UNC Officials Agree on Decision-Making Roles," *Raleigh News and Observer*, July 21, 1977; Jack Betts, "HEW Reported More Flexible on Integration," *Greensboro Daily News*, July 21, 1977; Lloyd, "Adams v. Califano," pp. 7–11; Tatel, testimony, UNC-HEW Case File, GA.

47. *Revised North Carolina State Plan . . . Phase II.*

48. In the fall of 1976, for example, about 27 percent of white students at North Carolina high schools enrolled as freshmen or transfers at the state's ten TWIs; the figure for blacks was slightly under 5 percent. A narrowing by 50 percent of this disparity would mean that over 11 percent of black high schools seniors would attend TWIs – a total of 2,288 black students or an increase of over 240 percent. A 150 percent increase would mean that 1,425 black entering freshmen and transfers attended TWIs by 1983.

49. *Revised North Carolina State Plan . . . Phase II.*

50. "Statement of President Friday to the Planning Committee, 14 August 1977," subgroup 1, ser. 1, file entitled "Black Institutions: Traditionally Black Institutions, 1977–1979," WCF Papers, UA/UNC; Rob Christiansen, "Friday Urges Rejection of Quota Plan," *Raleigh News and Observer,* August 15, 1977; Sherry Johnson, "UNC Unit Revises Desegregation Plan," *Greensboro Daily News,* August 15, 1977.

51. WCF to the Board of Governors, August 17, 1977, and Tatel, testimony, UNC-HEW Case File, GA; Raymond Dawson, "North Carolina's Response to the HEW Criteria," October 21, 1977, WCF Correspondence, GA; interview with Tatel, August 7, 1991.

52. WCF to Howe (August 18, 1977), Howe to WCF (August 25, 1977), and Jordan to Howe (August 25, 1977), WCF Correspondence, GA.

53. William A. Johnson, statement to the Board of Governors, August 22, 1977, ibid.

54. Board of Governors minutes, August 22, 1977, subgroup 2, ser. 2, subser. 3, WCF Papers, UA/UNC; "North Carolina University Clears Integration Plan," *New York Times,* August 23, 1977; "Chambers: Vestiges of Dual System Persist," *Greensboro Daily News,* September 26, 1980; Rob Christiansen, "Board OKs UNC Racial Plan," *Raleigh News and Observer,* August 23, 1977; Chambers, deposition, UNC-HEW Case File, GA; Sherry Johnson and Jack Betts, "UNC Plan Approved; Chambers Quits," *Greensboro Daily News,* August 23, 1977.

55. WCF to the Board of Governors (August 26, 1977), William A. Johnson to James B. Hunt (August 22, 1977), Hunt to Joseph A. Califano Jr. (September 2, 1977), and Orleans to WCF (August 25, 26 1977), WCF Correspondence, GA; Orleans, memo to the Adams File, October 18, 1977, WCF Correspondence, GA; Orleans, deposition, UNC-HEW Case File, GA.

56. "Initial Comments on the Revised North Carolina State Plan for the Further Elimination of Racial Duality in Public Higher Education, Phase Two, 1978–1983 (State Plan, Phase Two)," attached to David S. Tatel to WCF, November 7, 1977, WCF Correspondence, GA.

57. WCF, statement, attached to Board of Governors minutes, November 11, 1977, subgroup 2, ser. 2, subser. 3, WCF Papers, UA/UNC.

58. Dawson, testimony, UNC-HEW Case File, GA; interview with Dawson, June 20, 1991; WCF to Tatel, November 18, 1977, UNC-HEW Case File, GA.

59. The accounts of Tatel and Dawson differed significantly in one respect: Tatel asserted that Friday had maintained that autonomy on black campuses had impeded efforts to upgrade them. When this subsequently became public in the administrative hearings in September 1980, Friday, in the face of objections from TBI chancellors and trustees, strenuously denied it. Tatel, testimony, and Dawson, deposition, UNC-HEW Case File, GA.

60. WCF to members of the Planning Committee, November 28, 1977, WCF Correspondence, GA; "Comments on the North Carolina *State Plan, Phase II*" (December 5, 1977) and Tatel to L. H. Fountain (December 5, 1977), UNC-HEW Case File, GA; WCF, statement, Board of Governors minutes, December 30, 1977, subgroup 2, ser. 2, subser. 3, WCF Papers, UA/UNC.

61. Dawson, deposition, UNC-HEW Case File, GA; interview with Dawson, June 20, 1991. For OCR's comments, see Tatel to WCF, January 27, 1978, WCF Correspondence, GA.

62. Tatel, testimony, UNC-HEW Case File, GA; interview with Tatel, August 7, 1991.

63. Interview with Libassi, May 16, 1991; interview with Breneman, May 10, 1991; "Response to the Revised North Carolina State Plan for the Further Elimination of Racial Duality in Public Higher Education Systems, Phase II: 1978–1983," December 22, 1977, WCF Correspondence, GA; interview with Orleans, May 17, 1991.

64. Interview with Dawson, June 20, 1991; Dawson, deposition, January 16, 1981, UNC-HEW Case File, GA.

65. Interview with Dawson, June 20, 1991.

66. Ibid.; Friday to Tatel, January 23, 1978, WCF Correspondence, GA.

67. Friday to the Board of Governors, January 31, 1978, WCF Correspondence, GA; Tatel to Hunt, February 3, 1978, UNC-HEW Case File, GA; WCF, memorandum of record, February 2, 1978, WCF Correspondence, GA; interview with Libassi, May 16, 1991; WCF, statement, Board of Governors minutes, February 10, 1978, subgroup 2, ser. 2, subser. 3, WCF Papers, UA/UNC.

68. Geoffrey Mock, "Bill Friday Leaving Legacy at UNC," *Gastonia Gazette*, June 2, 1985. The story is repeated in David Perkins, "Conflict, Growth: A UNC Era Ends as Friday Retires," *Raleigh News and Observer*, March 2, 1986, in King, *Multicampus University of North Carolina*, p. 225, and in interview with WCF, February 20, 1991.

69. Interview with Libassi, May 16, 1991; interview with Breneman, May 10, 1991.

70. Interview with Tatel, August 7, 1991.

71. Interview with Gary Barnes, October 15, 1991; interview with Joseph J. Levin Jr., April 19, 1991.

72. Interview with Califano, April 5, 1991; Califano, *Governing America*, pp. 246–52; interview with Chambers, June 18, 1990; interview with Yoder, April 19, 1991.

73. Interview with Levin, April 19, 1991.

CHAPTER 11

1. Jimmy Carter, according to Califano, favored increasing the number of black students at TWIs, and he teased Juanita Kreps at the cabinet meeting of February 6, 1978, by asserting that she wanted to maintain Carolina, along with Duke and Wake Forest, as "fancy schools." The president later told Califano that when he said this to Kreps, he was "really trying to send a message to Bill Friday," who he said was "a great liberal until it begins to pinch him a little bit, just like the mayors of some of those Northern cities like Boston when desegregation was ordered." Califano, *Governing America*, pp. 246–52. In any event, Carter's influence over Califano was limited. The president instructed White House aide Ann Wexler to investigate the possibilities of compromise. Wexler then spoke with Peter Libassi, who remained the most accommodationist high-level HEW official, and he told her that there "was room to maneuver" and that litigation was unlikely. Subsequently, Libassi arranged a meeting with David Tatel and Califano to urge moderation and settlement. WCF, memorandum of record, February 14, 1978.

2. Dawson, memorandum of record, February 20, 1978; Orleans, memo to the Adams file, March 8, 1978, WCF Correspondence, GA; Tatel, testimony, September 22, 1980, UNC-HEW Case File, GA; WCF to Carl Kaysen, March 13, 1978, subgroup 1, ser. 8, file entitled "Sloan Commission: General, Feb.–June 1978," WCF Papers, UA/UNC. On February 13 Friday received a report from a black Board of Governors member, E. B. Turner, that a Califano aide had told the LDF, at a meeting in Alexandria, Va., that Friday was "not cooperative in solving this problem." WCF, memorandum of record, February 13, 1978.

3. Califano, *Governing America*, pp. 246–53; WCF, memorandum of record, March 21, 1978. Califano then called North Carolina congressman L. Richardson Preyer Jr. and asked him to urge Friday to become more conciliatory; he promised Preyer that he would telephone Governor Hunt. Preyer immediately reported the conversation to Friday, who called Hunt's office to ward off any political pressure to settle prematurely.

4. Califano, statement and transcript of press conference, March 22, 1978, UNC-HEW Case File, GA; Sherry Johnson, "HEW Process to Halt UNC Funds Started; Friday Sees Further Talks 'Questionable,'" *Greensboro Daily News*, March 23, 1978; Robert Hodierne and Susan Jetton, "HEW Moves to Cut Aid to UNC," *Charlotte Observer*, March 23, 1978.

5. Ferrel Guillory, "HEW Moves to Block Federal Funds to UNC" (March 23, 1978), Rob Christiansen, "Head of UNC Questions Further Talks with HEW" (March 23, 1978), and Christiansen, "Charges Anger UNC Officials" (March 24, 1978), *Raleigh News and Observer*.

6. Califano, transcript of press conference, March 22, 1978, UNC-HEW Case File, GA; "Califano Wants More Talks; UNC Still Considering Fight," *Greensboro Daily News*, March 25, 1978; Harold Warren, "UNC Can Use Jaworski Firm to Fight HEW, Hunt Says," *Charlotte Observer*, March 24, 1978; Rob Christiansen, "HEW Asks Renewed Talks," *Raleigh News and Observer*, March 25, 1978; William A. Johnson, statement, March 24, 1978, WCF Correspondence, GA.

7. Califano, *Governing America*, pp. 252–53.

8. "U. of North Carolina Fights for U.S. Funds," *New York Times*, April 13, 1978; Dawson, deposition, UNC-HEW Case File, GA.

9. Interview with Beattie, June 26, 1991; interview with Boyer, May 9, 1990. "As usual, I was deeply impressed by your great leadership and steady vision," Boyer later wrote Friday. "The food was absolutely tops, and the atmosphere so intimate and gracious." Boyer to WCF, May 2, 1978, WCF Correspondence, GA.

10. Dawson, deposition and testimony (March 16, 1981), UNC-HEW Case File, GA; interview with Beattie, June 26, 1991.

11. Dawson, testimony (March 16, 1981), and deposition, UNC-HEW Case File, GA.

12. Rob Christiansen, "UNC Board May Get HEW Decision Today," *Raleigh News and Observer*, May 12, 1978; Sherry Johnson, "UNC Gearing Up for Legal Action," *Greensboro Daily News*, May 12, 1978; Tatel, testimony, September 23, 1980, UNC-HEW Case File, GA.

13. Califano, *Governing America*, pp. 252–53; Rob Christiansen, "UNC Board May Get HEW Decision Today," *Raleigh News and Observer*, May 12, 1978; Robert Hodierne and Harold Warren, "UNC Plan Wins HEW Approval," *Charlotte Observer*, May 13, 1978. The key sentence of the agreement was: "The Board of Governors is committed to take appropriate actions that will, when combined with the other programs and steps described elsewhere in this plan, be intended to result by the academic year 1982–83 in the enrollment of a significant portion of students in unduplicated programs in traditionally white and traditionally black institutions." Rob Christiansen, "UNC-HEW Opinions Divided to End," *Raleigh News and Observer*, May 14, 1978.

14. *Revised North Carolina Plan . . . Supplemental Statement II* (May 12, 1978).

15. WCF, statement to the Board of Governors, May 12, 1978, WCF Correspondence, GA; Silard, "Motion for Issuance of Show Cause Order," May 16, 1978, UNC-HEW Case File, GA.

16. Board of Governors minutes, May 12, 1978, subgroup 2, ser. 2, subser. 3, WCF Papers, UA/UNC; WCF to Beattie, May 17, 1978, WCF Correspondence, GA; Rob Christiansen, "UNC Reaches Accord with HEW" (May 13, 1978), and Christiansen, "UNC-HEW Opinions Divided to End" (May 14, 1978), *Raleigh News and Observer*; Sherry Johnson and Paul Clancy, "HEW Accepts Desegregation Plan," *Greensboro Daily News*, May 13, 1978.

17. Christiansen, "UNC Reaches Accord"; Eizenstat to Ervin, July 24, 1978, Name File, Carter Papers, JCPL; WCF, memorandum of record, July 20, 1978; interview with WCF, December 3, 1990.

18. Interview with Tatel, August 7, 1991; Tatel, testimony, UNC-HEW Case File, GA.

19. Silard, "Motion for Issuance of Show Cause Order," May 16, 1978, UNC-HEW Case File, GA.

20. Tatel to Hunt (June 12, 1978), Tatel to WCF (June 21, July 10, 1978), WCF to Tatel (June 26, 1978), Califano to Hunt (July 11, 1978), and Dawson to Tatel (July 19, 1978), UNC-HEW Case File, GA; Dawson, testimony (March 16, 1981) and deposition, UNC-HEW Case File, GA.

21. "Settlement No Victory for UNC," editorial, *Raleigh News and Observer*, May 16, 1978.

22. Sherry Johnson, "Duplicate Programs Point of Contention for UNC and HEW" (September 10, 1978), and "Case Study: UNC-G, A&T Nursing Schools" (September 10, 1978), *Greensboro Daily News*.

23. Dawson, memorandum of record, September 27, 1978.

24. "UNC Fears HEW Rejection" (November 25, 1978), and William D. Snider, "UNC-HEW: Conflict Continues to Brew" (November 26, 1978), *Greensboro Daily News*.

25. Sherry Johnson, "Friday Lists Alternatives to Mergers" (November 18, 1978), and "UNC Fears Rejection" (November 25, 1978), *Greensboro Daily News*; interview with Orleans, May 17, 1991; Sherry Johnson, "Panel to Rule on UNC-G, A&T Duplication" (December 1, 1978), and Johnson, "UNC Adopts Studies of Duplication" (December 9, 1978), *Greensboro Daily News*; Harold Warren, "UNC Study Concludes Duplication Necessary," *Charlotte Observer*, December 2, 1978; *Comparative Study of . . . Program Offerings*; interview with Dawson, September 25, 1991.

26. Sherry Johnson, "UNC Duplications Defended in Study," and "UNC Adopts Studies of Duplication," *Greensboro Daily News*, December 9, 1978. The Greensboro paper agreed with Friday. From a "blissfully uncomplicated perspective," it appeared that the university was engaged in "foot-dragging." But it was "sheer educational madness" to adopt a radical solution of "summarily shuffling programs, faculty and students back and forth." The UNC position was a sound and principled one, consistent with the original intent of the Civil Rights Act of 1964; it was "the only stance any educator could embrace in good conscience." "UNC's Principled Stand," editorial, *Greensboro Daily News*, December 5, 1978.

27. Virginia's plan was accepted in January 1979, Georgia's in February 1979. Rob Christiansen, "Georgia Colleges Regretting HEW Pact," *Raleigh News and Observer*, July 8, 1979.

28. John Sanders to WCF, December 27, 1978, subgroup 1, ser. 5, file entitled "HEW: UNC System: General, 1973–1980," WCF Papers, UA/UNC; "HEW Source Says UNC Desegregation Plan Faces Rejection," *Greensboro Daily News*, January 10, 1979; Califano, *Governing America*, p. 254. Ray Dawson, in a memorandum of record, January 8, 1979, maintained that OCR wanted to settle with the other *Adams* states "so that North Carolina can again be isolated."

29. "Attorney Urges HEW to Block UNC Funds," *Greensboro Daily News*, January 12, 1979; Tatel, deposition and testimony (September 22, 1980), UNC-HEW Case File, GA; Roger Wilkins, "College Integration Plan Irks Black Leaders," *New York Times*, January 22, 1979; OCR staff analysis, in Tatel to WCF, January 18, 1979, UNC-HEW Case File; Califano, *Governing America*, p. 254.

30. WCF to Tatel, January 25, 1979, UNC-HEW Case File, GA.

31. Sherry Johnson, "Friday: No 'Cosmetic' Plan," *Greensboro Daily News*, January 23, 1979; Beattie to Eizenstat, February 1, 1979, Domestic Policy Staff Records, JCPL; WCF to Tatel (January 25, 1979), Tatel, testimony (September 22, 1980), and Tatel to WCF (February 16, 1979), UNC-HEW Case File, GA.

32. Sherry Johnson, "Califano Says UNC Plan Needs Program Changes," *Greensboro Daily News*, February 10, 1979.

33. WCF, memorandum of record, February 13, 1979; Sherry Johnson, "Califano Says UNC Plan Needs Program Changes," Johnson, "Black Chancellors Set Up HEW Parley" (February 4, 1979), and Johnson, "Encouragement Felt by Black Chancellors" (February 7, 1979), *Greensboro Daily News*; Edward C. Burke, "5 Black College Officials Oppose Integration Order," *New York Times*, February 5, 1979; Robert Hodierne, "Black-Campus Chancellors: HEW Wrong," *Charlotte Observer*, February 6, 1979; Berry, deposition (February 14, 1980), Sharpe, deposition, and Tatel, deposition and testimony (September 22, 1980), UNC-HEW Case File, GA; Califano, *Governing America*, pp. 254–55; interview with Tatel, August 7, 1991.

34. Interview with Tatel, August 7, 1991; Califano, *Governing America*, pp. 254–55; interview with Califano, April 5, 1991. Tatel confirmed Califano's account. The HEW secretary was concerned that the stalemate in negotiations had resulted from "inaccurate information" available to North Carolinians; the invitation from the TBI chancellors was "an opportunity to make the public in North Carolina through their newspapers aware of the conditions that existed on those campuses." Tatel, testimony, September 23, 1980, UNC-HEW Case File, GA; "UNC Black Campus Tour Federal Ploy – Testimony," *Greensboro Daily News*, September 24, 1980.

35. Tatel, deposition, UNC-HEW Case File, GA; interview with Tatel, August 7, 1991; Berry depositions, UNC-HEW Case File.

36. Berry deposition, February 14, 1980, UNC-HEW Case File, GA.

37. Ibid.; Sharpe deposition, UNC-HEW Case File, GA; Sherry Johnson, "HEW Officials to Visit State Next Week" (February 15, 1979), "Snow Postpones HEW Team Visit" (February 20, 1979), and "HEW to Begin UNC System Tour" (February 21, 1979), *Greensboro Daily News*.

38. Sherry Johnson, "Upgrading Black Colleges HEW's Aim," *Greensboro Daily News*, February 22, 1979; Robert Hodierne, "HEW Finds Black Colleges in Poor Shape," *Charlotte Observer*, February 22, 1979; interview with Tatel, August 7, 1991.

39. Sherry Johnson, "After Tour HEW Officials Call A&T 'Best of Any of the Black Schools,'" *Greensboro Daily News*, February 23, 1979.

40. Interview with Thompson, January 30, 1991. According to Berry, North Carolina Central had only broken autoclaves, Fayetteville State had none, UNCG had two, A&T had two, and N.C. State had forty. "Officials Say Schools 'Clearly Unequal,'" *Raleigh News and Observer*, February 23, 1979. Berry's statement at Elizabeth City State appears in Lloyd V. Hackley, deposition, UNC-HEW Case File, GA. Berry essentially admitted making the statement. According to her, she said that "that was nice, . . . but did they have any other things that they would like us to see, and were there any inadequacies on the campus?" Berry, deposition, March 18, 1980, UNC-HEW Case File.

41. Rob Christiansen and Joye Brown, "HEW Officials Leave Dim Hopes," *Raleigh News and Observer*, February 24, 1979; Robert Hodierne, "Chairman of UNC Pessimistic," *Charlotte Observer*, February 24, 1979; Sherry Johnson, "HEW Promises Further Talks on UNC," *Greensboro Daily News*, February 24, 1979; Sharpe, deposition, UNC-HEW Case File, GA; WCF, memorandum of record, February 26, 1979. Well in advance of the trip, OCR drafted a press release entitled "The University of North Carolina: Separate and Still Unequal" that was to be circulated at the conclusion of the visit. Tatel, testimony, September 23, 1980, UNC-HEW Case File. Subsequently, Califano maintained that he had seen Berry as "a Rauh messenger" while showing "more respect" for Tatel. Califano, comments, reported in Jay Jenkins to WCF,

September 7, 1979, subgroup 1, ser. 1, file entitled "Black Institutions: Traditionally Black Institutions, 1977–1979," WCF Papers, UA/UNC.

42. "Officials Say Schools 'Clearly Unequal,' " *Raleigh News and Observer*, February 23, 1979; Sherry Johnson, "HEW Visitors: Tar Heels, Too, Saw Inequities," *Greensboro Daily News*, February 25, 1979; Berry to Califano, February 27, 1979, attached to Berry, deposition, March 18, 1990, UNC-HEW Case File, GA.

43. Interview with Tatel, August 7, 1991; interview with Beattie, June 26, 1991; Jack Betts, "Hunt Admits Federal Prod Made State 'More Aware,' " *Greensboro Daily News*, February 23, 1979; Ned Cline and Robert Hodierne, "Hunt: HEW Pointed Out UNC Needs," *Charlotte Observer*, February 23, 1979; "HEW's Helpful Visit," editorial, *Greensboro Daily News*, February 25, 1979; "N.C. Black Campuses Still Poor," editorial, *Charlotte Observer*, February 23, 1979; Johnson, "HEW Visitors"; interview with Dawson, September 25, 1991.

44. Johnson, "HEW Visitors"; interview with Orleans, May 17, 1991; WCF, memorandum of record, February 22, 1979; Cline and Hodierne, "Hunt: HEW Pointed Out UNC Needs."

45. WCF, memorandum of record, February 26, 1979; interview with Roy Carroll, August 8, 1991. When LDF attorneys, earlier in February, had described UNC's position as "massive resistance to desegregation," Friday was deeply offended and so expressed himself to Joseph Rauh. "No, North Carolina is not engaging in massive resistance to desegregation," he wrote in March 1979. Beginning in 1972, when the TBIs became part of the restructured UNC system, the university had taken "positive steps . . . to eliminate racial duality." WCF to Rauh, March 14, 1979, WCF Correspondence, GA; see also Rauh to WCF, March 5, 1979, ibid.

46. WCF, memorandum of record, February 22, 1979; Dawson to Eizenstat (March 2, 1979) and Eizenstat to Jimmy Carter (March 5, 1979), Domestic Policy Staff Records, JCPL.

47. Eizenstat to Jimmy Carter, March 5, 1979; Califano, *Governing America*, pp. 255–56; WCF, memorandum of record, March 13, 1979; Robert Hodierne, "Califano Ignores N.C. Pleas," *Charlotte Observer*, March 23, 1978.

48. "Hew Offers UNC Compromise Plan," *Greensboro Daily News*, March 7, 1979.

49. Rob Christiansen, "UNC, HEW Resume Talks Today with New Proposals," *Raleigh News and Observer*, March 8, 1979; "HEW Offers UNC Compromise Plan," *Greensboro Daily News*, March 7, 1979; Sharpe, deposition, UNC-HEW Case File, GA.

50. Dawson, memorandum of record, March 8, 1979; Dawson, testimony, March 16, 1981, UNC-HEW Case File, GA; interview with Dawson, September 25, 1991; Robert Hodierne, "UNC Hears HEW Suggestions; No Solution at Hand," *Charlotte Observer*, March 9, 1979.

51. Tatel, deposition, Sharpe, deposition, and Pacht, deposition, March 13, 1980, UNC-HEW Case File, GA.

52. Dawson, testimony, March 16, 1981, UNC-HEW Case File, GA; interview with Dawson, September 25, 1991.

53. Dawson, memorandum of record, March 12, 1979; Joanne Hurley to Eizenstat (March 13, 1979) and Eizenstat to Gail Harrison (March 13, 1979), Domestic Policy Staff Records, JCPL; WCF, memorandum of record, March 13, 1979.

54. WCF, memorandum of record, March 13, 1979.

55. Ibid.

56. WCF, Joyner, Dawson, and Thompson, memorandum of record, March 13, 1979.

57. Ibid.; Dawson, deposition and testimony (March 16, 1981), and Tatel, deposition and testimony (September 22, 1980), UNC-HEW Case File, GA.

58. "Califano Accused of Neglect on Desegregation Deadline," *New York Times*, March 17, 1979; WCF, memorandum of record, March 15, 1979; Califano, *Governing America*, pp. 255–56.

59. Robert Hodierne and Ned Cline, "U.S. Plans More Talks with UNC on Stalemated Integration Issue," *Charlotte Observer*, March 16, 1979; WCF, memorandum of record, March 22, 1979.

60. "UNC, HEW Confer to Avert Cutoff" (March 16, 1979), and "UNC Conflict Hinges on Politics, Dollars" (March 18, 1979), *Greensboro Daily News*; Dawson, deposition, UNC-HEW Case File, GA; Jack Betts, "Hunt Says HEW's Feelers on Dispute 'Inappropriate,'" *Greensboro Daily News*, March 23, 1979.

61. Vic Gold, "This Time You SOB You've Gone Too Far," *The Washingtonian*, June 1979, pp. 112–15; Robert Hodierne, "UNC Hires Top Lawyer Just in Case," *Charlotte Observer*, March 17, 1979; interview with Roy Carroll, August 8, 1991.

62. Board of Governors minutes, March 16, 1979, subgroup 2, ser. 2, subser. 3, WCF Papers, UA/UNC; "UNC Officials Expect Plan to Be Rejected by Califano," *Greensboro Daily News*, March 17, 1979; interview with Orleans, May 17, 1991; interview with Jordan, November 18, 1991; interview with Joseph J. Levin Jr., April 19, 1991; interview with Richard Beattie, June 26, 1991.

63. "HEW Waiting to Plan Next UNC Move" (March 20, 1979), and "Panel Gives Friday Vote of Confidence" (March 21, 1979), *Greensboro Daily News*; interview with Levin, April 19, 1991; Richard H. Robinson to WCF, Dawson, and Joyner, March 22, 1979, WCF Correspondence, GA; Dawson to John A. Williams Jr., March 22, 1979, subgroup 1, ser. 1, file entitled "Black Institutions: Traditionally Black Institutions, 1977–1979," WCF Papers, UA/UNC.

64. Sherry Johnson, "HEW Rejects UNC Desegregation Plan," *Greensboro Daily News*, March 27, 1979; Robert Hodierne, "HEW Rejects UNC's Plan, Readies Cuts," *Charlotte Observer*, March 27, 1979; Karen De Witt, "Califano Acts to End Carolina College Aid on Segregation Issue," *New York Times*, March 27, 1979; Tatel, testimony, September 22, 1980, UNC-HEW Case File, GA.

65. "HEW's Shoe Drops," editorial (March 28, 1979), Sherry Johnson, "UNC to Continue Negotiations" (March 28, 1979), and "Hunt Pledges State Funds to Aid UNC" (March 30, 1979), *Greensboro Daily News*; Tatel, testimony, September 22, 1980, UNC-HEW Case File, GA; "U.S. Gives North Carolina Notice on Forfeiting Funds," *New York Times*, March 31, 1979; "HEW Gives UNC Hearing Notice," *Greensboro Daily News*, March 31, 1979.

66. Interview with Tatel, August 7, 1991.

67. Interview with Levin, April 19, 1991.

68. Interview with Jordan, November 18, 1991.

69. Eizenstat and Watson to Carter (April 10, 1979) and Califano to Carter (April 10, 1979), Domestic Policy Staff Records, JCPL.

70. Califano, *Governing America*, p. 257.

71. Interview with Orleans, May 17, 1991.

72. WCF Statement to the Board of Governors, April 20, 1979, WCF Correspondence, GA.

73. Tatel, testimony (September 22, 1980), and Dawson, deposition and testimony (March 16, 1981), UNC-HEW Case File, GA; WCF, statement to the Board of Governors, April 20, 1979, WCF Correspondence, GA; interview with Beattie, June 26, 1991.

74. Califano, *Governing America*, p. 256.

75. "Califano: UNC Plan Sabotaged," *Greensboro Daily News*, May 31, 1981; interview with Jordan, November 18, 1991. Friday claimed, at that point, not to have read the book. Jordan said in the interview in November 1991 that there might have been a proposed settlement but that he was not informed of it. Similarly, Philip Carson strongly denied Califano's assertion of a deal. Interview with Carson, July 18, 1991.

76. Interview with Richard Beattie, June 26, 1991; interview with Dawson, September 25, 1991; interview with Carroll, August 8, 1991.

77. Carter, handwritten note on Eizenstat, and Watson to Carter, April 10, 1979, Domestic Policy Staff Records, Carter Papers, JCPL. Carter's note was likely written some weeks after the receipt of the memorandum.

78. On April 18 the gap on the duplication issue remained. See "UNC Reported Holding Out for HEW Concession," *Greensboro Daily News*, April 19, 1979; Dawson, deposition, UNC-HEW Case File, GA.

79. Tatel, deposition and testimony, UNC-HEW Case File, GA (Tatel's source for this was Beattie, who in turn said that this information came from Friday himself); interview with Carroll, August 8, 1991; Dawson, deposition and testimony (March 16, 1981), UNC-HEW Case File.

80. WCF, statement to the Board of Governors, April 20, 1979, WCF Correspondence, GA.

81. Interview with Jeffrey H. Orleans, May 17, 1991.

82. Board of Governors resolution, April 20, 1979, attached to Robinson to William Johnson, April 23, 1979, WCF Correspondence, GA; Board of Governors minutes, April 20, 1979, subgroup 2, ser. 2, subser. 3, WCF Papers, UA/UNC.

CHAPTER 12

1. Interview with Carroll, August 8, 1991; interview with Dawson, August 1, 1991.

2. The suit challenged the constitutionality of federal intervention and asked the court to prevent a cutoff of federal funds that was scheduled to begin on May 2. UNC attorneys claimed that HEW officials had violated academic freedom and free speech by attempting to impose "an improper, illegal and unconstitutional racial balance at the university by shifting programs and students." The suit further asserted that the UNC system was not segregated by law and that Chapel Hill's record of integration was better than that of forty out of forty-eight research campuses nationally. "University Sues over Fund Cutoff," *New York Times*, April 25, 1979; Jack Betts, "UNC Sues HEW to Avert Cutoff," *Greensboro Daily News*, April 25, 1979; Rob Christiansen, "State Files Lawsuit to Block Cutoff of Federal Funds to UNC System" (April 25, 1979), and "Testing HEW's Limits . . . While Keeping Obligations," editorial (April 25, 1979), *Raleigh News and Observer*; Robert Hodierne, "How Much Is Enough? UNC Lawsuit Asks HEW" (April 28, 1979), and "UNC-HEW Dispute Goes to Court," editorial (April 29, 1979), *Charlotte Observer*.

3. Essentially the same enhancement package that had been offered to HEW negotiators, it promised $17.4 million for the renovation of buildings, $19 million for new buildings, and $1 million for new equipment. Of the total amount, the largest single share, almost $15 million, would go to A&T; most of this amount was for the establishment of an animal science facility that would operate in conjunction with N.C. State's new vet school. UNC freely admitted that the case against HEW and the enhancement package were linked. Although the appropriations request was being submitted on its own merits, commented Felix Joyner, "a man would be a fool to say this is not connected with HEW." "UNC Asks Money for Improving Black Campuses," *Charlotte Observer*, April 26, 1979.

4. Jack Betts, "UNC Loses Struggle to Stay Out of Court" (April 29, 1979), and Betts, "U.S. Wants to Transfer UNC Lawsuit" (May 2, 1979), *Greensboro Daily News*; interview with Andrew Vanore, June 13, 1991; "Judge Bars U.S. Aid Cutoff for U. of North Carolina," *New York*

Times, April 28, 1979; Jack Betts, "HEW Temporarily Halted from Cutting UNC Funds," *Greensboro Daily News*, April 28, 1979. The original temporary restraining order was for ten days; Dupree extended it three times. "H.E.W. Loses Plea to Act against North Carolina U.," *New York Times*, May 12, 1979; Jack Betts, "Fund Cutoff Order Extended by Judge" (May 16, 1979), and "Judge Extends Ban of UNC Fund Cutoff" (May 22, 1979), *Greensboro Daily News*.

5. Jack Betts, "UNC Suit to Remain in State," *Greensboro Daily News*, May 24, 1979.

6. *State of North Carolina et al.* v. *Department of Health, Education, and Welfare*; "Judge Halts Cutoff of Funds to U. of North Carolina," *New York Times*, June 9, 1979; Jack Betts, "Judge Allows HEW Review, Bars Funds Cutoff to UNC" (June 9, 1979), and "Judge Denies Cutoff of UNC Funding" (October 19, 1979), *Greensboro Daily News*.

7. "UNC, HEW Both Cheer," editorial, *Raleigh News and Observer*, June 12, 1979; "A Call to Reason," editorial, *Greensboro Daily News*, June 12, 1979.

8. The original judge in the case, Lewis F. Parker, an FTC arbitrator, eventually excused himself and was replaced by John Mathias. "Arbitrator from FTC to Hear UNC Case" (July 5, 1979), and Jack Betts, "HEW Trial against UNC Starts Jan. 7" (August 17, 1979), *Greensboro Daily News*; "Desegregation Trial Set Between H.E.W. and U. of North Carolina," *New York Times*, August 19, 1979.

9. "UNC Goes to Court," editorial, *Greensboro Daily News*, April 26, 1979.

10. "Still Separate in North Carolina," editorial, *New York Times*, April 7, 1979. Vernon Jordan, head of the National Urban League, criticized UNC for its countersuit at the Winston-Salem State commencement. "The best way to avoid federal intervention," he said, was "to get North Carolina's house of education in order and in equity." "Vernon Jordan Blasts UNC for Suing HEW," *Greensboro Daily News*, May 21, 1979.

11. Alan Pifer, for example, received a copy of UNC's motion against HEW. "What a tangled business this is in North Carolina," Pifer responded, "right against right!" Pifer to WCF, May 2, 1979, WCF Correspondence, GA.

12. Jack Betts, "UNC Asks $40 Million More to Improve Black Campuses" (April 26, 1979), "Friday: $40 Million May Convince HEW" (May 10, 1979), "Friday Pledges No Mergers among University System" (May 13, 1979), and "HEW Theory on Duplication Unfounded, Friday Tells Club" (August 31, 1979), *Greensboro Daily News*.

13. Interview with Levin, April 19, 1991; interview with Gary Barnes, October 15, 1991.

14. Interview with Jeffrey H. Orleans, May 17, 1991; "UNC Given Extra Time in HEW Case," *Greensboro Daily News*, July 28, 1979; Richard H. Robinson, memorandum of record, July 31, 1979, with Friday's notation.

15. Hurley to Eizenstat, with Eizenstat's notations, April 23, 1979, Domestic Policy Staff Records, JCPL; WCF, memorandum of record, April 24, 1979.

16. Joanne Hurley to Eizenstat, April 23, 1979, with Eizenstat's notations; WCF, memorandum of record, April 25, 1979.

17. Eizenstat and Watson to Carter, May 12, 1979, Domestic Policy Staff Records, JCPL; WCF, memorandum of record, May 24, 1979.

18. WCF, memorandum of record, May 24, 1979. Carter noted, on May 14, that Bill Johnson was going to Washington "re Univ integration." Carter, handwritten note, May 14, 1979, Domestic Policy Staff Records, JCPL. "Let's hope for the best," Eizenstat wrote two weeks later. Eizenstat to WCF, May 29, 1979, Name File, Carter Papers, JCPL.

19. WCF, memorandum of record, May 31, 1979.

20. The Board of Governors ad hoc lawyers' committee, again playing a significant role,

consulted with its attorneys about a settlement that would take the form of a consent decree under Dupree's supervision. Dawson traveled to Washington on July 2 to discuss a final version of the draft consent decree with Joe Levin, but OCR and the Justice Department, which was now involved in the case, quickly rejected it. Federal officials objected to UNC's proposed settlement. They preferred a Title VI process and continued OCR supervision rather than a consent decree, which would mean Justice Department supervision. HEW officials maintained that the UNC proposal represented no progress. David Tatel characterized it as "substantially less than what had been offered earlier," without many of the earlier commitments. He believed that it was, if anything, a "step backwards." WCF, memorandum of record, June 13, 1979; Dawson, testimony, March 16, 1981, and Tatel, testimony, September 22, 1980, UNC-HEW Case File, GA.

21. Jack Betts, "HEW Trial against UNC Starts Jan. 7," *Greensboro Daily News*, August 17, 1979; WCF, memorandum of record, July 30, 1979. At one point, Helms threatened to hold up Harris's confirmation hearings on the antismoking and desegregation issues. Richard Whittle, "Helms Pleased with HEW's Harris" (July 28, 1979), and "Helms vs. Harris, Briefly," editorial (July 29, 1979), *Raleigh News and Observer*.

22. WCF, memorandum of record, September 10, 25, 1979; Johnson to ad hoc committee, September 19, 1979, WCF Correspondence, GA; Dawson, deposition and testimony (March 16, 1981), and Tatel, testimony (September 22, 1980), UNC-HEW Case File, GA; interview with WCF, November 19, 1990.

23. Jack Betts, "Hunt Angry over HEW Treatment," *Greensboro Daily News*, October 13, 1979; interview with Levin, April 19, 1991; interview with Beattie, June 26, 1991; interview with Tatel, August 7, 1991.

24. Interview with Levin, April 19, 1991; interview with Tatel, August 7, 1991.

25. WCF, memorandum of record, October 3, 1979; interview with Joe Levin, April 19, 1991; "Harris Evaluates UNC Efforts," *Greensboro Daily News*, January 13, 1980; interview with WCF, December 3, 1990.

26. WCF, memoranda of record, October 3, 15, 1979; interview with Roy Carroll, August 8, 1991.

27. WCF, memorandum of record, October 15, 1979.

28. Betts, "Hunt Angry over HEW Treatment"; WCF, memoranda of record, October 19, 24, 1979.

29. WCF, memorandum of record, October 15, 1979.

30. Ibid.

31. "UNC Presents HEW Revised Mixing Plan," *Greensboro Daily News*, October 26, 1979; Sherry Johnson and Richard Whittle, "UNC Offers New Desegregation Plan," *Raleigh News and Observer*, October 26, 1979; Tatel, testimony, September 22, 1980, UNC-HEW Case File, GA; WCF, memoranda of record, December 3, 6, 1979; "UNC Desegregation Compromise Hopes Dim," *Greensboro Daily News*, November 15, 1979.

32. In pretrial maneuvering during the autumn of 1979, administrative judge Lewis Parker denied UNC's motion to dismiss the case while he also threw out an attempt by HEW attorneys to cut off UNC funding because, they claimed, the university had prevented its employees from testifying in the case. As witnesses from both sides were deposed during the winter of 1980, university attorneys sought delay; the withdrawal of Judge Parker in April 1980, because his daughter was applying for admission to Carolina, meant that a new judge, John Mathias, would have to become acquainted with the case. The result was that the proceedings

did not resume until the summer. As the pretrial preparations proceeded, the price tag for UNC grew larger: by February 1980 it had already spent $423,000 in legal fees and expenses. Chuck Morgan, Joe Levin, Ed Ashworth, and Richard Cohen were working on the case, although Levin – whom UNC officials found more congenial than the flamboyant Morgan – had assumed daily control of the litigation. In addition to the fees of these attorneys, North Carolina taxpayers were paying for numerous depositions, along with the expenses of Andy Vanore, who rented a Washington apartment. "UNC Will Face Trial in Federal Funding Dispute" (October 18, 1979), "U.S. Officials Claim UNC 'Coercive'" (November 1, 1979), "Friday Denies UNC Coercion" (November 2, 1979), "Judge Upholds Ruling on UNC 'Gag Rule'" (November 21, 1979), "UNC Asks Delay of Desegregation Hearing" (January 5, 1980), "Desegregation Hearing Delay Sought by UNC" (February 10, 1980), "Daughter on UNC List Forces Judge Off Case" (April 8, 1980), and "Judge Named for UNC Case" (April 11, 1980), *Greensboro Daily News*; interview with Gary Barnes, October 15, 1991; Jack Betts, "$1 Million Dispute?: UNC Court Case Costs State a Bundle," *Greensboro Daily News*, February 17, 1980.

33. "Briefs Outline Views in UNC Case" (June 29, 1980), and "Government, UNC Renew Legal Fight" (July 23, 1980), *Greensboro Daily News*.

34. Levin, opening statement, administrative hearings transcript, July 22, 1980, UNC-HEW Case File, GA.

35. Stymied in their ability to summon witnesses from within the UNC system, government attorneys called Watts Hill Jr., who testified on July 23–25, 1980, as a government expert witness on North Carolina higher education. While Hill testified how the TBIs had been historically underfunded and suffered from inferior facilities and faculties, Gregory Kannerstein, an associate dean at Haverford College, who had written a dissertation on desegregation strategies at Harvard, asserted that program shifts and mergers were viable methods of ending racial duality. Albert H. Berrian, president of the Washington-based Institute for Service to Education, testified that TWIs such as Appalachian State and UNC-Charlotte had progressed faster than the TBIs and that the vet school could have been located at A&T. "Black Colleges Said Underfunded" (July 25, 1980), "Thesis: Merge Grad Schools" (August 2, 1980), Jack Betts, "Hill Says Slip of Tongue Caused UNC Enmity" (August 3, 1980), and "Consultant Faults N.C. on Schools" (August 5, 1980), *Greensboro Daily News*; Dawson to Levin, Vanore, and Cohen, July 30, 1980, subgroup 1, ser. 1, file entitled "Black Institutions: Traditionally Black Institutions, 1980," WCF Papers, UA/UNC.

36. "Tatel Says UNC Cool" (September 23, 1980), "Chambers: Vestiges of Dual System Persist" (September 26, 1980), "Black Institutions Offer Less: Expert" (October 4, 1980), "UNC Lawyers Grill Dentler" (October 8, 1980), and "U.S. Offers Last Witness in UNC Case" (October 15, 1980), *Greensboro Daily News*. For Dentler and Baltzell's case against UNC, see Dentler, Baltzell, and Sullivan, *University on Trial*.

37. WCF to Sitton, memorandum, May 8, 1980, subgroup 1, ser. 1, file entitled "Black Institutions: Traditionally Black Institutions, 1980," WCF Papers, UA/UNC.

38. "UNC-HEW Case Soon to Become UNC-ED Case," *Greensboro Daily News*, December 30, 1979; WCF, memoranda of record, November 6, December 6, 1979.

39. Interview with Cater, May 9, 1991.

40. WCF, memorandum of record, June 13, 1980.

41. WCF, memoranda of record, June 13, July 14, 1980; WCF to Eizenstat, June 23, 1980, WCF Correspondence, GA.

42. Interview with Gary Barnes, October 15, 1991. Barnes noted that he learned later that

only Richard Foster, OCR's lead attorney in the administrative hearings, knew of the Kujovich channel.

43. WCF, memorandum of record, July 14, 1980; interview with Dawson, September 25, 1991.

44. Dawson, memorandum of record, July 22, 1980.

45. WCF, memorandum of record, July 21, 1980; interview with Dawson, September 25, 1991.

46. Dawson to WCF, memorandum, July 24, 1980, subgroup 1, ser. 1, file entitled "Black Institutions: Traditionally Black Institutions, 1980," WCF Papers, UA/UNC; WCF, memorandum of record, July 28, 1980.

47. WCF, memorandum of record, August 24, 1980.

48. Eizenstat to WCF, September 11, 1980, and WCF, memorandum of record, November 11, 1980. Kujovich visited Chapel Hill on July 14, 24, August 7, September 9–10, October 21, 30, November 6–7, and December 2.

49. Dawson to WCF, November 26, 1980, subgroup 1, ser. 1, file entitled "Black Institutions: Traditionally Black Institutions, 1980," WCF Papers, UA/UNC.

50. WCF, memorandum of record, December 5, 1980, and WCF to Hufstedler, December 27, 1980.

51. Interview with Dawson, September 25, 1991.

52. WCF to Hufstedler, December 27, 1980.

53. WCF, memorandum of record, December 15, 1980.

54. WCF, memorandum of record, December 17, 1980, Hufstedler to WCF, January 2, 1981, WCF to Eizenstat, January 8, 1981, and WCF, memorandum of record, January 19, 1981.

55. Dawson to WCF, Joyner, and Robinson, January 22, 1980.

56. "UNC's Brief," editorial (February 10, 1981), Charles Babington, "Hearings Resume Today" (February 23, 1981), "Conservative Testifies UNC Not Segregated" (March 6, 1981), and "Desegregation Hearings Move to Chapel Hill Today" (May 7, 1981), *Greensboro Daily News*.

57. Sharon Bond, "Friday Reserved about Outcome of Dispute," and Stan Swofford, "Chambers: Conservative Win May Halt UNC Case," *Greensboro Daily News*, November 15, 1980.

58. WCF, memorandum of record, January 16, 1981; Jack Betts, "UNC All Ears, Reagan Silent: Battle Still On," *Greensboro Daily News*, February 4, 1981; interview with Roy Carroll, August 8, 1991.

59. "Helms Promises Push to End UNC Dispute," *Greensboro Daily News*, January 16, 1981; Betts, "UNC All Ears."

60. WCF, memorandum of record, January 19, 1981; Jack Betts, "Education Chief 'Gets to Know' UNC Position," *Greensboro Daily News*, February 5, 1981; "Under the Dome" (February 5, 1981), and Sherry Johnson and Rob Christiansen, "Bell's Rise Helped Seal U.S. Break with UNC" (June 21, 1981), *Raleigh News and Observer*.

61. Interview with Dawson, September 25, 1991; interview with Levin, April 19, 1991; Johnson and Christiansen, "Bell's Rise Helped Seal U.S. Break with UNC."

62. WCF, memorandum of record, February 27, 1981; interview with WCF, March 11, 1991; Johnson and Christiansen, "Bell's Rise Helped Seal U.S. Break with UNC."

63. Bennett visited Chapel Hill on March 6, 21, May 11–12, and June 1–2. Zona Norwood to Dawson, June 16, 1981; Jack Betts, "UNC Board Vote Ends Long Battle," *Greensboro Daily News*, June 21, 1981; interview with Dawson, September 25, 1991; Johnson and Christiansen, "Bell's Rise Helped Seal U.S. Break with UNC."

64. Interview with Dawson, September 25, 1991.

65. Interview with Levin, April 19, 1991; interview with Dawson, September 25, 1991; Johnson and Christiansen, "Bell's Rise Helped Seal U.S. Break with UNC."

66. Interview with Levin, April 19, 1991.

67. Betts, "UNC Board Vote Ends Long Battle"; interview with Levin, April 19, 1991; interview with Barnes, October 15, 1991.

68. "NAACP Says UNC Settlement Imminent" (March 27, 1981), and Jack Scism and Charles Babington, "Lawyer Stands by 'Tip' on UNC" (March 28, 1981), *Greensboro Daily News*; Lee Weisbecker, "UNC Bias Settlement Isn't Near, Sources Say," *Charlotte Observer*, March 28, 1981.

69. Lee Weisbecker, "UNC Desegregation Talks Kept Secret," *Charlotte Observer*, June 21, 1981; WCF, memorandum of record, April 24, 1981; Betts, "UNC Board Vote Ends Long Battle"; interview with Dawson, September 25, 1991.

70. Interview with Levin, April 19, 1991.

71. Betts, "UNC Board Vote Ends Long Battle"; interview with WCF, March 11, 1991.

72. Betts, "Settlement Is at Hand in UNC Dispute," *Greensboro Daily News*, June 18, 1981; Sherry Johnson, "UNC Meeting Spurs Speculation about Desegregation Settlement," *Raleigh News and Observer*, June 18, 1981; Wendy Fox and Katherine White, "UNC Board to Consider U.S. Dispute," *Charlotte Observer*, June 19, 1981; Betts, "New Plan for UNC Sets Goals, Not Quotas," *Greensboro Daily News*, June 20, 1981; David McKinnon and Rob Christiansen, "UNC Accepts Proposed 'Goals' for Additional Desegregation," *Raleigh News and Observer*, June 21, 1981; Katherine White, "UNC Approves Desegregation Agreement," *Charlotte Observer*, June 21, 1981; Elizabeth Leland, "Judge Oks UNC Pact; Appeal Planned," *Raleigh News and Observer*, July 18, 1981; Dupree, memorandum of decision, July 17, 1981, WCF Correspondence, GA.

73. "Consent Decree *North Carolina* v. *Department of Education*," July 17, 1981, WCF Correspondence, GA.

74. Interview with Barnes, October 15, 1991.

75. Califano to WCF (June 25, 1981) and WCF to Califano (August 18, 1981), WCF Correspondence, GA.

76. Betts, "UNC Board Vote Ends Long Battle." Rauh later said that Friday was a "sad successor to the late great Frank Graham." Rauh to William A. Link, May 4, 1991, in author's possession.

77. Sue Anne Pressley, "UNC System Labors at Recasting Its Racial Character," *Charlotte Observer*, July 4, 1982; "Delay Sought in Integration of North Carolina Colleges" (June 30, 1981) and "Court of Appeals Clears Way for Carolina Integration Plan" (July 1, 1981,) *New York Times*; *Adams* v. *Bell*.

78. Joseph J. Levin to the editor, *New York Times*, July 29, 1981; interview with Dawson, August 1, 1991; John Coggins, "Friday Says CBS Report 'Inadequate,'" *Raleigh News and Observer*, September 14, 1981; "CBS Airs a Follow-Up to Desegregation Story," *New York Times*, September 21, 1981; John Coggins, "CBS Shows Friday in UNC Follow-Up," *Raleigh News and Observer*, September 21, 1981. For similar evidence of negative press, see Reginald Stuart, "New Trend in College Desegregation Emerges," *Raleigh News and Observer*, September 3, 1981.

79. See, for example, WCF to Eugene C. Lee (July 14, 1983), David Riesman to WCF (September 26, 1983), and WCF to Riesman (October 3, 1983), subgroup 1, ser. 1, files entitled "Black Institutions: Traditionally Black Institutions, 1983–1986" and "General, 1980–1986," WCF Papers, UA/UNC; *Marsha Artis et al. v. Board of Regents of University System of Georgia*,

unpublished opinion, Feb 23, 1981. Gary Barnes noted that, in the case of Tennessee, the merger of Tennessee State and the University of Tennessee-Nashville was a "disaster" and actually decreased the degree of desegregation. In Virginia, Norfolk State and Old Dominion created joint programs, providing transportation between the two schools. The program elevated the numbers of minorities, at least technically, but did little to desegregate. Interview with Barnes, October 15, 1991.

80. "Summaries of State Compliance, Higher Education Desegregation," February 10, 1988, in GA files.

81. I am indebted to Helen Jane Wettach of the UNC General Administration for supplying these figures, which are all part of the public record.

82. Interview with Levin, April 19, 1991.

83. *Knight* v. *State of Alabama*, 787 F. Supp. 103 (1991), 829 F. Supp. 1286 (1993); Linda Greenhouse, "Court, 8–1, Faults Mississippi on Bias in College System," and excerpts from White's opinion, *New York Times*, June 27, 1992.

84. *United States* v. *Fordice*, *New York Times*, June 27, 1992. Scalia's prediction seemed confirmed in October 1992, when the Mississippi Board of Trustees of the Institutions of Higher Learning, the state coordinating board, announced a plan in response to the *Fordice* decision. It called for the merger of TBI Mississippi Valley State with the TWI Delta State University, the merger of the TWI Mississippi University for Women with the University of Southern Mississippi, the merger of the TBI Alcorn State University with the TWI Mississippi State University, and the enhancement of the TBI Jackson State University. Joye Mercer, "Plan to Desegregate Higher Education in Mississippi Unites State's Colleges, Black and White Alike," *Chronicle of Higher Education*, November 4, 1992.

CONCLUSION

1. Interview with Roy Carroll, August 8, 1991.

2. Interview with King, March 4, 1991; interview with WCF, November 24, 1992.

3. Board of Governors minutes, October 14, 1983, subgroup 2, ser. 2, subser. 3, WCF Papers, UA/UNC; interview with WCF, December 1, 1992.

4. Interview with Jordan, November 18, 1991; interview with Arnold K. King, March 4, 1991; Elizabeth Leland, "UNC Board to Elect Chairman; No Clear Front-Runner Emerges," *Raleigh News and Observer*, July 27, 1984; Bernadette Hearne, "Factions Square Off in UNC Board Race," *Greensboro News and Record*, July 27, 1984.

5. Board of Governors minutes, July 27, 1984, subgroup 2, ser. 2, subser. 3, WCF Papers, UA/UNC; Elizabeth Leland, "Carson Elected UNC Board Chairman," *Raleigh News and Observer*, July 28, 1984; Bernadette Hearne, "UNC Board Elects Chairman in Close Vote" (July 28, 1984), "Shakeup on UNC's Board," editorial (July 28, 1984), and Hearne, "UNC Board Chief Hopes Spotlight Stays on University After Election" (August 2, 1984), *Greensboro News and Record*; interview with Jordan, November 18, 1991.

6. Interviews with WCF, March 11, 1991, November 24, 1992; Bernadette Hearne, "UNC Chief Not Talking on Retirement" (September 11, 1984), and Hearne, "Friday to Delay His Retirement until July '86" (September 15, 1984), *Greensboro News and Record*. The committee included Phil Carson, Wayne Corpening, Walter Davis, Bill Dees, Jake Froelich, James Holshouser, Bill Johnson, John R. Jordan Jr., Julia Morton, Louis Randolph, and David Whichard. Board of Governors minutes, March 8, 1985, subgroup 2, ser. 2, subser. 3, WCF Papers,

UA/UNC. See also Bernadette Hearne, "UNC Governors Hunt for Leader" (November 26, 1984), and "UNC's Search Begins" (November 27, 1984), *Greensboro News and Record*; Todd Cohen, "Spangler Elected UNC President," *Raleigh News and Observer*, February 1, 1986.

7. Interview with Jordan, November 18, 1991; "Paper Says Panel Split on Choice" (January 2, 1986), and John R. Alexander, "Advice on Picking a UNC President" (January 5, 1986), *Greensboro News and Record*; Cohen, "Spangler Elected"; David Perkins, "UNC Search Panel Chooses Spangler," *Raleigh News and Observer*, January 31, 1986. For a brief sketch of Fred Davison, see Dyer, *The University of Georgia*, pp. 344–45.

8. Chuck Alston, "Spangler Surprise at UNC," *Greensboro News and Record*, February 1, 1986; interviews with WCF, March 11, 1991, November 24, 1992; Board of Governors minutes, February 14, 1986, subgroup 2, ser. 2, subser. 3, WCF Papers, UA/UNC; Barbara Barnett, "Friday Says Goodbye to UNC System Board," *Charlotte Observer*, February 15, 1986; "Friday Explains Decision," *Rocky Mount Telegram*, March 20, 1986; interview with WCF, November 24, 1992.

9. Ingalls, "U. of North Carolina's Friday"; Dudley Clendinen, "Chapel Hill Welcomes New President," *New York Times*, October 18, 1986; Jonathan Yardley, "Taking Education a Step Higher," *Washington Post*, March 17, 1986.

10. "Friday's Resignation," editorial, *Durham Herald*, February 19, 1986; "Friday's Legacy Enriches State," editorial, *Wilmington Morning Star*, February 22, 1986. See also "A Distinguished Career," editorial, *High Point Enterprise*, February 26, 1986; "Presidential Comings and Goings," editorial, the *Daily Tar Heel*, February 28, 1986; "Bill Friday," editorial, *Richmond Journal*, March 3, 1986; "Friday's Vision," editorial, *Winston-Salem Journal*, March 4, 1986; "Congratulations to Friday," editorial, *Wilson Daily Times*, March 5, 1986; "Bill Friday Has Left Legacy of Excellence," editorial, *Asheville Times*, March 6, 1986; "Well Done, Dr. Friday, Well Done," editorial, *Henderson Dispatch*, March 8, 1986; "An Era Ends," editorial, *Anson Record*, March 11, 1986.

11. Barbara Barnett, "Big Imprint: Long, Important Era Ending in History of N.C. Campuses," *Charlotte Observer*, February 28, 1986; Bernadette Hearne, "Friday Clears President's Office for First New Face in 3 Decades," *Greensboro Daily News*, March 1, 1986; Barbara Barnett, "Friday's Era Ends at UNC," *Charlotte Observer*, March 1, 1986; Liz Lucas, "A Few Less Worries," *Chapel Hill News*, March 2, 1986. See also "Friday Leaves Office after Serving 30 Years," *Henderson Dispatch*, March 1, 1986; F. Alan Boyce, "UNC's Friday Leaves Office after 30 Years," *Shelby Daily Star*, March 1, 1986; Mike McLaughlin, "End of an Era: Friday Steps Down as University President," *Sanford Herald*, March 1, 1986; Art Eisenstadt, "End of an Era: Friday Looks Back with Pride on 30 Years at UNC," *Winston-Salem Journal*, March 1, 1986.

12. "Friday Says Goodbye to UNC Board," *Salisbury Post*, February 15, 1986; interview with WCF, March 11, 1991; Donald W. Patterson, "Friday Plans Years of Service," *Greensboro News and Record*, June 29, 1986.

13. Interview with IHF, October 4, 1990, SOHP; interview with James Graham, November 18, 1991; interview with Georgia Kyser, October 15, 1991.

14. "Thousands Turn Out to See H. Keith Brodie Inaugurated," *Greensboro News and Record*, September 29, 1985; Walter DeVries to WCF, April 25, 1985, WCF Correspondence, Kenan; interview with WCF, December 1, 1992.

15. Interview with WCF, December 1, 1992.

16. Chuck Alston, "UNC's Friday Puts Rumors of Senate Candidacy to Rest," *Greensboro News and Record*, October 25, 1985; "Friday Won't Resign Early for Candidacy" (October 4,

1985), Ken Eudy, "UNC's Friday Rules Out Senate Race" (October 25, 1985), and "Friday's Decision One of Humility" (April 17, 1986), *Charlotte Observer*; Todd Cohen, "Friday Requests He Not Be Considered as Democratic Candidate for Senate," *Raleigh News and Observer*, October 25, 1985; interview with WCF, December 1, 1992.

17. Interview with John R. Jordan Jr., November 18, 1991; interview with Gay Currie Fox, August 10, 1992; interview with Georgia Kyser, October 15, 1991; interview with WCF, December 1, 1992.

18. Interview with WCF, March 11, 1991; William R. Kenan Jr. Charitable Trust, *The First Twenty-Five Years.*

19. Executive Committee minutes, April 20, 1967, subgroup 2, ser. 1, subser. 3, WCF Papers, UA/UNC; WCF, memorandum of record, November 11, 1970, WCF Correspondence, Kenan; interview with WCF, March 11, 1991. See, for example, a $200,000 grant to Warren Wilson College, a Presbyterian college in western North Carolina. Arthur M. Bannerman to WCF (August 25, 1970) and William C. Archie to WCF (August 28, 1970), subgroup 1, ser. 1, file entitled "General, 1970–1974," WCF Papers, UA/UNC.

20. Interviews with WCF, March 11, 1991, November 24, 1992.

21. Interview with WCF, March 11, 1991.

22. Interviews with WCF, March 11, 1991, December 1, 1992.

23. WCF to Winfred Godwin and Karl Haigler (December 16, 1987) and U.S. Department of Education, press release (February 5, 1988), WCF Correspondence, Kenan; interview with WCF, March 11, 1991.

24. National Center for Family Literacy, *A Place to Start.*

25. Interviews with WCF, January 7, 14, 1991, December 1, 1992; Commission on the Future of North Carolina, *The Future of North Carolina.*

26. Southern Growth Policies Board, *Halfway Home.* According to William Winter, Friday played a major behind-the-scenes role in the report. Interview with Winter, October 5, 1992.

27. WCF, "Illiteracy: North Carolina's Hidden Danger" and "A Memo to the Class of '91," speech at N.C. State University Commencement, May 11, 1991, WCF Correspondence, Kenan.

28. Interview with Autry, June 20, 1991.

29. "Former UNC President Calls for Study of Poverty," *Greensboro News and Record*, May 30, 1986; interview with WCF, January 7, 1991; interview with Autry, June 20, 1991; WCF to E. B. Turner (April 9, 1986), Chamberlin to WCF (April 16, June 27, 1986), and Chamberlin to committee of fifteen (May 30, 1986), WCF Correspondence, Kenan; interview with Chamberlin, December 21, 1992.

30. "Report of the North Carolina Commission on Jobs and Economic Growth" (November 12, 1986) and "Rural Economic Development Center of North Carolina" (ca. 1986), WCF Correspondence, Kenan.

31. Interviews with WCF, January 7, 1991, December 1, 1992; Gerry Hancock to Jordan and Hall (August 15, 1986) and Hall to Jordan, WCF, Hancock, Bill Veeder, and George Autry (September 1986), Kenan; Kimberly Edens, "Friday Leads Project to Meet Rural Needs," *Daily Tar Heel*, October 3, 1986; "Bill Friday Leads Drive for Center," *Greensboro News and Record*, October 1, 1986; interview with Autry, June 20, 1991; MDC to REDC Steering Committee, May 11, 1987, WCF Correspondence, Kenan; interview with Winter, October 5, 1992.

32. Interview with Hall, May 30, 1991; interview with George Autry, June 20, 1991; Rural Economic Development Center, *Annual Report, 1988–89* and *1989–90.*

33. Interview with Hall, May 30, 1991.

34. WCF, speech before NCCBI, March 16, 1988, WCF Correspondence, Kenan. For a similar speech, see Jack Scism, "Rural Areas Don't Share Prosperity, Friday Says," *Greensboro News and Record*, December 9, 1986. See also "The 'Other' North Carolina," editorial, *Greensboro News and Record*, December 10, 1986.

35. Interview with James Goodmon, May 28, 1991. See also WCF, remarks in celebration of the 100th anniversary of the movement of Trinity College to Durham, September 26, 1992, WCF Correspondence, Kenan.

36. Interview with WCF, December 1, 1992; Tinker Ready, "N.C. Panel Pushes Health-Reform Plan," *Raleigh News and Observer*, November 24, 1992; *Universal Access at an Affordable Cost.*

37. Charles E. Young to WCF and others (July 12, 1982) and Derek Bok to WCF and others (August 13, 1982), subgroup 1, ser. 8, file entitled "ACE: Committee on Division I Intercollegiate Athletics, 1982," WCF Papers, UA/UNC. The ACE group consisted of twenty-one members.

38. Interviews with WCF, November 28, 1990, November 24, 1992.

39. Young's ad hoc committee supported ambitious reforms. It endorsed the reduction of athletic budgets and the limitation of sports scholarships on the basis of need, a major reduction in the number of football scholarships, and stricter limits on the size of coaching staffs. It also promoted the reimposition of academic integrity beyond what had already been accomplished in the NCAA's Proposition 48, which created minimum SAT scores that student-athletes had to receive in order to compete. The Young Committee considered proposing the elimination of intercollegiate competition for freshmen and a reduction in the number of games. In the autumn of 1986 the Young Committee agreed on an even more concrete set of proposals, developed in consultation with the NCAA's Presidents' Commission, calling for a reduction in the length of recruiting periods and in the visits for football and basketball recruiters, a shorter playing season in both of these sports, and fewer basketball and football coaches. Young to WCF et al. (August 22, 1986), Young to John Slaughter (September 30, 1986), WCF Correspondence, Kenan. See also Chip Alexander, "Inaction by NCAA Disappoints Friday," *Raleigh News and Observer*, October 6, 1986. On the NCAA's rejection of the ad hoc committee, see Charles Young to WCF et al., October 13, 1986, WCF Correspondence, Kenan.

40. WCF to Jack W. Peltason, July 6, 1987, WCF Correspondence, Kenan; Chip Alexander, "Slaughter Shirks the Helm in Athletic Reform Movement," *Raleigh News and Observer*, July 5, 1987; interview with Boyer, May 9, 1990; Creed C. Black to WCF, April 21, 1988, WCF Correspondence, Kenan.

41. On the origins of the Moyers special, see Moyers to Creed Black, August 14, 1989, WCF Correspondence, Kenan.

42. Knight Foundation Commission, *Keeping Faith with the Student-Athlete.*

43. Knight Foundation Commission, *A Solid Start*, p. 4.

44. Interview with WCF, December 1, 1992; Knight Foundation Commission, *A Solid Start.*

45. Interview with WCF, March 11, 1991.

Bibliography

MANUSCRIPT COLLECTIONS

Atlanta, Georgia
Jimmy Carter Presidential Library
  Jimmy Carter Papers

Chapel Hill, North Carolina
University Archives, UNC–Chapel Hill
  William B. Aycock Papers
  William D. Carmichael Jr. Papers
  William C. Friday Papers
  Paul F. Sharp Papers
  J. Carlyle Sitterson Papers
William R. Kenan Jr. Center
  William C. Friday Correspondence
Southern Historical Collection, UNC–Chapel Hill
  Frank Porter Graham Papers
  James Gordon Hanes Papers
  Lennox Polk McLendon Papers
  N. Hiden Ramsey Papers
  T. Clarence Stone Papers
  Thomas J. White Jr. Papers
UNC General Administration, Chapel Hill
  William C. Friday Correspondence
  UNC-HEW Case File
    Testimony (HEW Administrative Hearings)
      Dawson, Raymond, March 12–13, 16–17, 1981
      Hill, Watts, Jr., July 23–25, 1980
      Levin, Joseph, opening statement, July 22, 1980
      Tatel, David, September 22–23, 1980
    Depositions
      Berry, Mary Frances, February 14, 1980
      Chambers, Julius L., July 3, 1980
      Dawson, Raymond, January 16, 1981
      Gerry, Martin, January 13, 1977
      Hackley, Lloyd V., June 19, 1980
      Hill, Watts, Jr., April 15, 1980
      Howe, Harold, II, March 5, 1980
      Orleans, Jeffrey, May 15, 1980
      Pacht, Arline Burstein Mendelson, February 20, March 13, 1980
      Sharpe, Roger Dean, March 21, 1980

Tatel, David S., April 1, 1980
Affidavits
Friday, William C., September 13, 1979
Libassi, F. Peter, June 5, 1979
Pottinger, J. Stanley, June 20, 1970

Greensboro, North Carolina
Special Collections and University Archives, UNCG Library
James Sharborough Ferguson Papers
Edward Kidder Graham Jr. Papers
North Carolina Speaker Ban Collection

North Tarrytown, New York
Rockefeller Archive Center
General Education Board Papers
Rockefeller Foundation Archives

Raleigh, North Carolina
North Carolina Division of Archives and History
William Dallas Herring Papers (microfilm copy)
North Carolina Speaker Ban Study Commission Records
North Carolina State Board of Higher Education Records

Winston-Salem, North Carolina
North Carolina Baptist Historical Collection, Wake Forest University
Irving E. Carlyle Papers

INTERVIEWS

By author:
Allen, James, September 11, 1990
Allison, A. Douglass, May 14, 1991
Anderson, Anne, March 19, 1990
Anderson, Donald, March 19, 1990
Autry, George, June 20, 1991
Aycock, Elizabeth, June 13, 1991
Aycock, William B., April 11, 1990
Barnes, Gary, October 15, 1991
Beattie, Richard, June 26, 1991
Bennett, William J., April 24, 1991
Blitzer, Charles, April 17, 1991
Bostian, Carey T., March 11, 1991
Boyer, Ernest L., May 9, 1990
Breneman, David, May 10, 1991
Britt, David M., June 4, 1991
Caldwell, John Tyler, January 26, 1990
Califano, Joseph A., Jr., April 5, 1991
Carroll, Roy, August 8, 1991

Carson, Philip, July 18, 1991

Cater, Douglass, May 9, 1991

Chamberlin, Gordon, December 21, 1992

Chambers, Julius L., June 18, 1990

Clayton, Ivie, May 28, 1991

Coates, Gladys, June 10, 1991

Cochrane, William, April 19, 1991

Colvard, Dean W., January 29, 1990

Cromartie, William, May 23, 1991

Davis, Archie K., January 17, 1990

Dawson, Raymond, January 30, 1990; February 4, June 20, August 1, September 25, November 20, 1991; March 10, 1992

Dees, William, April 30, 1990

Fordham, Christopher, III, January 25, 1991

Fox, Gay Currie, August 10, 1992

Friday, Fran, April 27, 1994

Friday, Ida Howell, October 30, 1990, September 16, 1992

Friday, John R., November 8, 1993

Friday, Mary, October 4, 1992

Friday, William C., October 3, 24, 26, November 19, 26, 28, December 3, 1990; January 7, 14, 28, February 20, 25, March 6, 11, 13, April 1, 1991; January 30, February 13, 17, March 2, 18, April 9, 28, May 5, June 17, November 24, December 1, 1992

Gerry, Martin, August 6, 28, 1991

Godwin, Winfred, April 23, 1990

Goheen, Robert F., June 19, 1990

Goodmon, James, May 28, 1991

Graham, James, November 18, 1991

Guthrie, R. Claire, August 5, 1991

Hackley, Lloyd V., May 29, 1991

Hall, Billy Ray, May 30, 1991

Harris, Betty Friday, February 12, 1990

Henry, David, February 9, 1990

Herbert, George, May 13, 1991

Herring, William Dallas, February 2, 1990

Hesburgh, Theodore, June 7, 1990

Hill, Watts, Sr., May 30, 1990

Hinchman, James, April 18, 1991

Holmes, Peter E., April 18, 1991

Jenkins, Jay, May 30, 1991

Jenrette, Richard, May 8, 1990

Jordan, John R., Jr., November 18, 1991

Joyner, Felix, January 18, 1991

Kerr, Clark, April 6, 1990

King, Arnold K., February 7, 1990, March 4, 1991

Krochmal, Arnold, July 24, 1991

Kyser, Georgia, October 15, 1991

Lacy, Dan, May 8, 1990
Laupus, William, December 3, 1991
Lefort, Charles Romeo, January 26, 1990
Lehman, Paul H., Jr., May 10, 1990
Levin, Joseph J., Jr., April 19, 1991
Levine, Jules I., February 23, 1991
Libassi, F. Peter, May 16, 1991
Lindsay, Elizabeth, August 17, 1992
McMillan, R. D., May 14, 1991
Monroe, Edwin, June 11, 18, 1991
Morgan, John L., Jr., February 26, 1990
Morgan, Lucy S., and Eunice Tyler, July 24, 1991
Norwood, Zona, April 3, May 1, 1991
Orleans, Jeffrey H., May 17, 1991
Pate, Rudy, May 28, 1991
Pomerantz, Robert, March 21, 1990
Pratt, John H., April 18, 1991
Pritchett, Mebane, April 23, 1990
Robinson, Richard H., June 3, 1991
Sanders, John L., January 25, March 4, 1991
Sanford, Terry, April 17, 1991
Scott, Robert W., April 4, 1990
Shannon, Edgar, February 22, 1991
Sheps, Cecil, May 15, 1991
Sitterson, J. Carlyle, March 6, 1991
Smith, Edward A., November 27, 1992
Smith, Marshall, August 24, 1991
Snavely, Dick, May 28, 1991
Snider, William D., May 2, 1990
Stevens, John S., July 23, 1991
Stinson, Katherine, April 16, 1990
Stowe, Dalton, February 12, 1990
Summey, Robert F., November 20, 1992
Tatel, David, August 7, 1991
Thompson, Cleon, January 30, 1991
Thornburg, Wilma, February 12, 1990
Vanore, Andrew, June 13, 1991
Wharton, Clifton, May 8, 1990
White, Jess, May 10, 1991
White, Thomas J., Jr., April 30, 1990
Wilson, I. Glenn, May 6, 1991
Winter, William, October 5, 1992
Yoder, Edwin M., April 19, 1991

In the Centennial Oral History Collection, UNCG Library, Greensboro:
    Adams, Charles, April 6, 1990 (interview by Anne Phillips)
    Bardolph, Richard, May 14, 1991 (interview by Linda Danford)

Blackwell, Gordon W., November 12, 1990 (interview by William A. Link)

Burgess, M. Elaine, November 8, 1990 (interview by William A. Link)

Calhoon, Robert M., February 1, 1990 (interview by William A. Link)

Dickieson, George, March 20, 1990 (interview by William A. Link)

Eidenier, Betty Hobgood, March 29, 1991 (interview by Missy Foy)

Jester, Betty Brown, March 20, 22, 1990 (interviews by Missy Foy)

Russell, Donald, February 14, 1990 (interview by Anne Phillips)

Singletary, Otis, November 9, 1989 (interview by William A. Link)

Umstead, Betsy, December 7, 1989 (interview by William A. Link)

In the William C. Friday Papers, University Archives, UNC–Chapel Hill:
Friday, William C., June 4, 1971 (interview by Bill Williams); April 17, 1974 (interview by
    G. W. Hill); June 21, 1979 (interview by Dean W. Colvard)

In the Institute of Government Records, University Archives, UNC–Chapel Hill (all
interviews by Richie Leonard):
Andrews, Ike, July 3, 1972

Bryant, Victor S., May 1, 1972

Burney, John T., May 25, 1972

Caldwell, John T., April 21, 1972

Dees, William, April 24, 1972

Friday, William C., May 2, 1972

Hill, Watts, Jr., March 13, 1972

Hill, Watts, Sr., February 29, 1972

Huskins, J. P., March 15, 1972

Hyde, Wallace, March 16, 1972

Jenkins, Leo M., April 18, 1972

Jordan, Robert B. III, April 13, 1972

Lucas, Paul, March 29, 1972

McLendon, L. P., Jr., April 24, 1972

Scott, Robert, November 1, 1972

Sloan, Maceo, May 3, 1972

Warren, Lindsay, June 19, 1971

Wilson, Elise, May 3, 1972

In the Lyndon Baines Johnson Presidential Library, Austin, Texas:
Friday, William C., July 10, 1987 (interview by Janet Kerr-Tener)

In the Southern Oral History Program, UNC–Chapel Hill Library:
Aycock, William B., February 6, March 6, 8, 1990 (interviews by Frances Weaver)

Davis, Archie K., May 19, 1986 (interview by Anne Firor Scott)

Dobbins, Preston, December 4, 1974 (interview by Jacquelyn D. Hall)

Friday, Ida Howell, October 1, 4, 15, 1990 (interviews by Frances Weaver)

Friday, William C., December 14, 1973 (interview by Jack Bass and Walter DeVries),
    December 5, 1974 (interview by D'Ann Campbell), March 19, 1975 (interview by Steve
    Miller)

King, Arnold K., June 10–11, 1985 (interviews by J. Jenkins)

Lane, Mary Turner, September 9, 16, 1986, October 1, 28, 1987 (interviews by Pamela Dean)

Morgan, Lucy S., May 24, 1987 (interview by M. Turbeville)

Sanford, Terry, December 18, 1986 (interview by C. Cheatham), April 17, 1991 (interview by Brent Glass)

Scott, Ralph, April 22, 1974 (interview by Jacquelyn D. Hall and Bill Finger)

Sitterson, J. Carlyle, November 4, 6, 1987 (interviews by Pamela Dean)

White, Thomas J., Jr., May 2, 16, June 6, 1985 (interviews by Pamela Dean)

In the North Carolina Speaker Ban Collection, UNCG Library, Greensboro (all interviews by William A. Stewart Jr.):

Friday, William C., February 23, 1987

Medford, James, January 27, 1988

Morgan, Robert, March 24, 1987

LEGAL DOCUMENTS

Cases

Adams v. *Bell*, 711 F.2d 161 (1983)

Adams v. *Califano*, 430 F. Supp. 118 (1977)

Adams v. *Richardson*, 351 F. Supp. 636 (1972), 356 F. Supp. 92 (1972), 480 F.2d 1150 (1973)

Adams v. *Weinberger*, 391 F. Supp. 269 (1975)

Atkins v. *Scott*, 597 F.2d 872 (1979)

Dickson v. *Sitterson*, 280 F. Supp. 486 (1968)

Epps et al. v. *Carmichael*, 93 F. Supp. 327 (1950)

Frasier v. *Board of Trustees of the University of North Carolina*, 134 F. Supp. 589 (1955)

Knight v. *State of Alabama*, 787 F. Supp. 103 (1991), 829 F. Supp. 1286 (1993)

Mandel v. *U.S. Department of Health, Education, and Welfare*, 411 F. Supp. 542 (1976)

McKissick v. *Carmichael*, 187 F.2d 949 (1951)

State of North Carolina et al. v. *Department of Health, Education, and Welfare*, 480 F. Supp. 929 (1979)

United States v. *Fordice*, 112 S.Ct. 2727 (1992)

Other Documents

"Comments on the North Carolina *State Plan, Phase II*," December 5, 1977

"Consent Decree, *North Carolina* v. *Department of Education,* July 17, 1981"

"Motion for Further Relief and Points and Authorities in Support Thereof," August 1, 1975

"Motion for Leave to File Amicus Curiae Brief in Opposition to Plaintiffs Motion for Further Relief," March 21, 1976

"Statement by the National Association for Equal Opportunity in Higher Education," March 3, 1977

NEWSPAPERS AND PERIODICALS

The Agromeck

Anson Record

Asheville Citizen

Asheville Times

The Carolinian

Chapel Hill Weekly

Charlotte Observer

Chronicle of Higher Education

Daily Tar Heel

Durham Morning Herald

Durham Sun
Fayetteville Times
Gastonia Gazette
Greensboro Daily News
Greensboro News and Record
Henderson Dispatch
Hertford County News-Herald
High Point Enterprise
Lexington News-Gazette
New York Times
North Carolina State College News
Old Gold and Black
Raleigh News and Observer
Raleigh Times

Richmond Journal
Rocky Mount Telegram
Salisbury Post
Sanford Herald
Southern Pines Pilot
State College Record
The Technician
Wake Forest Howler, 1938
Washington Post
Washington Star
Wilmington Morning Star
Wilson Daily Times
Winston-Salem Journal
Yackety Yack

BOOKS, ARTICLES, AND THESES

Allen, Robert L. *The Port Chicago Mutiny*. New York: Warner Books, 1989.

Ashby, Warren. *Frank Porter Graham: A Southern Liberal*. Winston-Salem, N.C.: John Blair, 1980.

Ashmore, Harry S. *Unseasonable Truths: The Life of Robert Maynard Hutchins*. Boston: Little, Brown and Company, 1989.

Batchelor, John E. "Save Our Schools: Dallas Herring and the Governor's Special Advisory Committee on Education." M.A. thesis, University of North Carolina at Greensboro, 1983.

Blum, John Morton. *V Was for Victory: Politics and American Culture during World War II*. New York: Harcourt Brace Jovanovich, 1976.

Bratton, Mary Jo. *East Carolina University: The Formative Years, 1907–1982*. Greenville, N.C.: East Carolina Alumni Association, 1986.

Brint, Steven, and Jerome Karabel. *The Diverted Dream: Community Colleges and the Promise of Educational Opportunity in America, 1900–1985*. New York: Oxford University Press, 1989.

Brubacher, John S. *Higher Education in Transition: A History of American Colleges and Universities, 1636–1976*. New York: Harper and Row, 1976.

Building the Navy's Bases in World War II: A History of the Bureau of Yards and Docks and the Civil Engineer Corps, 1940–1946. 2 vols. Washington, D.C.: U.S. Government Printing Office, 1947.

Bulletin of Wake Forest College, 1937–1938. Wake Forest: N.p., n.d.

Burns, Augustus M., III. "Graduate Education for Blacks in North Carolina, 1930–1951." *Journal of Southern History* 46 (May 1980): 195–218.

Califano, Joseph A., Jr. *Governing America: An Insider's Report from the White House and the Cabinet*. New York: Simon and Schuster, 1981.

Carnegie Commission on Higher Education. *Priorities for Action: Final Report of the Carnegie Commission on Higher Education*. New York: McGraw-Hill, 1973.

Carpenter, William L., and Dean W. Colvard. *Knowledge Is Power: A History of the School of Agriculture and Life Sciences at North Carolina State University, 1877–1984*. Raleigh: North Carolina State University, 1987.

Chafe, William H. *Civilities and Civil Rights: The Black Struggle for Freedom in Greensboro, North Carolina*. New York: Oxford University Press, 1980.

——. *Never Stop Running: Allard Lowenstein and the Struggle to Save American Liberalism*. New York: Basic Books, 1993.

Cheek, Neal. "An Historical Study of the Administrative Actions in the Racial Desegregation of the University of North Carolina at Chapel Hill." Ph.D. dissertation, University of North Carolina at Chapel Hill, 1973.

Clotfelter, James, ed. *Frank Porter Graham: Service to North Carolina and the Nation.* Greensboro: North Carolina Service Project at the University of North Carolina at Greensboro, 1993.

Coates, Albert. "William Donald Carmichael, Jr." *Popular Government* 25 (October 1957): 6.

——. *What the University of North Carolina Meant to Me: A Report to the Chancellors and the Presidents and to the People with Whom I Have Lived and Worked from 1914 to 1969.* Richmond, Va.: William Byrd Press, 1969.

Commission on the Future of North Carolina. *The Future of North Carolina: Goals and Recommendations for the Year 2000.* Raleigh: Commission on the Future of North Carolina, 1984.

Comparative Study of Baccalaureate and Master's Program Offerings. Chapel Hill: UNC Board of Governors, December 6, 1978.

Conkin, Paul K. *Gone with the Ivy: A Biography of Vanderbilt University.* Knoxville: University of Tennessee Press, 1985.

——. "Bleak Outlook for Academic History Jobs." *Perspectives* 31 (April 1993): 1, 10–12.

Cope, Robert F., and Manley Wade Wellman. *The County of Gaston: Two Centuries of a North Carolina Region.* Gastonia: Gaston County Historical Society, 1961.

Crabtree, Beth G. *North Carolina Governors, 1585–1974.* Raleigh: North Carolina Division of Archives and History, 1974.

Crow, Jeffrey J., Paul D. Escott, and Flora J. Hatley. *A History of African Americans in North Carolina.* Raleigh: North Carolina Division of Archives and History, 1992.

Davenport, Harold Douglas. "A History of Linwood College." M.A. thesis, Appalachian State Teachers College, 1959.

Dentler, Robert A., D. Catherine Baltzell, and Daniel J. Sullivan. *University on Trial: The Case of the University of North Carolina.* Cambridge, Mass.: Abt Books, 1983.

Diggins, John. *The Proud Decades: America in War and Peace, 1941–1960.* New York: Norton, 1988.

Douglas, Davison McDowell. "Changing Times: The Desegregation of the Charlotte Schools, 1954–1975." Ph.D. dissertation, Yale University, 1992.

Dyer, Thomas G. *The University of Georgia: A Bicentennial History, 1785–1985.* Athens: University of Georgia Press, 1985.

Ehle, John. *Dr. Frank: Life with Frank Porter Graham.* Chapel Hill: Franklin Street Books, 1993.

Findings and Recommendations of the Personnel Security Board in the Case of Dr. J. Robert Oppenheimer. Washington, D.C.: Atomic Energy Commission, 1954.

Friday, William. *Frank Porter Graham and Human Rights.* Chapel Hill: Privately printed, 1983.

The Genealogy of Peter Heyl and His Descendants, 1100–1936. Shelby, N.C.: Zolliecoffer Jenks Thompson, 1938.

Goldman, Eric F. *The Tragedy of Lyndon Johnson.* New York: Knopf, 1969.

Gordon, Lynn. *Gender and Higher Education in the Progressive Era.* New Haven: Yale University Press, 1990.

Governor's Commission on Education beyond the High School. *Report of the Governor's Commission on Education beyond the High School.* Raleigh: N.p., 1962.

Graham, Hugh Davis. *The Uncertain Triumph: Federal Education Policy in the Kennedy and Johnson Years.* Chapel Hill: University of North Carolina Press, 1984.

———. "Structure and Governance in American Higher Education: Historical and Comparative Analysis in State Policy." *Journal of Policy History* 1 (1989): 80–107.

Gunther, Timothy. "No Reds in Blue Heaven: A Discourse on the Passage, Amendment, and Repeal of the North Carolina Communist Speaker Ban Law." Senior honors' thesis, University of North Carolina at Chapel Hill, 1985.

Hart, Thomas Roy. *The School of Textiles, N.C. State College: Its Past and Present.* Raleigh: North Carolina State College, 1951.

Henry, David Dodds. *Challenges Past, Challenges Present: An Analysis of American Higher Education since 1930.* San Francisco: Jossey-Bass Publishers, 1975.

Hershberg, James. *James B. Conant: Harvard to Hiroshima and the Making of the Nuclear Age.* New York: Knopf, 1993.

Hieb, Samuel A. "General Education, Edward Kidder Graham, and the Woman's College." Unpublished seminar paper, University of North Carolina at Greensboro, 1991.

Ingalls, Zoe. "U. of North Carolina's Friday on His 30 Years as President: 'I Just Learned as I Went Along.'" *Chronicle of Higher Education* 31, no. 24 (February 26, 1986): 3.

Jencks, Christopher, and David Riesman. *The Academic Revolution.* Garden City, N.Y.: Anchor Books, 1969.

Johnson, Leonard E., and Lloyd M. Smith. *Men of Achievement in the Carolinas: Their Contributions to the Rapid Development of the Two States.* Charlotte, N.C.: H. A. Stalls Company, 1952.

Junk, Cheryl Fradette. "The Waiting Task: The Concept of Service at Woman's College, 1919–1941." *Inquiry* 1 (Spring 1992): 1–14.

Kearney, Deirdre S. "All Out for Victory: Woman's College and the Impact of the War, 1937–1947." Unpublished seminar paper, University of North Carolina at Greensboro, May 1992.

Kerr, Clark. *The Great Transformation in Higher Education, 1960–1980.* Albany: State University of New York Press, 1991.

King, Arnold K. *The Multicampus University of North Carolina Comes of Age, 1956–1986.* Chapel Hill: University of North Carolina, 1986.

Knight Foundation Commission on Intercollegiate Athletics. *Keeping Faith with the Student-Athlete: A New Model for Intercollegiate Athletics.* N.p.: Knight Commission, 1991.

———. *A Solid Start: A Report on the Reform of Intercollegiate Athletics.* N.p.: Knight Commission, 1992.

Korstad, Robert Rodgers. *Dreaming of a Time: The School of Public Health, the University of North Carolina at Chapel Hill, 1939–1989.* Chapel Hill: UNC School of Public Health, 1990.

Lancaster, James M. "A Study of Statewide Higher Education Agencies." Ed.D. dissertation, University of North Carolina at Greensboro, 1985.

Larrabee, Charles X. *Many Missions: Research Triangle Institute's First 31 Years.* Research Triangle Park, N.C.: Research Triangle Institute, 1991.

Lee, Eugene, and Frank M. Bowen. *The Multicampus University: A Study in American Governance.* New York: McGraw-Hill, 1971.

Lee, Ulysses Grant. *The Employment of Negro Troops.* Washington, D.C.: Office of the Chief of Military History, U.S. Army, 1966.

Lefler, Hugh Talmage, and Albert Ray Newsome. *The History of a Southern State: North Carolina.* 3d ed. Chapel Hill: University of North Carolina Press, 1973.

Leonard, Richie. "The Reorganization of Public Senior Higher Education in North Carolina: The Legislative Phase, 1970–71." Unpublished paper, December 1973 (in author's possession).

Link, William A. *The Paradox of Southern Progressivism, 1880–1930.* Chapel Hill: University of North Carolina Press, 1993.

Lockmiller, David. *The Consolidation of the University of North Carolina.* Chapel Hill: University of North Carolina Press, 1942.

Luebke, Paul. *Tar Heel Politics: Myths and Realities.* Chapel Hill: University of North Carolina Press, 1990.

Mohr, Clarence L. "National Forces in Regional Perspective: The Metamorphosis of Southern Higher Education, 1945–1965." Unpublished paper delivered at the Porter L. Fortune Jr. Symposium in Southern History, University of Mississippi, October 1992.

Montgomery, James Riley, Stanley J. Folmsbee, and Lee Seifert Greene. *To Foster Knowledge: A History of the University of Tennessee, 1794–1970.* Knoxville: University of Tennessee Press, 1984.

Moose, Ruth, ed. *I Have Walked: Stories and Poems about Poverty.* Greensboro: North Carolina Poverty Project, Inc., 1989.

Morgan, Chester M. *Dearly Bought, Deeply Treasured: The University of Southern Mississippi, 1912–1987.* Oxford: University of Mississippi Press, 1990.

"Mr. Friday." *North Carolina State Alumni Magazine* 58, no. 4 (March 1986): 2–9.

Nalty, Bernard C. *Strength for the Fight: A History of Black Americans in the Military.* New York: The Free Press, 1986.

National Center for Family Literacy. *A Place to Start: The Kenan Trust Family Literacy Project.* Louisville, Ky.: National Center for Family Literacy, 1989.

Nelson, Dennis D. *The Integration of the Negro into the U.S. Navy.* New York: Farrar, Straus, and Young, 1951.

North Carolina Poverty Project, Inc. *How We Feed the Poor.* Greensboro: North Carolina Poverty Project, Inc., n.d.

North Carolina State Board of Higher Education. *State Supported Traditionally Negro Colleges in North Carolina.* Raleigh: North Carolina Board of Higher Education, 1967.

——. *Planning for Higher Education in North Carolina.* Raleigh: North Carolina Board of Higher Education, 1968.

The North Carolina State Plan for the Further Elimination of Racial Duality in the Public Post-Secondary Education Systems. Chapel Hill: UNC Board of Governors, 1974.

Official Handbook of the Student Body of Wake Forest College, 1937–1938 Edition. Wake Forest: Student Government Association, n.d.

Orfield, Gary. *Must We Bus? Segregated Schools and National Policy.* Washington, D.C.: The Brookings Institution, 1978.

Panetta, Leon E., and Peter Gall. *Bring Us Together: The Nixon Team and the Civil Rights Retreat.* Philadelphia: J. B. Lippincott Company, 1971.

Paschal, George Washington. *History of Wake Forest College.* 3 vols. Wake Forest, N.C.: Wake Forest College, 1943.

Pleasants, Julian M. "A Question of Loyalty: Frank Porter Graham and the Atomic Energy Commission." *North Carolina Historical Review* 69 (October 1992): 414–37.

Pleasants, Julian M., and Augustus M. Burns III. *Frank Porter Graham and the 1950 Senate Race in North Carolina.* Chapel Hill: University of North Carolina Press, 1990.

Polenberg, Richard. *War and Society: The United States, 1941–1945.* Philadelphia: J. B. Lippincott Company, 1972.

Pope, Liston. *Millhands and Preachers: A Study of Gastonia.* New Haven: Yale University Press, 1942.

Poverty Project Exploration Report to Participants. Greensboro: North Carolina Poverty Project, Inc., 1992.

Powell, William S. *The North Carolina Gazetteer.* Chapel Hill: University of North Carolina Press, 1968.

——, ed. *Dictionary of North Carolina Biography.* 5 vols. to date. Chapel Hill: University of North Carolina Press, 1979–.

Ravitch, Diane. *The Troubled Crusade: American Education, 1945–1980.* New York: Basic Books, 1983.

Rawlings, Florence Gibbs. "Dispatch Correspondent Finds Much There to Interest." In Mildred Searson Goeller, *Memories and Clippings.* N.p., 1984.

——. "The Early History of Raphine," April 21, 1908. In Mildred Searson Goeller, *Memories and Clippings.* N.p., 1984.

Reagan, Alice Elizabeth. *North Carolina State University: A Narrative History.* Raleigh: North Carolina State University Foundation, 1987.

Reddick, Lawrence D. "The Negro in the United States Navy during World War II." *Journal of Negro History* 32 (April 1947): 201–19.

The Revised North Carolina State Plan for the Further Elimination of Racial Duality in the Public Post-Secondary Education Systems. Chapel Hill: UNC Board of Governors, 1974.

The Revised North Carolina State Plan for the Further Elimination of Racial Duality in Public Higher Education Systems, Phase II: 1978–1983. Chapel Hill: UNC Board of Governors, 1977.

The Revised North Carolina State Plan for the Further Elimination of Racial Duality in Public Higher Education Systems, Phase II: Supplemental Statement, December 30, 1977. Chapel Hill: UNC Board of Governors, 1977.

The Revised North Carolina State Plan for the Further Elimination of Racial Duality in Public Higher Education Systems, Phase II: Supplemental Statement II. Chapel Hill: UNC Board of Governors, May 12, 1978.

Rhyne, Jenning J. *Some Southern Cotton Mill Workers and Their Villages.* Chapel Hill: University of North Carolina Press, 1930.

Riesman, David. *Abundance for What?* New York: Doubleday and Company, 1964.

Roberts, Nancy. *The Governor.* Charlotte, N.C.: McNally and Loftin, 1972.

Rural Economic Development Center. *North Carolina Rural Economic Development Center Annual Report, 1988–89.* Raleigh: Rural Economic Development Center, 1989.

——. *North Carolina Rural Economic Development Center Annual Report, 1989–90.* Raleigh: Rural Economic Development Center, 1990.

Sanders, John L. "The Evolution of the Idea of Making the Initial Board of Governors a Permanent Body." Unpublished paper, 1972 (in author's possession).

——. "The University of North Carolina: The Legislative Evolution of Public Higher Education." *Popular Government* 59 (Fall 1993): 13–21.

Sansing, David G. *Making Haste Slowly: The Troubled History of Higher Education in Mississippi.* Oxford: University of Mississippi Press, 1990.

Schrecker, Ellen W. *No Ivory Tower: McCarthyism and the Universities.* New York: Oxford
  University Press, 1986.
Session Laws and Resolutions Passed by the General Assembly at the Regular Session, 1955.
  Winston-Salem, N.C.: Winston Printing Company, 1955, 1959.
Shumaker, James. "Let Me Share This with You." *Carolina Alumni Review* 74, no. 2 (Winter
  1986): 27–28.
Snider, William D. "Twenty-Nine Tumultuous Years of Conflict and Accomplishment." *We
  the People of North Carolina* 43, no. 10 (October 1985): 15–16.
——. *Light on the Hill: A History of the University of North Carolina at Chapel Hill.* Chapel
  Hill: University of North Carolina Press, 1992.
Solomon, Barbara. *In the Company of Educated Women: A History of Women and Higher
  Education in America.* New Haven: Yale University Press, 1985.
Southern Growth Policies Board. *Halfway Home and a Long Way to Go.* Research Triangle
  Park, N.C.: Southern Growth Policies Board, 1986.
Spearman, Robert. Senior honors' thesis, University of North Carolina at Chapel Hill, 1965.
Speeches and Statements of William Brantley Aycock. Chapel Hill: Colonial Press, 1989.
*State Supported Higher Education in North Carolina: The Report of the Commission on Higher
  Education.* Raleigh: N.p., 1955.
State Supported Traditionally Negro Colleges in North Carolina. Raleigh: North Carolina Board
  of Higher Education, 1967.
Stern, Philip M., with the collaboration of Harold P. Green. *The Oppenheimer Case: Security
  on Trial.* New York: Harper and Row, 1969.
Stewart, William Allen. "The North Carolina Speaker Ban Law Episode: Its History and
  Implications for Higher Education." Ed.D. dissertation, University of North Carolina at
  Greensboro, 1988.
Stone, Richard. "The Graham Plan of 1935: An Aborted Crusade to De-emphasize College
  Athletics." *North Carolina Historical Review* 64 (July 1987): 274–93.
Strobel, Marian Elizabeth. "Ideology and Women's Higher Education, 1945–1960." Ph.D.
  dissertation, Duke University, 1975.
Synnott, Marcia G. "Federalism Vindicated: University Desegregation in South Carolina and
  Alabama, 1962–1963." *Journal of Policy History* 1 (1989): 292–318.
Tushnet, Mark V. *The NAACP's Legal Strategy against Segregated Education, 1925–1950.* Chapel
  Hill: University of North Carolina Press, 1987.
Universal Access at an Affordable Cost: Ensuring Health Care Services for All North Carolinians.
  Durham: North Carolina Institute of Medicine, 1993.
Vaughn, James Herbert, Jr. "The Integration of Negroes in the Law School of the University
  of North Carolina." M.A. thesis, University of North Carolina at Chapel Hill, 1952.
Waldorf, Rosemary. "It Was a Wonderful Life." *Carolina Alumni Review* 74 (Winter 1986): 32–
  34.
William R. Kenan Jr. Charitable Trust. *The First Twenty-Five Years, 1966–1991.* Chapel Hill:
  William R. Kenan Jr. Charitable Trust, 1991.
Williams, Derek John. " 'It Wasn't Slavery Time Anymore': Foodworkers' Strike at Chapel
  Hill, Spring 1969." M.A. thesis, University of North Carolina at Chapel Hill, 1979.
Wilson, Louis Round. *The University of North Carolina, 1900–1930: The Making of a Modern
  University.* Chapel Hill: University of North Carolina Press, 1957.
——. *The University of North Carolina under Consolidation, 1931–1963: History and Appraisal.*
  Chapel Hill: University of North Carolina Consolidated Office, 1964.

Acknowledgments

This book would not have been written were it not for the patience, encouragement, and support of a number of people. I am grateful to two directors of the University of North Carolina Press, Matthew N. Hodgson and Kate Douglas Torrey, for persuading me to undertake this book and for their steadfast enthusiasm. The William Rand Kenan Jr. Charitable Trust provided generous financial support without which this biography would not have been written, and I particularly appreciate the interest of Frank H. Kenan and Thomas S. Kenan III. The completion of this book also reflects the support of the UNCG administration, including Chancellor William E. Moran, Provost Donald V. DeRosa, Dean of the College and Sciences Walter H. Beale, Associate Director of Research Services Beverly B. Maddox-Britt, and History Department heads Allen W. Trelease and Steven F. Lawson. I am very grateful for the university's willingness to grant me time off from teaching to complete the manuscript.

I also must thank the subject of this biography, William C. Friday. He was infinitely patient in taking time to conduct the interviews that form the backbone of this biography and always accommodating to my needs, however imposing they might have been. Although I am sure that he would have liked to have known what was contained in the book before it was published, he encouraged me to follow my instincts as a scholar while he insisted that his own story be told truthfully. I hope that this book lives up to his own very high standards.

Friday family members cooperated fully, and I appreciate their grace despite the intrusion. I frequently imposed on the time and talents of Zona Norwood, Bill Friday's legendary assistant. She was generous with help, advice, and information, which she provided with balance and good humor. I am also grateful for the cheerful professionalism with which Helen Jane Wettach of the UNC General Administration aided my search for documents and records. Autumn Miller began the mammoth task of transcribing the interviews upon which much of this study is based. Karen Brady-Hill transcribed the remainder of interviews and did so with intelligence, interest, and skill. Bryant Hutson helped in editing transcripts and with the bibliography; Pat McGee and David Herr aided me in the last stages of the preparation of the manuscript. Judyth White was a constant, reliable, and skilled research assistant, and I was fortunate to have her help and support. Two members of the excellent editorial staff at the UNC Press, Pamela Upton and Stevie Champion, helped to guide the manuscript to completion, and I greatly appreciate their assistance.

This biography is largely based on interviews with a number of people, and I thank them for their willingness to participate in this project. Some of Friday's acquaintances declined to be interviewed, for their own reasons, and I regret not including their perspectives in this account. Although I do not have enough space to mention all of the interviewees, they are listed separately in the bibliography, and I profoundly appreciate their contributions to this book. I have donated all of the tapes and transcripts of these interviews to the Southern Oral History Program at the University of North Carolina at Chapel Hill Library, where they will be available to future students of Bill Friday and the University of North Carolina.

The help of numerous librarians and archivists was invaluable. I am grateful to Betty Carter and Emily C. Mills of the UNCG Special Collections and University Archives, and Kathryn M.

Crowe, Nancy C. Fogarty, and Catherine K. Levinson, along with other reference librarians at UNCG. At Chapel Hill, Mike Martin, David Molke-Hansen, Richard Shrader, and John White helped to guide me through the collections of the Southern Historical Collection and University Archives, while Bob Anthony and Alice Cotten of the North Carolina Collection helped me track down innumerable research leads. John R. Woodward of Wake Forest University Library and Maurice S. Toler of North Carolina State University Library provided help. Thomas Rosenbaum of the Rockefeller Archive Center also supplied invaluable aid. William Dallas Herring granted me access to his rich personal papers, and Jesse R. Lankford of the North Carolina Division of Archives and History made them available on microfilm.

A number of people took time out of their busy schedules to read and criticize drafts of this book. Robert M. Calhoon and Allen W. Trelease read several chapters, and I have profited from their advice. John D'Emilio and Steven F. Lawson read the entire manuscript and offered useful suggestions for greater clarity and brevity in a long manuscript. Davison M. Douglas, of the College of William and Mary Law School, shared his expertise about the history of desegregation in a critical but invaluable reading of the last portion of the manuscript. John Sanders also read the entire manuscript, and I have benefited from his considerable knowledge of recent North Carolina history. As readers for the UNC Press, Edward Holley, David Riesman, and Edwin M. Yoder made very important suggestions. Cheryl F. Junk skillfully critiqued an early version and offered indispensable advice about style and substance. I imposed on the time of other readers who also helped to make this a better book, although any errors or misrepresentations are mine alone. Zona Norwood, who read an early and long draft, offered constructive suggestions. Raymond H. Dawson submitted himself to a series of long interviews and was unfailingly helpful in my research. He also carefully examined the entire manuscript and provided a fair-minded and dispassionate critique, though he was an active participant in most of the events of the last third of this book.

As always, I have depended on the advice of my family, and I have exploited their editorial abilities as much as I have relied on their encouragement. Arthur S. Link and Margaret Douglas Link read the manuscript with their typical thoroughness and careful attention to language and clarity. Susannah J. Link not only spared subsequent readers conceptual confusion and awkward language, but she also provided both constancy and editorial skepticism. The dedication is for three Tar Heel natives, whose boundless faith in humanity and the spirit of the future is exemplified in the life of Bill Friday.

Index

desegregation during the 1950s, 82; initiates the *Adams* case, 253–54; Chambers elected president, 258; relations with OCR, 260, 287–88; and vet school controversy, 264–65, 273–74, 281; determination about UNC desegregation, 276, 278, 304; and *Comparative Study*, 280; new motion (1975) in *Adams*, 280–83; pressure on HEW and Education, 301, 313, 328, 349; and HEW administrative hearings, 348; and UNC-Education consent decree, 359, 362

Lehman, Paul H., Jr., 28, 30, 31, 33, 36, 38, 39, 42

Lenoir Hall, 71, 83, 145–51, 156

Lenoir-Rhyne College, 65

Leper, Brian, 17

Lepper, Mary, 257

Leventhal, Melvin, 287

Levi, Edward H., 204

Levin, Joseph J., Jr., 330–32, 339, 341–42, 345, 347, 351–52, 354, 356, 358–60, 362, 364–65

Levine, Jules, 229–31

Levy, Howard, 330

Lewis, Henry W., 153

Lewis, J. G., 27

Lewis, Mickey, 143

Lexington, Va., 4, 13

Liaison Committee on Medical Education (LCME), 222–25, 226–29, 231, 238–40, 242–43

Libassi, F. Peter, 285–93, 299, 302–3, 307

Library of Congress, 216

Lichtman, Elliott, 288

Lillington, N.C., 289

Litchfield, Terry, 104, 106

Little, William, 215

Long-range plan: established in 1976 for UNC campuses, 200

Loray strike, 10

Los Angeles State College, 104

Louisiana: higher education desegregation in, 253, 261

Louisville, Ky., 375–76

Lowell Textile School, 26

Lowenstein, Allard, 111–13

Lucas, Paul, 175

Luebke, Paul, xiii

Lumber River, 43

Lumberton, N.C., 43, 175, 233

Lumberton High School, 44

McAlester, Okla., 52

McCall, Fred B., 54

McCarthy, Joseph R., 79, 277

McClure's Drugstore (Lexington, Va.), 13

McCorkel, Roy James, Jr., 128–29, 131, 138

McCorkle Place, 137

McCoy, Reginald F., 232

McGraw, Harold, 216

McGraw-Hill, Inc., 216

McGuire, Frank, 99, 102, 107

Mackie, Ernest L., 62

McKinney, Claude, 215

McKinney, Roy, 270–71

McKissick, Floyd, 132

McKnight, C. A. ("Pete"), 270

McLendon, Lennox Polk, Jr. ("Mac"), 58, 176

McLendon, Lennox Polk, Sr. ("Major"), 165–67, 176

McMillan, James, 44, 339

McMillan, R. D., 185, 193, 245

McNamara, Robert, 202

Madison County, N.C., 375

Madison Square Garden, 103

Mandel, Marvin, 268

Mandel case, 268, 281

Manning Hall, 54, 58–59, 60, 146, 151–52

Manteo, N.C., 360

Marine Corps, 333

Marland, Sidney, 204

Marshall, John, 53

Marshall, Thurgood, 82

Marshall, Walter, 320

Martin, Jim, 218, 375

Martin, Perry, 116

Maryland: higher education desegregation in, 253, 261, 267–68

Massachusetts Institute of Technology (MIT), 210

North Carolina State College of Agriculture and Engineering: and UNC consolidation, 24–25, 68–69; Friday attends, 24–38, 48, 52, 55, 57–58, 61, 64; employs Friday (1941–42), 40–42; alumni giving at, 76; athletics at, 79–80, 84; desegregation of, 83–84, 249–50; nuclear reactor at, 85, 96; coeducation at, 86; Friday's inauguration at, 95–96; Helms attacks, 110; and civil rights revolution, 111; and BHE, 160; and name change, 160, 165, 167–68. *See also* North Carolina State University

North Carolina State Highway Patrol, 145, 151

North Carolina State University, 124; name change (1963), 160, 165, 167–68; doctoral status of, 200; engineering programs at, 200; and RTP, 212–13, 215; and vet school, 262–67, 273, 314; and UNC desegregation, 311; and Tatel-Berry tour, 320. *See also* North Carolina State College of Agriculture and Engineering

North Carolina Supreme Court, 95

North Street: Friday's apartment at, 55, 59–60

Norton, J. W. R., 222

Norwood, Zona, 187–88, 193–94, 198, 371

Notre Dame University: officer training at during World War II, 47; Hesburgh presidency, 201, 382

Oberlin Road, 31

O'Connor, Colleen, 320

Odum, Howard W., 56, 77

Office for Civil Rights (OCR): created, 251; and Panetta's letter, 252–53; enforces *Adams*, 255–62; and vet school controversy, 262–67, 270, 272–73; and pressure on Maryland and North Carolina (1975), 267–71, 273–76; and settlement (October 1975), 271–72; suspicions of UNC, 273–76; new leadership under Jimmy Carter, 278, 284–85; and *Comparative Study*, 278–80; deteriorating relations with UNC (1975–77), 281–83; and development of *Adams* criteria, 286–92;

response to *Phase II*, 299–304; and *Supplemental Statement II*, 311, 313–17; and the Tatel-Berry tour, 318–23; and UNC negotiations (Spring 1979), 324–39; and UNC countersuit, 341, 344, 347–49; and Kujovich negotiations, 350–54; mid-1980s task force, 363

Office of Economic Opportunity, 378

Ohio: House of Representatives of, 114

Ohio State University, 113, 198, 262

O'Keefe, Michael, 286, 289, 291

Oklahoma: higher education desegregation in, 253, 261, 303, 315, 363

Old Dominion University, 315

Old Gold and Black, 23

Old Providence Church, 3–4, 13

Old Well, the, 63, 71

O. Max Gardner Award, 70

Oppenheimer, J. Robert, 60; disloyalty charges against, 79

Orangeburg, S.C., 44, 142

Orange County, N.C., 112

Orleans, Jeffrey H., 289, 291, 299, 307, 316, 323, 330, 333, 336

Oxford, Miss., 285

Pacht, Arlene Mendelson, 286, 299, 301, 307, 324–26

Pamlico County, N.C., 113

Panetta, Leon, 252–53, 255, 266, 282

Parent and Child Education (PACE) program, 375

Parker, Ernest, 107

Parker, Janie, 42

Pasour, Marcus, 16

Paul, Dan, 40

Pearl Harbor: Japanese attack on, 40, 46

Pearsall, Tom, 161, 167

Pearsall Plan, 161–62

Pearson, Conrad O., 82

Peltason, Jack, 381

Pembroke State College: becomes university, 169

Pennsylvania: higher education desegregation in, 253, 261

Perry, Arnold, 137